T0134753

Communications
in Computer and Information Science

1766

Rationale

The CCIS series is devoted to the publication of proceedings of computer science conferences. Its aim is to efficiently disseminate original research results in informatics in printed and electronic form. While the focus is on publication of peer-reviewed full papers presenting mature work, inclusion of reviewed short papers reporting on work in progress is welcome, too. Besides globally relevant meetings with internationally representative program committees guaranteeing a strict peer-reviewing and paper selection process, conferences run by societies or of high regional or national relevance are also considered for publication.

Topics

The topical scope of CCIS spans the entire spectrum of informatics ranging from foundational topics in the theory of computing to information and communications science and technology and a broad variety of interdisciplinary application fields.

Information for Volume Editors and Authors

Publication in CCIS is free of charge. No royalties are paid, however, we offer registered conference participants temporary free access to the online version of the conference proceedings on SpringerLink (http://link.springer.com) by means of an http referrer from the conference website and/or a number of complimentary printed copies, as specified in the official acceptance email of the event.

CCIS proceedings can be published in time for distribution at conferences or as post-proceedings, and delivered in the form of printed books and/or electronically as USBs and/or e-content licenses for accessing proceedings at SpringerLink. Furthermore, CCIS proceedings are included in the CCIS electronic book series hosted in the SpringerLink digital library at http://link.springer.com/bookseries/7899. Conferences publishing in CCIS are allowed to use Online Conference Service (OCS) for managing the whole proceedings lifecycle (from submission and reviewing to preparing for publication) free of charge.

Publication process

The language of publication is exclusively English. Authors publishing in CCIS have to sign the Springer CCIS copyright transfer form, however, they are free to use their material published in CCIS for substantially changed, more elaborate subsequent publications elsewhere. For the preparation of the camera-ready papers/files, authors have to strictly adhere to the Springer CCIS Authors' Instructions and are strongly encouraged to use the CCIS LaTeX style files or templates.

Abstracting/Indexing

CCIS is abstracted/indexed in DBLP, Google Scholar, EI-Compendex, Mathematical Reviews, SCImago, Scopus. CCIS volumes are also submitted for the inclusion in ISI Proceedings.

How to start

To start the evaluation of your proposal for inclusion in the CCIS series, please send an e-mail to ccis@springer.com.

Guangtao Zhai · Jun Zhou · Hua Yang ·
Xiaokang Yang · Ping An · Jia Wang
Editors

Digital Multimedia Communications

19th International Forum, IFTC 2022
Shanghai, China, December 8–9, 2022
Revised Selected Papers

Editors
Guangtao Zhai (iD)
Shanghai Jiao Tong University
Shanghai, China

Hua Yang
Shanghai Jiao Tong University
Shanghai, China

Ping An (iD)
Shanghai University
Shanghai, China

Jun Zhou (iD)
Shanghai Jiao Tong University
Shanghai, China

Xiaokang Yang
Shanghai Jiao Tong University
Shanghai, China

Jia Wang
Shanghai Jiao Tong University
Shanghai, China

ISSN 1865-0929   ISSN 1865-0937 (electronic)
Communications in Computer and Information Science
ISBN 978-981-99-0855-4   ISBN 978-981-99-0856-1 (eBook)
https://doi.org/10.1007/978-981-99-0856-1

This Springer imprint is published by the registered company Springer Nature Singapore Pte Ltd.
The registered company address is: 152 Beach Road, #21-01/04 Gateway East, Singapore 189721, Singapore

Preface

This volume contains the selected papers presented at IFTC 2022, 19th International Forum of Digital Multimedia Communication, held in Shanghai, China, on December 9, 2022.

IFTC is a summit forum in the field of digital media communication. The 19th IFTC served as an international bridge for extensively exchanging the latest research advances in digital media communication around the world. The forum also aimed to promote technology, equipment, and applications in the field of digital media by comparing the characteristics, frameworks, and significant techniques and their maturity, analyzing the performance of various applications in terms of scalability, manageability, and portability, and discussing the interfaces among varieties of networks and platforms.

The conference program included invited talks focusing on AI and Media Quality delivered by four distinguished speakers from the University of Brasilia (Brazil), the National Institute of Applied Sciences (France), Sichuan University (China), and Shandong University (China). The conference oral and poster sessions had 8 and 32 papers respectively. Those 40 papers in this book were selected from the 112 submissions using single-blind review, with 3 reviews received for each paper. The topics of these papers range from audio/image/video processing to ratification intelligence as well as big data.

The proceedings editors wish to thank the authors for contributing their novel ideas and visions that are recorded in this book, and we thank all reviewers for their contributions. We also thank Springer for their trust and for publishing the proceedings of IFTC 2022.

IFTC 2022 was co-hosted by the Shanghai Image and Graphics Association (SIGA), the China International Industry Fair (CIIF 2022), and the Shanghai Association for Science and Technology, and it was co-sponsored by Shanghai Jiao Tong University (SJTU), Shanghai Telecom Company, the Shanghai Institute for Advanced Communication and Data Science (SICS), Shanghai University of Engineering Science, and the Shanghai Key Laboratory of Digital Media Processing and Transmission.

December 2022

Guangtao Zhai
Jun Zhou
Hua Yang
Ping An
Xiaokang Yang
Jia Wang

Organization

General Chairs

Xiaokang Yang	Shanghai Jiao Tong University, China
Ping An	Shanghai University, China
Guangtao Zhai	Shanghai Jiao Tong University, China

Program Chairs

Xiangyang Xue	Fudan University, China
Jun Zhou	Shanghai Jiao Tong University, China
Yue Lu	East China Normal University, China
Hua Yang	Shanghai Jiao Tong University, China
Jia Wang	Shanghai Jiao Tong University, China

Tutorial Chairs

Yugang Jiang	Fudan University, China
Yuming Fang	Jiangxi University of Finance and Economics, China
Jiantao Zhou	University of Macau, China

International Liaisons

Weisi Lin	Nanyang Technological University, Singapore
Patrick Le Callet	Nantes Université, France
Lu Zhang	INSA Rennes, France

Finance Chairs

Yi Xu	Shanghai Jiao Tong University, China
Hao Liu	Donghua University, China
Beibei Li	Shanghai Polytechnic University, China

Xuefei Song   Shanghai Ninth People's Hospital, China

Publications Chairs

Hong Lu   Fudan University, China
Feiniu Yuan   Shanghai Normal University, China
Xianming Liu   Harbin Institute of Technology, China
Liquan Shen   Shanghai University, China

Award Chairs

Zhijun Fang   Shanghai University of Engineering Science,
                                         China
Xiaolin Huang   Shanghai Jiao Tong University, China
Hanli Wang   Tongji University, China
Yu Zhu   East China University of Science and Technology,
                                         China

Publicity Chairs

Wenjun Zhang   Shanghai Jiao Tong University, China
Bo Yan   Fudan University, China
Gang Hou   Central Research Institute of INESA, China

Industrial Program Chairs

Yiyi Lu   China Telecom, Shanghai, China
Guozhong Wang   Shanghai University of Engineering Science,
                                         China
Chen Yao   Third Research Institute of the Ministry of Public
                                         Security, China
Yan Zhou   Renji Hospital, China

Arrangements Chair

Cheng Zhi   Shanghai Image and Graphics Assocication,
                             China

Program Committee

Ping An   Shanghai University, China
Zhenzhong Chen   Huazhong University of Science and Technology,
                             China
Weiling Chen   Fuzhou University, China
Chenwei Deng   Beijing Institute of Technology, China
Lianghui Ding   Shanghai Jiao Tong University, China
Huiyu Duan   Shanghai Jiao Tong University, China
Lu Fang   University of Science and Technology of China,
                             China
Yuming Fang   Jiangxi University of Finance and Economics,
                             China
Zhijun Fang   Shanghai University of Engineering Science,
                             China
Gui Feng   Huaqiao University, China
Shuang Fen   Communication University of China, China
Ke Gu   Beijing University of Technology, China
Jianling Hu   Soochow University, China
Menghan Hu   East China Normal University, China
Ruimin Hu   Wuhan University, China
Xiaolin Huang   Shanghai Jiao Tong University, China
Rongrong Ji   Xiamen University, China
Tingting Jiang   Peking University, China
Yugang Jiang   Fudan University, China
Beibei Li   Shanghai Polytechnic University, China
Hao Liu   Donghua University, China
Jiaying Liu   Peking University, China
Xianming Liu   Harbin Institute of Technology, China
Zhi Liu   Shandong University, China
Hong Lu   Fudan University, China
Yiyi Lu   China Telecom Shanghai Company, China
Yue Lu   East China Normal University, China
Ran Ma   Shanghai University, China
Siwei Ma   Peking University, China
Xiongkuo Min   Shanghai Jiao Tong University, China

Yi Niu	Xidian University, China
Da Pan	Communication University of China, China
Peng Qi	Tongji University, China
Feng Shao	Ningbo University, China
Liquan Shen	Shanghai University, China
Xiangmin Xu	South China University of Technology, China
Yi Xu	Shanghai Jiao Tong University, China
Qiudong Sun	Shanghai Second Polytechnical University, China
Shiliang Sun	East China Normal University, China
Wei Sun	Shanghai Jiao Tong University, China
Ci Wang	East China Normal University, China
Guozhong Wang	Shanghai University of Engineering Science, China
Hanli Wang	Tongji University, China
Jia Wang	Shanghai Jiao Tong University, China
Shigang Wang	Jilin University, China
Yongfang Wang	Shanghai University, China
Hongan Wei	Fuzhou University, China
Meng Wu	Northwestern Polytechnical University, China
Xiangyang Xue	Fudan University, China
Bo Yan	Fudan University, China
Chao Yang	Shandong University, China
Hua Yang	Shanghai Jiao Tong University, China
Jingyu Yang	Tianjing University, China
Xiaokang Yang	Shanghai Jiao Tong University, China
Chen Yao	Third Research Institute of the Ministry of Public Security, China
Long Ye	Communication University of China, China
Haibing Yin	Hangzhou Dianzi University, China
Feiniu Yuan	Shanghai Normal University, China
Guangtao Zhai	Shanghai Jiao Tong University, China
Xiaoli Zhao	Shanghai University of Engineering Science, China
Chengxu Zhou	Liaoning University of Technology, China
Jiantao Zhou	University of Macau, China
Jun Zhou	Shanghai Jiao Tong University, China
Yan Zhou	Renji Hospital, China
Wenhan Zhu	Shanghai Jiao Tong University, China
Yu Zhu	East China University of Science and Technology, China
Yucheng Zhu	Shanghai Jiao Tong University, China

Contents

Quality Assessment

Vidoeo Processing

Machine Learning

Audio and Speech Processing

Big Data

Computer Vision

Pedestrian Re-recognition Based on Memory Network and Graph Structure

Yunfeng Zhang[1], Jiaqi Cao[2], Xiaopeng Li[1], Jiarui Ou[3], Shihua Zhu[1],
Muzhou Hou[1], and Cong Cao[1]([✉])

[1] School of Mathematics and Statistics, Central South University, Changsha, China
{8201190307,182112006,zhushihua,hmzw,congcao}@csu.edu.cn
[2] Graduate School of Hebei University of Geosciences, Shijiazhuang, China
[3] Department of Dermatology of Xiangya Hospital, Central South University,
Changsha, China

Abstract. Computer interaction and public safety have great research significance and practical value. Because of the problem that the recurrent neural network used in the existing literature will produce gradient disappearance and gradient explosion when the video sequence is long. Then, we propose a Person Re-identification Network with ConvLSTM (CLPRN) network based on convolutional long and short-term memory networks to solve the short-term memory problem. And then, aiming at the problem of information fusion between frames, we propose a Person Re-identification Network with Graph Convolution (GCPRN) network based on the graph structure, introduce a multi-header attention mechanism, and measure the relationship between frames. The experimental results shows that the Rank 1 of the GCPRN network on iLIDS Video re-identification (iLIDS-VID) dataset reaches 70.58% and Rank 5 reached 81.20%, surpassing the Unsupervised Tracklet Association Learning (UTAL) and Temporal Knowledge Propagation (TKP) algorithm that reached a high level on the iLIDS-VID dataset.

Keywords: Long short-term memory networks · Graph neural network · Person re-identification

1 Introduction

Pedestrian re-recognition and target tracking, as advanced tasks of computer vision, involve many application scenarios such as automatic driving. Human-Person Re-identification also called pedestrian re-identification, abbreviated as Re-ID. Pedestrian re-identification is considered a pedestrian retrieval problem across cameras. Given a pedestrian to be retrieved, the task of pedestrian relocation is to determine whether the pedestrian appears under different cameras at the same time, or under the same camera at different times. The pedestrian to be retrieved may be an image, a video sequence, or even a text description. Due

G. Zhai et al. (Eds.): IFTC 2022, CCIS 1766, pp. 3–15, 2023.
https://doi.org/10.1007/978-981-99-0856-1_1

to the existence of more and more surveillance cameras in real life, as well as the public's demand for security, the research of intelligent monitoring systems has begun to have the necessity of research and strong practical significance.

At present, there have been made great progress in image-based person re-identification [1–3], and video-based person Re-ID has also attracted more attention, as the use of multiple images can provide a lot of temporal and spatial information [4,5]. For example, feature representation learning is a basic class of pedestrian re-identification methods that can be divided into four broad categories: global feature learning [6], local feature learning [7], auxiliary feature learning [8], and video feature learning [9]. These methods are all studied on single-frame images because single-frame images have relatively low requirements on hardware devices, which is the mainstream of pedestrian re-recognition research. However, due to the limitations of limited information in a single frame image, there is also a lot of research work focused on the use of video sequences to research pedestrian re-identification methods. Video sequence learning takes into account not only the spatial content information of pedestrians, but also the information of motion transformation between frames, but it also brings additional challenges. This paper mainly explores the effect of video sequences on pedestrian re-identification under different network structures.

Based on the initial challenge of accurately capturing temporal information, Dahjung et al. [10] added weight between spatial and temporal branches. [11] proposed a sequence fusion framework to fuse pedestrian-area feature representations at the frame level. Zhao et al. [12] used semantic information video feature separation and frame re-weighting. Because of the problem that the video is discontinuous and the pedestrian re-recognition across the camera leads to some frames being outlined, some scholars have successively proposed that the Attentive Spatial-Temporal Pooling Networks (ASTPN) selects representative information frames [13]. [14] proposed the attention module combined with segmentation detects significant and common frames. [15] used emissivity variations to handle anomalous frames in video sequences and used multi-frames to handle occluded areas. Another challenge is to deal with situations where video sequences vary in degree, Chen et al. [16] divided long video sequences into several short video sequences and then aggregate the top rankings to get a comprehensive set of embedded features. [4] have used temporal and spatial attention mechanisms to obtain a robust representation of features. [17] have incorporated both long and short relationships into the mechanism of self-attention.

However, how to better combine motion information between frames and frames, how to integrate the features between different frames, and how to measure the importance of different frames for pedestrian re-recognition has always been an important part of video sequence research. [18] have proposed a network to extract motion characteristics between frames. [19] used pose estimation to assist in judging the quality of the image, and the image with the complete pose point is a high-quality frame. Li et al. [20] proposed the concept of the most stable frames, which first used convolutional neural networks (CNN) to obtain the features of each frame image, and then calculated the distance between the features of each frame and the average frame features.

The research of these scholars has provided us with inspiration and ideas, and we have found that Long Short-Term Memory (LSTM) have natural time-series modeling capabilities, while graph neural networks have been widely used in major tasks of computer vision in recent years and have achieved good results. Based on this, we build different spatiotemporal feature fusion networks based on LSTM and graph structure and explore the differences in pedestrian spatiotemporal feature expression of video sequences under different network structures and the impact on pedestrian re-identification effect. Issues surrounding the expression of motion information between frames in a video sequence, as well as how different frames are fused and how important the frames are measured. The contributions of this paper are summarized as follows:

- We use LSTM to solve the gradient disappearance problem, and a Convolutional Long Short Term Memory (ConvLSTM) to build a network to process image sequences.
- Graph neural networks can well express the relationship between nodes and the global characteristics of the whole graph, so we build a network based on Graph Convolutional Network (GCN) structure to solve the pedestrian re-identification problem.
- Comparing the differences between the two different network structures in the pedestrian re-identification task on the dataset iLIDS-VID, the effectiveness of the proposed network is verified experimentally.

2   Preliminary

This section gives specific preparations and contains some details and introductions to ConvLSTM and graph neural networks.

2.1   The Details of ConLSTM

Much existing research used recurrent neural networks, and spatiotemporal attention mechanisms when processing video sequence data. However, these studies are either time-consuming and not robust or prone to gradient vanishing or gradient explosion problems. LSTM [21] can be seen as a variant of Recurrent Neural Network (RNN), ConvLSTM can be seen as a variant of LSTM, and the input of cell state makes our ConvLSTM has the ability to have long-term memory, ConvLSTM is often applied to video sequence data. The ConvLSTM structure is shown in Fig. 1.

2.2   The Details of Graph Neural Networks

In recent years, graph neural networks and their various variants have been widely and successfully used in various computer vision tasks due to their powerful relationship modeling capabilities. We use a space-based graph convolutional

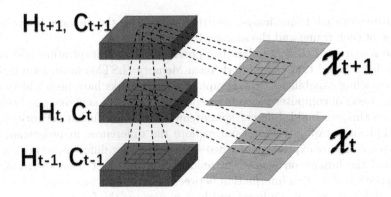

Fig. 1. The ConvLSTM structure.

neural network, based on the spatial relationship of nodes, and convolution of adjacent nodes, and spatially defines graph convolution operations. The adjacency matrix of the graph is denoted as A, so the propagation between layers can be used as shown in (Eq. 1):

$$H^{l+1} = \sigma \left(\tilde{D}^{-\frac{1}{2}} \tilde{A} \tilde{D}^{-\frac{1}{2}} H_l W_l \right) \tag{1}$$

where H is the feature of the l-layer graph, for the network inputs of the first layer are: $H^0 = X$; $\tilde{A} = A + I$, I is the identity matrix; $\tilde{D}$ is the degree matrix of $\tilde{A}$; $\tilde{D}_{ij} = \sum \tilde{A}_{ij}$ is the degree matrix stored on the diagonal, the rest of the position is 0; σ is the activation function; W^i is the network weight of the layer i. A typical network structure diagram of GCN is shown in Fig. 2.

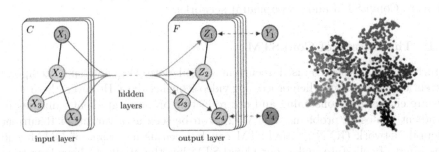

Fig. 2. GCN structure.

3   Proposed Methods

In this section, we give more details of our proposed Person Re-identification Network with ConvLSTM (CLPRN) network and Person Re-identification Network with Graph Convolution (GCPRN) network based on GCN framework.

3.1   ConvLSTM-Based CLPRN Network

We construct a CLPRN that is based on ConvLSTM to pedestrian re-identification. The details of this network is shown in Fig. 3. Each frame of the figure is processed by a CNN to extract the spatial features of pedestrians, which we called as SpatNets. For the sake of simplicity, we call the whole SpatNets function $f = C(x)$, which takes the image x as input and obtain a vector. Thus, each layer of a CNN can be represented as $C(s(t)) = Tanh(Maxpooloing(Conv(s(t))))$, which the first layer input $s(t)$ is the original image, and the input at a deeper level is the previous layer of the CNN. In the CLPRN networks, we uses $Effientnet - B0$ as SpatNets. The output f of SpatNets is a 1280-dimensional feature vector that contains the spatial characteristics of the pedestrian's entire body at t-time.

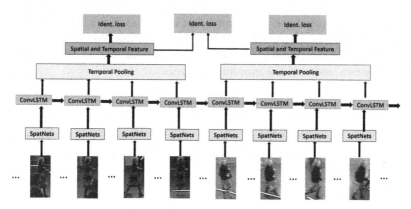

Fig. 3. CLPRN structure.

Then, f will be passed into the Convolutional Long Short-Term Memory Network (ConvLSTM), which will be mapped into the low-latitude feature space and fused with pedestrian information at previous moments. The LSTM network solves the short-term memory problem of the recurrent neural network when processing the image sequence, and avoids the occurrence of gradient disappearance and gradient explosion. At each step of the long-term short-term memory network, the cellular state of the previous moment will be combined to determine what to discard from the previous cell information, what to discard from the current cell information, and what to keep.

Because pedestrian re-identification requires the identification of a pedestrian from a video sequence, the use of long-term short-term memory networks can better capture the temporal information of pedestrians. By combining CNN and LSTM, our aim is expected to combine temporal and spatial information for pedestrians. Through the time domain pooling layer, the spatiotemporal feature vector of the sequence is obtained, and finally, the Softmax activation function is used, and the entire network structure of the CLPRN is completed.

3.2 Person Re-identification Network with Graph Convolution

GCPRN builds a graph model at the image level, each frame in the pedestrian video sequence is performed as a node in the graph model, to consider the relationship between the nodes, that is, the relationship between frames. GCN assigns the same weight to different neighbors for neighborhoods of the same order, which limits the ability of the graph to measure the degree of spatial relevance of the node. Then, we replaced the original GCN's normalized function with a neighbor node feature aggregation function that uses attention weights. In GCN, a combination of multiple self-attention structures is introduced, and each head is used to learn features in different spaces and has different attention focus, which makes the model have greater compatibility and capacity.

As shown in (Eq. 2), the characteristics of all nodes adjacent to each node together constitute the output characteristics of the node, and the characteristics of the neighboring nodes and the output characteristics of the node are obtained through the nonlinear activation function. Then, we can obtain the global geometric features of the graph structure by directly calculating the relationship between any two nodes in the graph structure.

$$H_i^\star = \sigma\left(\sum_{j \in N_i} \alpha_{ij} W \vec{h_j}\right)$$

$$\alpha_{ij} = \frac{\exp\left(\text{LeakyReLu}\left(\boldsymbol{a}_T[W]\vec{h_j}\|[W]\vec{h_j}\right)\right)}{\sum_{k \in N_i} \exp\left(\text{LeakyReLu}\left(\boldsymbol{a}_T[W]\vec{h_j}\|[W]\vec{h_k}\right)\right)} \tag{2}$$

where W is the weight matrix multiplied by the feature; α is the number of attention correlations calculated earlier; σ is nonlinear activation function; $j \in N_i$ represent all nodes that adjacent to i.

The detail framework of our GCPRN is shown in Fig. 4. Where $Graph(A, X)$ is the input to the GCPRN, containing the node feature X, which we mean the embedding obtained in the first stage, and the adjacency matrix A. We define the adjacency matrix by the similarity between features, when the Euclidean distance between any two nodes is greater than 0.5, there is an associated adjacency between the nodes, otherwise it is considered none. As shown in Fig. 4, the GCPRN network contains two attention convolutional networks, and the figure notes the definition of the graph convolution and gating mechanism is the same as augmenting GCN.

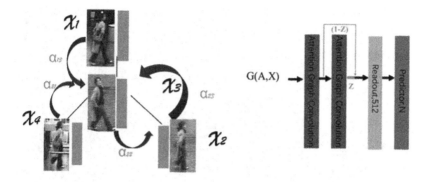

Fig. 4. GCPRN structure.

4   Experimental Results

The proposed CLPRN and GCPRN framework is used to perform the training and testing on a Dell server (hexa-core 3.20 GHz processor, 32 GB RAM and one NVIDIA GeForce GTX 2060 video card). The presented methods were implemented in Python using the TensorFlow framework.

4.1   Datasets Description

We conducted experimented with the iLIDS Video re-identification (iLIDS-VID) dataset, which was created from pedestrians captured in two non-overlapping camera views in the airport arrivals hall under a multi-camera CCTV network. There are 600 image sequences in the dataset containing 300 different individuals, each with a pair of image sequences from two camera views. The iLIDS-VID dataset is shown in Fig. 5. Also, the 300 individual image sequences vary in length, ranging from 23 to 92 image frames, with an average sequence length of 73.

4.2   Implementation Details

Since the image resolution of the iLIDS-VID dataset is 64×128 size, in order to adapt to the input requirements of the convolutional neural network, the experiment first expands the image resolution to 224×224 by using bilinear interpolation upsampling. Since the iLIDS-VID dataset is small compared to other datasets, experiments flip images horizontally with a probability size of 0.5. We use enhanced dithering with a color dither of 0.4, and to prevent the model from overfitting, the experiment uses label smoothing with a smoothing factor of 0.1, as defined in (Eq. 3):

$$P_i = \begin{cases} 1 - \theta, & \text{if } i = y \\ \frac{\theta}{K-1} & \text{otherwise} \end{cases} \tag{3}$$

Fig. 5. The iLIDS-VID dataset.

To facilitate the comparison of the effects of the model, we use Accuracy as an evaluation metric, as defined in (Eq. 4):

$$Acc = \frac{y_i^{tp} + y_i^{tn}}{y_i^{tp} + y_i^{tn} + y_i^{ft} + y_i^{fn}} \qquad (4)$$

where y_i^{tp}, y_i^{fp}, y_i^{tn} and y_i^{fn} are true positives, false positives, true negatives, and false negatives on the iLIDS-VID dataset of i.

In addition, we tried the effect of the number of blocks on the effect of the model, using the feature map of $576 \times 16 \times 16$ in Effientnet-B0 as input to ConvLSTM. The final nonlinear activation function uses Softmax, and the formula is defined as shown in (Eq. 5):

$$\text{Softmax}(x) = \frac{\exp(W * x)}{\sum_{c=1}^{C} \exp(W * x)} \qquad (5)$$

Our methods are implemented using Python and Keras. We use Adam (Eq. 6) as the optimizer, the learning rate starts at 0.001, β_1 starts at 0.9, and β_2 starts at 0.999, the ε parameter is $1e-8$. The training was performed with 100 epochs, and after 30 epochs, the learning rate decreased with an sqrt factor of 0.1.

$$E\left[g^2\right]_n = \beta_1 E\left[g^2\right]_{n-1} + (1 - \beta_1)\, g_n^2$$

$$E\left[\overline{g^2}\right]_n = \frac{E\left[g^2\right]_n}{(1 - \beta_1^n)}$$

$$E[\bar{g}]_n = \frac{E[g]_n}{(1 - \beta_2^n)} \tag{6}$$

$$\theta_n = \theta_{n-1} - \alpha\frac{E[\bar{g}]_n}{\sqrt{E\left[\overline{g^2}\right]_n + \epsilon}} g_n$$

When the learning rate drops to $0.5e - 6$, it no longer decreases. The evaluation index selects the validation set accuracy rate, and when the increased or decreased threshold exceeds 0.0001, the model effect is considered to have changed. The loss function that we used Cross-Entropy, as shown in (Eq. 7):

$$\text{Cross-Entropy}(Y, P) = -\frac{1}{N}\sum_{i=0}^{N-1}\sum_{k=0}^{K-1} y_{i,k}\log\left(p_{i,k}\right) \tag{7}$$

4.3 Experimental Results

Regarding the spatial feature classifier, we have selected five models, including Wide Residual Network (WRN), ResNet-34, SeResnet-50, MobileNet-V3, and EffientNet-B0, to classify pedestrian data. Among them, WRN tries to improve network performance by widening the residual network from the width of the network based on the residual network (ResNet). The structure of EffientNet-B0 is to include the inverted residuals and linear bottlenecks modules used in the MobileNet-V2 architecture, combined with the Squeeze-and-Excitation (SE) modules in SeResnet-50. However, EfficientNet proposes a complex correlation coefficient and adjusts it in three dimensions. To illustrate the performance differences between these five network structures, we experimented with these five models on the iLIDS-VID dataset. To verify the effectiveness of CLPRN and GCPRN for pedestrian re-identification, we experimented with the dataset iLIDS-VID.

To visualize the training process, a graph of the model loss and accuracy scores during CLPRN network training is plotted, as shown in Fig. 6. When the CLPRN network is trained to about 50 Epochs, the loss on the training set and the test set begins to gradually slow down and tends to converge; the accuracy rate on the training set and the test set no longer rises, and the model tends to converge. Moreover, CLPRN has an accuracy of 95.24% on the test set, no overfitting, and has a good generalization.

The model accuracy curves during the training of the GCPRN network are shown in Fig. 7. When the GCPRN network is trained to about 50 Epochs, the accuracy rate on the training set no longer rises, and the model tends to converge. Moreover, the accuracy rate of GCPRN in the training set is 99.18%.

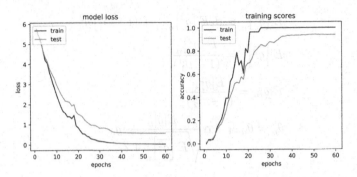

Fig. 6. The curve of CLPRN training process.

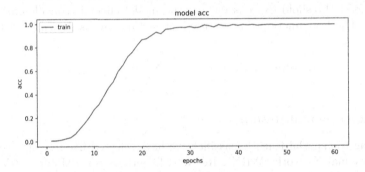

Fig. 7. The curve of GCPRN training process.

The experimental results are shown in Table 1, the accuracy of the CLPRN network is 95.24%, which is better than the EffientNet-B0 model, and the accuracy rate is improved by 5.49%. The accuracy of GCPRN is 99.19%, which is 9.44% higher than the Effientnet-B0 model, 3.95% higher than the CLPRN model, and 51.14% higher than the worst WRN model.

Next, we perform pedestrian matching on the dataset iLIDS-VID, and the experimental results are shown in Table 2. From the data in the table, CLPRN's Rank1 is 45.02% and Rank5 is 56.78%. It can be seen that the CLPRN method we propose in Rank1 is second only bad to the Temporal Knowledge Propagation (TKP) network, and the effect is significantly better than the other three contrast networks, which fully proves the effectiveness of the CLPRN network for image feature fusion in pedestrian re-recognition. In addition, we found that CLPRN is not as effective as other networks in rank5, and only better than the Sparsity for Re-Identification (SRID) network, indicating that the CLPRN effect needs to be improved. Therefore, we propose more advanced GCPRN networks with the precision of rank1 are 70.58% and Rank5 is 81.20%. As you can see, on Rank1, the GCPRN method we proposed is far ahead of other methods. Compared to the second-ranked Temporal Knowledge Propagation (TKP), it increased by 15.98%; compared to the third-ranked CLPRN, it increased by 25.56%. On Rank5, our

Table 1. Comparison with the classification results of different model.

Model	Accuracy GCPRN	**VS** Other models
WRN	48.05%	↑ **51.14%**
Resnet-34	55.56%	↑ 43.63%
SeResnet-50	60.09%	↑ 39.10%
MobileNet-V3	65.00%	↑ 34.19%
EffientNet-B0	89.75%	↑ 9.44%
CLPRN	95.24%	↑ **3.95%**
GCPRN	**99.19%**	–

Table 2. Comparison with the search results of different model.

Model	Rank1	Rank5	GCPRN ↑ (Rank1)	GCPRN ↑ (Rank5)
SRID [22]	24.90%	44.50%	↑ **45.68%**	↑ **36.70%**
STFV3D+KISSME [23]	44.30%	71.70%	↑ 26.28%	↑ 9.50%
UTAL [24]	35.10%	59.00%	↑ 35.48%	↑ 22.20%
TKP [25]	54.60%	79.40%	↑ **15.98%**	↑ **1.80%**
CLPRN	45.02%	56.78%	↑ 25.56%	↑ 24.42%
GCPRN	**70.58%**	**81.20%**	–	–

GCPRN approach also ranks first. Compared to the second-ranked Temporal Knowledge Propagation (TKP), GCPRN increased by 1.8%; compared to the third-ranked STFV3D (Spatio-temporal Fisher vector)+KISSME (keep it simple and straightforward metric), it increased by 9.5%. This experiment also fully demonstrates the effect of GCPRN in extracting pedestrian spatiotemporal features.

5   Conclusion

In this paper, two different aggregation networks CLPRN and GCPRN are proposed around different fusion methods between the same pedestrian frame. Among them, CLPRN is based on the LSTM network, which first uses EffientNet-B0 to extract the spatial features of pedestrians in the order of pedestrian video sequences, and then constructs a spatial feature combination based on ConvLSTM to extract pedestrians to determine pedestrian identifications. Experimental results have shown that CLPRN networks exceed the SRID in three contrasting algorithms, showing their feasibility. But this aggregation method is not an ideal way of fusion from an experimental point of view. Next, we proposed a GCPRN network based on a graph structure in an attempt to compensate for this shortcoming. The GCPRN network quantifies the weight size of different frames for pedestrian identification discrimination and measures the size of the correlation between frames. Experimental results showed that the GCPRN network surpasses all the other methods in classification accuracy, which proves that the GCPRN network is effective for the fusion of the overall video sequence.

Acknowledgements. This study was supported by the Hunan Province Natural Science Foundation (grant number 2022JJ30673).

References

1. Sun, Y., Zheng, L., Yang, Y., Tian, Q., Wang, S.: Beyond part models: person retrieval with refined part pooling (and a strong convolutional baseline). In: Ferrari, V., Hebert, M., Sminchisescu, C., Weiss, Y. (eds.) ECCV 2018. LNCS, vol. 11208, pp. 501–518. Springer, Cham (2018). https://doi.org/10.1007/978-3-030-01225-0_30
2. Wang, G.Z., Yuan, Y.F., Chen, X., Li, J.W., Zhou, X.: Learning discriminative features with multiple granularities for person re-identification. In: Proceedings of the 26th ACM International Conference on Multimedia, pp. 274–282. Association for Computing Machinery, New York (2018)
3. Jin, X., Lan, C.L., Zeng, W.J., Wei, G.Q., Chen, Z.B.: Semantics-aligned representation learning for person re-identification. In: Proceedings of the AAAI Conference on Artificial Intelligence, pp. 11173–11180. AAAI Press, Palo Alto (2020)
4. Fu, Y., Wang, X.Y., Wei, Y.C., Thomas, H.: STA: spatial-temporal attention for large-scale video-based person re-identification. In: Proceedings of the AAAI Conference on Artificial Intelligence, pp. 8287–8294. AAAI Press, Palo Alto (2019)
5. Chen, Z.Q., Zhou, Z.H., Huang, J.C., Zhang, P.Y., Li, B.: Frame-guided region-aligned representation for video person re-identification. In: Proceedings of the AAAI Conference on Artificial Intelligence, pp. 10591–10598. AAAI Press, Palo Alto (2020)
6. Chen, H.R., et al.: Deep transfer learning for person re-identification. In: 2018 IEEE Fourth International Conference on Multimedia Big Data (BigMM), pp. 1–5. IEEE (2018)
7. Wu, Y.M., et al.: Adaptive graph representation learning for video person re-identification. IEEE Trans. Image Process. **29**, 8821–8830 (2020)
8. Zhu, Z.H., et al.: Aware loss with angular regularization for person re-identification. In: Proceedings of the AAAI Conference on Artificial Intelligence, pp. 13114–13121. AAAI Press, Palo Alto (2020)
9. Zhang, G.Q., Chen, Y.H., Dai, Y., Zheng, Y.H., Wu, Y.: Reference-aided part-aligned feature disentangling for video person re-identification. In: 2021 IEEE International Conference on Multimedia and Expo (ICME), pp. 1–6. IEEE (2021)
10. Dahjung, C., Khalid, T., Edward, J.D.: A two stream siamese convolutional neural network for person re-identification. In: Proceedings of the IEEE International Conference on Computer Vision, pp. 1983–1991. IEEE (2017)
11. Wang, T., Gong, S., Zhu, X., Wang, S.: Person re-identification by video ranking. In: Fleet, D., Pajdla, T., Schiele, B., Tuytelaars, T. (eds.) ECCV 2014. LNCS, vol. 8692, pp. 688–703. Springer, Cham (2014). https://doi.org/10.1007/978-3-319-10593-2_45

12. Zhao, Y.R., Shen, X., Jin, Z.M., Lu, H.T., Hua, X.S.: Attribute-driven feature disentangling and temporal aggregation for video person re-identification. In: Proceedings of the IEEE/CVF Conference on Computer Vision and Pattern Recognition, pp. 4913–4922. IEEE (2019)

13. Xu, S.J., et al.: Jointly attentive spatial-temporal pooling networks for video-based person re-identification. In: Proceedings of the IEEE International Conference on Computer Vision, pp. 4733–4742. IEEE (2017)

14. Arulkumar, S., Athira, N., Anurag, M.: Co-segmentation inspired attention networks for video-based person re-identification. In: Proceedings of the IEEE/CVF International Conference on Computer Vision, ICCV, pp. 562–572 (2019)

15. Ma, Z.A., Xiang, Z.Y.: Robust object tracking with RGBD-based sparse learning. Front. Inf. Technol. Electron. Eng. **18**(7), 989–1001 (2017)

16. Chen, D.P., Li, H.S., Xiao, T., Yi, S., Wang, X.G.: Video person re-identification with competitive snippet-similarity aggregation and co-attentive snippet embedding. In: Proceedings of the IEEE Conference on Computer Vision and Pattern Recognition, pp. 1169–1178. IEEE (2018)

17. Li, J.N., Wang, J.D., Tian, Q., Gao, W., Zhang, S.L.: Global-local temporal representations for video person re-identification. In: Proceedings of the IEEE/CVF International Conference on Computer Vision, pp. 3958–3967. IEEE (2019)

18. Liu, H., et al.: Video-based person re-identification with accumulative motion context. IEEE Trans. Circ. Syst. Video Technol. **28**(10), 2788–2802 (2017)

19. Song, G., Leng, B., Liu, Y., Hetang, C., Cai, S.: Region-based quality estimation network for large-scale person re-identification. In: Proceedings of the AAAI Conference on Artificial Intelligence, pp. 7347–7354. AAAI Press, Palo Alto (2018)

20. Li, Y.J., et al.: Video-based person re-identification by deep feature guided pooling. In: Proceedings of the IEEE Conference on Computer Vision and Pattern Recognition Workshops, pp. 39–46. IEEE (2017)

21. Shi, X.J., et al.: Convolutional LSTM network: a machine learning approach for precipitation nowcasting. In: Proceedings of the Conference on Neural Information Processing Systems, pp. 802–810. Curran Associates, Inc (2015)

22. Karanam, S., Li, Y., Radke, R.J.: Sparse re-id: block sparsity for person re-identification. In: Proceedings of the IEEE Conference on Computer Vision and Pattern Recognition Workshops, pp. 33–40. IEEE (2015)

23. Klaser, A., Marszałek, M., Schmid, C.: A spatio-temporal descriptor based on 3d-gradients. In: BMVC 2008–19th British Machine Vision Conference, Leeds, United Kingdom, pp. 1–10 (2008)

24. Li, M.X., Zhu, X.T., Gong, S.G.: Unsupervised tracklet person re-identification. IEEE Trans. Pattern Anal. Mach. Intell. **42**(7), 1770–1782 (2019)

25. Gu, X.Q., Ma, B.P., Chang, H., Shan, S, G., Chen, X.L.: Temporal knowledge propagation for image-to-video person re-identification. In: Proceedings of the IEEE/CVF International Conference on Computer Vision, pp. 9647–9656. IEEE (2019)

Pedestrian Attribute Recognition Method Based on Multi-source Teacher Model Fusion

Zhengyan Ding[✉] and Yanfeng Shang

Research Center on Internet of Things, The Third Research Institute of the Ministry of Public Security, Shanghai 201204, China
dzy_wlw@163.com

Abstract. Existing pedestrian attribute recognition (PAR) methods usually use deep models to achieve attribute classification. However, the attribute recognition models trained on the public datasets have poor generalization ability and cannot be applied to complex scenarios. Also, through the traditional multi-label classification framework and a single network model, it is difficult for different attribute features to be effectively represented and fused. Aiming at the above problems, this paper proposes a novel knowledge distillation framework based on the fusion of multi-source prior teacher models. Focusing on the diversity of datasets, architectures and knowledge, different model training schemes are designed. For ensuring the diversity and accuracy of teacher models, this paper selects models through adaptive scoring mechanism and finally adopts active learning mechanism to achieve closed-loop model optimization. Tested on four common PAR benchmark datasets, experimental results show that under the condition that the complexity of the model is unchanged, the mean accuracy is improved by 2% to 5%, compared with the baseline model.

Keywords: Pedestrian attribute recognition · Multi-source · Knowledge distillation · Active learning

1 Introduction

Pedestrian attribute recognition (PAR) is always very important in the field of intelligent video analysis. By identifying the visual attributes of the pedestrian target, including semantic information such as gender, age, clothing, and so on, it is possible to provide a structured description and rapid retrieval of the specific target.

With the continuous development of deep learning technology, especially the widespread application of convolutional neural network models for image classification, researchers also proposed the PAR method based on deep network models [1] and made many improvements as follows. Zeng et al. [2] proposed a collaborative attention sharing mechanism for pedestrian multi-attribute recognition, which is different from the traditional feature linear fusion module to realize the adaptive selection of feature channels and spatial regions. Moghaddam et al. [3] further combined with semantic information to analyze the location of different parts of the target, reducing the interference of unrelated component features on specific attribute recognition tasks, and using a lightweight backbone network to achieve the improvement of PAR efficiency. In addition, by collecting pedestrian target data in different scenarios and labeling relevant attribute information, the researchers built multiple large-scale PAR datasets, such as PA100k [4], PETA [5], RAPv1 [6] and RAPv2 [7], etc. For example, the RAP-V2 dataset contains 54 attributes of pedestrian targets, covering various global and local attributes. Global attributes mainly include gender, age, etc. and local attributes mainly include head, upper body and lower body attributes.

However, due to the inconsistent region of interest (ROI) between different attribute recognition tasks, it is difficult to effectively and comprehensively characterize the features of various attributes through a single model using traditional multi-label classification framework [8], and the fusion of multiple classification models will lead to a significant increase in computational complexity [2]. On the other hand, due to the complexity and diversity of practical application scenarios, the PAR model trained by the above public dataset has poor generalization ability in actual scenarios, especially for some difficult samples, such as occlusion, truncation, blur, etc. The existing feature optimization method usually adopts a model structure similar to the feature pyramid [9], which will lead to a significant increase in model complexity compared with the original model, and since that no prior knowledge except for scale information is introduced, the feature representation ability of the PAR model still needs to be further improved. Especially for lightweight models, the recognition accuracy is reduced more, resulting in the inability to meet the application requirements.

Focused on the above problems, this paper proposes a novel PAR method based on the fusion of multi-source teacher models, for actual tasks under the video surveillance scenario:

1) For the diversity of datasets, this paper uses sample data of different scenario categories and statistical distributions, to train the teacher model that fits multi-source data.

2) For the diversity of architectures, this paper adopts model architectures of different backbone networks and training tasks, to train the teacher model with multi-source feature representation.

3) For the diversity of knowledge, this paper introduces prior knowledge from metric learning and self-supervised learning respectively, to train the teacher model translated from multi-source knowledge.

Through the knowledge distillation framework, the above teacher models are fused by adaptive scoring mechanism, which guarantees both the diversity and accuracy in the meantime. Then, using the active learning framework, the pseudo-label of massive unlabeled data is generated, in which only a small number of uncertain samples need manual correction and the teacher model is iterated with only a small annotation cost, to realize the closed-loop optimization mechanism of the model in actual surveillance application.

2 Baseline Model

2.1 Datasets

For baseline model, this paper uses the public PAR datasets for training and testing, as shown in Fig. 1, covering various global and local attributes.

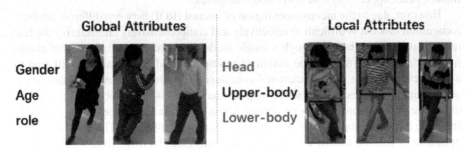

Fig. 1. Global attributes and local attributes in RAP-V2 dataset

2.2 Architecture

The multi-label classification framework is selected as baseline model architecture, in which the backbone network is ResNet50 and the specific training strategy and hyperparameter settings refer to [8].

2.3 Knowledge

In the training phase of baseline model, knowledge from attribute label information is acquired using the traditional supervised learning methods, which depend on dataset quality seriously.

3 Multi-source Datasets

3.1 Datasets of Different Scenario Categories

Considering that datasets of different scenario categories have obvious difference in lighting conditions, shooting angles, clarity, etc., this paper divides the existing training data into three different scenario categories (indoor, outdoor near and outdoor far), and integrates the scene type information as prior information into training different models, denoted as *Teacher_1_X*. The training process is shown in Fig. 2, and finally based on the fusion results of three models, the 1st teacher model is obtained through the knowledge distillation framework [10], which is recorded as *Teacher_1*.

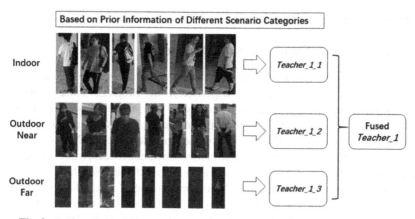

Fig. 2. Fusing multi-source teacher models based on different scenario categories

3.2 Datasets of Different Statistical Distributions

In the actual application, the PAR dataset has the problem of uneven statistical distribution, and different sampling process according to the label information for a specific attribute will lead to sample data with different statistical distributions, resulting in obvious differences in training results. Therefore, this paper takes the statistical distribution of sample data as a prior information, so as to obtain multi-source teacher models, denoted as *Teacher_2_X*. The training process is shown in Fig. 3, taking the two-categories attribute as example, three different sample distributions can be designed. Finally, the knowledge distillation framework is used for model fusion, and the 2nd teacher model is obtained, which is recorded as *Teacher_2*.

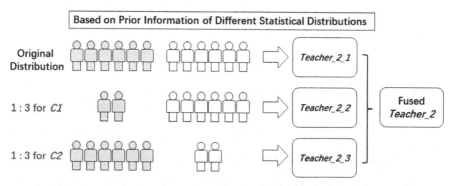

Fig. 3. Fusing multi-source teacher models based on different statistical distributions

4   Multi-source Architectures

4.1   Architectures of Different Backbone Networks

At present, the mainstream CNN networks mainly include ResNet series models [11] and Inception series models [12]. This paper selects the ResNet50 model as the baseline backbone network, and accordingly selects the InceptionV4 model as the second backbone network. In order to improve the difference of model structure, this paper further selects the ResNet50 model as the third backbone network. ResNet series models [13] are different from the traditional convolutional neural network, using Involution to replace the convolution operation. The self-attention mechanism similar to the Vision-Transformer structure [14] is integrated into the learning of visual features, so as to obtain a new type of efficient backbone network. As shown in Fig. 4, by using the model structure of three different backbone networks, a variety of teacher models are trained for heterogeneous feature representation, denoted as *Teacher_3_X*. Finally, the knowledge distillation framework is used for fusion to obtain the 3rd type of teacher model, which is recorded as *Teacher_3*.

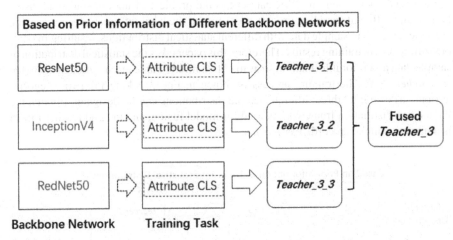

Fig. 4. Fusing multi-source teacher models based on different backbone networks

4.2   Architectures of Different Training Tasks

The PAR task is related to pedestrian key-point detection (denoted as *Extra_Task_1*) and pedestrian part segmentation (denoted as *Extra_Task_2*):

1) The visual features of PAR task rely on the spatial attention mechanism. For example, the vital features of upper body attribute are mainly located in the upper body of pedestrians, and the position information of the upper body can be judged exactly through *Extra_Task_1* and *Extra_Task_2*, thereby improving the relevant attribute recognition results, as shown in Fig. 5.

Relationship of Training Tasks: Spatial Attention Mechanism

Fig. 5. Relationship of training tasks based on spatial attention mechanism

2) The semantic features of PAR task rely on the spatial relation information between multiple local regions of the human body. For example, judging the lift-hand action through the spatial relation between the wrist and the shoulder, and combining the information of the carrying thing at the wrist position, the call-action attribute will be accurately identified, as shown in Fig. 6.

Relationship of Training Tasks: Spatial Relation Information

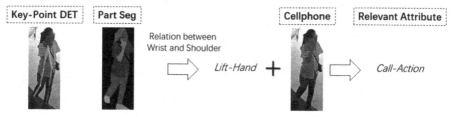

Fig. 6. Relationship of training tasks based on spatial relation information

Therefore, on the basis of the baseline model architecture (only attribute classification task), this paper further combines the two related tasks (key-point detection and part segmentation). As shown in Fig. 7, by using the combination of three different training tasks, a variety of models are trained for heterogeneous feature representation, denoted as *Teacher_4_X*. Finally, the knowledge distillation framework is used for fusion to obtain the 4th type of teacher model, which is recorded as *Teacher_4*.

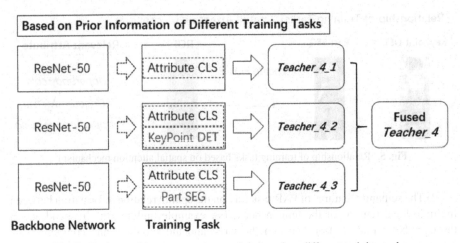

Fig. 7. Fusing multi-source teacher models based on different training tasks

5 Multi-source Knowledge

5.1 Knowledge from Metric Learning

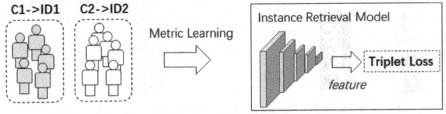

Fig. 8. Training Instance Retrieval Model Based on Metric Learning

As shown in Fig. 8, the original attribute categories are regarded as pedestrian ID information, and triplet loss is introduced to train instance retrieval model and calculate the feature similarity between pedestrian target images based on metric learning.

For actual application, the results of attribute classification model are usually limited by category knowledge from the labeled data. This paper uses the instance retrieval model to assist in mining knowledge from unlabeled data, as shown in the Fig. 9. For the massive unlabeled data, we select unsure samples of the classification model, which confidence is below the threshold (τ is 0.7), as query data, and the labeled data is used as gallery dataset. Then we obtain the pseudo-label information by voting of the top-50 results, according to the feature similarity. Finally, the data with pseudo-label information is fused with the original data to train the 5th teacher model, introducing prior knowledge from metric learning, which is recorded as *Teacher_5*.

5.2 Knowledge from Self-supervised Learning

This paper uses the Masked AutoEncoder (MAE) model [15] for data generation, as shown in Fig. 10. Firstly, we mask some regions in the original image randomly according

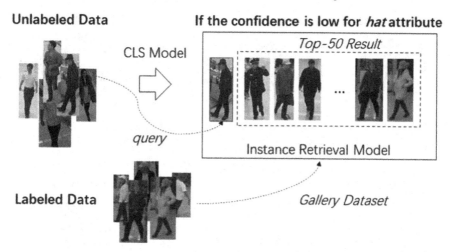

Fig. 9. Generate pseudo-label of unsure data by instance retrieval model

to a certain proportion, and then restore the image through an asymmetric encoder-decoder structure, in which the encoder module adopts the deep network model based on the Transformer structure [14] for feature coding, and the decoder module adopts a lightweight model. For the newly generated sample data, the attribute recognition model is used for classification, and only samples with consistent labels are retained, so that the key features related to the specific attribute are retained. The MAE model is trained by self-supervised learning on massive unlabeled data, so it can effectively achieve general feature representation of pedestrian targets. Finally, the newly generated data is fused with the original data, to train the 6th teacher model, introducing prior knowledge from self-supervised learning, which is recorded as *Teacher_6*.

6 Fusion of Multi-source Teacher Models

6.1 Scoring Mechanism for Model Accuracy

This paper refers to the mainstream evaluation methods for PAR task [8], and combines two metrics to score the model accuracy, as follows:

1) For attribute: mean accuracy of all attributes, denoted as *mA*.
2) For sample: F1 score of all samples, denoted as *F1_score*, representing the harmonic average of the mean accuracy and the mean recall.

In this paper, the *mA* and *F1_score* of the baseline model is used as reference value to select the teacher models. If the *mA* decreases by more than 10% or the *F1_score* decreases by more than 0.05, it is supposed that the teacher model does not meet the fusion requirements for model accuracy.

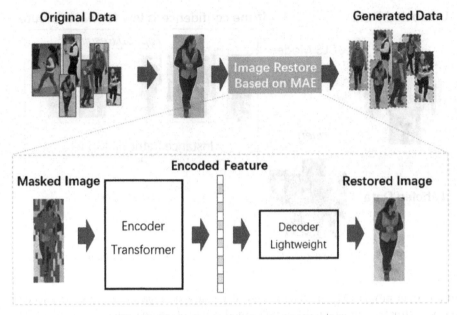

Fig. 10. Generate restored data by MAE model

6.2 Scoring Mechanism for Model Diversity

This paper refers to the mainstream evaluation methods for calculating distribution difference between model outputs [16], and uses JS divergence to score the model diversity. Compared with the baseline model, the teacher models are evaluated on the validation dataset, and the mean JS for all samples and all categories is taken as the metric for model diversity, denoted as *mJS*.

6.3 Adaptive Fusion Mechanism

Considering the accuracy and diversity requirements of the teacher model, this paper implements an adaptive fusion mechanism for multi-source teacher models, and the detailed pipeline is as follows:

Step 1: In the training phase for teacher models, we evaluate each model of different iteration cycles (the value of *epoch* varies from 1 to *max_epoch*), and select the model that meets the accuracy requirements based on *mA* and *F1_score* (see Sect. 6.1). Then the candidate model group is constructed, including all *Teacher_i* models that meet the accuracy requirements, denoted as *Group_i*. The value of *i* varies from 1 to 6, corresponding to the type number of multi-source teacher models.

Step 2: For the six different candidate model groups {*Group_i*}, the teacher models of each group are compared with the baseline model, and the model with the largest diversity is selected, that is, the value of *mJS* is the largest. Then the selected model is denoted as *BestTeacher_i*.

Step 3: For the six different best teacher models {*BestTeacher_i*}, the knowledge distillation framework is used for training, to obtain an adaptive fusion of multi-source teacher models.

6.4 Iteration Based on Active Learning

However, based on the fusion mechanism of multi-source teacher models proposed above, the optimized PAR model still has low accuracy in practical application scenarios, and data optimization needs to be realized, in which massive pseudo-label samples are supplemented. In order to reduce the labeling cost, this paper adopts an iterative optimization mechanism based on active learning, and selects the most informative samples to be labeled manually, so that the difficult samples are more focused on and the iteration efficiency is improved significantly. In this paper, a probabilistic model [17] is used to estimate the probability distribution of the output results of the PAR model and the uncertainty of the sample is calculated by combining the scoring function.

The whole iterative framework is shown in Fig. 11, only a small amount of manually corrected pseudo-label data is supplemented to achieve closed-loop optimization, from model to data.

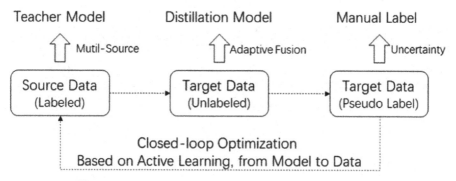

Fig. 11. The whole iterative framework based on active learning

7 Experiments

7.1 Experimental Settings

We conduct experiments on four common PAR benchmark datasets, PA100k [4], PETA [5], RAPv1 [6], RAPv2 [7]. The proposed methods are implemented with PyTorch, referring to the training parameters and evaluation metrics in [8]. As shown in Table 1, the settings of each benchmark dataset are consistent with [8].

Table 1. The settings of each benchmark dataset

Dataset	Attributes	Training Images	Testing Images
PA100k [4]	26	90,000	10,000
PETA [5]	35	11,400	7,600
RAPv1 [6]	51	33,268	8,317
PAPv2 [7]	54	67,943	16,985

7.2 Experimental Results

In the experiments, the metrics for attributes (mA) and samples (Precision, Recall, F1 score) are calculated, as shown in Tables 2, 3, 4 and 5. Compared with the existing PAR methods, our proposed method achieves a better performance, which outperforms the baseline model by 4.59%, 4.23%, 4.52%, 2.47% for mA in PA100k, PETA, RAPv1 and PARv2 respectively, under the condition that the complexity of the model is unchanged.

Table 2. Recognition results of different algorithms on the PA100k dataset (%)

Method	Backbone	mA	Precision	Recall	F1 score
DeepMAR [1]	CaffeNet	72.70	82.24	80.42	82.32
RPAR [8]	ResNet50	79.38	89.41	84.78	86.55
Baseline	ResNet50	79.00	89.17	84.71	86.49
Ours	**ResNet50**	**83.59**	90.58	89.41	**89.65**

Table 3. Recognition results of different algorithms on the PETA dataset (%)

Method	Backbone	mA	Precision	Recall	F1 score
DeepMAR [1]	CaffeNet	82.89	83.68	83.14	83.41
RPAR [8]	ResNet50	85.11	86.99	86.33	86.39
Baseline	ResNet50	83.10	90.72	82.40	85.77
Ours	**ResNet50**	**87.33**	90.01	88.52	**89.02**

Taking the RAPv2 dataset as an example, the attributes with the top-10 accuracy gain are shown in Fig. 12, and it is demonstrated that the accuracy of each attribute is improved by more than 10%, compared with baseline model.

Table 4. Recognition results of different algorithms on the RAPv1 dataset (%)

Method	Backbone	mA	Precision	Recall	F1 score
DeepMAR [1]	CaffeNet	73.79	74.92	76.21	75.56
RPAR [8]	ResNet50	78.48	82.84	76.25	78.94
Baseline	ResNet50	77.26	83.08	71.78	76.36
Ours	**ResNet50**	**81.78**	81.84	81.33	**81.53**

Table 5. Recognition results of different algorithms on the RAPv2 dataset (%)

Method	Backbone	mA	Precision	Recall	F1 score
RPAR [8]	ResNet50	78.28	77.96	79.38	78.30
Baseline	ResNet50	76.83	81.50	77.98	79.35
Ours	**ResNet50**	**79.30**	79.99	79.85	**79.91**

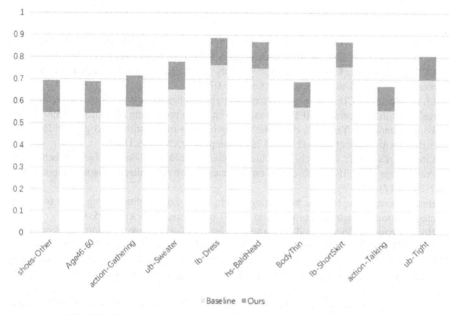

Fig. 12. The top-10 attributes for accuracy gain in the RAPv2 dataset

8 Conclusion

Focusing on the PAR task, this paper realizes the closed-loop optimization of the model by adaptive fusion of the multi-source teacher models and active learning mechanism, so as to effectively improve the feature representation ability of the recognition model.

Compared with the traditional model fusion method, this paper takes into account multi-source datasets, architectures and knowledge, which enhances the interpretability of model fusion. In the next step, this paper will further improve the diversity of model architectures, such as designing new model structures through AutoML methods.

Acknowledgements. This paper is sponsored by Shanghai Sailing Program 20YF1409300.

References

1. Li, D., Chen, X., Huang, K.: Multi-attribute learning for pedestrian attribute recognition in surveillance scenarios. In: Proceedings of the 2015 Asian Conference on Pattern Recognition. Piscataway: IEEE, pp. 111–115 (2015)
2. Zeng, H., Ai, H., Zhuang, Z., et al.: Multi-task learning via co-attentive sharing for pedestrian attribute recognition. In: 2020 IEEE International Conference on Multimedia and Expo (ICME). IEEE, pp. 1–6 (2020)
3. Moghaddam, M., Charmi, M., Hassanpoor, H.: Jointly human semantic parsing and attribute recognition with feature pyramid structure in EfficientNets. IET Image Processing (2021)
4. Liu, X., Zhao, H., Tian, M., et al.: Hydraplus-net: Attentive deep features for pedestrian analysis. In: Proceedings of the IEEE international conference on computer vision, pp. 350–359 (2017)
5. Deng, Y., Luo, P., Loy, C.C., et al.: Pedestrian attribute recognition at far distance. In: Proceedings of the 22nd ACM international conference on Multimedia, pp. 789–792 (2014)
6. Li, D., Zhang, Z., Chen, X., et al.: A richly annotated dataset for pedestrian attribute recognition (2016). arXiv preprint arXiv:1603.07054
7. Li, D., Zhang, Z., Chen, X., et al.: A richly annotated pedestrian dataset for person retrieval in real surveillance scenarios. IEEE transactions on image processing **28**(4), 1575–1590 (2018)
8. Jia, J., Huang, H., Yang, W., et al.: Rethinking of pedestrian attribute recognition: Realistic datasets with efficient method (2020). arXiv preprint arXiv:2005.11909
9. Lin, T.Y., Dollár, P., Girshick, R., et al.: Feature pyramid networks for object detection. In: Proceedings of the IEEE conference on computer vision and pattern recognition, pp. 2117–2125 (2017)
10. Bagherinezhad, H., Horton, M., Rastegari, M., et al.: Label refinery: Improving imagenet classification through label progression (2018). arXiv preprint arXiv:1805.02641
11. He, K., Zhang, X., Ren, S., et al.: Deep residual learning for image recognition. In: Proceedings of the IEEE conference on computer vision and pattern recognition, pp. 770–778 (2016)
12. Szegedy, C., Vanhoucke, V., Ioffe, S., et al.: Rethinking the inception architecture for computer vision. In: Proceedings of the IEEE conference on computer vision and pattern recognition, 2818–2826 (2016)
13. Li, D., Hu, J., Wang, C., et al.: Involution: Inverting the inherence of convolution for visual recognition. In: Proceedings of the IEEE/CVF Conference on Computer Vision and Pattern Recognition, pp. 12321–12330 (2021)
14. Dosovitskiy, A., Beyer, L., Kolesnikov, A., et al.: An image is worth 16x16 words: Transformers for image recognition at scale (2020). arXiv preprint arXiv:2010.11929
15. He, K., Chen, X., Xie, S., et al.: Masked autoencoders are scalable vision learners. In: Proceedings of the IEEE/CVF Conference on Computer Vision and Pattern Recognition, 16000–16009 (2022).

16. Cui, C., Guo, R., Du, Y., et al.: Beyond Self-Supervision: A Simple Yet Effective Network Distillation Alternative to Improve Backbones (2021). arXiv preprint arXiv:2103.05959
17. Choi, J., Elezi, I., Lee, H.J., et al.: Active learning for deep object detection via probabilistic modeling. In: Proceedings of the IEEE/CVF International Conference on Computer Vision, pp. 10264–10273 (2021)

Dense 3D Reconstruction of Non-cooperative Target Based on Pose Measurement

Jiasong Wang[1], Hao Wang[2(✉)], Yongen Zhao[3], Ronghao Yuan[2], and Fan Xu[2]

[1] Changchun Institute of Optics, Fine Mechanics and Physics, Chinese Academy of Sciences, Changchun 130000, China

[2] Aerospace System Engineering Shanghai, Shanghai Engineering Research Center of Space Robotics, Shanghai 201109, China
2938553020@qq.com

[3] School of Mechatronics Engineering, Harbin Institute of Technology, Harbin 150000, China

Abstract. To accurately identify the three-dimensional (3D) structure information of non-cooperative targets in on-orbit service tasks, this paper proposed a 3D reconstruction method combining pose measurement and dense reconstruction. Firstly, based on the depth camera, the Iterative Closest Point (ICP) algorithm is used to realize the pose measurement between each frame of the non-cooperative target. Then, the loopback detection based on the bag-of-words method is adopted to eliminate the cumulative error of pose measurement. At the same time, the sparse 3D model of the non-cooperative target can be obtained by combining feature point extraction and matching. Furthermore, secondary sampling is performed in the tracking and local mapping threads by increasing the dense mapping thread. Then, the loop thread is used to update the pose in turn. After the global pose optimization, a more accurate 3D reconstruction model can be obtained. By using point cloud optimization, the accurate dense 3D reconstruction model of a non-cooperative target is constructed. Finally, numerical simulations and experiments verify the accuracy and effectiveness of the proposed method.

Keywords: Pose measurement · Dense reconstruction · Non-cooperative target

1 Introduction

In the task of identification of non-cooperative targets, with the increase in the number of measurements, the focus of research has gradually shifted to improving the accuracy of algorithms, reducing the power consumption of on-board equipment, reducing the on-board computational burden, and improving the real-time performance of algorithms [1,2]. The 3D reconstruction technique is commonly used for non-cooperative target recognition tasks. The principle is

G. Zhai et al. (Eds.): IFTC 2022, CCIS 1766, pp. 30–43, 2023.
https://doi.org/10.1007/978-981-99-0856-1_3

the process of inscribing real scenes into mathematical models that conform to logical computer representations through depth data acquisition, image pre-processing, point cloud alignment and fusion, and surface generation [3,4]. It is mainly divided into contact 3D reconstruction and non-contact 3D reconstruction, among which, non-contact 3D reconstruction is an important research content in computer vision with higher accuracy [5].

The 3D reconstruction technology is divided into two methods, active and passive, according to the different principles [6–9]. Among them, active 3D reconstruction means to launch controllable signals to the target spacecraft to be measured, compare and analyze the launch and recovery signals, and get the depth of each point on the surface of the target spacecraft to be measured, which is divided into laser ranging method, structured light method, and signal interference method according to the difference of launch signal and launch equipment. The representative laser ranging method is the Time of flight method (TOF) [10,11]. In the early days, the TOF industrial cameras produced by German companies could obtain 3D point data within 13m by only one measurement, but the accuracy was low which only reached 1cm. The Kinect camera was used to achieve the 3D reconstruction of the target, but the Kinect is limited by the low-depth environment, which limits its application scenarios to a certain extent and makes it difficult to be practically applied in the in-orbit service missions [12].

Passive 3D reconstruction is divided into single-view measurement and multi-view measurement [13,14]. Based on the single-view measurement method, the equipment demand is small, and only one camera is needed. Without the help of other information, part of the three-dimensional reconstruction of the target can be completed. This method is mainly divided into the focal length method and the single-view image method. The focal length method is mainly divided into the focusing method and the defocusing method [15]. The focusing method requires a reasonable focal length adjustment of the camera on the service spacecraft to achieve the relative position of the camera and the target in focus. Then, using the known camera parameters, the depth between the camera and the observed point is calculated by the imaging model of the corresponding camera, which is usually centimeter-level accuracy and slow measurement speed. The defocusing rule is based on a pre-calibrated model to calculate the depth information of each point in the image [16–18]. On the other hand, the main process of 3D re-reconstruction based on multi-view images includes sparse reconstruction based on the structure from motion method (SFM) [19,20] and dense reconstruction based on multi-view stereo (MVS) [21,22].

Compared with other algorithms, the SFM algorithm can reconstruct the target and obtain the sparse point cloud model of the target only by obtaining the image captured by the camera in a different relative pose from the target. The 3D reconstruction method based on multi-view images has the following advantages. Firstly, it can acquire camera parameters automatically in the process of reconstruction. Secondly, not only the sparse point cloud of the target can be obtained, but also the dense point cloud model of the target can be obtained. Finally, the algorithm has high real-time performance. Lhuillier et al. proposed a high real-time 3D reconstruction quasi-dense method [23]. Furukawa et al. proposed a patch-based multi-view stereo vision algorithm, which performs well in the existing quasi-dense matching algorithms [24].

The 3D structure of a non-cooperative target is the key information for in-orbit services, and an algorithm for dense 3D reconstruction of the target needs to be studied in order to obtain accurate 3D structure information of the target. After obtaining the bit poses of feature points on the target, a sparse target point cloud based on feature points can be reconstructed, but recovering the 3D structure information of the target using only feature points will produce insufficient information. Therefore, this part requires secondary sampling of the image to get more structural information points, make the structural information points participate in the positional update and global optimization, then choose a suitable point cloud filtering method to process the point cloud, and finally get an accurate target dense 3D reconstruction model to pave the way for the subsequent in-orbit service. Nowadays, 3D reconstruction in space is seldom combined with dense 3D reconstruction and positional measurement algorithms. Therefore, it becomes a new research direction for on-orbit service of non-cooperative targets in space by choosing the SLAM algorithm framework and adopting suitable methods to obtain dense point clouds.

2   Pose Estimation of Non-cooperative Targets

2.1   Pose Estimation Based on ICP Algorithm

The camera used in this paper is a binocular camera or a depth camera, and the ICP algorithm based on Singular Value Decomposition (SVD) is implemented when estimating the motion based on the 3D points between two frames.

Suppose the coordinates of the set of points in a set of well-matched images is $P = \{p_1, \cdots, p_n\}$, $P' = \{p'_1, \cdots, p'_n\}$. The positional change between the two images can be expressed as Eq. (1).

$$p_i = Rp'_i + t \quad i = 1, 2, \cdots, n \tag{1}$$

where R is posture rotation matrix and t is translational vector. Define the error expression for the i-th pair of points as

$$e_i = p_i - \left(Rp'_i + t\right) \tag{2}$$

Convert the positional solution problem to a least squares problem by finding R and t such that the sum of squares of the errors is minimized.

$$\min_{R,t} \frac{1}{2} \sum_{i=1}^{n} \left\| \left(p_i - \left(Rp'_i + t\right)\right) \right\|_2^2 \tag{3}$$

To solve the above problem, define the centers of mass of the two sets of image points as follows

$$p = \frac{1}{n} \sum_{i=1}^{n} (p_i), \quad p' = \frac{1}{n} \sum_{i=1}^{n} (p'_i) \tag{4}$$

Substituting Eq. (4) into the optimization objective function Eq. (3), the simplified optimization problem can be obtained as

$$\min_{R,t} J = \frac{1}{2} \sum_{i=1}^{n} \|p_i - p - R(p'_i - p')\|^2 + \|p - Rp' - t\|^2 \tag{5}$$

To minimize the optimization objective function, it is sufficient to minimize the first term and zero the second term, so the ICP problem is transformed into the following steps:

Step 1. The center-of-mass position of the two frames is calculated, and then the coordinates of each point in the image after decentering are calculated. This yields

$$q_i = p_i - p, \quad q'_i = p'_i - p' \tag{6}$$

Step 2. Calculate the rotation matrix R as follows

$$R^* = \arg\min_{R} \frac{1}{2} \sum_{i=1}^{n} \|q_i - Rq'_i\|^2 = \frac{1}{2} \sum_{i=1}^{n} (q_i^T q_i + q_i^T R^T R q'_i - 2q_i^T R q'_i) \tag{7}$$

where

$$\sum_{i=1}^{n} -q_i^T R q'_i = \sum_{i=1}^{n} -tr\left(Rq'_i q_i^T\right) = -tr\left(R \sum_{i=1}^{n} q'_i q_i^T\right) \tag{8}$$

Define matrix $W = \sum_{i=1}^{n} q_i q_i'^T$ and perform singular value decomposition as

$$W = U\Sigma V^T \tag{9}$$

If the matrix W is full rank, the rotation matrix R can be obtained as

$$R = UV^T \tag{10}$$

Step 3. Based on the resulting rotation matrix, the translation vector t is calculated as

$$t^* = p - Rp' \tag{11}$$

2.2   Pose Error Compensation Based on Loop Detection

The ICP algorithm solves the frame-to-frame motion relationship, but it is not accurate enough to characterize the target spacecraft trajectory and determine the relative spacecraft poses only through the positional parameters obtained between adjacent frames. This is because by matching the relationship between adjacent frames only, the positional error obtained from each frame calculation will have a cumulative effect on all subsequent motion estimates. Therefore, the error will gradually increase during the continuous measurement of the target spacecraft's attitude, even until the measurement results diverge.

To solve the above problem, this section proposes the concept of loopback detection. When the spacecraft processes the image information obtained from the camera, it not only compares it with the previous frame, but also compares it with the historical frames to distinguish the similarities or even the similarities among them. In the absence of loopback, the spacecraft's attitude estimation is inaccurate due to the influence of errors in the historical frames on subsequent frames. With the addition of local loopback detection, certain constraints are added between multiple adjacent frames, and the errors can be reduced. However, in loopback detection, it is necessary to constantly determine whether the current relative position appears in the previous. To solve the above problem, the bag-of-words method [25] is used in this section. The principle is to describe an image using the types of features on the image and the number of each feature point, independent of the location where the features appear. The schematic diagram of the algorithm for the bag-of-words method to determine the loopback is shown in Fig. 1.

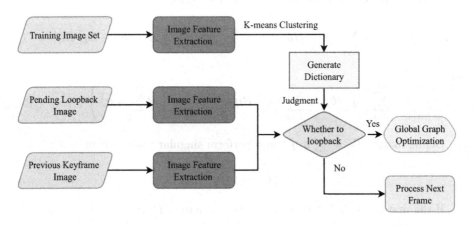

Fig. 1. Schematic diagram of loopback detection based on bag-of-words method

According to the principle of the bag-of-words method, the k-means cluster algorithm [26] is used to design the bag-of-words structure, and the image set of the European Space Agency is selected for training to get a dictionary book suitable for the task of positional measurement and dense 3D reconstruction facing non-cooperative targets in space. After getting the dictionary tree, the depth-first search algorithm can complete the frequency statistics of each feature in the two images and then perform loopback detection. If the loopback detection is passed, global graph optimization [27] is performed; otherwise, it is sufficient to continue the processing for the next frame. Ultimately, the overlap of point clouds is reduced, which makes the point clouds more accurate.

3   Dense 3D Reconstruction of Non-cooperative Target

In order to perform in-orbit servicing of failed spacecraft and space debris in space, it is necessary to obtain more accurate 3D model information of the target, including structure, dimensions, etc. Dense 3D reconstruction is a good solution to this need. Therefore, in this chapter, we will start from sparse 3D reconstruction and perform dense 3D reconstruction of the target by adding new threads, and the 3D model of the target will be post-processed with certain point clouds to finally obtain an accurate 3D reconstruction model of the target.

When the pose measurement is performed on the target, the 3D spatial information of the feature points on the target can be known, and then the feature point cloud model is formed, but the feature points are supposed to sparse the image, so the point cloud obtained is also a sparse point cloud model, as shown in Fig. 2.

Fig. 2. Sparse 3D reconstruction model

As can be seen from Fig. 2, the obtained sparse 3D reconstruction model can roughly determine the 3D dimensional information of the non-cooperative target, but the target structure and the load carried by the target are difficult to distinguish, making it difficult to continue the subsequent in-orbit service missions. Therefore, a dense 3D reconstruction of this target is needed. In this section, we first add the dense reconstruction threads to the original algorithm framework and then perform point cloud post-processing on the obtained dense point cloud to obtain an accurate 3D reconstruction model.

3.1 Algorithm Structure of Dense Reconstruction

To obtain the dense point cloud model of the target spacecraft, it is necessary to add the dense map building thread to the original program framework, and then obtain the dense 3D model of the target. The algorithm structure is shown in Fig. 3.

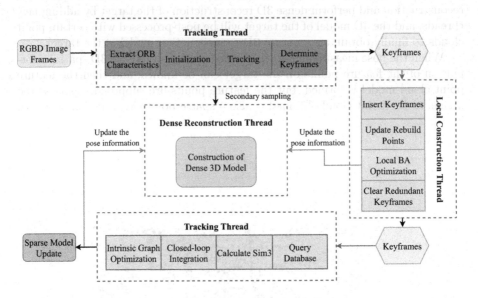

Fig. 3. Algorithm structure diagram for 3D dense reconstruction thread

As can be seen in Fig. 3, in the tracking thread, the images obtained by the camera are processed and rough positional measurements are obtained while the target image is sampled twice to obtain a dense point cloud. Then, in the local map building thread, the updated poses are passed to the second sampled point cloud, so that the point cloud is adjusted once for the poses to obtain a more accurate 3D point cloud model. Finally, in the closed-loop thread, after considering the closed-loop detection, the global poses are optimized and updated for the whole, and the updated poses are passed to the once updated point cloud model to obtain an accurate dense 3D reconstruction model of the target.

3.2 Point Cloud Post-Processing

In the process of building a map of the point cloud, it is necessary to filter the point cloud appropriately to obtain a better visual effect. In this section, three filters are used in turn: a statistical filter for outlier removal, a voxel filter based on voxel grid downsampling, and a radius filter for secondary removal of outlier points after downsampling.

The optimization strategies performed sequentially in the sampling process are as follows:

(1) When getting the point cloud generated in each frame, the points that exceed the valid range of depth values are eliminated. This is because if the points in the point cloud are outside the valid range of depth values, the confidence level of the depth values will decrease dramatically and affect the stability of the algorithm.

(2) Using statistical filtering to remove isolated noise points. That is, the statistical filter is used to count the distance information between each 3D point and the N points closest to the point. And by removing the points that are too far from the mean, the noise points isolated outside the point cloud are also deleted. Finally, the points in the main body of the point cloud are retained.

(3) Adopting voxel network filter to realize point cloud descending sampling. In the process of imaging non-cooperative targets by depth cameras, the point clouds of targets from different viewpoints are retained, and therefore, the fused point clouds will have some overlap. This overlap phenomenon not only greatly occupies the memory of the servicing spacecraft, but also deteriorates the visibility of the point clouds. The voxel filtering selects a cube of a certain size, i.e., a voxel, and within this voxel, a representative point is selected. Downsampling in the voxel space is achieved, which saves a lot of storage space and makes the 3D point cloud structure more clear.

(4) Remove outliers again with the radius filter. This filter performs secondary removal of outlier points from the point cloud after downsampling, and some of the regions with fewer features through the statistical filter after downsampling appear to have fewer point clouds after downsampling, making it difficult to determine whether they belong to the target spacecraft's own features, which has an impact on the target 3D reconstruction and subsequent recognition work. Therefore, this form of sparse point cloud is removed by the radius filter to make the 3D reconstructed point cloud clearer.

4   Experiment

The experiments in this section are divided into two part. The first part is to obtain non-cooperative spacecraft position information using ICP algorithm and loopback detection. The other part is to reconstruct the non-cooperative spacecraft using the dense 3D reconstruction algorithm.

Table 1. Environmental parameters of the experiment

Experimental environment	Environmental parameter
Time of duration	41.24 s
Actual trajectory length	14.795 m
Mean translational velocity	0.365 m/s
Mean angular velocity	27.891 deg/s
Trajectory size	17.1 m × 17.1 m × 17.1 m

The experiment uses the TUM dataset with the environmental parameters shown in Table 1. And the depth camera parameters are shown in Table 2.

Table 2. Camera parameters

Camera parameters	Value		
Camera internal reference matrix	$\begin{bmatrix} 517.3 & 0 & 318.6 \\ 0 & 516.5 & 255.3 \\ 0 & 0 & 1 \end{bmatrix}$		
Tangential distortion parameters	0.2624 00.9531 $-$ 0.0054		
Radial distortion parameters	0.0026 1.1633		

The position error of the non-cooperative spacecraft obtained from the optimized measurements using the ICP algorithm and loopback detection is shown in Fig. 4, and the attitude error is shown in Fig. 5.

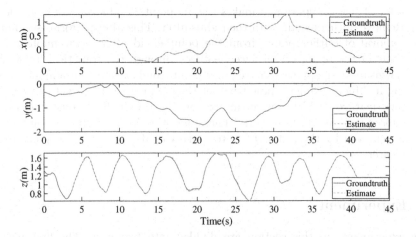

Fig. 4. Position comparison curve

From Fig. 4 and Fig. 5, it can be seen that the actual motion state information of the non-cooperative spacecraft can be well estimated by using the positional measurement method proposed in this paper. And the specific estimation errors are shown in Table 3 and Table 4.

In Table 3 and Table 4, the absolute errors reflect the direct difference between the estimated and true poses, which reflect the direct accuracy errors of the positional measurement as well as the global consistency. The relative errors mainly describe the precision of the difference between the poses of the target to be observed in the two frames at a certain time difference, which are equivalent to

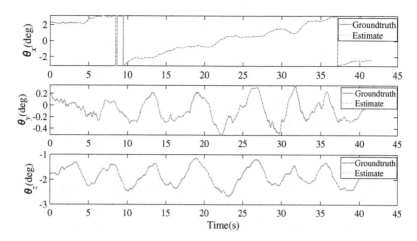

Fig. 5. Attitude comparison curve

Table 3. Position measurement error

Error type	Absolute position error/m	Relative position error/m
Max	0.044583	0.032203
Mean	0.012441	0.005417
Median	0.010770	0.004408
Min	0.0011881	0.000290
Rmse	0.014267	0.006592
Std	0.006982	0.003758

Table 4. Attitude measurement error

Error type	Average attitude Euler angular error /deg	Relative attitude Euler angular error /deg
Max	2.880826	1.615791
Mean	1.286589	0.312825
Median	1.258493	0.276258
Min	0.02909	0.018883
Rmse	1.351952	0.363415
Std	0.415287	0.184962

the visual odometry errors and reflect the accuracy of the positional measurement in the local time.

The method proposed in this article performs better on this dataset compared to other methods. The comparison results are shown in Table 5 for the absolute position as an example.

Table 5. Comparison of root mean square error under each algorithm

Algorithm	RMSE(translation)/m
Algorithm of this article	0.013809
Elastric Fusion(RGB-D)	0.020
Kintinuous Fusion	0.039
DVO-SLAM	0.022

From the results in Table 5, it can be seen that the method in this paper has a large improvement in the root mean square error reduction of 0.0062–0.0252m compared to other methods.

After obtaining the positional information and the sparse 3D model of the non-cooperative target, a dense 3D reconstruction is performed. The camera also adopts a depth camera. After dense 3D reconstruction, the reconstructed model before filtering is shown in Fig. 6. And the reconstructed model after filtering is shown in Fig. 7.

Fig. 6. Dense 3D reconstruction model before filtering

As can be seen in Fig. 6, the generated dense 3D point cloud effectively represents the characteristics of the target spacecraft, and the momentum wheels, gas storage equipment, heat transfer and other equipment on the satellite are clearly shown. In addition, the point cloud is uniformly distributed and the background is removed without residue. The 3D reconstructed model consists of 25230927 points before the point cloud filtering, which is reduced to 15150106 points after the filtering, and the number of point clouds is reduced by 40.0%. Before filtering, the upper layer of the target contains a large collection of noise points gathered together, but after filtering, the collection of noise points almost

Fig. 7. Dense 3D reconstruction model after filtering

disappears, and the number of discrete points around the target is also greatly reduced. Before and after filtering, no shape is lost.

In summary, after filtering, the noise points and outliers of the dense 3D reconstruction model are significantly reduced, and the structural and load information on the non-cooperative targets are clearly visible, which paves the way for the subsequent in-orbit service.

5   Conclusion

In this paper, we addressed the problem of accurate observation of non-cooperative targets in space by first solving the frame-to-frame measurement problem by ICP algorithm and using an optimization algorithm to obtain high-precision positional measurement information. Then the loopback detection algorithm was introduced to optimize the cumulative error problem caused by the long observation mission of the servicing spacecraft. On the other hand, based on the sparse 3D model about the feature points obtained from the pose measurement, the dense map building thread was added, and the coarse precision dense 3D point cloud is obtained by the secondary sampling of the tracking thread. Then, the initial update of the poses was performed in the local building thread to obtain a more accurate 3D point cloud. At the same time, in the closed-loop thread, the accurate positional values obtained by the closed-loop and global optimization were transferred to the point cloud model to obtain a dense 3D reconstruction model with accurate poses. Finally, this paper built a simulation environment for positional measurement and dense 3D reconstruction of the real object. A more accurate 3D model of the target was obtained, which layered the foundation for the possible subsequent work based on the 3D model.

References

1. Zhang, L., Wu, D.M., Ren, Y.: Pose measurement for non-cooperative target based on visual information. IEEE Access **7**, 106179–106194 (2019)
2. Liu, Y., Zhai, G., Gu, K., et al.: Reduced-reference image quality assessment in free-energy principle and sparse representation. IEEE Trans. Multimed. **20**(1), 379–391 (2017)
3. Peng, J., Xu, W., Liang, B., et al.: Virtual stereovision pose measurement of noncooperative space targets for a dual-arm space robot. IEEE Trans. Instrum. Measur. **69**(1), 76–88 (2019)
4. Liu, Y., Gu, K., Wang, S., et al.: Blind quality assessment of camera images based on low-level and high-level statistical features. IEEE Trans. Multimed. **21**(1), 135–146 (2018)
5. Kang, Z., Yang, J., Yang, Z., et al.: A review of techniques for 3D reconstruction of indoor environments. ISPRS Int. J. Geo-Inf. **9**(5), 330 (2020)
6. Gao, X.-H., Liang, B., Pan, L., Li, Z.-H., Zhang, Y.-C.: A monocular structured light vision method for pose determination of large non-cooperative satellites. Int. J. Control Autom. Syst. **14**(6), 1535–1549 (2016). https://doi.org/10.1007/s12555-014-0546-x
7. Liu, Y., Gu, K., Zhang, Y., et al.: Unsupervised blind image quality evaluation via statistical measurements of structure, naturalness, and perception. IEEE Trans. Circ. Syst. Video Technol. **30**(4), 929–9434 (2019)
8. Gibbs, J.A., Pound, M.P., French, A.P., et al.: Active vision and surface reconstruction for 3D plant shoot modelling. IEEE/ACM Trans. Comput. Biol. Bioinf. **17**(6), 1907–1917 (2019)
9. He, J., Yang, G., Liu, X., et al.: Spatio-temporal saliency-based motion vector refinement for frame rate up-conversion. ACM Trans. Multimed. Comput. Commun. Appl. (TOMM) **16**(2), 1–18 (2020)
10. Kolb, A., Barth, E., Koch, R., et al.: Time-of-flight cameras in computer graphics. In: Computer Graphics Forum, vol. 29, no. 1, pp. 141–159. Blackwell Publishing Ltd, Oxford (2010)
11. Liu, Y., Gu, K., Li, X., et al.: Blind image quality assessment by natural scene statistics and perceptual characteristics. ACM Trans. Multimed. Comput. Commun. Appl. (TOMM) **16**(3), 1–91 (2020)
12. Jalal, A., Kamal, S., Kim, D.: Shape and motion features approach for activity tracking and recognition from kinect video camera. In: 2015 IEEE 29th International Conference on Advanced Information Networking and Applications Workshops, pp. 445–450. IEEE (2015)
13. Liu, C., Li, J., Gao, J., et al.: Three-dimensional texture measurement using deep learning and multi-view pavement images. Measurement **172**, 108828 (2021)
14. Liu, Y., Gu, K., Zhai, G., et al.: Quality assessment for real out-of-focus blurred images. J. Vis. Commun. Image Representation **46**, 70–80 (2017)
15. Workman, S., Greenwell, C., Zhai, M., et al.: A method for direct focal length estimation. In: 2015 IEEE International Conference on Image Processing (ICIP), pp. 1369–1373. IEEE (2015)
16. Hu, H., Gao, J., Zhou, H., et al.: A combined binary defocusing technique with multi-frequency phase error compensation in 3D shape measurement. Optics Lasers Eng. **124**, 105806 (2020)
17. Hu, R., Liu, Y., Gu, K., et al.: Toward a no-reference quality metric for camera-captured images. IEEE Trans. Cybern. (2021)

18. Zheng, Y., Sugimoto, S., Sato, I., et al.: A general and simple method for camera pose and focal length determination. In: Proceedings of the IEEE Conference on Computer Vision and Pattern Recognition, pp. 430–437. IEEE (2014)
19. He, L., Wang, G., Hu, Z.: Learning depth from single images with deep neural network embedding focal length. IEEE Trans. Image Process. **27**(9), 4676–4689 (2018)
20. Liu, Y., Li, X.: No-reference quality assessment for contrast-distorted images. IEEE Access **8**, 84105–84115 (2020)
21. Wallace, L., Lucieer, A., Malenovský, Z., et al.: Assessment of forest structure using two UAV techniques: a comparison of airborne laser scanning and structure from motion (SfM) point clouds. Forests **7**(3), 62 (2016)
22. Gonçalves, G., Gonçalves, D., Gómez-Gutiérrez, Á., et al.: 3D reconstruction of coastal cliffs from fixed-wing and multi-rotor UAS: Impact of SfM-MVS processing parameters, image redundancy and acquisition geometry. Remote Sensing **13**(6), 1222 (2021)
23. Lhuillier, M., Quan, L.: A quasi-dense approach to surface reconstruction from uncalibrated images. IEEE Trans. Pattern Anal. Mach. Intell. **27**(3), 418–433 (2005)
24. Furukawa, Y., Ponce, J.: Accurate, dense, and robust multi-view stereopsis. IEEE Trans. Pattern Anal. Mach. Intell. **23**(8), 1362–1376 (2010)
25. Qader, W.A, Ameen, M.M., Ahmed, B.I.: An overview of bag of words; importance, implementation, applications, and challenges. In: International Engineering Conference (IEC), pp. 200–204. IEEE (2019)
26. Ahmed, M., Seraj, R., Islam, S.M.S.: The K-means algorithm: a comprehensive survey and performance evaluation. Electronics **9**(8), 1295 (2020)
27. Bai, F., Vidal-Calleja, T., Grisetti, G.: Sparse pose graph optimization in cycle space. IEEE Trans. Rob. **37**(5), 1381–1400 (2021)

River Turbidity Monitoring Based on Semi-supervised Transfer Learning

Shuangyi Xie[1,2,3,4,5], Xin Liao[1,2,3,4,5], Ruxue Bai[1,2,3,4,5],
Chengxu Zhou[1,2,3,4,5,6,7(✉)], and Ke Gu[1,2,3,4,5]

[1] Faculty of Information Technology, Beijing University of Technology, Beijing, China
[2] Engineering Research Center of Intelligent Perception and Autonomous Control, Ministry of Education, Beijing, China
[3] Beijing Laboratory of Smart Environmental Protection, Beijing, China
[4] Beijing Key Laboratory of Computational Intelligence and Intelligent System, Beijing, China
[5] Beijing Artificial Intelligence Institute, Beijing, China
[6] School of Electronic and Information Engineering, Liaoning University of Technology, Liaoning, China
zhouchengxu@lnut.edu.cn
[7] Key Laboratory of Intelligent Control and Optimization for Industrial Equipment of Ministry of Education, Dalian University of Technology, Dalian, China

Abstract. River turbidity is an important index to evaluate the quality of water environment, which is of great significance to environmental monitoring. Most of the existing monitoring methods rely on turbidity labels measured by river water quality monitoring stations. However, due to the limitation of spatial distribution of water quality monitoring stations, those turbidity data outside the monitoring range are difficult to obtain and the correlation of turbidity data between monitoring stations is poor. Using such data directly might weaken the generalization ability that the model has. In this paper, we propose a new river turbidity monitoring model based on semi-supervised transfer learning (RTMM-SSTL) to solve these problems. First, in the pre-training stage, we innovatively propose a semi-supervised training method combined with big data with pseudo labels for river turbidity monitoring to solve the problem of weakened model generalization ability. Then, the model is fine-tuned using GEE hyper spectral data with ground truth to further improve the monitoring capability of the model. Experiments conducted on the river turbidity monitoring task demonstrate that the proposed model is superior to the advanced learning models, and further proves that our semi-supervised transfer learning method performs better than the state-of-the-art supervision models.

This work was supported in part by the Beijing Natural Science Foundation under Grant JQ21014; in part by the National Science Foundation of China under Grant 62273011 and Grant 62076013; in part by the Industry-University-Research Innovation Fund for Chinese University - Blue Point Distributed Intelligent Computing Project under 2021LDA03003; in part by the Ministry of Education of China under Grant 202102535002, Grant 202102535012; in part by the Key Laboratory of Intelligent Control and Optimization for Industrial Equipment of Ministry of Education, Dalian University of Technology under Grant LICO2022TB03.

G. Zhai et al. (Eds.): IFTC 2022, CCIS 1766, pp. 44–58, 2023.
https://doi.org/10.1007/978-981-99-0856-1_4

Keywords: River turbidity monitoring · Remote sensing ·
Semi-supervised transfer learning

1   Introduction

The world is in a period of rapid population growth and rapid economic development. In this situation, human's destruction of nature, excessive exploitation and consumption of resources have brought about many environmental problems [1,2]. Water pollution, as one of the top ten environmental problems facing the world, has received widespread attention. A large amount of domestic wastewater and industrial wastewater without effective treatment are directly discharged into rivers, which might cause serious river pollution [3]. This not only harms the growth of aquatic organisms, but also may cause poisoning and bacterial gastrointestinal diseases after being ingested by human beings through drinking water or food chain [4–6]. In addition, it even hides the risk of large-scale infectious disease outbreak, threatening the survival of organisms [7]. Therefore, it is necessary to monitor the water pollution [8].

Turbidity is an important index to evaluate the quality of water, which reflects the obstruction degree of light passage by suspended matter or solute molecules in water [9], which is very necessary in the monitoring of drinking water and industrial water [10]. The suspended matter in turbid river water might cause certain damage to human health. At the same time, it is also easy to cause river siltation and affect the benefits of hydraulic engineering profit [11,12]. In addition, it also affects the industrial and agricultural production activities of downstream rivers [13,14]. However, when monitoring river turbidity, it may become more difficult due to the influence of water velocity, riverbed topography, climatic conditions and man-made wastewater discharge [15–17]. Therefore, river turbidity monitoring in the task of environmental monitoring [18–20] has attracted a growing number of attention from researchers.

According to the contact degree between the measured surface and the meter, the existing river turbidity monitoring methods are mainly divided into two kinds, namely, the monitoring methods based on sensor and the monitoring methods based on satellite remote sensing. Sensors are widely used because of their low cost, low power consumption and high sensitivity. Light scattering and absorption characteristics based on suspended particles, Adzuan et al. designed an infrared turbidity sensor using infrared LED and photodiode [21]. Wang et al. developed a turbidity sensor compatible with the Internet of Things by using the monitoring principles of transmitted light and orthogonal scattered light [22]. Kirkey et al. designed an optical backscatter transducer by using low-frequency square wave modulation to suppress the interference between ambient light and frequency electromagnetic radiation of power grid [23]. Jiang et al. developed a deep-sea in-situ turbidity sensor by measuring the amplitudes of diffuse light radiation using pseudo-random sequence modulation method, considering the structure of back-scattering light path [24]. However, this sensor-based method has obvious disadvantages. First, it needs to collect water samples in the field and analyze them in the laboratory, which is time-consuming. Second, due to special devices and structure characteristics, their output results are susceptible to environmental influences such as temperature and humidity, and noise interference from complex circuit structures. Third, their monitoring coverage is very limited, which means that wider catchment areas cannot be monitored.

In contrast, the non-contact method based on remote sensing satellites can make up for the shortcomings of sensor-based methods. Zhang et al. used optical and microwave data (Landsat TM and ERS-2 SAR) to construct an empirical neural network for estimating water quality [25]. Based on remote sensing reflectance and planetary reflectance data, Xing et al. used the exponential regression model to subtract adjacent bands to improve the accuracy of river turbidity monitoring [26]. Wu et al. used the method of multiple regression in neural network to find the relationship between turbidity and radiance [27]. Considering that water turbidity is affected by time and space, Chu et al. combined linear regression, geographically and temporally weighted regression to monitor water quality [28]. Subsequently, Gu et al. first proposed a random forest ensemble model (RFE-GEE), which makes full use of the spectral correlation information to generate feature groups that are highly correlated with the entire river through a full-combination subspace, and selects the base random forest to obtain more accurate turbidity measurement results [29].

As the rise of big data technology and the rapid growth of computing power, people have gradually found that performing supervised tasks directly on large-scale labeled data with high correlation and then performing transfer learning on the target tasks can make the model perform better. But this approach relies heavily on labels. In the monitoring task of river turbidity, river turbidity data are mostly measured by water quality monitoring stations, which can be regarded as ground truth of GEE hyper spectral data in the corresponding region. This also means that it is hard to collect river turbidity information outside the monitoring area. In addition, due to the uneven spatial distribution of water quality monitoring stations, the turbidity data correlation between the monitoring stations is low. The sparsity of the data reduces the availability of hyper spectral data, and easily leads the network to fall into local optimal solution and lack of generalization ability. To overcome these problems, Gu et al. introduced a new SMDLS framework, which mainly includes a new fractal module that can enhance the nonlinear capability, a new river-like generalized regression loss function that can enhance the robustness of distortion labels, and an ensemble-induced multichannel fusion method that can enhance the generalization ability and monitoring performance of the framework [30]. It is worth noting that when using training-based methods, image quality distortion [31–34] (i.e., compression) would affect the effect of DNN training [35]. Avoiding distortion in the process of hyper spectral image processing may be a potential way to improve the accuracy of river monitoring.

In view of the difficulty in obtaining ground truth and the low correlation of data, how to make full use of the limited number of labeled GEE hyper spectral data and massive unlabeled GEE hyper spectral data to enhance the performance of the model for river environment monitoring task has become a problem of great concern. In this paper, we propose a new model for training neural networks with a semi-supervised transfer learning method combining massive GEE hyper spectral images. The proposed model mainly consists of two stages. In the first stage, we used a small amount of GEE hyper spectral data with ground truth and massive GEE hyper spectral data without ground truth to generate pseudo labels and combined them to pre-train the CNN model. The generated pseudo labels can overcome the problem of low correlation between monitoring stations. In the second stage, considering that the difference between the pseudo-label and the ground truth may lead to poor model performance, we used the ground truth of 9 monitoring stations to fine-tune the model. After experimental verification, our model can further improve the performance of the original network and is superior to the advanced supervised method.

The main contributions of our paper can be summarized in the following three aspects:

1) We propose a semi-supervised pre-training method, which makes full use of labeled GEE hyper spectral data, unlabeled GEE hyper spectral data and generated pseudo-labels to train the network for improving the generalization capability of the monitoring model.
2) We construct a semi-supervised transfer learning model combined with big data for river turbidity monitoring, which overcomes the problem that the original data is sparse and is easy to produce local optimal solution to the model, and improves the performance of the monitoring task.
3) Compared with the supervised method, the proposed semi-supervised transfer model can improve the performance of the original supervised model.

The structure of the paper is arranged as follows: Sect. 2 introduces in detail the proposed river turbidity monitoring model based on semi-supervised transfer learning (RTMM-SSTL). Section 3 compares the performance of the proposed model with mainstream and state-of-the-art learning models to verify the superiority of our model. Section 4 summarizes the whole paper.

2   Methodology

Turbidity is an important index to evaluate the river environment, which plays an important role in river prevention of pollution and protection of human health. Existing sensor-based methods are susceptible to environmental noise and internal structure interference, and satellite-based methods have problems such as high cost. In addition, due to the weak correlation of turbidity data collected between monitoring stations, the model is easy to generate local optimal solution. How to make full use of low-cost massive unlabeled data to achieve accurate monitoring of river turbidity is still a problem we need to overcome. This section introduces our RTMM-SSTL model. First, we describe the network construction process of the proposed model. Second, we introduce a pseudo-label generation method based on big data and semi-supervised idea, which is used for pre-training to make up for the problem that the supervised model is dependent

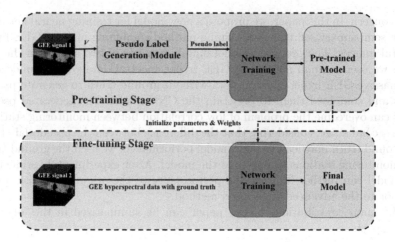

Fig. 1. The proposed RTPM-SSTL model structure. The input GEE signal 1 in the pre-training stage is composed of massive GEE hyper spectral data with few ground truth and is represented by V. GEE signal 2 in fine-tuning stage is GEE hyper spectral data with ground truth. It is noteworthy that the amount of hyper spectral data in GEE signal 1 is much more than that in GEE signal 2. However, many hyper spectral data in GEE signal 1 have no corresponding ground truth.

on labels but the existing labels are insufficient. Third, we use the ground truth to fine-tune the network for get the final network weight parameters. Figure 1 shows the structure of the proposed RTMM-SSTL model.

2.1 Network Construction

We choose the network proposed by [30] as the network structure of this model because it has shown good performance in the monitoring task of river turbidity. Its structure is shown in Fig. 2. The network uses two convolutional layers to expand the GEE signal. Four convolutional and batch normalization layers (ConvBNs) were used for feature selection. The skip connection based fractal module can adapt to self-organizing network structure. When multiple nested modules are used, the network deepens and has strong enough nonlinear mapping capability. At the same time, the fractal module can also force the ConvBN to fail through skip and sparse constraints in the convolutional layer, so as to reduce the network depth. This solves the problem of over-fitting and gradient disappearance caused by too deep network, while the problem of insufficient generalization ability of too shallow network. After considering the relationship between the performance saturation state and the number of fractal modules, four ConvBNs were selected. Subsequently, in order to make each subnetwork cooperate better, ensemble-induced multichannel fusion method is used to merge network blocks, which reduces the interference caused by outliers, avoids the phenomenon of network degradation, and increases the diversity of single channel networks to improve the robustness. Finally, a dense fully connected layer is used to estimate the turbidity of the river water.

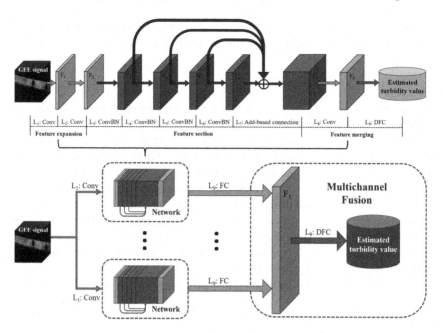

Fig. 2. Network structure of proposed model. 'Conv' stands for convolution operation. 'ConvBN' stands for the 'Conv' and batch normalization. 'DFC' stands for a dense fully connected layer. 'FC' stands for feature concatenation.

Due to the characteristics of the device and structure of the sensor itself, it is easy to be affected by environmental noise (small noise), which reduces the accuracy of the label. At the same time, the remote sensing signal in GEE is also easy to be affected by terrain and solar radiation (big noise). In order to overcome their interference from them in the training process and enhance the robustness of model, the loss function here uses riverway-like generalized regression loss:

$$
l_{RGR} = \begin{cases}
\dfrac{1}{H} \displaystyle\sum_{h=1}^{H} (y_l^h - y_p^h)^4 + \beta, & 0 < |y_l^h - y_p^h| < \varepsilon \\[3mm]
\dfrac{\alpha}{H} \displaystyle\sum_{h=1}^{H} (y_l^h - y_p^h)^2, & \varepsilon \leq |y_l^h - y_p^h| \leq \epsilon \\[3mm]
\dfrac{\theta}{H} |y_l^h - y_p^h| + \gamma, & \text{otherwise}
\end{cases}
\tag{1}
$$

where h represents the index. y_l^h is the ground truth of the h-th element, and y_p^h is the corresponding predicted value. H stands for the number of elements. $\beta = 0.1000, \alpha = 0.6325, \theta = 1.0000, \gamma = 0.5623$ were set to ensure the derivability of this loss function. Besides, ε and ϵ are used to distinguish different levels of noise. (1) combines the advantages of L_2 loss function, orthogonal function, and L_1 loss function: L_2 loss function can increase the stability of the network and accelerate its convergence [42]; Quadrature function can improve the anti-interference ability of small noise; L_1 loss function is robust to outliers.

2.2   Pseudo Label Generation

Semi-supervised pre-training of a limited number of hyper spectral data with ground truth and a large number of unlabeled hyper spectral images can inject information contained in ground truth into the pre-training model. Remote sensing technology based on hyper spectral has been widely used by researchers in river turbidity monitoring because of its high precision, multiple bands and rich information [36]. However, it is very expensive to obtain data from satellite-based remote sensing platforms, which is hard to meet the needs of users in practical applications. The free remote sensing data provided by Google cloud computing platform GEE (Google Earth Engine) can support the related research of river turbidity monitoring. [37,38]. Firstly, we collected a large number of GEE hyper spectral data through the GEE platform and limited ground truth provided by some water quality monitoring stations. The data consists of two parts: $V = [L, U] \in R^{d \times M}$, where $M = l + u$, L stands for labeled sample ($L = [v_1, v_2, ...v_l] \in R^{d \times l}$). U stands for unlabeled sample ($U = [v_{l+1}, v_{l+2}, ...v_l] \in R^{d \times l}$).

Considering the limited number of L and the weak correlation between them, we introduce the RFE-GEE method as the pseudo-label generation module, and use the generated river turbidity data as the pseudo-label of the unlabeled sample U. Its flow chart is shown in Fig. 3. First, we take 13 bands (13 features) in the hyper spectral data as input, and create m basis random forests using the full-combination subspace for them. Then, we use the error-minimization-based pruning algorithm to screen out n basis random forests with good performance. Finally, a regularized weight method is used to estimate the turbidity of river.

In the task of river turbidity monitoring, random subspace can skillfully combine the advantages of bootstrapping and aggregation to randomly generate feature combinations that are highly correlated with river turbidity. However, it only uses random partial features as independent training samples when training component learners. The full-combination subspace in RFE-GEE uses all feature combinations that may be highly correlated with river turbidity, where each subspace consists of a feature combination. This makes up for the unknown problem of the correlation between each band or their combination in hyper spectral data and river turbidity. Algorithm 1 introduces this full-combination subspace pseudocode. After n features of hyper spectral data are processed by this full-combination subspace, m base random forests are created. However, the obtained base random forest has different performance on ensemble [39]. The base random forest trained by the feature group with low correlation with river turbidity might reduce the overall output quality of the set. At this point, we cyclically pruned m base random forests according to the minimum error to remove poor-performing feature groups and reduce the complexity of the model, as described in Appendix A.

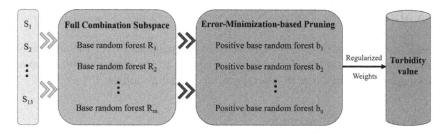

Fig. 3. Pseudo label generation module.

Algorithm 1. Framework of the Full Combination Subspace

Input: D: Data feature set; C: Component learners; m: Size of the data feature set;
Output: Multiple component learners $\{R_h|h = 1, ..., m\}$
1: initial $h = 1$;
2: **repeat**
3:    D_h=full combination from D;
4:    $R_h=C(D_h)$;
5:    $h = h + 1$;
6: **until** $h = m$

2.3   Fine-Tuning

After pre-training the model with large data V and pseudo labels, the model has a certain ability to extract the basic features of shallow layer and the abstract features of deep layer. However, the pseudo labels generated in the previous section are approximate labels, which means that they have error with the ground truth. Using the current model directly, the authenticity of the output results may be weak. Fortunately, these pseudo-labels improve the correlation between data and the number of available samples, which enhances the usability of pre-training.

Fine-tuning the pre-trained model to improve model performance is a common method in transfer learning. The fine-tuning avoids the time loss and computation loss when using massive data to retrain the model. In addition, using ground truth to further optimize the model can not only improve the monitoring performance and generalization capability of the model, but also avoid problems such as overfitting. Therefore, we retrain the model architecture and model initialization weights retained in the pre-training stage on labeled data. Here, we describe the training process of the RTPM-SSTL model again (see Fig. 1). First, we pre-train the network with the collected data V (including labeled data and unlabeled data) and the generated pseudo-labels. Then, we retrain the model architecture and model initialization weights retained in the pre-training phase on ground truth.

3   Validation

This section demonstrates the superiority of our proposed river turbidity monitoring model based on transfer learning according to the experimental setup and performance comparison with representative learning models.

3.1   Experimental Settings

Data Description. The experimental data are the open hyper spectral remote sensing data provided by the Sentinel-2 satellite acquired on the GEE platform from May 04, 2018 to March 26, 2019. In addition, we used accurate river turbidity data provided by multiple water quality monitoring stations as labels for hyper spectral images of the corresponding regions. It is worth noting that the ground truth used in fine-tuning were acquired near Juhe River, the Ch'Ao-pai River, and the Baoqiu River in Langfang, Hebei, China, with a total of 11681 Hyper spectral remote sensing data. Each data is composed of 13 bands as GEE input signals, and each band represents a dimension. According to the composition ratio of 6:2:2, the data were divided into training set, verification set and test set, respectively. In addition, a noise injection strategy [43] was used to improve the robustness of the RTPM-SSTL model, and increased the number of samples in the training set and the verification set by about 15 times.

Performance Indicators. To evaluate our river turbidity monitoring model based on transfer learning, mean square error (MSE), normalized mean gross error (NMGE) and peak signal-to-noise ratio (PSNR) are used as evaluation indices:

$$\text{MSE} = \frac{1}{n} \sum_{i=1}^{n} (q_i - \hat{q}_i)^2 \tag{2}$$

$$\text{NMGE} = \frac{\sum_{i=1}^{n} |q_i - \hat{q}_i|}{\sum_{i=1}^{n} q_i} \tag{3}$$

$$\text{PSNR} = 10 \log_{10} \left[\frac{nT^2}{\sum_{i=1}^{n} (q_i - \hat{q}_i)^2} \right] \tag{4}$$

where T represents the maximum of river turbidity. n stands for the total number of samples. q_i represents the river turbidity estimation value of the i-th sample, $\hat{q}_i$ is the corresponding label value. MSE can measure the absolute error between the ground truth and the estimation value. NMGE can be used to calculate the average error. PSNR can estimate the similarity between two input signals. When the MSE and NMGE are smaller, the PSNR value is larger and the RTMM-SSTL model presents better performance.

3.2   Performance Comparison with Representative Learning Models

To verify the performance superiority of our RTPM-SSTL model, we compare it with 9 learning models by using the above three indicators. The selected

Table 1. Performance comparison between our proposed model and nine representative models on the collected GEE hyper spectral dataset.

Model	RFR	SVR	ELM	DBN	BELM	SSEP	BLS	RFE-GEE	SMDLS	Proposed
MSE	80.722	88.579	144.38	134.84	141.69	79.403	91.025	67.133	**50.394**	40.438
NMGE	0.7139	0.7272	1.0596	0.9042	1.0549	0.6972	0.7374	0.5736	**0.5026**	0.4693
PSNR	8.8890	8.4870	6.3640	6.6610	6.4450	8.9300	8.3670	9.6890	**10.935**	11.891

models consist of two categories. The first category is four mainstream learning models: random-forest-based regression (RFR) [44], support vector regression (SVR) [45], extreme learning machine (ELM) [46] and deep belief network (DBN) [47]. The second category is the most advanced learning model: bidirectional ELM (BELM) [48], stacked selective ensemble predictor (SSEP) [39], generalized learning system (BLS) [49] and RFE-GEE [29]. The experimental results are shown in Table 1. We emphasize the best model in the comparison experiment in red, highlight the model with the suboptimal performance in bold, and underline the model with the third-best performance.

We comprehensively rank all the learning models involved in the comparison, and sort out the ranking: ELM < BELM < DBN < BLS < SVR < RFR < SSEP < RFE-GEE < SMDLS < RTMM-SSTL. Three key conclusions can be drawn from the analysis of the above experimental results. First, it is easy to observe that our model performs better than all the models participating in the comparative experiments on MSE, NMGE and PSNR metrics. Second, compared with the sub-optimal SMDLS, our model achieves a performance gain of 19.7% in MSE, 6.6% in NMGE and 8.7% in PSNR. The reason for this result may be that the RTPM-SSTL model adopts a method of combining big data and semi-supervised thinking in the pre-training stage, which improves the correlation between data, so as to better avoid the local optimal solution generated by the monitoring model and improve the generalization capability. Therefore, the performance of RTMM-SSTL with pre-training is much better than that of SMDLS without pre-training. Third, compared with the third-ranked RFE-GEE, our model achieves performance gains of 39.7%, 18.1%, and 22.7% on MSE, NMGE, and PSNR metrics, respectively. This may be due to the fact that we used the ground truth to fine-tune the pre-trained model, which to some extent overcomes the deviation problem between RFE-GEE output and the ground truth.

4   Conclusion

In this paper, we have proposed a novel RTMM-SSTL for river turbidity monitoring. According to the characteristics of river turbidity monitoring task, first of all, we have developed a semi-supervised pre-training method with pseudo labels to enhance the generalization capability of environmental monitoring mode. Then, we have applied the transfer learning method based on big data, and fine-tune the pre-trained model by ground truth for improving the model monitoring performance. Obviously, the number of labeled samples significantly affects the training results of the monitoring model. The model overcomes the overfitting and low correlation of river turbidity data, and enhances the generalization ability and monitoring ability of the model. Experimental results demonstrate that the RTPM-SSTL model is superior to the state-of-the-art models in monitoring performance. It is noteworthy that, in order to reduce the impact of image distortion on the model, we can try to improve the image quality [50,51] during image preprocessing.

Appendix A

Specifically, we first assume that the actual output of the i-th base random forest is $R_i(t)$, where $i \in [1, m]$, the probability density function at t is $P(t)$, and the output of the base random forest ensemble at t can be expressed as:

$$\hat{R}(x) = \sum_{i=1}^{m} \omega_i R_i(t) \tag{5}$$

where ω_i is the weight, $\omega_i \in [0, 1]$ and $\sum_{i=1}^{m} \omega_i = 1$. The generalization error of the i-th and ensemble base random forest on t are $G_i(t)$ and $\hat{G}(t)$. They can be obtained by the following equations:

$$G_i(t) = (R_i(t) - \bar{t})^2 \tag{6}$$

$$\hat{G}(t) = (\hat{R}_i(t) - \bar{t})^2 \tag{7}$$

where $\bar{t}$ is expected output of t. Combining Eq. (5) to Eq. (7), $\hat{G}(t)$ can be given by:

$$\hat{G}(t) = \left(\sum_{i=1}^{m} \omega_i R_i(t) - \bar{t} \right) \left(\sum_{j=1}^{m} \omega_j R_j(t) - \bar{t} \right) \tag{8}$$

Further, we assign equal significance to all the base random forests, namely $\omega = \frac{1}{m}$, we obtain:

$$\hat{G} = \sum_{i=1}^{m} \sum_{j=1}^{m} \omega_i \omega_j cor_{ij} \tag{9}$$

$$cor_{ij} = \int P(t)(R_i(t) - \bar{t})(R_j(t) - \bar{t})dt \tag{10}$$

where cor_{ij} stands for the correlation between the i-th and the j-th base random forest. It is easy to prove that $cor_{ij} = cor_{ji}$ and $cor_{ii} = er_i$.

Then, we evaluate each base random forest, selecting the ones with better performance and deleting the ones with poor performance. When testing whether the p-th learner needs to be excluded, we remove this learner and then recalculate the generalization error:

$$\widehat{G}^+ = \frac{1}{(m-1)^2} \sum_{\substack{i=1 \\ i \neq p}}^{m} \sum_{\substack{j=1 \\ j \neq p}}^{m} cor_{ij} \tag{11}$$

We believe that the final integration will be better if $\widehat{G}$ is greater than $\widehat{G}^+$ or equal to $\widehat{G}^+$ after removing the p-th base learner. According to this, we can deduce:

$$G_k \geq \frac{2m-1}{m^2} \sum_{i=1}^{m} \sum_{j=1}^{m} cor_{ij} - 2 \sum_{\substack{i=1 \\ i \neq p}}^{m} cor_{ip} = T_g \tag{12}$$

The right part of the inequality can be considered as a threshold T_g. When the generalization error is less than the base random forest, it should be removed. Then the output of the remaining n base random forest(i.e., $b = [b_1, b_2, ..., b_n]^T$) is aggregated to measure river turbidity:

$$B = \sum_{i=1}^{n} \omega_i b_i \tag{13}$$

where the weights for aggregation consists of ω_i. The least squares method can be directly used to calculate weights, but the results derived from it may have some problems such as over-fitting [40, 41]. Considering that the base random forest in b has a good effect on river turbidity measurement, there is a high correlation between them. Regularization based on L_2 is suitable for this problem. So the least square method and L_2 are considered in the loss function:

$$L(\omega) = ||B - w^T b|| + \lambda ||w||_2 \tag{14}$$

where λ represents the regularization parameter. w is a vector of weights for aggregation. We further derive the optimal weights by minimizing the loss function:

$$w^* = (b^T b + \lambda I)^{-1} b^T S \tag{15}$$

where I is an unit matrix. Finally, the river turbidity value can be obtained by combining Eq. (13) with Eq. (15).

References

1. Gu, K., Qiao, J., Li, X.: Highly efficient picture-based prediction of PM$_{2.5}$ concentration. IEEE Trans. Ind. Electron. **66**(4), 3176–3184 (2019)
2. Yue, G., Gu, K., Qiao, J.: Effective and efficient photo-based PM$_{2.5}$ concentration estimation. IEEE Trans. Instrum. Meas. **68**(10), 3962–3971 (2019)
3. Li, W., Sun, Y.: Automatic monitoring and control system of industrial sewage treatment. In: Proceedings of the Asia-Pacific Power Energy Engineering Conference, pp. 1–4 (2009)

4. Czajkowska, D., Witkowska-Gwiazdowska, A., Sikorska, I., Boszczyk-Maleszak, H., Horoch, M.: Survival of Escherichia coli serotype O157: H7 in water and in bottom-shore sediments. Pol. J. Environ. Stud. **14**(4), 423–430 (2005)
5. Zeigler, M., et al.: Outbreak of campylobacteriosis associated with a long-distance obstacle adventure race–Nevada, October 2012. Morb. Mortal. Wkly Rep. **63**(17), 375 (2014)
6. Cheng, R., et al.: Isolation and characterization of a salt-tolerant denitrifying bacterium Alishewanella sp. F2 from seawall muddy water. Sci. Rep. **10**(1), 1–11 (2020)
7. Yang, L., Yang, G., Li, H., Yuan, S.: Effects of rainfall intensities on sediment loss and phosphorus enrichment ratio from typical land use type in Taihu Basin, China. Environmental Science and Pollution Research **27**(12), 12866–12873 (2019). https://doi.org/10.1007/s11356-018-04067-0
8. Zhou, Y., Shi, S., Liu, H., Zhang, Y., Gu, K., Qiao, J.: Remote sensing inversion for river turbidity estimation based on noise injection and ensemble learning. In: Proceedings of the Chinese Association of Automation, pp. 6301–6305 (2021)
9. Kitchener, B.G., Wainwright, J., Parsons, A.J.: A review of the principles of turbidity measurement. Prog. Phys. Geogr. **41**(5), 620–642 (2017)
10. Mullins, D., Coburn, D., Hannon, L., Jones, E., Clifford, E., Glavin, M.: A novel image processing-based system for turbidity measurement in domestic and industrial wastewater. Water Sci. Technol. **77**(5), 1469–1482 (2018)
11. van Maren, D.S., Yang, S.L., He, Q.: The impact of silt trapping in large reservoirs on downstream morphology: the Yangtze River. Ocean Dyn. **63**(6), 691–707 (2013). https://doi.org/10.1007/s10236-013-0622-4
12. Sebastiaan van Maren, D., Yang, M., Wang, Z.B.: Predicting the morphodynamic response of silt-laden rivers to water and sediment release from reservoirs: Lower Yellow River, China. J. Hydraul. Eng. **137**(1), 90–99 (2011)
13. Jones, C.S., Schilling, K.E.: From agricultural intensification to conservation: sediment transport in the Raccoon River, Iowa, 1916–2009. J. Environ. Qual. **40**(6), 1911–1923 (2011)
14. Ni, J., Zhang, C., Ren, L., Yang, S.X.: Abrupt event monitoring for water environment system based on KPCA and SVM. IEEE Trans. Instrum. Meas. **61**(4), 980–989 (2012)
15. Herfort, L., et al.: Factors affecting the bacterial community composition and heterotrophic production of Columbia River estuarine turbidity maxima. MicrobiologyOpen **6**(6), e00522 (2017)
16. Jalón-Rojas, I., Schmidt, S., Sottolichio, A.: Turbidity in the fluvial Gironde estuary (southwest France) based on 10-year continuous monitoring: sensitivity to hydrological conditions. Hydrol. Earth Syst. Sci. **19**(6), 2805–2819 (2015)
17. Lee, C.S., Lee, Y.C., Chiang, H.M.: Abrupt state change of river water quality (turbidity): effect of extreme rainfalls and typhoons. Sci. Total Environ. **557**, 91–101 (2016)
18. Gu, K., Xia, Z., Qiao, J., Lin, W.: Deep dual-channel neural network for image-based smoke detection. IEEE Trans. Multimedia **22**(2), 311–323 (2020)
19. Gu, K., Zhang, Y., Qiao, J.: Ensemble meta learning for few-shot soot density recognition. IEEE Trans. Industr. Inform. **17**(3), 2261–2270 (2021)
20. Gu, K., Liu, H., Xia, Z., Qiao, J., Lin, W., Thalmann, D.: $PM_{2.5}$ monitoring: use information abundance measurement and wide and deep learning. IEEE Trans. Neural Netw. Learn. Syst. **32**(10), 4278–4290 (2021)

21. Adzuan, M.A., Rahiman, M.H.F., Azman, A.A.: Design and development of infrared turbidity sensor for Aluminium sulfate coagulant process. In: Proceedings of the IEEE 8th Control and System Graduate Research Colloquium, pp. 105–109 (2017)
22. Wang, Y., Rajib, S.S.M., Collins, C., Grieve, B.: Low-cost turbidity sensor for low-power wireless monitoring of fresh-water courses. IEEE Sens. J. **18**(11), 4689–4696 (2018)
23. Kirkey, W.D., Bonner, J.S., Fuller, C.B.: Low-cost submersible turbidity sensors using low-frequency source light modulation. IEEE Sens. J. **18**(22), 9151–9162 (2018)
24. Jiang, H., Hu, Y., Yang, H., Wang, Y., Ye, S.: A highly sensitive deep-sea in-situ turbidity sensor with spectrum optimization modulation-demodulation method. IEEE Sens. J. **20**(12), 6441–6449 (2020)
25. Zhang, Y., Pulliainen, J., Koponen, S., Hallikainen, M.: Application of an empirical neural network to surface water quality estimation in the Gulf of Finland using combined optical data and microwave data. Remote Sens. Environ. **81**(2–3), 327–336 (2002)
26. Xing, Q., Lou, M., Chen, C., Shi, P.: Using in situ and satellite hyperspectral data to estimate the surface suspended sediments concentrations in the Pearl River estuary. IEEE J. Sel. Topics Appl. Earth Obs. Remote Sens. **6**(2), 731–738 (2013)
27. Wu, J.L., Ho, C.R., Huang, C.C., Srivastav, A.L., Tzeng, J.H., Lin, Y.T.: Hyperspectral sensing for turbid water quality monitoring in freshwater rivers: empirical relationship between reflectance and turbidity and total solids. Sensors **14**(12), 22670–22688 (2014)
28. Chu, H.J., Kong, S.J., Chang, C.H.: Spatio-temporal water quality mapping from satellite images using geographically and temporally weighted regression. Int. J. Appl. Earth Obs. **65**, 1–11 (2018)
29. Gu, K., Zhang, Y., Qiao, J.: Random forest ensemble for river turbidity measurement from space remote sensing data. IEEE Trans. Instrum. Meas. **69**(11), 9028–9036 (2020)
30. Gu, K., Liu, J., Shi, S., Xie, S., Shi, T., Qiao, J.: Self-organizing multi-channel deep learning system for river turbidity monitoring. IEEE Trans. Instrum. Meas. **71**, 1–13 (2022)
31. Gu, K., Zhai, G., Yang, X., Zhang, W.: Hybrid no-reference quality metric for singly and multiply distorted images. IEEE Trans. Broadcast. **60**(3), 555–567 (2014)
32. Gu, K., Wang, S., Zhai, G., Ma, S., Lin, W.: Screen image quality assessment incorporating structural degradation measurement. In: Proceedings of the IEEE International Symposium on Circuits and Systems, pp. 125–128 (2015)
33. Yue, G., Hou, C., Gu, K., Zhou, T., Zhai, G.: Combining local and global measures for DIBR-synthesized image quality evaluation. IEEE Trans. Image Process. **28**(4), 2075–2088 (2019)
34. Sun, W., Gu, K., Ma, S., Zhu, W., Liu, N., Zhai, G.: A large-scale compressed 360-degree spherical image database: from subjective quality evaluation to objective model comparison. In: Proceedings of the IEEE International Workshop on Multimedia Signal Processing, pp. 1–6 (2018)
35. Dodge, S., Karam, L.: Understanding how image quality affects deep neural networks. In: Proceedings of the IEEE International Conference on Quality multimedia Experience, pp. 1–6 (2016)
36. Tarasov, M.K., Tutubalina, O.V.: Estimating the water turbidity in the Selenga river and adjacent waters of lake Baikal using remote sensing data.

Izv. Atmos. Ocean. Phys. **54**(9), 1353–1362 (2018). https://doi.org/10.1134/S0001433818090372

37. Govedarica, M., Jakovljević, G.: Monitoring spatial and temporal variation of water quality parameters using time series of open multispectral data. In: Proceedings of the International Conference on Remote Sensing and Geoinformation of the Environment, vol. 11174, pp. 298–307 (2019)

38. Zhou, Q., Wang, J., Tian, L., Feng, L., Li, J., Xing, Q.: Remotely sensed water turbidity dynamics and its potential driving factors in Wuhan, an urbanizing city of China. J. Hydrol. **593**, 125893 (2021)

39. Gu, K., Xia, Z., Qiao, J.: Stacked selective ensemble for $PM_{2.5}$ forecast. IEEE Trans. Instrum. Meas. **69**(3), 660–671 (2019)

40. Silva, T.C., Ribeiro, A.A., Periçaro, G.A.: A new accelerated algorithm for ill-conditioned ridge regression problems. Comput. Appl. Math. **37**(2), 1941–1958 (2018). https://doi.org/10.1007/s40314-017-0430-4

41. Gu, K., Zhou, J., Qiao, J.F., Zhai, G., Lin, W., Bovik, A.C.: No-reference quality assessment of screen content pictures. IEEE Trans. Image Process. **26**(8), 4005–4018 (2017)

42. Mao, X., Li, Q., Xie, H., Lau, R.Y., Wang, Z.: Multi-class generative adversarial networks with the L2 loss function. arXiv preprint arXiv:1611.04076, vol. 5, pp. 1057–7149 (2016)

43. Gu, K., Qiao, J., Lin, W.: Recurrent air quality predictor based on meteorology-and pollution-related factors. IEEE Trans. Industr. Inform. **14**(9), 3946–3955 (2018)

44. Breiman, L.: Random forests. Mach. Learn. **45**(1), 5–32 (2001). https://doi.org/10.1023/a:1010933404324

45. Smola, A.J., Schölkopf, B.: A tutorial on support vector regression. Stat. Comput. **14**(3), 199–222 (2004). https://doi.org/10.1023/B:STCO.0000035301.49549.88

46. Huang, G.B., Zhu, Q.Y., Siew, C.K.: Extreme learning machine: theory and applications. Neurocomputing **70**(1–3), 489–501 (2006)

47. Hinton, G.E.: Deep belief networks. Scholarpedia **4**(5), 5947 (2009)

48. Yang, Y., Wang, Y., Yuan, X.: Bidirectional extreme learning machine for regression problem and its learning effectiveness. IEEE Trans. Neural Netw. Learn. Syst. **23**(9), 1498–1505 (2012)

49. Chen, C.P., Liu, Z.: Broad learning system: an effective and efficient incremental learning system without the need for deep architecture. IEEE Trans. Neural Netw. Learn. Syst. **29**(1), 10–24 (2017)

50. Gu, K., Zhai, G., Yang, X., Zhang, W.: Deep learning network for blind image quality assessment. In: Proceedings of the IEEE International Conference on Image Processing, pp. 511–515, 2014

51. Gu, K., Li, L., Lu, H., Min, X., Lin, W.: A fast reliable image quality predictor by fusing micro-and macro-structures. IEEE Trans. Ind. Electron. **64**(5), 3903–3912 (2017)

The Fusion Oil Leakage Detection Model for Substation Oil-Filled Equipment

Zhenyu Chen[1]([✉]), Lutao Wang[1], Siyu Chen[1], and Jiangbin Yu[2]

[1] Big Data Center, State Grid Corporation of China, Beijing, China
czy9907@163.com
[2] Anhui Jiyuan Software Co., Ltd., Hefei, Anhui, China

Abstract. Under the condition of long-term high-load operation, substation equipment is prone to oil leakage, which affects the operation safety of substation equipment and the stability of the power system. This paper proposes an oil leakage detection technology based on the fusion of simple linear iterative clustering (SLIC) and Transformer sub-station equipment, which is used to solve the problem of intelligent identification of oil leakage in oil-filled equipment such as transformers and transformers in substations. This paper first uses the SLIC method to segment the image to obtain superpixel of image data, and then uses the DBSCAN method based on linear iterative clustering to cluster similar super-pixels. After training and learning, obtain the oil model with stable and accurate identification of oil leakage of substation oil-filled equipment. The experimental results show that the method proposed in this paper can efficiently identify oil leakage of substation equipment under the premise of ensuring stability, with an average recognition accuracy rate of 87.1%, which has high practicability and improves the detection and identification ability of oil leakage.

Keywords: Substation · Vision transformer · Simple linear iterative clustering · Oil leakage

1 Instruction

At present, most high-voltage equipment such as transformers, voltage/current transformers and capacitors in substations use insulating oil as insulating material, which can achieve insulation, cooling and arc extinguishing of high-voltage equip-ment. If the oil-filled equipment leaks oil, it will affect the safe and stable operation of the power grid and reduce the service life of the equipment. Therefore, it is necessary to study a method for detecting oil leakage of substation equipment, so as to realize the timely detection of oil leakage detection of equipment and improve the stability of power grid operation.

Substations are important nodes for stable and continuous power transmission. Traditional substation inspections rely on on-site inspections by professionals, result-ing in high inspection costs and low inspection efficiency. In addition, there are a lot of unsafe factors in the inspection process, which affects the personal safety of inspectors. With the use of monitoring and inspection robots in substation inspections, the pressure

G. Zhai et al. (Eds.): IFTC 2022, CCIS 1766, pp. 59–74, 2023.
https://doi.org/10.1007/978-981-99-0856-1_5

of manual inspections has been greatly reduced, but inspections rely on artificial intel-ligence recognition [1]. The combination of deep learning technology and substation inspection can greatly improve the detection efficiency [2]. Figure 1 above shows the oil leakage in several typical scenarios of the substation. The following problems can be summarized from the figure: (1) There are many equipment with oil leakage, including transformers, transformers, capacitors and other equipment. (2) The observable parts of oil leakage exist not only on the surface of the equipment, but also on the ground, with various shapes and transparency. (3) The leaking oil is transparent and similar to the shadow color of the equipment, and has no self-fixing characteristics.

Therefore, this paper proposes an oil leakage detection technology for substation equipment based on fusion SLIC, which can highlight the location of oil leakage, re-duce the influence of complex background, and improve the detection accuracy.

Fig. 1. Schematic diagram of oil leakage from substation equipment. In the picture, the background of the oil leakage part is complicated and the color is darker

At present, there are few researches on the detection of oil leakage from substation equipment. The traditional method relies on inspectors to irradiate easy-to-penetrate points such as casings and welds with flashlights, and make visual inspections through reflection, but this method has limitations in the inspection of warehouses and elevated equipment. Or regularly observe and judge through the oil level gauge, the timeliness is low.

Dong Baoguo [3] detected and segmented abnormal areas by difference method based on the color of leaking oil, and compared the color characteristics of abnormal areas in two images to obtain the result of oil leakage. However, this method relied on pictures taken when the leaking parts did not leak in the early stage for comparison. Wang Yan fused the OTSU algorithm with the detected oil leakage area by using the difference method and the segmentation method of monitoring target image, com-pared the images before and after oil leakage in the area, and analyzed and judged the oil leakage area by using the HS color histogram method. This method still relied on the images before and after oil leakage [4], which had limitations. In order to improve the detection rate of oil spill targets and reduce the influence of shadow lighting on the detection model, Huang Wenli et al. [5] proposed an attention segmentation network based on edge fusion, which made full use of the spatial background information of oil spill forms and proposed a self-attention mechanism to improve the detection rate of oil spill. Yang Minchen and Zhang Yan et al. [6] irradiated the oil leakage position with ultraviolet flashlight based on the fluorescence characteristics of the oil leakage. In a dark environment, the oil leakage position would be purple and prominent, but this method could only be detected in the dark and had limitations in the daytime sunshine conditions. Wu et al. [2] studied the detection method based on visible image information of oil leakage, used lightweight Mobilenet-SSD deep net-work model to train oil leakage pictures, and deployed them in edge equipment to achieve intelligent positioning and detection of oil leakage. This method has high practicability. Although machine learning is extremely capable of learning image features, it has limitations in the face of challenges such as the complex background and obscure features of oil seeps.

Image segmentation [7] provides an ideal method to solve images with complex back-ground interference and is one of the key technologies in CV field, especially color image segmentation [8], which can extract interesting or meaningful pixel sets and features in images [9]. Watershed segmentation algorithm [10], based on the similarity criterion, utilizes morphology and topological theory to traverses pixel sets and sub-merges pixels according to the threshold value. If the threshold value is greater than, a boundary will be formed to realize the classification of neighborhood pixels. This algorithm is susceptible to noise. In recent years, with the rapid development of artificial intelligence, image segmentation based on graph theory has also attracted widespread attention [11]. Image segmentation based on graph theory continuously optimizes the weight of pixel edge set after segmentation to achieve the purpose of minimum segmentation through opti-mization processing. GrabCut is a typical segmentation method based on graph theory [12–14]. Users input an bounding box as the seg-mentation target location to achieve the separation and segmentation of targets and complex backgrounds. However, this method has problems such as high time complexity and poor processing quality when targets and backgrounds are similar. Simple Linear Iterative Clustering (SLIC) algorithm shows advantages in generating subimages with good boundary compliance [15, 16]. SLIC is a super pixel algorithm based on K-means clustering, which has the advantages of low time complexity and better edge fitting [17]. In addition, density-based noise application spatial clustering (DBSCAN) [18, 19] performs well in grouping sub-images belonging to the same clus-ter.

Also, Vaswani et al. [20] proposed Transformer for the first time, establishing a new encoder-decoder architecture based on multi-head self-attention mechanism and feed-forward neural network. Then, Dosovitskiy et al. proposed the so-called ViT (Vision Transformer) [21], which is a complete Transformer, and has superior performance in image classification task when it is directly applied to image patch sequence. Additionally, the training process is also able to greatly simplified due to the unique advantage of the deep learning method [22–26].

In this paper, through the research of superpixel segmentation and oil leakage detection, the oil leakage detection of oil filling equipment in the substation scene is realized. Firstly, the method uses SLIC technology to perform super-pixel segmentation on oil leakage image and obtain the super-pixel segmentation result. Then, DBSCAN technology was used to cluster the segmentation results to highlight the oil leakage area. Then the image is recognized by ViT, and good recognition results are obtained. Finally, the effectiveness and feasibility of the proposed method are verified by experiments in substation scenarios. The flow of oil leakage identification method is shown in the figure below (Fig. 2).

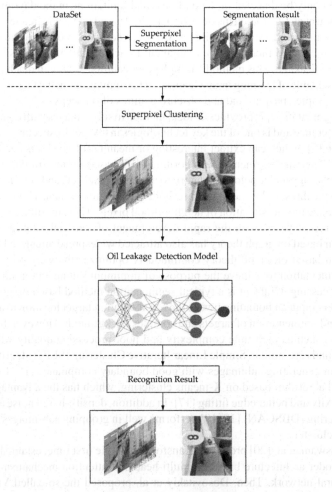

Fig. 2. Flowchart of the oil leakage detection

2   Oil Leakage Detection Based on Fusion SLIC and Transformer

2.1   Superpixel Segmentation Based on SLIC

The SLIC algorithm divides the image into superpixels, and each region has the same size and is named S. The geometric center of each region is considered as the center of the superpixel, and the coordinates of the center are updated at each iteration. Superpixels are grouped according to measurements of spatial distance d_s and d_c intensity (a measure of spatial and intensity distance).

$$d_s = \sqrt{(x_j - x_i)^2 + (y_j + y_i)^2} \tag{1}$$

$$d_c = \sqrt{(I_j - I_i)^2} \tag{2}$$

In the above formula, (x, y) represents the position of each pixel, and (I_j, I_i) represents the normalized pixel intensity.

Introducing the total distance of two measurement units d_s and d_c, calculated as follows:

$$D = \sqrt{d_c^2 + \left(\frac{d_s}{S}\right)^2 m^2} \tag{2}$$

In the above formula, m represents the compactness coefficient. The larger the parameter m, the more compact the generated superpixel area; on the contrary, the more superpixels fit the contour of the image, but the size and shape will be irregular. Figure 3 shows the results of oil leakage data based on SLIC superpixel segmentation.

2.2   Superixel Clustering Based On DBSCAN

The main idea of DBSCAN clustering is as follows: in two-dimensional space, the neighborhood within the radius of a given object is called Eps of the object, and if the Eps of the object contains at least the minimum threshold MinPts of objects with simi-lar attributes, the object is called core object. For any sample that is in the domain of the core object, it is called density direct. DBSCAN searches the cluster by examining Eps at each point in the data set. If the Eps of point p contains more than MinPts, a new cluster with p as the core object is created. DBSCAN then iteratively collects density-reachable objects directly from these core objects, which at the same time involves merging several density-reachable clusters. The process terminates when a new point cannot be added to any cluster.

The oil leakage image can be regarded as a special spatial data set, in which each pixel has a position coordinate and corresponding color value. By finding spatial clus-ters, clusters in the oil leakage image can be found effectively. Pixels with similar col-ors and spatial connections can be grouped together to form a segmented area. The difference between spatial clustering and pixel clustering lies in that image pixels are not only distributed in spatial space, but also in other feature Spaces such as color. The pixels

Fig. 3. Image super-segmentation results based on SLIC. (a) Pictures of oil leakage from equipment in substations; (b) Superpixel segmentation of images; (c) Local magnification of oil leakage

divided into a cluster should not only be spatially connected, but also similar in color. Table 1 shows the image clustering process of leaking oil based on DBSCAN.

Figure 4 shows the DBSCAN based superpixel clustering result. As can be seen from the figure, after DBSCAN clustering, oil stains with similar features are clustered together, eliminating other unrelated features and inhibiting complex background, which is conducive to the detection of oil leakage.

2.3 Oil Leakage Detection and Analysis Based on Transformer

In this paper, for the convenience of description, the service coding is simplified to X ($X = A, B, C...$), the service node coding is simplified to i ($i = 1, 2, 3...$), thus the service node identification is simplified to X_i ($X = A, B, C...; i = 1,2,3...$). The service overall topology diagram is shown in Fig. 1. The topology diagram involves four services, namely, A, B, C and D. The service A is provided by service node A_1. The service B can be provided by service node B_1, B_2, B_3, B_4, B_5. The service C is supplied by service node C_1, C_2 and C_3. The service D is provided by service node D_1 and D_2.

Table 1. Clustering process based on DBSCAN algorithm

Steps	Process
1	Input: Superpixel segmentation of images;
2	Get all pixels, assuming there are N;
3	Initialization parameters: ε, nb_min_points, $n = 0$;
4	For a new data point:
5	Find all reachable points using ε and nb_min_points;
6	Determine whether pixel n is an isolated point:
7	If yes, discard the noise point and go back to step 4;
9	If no, get a cluster;
10	Check if n is less than N:
11	If yes, go back to step 4 to continue execution;
12	If not, output the clustering result;
13	Output: Clustering results

Fig. 4. Superpixel clustering results based on DBSCAN. It can be seen from the figures that after DBSCAN pro-cessing, the background is weakened, and the oil leakage part is more prominent

The traditional Transformer is mainly composed of two parts: encoding and decoding. The multi-head attention mechanism is the core of the Transformer, which enables the model to remember the key information in the picture like the human visual attention. Refer to the image sequence processing method mentioned in the paper [21]. First, the image is cut, and the image is divided into several image blocks; secondly, the image block is sent to the trainable linear projection layer, and position encoding is performed.

Before sending the image to the encoder, the extracted image features need to be positioned. Coding, the position coding adopts the sine and cosine function to generate the position code, and then adds it to the feature image of the corresponding position. The position coding adopts the random initialization method, and the position coding function is:

$$PE(pos, 2i) = \sin\left(\frac{pos}{10000^{\frac{2i}{d_{\text{mod }el}}}}\right) \tag{4}$$

$$PE(pos, 2i+1) = \cos\left(\frac{pos}{10000^{\frac{2i}{d_{\text{mod }el}}}}\right) \tag{5}$$

In the above formula, pos is the absolute position of pixels in the feature graph, $d_{\text{mod }el}$ is the dimension of the image, $2i$ and $2i + 1$ represent parity.

The embedded patch and position encoding are superimposed to obtain an embedded vector, which is sent to the Transformer encoding layer for processing. Transformer encoding layer consists of multi-head attention and multi-layer perceptron. As shown in Fig. 5, multi-head attention contains multiple attention mechanisms, and a single attention contains query matrix, key matrix and value matrix, which are multiplied by the embedding vector The weight matrix is obtained:

$$Q = X \times W^Q \tag{6}$$

$$K = X \times W^K \tag{7}$$

$$V = X \times W^V \tag{8}$$

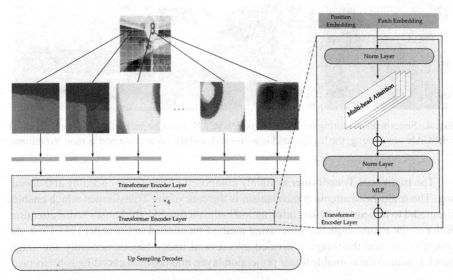

Fig. 5. Transformer Encoder structure

In the above formula, Q is query matrix, K is key matrix, V is value matrix, X is output embedding vector, W^Q, W^K and W^V corresponds to the weight matrix, respectively. The final output of the self-attention mechanism is:

$$Z = \text{soft max}\left(\frac{QK^T}{\sqrt{d_k}}\right)V \tag{9}$$

In the above formula, d_k is dimension of K.

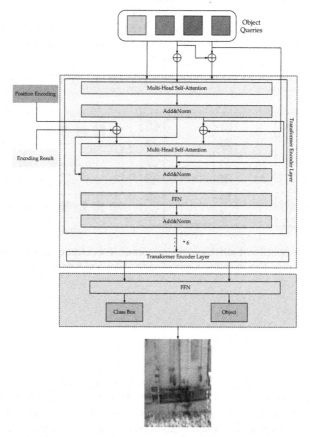

Fig. 6. Transformer Decoder structure diagram

Through the Transformer encoder, the features of the input image can be extracted. Unlike the RNN operation, there is no need for a convolutional neural network as the backbone network.

The key vector and value vector output by the encoder form a self-attention vector set, and the self-attention vector set is input to the decoding module to help the decoding module pay attention to which part of the input oil leakage image is the focus area. The decoder consists of multi-head attention and FNN layers, the location of oil leakage in the oil leakage image is obtained by three-layer linear transformation and ReLU in FFN, and the category of the object is obtained by a single linear layer. The decoder is shown in Fig. 6.

The entire oil leakage identification model is divided into three parts. The back-bone network extracts image features, the encoder-decoder performs information fu-sion, and the feedforward network performs prediction. As shown in Fig. 7 below, the backbone network is used to learn to extract the features of the original image.

The encoder reduces the dimension of the input feature image and converts the two-dimensional feature image into one-dimensional feature image structure. Finally, the output of the top encoder is an attention vector set containing key vector and value vector. The decoder uses a small number of fixed query vectors (N) as input, and dif-ferent query vectors correspond to different output vectors. The query vector is then decoded into box coordinates and class labels via FFN, resulting in N final predictions. The following figure shows the identification process of seepage oil based on ViT.

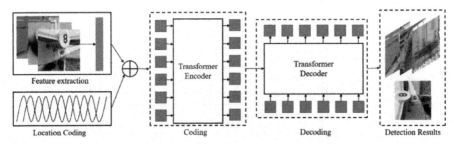

Fig. 7. Oil leakage detection results base on Transformer. The detection process includes n encod-ing modules and n decoding modules, 8 encoding modules and 8 decoding modules are used in this paper

3   Basis of Model Training

In this paper, the image recognition method based on the fusion SLIC method is adopted to verify the validity and accuracy of the image data of oil leakage from the substation end filling equipment. An image recognition experiment is designed to test the accuracy and difference between the proposed method and Transformer and faster-RCNN.

3.1   Software and Hardware

The test conditions of this paper are: CentOS 8, 64-bit operating system, Pytorch frame-work. Computer configuration: Desktop COMPUTER, NVIDIA TESLA P100, 32 GB video memory; E5-2680 V4 CPU processor, maximum main frequency 3.30 GHz, disk capacity 500 GB, Python programming language.

3.2 Path Planning

The original data set of this paper takes images for substation inspection, with a total of 4400 images of substation business scenes. In this paper, 220 images of about 5% of the 4400 images were randomly selected as the final test data, and the remaining 4180 images were used as the training data set. The original image contains two types of working conditions, oil seepage and oil leakage, which are not evenly distributed in the image. The image of the same scene is shot from multiple angles and the background is complex. The image data of oil leakage conditions of the two types of oil filling equipment used in this paper are as Fig. 8.

(a)   (b)

Fig. 8. Oil leakage images. (a) Oil spill image, Oil spills are mainly distributed on the ground; (b) Oil seepage image, Oil seepage is mainly distributed on the surface of the equipment

3.3 Experimental Results

Accuracy (*P*), Recall (*R*) and Average Precision (*AP*) are used as evaluation indexes to evaluate the proposed method. Among them, the calculation method of AP value refers to the calculation method of Everingham et al. The calculation formula of accuracy and recall rate is as follows:

$$P = \frac{TP}{TP + FP} \tag{10}$$

$$R = \frac{TP}{TP + FN} \tag{11}$$

where *TP* (True Position) is a positive sample that is predicted to be a positive sample, *FP* (False Position) is a Negative sample that is predicted to be a positive sample, and *FN* (False Negative) is a positive sample that is predicted to be a Negative sample.

In this paper, the data set of oil leakage working conditions of oil filling equipment in substation scenario is classified. The data set includes 4400 samples in total, and the number of samples of each working condition is shown as Table 2.

This paper first tests the difference of image classification results between the original sample and the expanded sample. Therefore, the image recognition models of the

Table 2. Number of samples of defect categories of electric oil-filled equipment

Type	Oil seepage images	Oil spill images
number	2300	2100

proposed method, Transformer and the Faster -RCNN method are trained by using the original data set and the expanded data set. The training data set of experiment 1 was 2200 original images, the training data set of Experiment 2 was an expanded image data set containing 3200 images, and the training data set of Experiment 3 was an expanded image data set containing 4400 images. For the data of the three experiments, 70% were selected as the training set and the remaining 30% as the verification set.

As can be seen from Table 3, Table 4 and Table 5, the method presented in this paper has shown excellent performance in experiments with different data amounts of 2200, 3200 and 4400. Among them, the identification accuracy of the method presented in this paper is 3.53% higher than Transformer on average and 11.50% higher than Faster-RCNN method on average. The identification accuracy of oil leakage is 2.00% higher than ViT and 15.9% higher than Faster-RCNN method on average. The proposed method has an average identification Precision of 4.93% higher than ViT, 16.27% higher than Faster-RCNN method, 12.53% higher than ViT and 11.70% higher than Faster-RCNN method in oil leakage category. The recognition recall rate of the proposed method in oil leakage class is 6.53% higher than ViT, 15.97% higher than Faster-RCNN method, 3.53% higher than ViT and 8.13% higher than Faster-RCNN method in oil leakage class (Figs. 9, 10 and 11).

Table 3. Accuracy comparison of table

Type	Oil seepage images (2200)	Oil seepage images (3200)	Oil seepage images (4400)	Oil spill images (2200)	Oil spill images (3200)	Oil spill images (4400)
Our method	88.3%	87.7%	89.1%	87.1%	86.5%	87.3%
ViT	84.6%	84.1%	85.8%	84.7%	84.9%	85.3%
Faster-RCNN	76.1%	77.4%	77.1%	69.5%	71.2%	72.5%

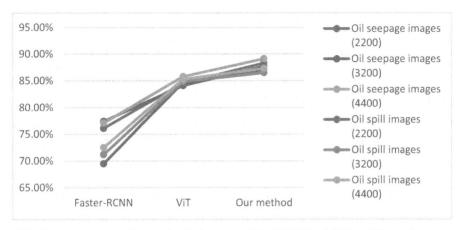

Fig. 9. The accuracy of our method is better than Fast-RCNN and ViT on different datasets

Table 4. Precision comparison of table

Type	Oil seepage images (2200)	Oil seepage images (3200)	Oil seepage images (4400)	Oil spill images (2200)	Oil spill images (3200)	Oil spill images (4400)
Our method	84.7%	86.3%	86.0%	86.6%	87.1%	87.1%
ViT	81.1%	80.4%	80.7%	74.9%	73.8%	74.5%
Faster-RCNN	69.3%	68.5%	70.4%	75.1%	75.4%	75.2%

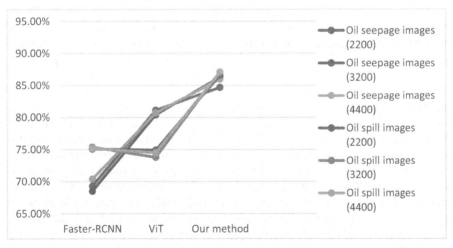

Fig. 10. The Precision of our method is better than Fast-RCNN and transformer on different datasets, while the oil spill detection based on transformer is lower than Fast-RCNN

Table 5. Recall comparison of table

Type	Oil seepage images (2200)	Oil seepage images (3200)	Oil seepage images (4400)	Oil spill images (2200)	Oil spill images (3200)	Oil spill images (4400)
Our method	82.4%	82.7%	83.4%	78.3%	78.7%	79.4%
ViT	76.7%	75.9%	76.3%	74.4%	75.8%	75.6%
Faster-RCNN	65.8%	66.7%	68.1%	69.9%	70.2%	71.9%

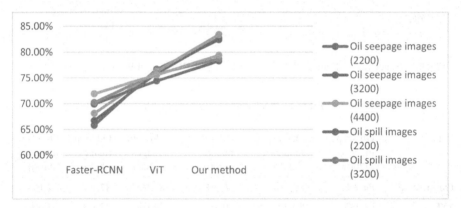

Fig. 11. On different datasets, recall comparison of our method outperforms Fast-RCNN and ViT

4 Conclusions

In this paper, aiming at the problems of difficult identification and detection of oil leakage from oil-filled equipment in daily inspection tasks of substations, the oil leakage detection technology of substation equipment based on fusion of SLIC is proposed. Firstly, the SLIC method is used to segment the image to obtain the super-pixel image data, and the oil leakage part is segmented from the background. Secondly, DBSCAN method based on linear iterative clustering was used to cluster similar superpixels to ensure accurate clustering of features of leaking oil condition images and remove the interference of background environment on leaking oil condition recognition. Finally, vision Transformer deep learning network is used to train and learn the oil leakage images collected in the substation field, and a stable and accurate oil leakage model is obtained. The oil leakage detection technology of substation equipment based on the fusion of SLIC proposed in this paper can effectively realize the accurate identification of oil leakage condition of oil-filled equipment in substation inspection task, and provide strong support for the intelligent application of power business.

Acknowledgements. This work was funded by the "Research on the key technology of intelligent annotation of power image based on image self-learning" program of the Big Data Center, State Grid Corporation of China.

References

1. Jianping, Z., Wenhai, Y., Xianhou, X., Dongfang, H.: Development and application of intelligent inspection robot in Substation. Energy and Environmental Protection **44**(01), 248–255 (2022)
2. Jianhua, W., Lihui, L., Zhe, Z., Yunpeng, L., Shaotong, P.: Oil leakage detection and recognition of substation equipment based on deep learning. Guangdong Electric Power **33**(11), 9–15 (2020)
3. Baoguo, D.: Transformer leakage oil detection based on image processing. Electric Power Construction **34**(11), 121–124 (2013)
4. Yan, W.: A Study on On-line Detection and Prevention of 35 kV Transformer Oil Leakage. Northeaat Petroleum University (2017)
5. Wenli, H., Liangjie, W., Tao, Z., et al.: A Leakage Oil Segmentation Network Based on Edge Information Fusion (2022)
6. Minchen, Y., Yan, Z., Lei, C., Jiajun, H.: Leakage oil detection method based on fluorescence characteristics of transformer oil. Electric World **59**(03), 32–34 (2018)
7. João Sousa, M., Moutinho, A., Almeida, M.: Classification of potential fire outbreaks: A fuzzy modeling approach based on thermal images. Expert Systems with Applications (2019)
8. Martin, E., Kriegel, H.P., et al. Incremental Clustering for Mining in a Data Warehousing Environment. Morgan Kaufmann Publishers Inc, pp. 323–333 (1998)
9. Yang, L., Ningning, Z.: Research on Image Segmentation Method based on SLIC. Comp. Technol. Develop. **29**(01), 75–79 (2019)
10. Parvati, K., Rao, B.S.P., Das, M.M.: Image segmentation using gray-scale morphology and marker-controlled watershed transformation. Discrete Dynamics in Nature and Society (2008)
11. Hou, Y.: Research on Image Segmentation Based on Graph Theory. Xidian University, Xi'an (2011)
12. Meng, T., Relickl, G., Veksler, O., et al.: GrabCut in one cut. IEEE international conference on computer vision. Sydney, NSW, Australia: IEEE, pp.1769–1776 (2013)
13. Meng, T., Ayed, I.B., Marin, D., et al.: Secrets of GrabCut and kernel k-means. In: IEEE international conference on computer vision. Santiago, Chile: IEEE, pp. 1555–1563 (2015)
14. Zhihua, J., Yu, N., Shibin, W., et al.: Improved GrabCut for human brain computerized tomography image segmentation. In: International conference on health information science, pp. 22–30 (2016)
15. Achanta, R., et al.: Slic superpixels. No. EPFL REPORT 149300 (2010)
16. Achanta, R., et al.: SLIC superpixels compared to state-of-the-artsuperpixel methods. Pattern Analysis and Machine Intelligence, IEEETransactions on **34**(11), 2274–2282 (2012)
17. Kanungo, T., Mount, D., Netanyahu, N., et al.: An efficient k-means clustering algorithm: analysis and implementation. IEEE Trans. Pattern Anal. Machi. Intel-lig. **24**(7), 881–892 (2000)
18. Bi, F.M., Wang, W.K., Long, C.: DBSCAN: Density-based spatial clustering of applications with noise. Journal of Nanjing University (Natural Sciences) **48**(4), 491–498 (2012)
19. Bryant, A., Cios, K.: RNN-DBSCAN: A density-based cluste-ring algorithm using reverse nearest neighbor density estimates. IEEE Trans. Knowle. Data Eng. **30**(6), 1109–1121 (2018)
20. Vaswani, A., Shazeer, N., Parmar, N., et al.: Attention is all you need. Advances in neural information processing systems, 30 (2017)
21. Dosovitskiy, A., et al.: An image is worth 16x16 words: Transformers for image recognition at scale. In ICLR (2021)
22. Gao, X.Y., Hoi Steven, C.H., Zhang, Y.D., et al.: Sparse online learning of image similarity. ACM Trans. Intellig. Sys. Technol. **8**(5), 64:1–64:22 (2017)

23. Zhang, Y., Gao, X.Y., et al.: Learning salient features to prevent model drift for correlation tracking. Neurocomputing **418**, 1–10 (2020)
24. Zhang, Y., Gao, X.Y., Chen, Z.Y., et al.: Mining spatial-temporal similarity for visual tracking. IEEE Trans. Image Processing **29**, 8107–8119 (2020)
25. Gao, X.Y., Xie, J.Y., Chen, Z.Y., et al.: Dilated convolution-based feature refinement network for crowd localization. ACM Transactions on Multimedia Computing, Communications, and Applications (2022)
26. Tang, G.Y., Gao, X.Y., et al.: Unsupervised adversarial domain adaptation with similarity diffusion for person re-identification. Neurocomputing **442**, 337–347 (2021)

A Generic Image Feature Extraction Method Towards Multiple Vision Tasks

Jiao Wei[1,2], Ping An[1,2(✉)], Kunqiang Huang[1,2], Chao Yang[1,2], and Ran Ma[1,2]

[1] School of Communication and Information Engineering, Shanghai University,
Shanghai 200444, China
anping@shu.edu.cn
[2] Key Laboratory for Advanced Display and System Application, Ministry of Education,
Shanghai 200072, China

Abstract. With the developments of artificial intelligence and image processing technology, the study of multiple vision tasks has become a hot topic in the field of computer vision, and the key to implementing vision tasks lies in the feature extraction of images. To meet the demands of modern life for multiple vision tasks and promote the deployment of artificial intelligence on edge devices, we propose an image feature extraction method applied to multiple vision tasks, which promotes the deployment of artificial intelligence on edge devices. Firstly, the function of the secondary task in multi-task learning is combined with a feature migration strategy to build a feature migration model for multiple vision tasks. Then, a generic feature extraction model based on feature fusion and feature migration is established under the guidance of image classification. The experimental results show that the proposed feature migration model with image classification as the secondary task can improve the mAP (mean average precision) of the target detection by 5.5%, and the feature migration model with target detection as the secondary task can improve the average accuracy of the image classification by 1%. The proposed generic feature extraction model can effectively implement the image classification and target detection tasks.

Keywords: Feature Extraction · Multiple Vision Tasks · Feature Migration · Feature Fusion

1 Introduction

With the booming development of cloud computing, big data, and artificial intelligence, there is an explosion of intelligent applications based on computer vision, such as intelligent surveillance, autonomous driving, medical image diagnosis, etc. It is necessary that these applications input images into algorithms for analysis and processing to achieve various vision tasks, such as image classification [1], target detection [2], semantic

This work was supported in part by the National Natural Science Foundation of China under Grants 62071287 and 61901252, Science and Technology Commission of Shanghai Municipality under Grants 20DZ2290100 and 22ZR1424300.

G. Zhai et al. (Eds.): IFTC 2022, CCIS 1766, pp. 75–84, 2023.
https://doi.org/10.1007/978-981-99-0856-1_6

segmentation [2], etc. However, traditional image processing techniques have difficulties dealing with a large number of vision tasks at the endpoints and deep learning models have shown ultra-high performance in computer vision tasks [3]. Therefore, the implementation of these vision tasks increasingly relies on deep neural networks (DNNs).

In recent years, deep learning has been applied to edge devices. Traditionally, deep learning models are deployed in the cloud, and image information is captured by image sensors on the edge devices, compressed and transmitted to the cloud computing center, and then analyzed and processed for various vision tasks, which is called "Compression-Then-Analysis, CTA" [4–6]. However, edge devices generate huge amounts of visual data, and transmitting in this mode not only puts a huge burden on the network but also causes congestion in the cloud computing center and network latency for the whole system. An effective way to solve such problems is to split the deep neural network and deploy part of it on the edge devices and the rest on the cloud, which is known as "Analysis-Then-Compression, ATC", also called "Collaborative Intelligence" (CI) [4, 7, 8].

The ATC paradigm generally requires three stages: feature extraction, feature compression, and feature transmission. And the visual task of the endpoint is often not a single task but multiple vision tasks, which require the extracted features to have high generalization capability. Besides, the features need to be compressed well during transmission. Wang [9] proposed an intermediate deep feature compression framework for multiple vision tasks, which obtains intermediate deep features with generalization capability by encoder and decoder network to implement image reconstruction and target detection tasks. For the compression and transmission of intermediate deep features in CI, [10, 11] proposed a lightweight compression method in which the codec only requires cropping, coarse quantization, binarization, and entropy coding, and [12] proposed a bit allocation algorithm according to the sensitivity of the channels in order to reduce the bit rate cost. In CI, for feature extraction towards multiple vision tasks, from the perspective of information entropy, [13–16] proposed a scalable framework that divides features into base and enhancement layers to implement multiple vision tasks. It can be seen that different vision tasks often have some identical feature information. Thus, in order to implement multiple vision tasks better, it is necessary to reduce information redundancy. In other words, it needs to extract generic features with high generalization capability.

Since feature extraction is the first step of the ATC paradigm, and the extracted features affect the performance of the vision tasks greatly, from the perspective of information entropy and feature migration, this paper proposes an image feature extraction method for multiple vision tasks including image classification and target detection. In order to select a suitable feature migration strategy and improve the performance of a single vision task, firstly, this paper combines the functions of secondary tasks in multi-task learning with feature migration strategies to build a feature migration model for multiple vision tasks. Then it is guided by the image classification task to build a generic feature extraction model based on feature fusion and feature migration, which enables the deployment of artificial intelligence on edge devices.

In this paper, Sect. 2 introduces the method proposed, and Sect. 3 gives the related experimental results. Finally, Sect. 4 concludes the whole paper.

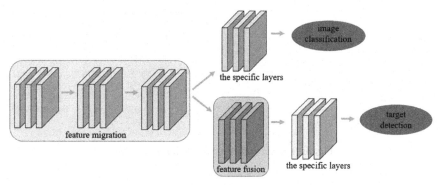

Fig. 1. The architecture of the generic feature extraction model based on feature fusion and feature migration

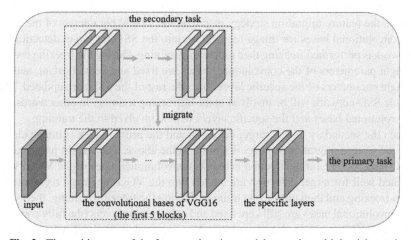

Fig. 2. The architecture of the feature migration model towards multiple vision tasks

2 Proposed Method

To realize the deployment of artificial intelligence on edge devices, the architecture of the generic feature extraction model based on feature fusion and feature migration proposed in this paper is shown in Fig. 1, where the feature migration is determined by the feature migration model towards multiple vision tasks.

The network used for image classification is the Visual Geometry Group (VGG) [17], which contains 5 blocks (convolutional bases) for feature extraction and fully connected layers for the classification task. The whole network consists of 13 convolutional layers, 5 max-pooling layers, 3 fully connected layers, and 1 output layer. The network used for target detection is Single Shot MultiBox Detector (SSD), whose backbone feature extraction network uses the convolutional bases of VGG (the first 5 blocks).

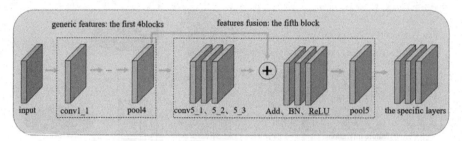

Fig. 3. The network structure of feature fusion

2.1 Feature Migration Model Towards Multiple Vision Tasks

The architecture of the feature migration model towards multiple vision tasks is shown in Fig. 2. When the secondary task is image classification and the primary task is target detection, the feature migration strategy is to load the weight parameters of the trained VGG convolutional bases for image recognition into the SSD for target detection, and the network is performed freezing then unfreezing training. During the freezing training, the weight parameters of the convolutional bases are fixed and kept constant, and only the weight parameters of the specific layers (i.e., the rest of the SSD) are updated. Then, the whole SSD network will be involved in the unfreezing training. In other words, both the convolutional bases and the specific layers will be involved in the training.

When the secondary task is target detection and the primary task is image classification, the feature migration strategy is similar to the above. The weight parameters of the SSD backbone feature extraction network (convolutional bases of the VGG) which are trained well for target detection are loaded into the VGG for image recognition to perform freezing and then unfreezing training. During the freezing training, the weights of the convolutional bases are still kept fixed and only specific layers (the fully connected layers of the VGG) are trained, and the whole VGG network is involved in the unfreezing training.

2.2 Generic Feature Extraction Model Based on Feature Fusion and Feature Migration

In Fig. 1, the feature extractor in the generic feature extraction model is still the convolutional bases of VGG (the first 5 blocks), and the feature migration is guided by the image classification task, mainly including the first 4 blocks of the convolutional bases. Besides, the feature fusion occurs in the 5th block. In this model, the specific layers pointing to the image classification are the 5th block of the original VGG and the fully connected layers. The specific layers pointing to the target detection are the rest of the SSD excluding the feature extraction network (the first 5 blocks).

In this model, the original VGG is used to implement the image classification task. When implementing the target detection task, the weights of the trained VGG's convolutional bases are loaded into the SSD by the feature migration strategy. The first 4 blocks are completely frozen to extract generic features with the same network structure and parameters. Moreover, only the feature fusion layers and specific layers are trained. For the target detection task, the extracted generic features are optimized by feature fusion. The feature fusion is performed by fusing the pool4 of the 4th block with the conv5_3 of the 5th block and followed by the BatchNormalization and LeakyReLU layers, which can increase the amount of information by feature reuse. And then the optimized generic features are input to the specific layers for processing. The network structure of the feature fusion part is shown in Fig. 3.

3 Experiments

The experiments are all implemented in a deep learning framework with Keras as the front-end and TensorFlow as the back-end, and the training and testing are performed on a GeForce RTX 2070GPU. The dataset used for target detection is a collection from voc2007 and voc2012 [19], containing 20 kinds of images. The dataset used for image classification in the feature migration model has 4159 images containing 10 kinds, which are aeroplane, bike, car, cat, dog, horse, leopards, motorbike, panda, and watch. Besides, the dataset used for image classification in the generic feature extraction model has 6891 images containing the same kinds as the target detection.

3.1 Experiments on Feature Migration Model Towards Multiple Vision Tasks

Firstly, image classification and target detection experiments are implemented by loading only the pre-trained weights obtained from the ImageNet dataset, respectively. In the image classification experiment, the input image size is set to 224×224. And the learning rate is $2e^{-3}$, whose decrement mode is "cos". Besides, the optimizer uses "SGD". The loss function uses "softmax loss", and the evaluation metric uses "top-1 accuracy". The experimental results are shown method A in Table 1, where the average accuracy is 0.98. In the target detection experiment, the input image size is 300×300, and the learning rate is $2e^{-3}$, whose decrement mode is "cos". Also, the optimizer uses "SGD", and the loss function is as follows:

$$L(x, c, l, g) = \frac{1}{N}(L_{cla}(x, c)) + \alpha L_{reg}(x, l, g) \tag{1}$$

where classification loss L_{cla} is "softmax loss", regression loss L_{reg} is "smooth L1 loss", N is the number of matches to the prior frame, α is the balance factor, l is the prior frame, g is the true frame, and c is the confidence level. Moreover, the evaluation metric uses "mean average precision (mAP)". The experimental results are shown in method A in Table 2, where the mAP is 81.3%.

Then the above already trained image classification and target detection tasks are used as secondary tasks for the experiments of the feature migration model, respectively. When target detection is the secondary task and image classification is the primary task, the convolutional bases' weight parameters of the above trained target detection model are loaded into the VGG for image classification and frozen. Only the fully connected layers of the VGG are trained, and the freezing training is set for 50 epochs, followed by the unfreeze training. When the model converges, the experimental results are shown in method B in Table 1, where the average accuracy is 0.99. The results of two methods that implement the image classification task are compared in Table 1. As can be seen from Table 1, both methods achieve high accuracy for image classification, but the image classification experiments implemented with the feature migration model show a little better performance improvement over the image classification experiments loaded with only ImageNet pre-training weights. It is obvious that the recognition accuracy for horse improves by 6% and the final average accuracy improves by 1%. It indicates that the performance of the image classification task can be improved by the feature migration model.

With image classification as the secondary task and target detection as the primary task, the convolutional bases' weight parameters of the above trained image classification model are loaded into the SSD for target detection and frozen. Only the rest layers of the SSD are trained, and the freezing training is set for 50 epochs, followed by the unfreezing training. When the model converges, the experimental results are shown in method B in Table 2, where the mAP is 86.8%. The results of the two methods to achieve the target detection experiments are compared in Table 2. The target detection experiments implemented with the feature migration model show a larger performance improvement than the target detection experiments loaded with only ImageNet pre-training weights with a 5.5% improvement in mAP. It indicates that with image classification as the secondary task, the performance of target detection can be effectively improved by feature migration.

These contrast experiments have shown that the feature migration model towards multiple vision tasks can effectively improve the performance of single vision tasks, especially when image classification is the secondary task and target detection is the primary task. The substance of the image classification task is to classify images, while the substance of the target detection task is to classify and locate targets contained in images. And it can be said that the target detection task is a more complex task based on the image classification task. Also, the same classification features exist between the two tasks. Therefore, the feature migration model through the image classification task can help the target detection task to extract more classification features. Meanwhile, in the feature migration strategy, the secondary task has a strong correlation with the primary task. On the one hand, the secondary task provides more feature information for the primary task. And on the other hand, features that are difficult to be learned by the primary task can be learned by the secondary task. This strategy alleviates the overfitting of the model to the primary task so that the model benefits from the regularization effect and finally improves the performance of the primary task.

3.2   Experiments on Generic Feature Extraction Model Based on Feature Fusion and Feature Migration

Firstly, the image classification experiment is conducted, and the experimental procedure is the same as the previous subsection. The experimental results are shown in Table 3, where the average accuracy is 0.97. The trained image classification experimental features are migrated to the target detection experiment and used as generic features. It means that the convolutional bases of the VGG for image classification are loaded into the original SSD and frozen completely, and only the specific layers are trained. The experimental results are shown in method A in Table 4, where the mAP is 61.4%.

Table 1. Comparison of the results of two methods for implementing image classification experiments, method A represents image classification experiments using ImageNet pre-trained weights loaded, and method B represents image classification experiments using the feature migration model

method	average accuracy	aeroplane	bicycle	car	cat	dog
A	0.98	0.99	1.00	0.99	0.99	0.92
B	**0.99**	1.00	1.00	1.00	1.00	0.92
method	-	horse	leopards	motorbike	panda	watch
A	-	0.92	1.00	1.00	1.00	0.98
B	-	**0.98**	1.00	1.00	0.99	0.98

Table 2. Comparison of the results of two methods for implementing target detection experiments, method A represents target detection experiments using ImageNet pre-trained weights loaded, and method B represents the results of target detection experiments using the feature migration model (Unit: %)

method	mAP	aeroplane	pottedplant	bird	diningtable	bottle
A	**81.3**	82	63	79	87	48
B	**86.8**	89	68	88	87	55
method	-	bus	car	cow	horse	sofa
A	-	89	82	81	92	91
B	-	93	90	93	95	91
method	-	tvmonitor	motorbike	boat	bicycle	person
A	-	83	87	72	89	75
B	-	89	91	81	93	83
method	-	sheep	cat	dog	train	chair
A	-	76	95	94	93	68
B	-	88	96	96	97	73

Then feature fusion is performed to optimize the above generic feature. The weights of the first 4 blocks in the convolutional bases of the VGG are loaded into the feature fused SSD and frozen completely. After that, only the fusion and specific layers are trained. The experimental results are shown in method B in Table 4, where the mAP is 65.1%.

The results of the above two target detection experiments are compared with each other, and the results are shown in Table 4. From Table 4, it can be seen that the mAP of generic features extracted by feature migration guided by image classification experiments is 61.4%, which can indicate that the generic features extracted by this method are

Table 3. Results of the image classification experiments

	aeroplane	bicycle	bird	boat	bottle
accuracy	0.99	0.96	1.00	0.97	0.98
	bus	car	cat	chair	cow
accuracy	1.00	0.91	0.98	0.90	0.93
	diningtable	dog	horse	motorbike	person
accuracy	1.00	0.98	1.00	1.00	0.97
	pottedplant	sheep	sofa	train	tvmonitor
accuracy	0.99	0.85	0.95	0.99	0.99

Table 4. Results of the target detection contrast experiments, method A denotes the SSD experimental method using feature migration to extract generic features, and method B denotes the SSD experiments after feature fusion based on A (Unit: %)

method	mAP	aeroplane	pottedplant	bird	diningtable	bottle
A	**61.4**	79	29	62	51	21
B	**65.1**	80	33	69	52	21
method	-	bus	car	cow	horse	sofa
A	-	70	65	60	75	58
B	-	78	67	60	82	59
method	-	tvmonitor	motorbike	boat	bicycle	person
A	-	66	75	51	74	65
B	-	68	79	55	79	68
method	-	sheep	cat	dog	train	chair
A	-	70	80	78	72	28
B	-	73	84	80	81	36

effective. Meanwhile, the mAP of the target detection experiment after feature fusion based on feature migration to extract generic features is 65.1%, which is a 3.7% improvement. It shows that the feature fusion method can effectively improve the performance of generic features in target detection. And furthermore, it shows that the generic feature extraction model based on feature fusion and feature migration can be applied to the image classification and target detection tasks simultaneously with good performance.

4 Conclusions

In this paper, we conduct a study on image feature extraction towards multiple vision tasks. The proposed feature migration model can improve the mAP of the target detection task by 5.5%, the average accuracy of the image classification task by 1%. Based on the experimental results derived from the feature migration model, using the image classification task as a guide, the proposed generic feature extraction model can effectively implement the image classification and target detection tasks to promote the deployment of artificial intelligence on edge devices. High-quality images are important for the successful usage of CI systems, and the feature extraction, the first step of CI, will greatly affect the generation of these high-quality images. In the future, we will continuously improve the performance of multiple vision tasks further. Besides, we will continue our research on feature compression and feature transmission subsequently to form a complete CI system.

References

1. Krizhevsky, A., Sutskever, I., Hinton, G.E.: ImageNet classification with deep convolutional neural networks[J]. Communications of the ACM **60**(6), 84–90 (2017)
2. Girshick, R., Donahue, J., Darrell, T., et al.: Region-based convolutional networks for accurate object detection and segmentation. IEEE Transactions on Pattern Analysis and Machine Intelligence (TPAMI) **38**(1), 142–158 (2016)
3. Hinton, G.E., Krizhevsky, A., Sutskever, I.: Imagenet classification with deep convolutional neural networks. Advances in neural information processing systems **25**(1106–1114), 1 (2012)
4. Redondi, A., Baroffio, L., Cesana, M., et al.: Compress-then-analyze vs. analyze-then-compress: Two paradigms for image analysis in visual sensor networks. In: 2013 IEEE 15th International Workshop on Multimedia Signal Processing (MMSP), pp. 278-282 (2013). https://doi.org/10.1109/MMSP.2013.6659301
5. Ding, L., Tian, Y., Fan, H., et al.: Joint coding of local and global deep features in videos for visual search. IEEE Trans. Image Proc. **29**, 3734–3749 (2020)
6. Duan, L., Lou, Y., Wang, S., et al.: AI-oriented large-scale video management for smart city: technologies, standards, and beyond. IEEE MultiMedia **26**(2), 8-20 (1 April-June 2019). https://doi.org/10.1109/MMUL.2018.2873564
7. Kang, Y., Hauswald, J., Gao, C., et al.: Neurosurgeon: collaborative intelligence between the cloud and mobile edge. ACM SIGARCH Computer Architecture News **45**(1), 615–629 (2017)
8. Bajić, I.V., Lin, W., Tian, Y.: Collaborative intelligence: challenges and opportunities. In: ICASSP 2021 - 2021 IEEE International Conference on Acoustics, Speech and Signal Processing (ICASSP), pp. 8493-8497 (2021). https://doi.org/10.1109/ICASSP39728.2021.9413943
9. Wang, W., An, P., Yang, C., et al.: Intermediate deep-feature compression for multitasking. In: Proceedings of SPIE/COS Photonics Asia 2019, Hangzhou, China(SPIE), pp. 33 (2019)
10. Cohen, R.A., Choi, H., Bajić, I.V., et al.: Lightweight compression of neural network feature tensors for collaborative intelligence. IEEE International Conference on Multimedia and Expo (ICME) **2020**, 1–6 (2020). https://doi.org/10.1109/ICME46284.2020.9102797
11. Cohen, R.A., Choi, H., Bajić, I.V., et al.: Lightweight compression of intermediate neural network features for collaborative intelligence. IEEE Open Journal of Circuits and Systems **2**, 350-362 (2021). https://doi.org/10.1109/OJCAS.2021.3072884
12. Hu, Y., Xia, S., Yang, W., et al.: Sensitivity-aware bit allocation for intermediate deep feature compression. IEEE International Conference on Visual Communications and Image Processing (VCIP) **2020**, 475–478 (2020). https://doi.org/10.1109/VCIP49819.2020.9301807
13. Choi, H., Bajić, I.V.: Scalable image coding for humans and machines. IEEE Transactions on Image Processing **31**, 2739-2754 (2022). https://doi.org/10.1109/TIP.2022.3160602

14. Choi, H., Bajić, I.V.: Latent-space scalability for multi-task collaborative intelligence. IEEE Int. Conf. Image Proce. (ICIP) **2021**, 3562–3566 (2021). https://doi.org/10.1109/ICIP42928.2021.9506712

15. Yang, S., Hu, Y., Yang, W., et al.: Towards coding for human and machine vision: scalable face image coding. IEEE Transactions on Multimedia **23**, pp. 2957-2971 (2021). https://doi.org/10.1109/TMM.2021.3068580

16. Hu, Y., Yang, S., Yang, W., et al.: Towards coding for human and machine vision: a scalable image coding approach. IEEE Int. Conf. Multim. Expo (ICME) **2020**, 1–6 (2020). https://doi.org/10.1109/ICME46284.2020.9102750

17. Simonyan, K., Zisserman, A.: Very deep convolutional networks for large-scale image recognition (2014). arXiv preprint arXiv:1409.1556

18. Liu, W., Anguelov, D., Erhan, D., et al.: SSD: Single shot multibox detector. In: European conference on computer vision (2016)

19. Everingham, M., Gool, L., Williams, C.K., et al.: The Pascal visual object classes (VOC) challenge. Int. J. Comp. Visi. **88**(2), 303-338 (2010)

Image Analysis

A Lightweight Segmentation Network Based on Weak Supervision for COVID-19 Detection

Fangfang Lu[1], Tianxiang Liu[1(✉)], Chi Tang[1], Zhihao Zhang[1], Guangtao Zhai[2], Xiongkuo Min[2], and Wei Sun[2]

[1] College of Computer Science and Technology,
Shanghai University of Electric Power, Shanghai, China
`lufangfang@shiep.edu.cn,`
`{liutianxiang,tangchi,zhangzhihao}@mail.shiep.edu.cn`
[2] Institute of Image Communication and Network Engineering,
Shanghai Jiao Tong University, Shanghai, China
`{zhaiguangtao,minxiongkuo,sunguwei}@sjtu.edu.cn`

Abstract. The Coronavirus Disease 2019 (COVID-19) outbreak in late 2019 threatens global health security. Computed tomography (CT) can provide richer information for the diagnosis and treatment of COVID-19. Unfortunately, labeling of COVID-19 lesion chest CT images is an expensive affair. We solved the challenge of chest CT labeling by simply marking point annotations to the lesion areas, i.e., by marking individual pixels for each lesion area in the chest CT scan. It takes only a few seconds to complete the labeling using this labeling strategy. We also designed a lightweight segmentation model with approximately 10% of the number of model parameters of the conventional model. So, the proposed model segmented the lesions of a single image in only 0.05 s. In order to obtain the shape and size of lesions from point labels, the convex-hull based segmentation (CHS) loss function is proposed in this paper, which enables the model to obtain an approximate fully supervised performance on point labels. The experiments were compared with the current state-of-the-art (SOTA) point label segmentation methods on the COVID-19-CT-Seg dataset, and our model showed a large improvement: IoU improved by 28.85%, DSC improved by 28.91%, Sens improved by 13.75%, Spes improved by 1.18%, and MAE decreased by 1.10%. Experiments on the dataset show that the proposed model combines the advantages of lightweight and weak supervision, resulting in more accurate COVID-19 lesion segmentation results while having only a 10% performance difference with the fully supervised approach.

Keywords: Weakly supervised segmentation · Lightweight · COVID-19

G. Zhai et al. (Eds.): IFTC 2022, CCIS 1766, pp. 87–105, 2023.
https://doi.org/10.1007/978-981-99-0856-1_7

1 Introduction

An outbreak of COVID-19 began in December 2019 and has since spread throughout the world [1]. In early 2020, the virus had spread to 33 countries and had begun a global pandemic. As of October 27 2022, more than 620 million confirmed cases of COVID-19 have been reported worldwide, with more than 6.5 million deaths, accounting for 1.0% of confirmed cases [2]. Clinical manifestations of the disease range from asymptomatic to the more severe acute respiratory distress syndrome (ARDS). The most common symptoms are fever, dry cough, and malaise. A small number of patients will develop dyspnea. Reverse transcription polymerase chain reaction (RT-PCR) is the gold standard for the diagnosis of COVID-19, but the quality of the RT-PCR sampling process affects the positive rate of the test, and RT-PCR requires a strict testing environment and testing equipment to ensure the correctness of the test results.

Although RT-PCR is the gold standard for COVID-19 diagnosis, its relatively low sensitivity and high specificity can lead to negative RT-PCR results in early-stage patients with no obvious symptoms [3]. The COVID-19 detection sensitivity of chest CT scan is relatively high. Chest CT scans accurately reflect the severity of COVID-19 patients, and radiologists can determine the type of patient based on the chest CT scan changes. Consequently, a chest CT scan can assist in the diagnosis of COVID-19. It has been shown to be effective in diagnosing the disease, as well as determining the prognosis for recovered patients, making it an important adjunct to the gold standard [4].

Typically, asymptomatic or mildly patients have no additional clinical symptoms. When the disease reaches a moderate or advanced stage, the chest CT image reveals a slight increase in lung tissue density, which is less than consolidation, with a blurred, cloudy appearance; however, the internal blood vessels and bronchial tissue are still visible, a phenomenon known as ground grass opacity (GGO). Additionally, chest CT scans can detect subpleural patchy shadows and interstitial pneumonia [3]. Pulmonary fibrosis can also be detected on CT scans of severe patients [5,6].

During the COVID-19 pandemic, there was a lack of experienced radiologists due to the high medical demand and physician shortage. Therefore, we required a computer-assisted system to assist radiologists in automatically analyzing chest CT scans and rapidly segmenting lesion areas to provide diagnostic clues to physicians, thereby alleviating the difficult problems of medical pressure and the shortage of physicians, which played a crucial role in preventing the spread of COVID-19 and treating patients promptly.

Fortunately, there have been numerous successful applications of deep learning techniques for computer-assisted COVID-19 screening. However, the use of conventional deep learning models to aid physicians in COVID-19 screening is suboptimal. Existing advanced models typically have a large number of parameters and calculation, which can lead to easy overfitting, slow inference, and inefficient deployment of the models, and is not conducive to practical applications;Second, the majority of the most widely used and effective models are fully supervised methods, which require complete labeling. However, labeled public datasets are scarce, and obtaining the complete labeling is laborious and time-consuming.

Given that we require a rapid screening method to effectively relieve medical pressure and to rapidly screen for COVID-19, it is urgent to design a COVID-19 screening system with low computation and rapid inference. In this paper, we are inspired by Gao et al. [7] to reduce the number of model channels to 256 and reduce the number of model parameters by group convolution and point-wise convolution using D-Block, a dilation convolution block. In order to avoid the problem of detail loss and model performance degradation caused by reducing the number of covariates, we also introduce the dilated convolution module D block, which enlarges the model's receptive field by adjusting the dilation rate. This improves the model's ability to learn multi-scale information without adding extra parameters, and we also add residual connections to address the issue of model performance degradation.

To compensate for the lack of publicly available data, we trained the model using point labels. According to Ma et al. [8], the fully supervised label annotator requires an average of 1.6 min to label a CT slice, however, the point label data annotator requires only 3 s to label a single pixel point in a lesion region, which greatly reduces the difficulty of acquiring point label data. However, point labels lack semantic information such as shape and size, and the prediction accuracy of the fully supervised model trained by them is low, making it challenging to use point labels to complete the semantic segmentation task effectively. Meanwhile, when the model is trained using a point-level loss function, the loss function only encourages the model to supervise a small number of pixel points, resulting in the model only predicting a very small region. Therefore, we refer to the novel loss function as convex-hull-based segmentation loss (CHS), which encourages the model to make accurate predictions by obtaining shape information from a small number of points in lesion regions. Our experiments on the point-annotation dataset demonstrate that our method outperforms the conventional point-level loss function, and we also demonstrate that this weakly supervised method performs similarly to the fully supervised method.

Our contribution is shown as follows:

1. In combination with D-Block, we proposed a weakly-point D-block network (WPDNet) for efficient and rapid segmentation of COVID-19 lesions on point-annotation datasets.
2. We propose the CHS loss function for point-annotation datasets, which can provide semantic information such as shape and size to the model and enhance segmentation performance.
3. We offer a method for labeling points that requires marking only a small number of points in each lesion area.

2   Related Work

In this section, we review the methods to accomplish COVID-19 segmentation on chest CT scans. Then, we discuss lightweight models and weakly supervised segmentation methods.

2.1   COVID-19 Segmentation Methodology

In recent years, the COVID-19 lesion segmentation method has become one of the most popular tasks within the field of medical image analysis due to its high application value. This task classifies each pixel of a chest CT image as either background or lesion, typically segmenting the lesion area from each CT slice, thereby providing the physician with the information required to diagnose the disease. Traditional lesion segmentation methods segment images using features such as the boundary gray gradient, gray value threshold, and image region.

Among them, the threshold-based [9–11] segmentation method utilizes the contrast information of CT images, which is the quickest but has a tendency to miss abnormal tissues and is suitable for segmenting images with a clear contrast between the object and the background. Region-based [12] segmentation methods are quick and produce more accurate segmentation results, but they are susceptible to noise, which can result in over segmentation and contour loss. Due to the robust feature extraction capability of deep learning, its image segmentation results are vastly superior to those of conventional methods; consequently, COVID-19 segmentation methods based on deep learning are widely used.

Due to the large variation of lesion size in COVID-19 chest CT images, multiscale learning plays a crucial role in COVID-19 segmentation. Therefore, SOTA deep learning methods aim to design fully convolutional networks to learn multiscale semantic information. Currently, U-Net [13] is one of the most popular medical image segmentation models. It proposes a symmetric encoder-decoder structure that employs skip-connections to fuse multi-scale information at different stages. Numerous COVID-19 segmentation methods are based on U-Net or its variants (Unet++ [14], Vnet [15], Attention-Unet [16], VBnet [17]). Wu et al. [18] designed a U-shaped COVID-19 segmentation network and proposed Enhanced Feature Module (EFM) and Attentional Feature Fusion (AFF) to improve the network feature representation, achieving a Dice score of 78.5%. Paluru et al. [19] proposed COVID-19 segmentation network with symmetric encoder-decoder structure using skip-connections to fuse multi-scale features at different levels to improve network performance, and the Dice score of this network was 79.8%.

The DeepLabs V2 [20] based segmentation methods has superior multi-scale learning capability because it uses the Atrous Spatial Pyramid Pooling (ASPP) module, which is comprised of dilated convolution with different dilatation rates, to learn abundant multi-scale semantic information from the input image. Xiao et al. [21] proposed SAUNet++ network segmentation COVID-19 based on Unet and Unet++ using ASPP and squeeze excitation residual (SER) modules and obtained a Dice score of 87.38%. In addition, Gao et al. [7] rethink the strategy for expanding the network's receptive field by designing a structure with two parallel 3×3 convolutions with different dilation rates and repeating this structure in the backbone to expand the network's receptive field without adding a context module after the backbone, while preserving the local information. Enshaei et al. [22] improved the model's multi-scale learning capability by incorporating the Content Perception Boosting Module (CPB) and achieved a Dice score performance of 80.69%.

In addition to the ROI (region of interest), there is a lot of redundant information in chest CT scan images. An attention mechanism is used to address this issue by instructing the models to concentrate on the most important data. Raj et al. [23] suggested using DenseNet rather than standard convolution and Attention Gate (AG) to ignore the background and increase segmentation accuracy. OuYang et al. [24] proposed a new dual-sampling attention network to automatically diagnose COVID-19, in which the attention module can effectively mitigate the imbalance problem in chest CT images. Feature fusion can synthesize multiple image features for complementary information and more robust and precise segmentation results. Shi et al. [25] trained 3DU-Net and 2D-UNet models with directional fields to fuse segment lesion features. Wu et al. [18] proposed a joint classification and segmentation (JCS) system for diagnosis that enhances robustness by fusing classification network information via the AFF module. These fully supervised methods are computationally intensive and time-consuming to deploy, despite their high accuracy. Some lightweight models are proposed to resolve this issue.

2.2 Lightweight Model

The design of lightweight models can solve two efficiency issues: (a) storage issues, as ordinary models require a great deal of storage space; (b) speed issues, as ordinary models are second-level and do not meet practical application requirements.

A common technique for lightweight design is model compression, in which trained models are pruned and quantized to solve storage and speed issues problems, but at the expense of performance. In recent years, the lightweight design of models has been considered mainly from a "computational approach" perspective. The "computational approach" for convolutional operations is divided into (a) spatial-based convolutional operations [26–28] and (b) shift-based convolutional operations [29,30], which reduces the number of parameters without affecting network performance. The shift convolution requires no additional parameters or operations and uses 1×1 convolution to simulate each type of convolution to reduce the number of parameters and computational complexity. Nevertheless, displacement convolution necessitates high-end hardware, and training results are not always optimal. Therefore, spatially-based convolution parameter methods are more common. Common spatial convolution operations include dilated convolution and depth wise separable convolution.

To achieve parametric reduction, many well-known network architectures, such as Inception networks [31], Xception [32], and MobileNets [33], use deep separable convolution. Among them, MobileNet V2 uses point-wise convolution (1×1 convolution) to further reduce the number of parameters and downscale the input feature channels. ESPNetV2 [28] employs depth wise separable dilated convolution instead of depth wise separable convolution and hierarchical feature fusion (HFF) to eliminate the grid residual problem, thereby reducing the network's computational complexity and enhancing its receptive field. Miniseg [34] employs dilated convolution in conjunction with point-wise convolution to decrease the model parameters while expanding the model's receptive field. Anam-Net [19] reduces the parameters using point-wise convolution and adds residual connections to prevent network performance degradation. Unfortunately, these methods require fully supervised labels, yet publicly available datasets are rare. To solve this problem, weakly supervised semantic segmentation is proposed.

2.3 Weakly Supervised Semantic Segmentation

Weakly supervised semantic segmentation can reduce the reliance on fully supervised labels. The common weakly supervised labels used for semantic segmentation are (a) image-level label [35,36]; (b) scribble label [37]; (c) bounding boxes [38,39]label; and (d) point label [40,41].

Weakly supervised segmentation utilizing image-level labels typically employs Class Activation Maps (CAM) to obtain initial lesion localization; however, this initial localization is imprecise and the final segmentation accuracy is low. Since CAM at different scales requires complex network structures and extensive post-processing, to solve this problem, Tang et al. [36] proposed the dual weakly supervised segmentation method M-SEAM-NAM, which proposes a Self-supervised Equivalent Attention Mechanism (SEAM) with Neighborhood Affinity Module (NAM) for exact segmentation. However, M-SEAM-NAM still has the problem of easily identifying the thoracic skeleton as a lesion. Scribble labels perform better than CAM in COVID-19 segmentation, but their acquisition time is relatively lengthy and there are no standard setting criteria. The acquisition of point labels for each image takes only 22.1 s, whereas the acquisition of fully annotated takes 239 s, which is an order of magnitude faster than the acquisition of point labels [42]. Laradji et al. [40] trained a COVID-19 segmentation network based on weakly supervised consistent learning (WSCL) on point labels, but the network showed over-segmentation. In order to solve this problem, this paper implements WPDNet and provides a point label setting method to complete COVID-19 semantic segmentation using weak supervision.

3   Materials and Methods

In this section, we first introduce the dataset used in this paper and then give the point label setting method. Then, the structure of our proposed WPDNet model is described in detail. Finally, our proposed loss function CHS for weakly supervised point label segmentation is introduced.

3.1   Data Collection

Since public datasets are relatively scarce and the majority of COVID-19 segmentation studies are based on private datasets, it is crucial to collect public datasets and evaluate the performance of various models.

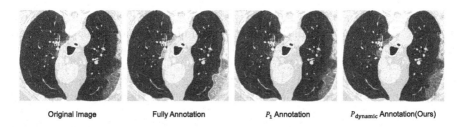

Original Image   Fully Annotation P_1 Annotation $P_{dynamic}$ Annotation(Ours)

Fig. 1. Different annotations strategy. We demonstrate the distinction between fully supervised labeling, P_1 labeling strategy, and $P_{dynamic}$ (ours) labeling strategy. Several points within the lesion region are labelled.

Dataset A. This dataset [43] contains the results of 110 CT scans of over 40 patient outcomes; the original images were downloaded from the public dataset of the Italian Society of Medical and Interventional Radiology and annotated using MedSeg by three radiologists.

Dataset B. This dataset [44] consists of over 800 CT slices from 9 patients on Radiopaedia, of which approximately 350 slices were determined positive by the radiologist and annotated using MedSeg, and over 700 slices were labeled for the lung parenchyma.

Dataset C. The dataset [45] consists of CT scans of 20 patients. Two radiologists labeled CT images of the left lung parenchyma, right lung parenchyma, and infected areas, which were then validated by experienced radiologists.

Dataset D. This dataset [46] contains anonymous chest CT scans provided by the Moscow Municipal Hospital in Moscow, Russia, with 50 labeled chest CT scans.

Point Label Setting. As point labeling gains popularity, there are already point labeling setup strategies [47,48] in place. Typically, they sample pixel points within the ROI and classify them as objects or backgrounds. Previous sampling strategies were manual [42,49,50] clicks by markers, but manual clicks are more subjective, and when the contrast between COVID-19 lesions and the surrounding background is low (especially in mild patients), markers may over focus on areas of significant contrast, which may result in monolithic data. According to Bearman et al. [51], random points on ground truth (GT) are more suitable than manual clicks for training weakly segmentation models.

The most common way to label is to mark one pixel in the center of the lesion, which is called P_1. COVID-19 lesion size varies frequently, and we want to reflect the lesion size on point labels. Therefore, we use a random sampling strategy to dynamically set the sampling points according to the area of each lesion region: two points are sampled when the number of lesion pixels is less than 288; four points are sampled when the number of lesion pixels is between 228 and 2386; and nine points are sampled when the number of lesion pixels is greater than 2386 (228 and 2386 are the lower quartile and upper quartile of all lesion areas, respectively). As depicted in Fig. 1, we refer to this method as $P_{dynamic}$ and mark only the focal pixels while ignoring the background pixels.

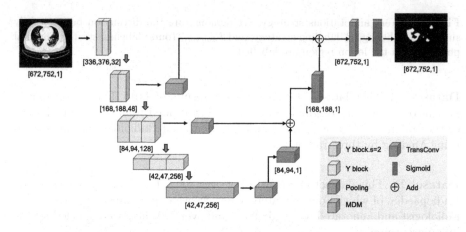

Fig. 2. Network structure. 10 Y blocks are used for feature extraction, where green block represents Y block when s = 2, and blue block represents Y block. D block is set with different dilation rates to improve the model receptive field. (Color figure online)

3.2   Network Structure

Our network backbone integrates the Y block and Multi-Scale D-Block Module (MDM), as shown in Fig. 2. In this section, we describe the main components of the model: the backbone and the MDM.

Backbone. The WPDNet network consists of five layers; the first four layers use the Y block in RegNet [52] to extract features, while the fifth layer employs the MDM module to expand the model's receptive field. As shown in Fig. 3, the Y block adds the SE block attention mechanism to remove redundant information after standard convolution and then uses point-wise convolution to combine weighted features in depth direction and adds point-wise convolution on residual connections to avoid noise interference while eliminating network performance degradation. The standard kernel size for convolutional is 3×3, and the number of channels increases from 32 to 256. In order to obtain spatial information at downsampling while boosting the size invariance of the encoder, we use a convolution with stride = 2 in the Y block while adding an average pooling with stride = 2 and a 1×1 convolution on the residual connection. This paper adds Multi-Scale D-block Module (MDM) to expand the encoder's receptive field without

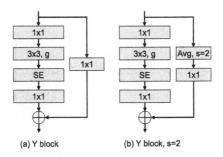

(a) Y block   (b) Y block, s=2

Fig. 3. Y block structure

sacrificing detail, as different receptive fields are required to extract features from different regions of an image. Finally, the segmentation results are obtained by fusing the features of different layers of the backbone during upsampling and restoring them to the original resolution.

Table 1. Multi-scale D-block module

Module	d1	Stride	Channels
MDM_1	2	1	256
MDM_4	4	1	256
MDM_6	8	1	256

Multi-scale D-Block Module. MDM consists primarily of D blocks; depending on how MDM is utilized at different network layers, different dilation rates and numbers of D blocks are set. We assume that the D block is repeated N times in MDM, we denote this as MDM_N, where $N \in \{1, 4, 6\}$. The D block is comprised of a parallel standard convolution and a dilated convolution, where the dilation rate of the dilated convolution can be set to various values depending on the MDM_N in which it is located, Table 1 shows their detailed parameter settings. When the stride of the D block is 2, the average pooling operation with stride $= 2$ is used at the jump connection. Figure 4 illustrates the MDM_4 with the D block structure.

3.3 Loss Function

Localization-based counting loss [47] (LC) is comprised of four components: image-level, point-level, split-level, and false-positive. Its primary application scenario is instance localization and counting, but it can force the model to predict the semantic segmentation label of each pixel in the image. To encourage

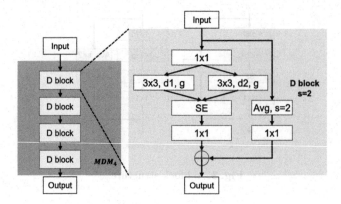

Fig. 4. D block structure.

the model to learn lesion information through point labels, the loss function CHS proposed in this paper is modified based on the LC loss function by adding convex-hull supervision and removing split-level supervision.

Given the output matrix X of the network after softmax, where X_{iy} denotes the probability that pixel i belongs to class y (lesion or background), Y denotes the point label matrix, where the object's position is 1 and all other positions are 0. Our proposed loss function can be expressed as follows:

$$\mathcal{L}(X,Y) = \underbrace{\mathcal{L}_I(X,Y)}_{Image-level\ loss} + \underbrace{\mathcal{L}_P(X,Y)}_{Point-level\ loss} + \underbrace{\mathcal{L}_F(X,Y)}_{False\ Positive\ loss} + \underbrace{\mathcal{L}_{CH}(X,Y)}_{Convex\ Hull\ loss} \quad (1)$$

Image-Level Loss. Let $\mathcal{C}$ denote the set of classes present in the image, the $\mathcal{C}'$ denote the set of classes not present in the image. The image-level loss is shown below:

$$\mathcal{L}_I(X,Y) = -\frac{1}{|\mathcal{C}|}\sum_{y\in\mathcal{C}}\log(X_{t_y y}) - \frac{1}{|\mathcal{C}'|}\sum_{y\in\mathcal{C}'}\log(1 - X_{t_y y}) \quad (2)$$

where $t_y = \arg\max_{j\in\mathcal{I}_a} X_{jy}$, $\mathcal{I}_a$ denote all pixels in the image. For each category present in the $\mathcal{C}$, at least one pixel should be labeled as that class; For each category present in the $\mathcal{C}'$, none of the pixels should belong to that class.

Point-Level Loss. $\mathcal{I}$ denotes the set of points in the point label. We apply the standard cross-entropy (CE) loss function to encourage the model to correctly predict the set of pixel points in $\mathcal{I}$. The point-level loss is shown below:

$$\mathcal{L}_P(X,Y) = -\sum_{j\in\mathcal{I}}\log(X_{jY_j}) \quad (3)$$

where X_{jY_j} denotes the probability that pixel j in the output matrix X belongs to the class of pixel j in the GT of the point label.

False Positive Loss. To reduce the number of false positive lesions, $\mathcal{L}_F$ discourages the network from predicting lesion regions without point annotations. The loss function is described as follows:

$$\mathcal{L}_F(X,Y) = -\sum_{j \in B} \log(X_{j0}) \tag{4}$$

where B represents the collection of all connected regions that lack point annotations and X_{i0} represents the probability that pixel i belongs to the background.

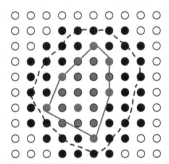

Fig. 5. Convex-Hull Loss Function. In a 10×10 network prediction output (the darker color represents the lesion prediction), the red color represents the GT of the point label, the blue line represents the boundary line obtained by convex hull of the point labels, and the blue pixels are all included in CH_i (the gray dashed line is only to suggest the true lesion area, it does not play any role in the actual work). (Color figure online)

Convex-Hull Loss. We define the set CH_i, $i \in \{1,\ldots,N\}$ where n is the number of lesions in the image. It is the collection of convex hull pixels generated by point labels in each lesion region, as depicted in Fig. 5. Then, we use a CE loss function to encourage the model's segmentation results to be as close as possible to the GT. The loss function is described as follows:

$$\mathcal{L}_{CH}(X,Y) = -\sum_{i=1}^{N} \sum_{j \in CH_i} \log(X_{jY_j}) \tag{5}$$

4   Experiments

In this section, we describe our experimental setup, evaluation metrics, and comparison experiments in detail.

4.1   Experimental Setup

Implementation Detail. We implemented the WPDNet model using the Pytorch framework and trained it on an Nvidia RTX 2080 Ti 11 GB GPU using the Adam optimizer, with a 1e−4 weight decay. 300 epochs were trained with the initial learning rate set to 1e−5 and the batch size set to 2. We use the same settings to train other networks on Dataset C to ensure fairness.

Evaluation Metrics. In this paper, we evaluated the COVID-19 segmentation methods using the following metrics:

Intersection over Union(IoU). To calculate the cross-merge ratio between the predicted and the GT:$IoU = \frac{TP}{TP+FP+FN}$, where TP, FP, and FN are the numbers of pixels of true positive, false positive, and false negative, respectively.

Dice Similarity Coefficient (DSC). Similar to IoU, DSC also calculates the similarity between prediction and GT, but the coefficient of TP in DSC is 2 rather than 1:$DSC = \frac{2*TP}{2*TP+FP+FN}$.

Sensitivity (Recall). To quantify the probability that the model predicts a lesion with a true positive GT:$Sens. = \frac{TP}{TP+TN}$.

Specificity. Measures the percentage of true negative in correct predictions: $Spec. = \frac{TN}{TN+FP}$.

4.2   Comparison

We compare the performance of the point-supervised loss function on various point label setting strategies, test the performance of our proposed loss function using different backbone networks. Finally, compare the WPDNet with image segmentation networks to conclude.

Table 2. Comparison of different point labeling strategies. The effect of different point labeling strategies on segmentation results was tested using our method (WPDNet) with FCN-8S, and the bolded part is our method.

Methods	Loss functions	Points strategy	Dice(%)	IoU(%)	Sens.(%)	Spec.(%)
FCN-8s	LC	P_1	67.74	60.09	63.99	99.95
FCN-8s	LC	$P_{dynamic}$	76.14	68.78	73.92	99.92
WPDNet	LC	P_1	69.33	61.80	66.41	99.94
WPDNet (Ours)	LC	$P_{dynamic}$	**76.18**	**69.01**	**79.14**	**99.80**

Points Number. As shown in Table 2, we evaluated the performance of two models, FCN-8s and WPDNet, using the same loss function for the two point labeling strategies. Notably, because the P_1 strategy cannot utilize the convex hull supervision in CHS, we evaluate the performance of both strategies using LC as a fairness benchmark. P_1 only labels a single pixel at the center of the lesion, whereas $P_{dynamic}$ labels points according to the area of each lesion, which can laterally reflect the size and shape of the lesion. Hence, Table 2 shows that our $P_{dynamic}$ strategy is almost comprehensively ahead of the P_1 strategy in both methods, with a maximum improvement of about 12% in the sensitivity metric when using WPDNet as the backbone and a different degree of lead for all other metrics.

Table 3. Comparison of different loss functions. The effect of LC and our loss function (CHS) on segmentation results was tested using our method (WPDNet) with FCN-8S, and each model's significant values are highlighted in bold.

Methods		Loss functions		Metrics(%)			
FCN-8s	WPDNet	LC	CHS	DSC	IoU	Sens.	Spec.
✓		✓		76.14	68.78	73.92	**99.92**
✓			✓	**80.15**	**73.18**	**88.32**	99.63
	✓	✓		76.18	69.01	79.14	**99.80**
	✓		✓	**81.00**	**73.44**	**95.44**	99.53

Loss Functions. As shown in Table 3, we evaluated the effect of our CHS loss function on FCN-8s and WPDNet, respectively, and found that our loss function provided superior performance compared to the point-supervised loss function LC. When FCN-8s used CHS, DSC, IoU, and Sens. improved by 4.01%, 4.4%, and 14.4%, respectively. With a maximum of 16.3%, the Sens. improvement was greatest when the WPDNet utilized CHS. Our CHS loss results in a more competitive performance for other metrics.

Figure 6 visualizes the segmentation results, comparing the LC loss with the CHS loss. Due to the fact that CHS adds convex-hull loss to LC to provide size and shape information to the model and removes split-level loss, it does not force the model to segment connected regions containing two or more point labels, allowing the network to learn more about the lesion. It can be observed that CHS improves the problem of more false negatives in LC and has better true positive results.

Quantitative Evaluation. To compare with SOTA methods, we constructed a performance comparison experiment using three fully supervised image segmentation models and two weakly supervised segmentation models, including Unet, AnamNet, COVID-Rate, WSCL, and M-SAME-NAM, COVID-Rate, AnamNet,

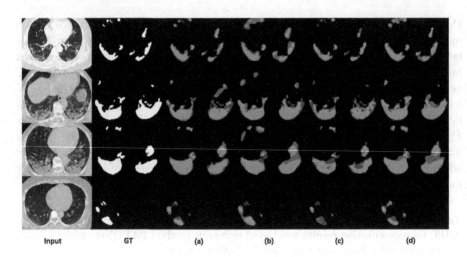

Fig. 6. Effect of loss function on segmentation performance. (a) WPDNet+LC; (b) WPDNet+CHS; (c) FCN-8s+LC; (d) FCN-8s+CHS; Red: false positive; green: true positive; blue: false negative. (Color figure online)

WSCL, and M-SAME-NAM are specifically designed for COVID-19 lesion segmentation, whereas M-SAME-NAM and WSCL are weakly supervised networks trained with classification labels and point labels, respectively.

Table 4. Compare the number of parameters, FLOPs, and inference speed of WPDNet with other SOTA methods.

Method	Backbone	#Param	FLOPs	Speed
Unet	–	31.04M	421.49G	16.3 fps
AnamNet	–	4.47M	196.12G	29.0 fps
COVID-Rate	–	14.38M	297.92G	19.2 fps
WSCL	FCN-8s	134.26M	317.25G	20.2 fps
M-SAME-NAM	ResNet38	106.40M	403.78G	2.8 fps
WPDNet	–	**11.03M**	**21.96G**	**24.6 fps**

The results of WPDNet compared with other networks in terms of number of parameters, FLOPs, and speed are shown in Table 4. These fully supervised segmentation networks (Unet, FCN8s, and Covid-Rate) have high accuracy, but the number of parameters and FLOPs of these methods are relatively high. Using more skip connections affects inference speed. The FLOPs of Unet reached 421 GFLOPs, and the inference speed was only 16.3 FPS (frames per second), while the FLOPs of Covid-Rate were only about half of those of Unet, but the inference speed was only increased by 2.9 FPS. AnamNet, a lightweight segmentation network, achieves the fastest inference speed of 29 FPS, but it requires fully supervised labeling, and the accuracy of the weakly supervised method presented in this paper is not significantly different. In the training phase, WSCL requires two FCN8s networks, so the training time is lengthy. Even though only one FCN8s is required to complete segmentation in the inference stage, the network's FLOPs still reach 317 GFLOPs, and the inference speed of 20 FPS is not dominant. M-SEAM-NAM needs to calculate the CAM and affinity matrix during inference and use the random walk algorithm to get the result, so its inference speed is only 2.8 FPS. WPDNet uses point-wise and D block to reduce the model parameters, and the FLOPs are only 21.96 GFLOPs while the inference speed reaches 24 FPS.

Table 5. Comparison of WPDNet with the advanced COVID-19 segmentation method, where the bolded black is the method in this paper.

Label	Methods	DSC(%)	IoU(%)	Sens.(%)	Spec.(%)
Full	Unet	87.58	82.23	86.11	99.93
	AnamNet	86.83	77.27	94.10	99.67
	COVID-Rate	83.79	80.13	88.22	99.85
Point	WSCL	52.09	44.59	81.69	98.35
Classification	M-SAME-NAM	51.00	50.13	53.50	80.19
Point	WPDNet **(Ours)**	**81.00**	**73.44**	**95.44**	**99.53**

A comparison of the evaluation metrics of WPDNet with the above networks is shown in Table 5. On DataSet C, WPDNet achieved the best results compared to other weakly supervised methods, with DSC and IOU leading by more than 29% and 28%, respectively, demonstrating the effectiveness of the weakly supervised method in this paper. Compared with the fully supervised method, the performance of WPDNet is slightly inferior; from the IoU point of view, the lowest difference of the method in this paper is only 3.8%, but the performance of Sens. in this paper is 9.3%, 1.3%, and 7.2%, respectively. Therefore, we can conclude that our method is rapid, effective, precise, simple to implement in practice, and crucial for assisting in the diagnosis of COVID-19.

Qualitative Comparison. In order to demonstrate the efficacy of WPDNet, this paper compares visually two weakly supervised methods and one fully supervised method. As depicted in Fig. 7, we chose some representative images from Dataset C for comparison, and it can be seen that the WSCL method suffers from over segmentation and that the numerous lesion regions are nearly connected. M-SEAM-NAM uses CAM combined with the affinity's segmentation method. Even though M-SEAM-NAM adds an attention mechanism for CAM to focus more on the lesion, it is still easy to misidentify the thoracic skeleton as a lesion. The segmentation results of this paper's method have the fewest false

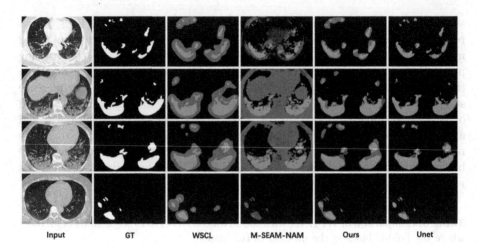

Input   GT   WSCL   M-SEAM-NAM   Ours   Unet

Fig. 7. The visualization comparison graphs of different segmentation methods. Red: false positive; green: true positive; blue: false negative. (Color figure online)

positives and are closest to GT, which is superior to the segmentation results of other weakly supervised methods. Compared to Unet, the segmentation results of this paper's method produce relatively more false positives, but are otherwise comparable to Unet.

5   Conclusion

Deep learning can lead to a detection and segmentation solution for COVID-19. In this paper, a lightweight, weakly-supervised point-label COVID-19 segmentation network called WPDNet is proposed.WPDNet fuses the D block into the network to expand the model's receptive field. The CHS loss function was designed based on LC to learn the shape and size of lesions under point labels.This paper presents a dynamic setting method for point labels, and experiments demonstrate that this method achieves the highest segmentation accuracy compared to the conventional method.In this paper, we used point-wise convolution and reduced the number of model channels, which significantly reduced the FLOPs of the model. Compared to other weakly supervised segmentations, the method described in this paper achieves the highest segmentation accuracy and is suitable for rapid COVID-19 lesion segmentation deployment.

References

1. Huang, C., et al.: Clinical features of patients infected with 2019 novel coronavirus in Wuhan, China. Lancet **395**(10223), 497–506 (2020)
2. Dong, E., Du, H., Gardner, L.: An interactive web-based dashboard to track COVID-19 in real time. Lancet. Infect. Dis **20**(5), 533–534 (2020)

3. Ai, T., et al.: Correlation of chest CT and RT-PCR testing in coronavirus disease 2019 (COVID-19) in china: a report of 1014 cases. Radiology **296**, E32–E40 (2020)
4. Zu, Z.Y., et al.: Coronavirus disease 2019 (COVID-19): a perspective from china. Radiology **296**(2), E15–E25 (2020)
5. Iqbal, A., et al.: The COVID-19 sequelae: a cross-sectional evaluation of post-recovery symptoms and the need for rehabilitation of COVID-19 survivors. Cureus **13**(2), e13080 (2021)
6. Froidure, A., et al.: Integrative respiratory follow-up of severe COVID-19 reveals common functional and lung imaging sequelae. Respir. Med. **181**, 106383 (2021)
7. Gao, R.: Rethink dilated convolution for real-time semantic segmentation. arXiv preprint arXiv:2111.09957 (2021)
8. Ma, J., et al.: Towards efficient COVID-19 CT annotation: a benchmark for lung and infection segmentation (2020). https://arxiv.org/abs/2004.12537v1
9. Abualigah, L., Diabat, A., Sumari, P., Gandomi, A.H.: A novel evolutionary arithmetic optimization algorithm for multilevel thresholding segmentation of COVID-19 CT images. Processes **9**(7), 1155 (2021)
10. Shen, C., et al.: Quantitative computed tomography analysis for stratifying the severity of coronavirus disease 2019. J. Pharm. Anal. **10**(2), 123–129 (2020)
11. Oulefki, A., Agaian, S., Trongtirakul, T., Laouar, A.K.: Automatic COVID-19 lung infected region segmentation and measurement using CT-scans images. Pattern Recogn. **114**, 107747 (2021)
12. Joshi, A., Khan, M.S., Soomro, S., Niaz, A., Han, B.S., Choi, K.N.: SRIS: saliency-based region detection and image segmentation of COVID-19 infected cases. IEEE Access **8**, 190487–190503 (2020)
13. Ronneberger, O., Fischer, P., Brox, T.: U-Net: convolutional networks for biomedical image segmentation. In: Navab, N., Hornegger, J., Wells, W.M., Frangi, A.F. (eds.) MICCAI 2015. LNCS, vol. 9351, pp. 234–241. Springer, Cham (2015). https://doi.org/10.1007/978-3-319-24574-4_28
14. Zhou, Z., Siddiquee, M.M.R., Tajbakhsh, N., Liang, J.: Unet++: redesigning skip connections to exploit multiscale features in image segmentation. IEEE Trans. Med. Imaging **39**(6), 1856–1867 (2019)
15. Milletari, F., Navab, N., Ahmadi, S.A.: V-Net: fully convolutional neural networks for volumetric medical image segmentation. In: 2016 Fourth International Conference on 3D Vision (3DV), pp. 565–571. IEEE (2016)
16. Oktay, O., et al.: Attention U-Net: learning where to look for the pancreas. arXiv preprint arXiv:1804.03999 (2018)
17. Han, M., et al.: Segmentation of Ct thoracic organs by multi-resolution VB-Nets. In: SegTHOR@ ISBI (2019)
18. Wu, Y.H., et al.: JCS: an explainable COVID-19 diagnosis system by joint classification and segmentation. IEEE Trans. Image Process. **30**, 3113–3126 (2021)
19. Paluru, N., et al.: ANAM-Net: anamorphic depth embedding-based lightweight CNN for segmentation of anomalies in COVID-19 chest CT images. IEEE Trans. Neural Netw. Learn. Syst. **32**(3), 932–946 (2021)
20. Chen, L.C., Papandreou, G., Kokkinos, I., Murphy, K., Yuille, A.L.: DeepLab: semantic image segmentation with deep convolutional nets, atrous convolution, and fully connected CRFs. IEEE Trans. Pattern Anal. Mach. Intell. **40**(4), 834–848 (2017)
21. Xiao, H., Ran, Z., Mabu, S., Li, Y., Li, L.: SauNet++: an automatic segmentation model of COVID-19 lesion from CT slices. Vis. Comput., 1–14 (2022). https://doi.org/10.1007/s00371-022-02414-4

22. Enshaei, N., et al.: COVID-rate: an automated framework for segmentation of COVID-19 lesions from chest CT images. Sci. Rep. **12**(1), 1–18 (2022)
23. Raj, A.N.J., et al.: ADID-UNET-a segmentation model for COVID-19 infection from lung CT scans. PeerJ Comput. Sci. **7**, e349 (2021)
24. Ouyang, X., et al.: Dual-sampling attention network for diagnosis of COVID-19 from community acquired pneumonia. IEEE Trans. Med. Imaging **39**(8), 2595–2605 (2020)
25. Shi, T., Cheng, F., Li, Z., Zheng, C., Xu, Y., Bai, X.: Automatic segmentation of COVID-19 infected regions in chest CT images based on 2D/3D model ensembling. Acta Automatica Sinica **47**(AAS-CN-2021-0400), 1 (2021). https://doi.org/10.16383/j.aas.c210400, https://www.aas.net.cn/cn/article/doi/10.16383/j.aas.c210400
26. Sandler, M., Howard, A., Zhu, M., Zhmoginov, A., Chen, L.C.: MobileNetV2: inverted residuals and linear bottlenecks. In: Proceedings of the IEEE Conference on Computer Vision and Pattern Recognition, pp. 4510–4520 (2018)
27. Ma, N., Zhang, X., Zheng, H.T., Sun, J.: ShuffleNetV2: practical guidelines for efficient CNN architecture design. In: Proceedings of the European Conference on Computer Vision (ECCV), pp. 116–131 (2018)
28. Mehta, S., Rastegari, M., Shapiro, L., Hajishirzi, H.: EspNetv2: a light-weight, power efficient, and general purpose convolutional neural network. In: Proceedings of the IEEE/CVF Conference on Computer Vision and Pattern Recognition, pp. 9190–9200 (2019)
29. Wu, B., et al.: Shift: A Zero FLOP, zero parameter alternative to spatial convolutions. In: Proceedings of the IEEE Conference on Computer Vision and Pattern Recognition, pp. 9127–9135 (2018)
30. Jeon, Y., Kim, J.: Constructing fast network through deconstruction of convolution. In: Advances in Neural Information Processing Systems, vol. 31 (2018)
31. Szegedy, C., et al.: Going deeper with convolutions. In: Proceedings of the IEEE Conference on Computer Vision and Pattern Recognition, pp. 1–9 (2015)
32. Chollet, F.: Xception: deep learning with depthwise separable convolutions. In: Proceedings of the IEEE Conference on Computer Vision and Pattern Recognition, pp. 1251–1258 (2017)
33. Howard, A.G., et al.: MobileNets: efficient convolutional neural networks for mobile vision applications. arXiv preprint arXiv:1704.04861 (2017)
34. Qiu, Y., Liu, Y., Li, S., Xu, J.: MiniSeg: an extremely minimum network for efficient COVID-19 segmentation. In: Proceedings of the AAAI Conference on Artificial Intelligence vol. 35(6), pp. 4846–4854 (2021). https://doi.org/10.1609/aaai.v35i6.16617
35. Zhou, Y., Zhu, Y., Ye, Q., Qiu, Q., Jiao, J.: Weakly supervised instance segmentation using class peak response. In: Proceedings of the IEEE Conference on Computer Vision and Pattern Recognition, pp. 3791–3800 (2018)
36. Tang, W., et al.: M-SEAM-NAM: multi-instance self-supervised equivalent attention mechanism with neighborhood affinity module for double weakly supervised segmentation of COVID-19. In: de Bruijne, M., et al. (eds.) MICCAI 2021. LNCS, vol. 12907, pp. 262–272. Springer, Cham (2021). https://doi.org/10.1007/978-3-030-87234-2_25
37. Liu, X., et al.: Weakly supervised segmentation of COVID-19 infection with scribble annotation on CT images. Pattern Recogn. **122**, 108341 (2022)
38. Khoreva, A., Benenson, R., Hosang, J., Hein, M., Schiele, B.: Simple does it: weakly supervised instance and semantic segmentation. In: Proceedings of the IEEE Conference on Computer Vision and Pattern Recognition, pp. 876–885 (2017)

39. Hsu, C.C., Hsu, K.J., Tsai, C.C., Lin, Y.Y., Chuang, Y.Y.: Weakly supervised instance segmentation using the bounding box tightness prior. In: Advances in Neural Information Processing Systems, vol. 32 (2019)
40. Laradji, I., et al.: A weakly supervised consistency-based learning method for COVID-19 segmentation in CT images. In: Proceedings of the IEEE/CVF Winter Conference on Applications of Computer Vision, pp. 2453–2462 (2021)
41. Laradji, I.H., Saleh, A., Rodriguez, P., Nowrouzezahrai, D., Azghadi, M.R., Vazquez, D.: Weakly supervised underwater fish segmentation using affinity LCFCN. Sci. Rep. **11**(1), 1–10 (2021)
42. Qian, R., Wei, Y., Shi, H., Li, J., Liu, J., Huang, T.: Weakly supervised scene parsing with point-based distance metric learning. In: Proceedings of the AAAI Conference on Artificial Intelligence, vol. 33(01), pp. 8843–8850 (2019). https://doi.org/10.1609/aaai.v33i01.33018843
43. MedSeg, Håvard, Bjørke, J., Tomas, S.: MedSeg COVID dataset 1 (2021). https://figshare.com/articles/dataset/MedSeg_Covid_Dataset_1/13521488
44. MedSeg, Håvard, Bjørke, J., Tomas, S.: Medseg COVID dataset 2 (2021). https://figshare.com/articles/dataset/Covid_Dataset_2/13521509
45. Ma, J., et al.: COVID-19 CT lung and infection segmentation dataset (2020). https://doi.org/10.5281/zenodo.3757476
46. Morozov, S.P., et al.: MosMedData: chest CT scans with COVID-19 related findings dataset. arXiv preprint arXiv:2005.06465 (2020)
47. Laradji, I.H., Rostamzadeh, N., Pinheiro, P.O., Vazquez, D., Schmidt, M.: Where are the blobs: counting by localization with point supervision. In: Proceedings of the European Conference on Computer Vision (ECCV), pp. 547–562 (2018)
48. Cheng, B., Parkhi, O., Kirillov, A.: Pointly-supervised instance segmentation. In: Proceedings of the IEEE/CVF Conference on Computer Vision and Pattern Recognition, pp. 2617–2626 (2022)
49. Mettes, P., van Gemert, J.C., Snoek, C.G.M.: Spot on: action localization from pointly-supervised proposals. In: Leibe, B., Matas, J., Sebe, N., Welling, M. (eds.) ECCV 2016. LNCS, vol. 9909, pp. 437–453. Springer, Cham (2016). https://doi.org/10.1007/978-3-319-46454-1_27
50. Papadopoulos, D.P., Uijlings, J.R., Keller, F., Ferrari, V.: Training object class detectors with click supervision. In: Proceedings of the IEEE Conference on Computer Vision and Pattern Recognition, pp. 6374–6383 (2017)
51. Bearman, A., Russakovsky, O., Ferrari, V., Fei-Fei, L.: What's the point: semantic segmentation with point supervision. In: Leibe, B., Matas, J., Sebe, N., Welling, M. (eds.) ECCV 2016. LNCS, vol. 9911, pp. 549–565. Springer, Cham (2016). https://doi.org/10.1007/978-3-319-46478-7_34
52. Radosavovic, I., Kosaraju, R.P., Girshick, R., He, K., Dollár, P.: Designing network design spaces. In: Proceedings of the IEEE/CVF Conference on Computer Vision and Pattern Recognition, pp. 10428–10436 (2020)

Bit-Depth Enhancement with Distortion Sensitivity

Jing Liu$^{(\boxtimes)}$, Xin Li, Xiaofeng Mi, and Yuting Su

School of Electrical and Information Engineering, Tianjin University, 92 Weijin Road,
Tianjin, China
jliu_tju@tju.edu.cn

Abstract. Displaying low bit-depth (LBD) images in high bit-depth
(HBD) monitors will cause structural distortions, resulting in the explosion of advanced bit-depth enhancement (BDE) methods. Despite the
recent progress, current BDE works cannot entirely remove false contours
and color shifts as they focus on the overall image quality while leaving
these visually sensitive distorted regions uncared. Thus, in this paper, we
propose a bit-depth enhancement algorithm with distortion sensitivity to
explicitly pay extra attention to the visually sensitive distorted regions
indicated by the predicted quantization distortion. Concretely, we propose a Distortion Sensitivity Network (DSN) working in multiple recurrent stages with shared parameters to extract the distortion-guided features from the input LBD image. A Distortion-Guided (DG) module and
a Distortion-Guided Mutual Attention (DGMA) module are designed to
leverage the predicted distortion as well as its gradient at different scales.
Experimental results on two widely used datasets demonstrate the superiority of the proposed methods compared with state-of-the-art methods.

Keywords: Bit depth enhancement · Distortion sensitivity · Attention
mechanism

1 Introduction

Image bit-depth is the number of bits used to represent each color channel of a
pixel. Although the high dynamic range (HDR) monitors support 10 or even
higher bits per pixel (e.g., 12, 14 bits) [1,2]–as opposed to standard 8 bits
per pixel–to show more realistic and natural colors of real pixels, the lack of
the high bit-depth images that the modern monitors are capable of rendering
is non-negligible. Displaying low bit-depth (LBD) images in an HDR monitor
directly will cause annoying false contour and color shift problems in a wide range
of smooth areas as shown in Fig 1(b). Hence, effective bit-depth enhancement
(BDE) methods have drawn great attention to improve the display performance.

The traditional algorithms predict the Least Significant Bits (LSBs) of each
pixel either based on independent pixels (such as zero padding and Bit Replica-
tion [3]) or dependent on the neighborhood pixels [4–12]. However, due to the

lack of semantic information, these methods can neither effectively distinguish the serious distortion areas from the normal regions, nor reasonably eliminate the distorted areas, that is, suffering from severe false contour and color shift distortions.

Later, deep learning brings a performance leap in this field. BE-CNN [13] is the first to use convolution neural network for image BDE. Subsequently, BitNet [14] improved the encoder-decoder structure to take advantages of multi-scale features and reduce computational complexity. The dense feature fusion operation used in BE-CALF [15] is conducive to more stable convergence during model training and more sufficient fusion of features at all levels of the network. LBDEN [16] proposed a lightweight network model with excellent image reconstruction ability, aiming at solving the problems of poor performance and long inference time of the existing deep learning based BDE algorithms. Regardless of the diverse model structures, these deep learning based methods are optimized to directly predict the pixel values of real HBD image or to indirectly predict the quantization residual between the input LBD image and real HBD image. These end-to-end prediction manners optimized by pixel-wise loss function (e.g., MSE or VGG-based perceptual loss) obviously ignore the visual sensitivity difference of diverse image structures and tend to overlook the sensitive structural and common artifacts like false contours and color shifts in smooth color transition areas.

To tackle the annoying artifacts, we pay specific attention to the visually sensitive distorted areas by making use of the predicted quantization distortion. As we all know, the quantization distortion will appear when we transform a continuous brightness signal or a fine-quantized discrete signal into a coarse-quantized representation, which always happens with AD conversion or later compression in ISP pipeline. When the degraded images are displayed in HDR monitors, the quantization distortion appears as the false contours or color shifts inevitably. Figure 1 shows two original HBD images, corresponding LBD images, quantization distortion maps, and quantization distortion gradient maps in sequence. Compared with the fine-quantized HBD images, the coarse-quantized LBD images have obvious wave-like false contours and disharmonious color shifts. For example, in figure (b), there are unnatural color differences emerging on the large scale snow background and the black rocks in the bottom right corner. We found that the visually sensitive artifacts in (b) have close correlation with the spatial variant quantization distortions in (c) and the gradient map in (d). The quantization distortions in (c) can be considered as the residual between the fine-quantized HBD image and the coarse-quantized LBD image, while the gradient maps in (d) reflect the spatial change of quantization distortions. It is observed that large quantization distortion generally indicates color shift while the abrupt change of quantization distortion generally indicates the false contours. Noticing this, in this paper, we adopt the quantization distortion and its gradient as two types of auxiliary indicators to the visually sensitive distortion and use them to explicitly guide the network to adaptively enhance the image distortion areas.

(a)   (b)   (c)   (d)

Fig. 1. The relationship diagram between the HBD images and their corresponding LBD images. (a) original HBD image, (b) LBD image, (c) the quantization distortion map between HBD (a) and LBD (b) image, (d) the gradient map of (c). The upper pictures show the distant mountains rendering the flat and vast sky indistinctly with a cluster of leafs occupying corner of sight. The lower pictures are large scale snows with some black rocks and a shadowy figure out of the fog.

In this paper, we focus on the visual sensitivity and propose the bit-depth enhancement with distortion sensitivity (BEDS). The quantization distortion map and the gradient map are fully exploited to indicate the distorted areas. To predict the quantization distortion maps accurately, we design a novel network inspired by SRFBN [17] that has multi recurrent working stages with shared parameters. Specifically, a quantization distortion map is predicted in the first stage and then used as an additional auxiliary guidance in the next stage to further optimize the distortion-guided feature maps. Besides, we also calculate the gradient map as another auxiliary information. The multi-stage training method can gradually refine the predicted quantization distortion map for better reconstruction performance without too much computation. Actually, we design a Distortion Sensitivity Network (DSN) in each stage to predict and refine the quantization distortion maps, which uses a U-Net like structure [18] as backbone. In the DSN, the input LBD image and its corresponding quantization distortion information are gradually up- and down-sampled in convolution layers to extract and fuse multi-scale features. We propose a Distortion-Guided (DS) module as one of the key components of DSN, which is applied to convolution layers with higher spatial dimension. The DS module contains two branches to fuse the feature maps modulated by different distortion information. And motivated by CCNet [19], we also propose a Distortion-Guided Mutual Attention (DGMA) module to gather contextual information from different branches. DGMA module is used only in coarse scale in order to avoid huge computational burden caused by the complex attention mechanism. The main contributions of this work are listed as follows:

1) We innovatively explore the quantization distortion map and its gradient map to indicate the visually sensitive distorted areas. They are used to enhance the feature extraction and help to reconstruct the distorted regions.
2) We propose a Distortion Sensitivity Network (DSN) working in multi recurrent stages to predict and optimize the quantization distortion map between the original HBD images and its degraded LBD images. All the stages share the same parameters to ensure relatively lower complexity.
3) We propose a Distortion-Guided (DG) module and a Distortion-Guided Mutual Attention (DGMA) module to facilitate distortion guidance at different scales in the light-weight DSN.
4) Experimental results show that our proposed BEDS achieves state-of-the-art performance with competitive inference speed, and numerous ablation studies verify the effectiveness of the key components.

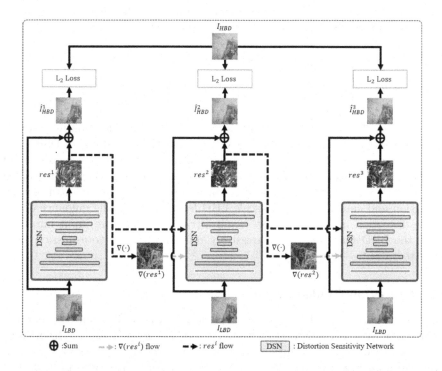

Fig. 2. The illustration of overall framework of proposed BEDS method.

2   The Proposed Algorithm

2.1   Distortion Sensitivity Network

The total pipeline of our proposed BEDS shown in Fig. 2 adopts a multi-stage training method motivated by SRFBN [17] in order to obtain the reconstructed HBD images with better visual effect without adding additional parameters or causing greater computational burden. We set the number of stages as I, and each stage i is temporally ordered from 1 to I. Working at each stage are the subnets with shared parameters and settings, whose key component is a Distortion Sensitivity Network (DSN) shown in Fig. 3, which can predicts the quantization distortion map res^i by a skip connection [15] according to the LBD images and the coarse distortion features. We provide a LBD image I_{LBD} and an original HBD image I_{HBD} to all stages and apply L_2 loss on the reconstructed HBD images $\hat{I}_{HBD}$ to supervise the training process.

To predict the distortion information more accurately, we introduce the res^i and its gradient map $\nabla(res^i)$ which can reveal extra guidance information into DSN in stage $i+1$. For the first stage, we just feed the LBD image to predict the most coarse quantization distortion map res^1 initially. Therefore, We formulate the reconstructed HBD image $\hat{I}_{HBD}^i$ in each stage as:

$$\hat{I}_{HBD}^i = \begin{cases} DSN(I_{LBD}) + I_{LBD} & i = 1 \\ DSN(I_{LBD},\ res^{i-1},\ \nabla(res^{i-1})) + I_{LBD} & 2 \leq i \leq I \end{cases} \tag{1}$$

where, $\nabla(res^{i-1})$ stands for gradient of the quantization distortion map res^{i-1} calculated by Sobel operator [20]. $DSN(\cdot)$ denotes the operations of DSEN.

Our proposed DSN adopts a U-Net like multi-scale framework, consisting of two key components, Distortion-Guided (DG) module and Distortion-Guided Mutual Attention (DGMA) module, which are working at different spatial dimension and can extract multi-scale LBD features. With the guidance of the coarse distortion information res^{i-1} and $\nabla(res^{i-1})$ which are input into each layer, the LBD features are progressively refined with the transmission from input to output.

2.2   Distortion-Guided Module

The Distortion-Guide (DG) module is shown in Fig. 4. We can see that the quantization distortion map res^{i-1} and its gradient map $\nabla(res^{i-1})$ from stage $i-1$ pass through a convolution layer firstly to generate corresponding adaptive spatial attention maps. Then a point-wise multiplication is applied on two branches to refine the LBD feature map f transmitted to the current layer with the guidance of res^{i-1} and $\nabla(res^{i-1})$, respectively. Finally, we concatenate the two different distortion-guided feature maps, named f^1 and f^2, and import them to the subsequent layer. The two auxiliary maps indicate the distortions in different aspects, so after being modulated with them, the refined feature map pays

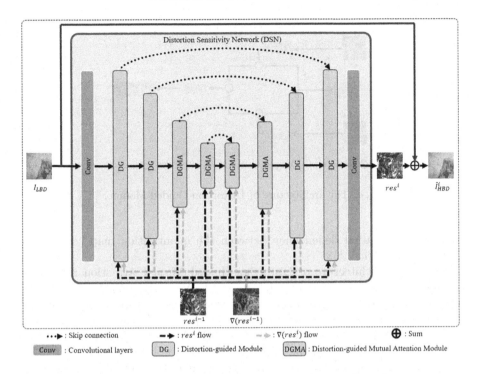

Fig. 3. The architecture of Distortion Sensitivity Network.

more attention to the distorted regions, leading to higher quality HBD image. The whole process is formulated as below:

$$f^1 = Conv(res^{i-1}) \odot f; \tag{2}$$

$$f^2 = Conv(\nabla(res^{i-1})) \odot f; \tag{3}$$

$$f' = Conv(Concat(f^1, f^2)). \tag{4}$$

where $Conv$ denotes convolution layers, and $Concat$ represents concatenation operation.

To further utilize the quantization distortion map res^{i-1} and its gradient map $\nabla(res^{i-1})$, on the basic of DG module, we introduce a mutual attention (MA) operation which adopts the architecture of criss-cross attention module in [19] to capture the mutual dependency between two branches. While one criss-cross attention module can just collect contextual information in horizontal and vertical, two cascaded modules can capture the dense and global contextual information with the cost of a minor computation increment. Therefore, instead of using dense attention [21,22], we concatenate two criss-cross attention to

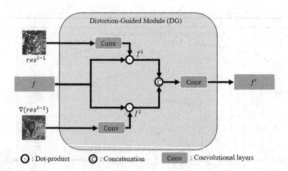

Fig. 4. The architecture of Distortion-Guided Module.

aggregate the mutual dependency between the quantization map res^{i-1} and gradient map $\nabla(res^{i-1})$.

The whole architecture of Distortion-Guided Mutual Attention module is shown in Fig. 5, named DGMA module for short. We firstly applied a convolution layer separately on the quantization distortion guided feature map f^1 and the gradient guided feature map f^2 to obtain q^t (query), k^t (key) and v^t (value), where t represents index of each branch in DGMA module. We then input the q^1, k^2 and v^2 to the MA of the upper branch, and input q^2, k^1 and v^1 to MA of the lower branch. As shown in Fig. 5, we calculate the mutual attention map and extract the fused features by performing the above operations. Finally, we concatenate the fused features from the two branches to generate the output feature map f' and transmit it into the next layer. The output feature map f' can be formulated as below:

$$f' = Conv(Concat(MA(q^1,\ k^2,\ v^2), MA(q^2,\ k^1,\ v^1))). \qquad (5)$$

where MA denotes the operation of mutual attention module.

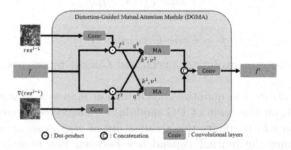

Fig. 5. The architecture of Distortion-Guided Mutual Attention Module.

2.3   Loss Function

Loss function is critical in deep learning methods, for it supervises the optimization of parameters in the network. L_2 loss function is a pixel-wise mean square error loss between the output image and the ground truth, which can be called reconstructed loss function in image enhancement field. We adopt the reconstruction loss into each stage as shown in Fig. 2 to calculate the difference between the reconstructed HBD images $\hat{I}_{HBD}$ and the original HBD images I_{HBD} pixel by pixel. With the supervision of reconstruction loss, the robustness and results' quality of the network can be ensured. The reconstruction loss function can be formulated as follows:

$$L_2 = \sum_{i=1}^{M}\sum_{j=1}^{N}\sum_{k=1}^{C}\left(\hat{I}_{HBD} - I_{HBD}\right)^2 \tag{6}$$

where, M, N, C are respectively the width, height and number of color channels of the image, $\hat{I}_{HBD}$ is the reconstructed image of LBD image, and I_{HBD} is the corresponding HBD ground truth.

3   Experiments

3.1   Experiment Settings

Our method is trained and tested in Sintel [23] and MIT-Adobe 5 K [24] datasets. The images in Sintel dataset [23] are extracted from the animated film *Sintel* which is synthesized by computers and has smooth content texture and high visual quality. In this paper, 1000 images are randomly selected from the original video frame sequence as the original training set, and then 50 images are randomly selected as test samples from the remaining video frame sequence. MIT Adobe 5 K [24] is composed of 5000 natural images captured by a group of different photographers using different brands of cameras. The process of extracting training and testing images in MIT Adob 5 K is similar to that of Sintel dataset, with 1000 training samples and 40 testing samples taken in a non-overlapping manner. All the training samples above are cropped to 128 × 128 and image augmentation methods (e.g. rotation and flip) are adopted when training.

We trained our network with Adam optimizer [25] ($\beta_1 = 0.9$, $\beta_2 = 0.999$, $\epsilon = 1 \times 10^{-8}$, weight decay 0). The proposed BEDS was trained by L_2 loss for 31 epochs with the learning rate 1×10^{-4} and batch size 18. All the experiments were performed on an NVIDIA GTX 2080Ti GPU.

3.2   Quantitative Results

We compared our method with three traditional methods: ZP, MIG, IPAD [8] and three deep learning based methods: BE-CALF [15], BitNet [14], ALBM-D4 [26] on Sintel dataset [23] and MIT-Adobe 5 K dataset [24]. The above methods were trained and tested on 4-bits to 8- and 16-bits image enhancement tasks.

The peak signal to noise ratio (PSNR) and the structural similarity (SSIM) [27] between the original HBD images and reconstructed images were employed as quantitative metrics.

Table 1 shows the test results on the Sintel and MIT-Adobe 5 K datasets. Our method outperforms other existing methods in all cases, reaching the state-of-the-art results. Specifically, compared with the sub-optimal method ALBM-D4, our method shows a significant improvement on Sintel dataset. For the BDE task from 4-bits to 8-bits, our method has an average PSNR and SSIM gain as high as 0.36 dB and 0.0045 compared with ALBM-D4. And for the more difficult BDE task from 4-bits to 16-bits, our method is better than ALBM-D4 with the average performance gain as high as 0.37 dB in PSNR and 0.0042 in SSIM. On the MIT-Adobe 5 K dataset, the average gain of our method over the sub-optimal method BitNet is 0.99 dB and 0.0118 in PSNR and SSIM respectively for the BDE task from 4-bits to 8-bits. Additionally, for the BDE task from 4-bits to 16-bits, the performance of our method are 1.02 dB and 0.0123 higher in PSNR and SSIM than BitNet, respectively. Besides, compared with the traditional methods, our method shows obviously much higher performances in all cases, it is because the traditional methods ignore the local contexts and semantics, leading to the existence of false contours and color shifts.

Table 1. Performance comparison with other BDE methods on Sintel and MIT-Adobe 5 K datasets. The best results is highlighted in **bold**.

	Sintel		MIT-Adobe 5 K	
	4–8 bit	4–16 bit	4–8 bit	4–16 bit
	PSNR/SSIM	PSNR/SSIM	PSNR/SSIM	PSNR/SSIM
ZP	29.68/0.7991	29.25/0.7892	29.64/0.8718	29.22/0.8684
MIG	31.61/0.7992	31.27/0.7896	32.54/0.8692	32.28/0.8658
IPAD [8]	35.71/0.8978	35.75/0.9056	35.31/0.8892	35.25/0.8904
BE-CALF [15]	39.65/0.9422	39.70/0.9486	37.03/0.9125	36.97/0.9131
BitNet [14]	39.14/0.9407	39.19/0.9463	38.99/0.9481	39.00/0.9479
ALBM-D4 [26]	40.46/0.9527	40.53/0.9575	38.17/0.9290	38.13/0.9284
Ours	**40.82/0.9572**	**40.90/0.9617**	**39.98/0.9599**	**40.02/0.9602**

Table 2. Average execution time per image on Sintel dataset.

Methods	MIG	IPAD [8]	BE-CALF [15]	BitNet [14]	ALBM-D4 [26]	Ours
Time(s)	0.009	33.293	0.563	0.109	0.946	0.376

3.3 Computational Complexity Analysis

In order to compare the inference speed of our method with others, we tested our BEDS and other methods on Sintel dataset in BDE from 4-bits to 16-bits and measured the average execution time per image. As showed in Table 2, though some previous traditional algorithms, such as MIG, have short execution time due to simply reconstructing the LSBs according to the independent pixel values, their visual effect and quantitative evaluation results are terrible. For some context-aware traditional methods such as IPAD, who has relatively good performance but very slow inference speed, our algorithm is nearly 300 times faster than it, taking only 0.376 s per image. Moreover, our method has the inference speed comparable to the SOTA methods, such as BE-CALF [15], BitNet [14] and ALBM-D4 [26], while maintaining a great reconstruction effect.

3.4 Qualitative Results

To subjectively evaluate our proposed method and other six methods mentioned, we compared the test results of BDE from 4-bits to 8-bits on Sintel dataset and MIT-Adobe 5 K dataset respectively. The images in the test datasets have smooth gradient areas and flat background such as the sky and cloud.

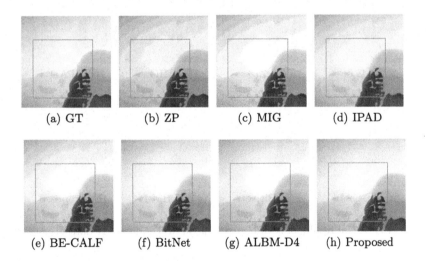

    (a) GT   (b) ZP   (c) MIG   (d) IPAD

(e) BE-CALF   (f) BitNet   (g) ALBM-D4   (h) Proposed

Fig. 6. Visual results of several methods on Sinte dataset.

Figure 6 shows the ground truth HBD image in the Sintel dataset and the reconstructed HBD images with different methods. As shown in the Fig. 6(h), our method effectively removes the false contours in the sky and copes with chromatic distortion problem, reconstructing a HBD image extremely similar with the ground truth. On the contrary, the traditional algorithms like ZP, MIG and IPAD fail to restore the color shifts or remove severe false contours. They handle each RGB channel separately, ignoring the local structural characteristic and leading to poor visual quality. The earlier deep learning based method BE-CALF suppresses the false contours well, but it is still visually unsatisfactory as shown by some shallow artifacts existing in the left corner of the sky. The subsequently proposed deep learning based algorithm ALBM-D4 [26] predicts the unknown bit plane in where the pixels have the same bit-depth to reconstruct a better HBD image. We can observe that our method has the performance like BitNet and ALBM-D4 which are state-of-the-art.

Figure 7 shows the ground truth HBD image in MIT-Adobe 5 K dataset and the reconstructed HBD images with different methods. The visual effects are similar to that in Sintel dataset. As shown in the Fig. 7(b), the most classical BDE method ZP just reconstruct the LBD images by padding zeros into the expansion bits, which will produces the artifacts like clouds. Another two traditional methods cannot improve the situations, while the clouds-like artifacts are greatly removed by the learning based methods as well as our BEDS. Generally, our proposed method can reconstruct HBD images with performance as excellent as the best methods have.

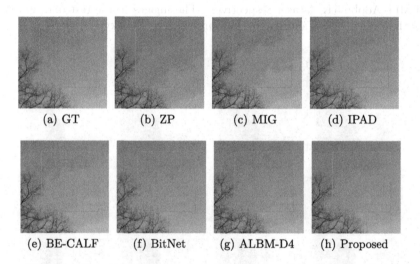

(a) GT   (b) ZP   (c) MIG   (d) IPAD

(e) BE-CALF   (f) BitNet   (g) ALBM-D4   (h) Proposed

Fig. 7. Visual results of several methods on MIT-Adobe 5 K dataset [24].

3.5 Ablation Studies

To evaluate the effectiveness of each key component of our proposed method, we trained our method and several variants and tested on the BDE from 4-bits to 16-bits using the Sintel dataset. We then calculated the PSNR and SSIM values between the ground truth image and the reconstructed image to evaluate the performance quantitatively.

Number of Stages. We conducted ablation experiments to explore the influence of the number of working stages (denoted as I). We set I as 1, 2 and 3 orderly. The results are shown in Table 3. We can observe that the reconstruction quality is significantly improved from 38.39 dB to 40.85 dB in PSNR when I increases from one to two, the gain in PSNR is 2.46 dB. In addition, as I continues to increase, the reconstruction performance keeps rising while the gain of performance gradually becomes smaller because of overfitting. Therefore, we set I as 3 for the best enhancement effect.

Table 3. Ablation study with different stage number on Sintel datasets.

Stage num	1	2	3
PSNR(dB)/SSIM	38.39/0.9495	40.85/0.9615	40.90/0.9617

The Effect of Auxiliary Information. We have input the quantization distortion map and the quantization distortion gradient map into each working stage as the auxiliary information. Therefore, in this section, we explored the effects of these two auxiliary information, and reported the quantitative results in Table 4. The first three lines demonstrate the separate effect of the quantization distortion (denoted as res) and the gradient of quantization distortion (denoted as $\nabla(res)$). According to the experiments, we observe that both of the two types of auxiliary information improve the quality of the total pipeline network, while the gradient information indicates the areas with large reconstruction difficulty, it can directly guide the feature map to pay more attention to these regions, reconstructing HBD images with better performance. To confirm the benefits of using distortion information to explicitly guide the network, we replace res and $\nabla(res)$ with the reconstructed $\hat{I}_{HBD}$ image and its gradient map $\nabla(\hat{I}_{HBD})$ as another variant. The results are shown in the last line. The HBD images can't indicate the distortion regions directly, thus fail to help the network to refine the details of severe degraded areas like the distortion maps, which validates the necessary of our proposed distortion sensitivity based method.

Table 4. Ablation study of auxiliary information on Sintel dataset. The best results is highlighted in **bold**.

res	$\nabla(res)$	$\hat{I}_{HBD}$	$\nabla(\hat{I}_{HBD})$	PSNR(dB)/SSIM
✓				40.34/0.9593
	✓			40.46/0.9527
✓	✓			**40.90/0.9617**
		✓	✓	40.76/0.9579

Table 5. Ablation study on the effect of mutual attention. The best results is highlighted in **bold**.

Self attention	Mutual attention	PSNR(dB)/SSIM
		40.56/0.9576
✓		40.65/0.9592
	✓	**40.90/0.9617**

The Effect of Mutual Attention. The mutual attention (MA) operation in DGMA module fuse the mutual dependency between the quantization distortion map and the gradient map. To evaluate the effectiveness of MA, we calculate the self-attention instead of the mutual attention by still using the architecture of criss-cross attention module [19]. Compared with the second line in Table 5, our method has higher values in PSNR and SSIM, which indicates the superiority of our innovation. Additionally, we remove the attention operation to train the network and the results are reported in the first line in Table 5. It is obvious that our method shows significant improvements in both PSNR and SSIM with the gain of 0.34 dB and 0.0041, respectively. Attention mechanism is beneficial to process large amount of information with finite resources, and mutual attention can capture different features to enrich the details of distorted regions.

4   Conclusion

In this paper, we proposed a novel bit-depth enhancement algorithm with distortion sensitivity to take full advantage of the predicted quantization distortion and its gradient to reconstruct high quality HBD images. Specifically, a multi-stage framework was designed to gradually refine the predicted quantization distortion map. In each stage, DSN with shared parameters was employed to obtain multiscale features, and in which two key components, DG and DGMA, were designed to extract and concatenate the distortion-guided features. Finally, the quantitative results and qualitative results on Sintel and MIT-Adobe 5 K datasets show the excellent performance of our proposed method.

Acknowledgments. This work was supported by the National Science Foundation of China under Grant 61701341.

References

1. Mantiuk, R., Krawczyk, G., Myszkowski, K., Seidel, H.P.: Perception-motivated high dynamic range video encoding. ACM Trans. Graph. (TOG) **23**(3), 733–741 (2004)
2. Banterle, F., Artusi, A., Debattista, K., Chalmers, A.: Advanced High Dynamic Range Imaging. AK Peters/CRC Press, Cambridge (2017)

3. Simonyan, K., Zisserman, A.: Very deep convolutional networks for large-scale image recognition. arXiv preprint arXiv:1409.1556 (2014)
4. Mittal, G., Jakhetiya, V., Jaiswal, S.P., Au, O.C., Tiwari, A.K., Wei, D.: Bit-depth expansion using minimum risk based classification. In: 2012 Visual Communications and Image Processing, pp. 1–5. IEEE (2012)
5. Cheng, C.H., Au, O.C., Liu, C.H., Yip, K.Y.: Bit-depth expansion by contour region reconstruction. In: 2009 IEEE International Symposium on Circuits and Systems, pp. 944–947. IEEE (2009)
6. Wan, P., Au, O.C., Tang, K., Guo, Y., Fang, L.: From 2D extrapolation to 1D interpolation: content adaptive image bit-depth expansion. In: 2012 IEEE International Conference on Multimedia and Expo, pp. 170–175. IEEE (2012)
7. Wan, P., Cheung, G., Florencio, D., Zhang, C., Au, Ȯ.C.: Image bit-depth enhancement via maximum-a-posteriori estimation of graph ac component. In: 2014 IEEE International Conference on Image Processing (ICIP), pp. 4052–4056. IEEE (2014)
8. Liu, J., Zhai, G., Liu, A., Yang, X., Zhao, X., Chen, C.W.: IPAD: intensity potential for adaptive de-quantization. IEEE Trans. Image Process. **27**(10), 4860–4872 (2018)
9. Liu, C.H., Au, O.C., Wong, P.H., Kung, M.C., Chao, S.C.: Bit-depth expansion by adaptive filter. In: 2008 IEEE International Symposium on Circuits and Systems (ISCAS), pp. 496–499. IEEE (2008)
10. Daly, S.J., Feng, X.: Decontouring: prevention and removal of false contour artifacts. In: Human Vision and Electronic Imaging IX, vol. 5292, pp. 130–149. SPIE (2004)
11. Ahn, W., Kim, J.S.: Flat-region detection and false contour removal in the digital tv display. In: 2005 IEEE International Conference on Multimedia and Expo, pp. 1338–1341. IEEE (2005)
12. Peng, C., Xia, M., Fu, Z., Xu, J., Li, X.: Bilateral false contour elimination filter-based image bit-depth enhancement. IEEE Signal Process. Lett. **28**, 1585–1589 (2021)
13. Liu, J., Sun, W., Liu, Y.: Bit-depth enhancement via convolutional neural network. In: Zhai, G., Zhou, J., Yang, X. (eds.) IFTC 2017. CCIS, vol. 815, pp. 255–264. Springer, Singapore (2018). https://doi.org/10.1007/978-981-10-8108-8_24
14. Byun, J., Shim, K., Kim, C.: BitNet: learning-based bit-depth expansion. In: Jawahar, C.V., Li, H., Mori, G., Schindler, K. (eds.) ACCV 2018. LNCS, vol. 11362, pp. 67–82. Springer, Cham (2019). https://doi.org/10.1007/978-3-030-20890-5_5
15. Liu, J., Sun, W., Su, Y., Jing, P., Yang, X.: Be-calf: bit-depth enhancement by concatenating all level features of DNN. IEEE Trans. Image Process. **28**(10), 4926–4940 (2019)
16. Zhao, Y., Wang, R., Chen, Y., Jia, W., Liu, X., Gao, W.: Lighter but efficient bit-depth expansion network. IEEE Trans. Circuits Syst. Video Technol. **31**(5), 2063–2069 (2020)
17. Li, Z., Yang, J., Liu, Z., Yang, X., Jeon, G., Wu, W.: Feedback network for image super-resolution. In: Proceedings of the IEEE/CVF Conference on Computer Vision and Pattern Recognition, pp. 3867–3876 (2019)
18. Ronneberger, O., Fischer, P., Brox, T.: U-Net: convolutional networks for biomedical image segmentation. In: Navab, N., Hornegger, J., Wells, W.M., Frangi, A.F. (eds.) MICCAI 2015. LNCS, vol. 9351, pp. 234–241. Springer, Cham (2015). https://doi.org/10.1007/978-3-319-24574-4_28
19. Huang, Z., Wang, X., Huang, L., Huang, C., Wei, Y., Liu, W.: CCNet: Criss-cross attention for semantic segmentation. In: Proceedings of the IEEE/CVF International Conference on Computer Vision, pp. 603–612 (2019)

20. Kanopoulos, N., Vasanthavada, N., Baker, R.L.: Design of an image edge detection filter using the Sobel operator. IEEE J. Solid-State Circuits **23**(2), 358–367 (1988)
21. Vaswani, A., et al.: Attention is all you need. In: Advances in Neural Information Processing Systems, vol. 30 (2017)
22. Dosovitskiy, A., et al.: An image is worth 16x16 words: Transformers for image recognition at scale. arXiv preprint arXiv:2010.11929 (2020)
23. Roosendaal, T.: Sintel. In: ACM SIGGRAPH 2011 Computer Animation Festival, p. 71 (2011)
24. Bychkovsky, V., Paris, S., Chan, E., Durand, F.: Learning photographic global tonal adjustment with a database of input/output image pairs. In: CVPR 2011, pp. 97–104. IEEE (2011)
25. Kingma, D.P., Ba, J.: Adam: a method for stochastic optimization. arXiv preprint arXiv:1412.6980 (2014)
26. Punnappurath, A., Brown, M.S.: A little bit more: Bitplane-wise bit-depth recovery. IEEE Trans. Pattern Anal. Mach. Intell. **44**, 9718–9724 (2021)
27. Wang, Z., Bovik, A.C., Sheikh, H.R., Simoncelli, E.P.: Image quality assessment: from error visibility to structural similarity. IEEE Trans. Image Process. **13**(4), 600–612 (2004)

Combining Transformer and Convolutional Neural Network for Smoke Detection

Yafei Gong[1,2,3,4,5], Xinkang Lian[1,2,3,4,5], Xuanchao Ma[1,2,3,4,5], Zhifang Xia[1,2,3,4,5,6], and Chengxu Zhou[1,2,3,4,5,7,8]($\boxtimes$)

[1] Faculty of Information Technology, Beijing University of Technology, Beijing, China
zhouchengxu@lnut.edu.cn
[2] Engineering Research Center of Intelligent Perception and Autonomous Control, Ministry of Education, Beijing, China
[3] Beijing Laboratory of Smart Environmental Protection, Beijing, China
[4] Beijing Key Laboratory of Computational Intelligence and Intelligent System, Beijing, China
[5] Beijing Artificial Intelligence Institute, Beijing, China
[6] National Information Center, Beijing, China
[7] School of Electronic and Information Engineering, Liaoning University of Technology, Jinzhou, Liaoning, China
[8] Key Laboratory of Intelligent Control and Optimization for Industrial Equipment of Ministry of Education, Dalian University of Technology, Dalian, China

Abstract. Smoke detection plays a crucial role in the safety production of petrochemical enterprises and fire prevention. Image-based machine learning and deep learning methods have been widely studied. Recently, many works have applied the transformer to solve problems faced by computer vision tasks (such as classification and object detection). To our knowledge, there are few studies using the transformer structure to detect smoke. In order to research the application potential and improve the performance of the transformer in the smoke detection field, we propose a model consisting of two transformer encoders and a convolutional neural network (CNN) module. The first transformer encoder can be used to establish the global relationship of an image, and the CNN structure can provide additional local information to the transformer. The fusion of global information and local information is conducive to the second transfer encoder to make better decisions. Experiments results on

This work was supported in part by the National Science Foundation of China under Grant 62273011 and Grant 62076013; in part by the Beijing Natural Science Foundation under Grant JQ21014; in part by the Industry-University-Research Innovation Fund for Chinese University - Blue Point Distributed Intelligent Computing Project under 2021LDA03003; in part by the Ministry of Education of China under Grant 202102535002, Grant 202102535012; in part by the Key Laboratory of Intelligent Control and Optimization for Industrial Equipment of Ministry of Education, Dalian University of Technology under Grant LICO2022TB03.

G. Zhai et al. (Eds.): IFTC 2022, CCIS 1766, pp. 121–135, 2023.
https://doi.org/10.1007/978-981-99-0856-1_9

122   Y. Gong et al.

large-size dataset for industrial smoke detection illustrate the effectiveness of the proposed model.

Keywords: Smoke detection · Transformer · Convolutional network · Classification

1 Introduction

Petrochemical enterprises are the foundation and pillar industry of China's economy. The pollutants emitted in the production process are one of the primary sources of petrochemical pollution, which will deteriorate air quality and endanger human health [1–3]. Gu [4] proposed a heuristic recirculating air quality predictor (RAOP) to predict future air quality. Smoke detection in petrochemical enterprises is significant for regulating the production process and reducing pollution emissions. Moreover, smoke detection is required in wildfire detection and compartment fire prevention, which makes the research on smoke detection has high practical value and remains an important research direction.

Sensor-based systems have been used in various production and living environments with the aid of computer vision over the years. The sensor can work well in some cases where the indoor environment or background are usually the same. However, in the flare stack system of petrochemical enterprises, the ambient temperature is high, and the state variable changes rapidly, which makes the sensor show unacceptable problems such as low accuracy and high hysteresis. In addition, the sensors have limited range. Overall, sensor based methods are difficult to satisfying the requirements of today's industrial process.

With the development of artificial intelligence, smoke detection methods based on images have received extensive attention and the research on it has grown significantly. Methods of smoke detection can be broadly devided into two categories, which are based on traditional machine learing (ML) methods and deep learning (DL) methods. The first methods identifies smoke areas based on the features that can represent smoke such as color, shape and texture. Those features are manually selected and processed and do not require the learning process. Some of these methods transfer the extracted features to classifiers for smoke detection. The ML methods might encounter a bottleneck because it is difficult for the head-extracted features to characterize the smoke in an image, which makes them have a high false alarm rate (FAR). Compared with traditional ML methods, the DL-based methods utilize complex networks to perform feature extraction and prediction [5–15]. Those networks are usually implemented using convolutional layers, pooling layers, and fully-connected layers, which provide a powerful tool and a new solution for smoke detection.

In recent years, transformer architecture has made significant progress in the field of NLP. Inspired by this, researchers also attempt to transfer it to computer vision tasks and have achieved excellent performance in image classification, object detection [16,17], semantic segmentation [18] and image processing [19]. Previous research has shown that the transformer structure requires more data than the CNN structure. Transfer learning is often used on smaller datasets, which limits the application of transformers when transfer learning is not available on specific tasks. From what we know, there are few research and applications based on transformers in the direction of smoke detection. Therefore, it is imperative to explore the performance of the transformer in smoke detection.

In this paper, we designed a model for smoke detection that combines the transformer and CNN structure. First, we proposed a model consisting of only the transformer layer to detect smoke. For an input image, we designed a patch embedding method that shifts and stacks the image to increase the amount of information of each token. A learnable smoothing factor was designed for the self-attention mechanism of the transformer layer to make the model more adaptive to the dataset. Subsequently, we designed a CNN module containing six convolutional layers and three pooling layers to provide the local features for the original model, which is beneficial for the model to obtain better performance. Finally, with the proper model configurations and parameter settings, our model achieved the best performance on the experimental dataset.

The structure of the paper is arranged as follows. Section 2 introduces the technical developments in smoke detection. Section 3 gives the proposed model's detailed composition. Section 4 details the experimental parameter settings and results. In the end, Sect. 5 summarizes the main conclusion of this article.

2   Background and Related Work

The problem of smoke detection is extremely challenging because of the complex background and serious noise interference in the venting flares of petrochemical enterprises. The primary methods for achieving smoke detection mainly include manual observation and electrochemical sensor monitoring. The method of manual observation is affected by subjective factors and cannot be used for long-term smoke monitoring. On the other hand, the sensor-based methods are affected by the flare gas's high temperature and complex composition, resulting in low accuracy and severe time delay. With the development of image processing and machine learning, researchers have devoted a lot of energy to the study of image-based recognition technology to enrich the limited sensor-based methods over the past years [20–25].

Traditional smoke detection methods usually use image processing algorithms to extract features, and use machine learning techniques for smoke classification. Cui [26] designed a classifier to determine whether there is smoke texture. The texture features was extraction by using wavelet transform and gray level co-occurrence matrices (GLCM), and a two layer neural network was trained to judge whether there was smoke texture in the image. Gubbi [27] used wavelet transform to represent smoke features and performed support vector machine to detect smoke. In order to obtain the amount of smoke in the image, Vidal-Calleja [28] designed a smoke detection method based on bag-of-words paradigm of LDA model. Yuan [29] designed a video smoke detection model and built a pyramid based on histograms of the local binary pattern (LBP) and local binary pattern variance (LBPV). The model used LBP to extract local information and image pyramid to extract global texture information. In [30], Yuan combined LBP, kernerl principal component analysis, and Gaussian process regression to proposed a method for smoke detection. Recently, Gu [31] designed a smoke detection model based on vision. The method first locates the flame in an image by using the broadly tuned color channel. Then, K-means is used for fast saliency detection to refine the flame position. Finally, the potential flare soot region is searched centered on the flame area and identified by the background color channel. Affected by the variability of lighting conditions, smoke density, and background clutter, it is not easy to achieve high-precision smoke identification only using artificially designed features and ML.

Compared with manually designing features, deep learning-based methods use complex networks to automatically extract features. In recent years, a lot of deep neural networks appear and are applied in variety fields. Such as Resnet [32], Googlenet [34], Densenet [33]. Those networks are used for classified tasks or as backbones for more complex tasks, and perform excellent on benchmark datasets. Inspired by the design of those models, several researchers have designed the deep convolutional neural network to solve the problem of smoke classification. In [35], Yin proposed a model, namely DNCNN, by combining convolution and batch normalization for smoke detection task. The model adopted data enhancement technology to alleviate the data imbalance problem and achieved more than 96.37% detection rate. Gu [36] designed a deep dual-channel network having two sub-networks for smoke detection. SBNN is a subnetwork to extract texture information, another subnetwork is SCNN which is used to extract contour information of smoke image. The network performs well when the image has rich smoke texture information. To this end, Gu [37]- [40] designed a variety of image quality evaluation networks. Liu [41] proposed another dual-channel network based on RGB information and dark channel features. One of the subnetworks extracts low-level RGB information using the residual connection mechanism, and the other is designed to extract dark channel features. Finally, the output of the two subnetworks is fused to obtain the final prediction result. Based on Resnet-50, You [42] designed a model for smoke detection and applied spatial attention and channel attention module which enhanced the ability to extract key smoke features. Khan [43] also applied spatial attention and channel attention mechanism to design the model. The model used the feature pyramid to enhance the edge texture features and deep semantic information.

In visual application tasks, convolutional neural network is usually considered as the fundamental component of the network. Transformer has shown its potential as a alternative to CNN in recent years. Vision transformer (Vit) [11] is a pure transformer that directly processes image patches sequences for image classification. Vit has yeild excellent performance on large datasets, but achieved lower performance than ResNets of comparable size on mid-sized datasets. The transformer lacks the inherent inductive biases of CNN, such as translation invariance and locality, so it requires a larger amount of data for better performance. To improve transformer performance for visual tasks, many Vit variants have been designed. These methods mainly include improving locality, enhancing self-attention and structural design [44–47]. Another way to bring the power of convolution into Vit is to use convolution and Vit together. For example, networks (such as CVT, Ceit and LocalVit) have introduced convolution layers into the transformer structure to improve the ablility of extracting local information [48–50].

Numerous works have applied transformers to visual tasks, but as far as we know, its research in the direction of smoke classification is not much. Therefore, it is necessary to explore the application performance of transformers in smoke classification. We design a model combining the transformer and CNN structures for smoke classification, and the detail of network design will be described in section three.

3   Method

3.1   Preliminary

Before introducing the model proposed in the paper, this section briefly reviews the self-attention mechanism and standard components of standard Vit.

Tokenization. Let the input image of the model $x \in R^{C \times H \times W}$. Here, C, H, and W correspond to the image's channel, height, and width, respectively. The transformer model requires sequence data, so it is necessary to convert image data into sequence data. The main idea of this process is to first split the image into non-overlapping image patches, and then platten these patches to acquire sequence data (patches). The sequence data can be defined as:

$$V(x) = \{x_1, x_2, \ldots, x_n\} \tag{1}$$

where $x_i \in R^{P^2 \times C}$ stand for the i-th flattened data, P is patch size, and n represents the number of patches. x_i usually comes from an image patch surrounded by a square with a side length of patch size. Then, tokenization operation is carried out, that is, patch is transformed into the hidden dimension space of transformer layer to obtain the token. This can be described by:

$$T(x) = V(x)E_t \tag{2}$$

where $E_t \in R^{(P^2 \cdot C) \times d}$ is a learnable parameter that maps each patch into the hidden dimension space of the transformer encoder, and d stand for hidden dimension of the transformer encoder.

Position Embedding. After the image is converted into tokens, the inherent position information in the image will be lost. Previous studies have proved that the position information is of great significance in transformers. Therefore, it is crucial to add positional information to patch embeddings. There are many ways to achieve this goal, such as learnable position embedding, 1D position embedding, 2D sin-cos position embedding, and zero-padding. The following equations can express the 2D sin-cos position embedding:

$$PE_{(index,2j)} = \sin\left(index/10000^{2j/dim}\right)$$
$$PE_{(index,2j+1)} = \cos\left(index/10000^{2j/dim}\right) \tag{3}$$

where $index$ represents the position of x_i in the entire sequence, dim stands for the dimension of the patch embedding, and j belongs to $[0, dim/2)$. Then, each token is superposed with the position embedding and sent to the transformer encoder to establish the global relationship. The final input of transformer encoder is defined by:

$$I(x) = f(\mathcal{T}(x), PE) \tag{4}$$

where PE and $\mathcal{T}(x)$ stand for position embeddings and tokens, respectively, and $f()$ is a function that adds position information to tokens and is usually achieved by element-add.

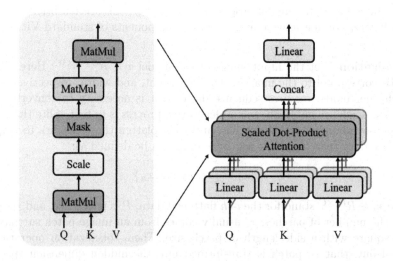

Fig. 1. Self-attention (left), multi-head self-attention (right)

Self-attention. The self-attention mechanism is the core part of Transformer. For input $I(x)$, a learnable linear projection is performed on each token to obtain Q (Query), K (Key), and V (Value), respectively. Then, use Q and K to calculate the similarity matrix M, which is realized by matrix multiplication of Q and K. The similarity matrix M is described as follows:

$$M = I(x)E_q\left(I(x)E_k\right)^{\top} \tag{5}$$

where $E(q) \in R^{d \times d_q}$ and $E(k) \in R^{d \times d_k}$, which has the same function as E_t, that is, indicating the learnable linear projection, d_q is the dimension of Q, d_k is the dimension of K. And $M \in R^{n \times n}$ stands for the semantic relation between tokens. Then, self-attention can be acquired by applying the matrix multiplication of M and V, defined in follows:

$$SA(x) = \text{softmax}\left(M/\sqrt{d_k}\right)(I(x)E_v) \tag{6}$$

where $E(v) \in R^{d \times d_v}$ represents a linear projection for V, and d_q stands for the dimension of V. In summary, the process of calculating self-attention can be summarized into the follows:

$$\text{Attention}(Q, K, V) = \text{softmax}\left(\frac{Q \cdot K^\top}{\sqrt{d_k}}\right) \cdot V \tag{7}$$

Multi-head attention is a mechanism that utilizes information from multiple-dimensional subspaces to improve self-attention performance. It is a common condition that a token usually has a strong relationship with multiple tokens. Self-attention mechanism limits a token's ability to treat other essential tokens equally while focusing on one or some special tokens. Multi-head attention is achieved by assigning different subspaces to each layer, and different layers use different Q, K, and V to calculate the self-attention under different subspaces. The left side of Fig. 1 shows the calculation process of self-attention, and the right side of Fig. 1 shows the multi-head self-attention calculation process.

3.2   Model Details

The detailed structure of the proposed model is shown in Fig. 2. The network consists of a CNN module, two transformer encoders, and an MLP head. First, the CNN module extracts the local information to the transformer encoder, and the transformer encoder will play its part by building the global relationship. Finally, the classification results are obtained through the MLP head.

CNN Module. In order to take advantage of the CNN inductive biases, a CNN module is designed to extranct local and translation invariant features. This CNN module contains six convolution layers and three max-pooling layersm, and every two convolution layers are fallowed by a max-pooling layer for down sampling the feature map. Each convolution layer's kernel size and stride are 3 and 1, respectively, and the kernel size of max-pooling layer and the stride are both 2. For the input image $x \in R^{C \times H \times W}$, the size of the feature maps obtained through the CNN module is one eighth of the imput image. The receptive field of a network is defined as follows:

$$RF_n = RF_{n-1} + (k_n - 1) \times \prod_{i=1}^{n-1} s_i \tag{8}$$

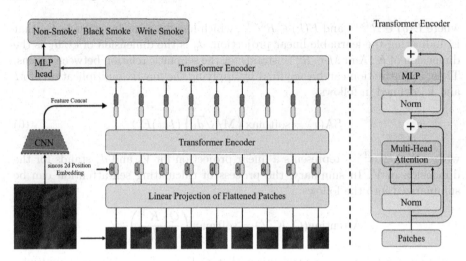

Fig. 2. The architecture of the designed model, including two transformer encoders and a CNN module.

Here, RF_n is the receptive field of the $n\text{-}th$ layer, k represents the kernel size of convolution and pooling layer, and the stride of convolution and pooling layer is represented by s_i. The receptive field of the designed CNN model is 36 according to Eq. (8), where the receptive field refers to the theoretical receptive fields, which is not equal to the actual receptive field obeying the Gaussian distribution. Each pixel in the feature maps contributes differently to the receptive of the next layer, and the contirbution drops sharply from the centor to the edge.

Patch Embedding. It is regarded as a common patch embedding method to divide the input image into non-overlapping patches, as described in Eq. (1). For the standard Vit, the patch size is 16 or 32 in most cases. For the dataset in this paper(will be described in section four), the image resolution is $48 \times 48 \times 3$, and the experiment results show that the parameters of standard vit, that is, when the image size is 224 and the patch size is 16, it cannot be directly transferred to the dataset. So, configure the image size to 96 and the patch size to 8. As a result, the receptive field of the transformer encoder is equal to 8 due the patch size determines the receptive field of the transformer encoder. At the same time, the information in each token is insufficient because of the smaller patch size. We designed a method that shifts and stacks the image to increase each token's receptive field and information. First, the input image is shifted in four directions (right-up, left-up, right-down, and left-down) at a distance of half the block size. Then, the new image is obtained by concatenating the original and shifted images:

$$x = \text{Concat}[x, x_{left-up}, x_{right\_up}, x_{left-down}, x_{right-down}] \qquad (9)$$

where x, $x_{left-up}$, x_{right_up}, $x_{left-down}$, and $x_{right-down}$ have the same dimension $R^{H \times W \times C}$. Finally, the tokens can be obtained throught Eq. (1) and Eq. (2), at which x_i in Eq. (1) becomes to $R^{P^2 \times 5 \times C}$ and E_t in Eq. (2) becomes to $R^{(P^2 \times 5 \times C) \times d}$.

Transformer Encoder. The proposed model includes two transformer encoders, and each transformer encoder consists of three transformer layers. The first transformer encoder directly established the global relationship to the tokens. Then, the features extracted by the CNN module and the first's encoder outputs are fused and used as the input features of the second transformer encoder. Although it is difficult to calculate the actual receptive field from the theoretical receptive field, CNN module provides rich local information to the transformer encoder. Moreover, a theoretical receptive field with a size of 36 also provides the possibility of expanding the receptive field of each token. The structure of the transformer in the designed model is the same as described in subsection Preliminary, except that the $\sqrt{d_k}$ in Eq. (6) is modified to a learnable parameter and initialized as $\sqrt{d_k}$. The parameter of $\sqrt{d_k}$ can adjust the distribution of the attention score matrix. The higher the value, the smoother the distribution of the attention score matrix. For small datasets such as CIFAR10 and Tiny-ImageNet, a lower $\sqrt{d_k}$ lead to better results. Therefore, we made $\sqrt{d_k}$ a learnable parameter that changes adaptively based on the dataset.

4   Experiments

4.1   Settings

DataSet. The dataset used in our paper is from [51], which aimed to detect the industrial flare stack smoke. The dataset used smoke-less, black, and white smoke to represent the normal operation conditions, insufficient combustion, and excessive combustion-supporting steam in the production process. The training set, validation set, and test set have 26538, 26483, and 17328 images, respectively, and the resolution size of the images is $48 \times 48 \times 3$. The Pytorch is used to implement the model and train the model. The experimental environment is a Windows computer with the Inter(R) Xeon(R) E5-2620X CPU at 2.10 GHz and four NVIDIA TITAN Xp.

Hyper Parameters Settings. For training all CNN models, we used SGD with momentum = 0.9, set weight decay to 1e−5, and set batch size to 128. The initial learning rate is 0.01 and linearly decreased to the end learning rate 1e−4. For training all transformer models, we also used SGD with momentum = 0.9, set weight decay to 1e−4, and set batch size to 128. The Adam and the Adamw optimizer with different hyperparameters were applied in our experiment, but SGD worked slightly better than Adam or Adamw. The cosine learning rate decay and the linear learning rate warm-up were used to train all transformer models. The initial warm-up learning rate is set to 1e−4, changed to the base learning rate of 0.001 with warm-up epoch = 10, and the end learning rate of 1e−5 with epoch = 150.

Model Configurations. The image size was set to 96, and patch size was set to 8 in our model. The configurations of these networks were slightly different from the corresponding papers except for the Levit. Specifically, the hidden dimension was set to 256, set the depth to six, set the number of heads to eight, and set the dimension of each head to 64. In addition, CNN models are also used for performance comparison. These models, which include five versions of Resnet, MobileNet-v1, MobileNet-v2, densenet, DCNN, vit and svit, are implemented using the official code provided by PyTorch or using the descriptions in the corresponding papers.

4.2   Evaluation Criteria

In classification tasks, four indicators are often used to measure model perfor-mance, namely accuracy, precision, recall rate, and f1-score. We used the Marco average method to calculate the precision, recall, and f1-score because the task processed is a three-classification task. These metrics are mainly defined from confusion matrix. The prediction results can be divided into True Positive (TP), False Positive (FP), False Nagetive (FN), and True Nagetive (TN) accoriding to their predicted categories and actual categories. TP represents a positive sample that is correctly predicted to be positive and TN represents a nagitiva sam-ple corrently predicted as nagitive. FN stands for a positive sample pridected as nagative, and a nagative sample is miss-classified as positive is called FP. Accuracy refers to the proportion of the number predicted correctly to the total:

$$Accuracy = \frac{TP+FP}{TP+TN+FP+FN} \tag{10}$$

Precision is defined as ratio of TP to the total number of samples that pridicted as positives:

$$Precision = \frac{TP}{TP+FP} \tag{11}$$

Recall is the ratio of TP to samples labeled as positives.

$$Recall = \frac{TP}{TP+FN} \tag{12}$$

F1-score is calculated by a weighted average of precision and recall.

$$F1\text{-socre} = 2 \times \frac{precision \times recall}{precision + recall} \tag{13}$$

4.3   Performance Comparison

The experimental results of each model are listed in Table 1. The proposed model (named Prop for convenience) obtained a desirable performance. The first nine rows in the table are the results of the CNN models. MobileNet achieved a tie for first place among all CNN models. The tenth to eleventh rows are the results of the vit architecture models, which used the parameter configuration described in subsection Settings. In the smoke classification field, there is no large-sized dataset like ImageNet to obtain the pre-training weights that can be fine-tuned on the downstream mid-sized datasets. Therefore, all models were directly trained on the smoke dataset used in this paper. As shown in Table 1, there were some gaps between the performance of the vision transformer models and CNN models.

The input image was resized to 96, and the patch size was set to 8. Then, we applied the patch embedding method proposed in Sect. 3.2 to process the input image for augmenting the information in each token, and we set the hidden dimension to 384. The above operations obtained an accuracy of 90.8%. Insufficient data and complex models may lead to the shortcoming of overfitting. Therefore, reducing model complexity may weaken this effect. We reduced the hidden dimension to 256, which brought about a 1.2% performance improvement. Subsequently, we further reduced the hidden dimension to 128 and the depth of networks to 4, then to 2, while we kept the number of heads unchanged or increased the number of heads, which generally led to performance degradation. Furthermore, we replaced the learnable position embedding with cos-sin position embedding and obtained results by fusing the outputs of the transformer instead of using a class token, which was beneficial to the network. In addition, the SGD optimizer achieved better performance than the Adam or the Adamw optimizer. The model configurations described in Sect. 4.1 is decided through experiments, and by using the configuration, we obtained the model PropVit. It performed better than the original Vit but still had gaps with CNN models.

Table 1. Results comparison of different models on smoke dataset

Model	Accuracy	Recall	Precision	F1-socre	Params (MB)
Resnet18	91.41	89.45	90.78	90.08	44.8
Resnet34	91.79	91.86	89.56	90.62	85.2
Resnet50	92.01	91.78	90.26	90.98	94.4
Resnet101	92.07	91.56	90.39	90.95	170.4
Resnet152	91.98	91.76	90.52	91.11	233.6
MobileNet-v1	91.08	91.03	89.67	90.32	12.8
MobileNet-v2	91.79	91.47	90.19	90.79	9.2
densenet	91.34	92.09	88.74	90.22	28.0
DCNN	92.32	92.02	90.54	91.27	7.6
vit	88.21	86.61	97.40	90.04	19.6
svit	92.00	90.60	90.33	90.46	23.2
PropVit	**93.21**	**92.26**	**91.71**	**91.98**	**19.9**

5   Conclusion

In this paper, we designed a network, which combinesthe transformer and CNN structure for smoke detection. The dataset used is for smoke detection in petrochemical enterprises' flare stack. First, The image size and patch size were set according to the dataset characteristics. Then, the input images were shifted and stacked to increase the information of each token. A learnable temperature parameter $\sqrt{d_k}$ was applied to replace the original fixed value $\sqrt{d_k}$, which makes the self-attention mechanism more adaptive to the dataset. The proposed Vit model has achieved better performance than the original Vit model through appropriate model design and configurations. Finally, we designed a CNN module to provide the local information to the Vit model to improve its performance. The features extracted by the CNN module and the information learned by the first transformer encoder were fused and processed by the second transformer encoder. The classification result was obtained through the MLP head. The proposed Vit model combined with a CNN branch achieved the best performance among all models. In future work, we will make an effort to integrate the capabilities of CNN structure into the Vit model in different ways to improve its performance in the smoke detection field.

References

1. Atkinson, R.: Atmospheric chemistry of VOCs and NOx. Atmos. Environ. **34**(12–14), 2063–2101 (2000)
2. Song, Y., et al.: Source apportionment of $PM_{2.5}$ in Beijing by positive matrix factorization. Atmos. Environ. **40**(8), 1526–1537 (2006)
3. Motte, J., Alvarenga, R.A., Thybaut, J.W., Dewulf, J.: Quantification of the global and regional impacts of gas flaring on human health via spatial differentiation. Environ. Pollut. **291**, 118213 (2021)
4. Gu, K., Qiao, J., Lin, W.: Recurrent air quality predictor based on meteorology- and pollution-related factors. IEEE Trans. Industr. Inform. **14**(9), 3946–3955 (2018)
5. Soh, P.-W., Chang, J.-W., Huang, J.-W.: Adaptive deep learning-based air quality prediction model using the most relevant spatial-temporal relations. IEEE Access **6**, 38186–38199 (2018)
6. Gu, K., Qiao, J., Li, X.: Highly efficient picture-based prediction of $PM_{2.5}$ concentration. IEEE Trans. Ind. Electron. **66**(4), 3176–3184 (2019)
7. Lee, S.H., Lee, S., Song, B.C.: Vision transformer for small-size datasets. arXiv preprint arXiv:2112.13492 (2021)
8. Gu, K., Liu, H., Xia, Z., Qiao, J., Lin, W., Thalmann, D.: $PM_{2.5}$ monitoring: use information abundance measurement and wide and deep learning. IEEE Trans. Neural Netw. Learn. Syst. **32**(10), 4278–4290 (2021)
9. Yue, G., Gu, K., Qiao, J.: Effective and efficient photo-based concentration estimation. IEEE Trans. Instrum. Meas. **68**(10), 396–3971 (2019)
10. Gu, K., Liu, J., Shi, S., Xie, S., Shi, T., Qiao, J.: Self-organizing multi-channel deep learning system for river turbidity monitoring. IEEE Trans. Instrum. Meas. **71**, 1–13 (2022)

11. Dosovitskiy, A., et al.: An image is worth 16x16 words: transformers for image recognition at scale. arXiv preprint arXiv:2010.11929 (2020)
12. Gu, K., Xia, Z., Qiao, J.: Stacked selective ensemble for $PM_{2.5}$ forecast. IEEE Trans. Instrum. Meas. **69**(3), 660–671 (2019)
13. Gu, K., Xia, Z., Qiao, J., Lin, W.: Deep dual-channel neural network for image-based smoke detection. IEEE Trans. Multimedia **22**(2), 311–323 (2020)
14. Graham, B., et al.: Levit: a vision transformer in ConvNet's clothing for faster inference. In: Proceedings IEEE International Conference on Computer Vision, pp. 12259–12269 (2021)
15. Gu, K., Zhang, Y., Qiao, J.: Ensemble meta learning for few-shot soot density recognition. IEEE Trans. Industr. Inform. **17**(3), 2261–2270 (2021)
16. Carion, N., Massa, F., Synnaeve, G., Usunier, N., Kirillov, A., Zagoruyko, S.: End-to-end object detection with transformers. In: Vedaldi, A., Bischof, H., Brox, T., Frahm, J.-M. (eds.) ECCV 2020. LNCS, vol. 12346, pp. 213–229. Springer, Cham (2020). https://doi.org/10.1007/978-3-030-58452-8_13
17. Zhu, X., Su, W., Lu, L., Li, B., Wang, X., Dai, J.: Deformable DETR: deformable transformers for end-to-end object detection. arXiv preprint arXiv:2010.04159 (2020)
18. Zheng, S., et al.: Rethinking semantic segmentation from a sequence-to-sequence perspective with transformers. In: Proceedings IEEE/CVF Conference Computer Vision Pattern Recognition, pp. 6881–6890 (2021)
19. Chen, H., et al.: Pre-trained image processing transformer. In: Proceedings IEEE/CVF Conference on Computer Vision and Pattern Recognition, pp. 12299–12310 (2021)
20. Ojo, J.A., Oladosu, J.A.: Video-based smoke detection algorithms: a chronological survey. In: Proceedings International Institute for Science, Technology and Education, pp. 2222–1719 (2014)
21. Gu, K., Li, L., Lu, H., Min, X., Lin, W.: A fast reliable image quality predictor by fusing micro-and macro-structures. IEEE Trans. Ind. Electron. **64**(5), 3903–3912 (2017)
22. Kaabi, R., Frizzi, S., Bouchouicha, M., Fnaiech, F., Moreau, E.: Video smoke detection review: State of the art of smoke detection in visible and IR range. In: Proceedings International Conference on Smart, Monitored and Controlled Cities, pp. 81–86 (2017)
23. Gu, K., Zhang, Y., Qiao, J.: Ensemble meta-learning for few-shot soot density recognition. IEEE Trans. Industr. Inform. **17**(3), 2261–2270 (2020)
24. Gaur, A., Singh, A., Kumar, A., Kumar, A., Kapoor, K.: Video flame and smoke based fire detection algorithms: a literature review. Fire Technol. **56**(5), 1943–1980 (2020)
25. Gu, K., Zhai, G., Yang, X., Zhang, W.: Hybrid no-reference quality metric for singly and multiply distorted images. IEEE Trans. Broadcast. **60**(3), 555–567 (2014)
26. Cui, Y., Dong, H., Zhou, E.: An early fire detection method based on smoke texture analysis and discrimination. In: Proceedings Congress Image Signal Processing, vol. 3, pp. 95–99 (2008)
27. Gubbi, J., Marusic, S., Palaniswami, M.: Smoke detection in video using wavelets and support vector machines. Fire Saf. J. **44**(8), 1110–1115 (2009)
28. Vidal-Calleja, T.A., Agammenoni, G.: Integrated probabilistic generative model for detecting smoke on visual images. In: Proceedings International Conference on Robotics and Automation, pp. 2183–2188 (2012)
29. Yuan, F.: Video-based smoke detection with histogram sequence of LBP and LBPV pyramids. Fire Saf. J. **46**(3), 132–139 (2011)

30. Yuan, F., Xia, X., Shi, J., Li, H., Li, G.: Non-linear dimensionality reduction and Gaussian process based classification method for smoke detection. IEEE Access **5**, 6833–6841 (2017)
31. Gu, K., Zhang, Y., Qiao, J.: Vision-based monitoring of flare soot. IEEE Trans. Instrum. Meas. **69**(9), 7136–7145 (2020)
32. He, K., Zhang, X., Ren, S., Sun, J.: Deep residual learning for image recognition. In: Proceedings IEEE Conference on Computer Vision and Pattern Recognition, pp. 770–778 (2016)
33. Huang, G., Liu, Z., Van Der Maaten, L., Weinberger, K.Q.: Densely connected convolutional networks. In: Proceedings IEEE Conference on Computer Vision and Pattern Recognition, pp. 4700–4708 (2017)
34. Szegedy, C., et al.: Going deeper with convolutions. In: Proceedings IEEE Conference on Computer Vision and Pattern Recognition, pp. 1–9 (2015)
35. Yin, Z., Wan, B., Yuan, F., Xia, X., Shi, J.: A deep normalization and convolutional neural network for image smoke detection. IEEE Access **5**, 18429–18438 (2017)
36. Gu, K., Xia, Z., Qiao, J., Lin, W.: Deep dual-channel neural network for image-based smoke detection. IEEE Trans. Multimedia **22**(2), 311–323 (2019)
37. Gu, K., Wang, S., Zhai, G., Ma, S., Lin, W.: Screen image quality assessment incorporating structural degradation measurement. In: Proceedings IEEE International Symposium on Circuits and Systems, pp. 125–128 (2015)
38. Yue, G., Hou, C., Gu, K., Zhou, T., Zhai, G.: Combining local and global measures for DIBR-synthesized image quality evaluation. IEEE Trans. Image Process. **28**(4), 2075–2088 (2019)
39. Gu, K., Zhai, G., Yang, X., Zhang, W.: Deep learning network for blind image quality assessment. In: Proceedings IEEE International Conference on Image Processing, pp. 511–515 (2014)
40. Sun, W., Gu, K., Ma, S., Zhu, W., Liu, N., Zhai, G.: A large-scale compressed 360-degree spherical image database: from subjective quality evaluation to objective model comparison. In: Proceedings IEEE International Workshop on Multimedia Signal Processing, pp. 1–6 (2018)
41. Liu, Y., Qin, W., Liu, K., Zhang, F., Xiao, Z.: A dual convolution network using dark channel prior for image smoke classification. IEEE Access **7**, 60697–60706 (2019)
42. You, C., Li, Z., Li, M., Gao, Z., Li, W.: Db-net: dual attention network with bilinear pooling for fire-smoke image classification. J. Phys: Conf. Ser. **1631**, 012054 (2020)
43. He, L., Gong, X., Zhang, S., Wang, L., Li, F.: Efficient attention based deep fusion CNN for smoke detection in fog environment. Neurocomputing **434**, 224–238 (2021)
44. Han, K., Xiao, A., Wu, E., Guo, J., Xu, C., Wang, Y.: Transformer in transformer. In: Advances in Neural Information Processing Systems, vol. 34, pp. 15908–15919 (2021)
45. Liu, Z., et al.: Swin transformer: hierarchical vision transformer using shifted windows. In: Proceedings IEEE/CVF International Conference on Computer Vision, pp. 10012–10022 (2021)
46. Ali, A., et al.: XCiT: cross-covariance image transformers. In: Advances in Neural Information Processing Systems, vol. 34, pp. 20014–20027 (2021)
47. Yuan, L., et al.: Tokens-to-token VIT: training vision transformers from scratch on ImageNet. In: Proceedings IEEE International Conference on Computer Vision, pp. 558–567 (2021)
48. Wu, H., et al.: CvT: introducing convolutions to vision transformers. In: Proceedings IEEE International Conference on Computer Vision, pp. 22–31 (2021)

49. Yuan, K., Guo, S., Liu, Z., Zhou, A., Yu, F., Wu, W.: Incorporating convolution designs into visual transformers. In: Proceedings IEEE International Conference on Computer Vision, pp. 579–588 (2021)
50. Li, Y., Zhang, K., Cao, J., Timofte, R., Van Gool, L.: Localvit: bringing locality to vision transformers. arXiv preprint arXiv:2104.05707 (2021)
51. Gong, Y., Ma, X.: Multiple categories of visual smoke detection database. arXiv preprint arXiv:2208.00210 (2022)

Generative Model Watermarking Based on Human Visual System

Li Zhang[1], Yong Liu[1], Shaoteng Liu[2], Tianshu Yang[2], Yexin Wang[3], Xinpeng Zhang[1], and Hanzhou Wu[1(✉)]

[1] School of Communication and Information Engineering, Shanghai University, Shanghai 200444, China
{jmzhangli,xzhang}@shu.edu.cn, h.wu.phd@ieee.org
[2] AI Technology Center, Tencent Inc., Beijing 100080, China
{shaotengliu,gracetsyang}@tencent.com
[3] AI Technology Center, Tencent Inc., Shenzhen 518000, Guangdong, China
yexinwang@tencent.com

Abstract. Intellectual property protection of deep neural networks is receiving attention from more and more researchers, and the latest research applies model watermarking to generative models for image processing. However, the existing watermarking methods designed for generative models do not take into account the effects of different channels of sample images on watermarking. As a result, the watermarking performance is still limited. To tackle this problem, in this paper, we first analyze the effects of embedding watermark information on different channels. Then, based on the characteristics of human visual system (HVS), we introduce two HVS-based generative model watermarking methods, which are realized in RGB color space and YUV color space respectively. In RGB color space, the watermark is embedded into the R and B channels based on the fact that HVS is more sensitive to G channel. In YUV color space, the watermark is embedded into the DCT domain of U and V channels based on the fact that HVS is more sensitive to brightness changes. Experimental results demonstrate the effectiveness of the proposed work, which improves the fidelity of the model to be protected and has good universality compared with previous methods.

Keywords: Model watermarking · Deep learning · Human visual system

1 Introduction

Deep learning (DL) [1] has been applied in many application fields such as computer vision [2] and natural language processing [3]. It is foreseen that DL will continue bringing profound changes to our daily life. However, it is known that training a powerful DL model requires lots of computational resources and

---

L. Zhang and Y. Liu—Equally contributed authors.

© The Author(s), under exclusive license to Springer Nature Singapore Pte Ltd. 2023
G. Zhai et al. (Eds.): IFTC 2022, CCIS 1766, pp. 136–149, 2023.
https://doi.org/10.1007/978-981-99-0856-1_10

well-labelled data. As a result, the trained DL model should be regarded as an important digital asset and should be protected from intellectual property (IP) infringement. Therefore, how to protect the IP of DL models has become a new technical challenge. It motivates researchers and engineers from both academia and industry to exploit *digital watermarking* [4] for IP protection of DL models [5], which is typically referred to as *model watermarking*. However, unlike conventional media watermarking that often treats the host signal as static data, DL models possess the ability of accomplishing a particular task, indicating that the algorithmic design of model watermarking should take into account the functionality of DL models.

An increasing number of model watermarking schemes are proposed in recent years. By reviewing the mainstream algorithms, advanced strategies realizing model watermarking can be roughly divided into three main categories, i.e., network based model watermarking, trigger based model watermarking, and dataset based model watermarking. Network based model watermarking algorithms aim at covertly embedding a watermark into the internal network weights [5–7] or network structures [8]. As a result, the watermark decoder should access the internal details fully or partly of the target DL model. Though trigger based model watermarking algorithms often change the internal parameters of the DL model through training from scratch or fine-tuning, the zero-bit watermark is carried by the mapping relationship between a set of trigger samples and their pre-specified labels. As a result, the watermark is extracted by analyzing the consistency between the labels and the prediction results of the target DL given a set of trigger samples [9,10]. Dataset based model watermarking algorithms exploit the entangled relationship between the DL model and a dataset related to the task of the DL model to construct a fingerprint of the DL model, which may be realized via a lossless way (i.e., without modifying the original model to be protected) to guarantee high security such as [11–13].

Recently, Wu *et al.* [14] propose a general watermarking framework for deep generative models. By optimizing a combined loss function, the trained model not only performs very well on its original task, but also automatically inserts a watermark into any image outputted by the model. In the work, the watermark is embedded into the model through watermark-loss back-propagation. As a result, by extracting the watermark from the outputted image, the ownership of the target model can be identified without interacting directly with the model. Yet another similar work is introduced by Zhang *et al.* [15], which was originally designed to resist surrogate attacks and also allows us to extract a watermark from the outputted image. Though [14] and [15] have demonstrated satisfactory watermark verification performance as reported in the papers, they both do not consider the characteristics of the human visual system (HVS). As a result, the visual quality may not be satisfactory from a broader perspective.

To tackle the aforementioned problem, we utilize the characteristics of HVS for system design of model watermarking. To this end, we propose two HVS based frameworks for generative model watermarking, i.e., HVS-RGB based generative model watermarking and HVS-YUV based generative model watermarking. Since the proposed two frameworks take into account the HVS characteris-

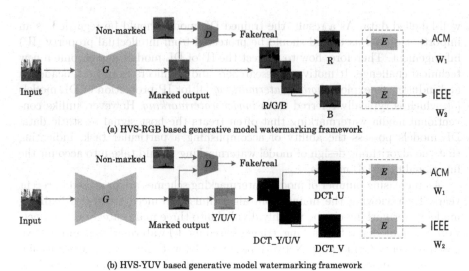

(a) HVS-RGB based generative model watermarking framework

(b) HVS-YUV based generative model watermarking framework

Fig. 1. The proposed two HVS based frameworks for generative model watermarking. For better understanding, the original task of G here is set to semantic segmentation.

tics, the generated *marked* images are more compatible with the HVS, thereby improving the fidelity of the network and the invisibility of the watermark. In summary, the main contributions of this paper include:

- We have analyzed the impact of embedding watermark on different channels of the generated images in the generative model watermarking by combining the HVS characteristics. Based on this analysis, we propose two HVS-based multi-channel generative model watermarking frameworks that improve the fidelity of the network while maintaining the fidelity of the watermark.
- Through convinced experiments on semantic segmentation, the results demonstrate the applicability and superiority of the proposed work.

The rest structure of this paper is organized as follows. In Sect. 2, we give the details of the proposed work. Then, we provide experiments and analysis in Sect. 3. Finally, we conclude this paper and provide discussion in Sect. 4.

2 Proposed Method

2.1 HVS Characteristics

HVS is one of the most complex biological systems [16–18] and typically includes the following characteristics:

- *Spectral characteristics:* The sensitivity of HVS to color is green, red, blue in descending order. Therefore, embedding a watermark in the green channel of a color image will affect the visual quality of the image more than the others. It is desirable to preferentially embed the watermark into the blue channel and then the red channel. The green component can be changed with the least degree in order to improve the invisibility of the watermark.

- *Brightness characteristics:* The HVS is more sensitive to changes in brightness. Therefore, in YUV color space, embedding the watermark into U or V chromatic aberration channel results in better visual quality than Y channel.

The brightness and spectral characteristics of HVS illustrate the effects of embedding the watermark into different channels of the image. In conventional image watermarking, there are already methods verifying that HVS characteristics are helpful for developing high fidelity watermarking systems such as [18,19]. In this paper, we mainly combine the spectral and brightness characteristics to analyze the effects of watermark embedding in different channels of the generated image in generative model watermarking. In the later experiments, we will analyze the visual quality of the generated images after embedding the watermark in different channels, and analyze the results of the experiments by combining the spectral and brightness characteristics of HVS. It is proved that the HVS characteristics still hold in the generative model watermarking. Therefore, the HVS characteristics can guide us to design model watermarking methods that better match the characteristics of human visual perception system.

2.2   HVS-Based Generative Model Watermarking Frameworks

We propose two HVS-based generative model watermarking (GMW) frameworks, which are shown in Fig. 1. Below, we first provide the overview and then describe the watermark embedding and extraction process.

HVS-RGB Based GMW Framework: As mentioned above, human beings are more sensitive to the green color. Reducing the modifications to the green (G) channel results in better visual quality of the image, which inspires us to preferentially embed the watermark information into the red (R) channel and/or the blue (B) channel. Motivated by this insight, we propose a framework to embed two watermarks into the R channel and the B channel respectively. As shown in Fig. 1, the process can be described as follows. Given the generative model G to be protected, we train G in such a way that the image outputted by G is always marked. The watermark information is carried by the R channel and the B channel of the marked image. Specifically, we determine the R/G/B channels of the image outputted by G. The R channel of the image is used to carry a watermark W_1 and the B channel is used to carry another watermark W_2. To realize this purpose, a neural network E is trained together with G through loss optimization so that W_1 can be extracted from the R channel, and W_2 can be extracted from the B channel. To ensure that G has good performance on its original task, the image outputted by G may be fed to a discriminator D. Though we consider W_1 and W_2 as two different watermarks in this paper, one may consider them as a whole, which will not cause any problem.

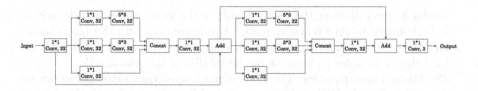

Fig. 2. Structural information for the watermark-extraction network E.

HVS-YUV Based GMW Framework: Similarly, human beings are more sensitive to changes in brightness. Therefore, by representing an image in the YUV color space, it is suggested to embed the watermark information in the U/V channels to not arouse noticeable artifacts. However, directly embedding watermark information into the U/V channels in the spatial domain may lead to significant distortion to the chroma. To address this problem, we propose to embed the watermark information into the U/V channels in the discrete cosine transform (DCT) domain. In this way, the entire process is similar to the above HVS-RGB based framework. The only one difference is that the image outputted by G should be converted to the Y/U/V color space. Then, the U channel and the V channel are processed by DCT. The transformed data can be expressed as DCT_U and DCT_V. Thereafter, DCT_U and DCT_V are fed to E for watermark embedding and watermark extraction.

Both frameworks are similar to each other according to the above analysis. For the two frameworks, we are now ready to describe the watermark embedding and extraction procedure for the host network G as follows:

- *Watermark embedding:* The watermark information is embedded into G by marking the output of G through optimizing a combined loss that will be detailed later. In other words, G is marked during joint training. The networks to be jointly trained include G, E and D, where D is optional.
- *Watermark extraction:* After training, G is deemed marked. By retrieving the watermark information from any image outputted by G with E, we are able to trace the source of the image and identify the ownership of the image and the target model. As multiple watermarks can be embedded, multiple purposes can be achieved.

2.3 Structural Design

G can perform any task outputting color images as results. In this paper, without the loss of generalization, we use the backbone network introduced in [20] as the host network G to be protected. The network structure is inspired by U-net [2]. The original task of G is limited to image semantic segmentation, whose goal is to cluster parts of an image together which belong to the same object class. The input and the output have the same size in this paper.

The objective of E is to extract the corresponding watermark from the corresponding channel (involving R, B, DCT_U, DCT_V). E accepts a single channel as input and then outputs the corresponding watermark (that may be either a binary/gray-scale image or a color one). It is free to design the network structure of E. In this paper, the structure of E is inspired by [14,21]. ReLU [22] is applied as the activation function for the internal layers, except that the output layer uses TanH. The details of E are shown in Fig. 2. In addition, G can be optionally optimized by a discriminator D. For example, we may use PatchGAN [23] to serve as D shown in Fig. 1.

2.4   Loss Function

Based on the aforementioned analysis, we are now ready to design the loss function for each watermarking framework. We use S_0 to denote the set of images not generated by G and S_1 to denote the set of images generated by G.

Loss Function for HVS-RGB Based GMW Framework: For the watermarking task, we hope that E can extract the corresponding watermark given the corresponding input, which can be expressed as:

$$L_1 = \frac{1}{|S_1|} \sum_{G(x) \in S_1} ||E(G(x)_{\mathrm{R}}) - W_1|| \tag{1}$$

and

$$L_2 = \frac{1}{|S_1|} \sum_{G(x) \in S_1} ||E(G(x)_{\mathrm{B}}) - W_2|| \tag{2}$$

where x is the input image of G, $G(x)_{\mathrm{R}}$ and $G(x)_{\mathrm{B}}$ represent the R component and the B component of the outputted image $G(x)$, respectively. On the other hand, we hope that random noise can be extracted from images not generated by G, which requires us to minimize:

$$L_3 = \frac{1}{|S_0|} \sum_{y \in S_0} ||E(y_{\mathrm{R}}) - W_z|| \tag{3}$$

and

$$L_4 = \frac{1}{|S_0|} \sum_{y \in S_0} ||E(y_{\mathrm{B}}) - W_z|| \tag{4}$$

where y_{R} and y_{B} represent the R component and the B component of the image $y \in S_0$, and, W_z is a noise image randomly generated in advance. For the original task of G, it is expected that the *marked* image generated by G is close to the ground-truth image. Typically, to accomplish the task, we expect to minimize:

$$L_5 = \frac{1}{|S_1|} \sum_{G(x) \in S_1} ||G(x) - T[G(x)]|| \tag{5}$$

where $T[G(x)]$ means the ground-truth image of $G(x)$. Since the R component and the B component of $G(x)$ will be used to carry the additional information, distortion will be introduced. To reduce the impact of watermark embedding, it is desirable to further control the distortion in the R channel and the B channel, i.e., we hope to minimize:

$$L_6 = \frac{1}{|S_1|} \sum_{G(x) \in S_1} ||G(x)_{\mathrm{R}} - T_{\mathrm{R}}[G(x)]|| \qquad (6)$$

and

$$L_7 = \frac{1}{|S_1|} \sum_{G(x) \in S_1} ||G(x)_{\mathrm{B}} - T_{\mathrm{B}}[G(x)]|| \qquad (7)$$

where $T_{\mathrm{R}}[G(x)]$ and $T_{\mathrm{B}}[G(x)]$ represent the R component and the B component of $T[G(x)]$. Simply minimizing the above losses may not well maintain the structural information of the image, to deal with this problem, we further introduce structural loss for improving the image quality. Namely, we want to minimize:

$$L_8 = \frac{1}{|S_1|} \sum_{G(x) \in S_1} (1 - \frac{\mathrm{SSIM}(G(x), T[G(x)]) + \mathrm{MS\text{-}SSIM}(G(x), T[G(x)])}{2}) \qquad (8)$$

where $\mathrm{SSIM}(\cdot, \cdot)$ [24] and $\mathrm{MS\text{-}SSIM}(\cdot, \cdot)$ [25] are two indicators representing the structural similarity between two images. The entire loss function is then:

$$L_{\mathrm{HVS\text{-}RGB}} = \alpha(L_1 + L_2) + \beta(L_3 + L_4) + (L_5 + L_6 + L_7 + L_8) \qquad (9)$$

where α and β are pre-determined parameters balancing the losses.

Loss Function for HVS-YUV Based GMW Framework: Similarly, the entire loss function can be divided into two parts, i.e., the watermarking loss and task loss. Referring to the loss function for HVS-RGB based GMW framework, the components of watermarking loss function include:

$$L_9 = \frac{1}{|S_1|} \sum_{G(x) \in S_1} ||E(G(x)_{\mathrm{DCT\_U}}) - W_1|| \qquad (10)$$

$$L_{10} = \frac{1}{|S_1|} \sum_{G(x) \in S_1} ||E(G(x)_{\mathrm{DCT\_V}}) - W_2|| \qquad (11)$$

$$L_{11} = \frac{1}{|S_0|} \sum_{y \in S_0} ||E(y_{\mathrm{DCT\_U}}) - W_z|| \qquad (12)$$

$$L_{12} = \frac{1}{|S_0|} \sum_{y \in S_0} ||E(y_{\mathrm{DCT\_V}}) - W_z|| \qquad (13)$$

where $G(x)_{\mathrm{DCT\_U}}$ and $G(x)_{\mathrm{DCT\_V}}$ represent the U channel and the V channel in the DCT domain for $G(x)$, respectively. $y_{\mathrm{DCT\_U}}$ and $y_{\mathrm{DCT\_V}}$ are the U channel and the V channel in the DCT domain for y. On the other hand, the task loss function involves L_5, L_8 and

$$L_{13} = \frac{1}{|S_1|} \sum_{G(x) \in S_1} ||G(x)_{\mathrm{DCT\_U}} - T_{\mathrm{DCT\_U}}[G(x)]|| \qquad (14)$$

$$L_{14} = \frac{1}{|S_1|} \sum_{G(x) \in S_1} ||G(x)_{\mathrm{DCT\_V}} - T_{\mathrm{DCT\_V}}[G(x)]|| \qquad (15)$$

Table 1. Quality evaluation for the marked images generated by the host network.

Channel	Average PSNR (dB)	Average SSIM	Average MS-SSIM
R	23.74	0.798	0.853
G	22.92	0.782	0.842
B	23.63	0.801	0.858
DCT_Y	22.85	0.781	0.840
DCT_U	23.49	0.794	0.848
DCT_V	23.60	0.793	0.853

where $T_{\mathrm{DCT\_U}}[G(x)]$ and $T_{\mathrm{DCT\_V}}[G(x)]$ represent the U component and the V component of $T[G(x)]$ in the DCT domain. So, the entire loss function is:

$$L_{\mathrm{HVS\text{-}YUV}} = \alpha(L_9 + L_{10}) + \beta(L_{11} + L_{12}) + (L_5 + L_8 + L_{13} + L_{14}). \qquad (16)$$

Remark: There are two choices for determining the network parameters of G and E. One is to train G and E together from scratch according to the entire loss function. The other is to train G and E from scratch according to the task loss of G and the watermark-extraction loss corresponding to W_1. Then, G and E can be fine-tuned with the entire loss function. We use the latter strategy due to the relatively lower computational complexity.

3   Experimental Results and Analysis

3.1   Setup

As mentioned previously, we limit the task of G to image semantic segmentation. And, the structure of G is similar to U-net. However, it should be admitted that it is always free to design the network structure of G and specify the task of G. Since our purpose is not to develop G, it is true that the network structure used in this paper is not optimal in terms of the task performance, which, however, does not affect the contribution of this work. We use the dataset mentioned in [26] for experiments, where 4,000 images are used for model training, 500 images are used for validation and another 500 images are used for testing. The size of input and the size of output are set to $256 \times 256 \times 3$ for the host network. For W_1, W_2 and W_z, their sizes are all equal to $256 \times 256 \times 3$ since the watermark-extraction network in Fig. 2 keeps the size of the output same as the size of the input, indicating that the size of the output should be identical to that of the image outputted by G as the latter will be fed into the network in Fig. 2.

During model training, we empirically applied $\alpha = 1$ and $\beta = 0.5$. The Adam optimizer was used to iteratively update the network parameters. The learning rate was set to 2×10^{-4}. Our implementation used TensorFlow trained on a single RTX 3090 GPU. We use three evaluation metrics, i.e., peak signal-to-noise ratio (PSNR), structural similarity (SSIM) [24] and multi-scale structural similarity

Table 2. Quality evaluation for the marked images and the extracted watermarks.

Method	Mean PSNR	Mean SSIM	Mean MS-SSIM	Mean BER$_1$	Mean BER$_2$
HVS-RGB	23.12	0.807	0.857	0.0024	0.0029
HVS-YUV	22.83	0.799	0.852	0.0026	0.0031
[14]	20.83	0.738	0.816	0.0020	0.0028

(MS-SSIM) [25] for evaluation. For all of these widely used indicators, a higher value demonstrates the better quality of the image. In this paper, we limit W_1 to the logo image "ACM" and W_2 to the logo image "IEEE" (refer to Fig. 1). Besides, W_z is a randomly generated noise image. ℓ_1 norm is applied to all the loss functions, which can speed up convergence during training.

3.2 Analysis of Watermark Embedding in Different Channels

Before reporting experimental results, we first analyze the effects of watermark embedding on different channels of the image by taking into account the afore-mentioned spectral and brightness characteristics. To this purpose, we separate three channels from the image generated by the host network and feed each of the channels into the watermark-extraction network. For each channel, the host network together with the watermark-extraction network are trained together so that the image outputted by the host network carries a watermark that can be extracted by the watermark-extraction network. It is pointed that we here only tested the watermark W_1, where W_2 was not used for simplicity. In other words, all the channels independently carry the same watermark for fair comparison.

Table 1 provides the experimental results of image quality evaluation. It can be found that even though different color channels result in different performance in terms of image quality, overall, R/B and DCT_U/DCT_V are superior to G and DCT_Y, respectively. This indicates that from the viewpoint of watermark embedding, it is quite desirable to preferentially embed the watermark data into the R/B and DCT_U/DCT_V channels, rather than the G and DCT_Y channels.

3.3 Main Results

The main contribution of this paper is to improve the visual quality of the marked images generated by the host network by taking into account the characteristics of HVS. Therefore, in this subsection, we have to measure the difference between the generated marked images and the ground-truth images. It is necessary that the embedded watermark information should be extracted with high fidelity for reliable ownership verification. Accordingly, the difference between the extracted watermark and the corresponding ground-truth should be analyzed as well.

We use PSNR, SSIM and MS-SSIM to quantify the visual difference between the images generated by the marked network and the ground-truth images. As shown in Fig. 1, two watermarks are embedded into the generated image. To quantify the watermarking performance, bit error rate (BER) is used for both

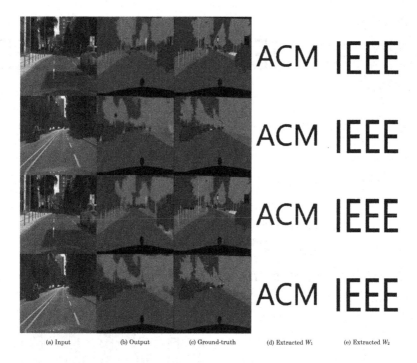

Fig. 3. Visual examples for the marked images and the extracted watermarks. The first two rows correspond to the HVS-RGB framework and the last two rows correspond to the HVS-YUV framework. Notice that, the input in the first row is identical to that in the third row, and the input in the second row is identical to that in the fourth row.

W_1 and W_2. For fair comparison, we also realize a baseline watermarking system based on [14] (without secret key), which feeds the image outputted by G directly into the watermark-extraction network to reconstruct either W_1 or W_2.

Table 2 shows the experimental results, where "mean BER_1" is used for W_1 and "mean BER_2" is used for W_2. The others are used for the images generated by the marked neural network. It is observed from Table 2 that the BER difference between the proposed strategy and the strategy in [14] is very low, which indicates that the proposed strategy does not impair the watermark fidelity. On the other hand, the proposed two frameworks significantly improve the quality of the image generated by the network. It means that the introduction of HVS is indeed helpful for enhancing the performance of generative model watermarking. Figure 3 further provides some examples, from which we can infer that the images are with satisfactory quality, which verifies the applicability.

3.4   Robustness and Ablation Study

In application scenarios, the marked images generated by the host network may be attacked. It is necessary to evaluate the robustness of the proposed two frameworks against common attacks. To deal with this problem, it is suggested to

(a) Noised image   (b) Extracted W_1 (c) Extracted W_2 (d) Noised image   (e) Extracted W_1 (f) Extracted W_2

Fig. 4. Visual examples for the noised images (marked) and the extracted watermarks. (a–c) HVS-RGB based framework and (d–f) HVS-YUV based framework. Here, $\sigma = 0.4$.

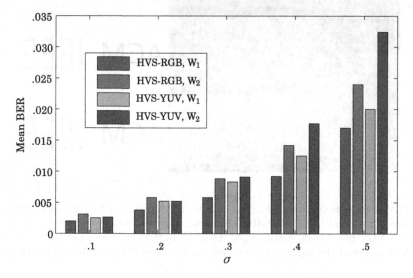

Fig. 5. The mean BERs due to different degrees of noise addition.

mimic the real-world attack to the images generated by the host network during model training, which has been proven to be effective in improving the robustness of DL models. To this end, to evaluate the robustness, during model training, we mimic the real-world attack to the images generated by the host network and feed them into the watermark-extraction network for watermark extraction. We consider one of the most representative attacks, i.e., noise addition, for simplicity.

Specifically, during model training, we add the Gaussian noise to every image generated by the host network by applying $\mu = 0$ and random $\sigma \in (0, 0.5)$. The noised image is then fed into the watermark-extraction network for watermark extraction. As a result, the trained model has the ability to resist noise addition. In this way, we are able to evaluate the robustness of the trained model by using BER. Figure 4 provides an example of noise addition, from which we can infer that the visual quality of the marked image is significantly distorted, but the embedded watermark can be extracted with satisfactory quality. Figure 5 further provides the BERs due to different degrees of noise addition. It can be observed that the BER tends to increase as the degree of noise addition

Table 3. Performance comparison by applying different loss functions. The experimental results in this table are mean values.

Method	SSIM Loss	MS-SSIM Loss	PSNR	SSIM	MS-SSIM	BER$_1$	BER$_2$
HVS-RGB			23.01	0.779	0.839	0.0029	0.0028
HVS-RGB	✓		23.05	0.801	0.846	0.0031	0.0030
HVS-RGB		✓	22.99	0.788	0.852	0.0026	0.0034
HVS-RGB	✓	✓	**23.12**	**0.807**	**0.857**	0.0024	0.0029
HVS-YUV			22.57	0.778	0.835	0.0022	0.0025
HVS-YUV	✓		22.79	0.784	0.838	0.0029	0.0034
HVS-YUV		✓	22.76	0.781	0.844	0.0026	0.0027
HVS-YUV	✓	✓	**22.83**	**0.799**	**0.852**	0.0026	0.0031

increases, which is reasonable because a larger degree of noise addition reduces the watermark information carried by the generated image, thereby resulting in a higher BER. However, overall, the BERs are in a low level. It indicates that by combining robustness enhancement strategies, the proposed two frameworks have satisfactory ability to resist against malicious attacks.

In addition, in order to achieve better visual performance, the proposed work applies structural loss to model training. In order to demonstrate its effectiveness, we analyze the experimental results on both the original task and the watermark task caused by applying different loss functions. In detail, L_8 indicates that both SSIM and MS-SSIM are used for model training. If L_8 is removed from Eq. (9) and Eq. (16), it means to skip the structural loss. By modifying L_8 as

$$\frac{1}{|S_1|} \sum_{G(x) \in S_1} (1 - \mathrm{SSIM}(G(x), T[G(x)])),$$

it means to only use the SSIM loss. By modifying L_8 as

$$\frac{1}{|S_1|} \sum_{G(x) \in S_1} (1 - \mathrm{MS\text{-}SSIM}(G(x), T[G(x)])),$$

it means to only use the MS-SSIM loss. Experimental results are shown in Table 3. It can be inferred from Table 3 that using SSIM and MS-SSIM as part of the entire loss function indeed has the ability to further improve the visual quality of the marked images. Meanwhile, the BER differences are all low, meaning that the introduction of structural loss will not significantly impair the watermarking performance. In summary, the proposed two frameworks are suitable for practice.

4   Conclusion and Discussion

In this paper, we propose two watermarking frameworks based on HVS for generative models that output color images as the results. Unlike the previous methods that embed a watermark into the generated image directly, the proposed two frameworks select the more suitable channel of the image generated by the host network according to the characteristics of HVS for watermark embedding and watermark extraction. As a result, the marked image generated by the trained network has better quality compared with the previous art without impairing the watermark according to the reported experimental results. Though the structure and task of the host network are specified in our experiments, it is open for us to apply the proposed two frameworks to many other networks, indicating that this work has good universality.

On the other hand, as reported in the experimental section, we should admit that the binary watermarks may not be extracted perfectly. This is due to the reason that neural network learns knowledge from given data, which makes the neural network fall into the local optimum point that cannot perfectly model the mapping relationship between the marked image and the watermark. However, despite this, the BER can be kept very low, implying that by introducing error-correcting codes, the original watermark can be actually perfectly reconstructed.

From the viewpoint of robustness, even though augmenting the training data samples through mimicking attacks can improve the robustness of the model, real attacks are actually very complex and unpredictable. It is therefore necessary to further enhance the robustness of the model from the perspective of structural design and loss function design. It may also be very helpful by incorporating the interpretability theory of neural networks, which will be investigated in future.

Acknowledgement. This work was supported by the CCF-Tencent Open Fund, and the Shanghai "Chen Guang" project supported by Shanghai Municipal Education Commission and Shanghai Education Development Foundation.

References

1. LeCun, Y., Bengio, Y., Hinton, G.: Deep learning. Nature **521**(7553), 436–444 (2015)
2. Ronneberger, O., Fischer, P., Brox, T.: U-Net: convolutional networks for biomedical image segmentation. In: Navab, N., Hornegger, J., Wells, W.M., Frangi, A.F. (eds.) MICCAI 2015. LNCS, vol. 9351, pp. 234–241. Springer, Cham (2015). https://doi.org/10.1007/978-3-319-24574-4_28
3. Hinton, G., et al.: Deep neural networks for acoustic modeling in speech recognition: the shared views of four research groups. IEEE Signal Process. Mag. **29**(6), 82–97 (2012)
4. Cox, I., Miller, M., Bloom, J., Fridrich, J., Kalker, T.: Digital Watermarking and Steganography. Morgan Kaufmann, Burlington (2007)
5. Uchida, Y., Nagai, Y., Sakazawa, S., Satoh, S.: Embedding watermarks into deep neural networks. In: Proceedings of the ACM International Conference on Multimedia Retrieval, pp. 269–277 (2017)
6. Li, Y., Wang, H., Barni, M.: Spread-transform dither modulation watermarking of deep neural network. J. Inf. Secur. Appl. **63**, 103004 (2021)
7. Wang, J., Wu, H., Zhang, X., Yao, Y.: Watermarking in deep neural networks via error back-propagation. In: Proceedings of the IS&T Electronic Imaging, Media Watermarking, Security, and Forensics, pp. 22-1-22-9(9) (2020)

8. Zhao, X., Yao, Y., Wu, H., Zhang, X.: Structural watermarking to deep neural networks via network channel pruning. In: Proceedings of the IEEE International Workshop on Information Forensics and Security, pp. 1–6 (2021)
9. Adi, Y., Baum, C., Cisse, M., Pinkas, B., Keshet, J.: Turning your weakness into a strength: watermarking deep neural networks by backdooring. In: Proceedings of the USENIX Conference on Security Symposium, pp. 1615–1631 (2018)
10. Zhao, X., Wu, H., Zhang, X.: Watermarking graph neural networks by random graphs. In: Proceedings of the IEEE International Symposium on Digital Forensics and Security, pp. 1–6 (2021)
11. Liu, G., Xu, T., Ma, X., Wang, C.: Your model trains on my data? Protecting intellectual property of training data via membership fingerprint authentication. IEEE Trans. Inf. Forensics Secur. **17**, 1024–1037 (2022)
12. Lin, L., Wu, H.: Verifying integrity of deep ensemble models by lossless black-box watermarking with sensitive samples. In: Proceedings of the IEEE International Symposium on Digital Forensics and Security, pp. 1–6 (2022)
13. Wu, H.: Robust and lossless fingerprinting of deep neural networks via pooled membership inference. arXiv preprint arXiv:2209.04113 (2022)
14. Wu, H., Liu, G., Yao, Y., Zhang, X.: Watermarking neural networks with watermarked images. IEEE Trans. Circuits Syst. Video Technol. **31**(7), 2591–2601 (2021)
15. Zhang, J., et al.: Model watermarking for image processing networks. In: Proceedings AAAI Conference on Artificial Intelligence, pp. 12805–12812 (2020)
16. Lewis, A.S., Knowles, G.: Image compression using the 2-D wavelet transform. IEEE Trans. Image Process. **1**(2), 244–250 (1992)
17. Levicky, D., Foris, P.: Human visual system models in digital image watermarking. Radio Eng. **13**(4), 1123–1126 (2004)
18. Barni, M., Bartolini, F., Piva, A.: Improved wavelet-based watermarking through pixel-wise masking. IEEE Trans. Image Process. **10**(5), 783–791 (2001)
19. Kutter, M., Winkler, S.: A vision-based masking model for spread-spectrum image watermarking. IEEE Trans. Image Process. **11**(1), 16–25 (2002)
20. Wu, H., Liu, G., Zhang, X.: Hiding data hiding. arXiv:2102.06826 (2021)
21. Szegedy, C., Ioffe, S., Vanhoucke, V., Alemi, A.A.: Inception-v4, inception-ResNet and the impact of residual connections on learning. In: Proceedings of the AAAI Conference on Artificial Intelligence, pp. 4278–4284 (2017)
22. Nair, V., Hinton, G.E.: Rectified linear units improve restricted Boltzmann machines. In: Proceedings of the International Conference on Machine Learning (2010)
23. Isola, P., Zhu, J.-Y., Zhou, T., Efros, A.A.: Image-to-image translation with conditional adversarial networks. In: Proceedings of the IEEE Conference on Computer Vision and Pattern Recognition, pp. 5967–5976 (2017)
24. Wang, Z., Bovik, A.C., Sheikh, H.R., Simoncelli, E.P.: Image quality assessment: from error visibility to structural similarity. IEEE Trans. Image Process. **13**(4), 600–612 (2004)
25. Wang, Z., Simoncelli, E.P., Bovik, A.C.: Multiscale structural similarity for image quality assessment. In: Proceedings of the IEEE Asilomar Conference on Signals, Systems & Computers, pp. 1398–1402 (2003)
26. Cordts, M., et al.: The cityscapes dataset for semantic urban scene understanding. In: Proceedings of the IEEE Conference on Computer Vision and Pattern Recognition, pp. 3213–3223 (2016)

Feature Adaptation Predictive Coding
for Quantized Block Compressive Sensing
of COVID-19 X-Ray Images

Haoran Zheng, Hao Liu[✉], and Genlong Chen

College of Information Science and Technology, Donghua University, Shanghai 201620, China
liuhao@dhu.edu.cn

Abstract. With the development of remote X-ray detection for Corona Virus Disease 2019 (COVID-19), the quantized block compressive sensing technology plays an important role when remotely acquiring the chest X-ray images of COVID-19 infected people and significantly promoting the portable telemedicine imaging applications. In order to improve the encoding performance of quantized block compressive sensing, a feature adaptation predictive coding (FAPC) method is proposed for the remote transmission of COVID-19 X-ray images. The proposed FAPC method can adaptively calculate the block-wise prediction coefficients according to the main features of COVID-19 X-ray images, and thus provide the optimal prediction candidate from the feature-guided candidate set. The proposed method can implement the high-efficiency encoding of X-ray images, and then swiftly transmit the telemedicine-oriented chest images. The experimental results show that compared with the state-of-the-art predictive coding methods, both rate-distortion and complexity performance of our FAPC method have enough competitive advantages.

Keywords: Compressive sensing · Predictive coding · COVID-19 X-ray · Feature adaptation

1 Introduction

In recent years, the Corona Virus Disease 2019 (COVID-19) pneumonia is a global pandemic which involves more than 200 countries and regions [1]. With the development of portable telemedicine imaging applications, the chest imagery will play a key role in COVID-19 diagnosis and adjuvant therapy, whose difficulty lies in the lack of high-efficiency transmission for remote X-ray images. The compressive imaging has become one cross-research field between computer science and medical science [2]. For effective communication of sparse or compressible signals, the block compressive sensing (BCS) can obtain a modicum of measurement data by implementing the random projection, and then reconstruct the original signal through nonlinear optimization with high probability [3]. To realize the high-efficiency transmission of sensed images, some communication systems are proposed for quantized block compressive sensing (QBCS) which consists of a BCS measuring end and a reconstruction end [4–8], where

G. Zhai et al. (Eds.): IFTC 2022, CCIS 1766, pp. 150–162, 2023.
https://doi.org/10.1007/978-981-99-0856-1_11

the reconstruction end usually reconstructs the original image by the smooth projected Landweber (SPL) algorithm [9].

At a QBCS measuring end, the low-dimensional measurements are the random projection of high-dimensional signal, and the measuring process can be regarded as both data acquisition and data compression at the same time. However, in the strict sense of information theory, the measuring process will not bring true compression, because it cannot generate a bitstream directly from any measuring end, and it can only be considered as a dimension reduction [10]. The actual compressive sensing needs to generate the final bitstream from a sensed image, which cooperates with the quantization and entropy encoder modules. In the absence of effective quantization, the rate-distortion performance of image compressive sensing is low [11]. The very complex quantization mechanism only achieves a marginal rate-distortion gain, which is not suitable for the low-power measuring end [12–14]. Therefore, it is very popular to apply scalar quantization (SQ) to measurements.

Inspired by the success of hybrid video coding, researchers tentatively add the intra-prediction coding technology to the technical framework of QBCS. For the QBCS predictive coding of natural images, Mun and Fowler proposed differential-pulse-code-modulation (DPCM) with uniform scalar quantization [15]. In order to consider the nonstationary of natural images, Zhang *et al.* extended the DPCM-based predictive coding, and proposed a spatial directional predictive coding (SDPC) method, which further explored the relationship between internal spatial correlation and adjacent measurements of natural images [16]. For each block, the best prediction candidate is selected from multiple prediction candidates in four prediction directional modes. Different from SDPC, Li *et al.* designed a median filtering prediction quantization (MFPQ) method [17], and used the median value of several adjacent reconstructed blocks as the best prediction candidate of the current measurement vector. The rate-distortion performance of MFPQ is below that of SDPC, but the computational complexity of MFPQ is below that of SDPC, and error resilience can be obtained. Although the computational complexity increases, the SDPC method realizes more accurate measurement-domain prediction than DPCM, and thus the SDPC method can achieve good rate-distortion performance.

Zhou *et al.* further proposed the angular intra prediction of measurement encoding for compressive sensing [18], where more structural lines are designed in the random observation matrix, so that the accuracy of adjacent boundary information increases, but more calculations are also required due to such operation. As compared with the traditional raster scan coding, the spiral predictive coding (SPC) method can cut down the impression of image edges [19]. Because all available modes are computed, the SPC method is not enough energy-efficient. Further, Chen *et al.* proposed a multi-class weighted prediction (MCWP) method according to the asymptotic random matrix spectral analysis theory [20], where the quantity of prediction candidates can be increased by linearly weighting four adjacent directions. Generally, these predictive coding methods perform the block-by-block scalar quantization with the same quality factor. By analyzing the contexts of blocks, Li *et al.* proposed a zero-padding DPCM (ZP-DPCM) method which ensures that the previous measurements are always used for predictive coding [21].

Overall, the existing predictive coding methods often utilize the prediction mechanism of fixed directional modes, and the gains of this mechanism are limited. Due to low-complexity requirement, it is difficult for predictive coding to further increase the quantity of prediction candidates or directional modes. Because the X-ray image is relatively monotonous, the prediction coefficients of the adjacent blocks are closely relevant. The closer the sparse energy is, the more similar two blocks are. Therefore, the energy distribution of an X-ray image may be used to estimate the structural features of the image. For the current block, the prediction modes are defined by its adjacent blocks, and the average energy of each block is adaptively weighted for predictive coding. According to the main features of COVID-19 X-ray images, the weighted predictive coding can be further improved by adjusting the coefficient weights in the measurement domain. To implement the high-efficiency encoding at a measuring end, this paper proposes a feature adaptation predictive coding (FAPC) method for quantized block compressive sensing of COVID-19 X-ray images. The proposed method will adaptively calculate the prediction coefficients according to the average energy of block-wise measurements.

The rest of the paper is organized as follows: Sect. 2 briefly reviews the telemedicine-oriented QBCS system. The proposed method is described detailly in Sect. 3. Section 4 gives the experimental results and analysis, and Sect. 5 draws a conclusion.

2   Telemedicine-Oriented QBCS System

Towards a real-time and low-complexity implementation, Fig. 1 illustrates the main functional modules and vectors at the measuring end of a telemedicine-oriented QBCS system. In the BCS module, an original image is divided into non-overlapping blocks, and all blocks are consistently measured at a subrate. Although the quantization module and the dequantization module cause the additional complexity, the two modules are not a substantial burden [9]. In these modules of Fig. 1, the prediction module takes up the main computational complexity. After scalar quantization, the entropy encoder module is used to generate the binary bitstream for data transmission or storage. At the same time, the dequantization vector is cached as the subsequent candidates. After receiving the bitstream, the reconstruction end may utilize any image reconstruction algorithm to recover each image.

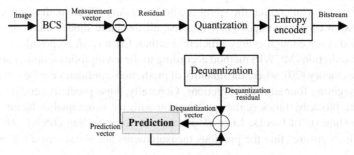

Fig. 1. Module diagram at the QBCS measuring end

At the measuring end, an original image x is sequentially delimit N non-overlapping blocks. The size of block is the B^2 pixels. Then, all measurement vectors are obtained by a block-level observation matrix. The block-level observation matrix Φ_B is a Gaussian random matrix with the size $M_B \times B^2$, and M_B is much smaller than B^2. At a subrate, the image-level observation matrix Φ consists of multiple Φ_B along the diagonal, i.e., $\Phi = \text{diag}([\Phi_B, \Phi_B, \cdots, \Phi_B])$. All blocks are numbered in a certain order, and most of the existing methods use the raster scan order. Here, i denotes the block number, $i = 1,2,...,$ N. x_i denotes the ith block in the image x. y_i denotes the ith measurement vector. At the subrate $S = M_B/B^2$, the ith block x_i is independently measured by Φ_B to generate its measurement vector y_i. Then, the block-by-block observation process can be expressed by:

$$y_i = \Phi_B \cdot x_i \tag{1}$$

A measuring end only needs to store the same Φ_B, instead of the entire Φ. Due to local correlation between adjacent blocks, the measurement-domain prediction technique can reduce the redundancy of measurement vectors. At a measuring end, $\tilde{y}_i$ denotes the dequantization vector of the ith block in the image x, and $\tilde{y}_i^p$ denotes the prediction vector of the ith block. $\tilde{y}_i^p$ is selected from previous dequantization vectors. Thus, the residual d_i can be calculated as follows:

$$d_i = y_i - \tilde{y}_i^p \tag{2}$$

Since d_i is a real value, it needs to be quantized. As compared with the quantization parameter of other coding standards, the quality factor of compressive sensing should be fine-grained due to random observation [22]. With a quality factor, the quantization value S_i is obtained by quantizing the residual d_i. Then, the entropy encoder is performed on the quantization value S_i. Here, $\tilde{d}_i$ denotes the dequantization residual of the ith block. By adding $\tilde{d}_i$ to the prediction vector $\tilde{y}_i^p$ for subsequent steps, the dequantization vector $\tilde{y}_i$ can be expressed by:

$$\tilde{y}_i = \tilde{d}_i + \tilde{y}_i^p \tag{3}$$

3   Feature Adaptation Predictive Coding

The block-by-block observation process is applied for all blocks in the image x. If the current block has better candidates, its prediction vector may be closer to its measurement vector. For the current measurement vector, its candidates will consist of one or more dequantization vectors in its neighborhood. Based on these candidates, the existing QBCS predictive coding methods calculate the correlation between the current measurement vector and each candidate, and then choose a prediction vector with the maximum correlation. To increase the accuracy and quality of prediction candidates, it is necessary to adaptively obtain the prediction candidates by combining the local feature and hierarchical feature.

According to clinical experiences, the COVID-19 chest images are almost white on X-ray chest film, and the lung shadow is an imaging terminology. The basic principle of

X-ray compressive imaging is that the X-ray penetrates the tissue and forms an image on the chest film or bottom plate, which is basically black and white. The lung of a normal person is a relatively black area. In case of lung shadow, the penetration of X-ray will be weakened, and it will appear as a white region on X-ray chest film. In this work, we utilize the typical COVID-19 X-ray image dataset: tawsifur [23, 24], and Fig. 2 shows three typical test images in the tawsifur dataset.

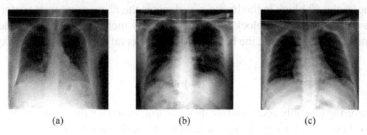

(a)   (b)   (c)

Fig. 2. COVID-19 X-ray images for experiment testing

Under the feature guidance of COVID-19 X-ray image, the QBCS predictive coding needs to obtain the features of ground glass changes or small patches in the lung image. The X-ray manifestations of common pneumonia are inflammatory exudative changes, such as increased, thickened and disordered lung markings. There is a probability of one or both sides, and the disease generally develops slowly. However, the COVID-19 X-ray images still have some empirical statistical characteristics, such as multiple small class flake shadows and interstitial changes at the beginning, mainly in the lateral zone of the lung. With the rapid progress of the disease, it can develop into ground glass shadows and sleeping shadows of both lungs, which shows the lung consolidation in serious cases. The lung examination of COVID-19 will show some ground glass shadows or infiltrating shadows, while the lung texture of common pneumonia is thickened in an X-ray image.

In order to highlight the convenience of the telemedicine-oriented QBCS system, the predictive coding should achieve the goal of low complexity and high fidelity. Each block is not independent of each other. They have a certain relationship with the surrounding eight blocks in terms of feature correlation. The sparsity of the block can be used to estimate the complexity of block structure. Since the sparse energy changes around those blocks where the ground glass phenomenon occurs in the lung are more obvious in a COVID-19 X-ray image, the feature-guided predictive coding will utilize the feature correlation between each measurement and the surrounding measurements. Due to the non-stationarity of X-ray images, the correlation coefficient of a measurement vector is different from its adjacent measurement vectors in different directions. For the current measurement vector, the optimal prediction candidate is selected from the adjacent dequantization vectors. If more prediction candidates are selected for the present measurement vector, the optimal prediction candidate is more approach to the current measurement. Figure 3 illustrates the construct of feature-guided predictive coding.

At one measuring end, the BCS measurements are compressed into a bitstream by quantization and entropy encoder. The scalar quantization may ignore the energy features of measurement signal and reduce the encoding distortion. At present, there are

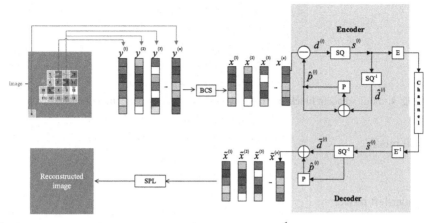

Fig. 3. Architecture of feature-guided predictive coding: SQ^{-1} is inverse scalar quantization; P is a prediction module; E is an entropy encoder; E^{-1} is an entropy decoder

some QBCS predictive coding methods, which can be regarded as specific extension of predictive coding. In order to find better prediction coefficients, the proposed method will adaptively calculate the block-wise prediction coefficients according to the average energy of the measurements, and dynamically adjust the weight values. In the measurement domain, a COVID-19 X-ray image itself is not a sparse signal. By background subtraction technology [25], it can be divided into two parts: foreground and background. Usually, the background part is fixed, while the foreground part is usually sparse due to the energy features of a COVID-19 X-ray image. Then, the appropriate quality factors are allocated to obtain the image features. The mean and variance of each image block are estimated for the foreground block and the background block, and thus the blocks are classified. Due to no isolated relationship between blocks of X-ray images, there is inherent feature correlation between adjacent blocks. Each measurement block has a high correlation with its adjacent blocks. It is necessary for a QBCS measuring end to apply the predictive coding. By using the sparsity of X-ray images, the novel predictive coding is used to make full use of the feature correlation of X-ray images.

In order to ensure the diversity of prediction candidates, the foreground blocks and background blocks are separated firstly, and four prediction modes are firstly defined for each adjacent block: top left, bottom left, bottom and top. Moreover, the background blocks use fewer prediction candidates, and the foreground blocks use more prediction candidates. During the QBCS predictive coding, Fig. 4 illustrates the four adjacent blocks for the measurement-domain prediction of current block, where a four-block neighborhood of current block includes four adjacent blocks as possible candidates, and the dequantization vectors of up to four adjacent blocks will be available for a give block at the reconstruction end. For the current block, these four prediction blocks are defined as A, B, C and D, respectively.

The following Eqs. (4)–(7) are the four prediction modes of adjacent blocks.

Up-left mode:

$$\hat{y}_{Up-L}^{(Cur)} = \tilde{y}^{(A)} \tag{4}$$

Fig. 4. Four adjacent blocks for the measurement-domain prediction of current block

Left mode:

$$\hat{y}_L^{(Cur)} = \tilde{y}^{(B)} \tag{5}$$

Under-left mode:

$$\hat{y}_{Un-L}^{(Cur)} = \tilde{y}^{(C)} \tag{6}$$

Up mode:

$$\hat{y}_{Up}^{(Cur)} = \tilde{y}^{(D)} \tag{7}$$

During block-by-block spiral scan, the earlier a block is referenced, the more important it is. On the other hand, the spatially closer block is more important. According to the reference order and the availability of dequantization vectors, four adjacent blocks around the current block are sorted from 1 to 4, where the smaller the serial number is, the more important it is for measurement-domain prediction. Under low-complexity constraint, the existing predictive coding methods almost select three or four candidates. In ascending order of serial number, the proposed FAPC method only selects up to two prediction candidates from the dequantization vectors of adjacent blocks around the current block, that is, the B and D blocks in vertical and horizontal directions, and thus obtain a basic candidate set for the current block. A block only needs one supplementary bit, and the FAPC method can improve the prediction quality when there is a small quantity of candidates.

Because that the residual sparsity is related to the block-wise similarity, the prediction coefficients of adjacent blocks closer to the sparsity of current block should be more significant. Based on asymptotic random matrix spectrum analysis theory, the signal sparsity can be estimated by the average energy of the measurements. The average energy of the measurements is defined as

$$E = \Sigma_{i=1}^{M} y_i^2 / M \tag{8}$$

where M is the dimension of the measurement vector y. To ensure that the reconstruction end and the measuring end can calculate the same weight coefficients, we can only use the information of $\tilde{y}^{(B)}$ and $\tilde{y}^{(D)}$. First, we estimate the energy of current block by:

$$\tilde{E}^{(Cur)} = \frac{\left(\frac{E^{(B)}}{L_B} + \frac{E^{(D)}}{L_D}\right)}{2} \tag{9}$$

where $E^{(B)}$ and $E^{(D)}$ represent the average energy of $\tilde{y}^{(B)}$ and $\tilde{y}^{(D)}$, respectively; L_B and L_D represent the distance between $\tilde{y}^{(Cur)}$ and $\tilde{y}^{(B)}$, $\tilde{y}^{(D)}$ respectively. Here, we set $L_B = L_D = 1$. The farther the distance between the adjacent block and the current block, the adjacent block has a smaller influence on the current block. So, we utilize the reciprocal of the distance as the weight of the average energy, and then calculate the error between $\frac{E^{[i]}}{li}$ and $\tilde{E}^{(Cur)}$.

$$\Delta_i = \left| \frac{E^{(i)}}{li} - \tilde{E}^{(Cur)} \right|, i \in \{B, D\} \tag{10}$$

Let $S = \Delta_B + \Delta_D$, we build an adaptive prediction mode:

$$\hat{y}_{FA}^{(cur)} = \frac{w \left(\frac{\Delta B}{L_B} \tilde{y}^{(B)} + \frac{\Delta D}{L_D} \tilde{y}^{(D)} \right)}{S} \tag{11}$$

where w is the overall coefficients adjustment factor, empirically $w = 0.9$. By combing three modes, we define a feature-guided candidate set as follow:

$$P_{FA} = \left\{ \hat{y}_L^{(Cur)}, \hat{y}_{Up}^{(Cur)}, \hat{y}_{FA}^{(Cur)} \right\} \tag{12}$$

For the current measurement vector $y^{(Cur)}$, the best prediction $\hat{y}_{FA-best}^{(Cur)}$ is determined by minimizing residuals between $y^{(Cur)}$ with the prediction candidates in the feature-guided candidate set P_{FA}, i.e.,

$$\hat{y}_{FA-best}^{(Cur)} = \underset{y \in P_{FA}}{\arg \min} ||y - y^{(Cur)}||_{l1} \tag{13}$$

When obtaining the optimal prediction $\hat{y}_{FA-best}^{(Cur)}$, the residual can be calculated by $d^{(Cur)} = y^{(Cur)} - \hat{y}_{FA-best}^{(Cur)}$, which is then scalar-quantized to obtain the quantization index $e^{(Cur)} = Q[d^{(Cur)}]$. Then the proposed method dequantizes $e^{(Cur)}$ to get $\tilde{d}^{(Cur)}$, and reconstructs the current measurement vector through $\tilde{y}^{(Cur)} = \hat{y}_{FA-best}^{(Cur)} + \tilde{d}^{(Cur)}$, which is ready for further predictive coding. Under a telemedicine-oriented QBCS system, the feature adaptation predictive coding with SQ is still abbreviated as FAPC.

According to Eqs. (8) and (9), it is possible to focus on the obvious energy change of different blocks when the ground glass phenomenon occurs in a COVID-19 X-ray image, because the correlation between the blocks where the ground glass phenomenon occurs is stronger, which is conducive to better analysis of the weight values in all directions, and the block-wise prediction quality in ground glass area will also increase.

4   Experimental Results

To verify the advantages of the proposed predictive coding method for quantized block compressive sensing. The rate-distortion performance of the proposed FAPC method is compared with DPCM [15], SDPC [16], MCWP [17] and ZP-DPCM [21]. The SPL algorithm is used to reconstruct each image from the decoded measurements which are generated by different predictive coding methods [9]. Extensive experiments are performed to compare the proposed method and other predictive coding methods whose implementations can be found at the corresponding websites.

At the QBCS measuring end, the block-level observation matrix Φ_B is an orthogonal random Gaussian matrix, and the block size B^2 is typically 16×16. The typical combinations of subrate (S) and quality factor (Q) are selected for each predictive coding method. The subrate is from 0.1 to 1.0, and the quality factor is from 1 to 8. In the tawsifur dataset [23, 24], all 362 test images are respectively measured and encoded by changing the (S,Q) combination. When the (S,Q) combinations are respectively (0.3,3), (0.5,6) and (0.7,8), Fig. 5 shows the reconstructed images of X-ray compressive imaging by executing the FAPC method, where a COVID-19 X-ray image, named Covid-test1, is selected from the tawsifur dataset. The subjective evaluation indicates that the larger subrate or quality factor can produce the more visual-pleasing reconstructed images. With (S,Q) = (0.3,3), some areas are blurred in the reconstructed image. With (S,Q) = (0.7,8), the reconstructed image has the good layering, contrast, and detail levels.

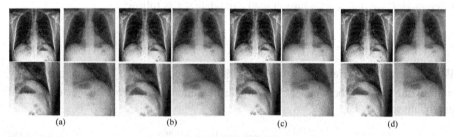

(a)   (b)   (c)   (d)

Fig. 5. Reconstructed images of chest COVID-19 X-ray image Covid-test1 under typical (S,Q) combinations: (a) original; (b) (0.3,3); (c) (0.5,6); (d) (0.7,8)

For the Covid-test1 image, Fig. 6(a) shows the rate-distortion curves of five predictive coding methods. To better viewing, Fig. 6(b) shows the detailed comparison after amplification. The higher the rate-distortion curve, the better its rate-distortion performance. To consistently demonstrate the data, we linearly interpolate the experimental data to obtain the PSNR values when the bitrate is 0.1–1.0 bpp (bits per pixel), as given in Table 1.

Figure 7(a) shows the average rate-distortion curves of all images in the tawsifur dataset, and Fig. 7(b) shows the detailed comparison after amplification. Table 2 gives the PSNR values at each bitrate of 0.1–1.0 bpp. The computational complexity of FAPC is lower than that of SDPC and MCWP. By fully utilizing the correlation among BCS measurements, the proposed FAPC method can consistently reduce the encoding distortion, and achieve superior restoration quality with low complexity.

Further, the Bjontegaard Delta PSNR (BD-PSNR) can quantitatively analyze the results in Fig. 6. Compared with the DPCM method, the SDPC, ZP-DPCM, MCWP, and FAPC methods can achieve the BD-PSNR gains of 0.51 dB, 0.54 dB, 0.58 dB, 0.64 dB, respectively. More prediction candidates will weaken the use of COVID-19 image features, and the FAPC method with fine prediction candidates can obtain better rate distortion performance. While maintaining the quantity of prediction candidates, the

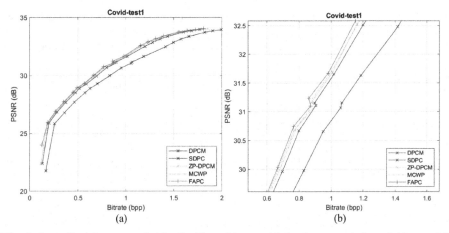

Fig. 6. Rate-distortion curves for the Covid-test1 image: (a) the data range is from 0.1 bpp to 2.0 bpp; (b) the data range is from 0.6 bpp to 1.4 bpp

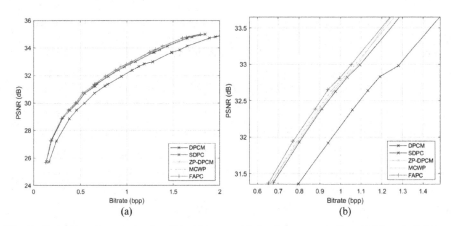

Fig. 7. Rate-distortion curves for all test images: (a) the data range is from 0.1 bpp to 2.0 bpp; (b) the data range is from 0.6 bpp to 1.4 bpp

proposed FAPC method can reduce the encoding distortion of X-ray images and obtain the best restoration quality with low complexity.

Table 1. Performance comparison for five predictive coding methods on the Covid-test1 image

Bitrate (bpp)	DPCM	SDPC	ZP-DPCM	MCWP	FAPC
0.1	23.52	25.07	25.43	25.23	25.55
0.2	23.86	25.93	26.32	26.06	26.18
0.3	26.44	26.96	27.74	27.09	27.24
0.4	27.12	27.93	28.56	28.07	28.13
0.5	28.02	28.76	28.94	28.92	29.02
0.6	28.71	29.33	29.58	29.42	29.53
0.7	29.27	29.99	30.09	30.12	30.24
0.8	29.79	30.68	30.80	30.91	30.93
0.9	30.43	31.13	31.07	31.02	31.12
1.0	30.74	31.50	31.70	31.70	31.84

Table 2. Performance comparison for five predictive coding methods on all test images

Bitrate (bpp)	DPCM	SDPC	ZP-DPCM	MCWP	FAPC
0.1	26.15	26.40	26.43	26.22	26.41
0.2	26.82	27.04	27.32	27.23	27.25
0.3	28.09	28.69	28.74	28.83	28.89
0.4	29.12	29.49	29.56	29.65	29.65
0.5	29.86	30.34	30.44	30.51	30.56
0.6	30.54	30.89	30.98	31.01	31.04
0.7	31.02	31.44	31.56	31.63	31.70
0.8	31.57	32.00	31.10	32.14	32.22
0.9	32.01	32.41	32.47	32.51	32.54
1.0	32.42	32.63	32.70	32.79	32.88

5   Conclusion

To improve the encoding performance of quantized block compressive sensing, a feature adaptation predictive coding method is proposed for telemedicine-oriented COVID-19 X-ray images. The proposed method can calculate the block-wise prediction coefficients according to main features of COVID-19 X-ray images, and thus realize the high-efficiency prediction, and the proposed method can obtain better rate-distortion performance when the candidate set is adaptively expanded. The experimental results show that as compared with the state-of-the-art methods, the proposed method has good rate-distortion performance and low complexity for COVID-19 X-ray compressive imaging. The proposed method can well adapt to the predictive coding of X-ray images, and promote the development of portable telemedicine imaging applications.

References

1. Dong, D., et al.: The role of imaging in the detection and management of COVID-19: a review. IEEE Rev. Biomed. Eng. **14**, 16–29 (2021)
2. Trevisi, M., Akbari, A., Trocan, M., Rodrmíguez-Vázquez, Á., Carmona-Galán, R.: Compressive imaging using RIP-compliant CMOS imager architecture and Landweber reconstruction. IEEE Trans. Circuits Syst. Video Technol. **30**(2), 387–399 (2020)
3. Zhang, H.P., Li, K., Zhao, C.Z., Tang, J., Xiao, T.Q.: Efficient implementation of X-ray ghost imaging based on a modified compressive sensing algorithm. Chin. Phys. B **31**(6), 064202 (2022)
4. Kulkarni, K., Lohit, S., Turaga, P., Kerviche, R., Ashok, A.: ReconNet: non-iterative reconstruction of images from compressively sensed random measurements. In: IEEE Conference on Computer Vision and Pattern Recognition (CVPR), Las Vegas, pp. 449–458 (2016)
5. Amit, S.U., Deepthi, P.: Rate-distortion analysis of structured sensing matrices for block compressive sensing of images. Signal Process. Image Commun. **65**, 115–127 (2018)
6. Xie, X.M., Wang, C., Du, J., Shi, G.M.: Full image recover for block-based compressive sensing. In: International Conference on Multimedia & Expo, San Diego, pp. 1–6 (2018)
7. Liu, Y., Yuan, X., Suo, J.L., Brady, D., Dai, Q.H.: Rank minimization for snapshot compressive imaging. IEEE Trans. Pattern Anal. Mach. Intell. **41**(12), 2990–3006 (2019)
8. Liu, X.M., Zhai, D.M., Zhou, J.T., Zhang, X.F., Zhao, D.B., Gao, W.: Compressive sampling-based image coding for resource-deficient visual communication. IEEE Trans. Image Process. **25**(6), 2844–2855 (2016)
9. Fowler, J.E., Mun, S., Tramel, E.W.: Block-based compressed sensing of images and video. Found. Trends Signal Process. **4**(4), 297–416 (2012)
10. Chen, Z., et al.: Compressive sensing multi-layer residual coefficients for image coding. IEEE Trans. Circuits Syst. Video Technol. **30**(4), 1109–1120 (2020)
11. Jacques, L., Hammond, D.K., Fadili, J.M.: Dequantizing compressed sensing: when oversampling and non-Gaussian constraints combine. IEEE Trans. Inf. Theory **57**(1), 559–571 (2011)
12. Sun, J.Z., Goyal, V.K.: Optimal quantization of random measurements in compressed sensing. In: IEEE International Symposium on Information Theory, Seoul, pp. 6–10 (2009)
13. Wang, L.J., Wu, X.L., Shi, G.M.: Binned progressive quantization for compressive sensing. IEEE Trans. Image Process. **21**(6), 2980–2990 (2012)
14. Ahn, J.H., Jiang, H.: Architecture and noise analysis for block-based compressive imaging. In: International Conference on Image Processing, Athens, pp. 31–35 (2018)
15. Mun, S., Fowler, J.E.: DPCM for quantized block-based compressed sensing of images. In: 20th European Signal Processing Conference, Bucharest, pp. 1424–1428 (2012)
16. Zhang, J., Zhao, D.B., Jiang, F.: Spatially directional predictive coding for block-based compressive sensing of natural images. In: IEEE International Conference on Image Processing, Melbourne, pp. 1021–1025 (2014)
17. Li, R., Liu, H.B., He, W.: Space-time quantization and motion-aligned reconstruction for block-based compressive video sensing. KSII Trans. Internet Inf. Syst. **10**(1), 321–340 (2017)
18. Zhou, J.B., Zhou, J.J., Guo, L.: Angular intra prediction based measurement coding algorithm for compressively sensed image. In: IEEE International Conference on Multimedia & Expo, San Diego, pp. 1–6 (2018)

19. Tian, W., Liu, H.: Measurement-domain spiral predictive coding for block-based image compressive sensing. In: International Conference on Image and Graphics, Beijing, pp. 3–12 (2019)
20. Chen, Q.L., Chen, D.R., Gong, J.L., Weighted predictive coding methods for block-based compressive sensing of images. In: 3rd International Conference on Unmanned Systems, Harbin, pp. 587–591 (2020)
21. Li, R., Yang, Y.H., Sun, F.Y.: Green visual sensor of plant: an energy-efficient compressive video sensing in the internet of things. Front. Plant Sci. **13**, 849606 (2022)
22. Mun, S., Fowler, J.E.: Motion-compensated compressed-sensing reconstruction for dynamic MRI. In: IEEE International Conference on Image Processing, pp. 1006–1010 (2013)
23. Chowdhury, M.E.H., Rahman, T., Khandakar, A., et al.: Can AI help in screening viral and COVID-19 pneumonia? IEEE Access **8**, 132665–132676 (2020)
24. Rahman, T., Khandakar, A., Qiblawey, Y., et al.: Exploring the effect of image enhancement techniques on COVID-19 detection using chest X-ray images. Comput. Biol. Med. **132**, 104319 (2021)
25. Wang, J., Wang, W., Chen, J.: Adaptive rate block compressive sensing based on statistical characteristics estimation. IEEE Trans. Image Process. **31**, 734–747 (2022)

Deep Fourier Kernel Exploitation in Blind Image Super-Resolution

Yu Fu, Xiaoyun Zhang[✉], Yixuan Huang, Ya Zhang, and Yanfeng Wang

Cooperative Medianet Innovation Center, Shanghai Jiao Tong University,
Shanghai, China
{fyuu11,xiaoyun.zhang,huangyixuan,ya_zhang,wangyanfeng}@sjtu.edu.cn

Abstract. Blind image super-resolution (SR) has achieved great progress through estimating and utilizing blur kernels. However, current predefined dimension-stretching strategy based methods trivially concatenate or modulate the vectorized blur kernel with the low-resolution image, resulting in raw blur kernels under-utilized and also limiting generalization. This paper proposes a deep Fourier kernel exploitation framework to model the explicit correlation between raw blur kernels and images without dimensionality reduction. Specifically, based on the acknowledged degradation model, we decouple the effects of downsampling and the blur kernel, and reverse them by the upsampling and deconvolution modules accordingly, via introducing a transitional SR image. Then we design a novel Kernel Fast Fourier Convolution (KFFC) to filter the image feature of the transitional image with the raw blur kernel in the frequency domain. Extensive experiments show that our methods achieve favorable and robust results.

Keywords: Blind image super-resolution · Blur kernel · Fourier convolution network

1 Introduction

Single Image Super-Resolution (SISR) aims to reconstruct the High-Resolution (HR) image from the given Low-Resolution (LR) counterpart. In past decades, it has been widely used in surveillance imaging, astronomy imaging, and medical imaging. As SISR is an extremely ill-posed task, early learning-based methods [8, 15, 37] make plain exploration, *i.e.* assume that the blur kernel in the degradation is predefined/known (e.g. Bicubic kernel). For more powerful generalization [3, 27], the blind SR task [5, 10, 21, 25, 30, 36], which handles LR images underlying unknown blur kernels, draws increasing attention. Most of these methods focus on accurate blur kernel estimation [3, 18], fully kernel exploitation [25, 33, 36], or combining both [10, 12]. This work focuses on fully exploiting the blur kernel in the blind SR task.

Given explicit raw blur kernels, the core of blind SR lies in how to properly introduce and fully utilize the information in them. The existing methods adopt

G. Zhai et al. (Eds.): IFTC 2022, CCIS 1766, pp. 163–179, 2023.
https://doi.org/10.1007/978-981-99-0856-1_12

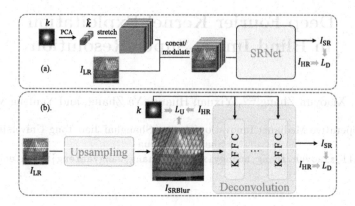

Fig. 1. Framework comparison on kernel exploitation super-resolution task, assuming the blur kernel is estimated or handcrafted. (a) Existing dimensionality reduction based framework; (b) Our deep Fourier kernel exploitation framework.

dimensionality reduction manners, ignoring the physical meaning of the blur kernel. As shown in Fig. 1(a), they use a predefined principal component analysis (PCA) to project the raw blur kernel into a discriminative domain vector $\hat{k}$, then $\hat{k}$ is stretched and trivially concatenated [25,36] or modulated [10,12,30,33] with the LR image. Such dimensionality reduction based methods suffer from two major flaws. (1) The PCA matrix inevitably discards part of the blur kernel information, and the predefined strategy severely limits generalization, since it is helpless when dealing with unseen kernels [7,19]. (2) Simply relying on the SR network to implicitly model the correlation between the blur kernel and the image makes the blur kernel under-utilized, and also lacks interpretability.

To tackle these problems and fully exploit the blur kernel information, without predefined dimensionality reduction, we revisit the degradation model, to decouple the effects of the raw blur kernel and the downsampling. Specifically, in the degradation model, we observe that the blur kernel and downsampling are independent. Hence, we propose to decouple the blind SR task into **upsampling** and **deconvolution** modules, via introducing a transitional SR image. As shown in Fig. 1(b), the upsampling module is only fed with the LR image, to produce the transitional SR image I_{SRBlur}, which has the same size as the HR image, but with coarse details. I_{SRBlur} is the approximation of convolving the HR image with the blur kernel k, thus it eliminates the effects of downsampling in the LR image, and naturally avoids poor generalization caused by introducing the predefined PCA. Given the transitional SR image, the deconvolution module aims to reverse the effects of k. To fully explore the kernel information, we here model the explicit correlation between the raw blur kernel and the image, instead of concatenating or modulation. We design a novel Kernel Fast Fourier Convolution (KFFC) to achieve efficient filtering via Fourier transform, considering that the convolving can be well reversed in the frequency domain with good interpretability [9]. Specifically, the proposed KFFC explicitly filters the image features of I_{SRBlur} through k in the frequency domain. We train the whole framework end-to-end and conduct extensive experiments and comprehensive ablation studies in both non-blind and blind settings to evaluate the state-of-the-art performance.

2   Related Work

2.1   Kernel Exploitation

Kernel exploitation in blind super-resolution (SR) aims to reconstruct super-resolved (SR) images from given low-resolution(LR) images with known degradation, which is also called the non-blind SR setting. Generally speaking, there are two definitions of the non-blind SR setting in the literature.

The one is training an SR model for one single degradation blur kernel and evaluating the model with the synthetic dataset based on the predefined kernel [2, 8,15,31,37]. For instance, Dong et al. [8] proposed the first learning-based CNN model for image super-resolution. Kim et al. [15] and Zhang et al. [37] employed a very deep CNN and attention mechanism, which improved the SISR performance by a large margin. Although they show superiority compared with traditional interpolation-based and model-based methods, all of them assume the LR images are degraded from the HR images through bicubic downsampling, therefore, they construct paired LR-HR training dataset through bicubic downsampling and conduct experiments with the predefined bicubic kernel for evaluation. One can see that degradation in a real-world scenario is complicated and unknown which can not be described by a simple bicubic kernel, and the models trained with a bicubic dataset will suffer from severe performance drop when the degradation is different from the bicubic kernel.

The other is that reconstruct the SR image from both the LR image and the corresponding blur kernel [10,25,33,36]. Following the acknowledged degradation model 1, these types of kernel exploitation methods focus on fully utilizing blur kernel for reconstructing SR images. Compared with former methods which are trained with a paired bicubic dataset, these types of methods take blur kernels into account and obtain better performance than the former methods when given an estimated or handcrafted blur kernel. Nevertheless, these kernel exploitation methods introduce the blur kernel through a dimension-stretching strategy, which underutilizes the blur kernel and limits the generalization. Specifically, they use a predefined principal component analysis (PCA) matrix to project the raw blur kernel into a discriminative domain vector and model the correlation between the blur kernel and the image through direct concatenation or modulation. In this paper, we focus on modeling the explicit correlation of the raw blur kernel and the image, which can remedy the kernel underutilization and limited generalization problems.

2.2   Blind SR

To tackle the blind SR task, which reconstructs SR image from only LR image with unknown degradation, a lot of works are proposed and achieve encouraging performance [3, 7, 10, 12, 14, 18, 28]. Most blind SR methods follow a two-step manner. Firstly, estimating the blur kernel from the given LR image. Bell-Kligler et al. [3] estimates the degradation kernel by utilizing an internal generative adversarial network (GAN) on a single LR image. Tao et al. [28] estimate the blur kernel in the frequency domain. Liang et al. [18] and Xiao et al. [32] try to estimate a spatial variant blur kernel for real-world images.

Given the estimated blur kernel and the LR image, the core of blind SR lies in utilizing blur kernels. As mentioned before, the kernel exploitation approaches can solve the blind SR task by introducing the estimated blur kernel. There also exist two types of methods that can combine the kernel estimating network. The one is to synthesis paired training datasets based on the estimated blur kernels, and then train a new non-blind SR model to enhance the performance on real datasets [3, 28]. However, one can see that these methods are time-consuming for training a new model and indirectly use the estimated blur kernel.

The other is that introduce the estimated blur kernel to the kernel exploiting SR network directly [10, 25, 33, 36]. Furthermore, some approaches tried to solve the two-step blind SR task in an end-to-end manner [7, 10, 12, 30] and proposed some new training strategies to enhance the performance. For example, Gu et al. [10] proposed an iterative mechanism to refine the estimated blur kernel based on the super-resolved image. Luo et al. [12] alternatively optimized the blur kernel estimation and kernel exploitation. It is worth pointing out that the proposed method focuses on fully exploiting the blur kernel for blind SR and could be combined with most kernel estimation and training strategies.

2.3　Other SR Methods

Beyond these methods aforementioned, there are other related methods that do not explicitly estimate blur kernels, such as degradation-modeling SR [20], They try to introduce more types of degradation, like jpeg compression, and design a sophisticated degradation model. Then they synthesize paired datasets for training, the whole process is time-consuming and still tends to generate over-smoothed results when meeting slight degradation [20]. Unpaired SR [13, 21] learns the degradation in real-world images based on the cycleGAN [38], which usually suffer from unstable training and pixel misalignment problems. Zero-shot SR [27] utilizes the similarity of patches across scales to reconstruct SR image from single LR image input, which has in-born problems that it can not learn a good prior of HR datasets.

3　Methodology

3.1　Blur Kernels in Blind Super-Resolution Task

Given the low-resolution image I_{LR} and the corresponding blur kernel k, the core of the blind SR task lies in fully exploiting the blur kernel information

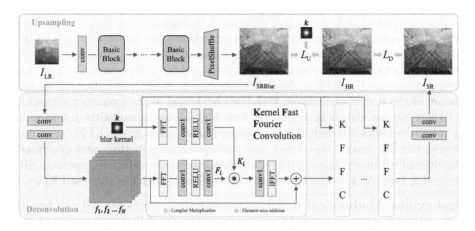

Fig. 2. Framework Overview. Given the LR image and the corresponding blur kernel, we decouple the kernel exploitation task into upsampling and deconvolution modules based on the degradation model. The **Upsampling** module reconstructs the SRBlur image under the constraints of the HR image and the blur kernel. The **Deconvolution** module is fed with the resultant image SRBlur and the blur kernel, and recovers the super-resolved image through our Kernel Fast Fourier Convolution which can model the explicit correlation between the blur kernel and the SRBlur image in the frequency domain. The whole framework is trained end-to-end.

to reconstruct the super-resolved image I_{SR}, compared with general SR tasks. Firstly, the acknowledged degradation model can be formulated as:

$$I_{LR} = (I_{HR} * k) \downarrow_\alpha + n, \tag{1}$$

where $*$ is a convolution operation, $\downarrow_\alpha$ is a downsampling operation with the scale factor α, and n is the additive Gaussian noise. Following [10,12,25], we assume noise can be reduced by [34]. And the degradation model can be divided into: convolving $(I_{HR} * k)$ and independent downsampling $\downarrow_\alpha$. The former means information blending of I_{HR} via k, and the latter denotes irreversible information lost, which is irrelevant with k. Thus, k only has a direct effect on the HR scale.

3.2 Deep Fourier Kernel Exploitation Framework

Motivation: Although existing dimension-stretching strategy based kernel exploitation methods in blind SR show superiority, they still pose two main flaws.

Firstly, the used PCA matrix inevitably discards part of the blur kernel information, and the predefined strategy severely limits generalization. To solve this, without using predefined PCA, we introduce the raw blur kernel to the SR network. The degradation model in Sect. 3.1 shows the independent downsampling impedes applying the raw blur kernel to the LR image directly. We hence decouple the effects of downsampling and the blur kernel, and reverse them by the upsampling and deconvolution modules accordingly. The two modules are bridged through a transitional SR image.

Secondly, simply relying on the SR network to implicitly interact the blur kernel and the image, under-utilizes the blur kernel, and also lacks interpretability. To address these problems, in the deconvolution module, we model the explicit correlation between the transitional SR images and raw blur kernels through the proposed module Kernel Fast Fourier Convolution (KFFC), to filter the image feature of the transitional image with the blur kernel in the frequency domain.

Therefore, as shown in Fig. 2, the raw blur kernel is explicitly introduced to the SR network through the decoupling framework and the KFFC module. Firstly, the LR image I_{LR} is fed into the upsampling module and generates transitional SR image I_{SRBlur}. Then, the deconvolution module reconstructs SR image I_{SR} from I_{SRBlur} and the raw blur kernel k through the proposed KFFC.

Upsampling Module is designed to generate the transitional HR-size image I_{SRBlur}, which is an approximation of convolving the HR image and the blur kernel k. Compared to directly recovering the original SR image I_{SR} from I_{LR}, the objective of the upsampling module is easier. Hence, for simplicity, we adopt the trivial SISR network as the module architecture. Specifically, we use several convolution layers to extract features from I_{LR}; then forward features to several cascaded basic blocks, which follows Residual in Residual Dense Block (RRDB) [31], to enhance the non-linear ability; and finally, upsample features via the PixelShuffle layer [26]. Note that, the architecture of upsampling module is flexible to the existing SISR network.

To supervise the upsampling module $\mathcal{U}$, we first calculate $(I_{HR} * k)$ as the ground-truth of I_{SRBlur}; then use the L_1 constraint to achieve reverse downsampling:

$$L_U = L_1(I_{HR} * k, \ I_{SRBlur}) = L_1(I_{HR} * k, \ \mathcal{U}(I_{LR})) \tag{2}$$

Deconvolution Module aims to reverse $(I_{HR} * k)$, $i.e.$ generate the SR image I_{SR}, given the transitional image I_{SRBlur} and blur kernel k. A trivial way is to concatenate or modulate k into the SR network like existing methods, we experimentally find that it only sharps images without reconstructing high-frequency details, thus under-utilizes blur kernel information (see Sect. 4.4). To solve this problem, we propose to model an explicit correlation between k and I_{SRBlur}. Since I_{SRBlur} is the approximation of convolving I_{HR} and k, we can regard deconvolution as deblurring I_{SRBlur} given k. Considering that, there exists a huge gap between I_{SRBlur} and ground-truth $(I_{HR} * k)$, directly restoring SR images by the inverse filter is impracticable. We hence regard the gap as independent noise, which is termed as $I_{SRBlur} = (I_{HR} * k) + n$; then, treat the task of the deconvolution module as deblurring images with noise.

Like inverse filters and Wiener filters, considering that convolution can be well reversed in the frequency domain, which has good interpretability [9], we here handle the deconvolution task via Fourier Transform. Inspired by Fast Fourier Convolution (FFC) [6] which is designed to capture a large reception field in shallow layers of the network for high-level tasks, we design a module called Kernel Fast Fourier Convolution (KFFC), to filter the transitional image with corresponding blur kernel k in the frequency domain.

Concretely, as shown in Fig. 2, we first use some CNN layers to extract the image feature of I_SRBlur, denoted as $\{f_i\}_{i=1}^N$; and then transform both feature maps $\{f_i\}_{i=1}^N$ and the blur kernel k into frequency domain through fast Fourier transform $\mathcal{F}$; next adopt two individual compilations of 1×1 convolution and Leaky ReLU $\mathcal{T}_F$, $\mathcal{T}_K$ to achieve non-linearly transformation. Based on the property of Fourier Transform, we can conduct filtering through complex multiplication in the frequency domain. Sequentially, we empirically use an extra 1×1 convolution to refine the filtered feature. Eventually, the filtered feature maps are converted back to the spatial domain through Inverse Fourier Transform $\mathcal{F}^{-1}$. The whole procedure of KFFC can be formulated as follows:

$$\begin{aligned}
\text{KFFC}(f_i, k) = \mathcal{F}^{-1}[(\Re(\boldsymbol{F}_i) \odot \Re(\boldsymbol{K}_i) - \Im(\boldsymbol{F}_i) \odot \Im(\boldsymbol{K}_i)) \\
+ i(\Im(\boldsymbol{F}_i) \odot \Re(\boldsymbol{K}_i) + \Re(\boldsymbol{F}_i) \odot \Im(\boldsymbol{K}_i)]
\end{aligned} \tag{3}$$

where $\boldsymbol{F}_i = \mathcal{T}_F(\mathcal{F}(f_i))$, $\boldsymbol{K}_i = \mathcal{T}_K(\mathcal{F}(k))$, $\odot$ denotes the Hadamard product. $\Re$ and $\Im$ denotes the real and the imaginary part respectively. Note that we adopt real Fourier Transform to simplify computation because applying Fourier Transform on real signal is perfectly conjugate symmetric. To enhance performance, we also cascade multiple KFFC structures, then use two convolution layers to output the SR image I_SR.

To supervise the deconvolution module $\mathcal{D}$, we leverage the L_1 constraint, which can be formulated as:

$$L_D = L_1(I_\text{HR}, I_\text{SR}) = L_1(I_\text{HR}, \mathcal{D}(I_\text{SRBlur}, k)) \tag{4}$$

The whole framework is end-to-end trained with a total loss of $L_\text{D} + \lambda L_\text{U}$, and λ is a weight term which is set as 1 in our experiments.

4 Experiments

4.1 Datasets and Implementations

The training data is synthesized based on Eq. 1. 3450 2K HR images are collected from DIV2K [1] and Flickr2K [29] for training. We use isotropic blur kernels following [10,12,33,36]. The kernel width is uniformly sampled in [0.2, 2.0], [0.2, 3.0] and [0.2, 4.0] for scale factors 2, 3, 4, respectively. The kernel size is fixed to 21×21. We also augment data by randomly horizontal flipping, vertical flipping, and $90°$ rotating.

Implementation Details: For all experiments, we use 6 RRDB blocks [31] in the upsampling module and 7 KFFCs in the deconvolution module with 64 channels. During training, we crop and degrade HR images to 64×64 LR patches for all scale factors. For optimization, we use Adam [16] with $\beta_1 = 0.9$, $\beta_2 = 0.999$, and a mini-batch size of 32. The learning rate is initialized to 4×10^{-4} and decayed by half at 1×10^5 iterations. We evaluate on five benchmarks: Set5 [4], Set14 [35], BSDS100 [22], Urban100 [11] and Manga109 [23]. All models are trained on RGB space, PSNR and SSIM are evaluated on Y channel of transformed YCrCb space.

Table 1. Quantitative performance comparison of the proposed method with other SOTAs on non-blind SR setting. The comparison is conducted using three different isotropic Gaussian blur kernels on Set5, Set14, and BSD100 datasets. We provide the ground-truth kernel(GTker) for all the listed methods in this table, as the original setting in SRCNN-CAB [25], SRMDNF [36] and UDVD [33]. As for SFTMD [10] and ZSSR [27], we also compare them by giving the GTker although they can solve the blind SR task through a kernel estimation network or bicubic downsampling. The best two results are highlighted in red and blue colors.

Method	Kernel Width	Set5 [4]			Set14 [35]			BSD100 [22]		
		x2	x3	x4	x2	x3	x4	x2	x3	x4
GTKer+ZSSR [27]		34.94	29.29	28.87	31.04	28.05	27.15	31.42	28.24	26.68
SRCNN-CAB [25]		33.27	31.03	29.31	30.29	28.29	26.91	28.98	27.65	25.51
SRMDNF [36]		37.79	34.13	31.96	33.33	30.04	28.35	32.05	28.97	27.49
SFTMD [10]	0.2	38.00	34.57	32.39	33.68	30.47	28.77	32.09	29.09	27.58
UDVD [33]		38.01	34.49	32.31	33.64	30.44	28.78	32.19	29.18	27.70
Ours		38.17	34.63	32.45	33.82	30.52	28.85	32.33	29.23	27.74
GTKer+ZSSR [27]		33.37	28.67	27.44	31.31	27.34	26.15	30.31	27.30	25.95
SRCNN-CAB [25]		33.42	31.14	29.50	30.51	28.34	27.02	29.02	27.91	25.66
SRMDNF [36]		37.44	34.17	32.00	33.20	30.08	28.42	31.98	29.03	27.53
SFTMD [10]	1.3	37.46	34.53	32.41	33.39	30.55	28.82	32.06	29.15	27.64
UDVD [33]		37.36	34.52	32.37	33.39	30.50	28.85	32.00	29.23	27.75
Ours		37.77	34.71	32.56	33.70	30.58	28.93	33.20	29.32	27.81
GTKer+ZSSR [27]		29.89	27.80	27.69	27.72	26.42	26.06	27.32	26.47	25.92
SRCNN-CAB [25]		32.21	30.82	28.81	29.74	27.83	26.15	28.35	26.63	25.13
SRMDNF [36]		34.12	33.02	31.77	30.25	29.33	28.26	29.23	28.35	27.43
SFTMD [10]	2.6	34.27	33.22	32.05	30.38	29.63	28.55	29.35	28.41	27.47
UDVD [33]		33.74	33.15	31.99	30.08	29.58	28.55	28.93	28.49	27.55
Ours		33.67	33.31	32.18	29.92	29.64	28.68	28.81	28.48	27.64

4.2 Experiments on Non-Blind Setting

We first evaluate the performance of the proposed method on the non-blind SR setting, which reconstructs the super-resolved image under the given low-resolution image and a corresponding known blur kernel. Following [10,33,36], we only consider isotropic Gaussian blur for simplicity, the kernel widths are set to 0.2, 1.3, 2.6, and the kernel sizes are 21×21 for all scale factors. Table 1 makes a comparison with SOTA methods under different kernel settings. We provide ground-truth kernels for all the listed methods in Table 1, as the original setting in SRCNN-CAB [8], SRMDNF [36], and UDVD [33]. As for SFTMD [10] and ZSSR [27], we also compare them by giving the ground-truth kernel, although they solve the blind SR task through a kernel estimation network [10] or bicubic downsampling [27].

The results in Table 1 show that our method performs best on most benchmarks, regardless of the degradation degree and scale factors. We surpass all competitors in most experimental settings and have a large gain of 0.31 dB for Set14 with kernel width 1.3. Interestingly, as the scale factor increases, the gain

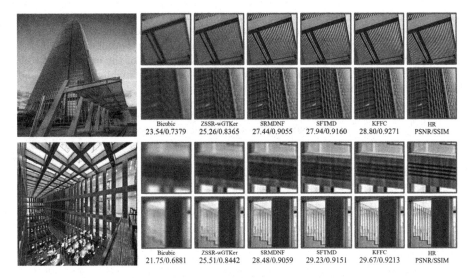

Fig. 3. Visual results of $img046, img049$ from Urban100, for different methods in non-blind setting. The SR factor is 2 and kernel width is 1.3.

of the proposed method gradually declines. We conjecture this is because the increasing scale factor reduces the effectiveness of blur kernels. In other words, the information loss in the downsampling process impedes the reconstruction. Figure 3 also shows visual comparisons. Our method yields better results on the recurring and regular textures such as the fine stripes, and reconstructs high quality fine details with fewer artifacts. All the above results reveal the superiority of our method quantitatively and qualitatively.

4.3   Experiments on Blind Setting

We also conduct blind SR settings to evaluate the effectiveness of the proposed method, which reconstruct super-resolved image under unknown degradation. Since determined blur kernels are needed for reasonable comparison, following in [10,12,14], we uniformly sample 8 kernels from range [1.8, 3.2], [1.35, 2.40] and [0.8, 1.6] for scale factor ×4, ×3, and ×2 respectively, which is also referred to *Gaussian8*. We compare our method with other SOTAs blind SR approaches including ZSSR [27](with bicubic kernel), IKC [10], DAN [12], AdaTarget [14]. Following [10,12], we also conduct comparisons with CARN [2] and its variants of performing the deblurring method before and after CARN. For all compared methods, we use their official implementation and pre-trained model except special remarks. It is worth pointing out that owing to our proposed method assuming the blur kernel is known, we conduct a comparison in a blind SR setting through integrating our method into IKC [10] and DAN [12]. Specifically, we replace the kernel exploitation part in the original methods with our proposed method and preserve the original training strategy such as iterative refining.

Table 2. Quantitative comparison of the proposed method with other SOTAs on various datasets in blind SR setting. The comparison is conducted using *Gaussian8* kernels on five benchmark datasets. We integrate our proposed method into IKC [10] and DAN [12], which means replacing the kernel exploitation part of the original network and preserving their training strategy. The best two results are highlighted in red and blue colors respectively.

Method	Scale	Set5 [4] PSNR	Set5 [4] SSIM	Set14 [35] PSNR	Set14 [35] SSIM	BSD100 [22] PSNR	BSD100 [22] SSIM	Urban100 [11] PSNR	Urban100 [11] SSIM	Manga109 [23] PSNR	Manga109 [23] SSIM
Bicubic		28.82	0.8577	26.02	0.7634	25.92	0.7310	23.14	0.7258	25.60	0.8498
CARN [2]		30.99	0.8779	28.10	0.7879	26.78	0.7286	25.27	0.7630	26.86	0.8606
Bicubic+ZSSR [27]		31.08	0.8786	28.35	0.7933	27.92	0.7632	25.25	0.7618	28.05	0.8769
[24]+CARN [2]		24.20	0.7496	21.12	0.6170	22.69	0.6471	18.89	0.5895	21.54	0.7946
CARN [2]+ [24]	x2	31.27	0.8974	29.03	0.8267	28.72	0.8033	25.62	0.7981	29.58	0.9134
IKC [10]		37.19	0.9526	32.94	0.9024	31.51	0.8790	29.85	0.8928	36.93	0.9667
DAN [12]		37.34	0.9526	33.08	0.9041	31.76	0.8858	30.60	0.9060	37.23	0.9710
DASR [30]		37.00	0.9508	32.61	0.8958	31.59	0.8813	30.26	0.9015	36.20	0.9686
IKC [10] + Ours		37.60	0.9562	33.31	0.9105	31.84	0.8880	30.66	0.9090	38.07	0.9718
DAN [12] + Ours		37.55	0.9547	33.26	0.9074	31.96	0.8897	31.20	0.9144	37.83	0.9726
Bicubic		26.21	0.7766	24.01	0.6662	24.25	0.6356	21.39	0.6203	22.98	0.7576
CARN [2]		27.26	0.7855	25.06	0.6676	25.85	0.6566	22.67	0.6323	23.85	0.7620
Bicubic+ZSSR [27]		28.25	0.7989	26.15	0.6942	26.06	0.6633	23.26	0.6534	25.19	0.7914
[24]+CARN [2]		19.05	0.5226	17.61	0.4558	20.51	0.5331	16.72	0.5895	18.38	0.6118
CARN [2]+ [24]	x3	30.31	0.8562	27.57	0.7531	27.14	0.7152	24.45	0.7241	27.67	0.8592
IKC [10]		33.06	0.9146	29.38	0.8233	28.53	0.7899	24.43	0.8302	32.43	0.9316
DAN [12]		34.04	0.9199	30.09	0.8287	28.94	0.7919	27.65	0.8352	33.16	0.9382
DASR [30]		33.53	0.9150	29.64	0.8143	28.64	0.7825	27.26	0.8269	32.05	0.9290
IKC [10] + Ours		33.51	0.9170	30.11	0.8313	28.84	0.7931	27.53	0.8344	32.90	0.9369
DAN [12] + Ours		34.11	0.9205	30.15	0.8303	28.98	0.7925	27.78	0.8380	33.20	0.9389
Bicubic		24.57	0.7108	22.79	0.6032	23.29	0.5786	20.35	0.5532	21.50	0.6933
CARN [2]		26.57	0.7420	24.62	0.6226	24.79	0.5963	22.17	0.5865	21.85	0.6834
Bicubic+ZSSR [27]		26.45	0.7279	24.78	0.6268	24.97	0.5989	22.11	0.5805	23.53	0.7240
[24]+CARN [2]		18.10	0.4843	16.59	0.3994	18.46	0.4481	15.47	0.3872	16.78	0.5371
CARN [2]+ [24]	x4	28.69	0.8092	26.40	0.6926	26.10	0.6528	23.46	0.6597	25.84	0.8035
IKC [10]		31.67	0.8829	28.31	0.7643	27.37	0.7192	25.33	0.7504	28.91	0.8782
DAN [12]		31.89	0.8864	28.42	0.7687	27.51	0.7248	25.86	0.7721	30.50	0.9037
AdaTarget [14]		31.58	0.8814	28.14	0.7626	27.43	0.7216	25.72	0.7683	29.97	0.8955
DASR [30]		31.55	0.8822	28.13	0.7597	27.36	0.7186	25.35	0.7538	29.80	0.8929
IKC [10] + Ours		31.96	0.8858	28.35	0.7661	27.39	0.7210	25.68	0.7634	30.29	0.8994
DAN [12] + Ours		31.98	0.8877	28.42	0.7676	27.54	0.7249	25.90	0.7729	30.41	0.9016

Table 2 shows the PSNR and SSIM results on five widely-used benchmark datasets. As one can see, the traditional interpolation-based method and non-blind SR methods suffer severe performance drop when the degradation is unknown or different from the predefined bicubic kernel. Although ZSSR also assumes the bicubic kernel, it achieves better performance than CARN because ZSSR trains a specific network for each single test image by utilizing the internal patch recurrence. However, ZSSR has in-born flaws: it can not learn a good prior of HR datasets because the train samplings are sampled from one single LR

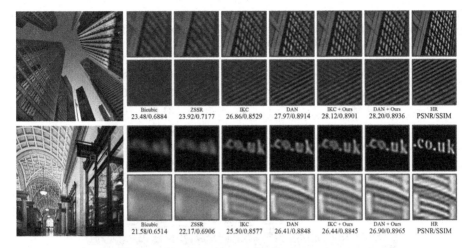

Fig. 4. Visual results of $img012, img083$ from Urban100, for different methods in blind setting. The σ of blur kernel is 1.25.

image. By taking the degradation kernel into account, the performance of CARN is largely improved when combined with a deblurring method. IKC and DAN are both two-step blind SR methods and can largely improve the results. IKC refined the estimated kernel through an iterative manner based on the last estimated kernel and super-resolved image. Furthermore, DAN optimizes the blur kernel estimation and super-resolution alternatively, which obtains better performance than IKC. Nevertheless, both of them adopt a kernel-stretching strategy for introducing the estimated blur kernel to the reconstruction network, which under-utilizes the blur kernel and limits generalization. Therefore, we integrate our proposed method into IKC and DAN to remedy the kernel underutilizing problem. As one can see, when combined with our proposed model, both the performance of IKC and DAN improve by a large margin. Our method leads to the best performance over most datasets, which proves that our methods achieve better kernel utilization. The qualitative results are shown in Fig. 4, which illustrates that our method can reconstruct sharp and clear repetitive texture or edges with fewer artifacts.

4.4 Ablation Study

We conduct ablation studies on vital components of the proposed method: the decoupling framework and the proposed KFFC module. The quantitative results are listed in Table 3. Following [10,36], we first project the raw blur kernel k of size $p \times p$ to a t-dimensional kernel vector $\hat{k}$ through a predefined PCA matrix. Note that p is 21 and t is set to 15 by default. And then we introduce $\hat{k}$ to the reconstruction network and interact the blur kernel and the LR image by directly concatenating or modulating, which is denoted as Base_Cat and Base_Mod respectively. We adopt our proposed decoupling architecture but still concatenate or modulate corresponding $\hat{k}$ in the deconvolution module for

Table 3. Ablation study results of network architectures. Results are reported in non-blind setting and the test dataset is Urban100. With both the decouple architecture and KFFC module, our method performs best.

Method	Decouple	Cat	Mod	KFFC	PSNR↑	SSIM↑
Base_Cat		✓			30.84	0.9111
Base_Mod			✓		31.61	0.9189
Dec_Cat	✓	✓			31.64	0.9193
Dec_Mod	✓		✓		31.68	0.9196
Ours$_{w/o}$	✓			✓	29.98	0.9136
Ours	✓			✓	**31.96**	**0.9233**

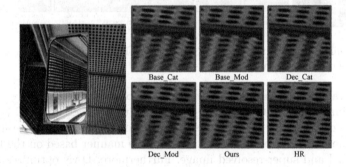

Fig. 5. Ablation visualization on Urban100. Our complete method reconstructs more clear and correct texture.

introducing the blur kernel, and term these methods as Dec_Cat and Dec_Mod respectively in Table 3. As one can see, compared to introducing the blur kernel in the LR scale, the decoupling architecture improves the performance quantitatively, which is consistent with our analysis that the blur kernel should only have an impact on the high-resolution scale based on the degradation model Sect. 3.1. Furthermore, one can see modeling the explicit correlation between the raw blur kernel and images in the frequency domain based on the proposed KFFC module gains significant improvements by about 0.35db by a large margin quantitatively, which demonstrates that the proposed KFFC utilizes the blur kernel more effectively. Moreover, we also evaluate our method without the blur kernel (denoted as Ours w/o). Its inferior is strong evidence that gains come from both the proposed method and the utilization of blur kernels. Qualitative results are shown in Fig. 5, our proposed method reconstructs more clear and correct texture when enabling all the vital components.

4.5   Generalization Evaluation

As mentioned in Sect. 3.2, the predefined PCA matrix will limit the generalization. Specifically, the previous dimension-stretching-strategy based kernel

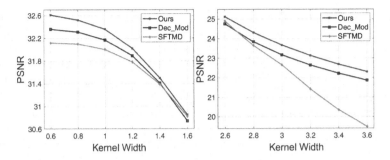

Fig. 6. In-distribution (left) and out-of-distribution (right) degradation results. Our method performs robustly under both settings.

SFTMD/25.78/0.8107   Dec_Mod/26.19/0.8160   Ours/26.62/0.8171   HR/PSNR/SSIM

Fig. 7. Visualization on unseen blur kernel. The quantitative results of the whole benchmark DIV2KRK [3] are listed below directly. Our method generates visual pleasant result with less artifacts.

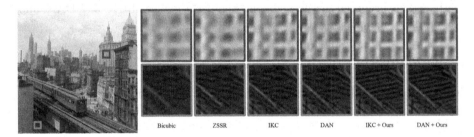

Bicubic   ZSSR   IKC   DAN   IKC + Ours   DAN + Ours

Fig. 8. SISR performance comparison of different methods with SR factor 2 on a real historical image [17].

exploitation methods [10,12,25,33,36] project the raw blur kernel into a kernel vector through a predefined PCA matrix. When the predefined PCA matrix meets unknown raw blur kernels, it will generate a wrong kernel vector, which means the whole SR network needs to be retrained again. Therefore, we conduct two experiments to evaluate the generalization of the proposed method: *i.e.*, out-of-distribution degradation, and unseen blur kernels. At last, we conduct an experiment on a real degradation dataset where the ground-truth HR image and the blur kernel are not available.

Out-of-Distribution Degradation: During training, we shrink the kernel widths of seen blur kernels from range $[0, 2, 2]$, and then evaluate the model on two parameter ranges of blur kernel widths. The in-distribution kernel width ranges from 0.6 to 1.6, while the out-of-distribution kernel width ranges from 2.6 to 3.6. Figure 6 shows quantitative results. The decoupling architecture limits the effect of the blur kernel on the HR scale, it alleviates the influence of the wrong kernel vector. As one can see, for both in and out distribution settings, our method performs better than other methods because we utilize the raw blur kernel and explicitly interact with raw blur kernels and images in the frequency domain.

Unseen Blur Kernels: We investigate the proposed method on DIV2KRK [3]. It sets the blur kernel to an anisotropic Gaussian kernel, randomly samples the kernel width from $[0.6, 5]$, and adopts uniform multiplicative noise. As shown in Fig. 7, all the performance suffers from severe performance drop because blur kernels in DIV2KRK are different from the isotropic Gaussian kernel in training settings. Nonetheless, our method still achieves better performance than existing methods both quantitatively and qualitatively. Here, quantitative results of the total dataset are recorded under the image directly.

Performance on Real Degradation: To further demonstrate the effectiveness of the proposed method. We conduct an experiment on a real degradation dataset where the ground-truth image and the blur kernel are not available. The qualitative comparison is shown in Fig. 8. Compared with other blind SR methods, our proposed method enhance the performance of IKC and DAN, and recover clear and sharp texture.

5   Conclusion

In this paper, we demonstrate the flaws in existing blind SR methods. Current blind SR methods adopt a two-step framework including kernel estimation and kernel exploitation. However, they adopt a dimension-stretching strategy for kernel exploitation when the blur kernel is estimated. Specifically, the estimated raw blur kernel will be projected into a kernel vector through a predefined PCA matrix, and they interact the blur kernel with LR images by direct concatenation or modulation, which underutilizes the raw blur kernel and limit the generalization. To tackle these problems, we decouple the kernel exploitation task into the upsampling and deconvolution modules. To fully explore the blur kernel information, we also design a feature-based kernel fast Fourier convolution, for filtering image features in the frequency domain. Comprehensive experiments and ablation studies in both non-blind and blind settings are conducted to show our gratifying performance.

Acknowledgement. This work is supported by National Natural Science Foundation of China (62271308), STCSM (No. 22511105700, No. 18DZ2270700), 111 plan (No. BP0719010), and State Key Laboratory of UHD Video and Audio Production and Presentation.

References

1. Agustsson, E., Timofte, R.: NTIRE 2017 challenge on single image super-resolution: dataset and study. In: Proceedings of the IEEE Conference on Computer Vision and Pattern Recognition Workshops, pp. 1122–1131 (2017)
2. Ahn, N., Kang, B., Sohn, K.A.: Fast, accurate, and lightweight super-resolution with cascading residual network. In: Proceedings of the European Conference on Computer Vision, pp. 252–268 (2018)
3. Bell-Kligler, S., Shocher, A., Irani, M.: Blind super-resolution kernel estimation using an internal-GAN. In: Advances in Neural Information Processing Systems, vol. 32 (2019)
4. Bevilacqua, M., Roumy, A., Guillemot, C., Alberi Morel, M.L.: Low-complexity single-image super-resolution based on nonnegative neighbor embedding. In: Proceedings of the British Machine Vision Conference, pp. 135.1–135.10 (2012)
5. Chen, H., et al.: Real-world single image super-resolution: a brief review. Inf. Fusion **79**, 124–145 (2021)
6. Chi, L., Jiang, B., Mu, Y.: Fast Fourier convolution. In: Advances in Neural Information Processing Systems, pp. 4479–4488 (2020)
7. Cornillere, V., Djelouah, A., Yifan, W., Sorkine-Hornung, O., Schroers, C.: Blind image super-resolution with spatially variant degradations. ACM Trans. Graph. **38**(6), 1–13 (2019)
8. Dong, C., Loy, C.C., He, K., Tang, X.: Image super-resolution using deep convolutional networks. IEEE Trans. Pattern Anal. Mach. Intell. **38**(2), 295–307 (2015)
9. Dong, J., Roth, S., Schiele, B.: Deep wiener deconvolution: wiener meets deep learning for image deblurring. In: Advances in Neural Information Processing Systems, vol. 33, pp. 1048–1059 (2020)
10. Gu, J., Lu, H., Zuo, W., Dong, C.: Blind super-resolution with iterative kernel correction. In: Proceedings of the IEEE/CVF Conference on Computer Vision and Pattern Recognition, pp. 1604–1613 (2019)
11. Huang, J.B., Singh, A., Ahuja, N.: Single image super-resolution from transformed self-exemplars. In: Proceedings of the IEEE Conference on Computer Vision and Pattern Recognition, pp. 5197–5206 (2015)
12. Huang, Y., Li, S., Wang, L., Tan, T., et al.: Unfolding the alternating optimization for blind super resolution. In: Advances in Neural Information Processing Systems, vol. 33, pp. 5632–5643 (2020)
13. Ji, X., Cao, Y., Tai, Y., Wang, C., Li, J., Huang, F.: Real-world super-resolution via kernel estimation and noise injection. In: Proceedings of the IEEE/CVF Conference on Computer Vision and Pattern Recognition Workshops, pp. 466–467 (2020)
14. Jo, Y., Oh, S.W., Vajda, P., Kim, S.J.: Tackling the ill-posedness of super-resolution through adaptive target generation. In: Proceedings of the IEEE/CVF Conference on Computer Vision and Pattern Recognition, pp. 16236–16245 (2021)
15. Kim, J., Lee, J.K., Lee, K.M.: Accurate image super-resolution using very deep convolutional networks. In: Proceedings of the IEEE Conference on Computer Vision and Pattern Recognition, pp. 1646–1654 (2016)
16. Kingma, D.P., Ba, J.: Adam: a method for stochastic optimization. In: 3rd International Conference on Learning Representations (2015)
17. Lai, W.S., Huang, J.B., Ahuja, N., Yang, M.H.: Deep Laplacian pyramid networks for fast and accurate super-resolution. In: Proceedings of the IEEE Conference on Computer Vision and Pattern Recognition, pp. 624–632 (2017)

18. Liang, J., Sun, G., Zhang, K., et al.: Mutual affine network for spatially variant kernel estimation in blind image super-resolution. In: Proceedings of the IEEE/CVF International Conference on Computer Vision, pp. 4096–4105 (2021)

19. López-Tapia, S., de la Blanca, N.P.: Fast and robust cascade model for multiple degradation single image super-resolution. IEEE Trans. Image Process. **30**, 4747–4759 (2021)

20. Luo, Z., Huang, Y., Li, S., Wang, L., Tan, T.: Learning the degradation distribution for blind image super-resolution. In: Proceedings of the IEEE/CVF Conference on Computer Vision and Pattern Recognition, pp. 6063–6072 (2022)

21. Maeda, S.: Unpaired image super-resolution using pseudo-supervision. In: Proceedings of the IEEE/CVF Conference on Computer Vision and Pattern Recognition, pp. 291–300 (2020)

22. Martin, D., Fowlkes, C., Tal, D., Malik, J.: A database of human segmented natural images and its application to evaluating segmentation algorithms and measuring ecological statistics. In: Proceedings Eighth IEEE International Conference on Computer Vision, vol. 2, pp. 416–423 (2001)

23. Matsui, Y., et al.: Sketch-based manga retrieval using manga109 dataset. Multimed. Tools Appl. **76**(20), 21811–21838 (2017)

24. Pan, J., Sun, D., Pfister, H., Yang, M.H.: Deblurring images via dark channel prior. IEEE Trans. Pattern Anal. Mach. Intell. **40**, 2315–2328 (2017)

25. Riegler, G., Schulter, S., Ruther, M., Bischof, H.: Conditioned regression models for non-blind single image super-resolution. In: Proceedings of the IEEE International Conference on Computer Vision, pp. 522–530 (2015)

26. Shi, W., et al.: Real-time single image and video super-resolution using an efficient sub-pixel convolutional neural network. In: Proceedings of the IEEE Conference on Computer Vision and Pattern Recognition, pp. 1874–1883 (2016)

27. Shocher, A., Cohen, N., Irani, M.: "Zero-shot" super-resolution using deep internal learning. In: Proceedings of the IEEE Conference on Computer Vision and Pattern Recognition, pp. 3118–3126 (2018)

28. Tao, G., et al.: Spectrum-to-kernel translation for accurate blind image super-resolution. In: Advances in Neural Information Processing Systems, vol. 34, pp. 22643–22654 (2021)

29. Timofte, R., Agustsson, E., Van Gool, L., Yang, M.H., Zhang, L.: NTIRE 2017 challenge on single image super-resolution: methods and results. In: Proceedings of the IEEE Conference on Computer Vision and Pattern Recognition Workshops, pp. 114–125 (2017)

30. Wang, L., et al.: Unsupervised degradation representation learning for blind super-resolution. In: Proceedings of the IEEE/CVF Conference on Computer Vision and Pattern Recognition, pp. 10581–10590 (2021)

31. Wang, X., et al.: ESRGAN: enhanced super-resolution generative adversarial networks. In: Proceedings of the European Conference on Computer Vision Workshops (2018)

32. Xiao, J., Yong, H., Zhang, L.: Degradation model learning for real-world single image super-resolution. In: ACCV (2020)

33. Xu, Y.S., Tseng, S.Y.R., Tseng, Y., Kuo, H.K., Tsai, Y.M.: Unified dynamic convolutional network for super-resolution with variational degradations. In: Proceedings of the IEEE/CVF Conference on Computer Vision and Pattern Recognition, pp. 12496–12505 (2020)

34. Zamir, S.W., et al.: CycleISP: real image restoration via improved data synthesis. In: CVPR (2020)

35. Zeyde, R., Elad, M., Protter, M.: On single image scale-up using sparse-representations. In: Boissonnat, J.-D., et al. (eds.) Curves and Surfaces 2010. LNCS, vol. 6920, pp. 711–730. Springer, Heidelberg (2012). https://doi.org/10. 1007/978-3-642-27413-8_47

36. Zhang, K., Zuo, W., Zhang, L.: Learning a single convolutional super-resolution network for multiple degradations. In: Proceedings of the IEEE Conference on Computer Vision and Pattern Recognition, pp. 3262–3271 (2018)

37. Zhang, Y., Li, K., Li, K., Wang, L., Zhong, B., Fu, Y.: Image super-resolution using very deep residual channel attention networks. In: Proceedings of the European Conference on Computer Vision (ECCV), pp. 286–301 (2018)

38. Zhu, J.Y., Park, T., Isola, P., Efros, A.A.: Unpaired image-to-image translation using cycle-consistent adversarial networks. In: Proceedings of the IEEE International Conference on Computer Vision, pp. 2223–2232 (2017)

Pyramid Channel Attention Combined Adaptive Multi-column Network for SISR

Yingjie Yang[1], Yongfang Wang[1(✉)], Junjie Lian[1], and Zhijun Fang[2]

[1] School of Communication and Information Engineering, Shanghai University,
Shanghai 200444, China
yfw@shu.edu.cn

[2] School Computer Science and Technology, Donghua University, Shanghai 201620, China

Abstract. Deep convolutional neural networks (CNN) have achieved excellent performance in the single image super-resolution (SISR) task. Blindly stacking network depth cannot effectively utilize the shallow features and equal treatment of features from different stages seriously hinders network's representational ability. To address the problems, we present a novel network structure called pyramid channel attention combined adaptive multi-column network (PCA-AMCN) for SISR. Specifically, adaptive multi-column block (AMCB) is proposed to extract local features and adaptively handle the interlayer and interlayer features, which contains three columns made up from different convolution kernels, and each column is weighted by a learnable adaptive parameter in the same receptive field and eventually fused by residual skip connection. Furthermore, pyramid channel attention (PCA) is designed to implement channel attention mechanism, which can progressively infer attention weights more accurately through the pyramid structure. The experimental results on benchmark datasets demonstrate the superiority of PCA-AMCN in comparison with other state-of-the-art methods.

Keywords: Single image super-resolution · Pyramid channel attention · Convolutional Neural Network (CNN) · Adaptive multi-column network

1 Introduction

Single image super-resolution (SISR) has numerous useful applications. Its purpose is to get the high-resolution (HR) image by appropriate nonlinear mapping. While image super-resolution (SR) is inverse problem with serious ill-posed procedure, one LR image could have several corresponding HR results.

Convolutional neural network (CNN) demonstrates great progress in SISR. Among them, Dong et al. [1] combined CNN with SR task that called SRCNN which learned end-to-end mapping between bicubic interpolation low-resolution images and high-resolution images. Kim et al. [2] proposed VDSR and introduced residual learning mechanism. In DRCN [3], Kim et al. proposed the single state recurrent neural network (RNN) to demonstrate that deep network can effectively improve performance. Shi et al. [4] introduced the concept of subpixel into SR and added subpixel layer into network structure for up-sampling. Inspired by the depth of the architecture, EDSR

G. Zhai et al. (Eds.): IFTC 2022, CCIS 1766, pp. 180–190, 2023.
https://doi.org/10.1007/978-981-99-0856-1_13

[5] achieved excellent performance by stacking extremely deep networks with residual blocks. SRGAN [6] generated better visual experience images through generative adversarial network (GAN). Recently, attention mechanism attracts wide attention in SR task, such as RCAN [7], LFFN [8]. The attention mechanism of image task may consists of spatial attention (SA) and channel attention (CA) [9], which can efficiently increase representation power of network.

Due to strong correlation information between LR input and reconstructed HR image, shallow features extracted from network are more significant to SR task than other computer vision tasks. Researchers [2, 5] find that stacking layers of CNN can improve the performance, but excessively deep network leads to feature redundancy and shallow features gradually disappear in transmission. So many researches improve learning ability by widening network instead of deepening network such as [10–12].

Among them, features extracted from different branches are equally treated, which is obviously inefficient for feature utilization and fusion. In addition, compared to SA mechanism, CA mechanism is more abstract. However, previous CA mechanism was simply handled by pooling and other operations directly from original feature maps to generate attention weights. This makes it difficult to implement the CA mechanism precisely.

In order to solve those problems, this paper propose a pyramid channel attention combined adaptive multi-column network (PCA-AMCN) for SISR. We design adaptive multi-column block (AMCB) which contains three columns of different convolution kernels with learnable adaptive parameters. Different convolution kernels have different characteristics and the extracted features can be complementary to each other [13]. In the same receptive field, we weight each column with adaptive learnable parameter to deal with the relationship between interlayer and interlayer features. We also propose pyramid channel attention (PCA) to complete CA mechanism more accurately. In object recognition [14] and other fields, pyramid structure is widely implemented. Because it can extract abstract high-level features. This paper proposes to use pyramid structure to abstract features layer by layer and speculate CA weight from higher to lower levels of feature abstraction. Furthermore, qualitative and quantitative experiment results demonstrate effectiveness of proposed model.

2 Proposed Method

2.1 Network Structure

Our PCA-AMCN could be decomposed into four parts: shallow feature extraction module, adaptive multi-column blocks (AMCB), pyramid channel attention (PCA), and reconstruction module (as shown in Fig. 1). We denote I_{LR} and I_{SR} as the input and output of PCA-AMCN respectively. The network should learn to accurately reconstruct HR image I_{HR} from input image I_{LR}.

As shown in the following equation, one 3×3 convolution layer constitutes our shallow feature extraction module.

$$F_0 = f_{SF}(I_{LR}) \tag{1}$$

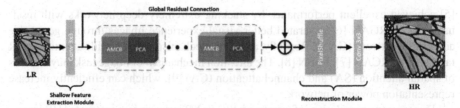

Fig. 1. The architecture of proposed pyramid channel attention combined adaptive multi-column network (PCA-AMCN).

where f_{SF} is convolution operation to input I_{LR} and F_0 is the extracted shallow features.

Then the deep features are obtained through a series of AMCB and PCA, which can be defined as

$$F_n = f_{PCA}^n \left(f_{AMCB}^n \left(\cdots f_{PCA}^1 \left(f_{AMCB}^1 (F_0) \right) \cdots \right) \right) \tag{2}$$

where f_{AMCB}^n and f_{PCA}^n respectively represents the nth block of proposed AMCB and PCA and F_n denotes the nth block's feature. Notice that proposed AMCB and PCA operate alternately in the network.

Before entering reconstruction module, global residual connection is used to combine the shallow features F_0 and deep features F_n. The reconstruction process is implemented by stacking one pixel-shuffle layer for up-sampling and one convolution layer to adjust the channel, given by:

$$I_{SR} = f_{RE}(F_0 + F_n), \tag{3}$$

where f_{RE} represents the reconstruction module and I_{SR} is the finally reconstructed high resolution image.

2.2 Adaptive Multi-Column Block (AMCB)

The proposed AMCB contains three columns with corresponding adaptive weights and residual skip connection (as shown in Fig. 2).

In terms of SR task, because final result's SR is similar with low-resolution images, image's shallow feature will be very important for the process of reconstruction. In order not to lose image shallow feature due to over stacked network, we choose to widen the network rather than lengthen it to improve the ability to extract deep features.

We utilize the properties of different convolution kernels to construct the three columns of AMCB, so that the features of each column can be complementary. The features between three columns are weighted respectively by learnable adaptive parameters. Meanwhile, these parameters also participate in the fusion with the pervious block features.

Compared with treating features equally in most of previous works, our approach allows for more efficient feature fusion and utilization by fully learning the relationship between interlayer and interlayer features. Note that we weight each column on the same receptive field, which is more conducive to feature fusion. Details can be found in Table 1.

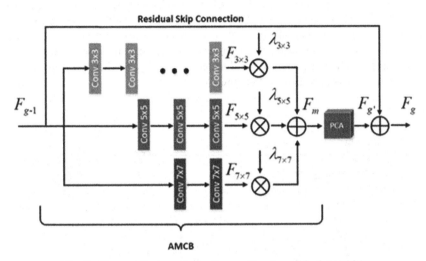

Fig. 2. The architecture of adaptive multi-column block (AMCB)

Table 1. Detail settings of each column in AMCB.

Kernel Size	Number	Padding	Receptive field
3×3	6	1	13
5×5	3	2	13
7×7	2	3	13

We define the n-th convolution with kernel size s to be $C_{s \times s}^n$. The input is F_{g-1} and the output of three columns is separately $F_{3\times3}$, $F_{5\times5}$, $F_{7\times7}$.

$$F_{3\times3} = C_{3\times3}^6(C_{3\times3}^5(\dots C_{3\times3}^1(F_{g-1})\dots)),$$
$$F_{5\times5} = C_{5\times5}^3(C_{5\times5}^2(C_{5\times5}^1(F_{g-1}))),$$
$$F_{7\times7} = C_{7\times7}^2(C_{7\times7}^1(F_{g-1})).$$

(4)

Then we weight the three columns with three learnable adaptive parameters $\lambda_{3\times3}$, $\lambda_{5\times5}$, $\lambda_{7\times7}$.

$$F_m = (\lambda_{3\times3} \times F_{3\times3} + \lambda_{5\times5} \times F_{5\times5} + \lambda_{7\times7} \times F_{7\times7}), \tag{5}$$

where F_m denotes the fusion feature of three columns and will be enter into the PCA as input.

2.3 Pyramid Channel Attention (PCA)

Figure 3 shows details of proposed PCA. Since CA mechanism is more abstract than SA mechanism, we build pyramid structure to infer CA accurately. Feature compression can effectively extract high-level semantic features in deep network, which is usually implemented in target detection, high dynamic range reconstruction and so on. Here, we use 3×3 convolution with stride of 2 to implement feature compression and selectively filter features. Pyramid structure is used to realize the CA mechanism from coarse to fine through different abstract level features.

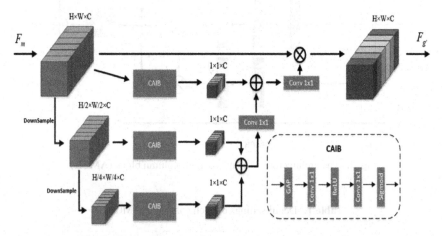

Fig. 3. The architecture of pyramid channel attention (PCA).

F_m is the input of the PCA and the operation of down-sampling is f_D. We will get two down-sampling feature maps F_m^1 and F_m^2, which can be described as

$$F_m^1 = f_D(F_m), \quad F_m^2 = f_D\left(F_m^1\right). \tag{6}$$

In order to get accurate CA map, we design a method to abstract feature in a coarse-to-fine way. At first, the most abstract features at the bottom of the pyramid will be used to infer the CA map, and gradually merge with the inferences at the top to complete the refinement work. Our channel attention inference block (CAIB) is composed of global average pooling (GAP), convolution with 1×1 kernel, ReLU and sigmoid function

$$F_{CA}^1 = f_{CA}(F_m), \quad F_{CA}^2 = f_{CA}\left(F_m^1\right), \quad F_{CA}^3 = f_{CA}\left(F_m^2\right), \tag{7}$$

where f_{CA} is CAIB, $F_{CA}^1, F_{CA}^2, F_{CA}^3$ denote CA map from different abstract level features, respectively. Then they are fused step by step through 1×1 convolution f_{fuse} to get final map F_{CA}, which is weighted to the input to complete CA mechanism. $F_{g'}$ is the final output of the PCA.

$$F_{CA} = f_{fuse}\left(f_{fuse}\left(F_{CA}^3 + F_{CA}^2\right) + F_{CA}^1\right)$$
$$F_{g'} = F_{CA} \times F_m \tag{8}$$

3 Proposed Method

3.1 Datasets and Metrics

With most of the previous work, we select DIV2K [15] as our training set. It contains 800 pairs of training images, 100 validation images and 100 test images. Here this paper is only trained by DIV2K's training data. For testing, five benchmark datasets are used: Set5 [16], Set14 [17], B100 [18], Urban100 [19] and Manga109 [20]. We have evaluated our network's results with PSNR and SSIM [21] on the Y channel in YCbCr space. Greater values of all indicators show a better performance.

3.2 Implementation Details

Data augmentations including flipping and rotation are randomly performed in model input before entering into the network. The low-resolution input will be cropped into 48×48 patches randomly. The network's batch size is set as 16. The learnable adaptive parameter of each column in AMCB is initialized to 0.3333, where the sum of the parameters of three columns is near to 1. We use L1 loss to train our model based on ADAM [22]. At the beginning, learning rate is set as 10^{-4} which will decrease to half after every 2×10^5 iterations. Our model is implemented in PyTorch framework based on RTX 2070 GPU.

3.3 Ablation Study

In order to demonstrate effectiveness of proposed network, we have made many ablation experiments. We define a cascade of AMCB and PCA as one module in ablation experiments. The ablation results with effects of proposed AMCB and PCA is shown in Table 2. 8 modules are used in the network structure and experiments are carried out on Set5 for the scale factor ×4.

In the first row, PCA is eliminated. In the second row, we use CA structure in [7] to replace our PCA structure and in the third row, basic residual unit is used to replace the proposed AMCB. Compared to AMCB only, PCA improves PSNR from 32.29 to 32.37 and SSIM from 0.8965 to 0.8968. Compared with CA structure in [7], our PCA structure achieves improvement, which proves that PCA can implement CA mechanism more accurately. Accordingly, we find that both PCA and AMCB perform better than basic residual unit. These comparisons prove the effectiveness of the proposed PCA-AMCN.

Furthermore, we conduct experiments on the number of modules in order to demonstrate influence of network depth. These experiments are also conducted on the scale factor of 4 and the benchmark dataset is Set5. From Table 3, with the number of modules increases and the network deepens, PSNR and SSIM achieve considerable improvement. Compared to model with 4 modules, model with 10 modules achieves 0.18 dB improvement in PSNR. This manifests that our model has good extensibility and the performance improvement based on increasing the number of modules is in a certain extent.

Table 2. Ablation experiment on effects of AMCB and PCA.

AMCB	✓	✓	×	✓
PCA	×	–	✓	✓
PSNR	32.29	32.31	32.26	32.37
SSIM	0.8965	0.8966	0.8960	0.8968

Table 3. Ablation Experiment on number of modules.

Module Number	4	6	8	10
PSNR	32.23	32.29	32.37	32.41
SSIM	0.8957	0.8962	0.8968	0.8976

3.4 Comparison with State-of-the-Art Methods

We compare proposed PCA-AMCN with several state-of-the-art SISR methods: SRCNN [1], VDSR [2], LapSRN [23], DRRN [24], MemNet [25], IDN [26], CARN [27], FALSR [28], LFFN [8].

Quantitative evaluation results in scale factor of $\times 2$, $\times 3$, $\times 4$ are shown in Table 4. The best algorithm is highlighted in red and the second-best performance is indicated in blue. Our proposed PCA-AMCN achieves the best quantitative results over other previous work. When SR is applied in complex images (Urban100), our model outperforms LFFN [8] with PSNR improvement of 0.20 dB, 0.22 dB, 0.09 dB in scale $\times 2$, $\times 3$, $\times 4$ on Uban100 respectively.

Moreover, we present visual qualitative comparison results in scale $\times 4$, as shown in Fig. 4. We can observe that our model has ability to accurately repair shape edges without blurring artifacts.

In the upper left corner of Image 019, our reconstructed image recovers clear textures while other methods have distortions. In high frequency details reconstruction such as Image 073, which contains dense structures and textures, our method can effectively suppress the artificial ambiguity better. Meanwhile, our method can provide a better visual experience such as Image 87. Our method reconstructs the HR image has shaper edges and more uniform colors in flat areas.

Table 4. Quantitative comparisons of state-of-the-art methods on benchmark datasets.

Method	scale	Set5		Set14		BDS100		Urban100		Manga109	
		PSNR	SSIM	PSNR	SSIM	PSNR	SSIM	PSNR	SSIM	PSNR	SSIM
Bicubic.	2	33.66	0.9299	30.24	0.8688	29.56	0.8431	26.88	0.8403	30.30	0.9339
SRCNN[1].	2	36.66	0.9542	32.45	0.9067	31.36	0.8879	29.50	0.8946	35.60	0.9663
VDSR[2].	2	37.53	0.9590	33.05	0.9130	31.90	0.8960	30.77	0.9140	37.22	0.9750
LapSRN[23].	2	37.52	0.9591	33.08	0.9130	31.80	0.8950	30.41	0.9101	37.27	0.9740
DRRN[24]	2	37.74	0.9591	33.23	0.9136	32.05	0.8973	31.23	0.9188	37.60	0.9736
MemNet[25].	2	37.78	0.9597	33.28	0.9142	32.08	0.8979	31.31	0.9195	37.72	0.9740
IDN[26].	2	37.83	0.9600	33.30	0.9148	32.08	0.8985	31.27	0.9196	-	-
CARN[27].	2	37.76	0.9590	33.52	0.9166	32.09	0.8978	31.92	0.9256	-	-
FALSR-A[28].	2	37.82	0.9595	33.55	0.9168	32.12	0.8987	31.93	0.9256	-	-
LFFN[8].	2	37.95	0.9597	-	-	32.20	0.8994	32.39	0.9299	38.73	0.9765
Ours.	2	38.04	0.9609	33.74	0.9190	32.23	0.9008	32.59	0.9329	38.84	0.9776
Bicubic.	3	30.39	0.8682	27.55	0.7742	27.21	0.7385	24.46	0.7349	26.95	0.8556
SRCNN[1].	3	32.75	0.9090	29.28	0.8209	28.41	0.7863	26.24	0.7989	30.59	0.9107
VDSR[2].	3	33.66	0.9213	29.77	0.8314	28.82	0.7976	27.14	0.8279	32.01	0.9310
DRRN[24].	3	34.03	0.9244	29.96	0.8349	28.95	0.8004	27.53	0.8378	32.74	0.9390
MemNet[25]	3	34.09	0.9248	30.00	0.8350	28.96	0.8001	27.56	0.8376	-	-
IDN[26]	3	34.11	0.9253	29.99	0.8354	28.95	0.8013	27.42	0.8359	-	-
CARN[27]	3	34.29	0.9255	30.29	0.8407	29.06	0.8034	28.06	0.8493	-	-
LFFN[8].	3	34.43	0.9266	-	-	29.13	0.8059	28.34	0.8558	33.65	0.9445
Ours.	3	34.59	0.9289	30.44	0.8450	29.18	0.8079	28.56	0.8610	33.94	0.9470
Bicubic.	4	28.42	0.8104	26.00	0.7027	25.96	0.6675	23.14	0.6577	24.89	0.7866
SRCNN[1].	4	30.48	0.8628	27.49	0.7503	26.90	0.7101	24.52	0.7221	27.66	0.8505
VDSR[2]	4	31.35	0.8838	28.01	0.7674	27.29	0.7251	25.18	0.7524	28.83	0.8890
LapSRN[23]	4	31.54	0.8850	28.19	0.7720	27.32	0.7280	25.21	0.7560	29.09	0.8845
DRRN[24].	4	31.68	0.8888	28.21	0.7720	27.38	0.7284	25.44	0.7638	29.46	0.8960
MemNet[25].	4	31.74	0.8893	28.26	0.7723	27.40	0.7281	25.50	0.7630	-	-
IDN[26].	4	31.82	0.8903	28.25	0.7730	27.41	0.7297	25.41	0.7632	-	-
CARN[27].	4	32.13	0.8937	28.60	0.7806	27.58	0.7349	26.07	0.7837	-	-
LFFN[8].	4	32.15	0.8945	-	-	27.52	0.7377	26.24	0.7902	30.66	0.9099
Ours.	4	32.41	0.8976	28.68	0.7847	27.64	0.7389	26.33	0.7944	30.73	0.9116

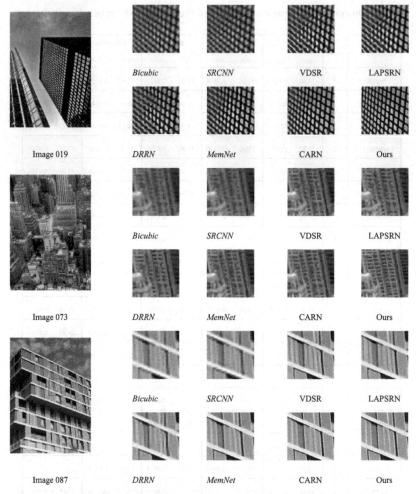

Fig. 4. Visual qualitative comparison for ×4 scale on "Image 019", "Image 073", "Image 087" from Urban100 dataset.

4   Conclusion

In this paper, we propose a pyramid channel attention combined adaptive multi-column network (PCA-AMCN) for accurate SISR. This paper also designs adaptive multi-column block (AMCB) in order to utilize properties of different convolution kernels to extract features, where interlayer and intralayer feature fusion is carried out through learnable adaptive parameters.

In addition, pyramid channel attention (PCA) is proposed to progressively abstract features by pyramid structure. PCA infer attention weights from extracted features with different abstraction level to complete CA mechanism more precisely. Comprehensive experiment results demonstrate the effectiveness of proposed model.

Acknowledgement. This work was supported by Natural Science Foundation of China under Grant No. 61671283, U2033218.

References

1. Dong, C., Loy, C.C., He, K., et al.: Learning a deep convolutional network for image super-resolution. In: European Conference on Computer Vision, pp. 184–199. Zurich (2014)
2. Kim, J., Kwon Lee, J., Mu Lee, K.: Accurate image super-resolution using very deep convolutional networks. In: Proceedings of the IEEE Conference on Computer Vision and Pattern Recognition, pp. 1646–1654. Las Vegas (2016)
3. Kim, J., Kwon Lee, J., Mu Lee, K.: Deeply-recursive convolutional network for image super-resolution. In: Proceedings of the IEEE Conference on Computer Vision and Pattern Recognition, pp. 1637–1645. Las Vegas (2016)
4. Shi, W., et al.: Real-time single image and video super-resolution using an efficient sub-pixel convolutional neural network. In: Proceedings of the IEEE Conference on Computer Vision and Pattern Recognition, pp. 1874–1883. Las Vegas (2016)
5. Lim, B., Son, S., Kim, H., Nah, S., Mu Lee, K.: Enhanced deep residual networks for single image super-resolution. In: Proceedings of the IEEE Conference on Computer Vision and Pattern Recognition Workshops, pp. 136–144. Honolulu (2017)
6. Ledig, C., et al.: Photo-realistic single image super-resolution using a generative adversarial network. In: Proceedings of the IEEE Conference on Computer Vision and Pattern Recognition, pp. 4681–4690. Honolulu (2017)
7. Zhang, Y., Li, K, Wang, L., Zhong, B., Fu, Y.: Image super-resolution using very deep residual channel attention networks. In: P Proceedings of the European Conference on Computer Vision (ECCV), pp. 286-301. Munich (2018).
8. Yang, W., Wang, W., Zhang, X., Sun, S., Liao, Q.: Lightweight feature fusion network for single image super-resolution. IEEE Signal Process. Lett. **26**(4), 538–542 (2019)
9. Woo, S., Park, J., Lee, J.Y., So Kweon, S., Alemi, A.A.: CBAM: Convolutional block attention module. In: Proceedings of the European Conference on Computer Vision (ECCV), pp. 3-19. Munich (2018)
10. Szegedy, C., Ioffe, S., Vanhoucke, V., So Kweon, S., Mu Lee, I.: Inception-v4, inception-resnet and the impact of residual connections on learning. In: Thirty-First AAAI Conference on Artificial Intelligence, San Francisco (2017)
11. Chen, L.C., Zhu, Y., Papandreou, G., Schroff, F., Adam, H.: Encoder-decoder with atrous separable convolution for semantic image segmentation. In: Proceedings of the European Conference on Computer Vision (ECCV), pp. 801-818. Munich (2018)
12. Xie, S., Girshick, R., Dollár, P., Tu, Z., He, K.: Aggregated residual transformations for deep neural networks. In: Proceedings of the IEEE Conference on Computer Vision and Pattern Recognition, pp. 1492–1500. Honolulu (2017)
13. Li, J., Fang, F., Mei, K., Zhang, G.: Multi-scale residual network for image super-resolution. In: Proceedings of the European Conference on Computer Vision (ECCV), pp. 517-532. Munich (2018)
14. Ghiasi, G., Lin, T.Y., Le, Q.V.: NAS-FPN: Learning scalable feature pyramid architecture for object detection. In: Proceedings of the IEEE Conference on Computer Vision and Pattern Recognition, pp. 7036–7045. Long Beach (2019)
15. Agustsson, E., Timofte, R.: Ntire 2017 challenge on single image super-resolution: Dataset and study. In: Proceedings of the IEEE Conference on Computer Vision and Pattern Recognition Workshops, pp. 126–135. Honolulu (2017)

16. Bevilacqua, M., Roumy, A., Guillemot, C., Alberi-Morel, M.L.: Low-complexity single-image super-resolution based on nonnegative neighbor embedding. In: Proceedings of British Machine Vision Conference, pp. 1–10. British (2012)

17. Zeyde, R., Elad, M., Protter, M.: On single image scale-up using sparse-representations. In: International Conference on Curves and Surfaces, pp. 711–730. Avignon (2010)

18. Martin, D., Fowlkes, C. , Tal, D. , Malik, J.: A database of human segmented natural images and its application to evaluating segmentation algorithms and measuring ecological statistics. In: IEEE International Conference on Computer Vision, Barcelona (2002)

19. Huang, J.B., Singh, A., Ahuja, N.: Single image super-resolution from transformed self-exemplars. In: Proceedings of the IEEE Conference on Computer Vision and Pattern Recognition, pp. 5197–5206. Boston (2015)

20. Matsui, Y., et al.: Sketch-based manga retrieval using manga109 dataset. Multimed. Tools Appl. 76(20), 21811–21838 (2016). https://doi.org/10.1007/s11042-016-4020-z

21. Wang, C., Bovik, A.C., Sheikh, H.R.: Simoncelli, Image quality assessment: from error visibility to structural similarity. IEEE Trans. Image Process. 13(4), 600–612 (2004)

22. Kingma, D.P., Ba, J.: Adam: a method for stochastic optimization. arXiv preprint arXiv:1412.6980 (2014)

23. Lai, W.S., Huang, J.B., Ahuja, N., Yang, M.H.: Deep Laplacian pyramid networks for fast and accurate super-resolution. In: Proceedings of the IEEE Conference on Computer Vision and Pattern Recognition, pp. 624–632. Honolulu (2017)

24. Tai, Y., Yang, J., Liu, X.: Image super-resolution via deep recursive residual network. In: Proceedings of the IEEE Conference on Computer Vision and Pattern Recognition, pp. 3147–3155. Honolulu (2017)

25. Tai, Y., Yang, J., Liu, X., Xu, C.: MemNet: A persistent memory network for image restoration. In: Proceedings of the IEEE International Conference on Computer Vision, pp. 4539–4547. Venice (2017)

26. Hui, Z., Wang, X., Gao, X.: Fast and accurate single image super-resolution via information distillation network. In: Proceedings of the IEEE Conference on Computer Vision and Pattern Recognition, pp. 723–731. Salt Lake City (2018)

27. Ahn, N., Kang, B., Sohn, K.A.: Fast, accurate, and lightweight super-resolution with cascading residual network. In: Proceedings of the European Conference on Computer Vision (ECCV), pp. 252-268. Munich (2018)

28. Chu, X., Zhang, B., Ma, H., Xu, R., Li, J., Li, Q.: Fast, accurate and lightweight super-resolution with neural architecture search. arXiv preprint arXiv:1901.07261 (2019)

FPGA-Based Hardware Implementation of JPEG XS Encoder

Dong Yang[ID] and Li Chen[✉][ID]

Institute of Image Communication and Network Engineering,
Shanghai Jiao Tong University, Shanghai, China
{ydajwz123,hilichen}@sjtu.edu.cn

Abstract. JPEG (Joint Photographic Experts Group) XS is a new international standard targeting mezzanine compression with features of low complexity and low latency. It is designed extremely parallelizable and simple to implement on modern CPU, GPU, FPGA and ASIC. This paper proposes an efficient hardware JPEG XS encoder implementation. In this design, JPEG XS encoder is clearly decoupled into submodules that are pipelined and parallelized to effectively increase system throughput. The carefully crafted Rate Control module takes up a few cycles while reducing the use of hardware resources. The well-designed hardware architecture is suitable to be implemented using Xilinx HLS Tool and operates at 196 MHz on Alveo U50, achieving encoding speed of 8K 42 fps. The restored images usually yield a PSNR over 50 dB when bitrate is larger than 8.0 bpp.

Keywords: Image encoder · FPGA Implementation · Low latency codec

1 Introduction

JPEG XS [1] is a new wavelet-based still image coding standard featuring low latency and complexity while keeping visually lossless.

The primary use case is to reduce the bitrate during transmission in professional studios with a compression rate about 10:1, while maintaining the video quality through successive generations of infrastructures and protocols [2].

The vast majority of broadcasting equipment currently uses serial digital interface (SDI) to transmit video. As the demand for higher resolution, bit depth and even higher frame rate growing fast, the original HD-SDI (1.5Gbps) is extended to 3G-SDI (3 Gbps), in addition, 12G-SDI (12 Gbps) for UHD-4K video. However, UHD-8K video is hard to deploy with such a bandwidth. Cable extension is an expensive solution and that means all existing infrastructures aimed to UHD-4K are useless. Therefore, mezzanine compression is needed to fit data in 12G-SDI or even 10Gbps-Ethernet. Moreover, video-over-IP [3] reuses generic-purpose Ethernet, which is more flexible than dedicated SDI.

Other than existing popular video or image codecs, such as JPEG2000 [4], ProRes [5], DSC [6], HEVC [7], JPEG XS allows for increasing data rate of videos while preserving the superiorities of uncompressed videos, such as transparent quality, low power consumption, low latency, ease to implement and deploy, low complexity, high throughput [2]. As the standard of JPEG XS maturing, researchers gradually explore the implementation of the codec. Richter [8] discussed the parallelizability and performance of the entropy coding. Bruns [9] analyzed the coding procedures and designed a decoder on GPU. Also, intoPIX, a commercial company, demonstrates the product of JPEG XS commercially without discussing any technical details in public. The tremendous amount of video data in professional AV market usually require codecs implemented on hardware to obtain low latency as well as stability. Field-programmable gate array (FPGA) serves as a flexible hardware platform for implementation, since it is embedded into the processing pipeline and can be re-configured as codecs evolving.

In this paper, we propose a hardware-friendly JPEG XS encoding algorithm and design a feasible hardware architecture, which can be implemented by Xilinx High-Level Synthesis (HLS) Tool efficiently. The algorithm and hardware design will be illustrated together in the following sections. The rest of the paper is composed of four parts. Section Two gives readers a basic idea of JPEG XS encoding pipeline. Section Three demonstrates the hardware architecture of the proposed JPEG XS encoder and clarifies some critical designs in detail. Section Four shows experiment results to prove the encoder perform as expected and reports the hardware resources required for the design. Section Five summarizes the paper and discusses the possible future work.

2   JPEG XS Overview

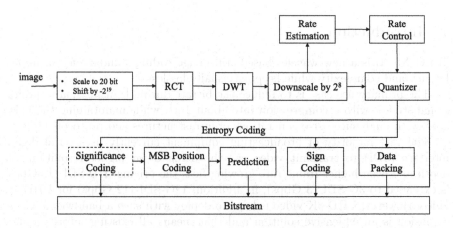

Fig. 1. Architecture overview of JPEG XS

JPEG XS is easier to be described in the encoder's perspective [9]. The coding pipeline is summarized as Fig. 1. Image data is pre-processed by scaling and DC level shifting, and is followed by a reversible color transformation (RCT), which maps the data from red, green, blue components to luma and two chroma signals. RCT is aimed to decorrelate the image components and can be bypassed according to the coding config.

Discrete wavelet transformation (DWT) is applied to each channel of the image for intra-component decorrelation. The transformation usually takes five decompositions in horizontal direction and at most two decompositions vertically. The main profile [2] of JPEG XS suggests one vertical decomposition for common scenarios. Therefore, a precinct, the basic coding unit, depends on merely two lines of DWT coefficients, corresponding to only several lines of original image data. The small number of vertical decompositions makes low-latency possible from the perspective of data. Further, precincts are gathered to form a slice, usually 16 lines of data, and JPEG XS guarantees there is no prediction between slices, such that they can be processed independently, indicating potential parallelism. Rate is allocated and controlled for each precinct. DWT coefficients of subbands are pre-quantized in this stage to estimate budget. The budget depends on truncation positions of subbands, which is actually calculated by two variables Q, R and two pre-defined arrays Gains and Refinements. Q stands for quantization and R represents refinement. The truncated length for each subbands can be calculated as below:

$$t_b = max\left(Q - \text{Gains}\left[b\right] - \mathbb{1}_{\text{Refinements}[b]<R}, 0\right) \qquad (1)$$

b is the index of the subband. Intuitively, the array of Gains represents the importance of each subband. Refinements array allows JPEG XS to allocate bits more precisely. Since refined subband preserves one more bit for each DWT coefficient to make use of surplus bits in this precinct.

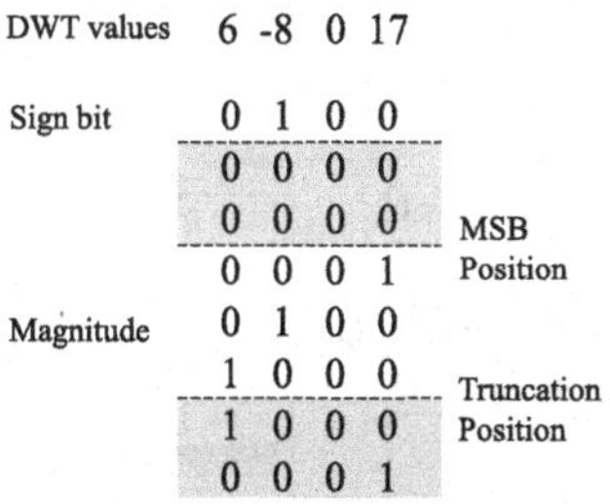

Fig. 2. Coding group in JPEG XS

Entropy coding is utilized to compress the DWT coefficients. The values are represented in the form of sign bits and magnitudes for the convenience of entropy encoding. Each four consecutive DWT coefficients forms a coding group [10] as Fig. 2. Most significant bit (MSB) positions of all groups are encoded by variable length unary code, denoted as bounded code [9]. Further, significance flags (sigf) help aggregate continuous zero MSB positions. Eight MSB position

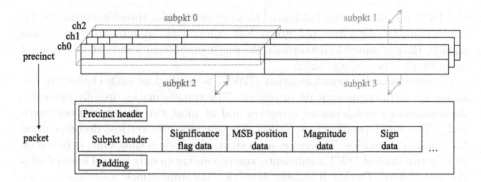

Fig. 3. Structure of JPEG XS packet

values forms a significance flag group, which saves bits for MSB positions with an extra significance flag bit if all quantized values are zeros in this group. As for bit-plane data, they are emitted after quantization directly without any complex coding procedure. Sign packing is usually applied for its relatively negligible complexity.

The entropy coding results are ordered as Fig. 3 to form the bitstream. All parts are aligned to 8 bit or 16 bit as needed. There are several sub-packets in one precinct with their own headers. Also, there is global information in the image header, which defines image attributes and configs, including Gains and Refinements array mentioned above.

3   Hardware Architecture and Implementation

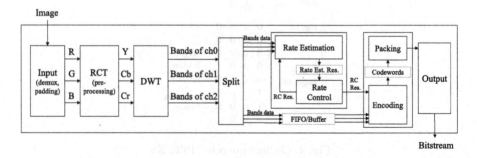

Fig. 4. The hardware system architecture of JPEG XS encoder

The hardware system architecture of JPEG XS Encoder is shown in Fig. 4, consisting of IO, RCT, DWT, Rate Estimation, Rate Control, Encoding and Packing sub-modules.

Image data is prepared by the Input module, which generates three streams for each image channel. The following RCT module pre-processes individual pixels and applies inter component decorrelation to the image. Multiple filtering engines are utilized in DWT module to ensure that the data flows without blocking. Rate Estimation is fully pipelined and stores bit budget information as a reference for Rate Control module. The Rate Estimation does not move on to next precinct until the rate control module decides RC result for the current precinct. The RC result together with bypassed DWT data is consumed by the Encoding module as soon as possible. Moreover, the intermediate codewords is double buffered and Packing module always processes data much faster than the Encoding module. Finally, the packets are aggregated to create the bitstream.

3.1   IO and Pre-processing

The layout of input image is CHW or HWC. For HWC layout, a small demux module is needed to separate three channels. Also, the input image can be monochromic, occupying only one channel in the following procedures. For convenience, the image data in each line is padded to a proper size that can be modded by the number of pixel consumed per cycle. The image data is scaled and shifted before fed into the transformation module. To ensure lossless for transformation, the data is scaled to 20 bit and shifted by -2^{19}.

3.2   Reversible Color Transformation

JPEG XS utilizes Reversible Color Transformation (RCT) to map color from RGB domain to YUV domain. Integer-based transformation is reversible and makes it possible to decorrelate color through shifting bits rather than division operation. Also, the module can be bypassed if input image is YUV data or the pre-defined quantization scheme is aimed to RGB data originally.

3.3   LeGall 5/3 DWT

The wavelet-transformation used in the design is LeGall 5/3 DWT, as shown in Fig. 5. Only one vertical decomposition is required for the Main Profile. And several line buffers are used for vertical filtering.

The average data rate between these filtering engine is not the same, since the filtering stride is two. For example, if the input data rate is eight pixels per cycle, then the vertical filtering engine emits data at a speed of average four pixels per cycle in both high frequency out port and low frequency port. Width-Converter is needed and the parallelism, which means computation ability, of these filtering engines are different according to their levels.

For filtering, each engine uses two kinds of filters to extract high frequency and low frequency information along vertical as well as horizontal direction. The high pass filter and low pass filter are show as below:

Y/Cb/Cr

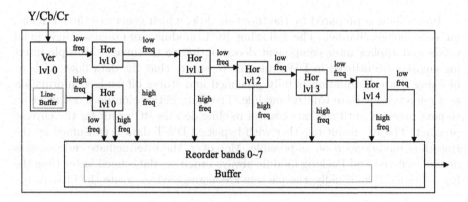

Fig. 5. Block diagram of the DWT module with 1 level vertical filtering and 5 levels horizontal filtering

- high-pass filter: $\{-\frac{1}{2}, 1, -\frac{1}{2}\}$
- low-pass filter: $\{-\frac{1}{8}, \frac{1}{4}, \frac{3}{4}, \frac{1}{4}, -\frac{1}{8}\}$

Actually, lifting version of DWT is applied when implementing filtering, such that only shifting and addition operation is required for this task. The result is obtained by following equations:

$$hf[n] = x[2n+1] - \frac{x[2n] + x[2n+2]}{2} \tag{2}$$

$$lf[n] = x[2n] + \frac{hf[n-1] + hf[n] + 2}{4} \tag{3}$$

hf and lf stand for high and low frequency results respectively. And division in the equation can be implemented by arithmetic shifting easily.

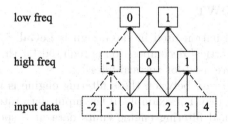

Fig. 6. Data dependency of lifting 5/3 DWT. Dash line indicates symmetric padding.

To be more specific, Fig. 6 shows the dependency among high frequency, low frequency data, input data and padded data. For the vertical filter in the DWT module, four-line buffer is required for each image channel, since 5/3 DWT obtain low frequency information from five image lines.

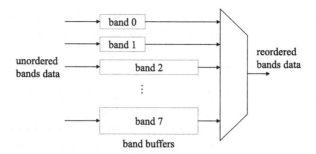

Fig. 7. Reordering DWT bands data. Note that different bands requires various size of buffer to store one line of data.

DWT coefficients of different bands arrives just in the reversed order as needed. Therefore, as shown in Fig. 7, reordering is applied to simplify control signals in the following sub-modules.

3.4 Rate Control

JPEG XS are usually used in strictly constant bitrate mode. And bits are allocated in the granularity of precinct. The bits consumed in one precinct is determined by two variables Q and R and two pre-defined arrays Gains and Refinements, which result in truncated position for each band.

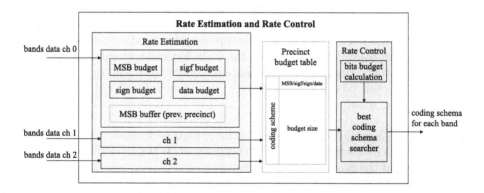

Fig. 8. Block diagram of the Rate Estimation and Rate Control module

The overview of the RC module is demonstrated as Fig. 8. DWT coefficients are fed into Rate Estimation module, where the unit pre-calculates the bits needed for each coding scheme. Further, the estimated budget guides the Rate Control Unit to find best coding scheme and emit the RC results.

The coding scheme refers to mode (whether to use significance flag and whether to use prediction) and truncated position in each band. The budgets are classified according to the bitstream structure. The estimation focuses on four kinds of budgets, since header related information are fixed bit length. MSB, sigf, sign, data in the figure represents MSB position, significance flag, sign bit and magnitude of the DWT coefficient. These four budgets are calculated and accumulated in parallel as the DWT coefficients flowing through this unit. And some intermediate variables, such as MSB position, are stored in buffer.

All the budget size related information is temporarily stored in a precinct budget table (PBT). Intuitively, budget of all modes and truncation position is needed as a reference. The precinct budget table can be formulated as a lookup function:

$$pbt(band, mode, truc\_pos) = MSB/sigf/sign/data \text{ budget size} \qquad (4)$$

However, if all situations are taken into consideration, the dimension of the table is too large to hold in on-chip SRAM. And the parallelism depends on the number of modes and truncation positions. Then, too many truncation positions consume multiple computation resource as well as the storage resource. Data of different subbands in one channel flows through the module sequentially. Therefore, the number of bands do not contribute to the need of parallelism.

It is noticed that JPEG XS targets visually lossless. Images for human eyes are usually continuous among lines. The design only considers the truncation length in the neighbor of that of the previous precinct. The neighbor size, denoted as N_t could be adjusted in the trade-off between hardware resource and coding performance. And a situation with high truncation position is preserved because JPEG XS requires a strict CBR mode. This backup truncation length is used in case that bits are not enough for all values in neighborhood.

Such a rate control scheme makes the Rate Estimation and Rate Control module run serially. Because Rate Estimation module needs the truncation position of the previous precinct. And the Rate Control module will not begin to find the best coding scheme until the PBT is filled by the Rate Estimation module.

The Rate Estimation module itself is fully pipelined and it consumes specific number of pixels each cycle. In order to achieve high performance, Rate Control module pre-calculates target budget for this precinct. When the PBT is available, it starts to find the proper coding scheme.

As shown in Fig. 9, RC model takes two stages to find the best Q and R, named STATE_Q and STATE_R in the state machine. When RC result is feasible and Q is still in the neighbor of the previous one, STATE_Q just loops. And if Q reaches upper bound and the budget still exceeds target bits, STATE_R is skipped.

Because shorter truncation length always results in more bits consumed. Binary search is applied to locate the best Q, corresponding to the loop of STATE_Q. The green part of the Fig. 9 aggregates all budgets for (Q, R), including MSB, sigf, data and sign budgets. During the stage, estimated best budgets of each bands are emitted and also buffered. Further, they are compared with

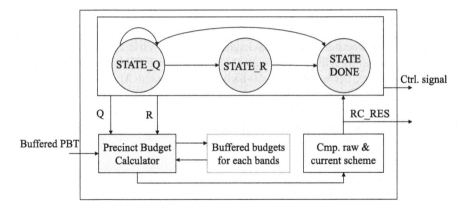

Fig. 9. Block diagram of the RC searcher module, searching for best coding scheme (Color figure online)

raw coding budget. If the naive coding is better, sometimes in scenario of very low compression rate, a raw fallback bit is signalled.

Although budgets in different truncation situation can be calculated simultaneously, it requires more than N_t times resource but saves only dozens of cycles for one precinct. The green part of the Fig. 9 is fully pipelined and takes around one hundred cycles to accomplish, which is tolerant in contrast to the speed of Rate Estimation module.

3.5 Bitstream Packaging

Encoding module takes the rate control result to do entropy coding. The codewords, including MSB positions, significance flags, magnitudes and signs, are all double buffered.

The encoding module consumes DWT data much more fast than the Rate Estimation module. Since there is three engines in the rate estimation, while only one in the Encoding module, processing data in the order of band numbers. Therefore, the parallelism of the Encoding engine is four times as that of Rate Estimation.

The double buffer of codewords makes Encoding module be able to process the next sub-packet before Packing module has finished packing the current one. And each coding group can be encoded separately. Further, they can be stacked by shifting operations to form a part of bitstream. Finally all the parts are ordered by Packing module and be delivered to IO module.

4   Experiments

The design was synthesized and packaged by Xilinx Vitis HLS 2022.1, and be placed and routed by Xilinx Vivado 2022.1. The target FPGA used in the experiments was a Xilinx Ultrascale+ xcu50-fsvh2104-2-E on the Alveo U50 data center accelerator card. The parallelism of the JPEG XS IP core is set to 8. In other words, the encoder consumes eight pixels per cycle. And the neighbor size N_t mentioned in Rate Control module is set to 5.

The functionality can be summarized as below:

- Colorspace: Supporting RGB, YCbCr
- Sampling: Supporting 4:4:4, 4:2:2
- Bitdepth: Supporting 12, 10, 8 bit
- Resolution: Supporting maximal width of 8192
- Rate Control: Supporting CBR, ranging from 1.0 to 10.0 bpp

Table 1. Hardware resource for JPEG XS encoder

Resource	Used	Available	Utilization %
LUT	172196	745249	23.11
LUTRAM	6411	392816	1.63
FF	84865	1579157	5.37
BRAM	240	1163	20.64
URAM	24	636	3.77
DSP	43	5948	0.72

The hardware resources usage is listed in Table 1. The LUT usage is acceptable for majority of Xilinx Virtex and Xilinx Kintex FPGAs and is even supported by some Spartan devices. The on-chip RAM usage is related to the line-buffers and precinct buffers, which means it shrinks when the maximal width of image is small. The DSP usage is close to zero because all the calculation is based on fixed-width integer and usually only shifting and addition operations are used to manipulate the data.

Table 2. Encoding speed of the JPEG XS encoder for 12 bit RGB444 images on Alveo U50

Frequency	4K(3840 × 2160)	8K(7680 × 4320)
158 MHz	8.14 ms/122 fps	29.57 ms/33 fps
196 MHz	6.57 ms/152 fps	23.72 ms/42 fps

Another benchmark was also conducted to test the speed of the encoder. The program was developed under the framework of Vitis Unified Software Platform.

The image data is pre-fetched to on-board HBM. And we run the encoding kernel 1000 times to calculate the average encoding speed. The result are shown in Table 2, indicating that 158 MHz is enough for 4K 120 fps as well as 8K 30 fps. Although the number of pixels in 8K image is just four times as that of 4K image, the consumed time is not in that way. Because the design requires an extra serial rate control operation for each precinct. As this time is almost fixed, the large number of pixels is more likely to cover this decision time.

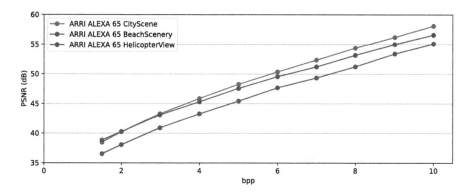

Fig. 10. The image quality of the encoder measured on 12 bit RGB444 ARRI Alexa 65 sequences

Table 3. Comparison between the encoder and JPEG XS reference software on 12 bit RGB444 ARRI Alexa 65 sequences

BPP		1.5	2.0	3.0	4.0	5.0	6.0	7.0	8.0	9.0	10.0
CityScene	HW	38.46	40.23	43.29	45.87	48.27	50.35	52.35	54.38	56.20	58.10
	SW	38.46	40.23	43.29	45.87	48.27	50.36	52.35	54.39	56.22	58.11
BeachScenery	HW	38.83	40.27	43.10	45.32	47.57	49.55	51.21	53.16	54.99	56.59
	SW	38.84	40.27	43.09	45.33	47.57	49.56	51.21	53.17	55.00	56.59
HelicopterView	HW	36.53	38.06	40.90	43.28	45.44	47.68	49.34	51.22	53.40	55.08
	SW	36.53	38.07	40.90	43.28	45.45	47.69	49.34	51.21	53.42	55.08

The dataset for testing image quality comes from ARRI ALEXA 65 sample footage [11]. Figure 10 depicts the performance of the encoder on 12 bit UHD image sequences. The sequences rendered by ARRI official tool are in size 6560 × 3100, 12 bit. Image quality can be usually well preserved when bitrate is larger than 8.0 bpp, which yields a PSNR over 50dB. And high compression rate, such as 24:1 (1.5bpp), leads to a relative small PSNR. However, image with a PSNR around 40dB can still maintain good visual quality. As described in Table 3, the image quality is almost the same with that of JPEG XS reference software in Main profile [12]. The difference comes from some approximations in RC module and is negligible. And the hardware implementation makes it encoding at a real-time speed.

5   Conclusion

This paper presents an JPEG XS encoder design that can be efficiently implemented by Xilinx HLS. The encoder is highly pipelined with only rate control sub-module running sequentially. No off-chip memory accessing means almost fixed latency on hardware, making it suitable for video streaming. The high parallelism of pixels let the encoder achieve processing speed of 4K 152fps or 8K 42fps at 196 MHz frequency. And PSNR of the encoded image usually can reach 50dB at 8.0 bpp. In summary, the encoder is easy to be implemented while achieves impressive performance with limited resource. The encoder can also serve as a reference for the decoder design, since JPEG XS is almost symmetric in encoder and decoder sides except for the rate estimation module.

References

1. Richter, T., Descampe, A., Keinert, J., Rouvroy, G.: Information technology—JPEG XS low-latency lightweight image coding system, Part 1: Core coding system. Standard, International Organization for Standardization, Geneva, CH (2022)
2. Descampe, A., et al.: JPEG XS—a new standard for visually lossless low-latency lightweight image coding. Proc. IEEE **109**(9), 1559–1577 (2021)
3. SMPTE Standard: Transport of high bit rate media signals over IP networks (HBRMT). The Society of Motion Picture and Television Engineers 16 (2022)
4. ISO, I.S., JTC, I., et al.: Information technology-jpeg 2000 image coding system-part 1: Core coding system. ISO/IEC 15444-1 (2001)
5. RDD 36:2015 - SMPTE registered disclosure doc - apple prores bitstream syntax and decoding process. RDD 36:2015, pp. 1–39 (2016)
6. Walls, F.G., MacInnis, A.S.: Vesa display stream compression for television and cinema applications. IEEE J. Emerg. Sel. Top. Circuits Syst. **6**(4), 460–470 (2016)
7. Sullivan, G.J., Ohm, J.R., Han, W.J., Wiegand, T.: Overview of the high efficiency video coding (HEVC) standard. IEEE Trans. Circuits Syst. Video Technol. **22**(12), 1649–1668 (2012)
8. Richter, T., Keinert, J., Descampe, A., Rouvroy, G.: Entropy coding and entropy coding improvements of JPEG XS. In: 2018 Data Compression Conference, pp. 87–96. IEEE (2018)
9. Bruns, V., Richter, T., Ahmed, B., Keinert, J., Fößel, S.: Decoding JPEG XS on a GPU. In: 2018 Picture Coding Symposium (PCS), pp. 111–115. IEEE (2018)
10. Keinert, J., Lorent, J., Descampe, A., Rouvroy, G., Fößel, S.: Introduction to JPEG XS-the new low complexity codec standard for professional video production. IBC Technical Paper (2017)
11. Kiku, D., Monno, Y., Tanaka, M., Okutomi, M.: Beyond color difference: residual interpolation for color image demosaicking. IEEE Trans. Image Process. **25**(3), 1288–1300 (2016)
12. Richter, T., Descampe, A., Keinert, J., Rouvroy, G.: Information technology—JPEG XS low-latency lightweight image coding system—Part 5: Reference software. Standard, International Organization for Standardization, Geneva, CH (2020)

A Correction-Based Dynamic Enhancement Framework Towards Underwater Detection

Yanling Qiu, Qianxue Feng, Boqin Cai, Hongan Wei, and Weiling Chen[✉]

Fujian Key Lab for Intelligent Processing and Wireless Transmission
of Media Information, Fuzhou University, Fuzhou 350108, China
{201120096,211120125,221120099,weihongan,weiling.chen}@fzu.edu.cn

Abstract. To assist underwater object detection for better performance, image enhancement technology is often used as a pre-processing step. However, most of the existing enhancement methods tend to pursue the visual quality of an image, instead of providing effective help for detection tasks. In fact, image enhancement algorithms should be optimized with the goal of utility improvement. In this paper, to adapt to the underwater detection tasks, we proposed a lightweight dynamic enhancement algorithm using a contribution dictionary to guide low-level corrections. Dynamic solutions are designed to capture differences in detection preferences. In addition, it can also balance the inconsistency between the contribution of correction operations and their time complexity. Experimental results in real underwater object detection tasks show the superiority of our proposed method in both generalization and real-time performance.

Keywords: Object detection · Underwater image enhancement · Image utility quality · Low-level corrections · Contribution dictionary

1 Introduction

Underwater object detection, which plays an important role in underwater intelligent applications such as marine ecological monitoring, ocean exploration, and geological mapping, has drawn considerable attention [1]. However, due to the limits of underwater imaging, the underwater image always appears to be degraded. Figure 1 shows underwater images with typical distortions. Unideal light sources and uneven lightwave attenuation can cause non-uniform illumination and color degradation. Suspended small particles and camera equipment jitter may result in ocean snow noise and motion blur. The negative consequence of these degradation phenomena is reflected in the absence of target contours, the lack of effective details, and the corruption of high-level semantic information. Therefore, underwater images should be enhanced to support subsequent underwater object detection tasks.

In recent years, research on underwater image enhancement is focused on enhancing image visual quality. The research strategies can be broadly classified

G. Zhai et al. (Eds.): IFTC 2022, CCIS 1766, pp. 203–216, 2023.
https://doi.org/10.1007/978-981-99-0856-1_15

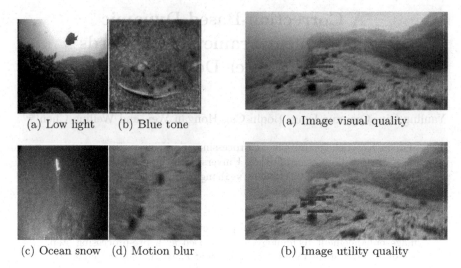

(a) Low light   (b) Blue tone   (a) Image visual quality

(c) Ocean snow   (d) Motion blur   (b) Image utility quality

Fig. 1. Degraded underwater images.   **Fig. 2.** Comparison on visual to utility.

into two categories: physical model-based and deep learning-based strategies. In the first strategy, researchers usually start with a physical degradation model based on underwater imaging principles, then estimate unknown model parameters through prior assumptions. Researchers investigate various prior assumptions including underwater dark channel prior (UDCP) [2] and underwater light attenuation prior (ULAP) [3] and color space dimensionality reduction prior (CSDRP) [4]. The second strategy almost relies on the amount of paired training data and the learning ability of deep neural networks. References [5] and [6] synthesized a large number of undistorted underwater images via generative adversarial networks (GAN) to acquire enough data to train enhancement algorithms. Based on massive data, references [7] and [8] build a series of end-to-end enhancement networks to learn features from various underwater image domains. These enhancement methods can help to improve image quality towards human commonsense and aesthetics, however, may not always contribute to detection accuracy [9].

As shown in Fig. 2, image utility quality is distinct from image visual quality. The richness of effective information, which is helpful to recall and precision of detection task, determines image utility quality. Reference [10] states that reducing noise and removing blur are effective approaches to increase classification accuracy. Since low-light images hurt detection performance, reference [11] develops an unsupervised bio-inspired two-path network (BITPNet) for enhancing nighttime traffic images. As weak contrast and insufficient color may weaken high-level semantic information, references [12] and [13] guide the training of the enhancement network through the feedback information provided by a detection model.

Nevertheless, current studies on image utility quality enhancement cannot be generalized to underwater scenes. Different from the atmospheric environment, the imaging conditions of underwater images are severe. These enhancement methods perform poorly in degraded underwater images. Meanwhile, existing works, that are optimized for a fixed classifier or detector only, cannot fully improve the performance of different detectors. The limited capacity of underwater delivery equipment and high real-time requirements for underwater object detection tasks bring great challenges to underwater image utility quality enhancement.

To address these concerns, a task-oriented dynamic enhancement framework based on low-level corrections is proposed to back up detection tasks. Our unique contribution can be summarized as follows:

- We propose a framework for underwater image utility quality enhancement based on low-level corrections. The utility quality strategy and lightweight corrections can achieve real-time detection performance improvement in diverse underwater applications.
- We investigate different contributions of image features to the image utility quality and construct a contribution dictionary based on various detection network architectures. The dynamic method can be widely applied before object detection tasks or other high-level vision tasks.

2   Method

2.1   Low-Level Corrections

Low-level information distortion will cause changes in high-level semantic information. The primary reason for detector inaccuracy is the degradation of underwater images, including distortions in brightness, color, clarity, and contrast. In the case of low brightness, insufficient luminance may lead to the loss of edge and contour information, making object localization difficult; in the case of excessive brightness or overexposure, detail information is lacking, making accurate object classification difficult. Similarly, color distortion can make it difficult to match the real color features, thus dramatically reducing classification accuracy. Lower clarity and contrast can weaken the high-level semantic information of an image, thus affecting detection performance.

Therefore, this paper focuses on the following low-level corrections, and the detailed operations are shown in Table 1.

- Gamma transformation is performed for brightness distortion. A nonlinear mapping of gray levels is used to achieve brightness equalization. The parameter of gamma transformation is set to 0.5 for stretching gray values in dark areas for low-light underwater images.
- White balance is employed for color distortion. White balance processes the RGB channels of an image to eliminate the effects of underwater environments and restore color information.

Table 1. Distortions/Corrections/Features

Distortion	Correction	Feature
Brightness	Gamma transformation	Brightness
Color	White balance	Saturation
Clarity	Median filter	Entropy
Contrast	Contrast-limited adaptive histogram equalization	Gradient

(a) Brightness   (b) Color   (c) Clarity   (d) Contrast   (e) Contrast

Fig. 3. Results of low-level corrections. Raw images are in the top row, enhanced images are in the bottom row.

- Median filtering is performed for clarity distortion. The filter sets each pixel point's gray value to the median of all pixel points in its neighboring window, enabling image pixel values closer to their true values. Noise impact is relieved by clearing up isolated points.
- Contrast-limited adaptive histogram equalization (CLAHE) is used for contrast distortion. CLAHE achieves global contrast enhancement by using the mapping curve determined by the histogram of grayscale distribution.

As shown in Fig. 3, low-level corrections can help to reduce the number of missed objects and increase confidence in correct objects. Compared to the other correction operations, clarity correction only improves the confidence of correct objects which helps a little with detection. Moreover, excessive corrections can instead lead image features to become more unfavorable to be detected. For instance, over-contrast correction introduces additional noise.

2.2   Image Utility Quality

In this paper, we use image utility quality to quantify the degree of underwater image distortion.

Image utility quality represents the richness of valid information that is concerned with machine vision tasks. In object detection tasks, the image utility quality of the entire dataset is reflected as the mean average precision (mAP), which is formulated as:

$$mAP = \frac{1}{k}\sum_{i=1}^{k}\sum_{i=1}^{n-1}(R_{i+1} - R_i)P_{inter}(R_i + 1) \tag{1}$$

where,

$$P = \frac{TP}{TP + FP} \tag{2}$$

$$R = \frac{TP}{TP + FN} \tag{3}$$

TP is the number of true positives, FP is the number of false positives, and FN is the number of false negatives. AP represents the area under the Precision-Recall curves. However, mAP is insufficient for describing the utility quality of a single image. Due to the influence of isolated variables, image utility quality cannot be exactly quantified. The Precision-Recall curve fluctuates greatly, and the results of mAP are inconsistent in the whole image dataset and a single image. For a more correct definition of image utility quality, detailed elements in the mAP equation were introduced to calculate the image utility quality score.

$$Q = mAP - \frac{FN}{GT} + C_{TP} - C_{FP} \tag{4}$$

where, GT is the number of ground truths. C_{TP} denotes the smallest confidence value in the TP list and C_{FP} denotes the largest confidence value in the FP list. Reducing FP, increasing C_{TP}, or decreasing C_{FP} are effective solutions that can improve image utility quality. With this, each correction can split the image dataset into two categories. One type is required to implement the correction, whereas the other is not required.

Therefore, low-level corrections that reduced underwater image distortions can improve image features, enhance image utility quality, and boost the performance of detection tasks.

2.3   Contribution Dictionary

High real-time performance is required for object detection tasks. Tasks background can be classified into two types: one is the direct application of intelligence to the acquired images in complicated and changing underwater scenes. Underwater equipment, however, has limited carrying capacity for complex computing operations. The other is to apply the underwater images after transmitting them to land via an underwater channel. However, underwater channels suffer from restricted bandwidth, multipath, quick fading, and other defects. The transmission delay makes it impossible to respond to underwater changes promptly. As a result, as a pre-processing step, the image utility quality enhancement must focus on another major indicator of detection performance: time complexity. It is essential to balance the improvement contribution and time consumption introduced by correction operations.

Table 2. Popular detector

Method	Backbone
SSD [14]	VGG-16
Efficientdet [15]	EfficientNet-B0
Centernet [16]	ResNet-50
YOLOX [17]	CSPDarknet

(a) Centernet   (b) YOLOX

Fig. 4. Prediction feature maps.

Table 2 shows the popular object detection networks for underwater tasks. For feature extraction, the network backbone varies. For feature matching, the anchor strategy differs. In general, for the anchor-free strategy, the predicted feature maps with key points focus more on global features. For shallower backbones, with the small respective field, will extract more fine-grained features from an image. As the number of downsampling or convolution increases, the respective field gradually expands, so more high-level semantic features can be extracted to form the final prediction feature map. The prediction feature maps of different detectors are shown in Fig. 4.

Even for the same image, utility quality can vary dramatically due to the differences in image features used. Equation 4 also supports this conclusion. Since detectors pay different attention to image features, this paper tends to construct a contribution dictionary for indicting the correlation between image features and image utility quality. The contribution dictionary can be determined as follows:

$$I = \omega * \xi(C, D) \tag{5}$$

where, ω refers to the contribution label corresponding to correction operation. When the image feature value matches the applicable range, the contribution label is set to 1. Otherwise, set the contribution label to 0. ξ refers to the contribution weight of this correction operation. The contribution weight is the normalized correlation coefficient. The stronger the correlation between image feature and image utility quality, the higher the weight. Hence, the contribution dictionary can be determined by the low-level corrections: C and the detector: D.

In general, ξ of each correction is ranked as contrast correction, color correction, clarity correction, and brightness correction. According to this order, the enhancement framework first cascades correction operations.

$$B = \frac{I}{T} \tag{6}$$

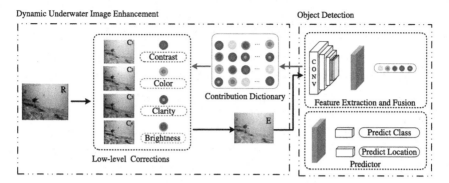

Fig. 5. Image utility quality enhancement framework for underwater object detection.

I is the contribution gains calculated from Eq. 5. T is the time complexity obtained from prior knowledge. Since gradient always be a key feature in image utility quality, the initial benchmark of B value is calculated by contrast correction. When the new correction operation gets a higher B value, the operation will be performed and its parameters will be updated to be a new benchmark later. Finally, an optimal combination of corrections can be generated.

2.4 The Overview of the Proposed Framework

The underwater image utility quality enhancement framework proposed in this paper is shown in Fig. 5. The implementation of the dynamic low-level corrections is guided by a contribution dictionary based on detection prior. The original underwater images are first pre-processed by the image enhancement module to enhance image utility quality and generate enhanced images before being sent into the object detection module. In the image enhancement module, according to the analysis of the underwater degradation, low-level correction operations consist of contrast correction, color correction, clarity correction, and brightness correction. In the object detection module, the detector does not refer to a fixed detection model, but to detection models used in specific tasks.

Our method is task-oriented, aiming to improve the image utility quality. With the work above, the framework provides dynamic and optimal enhancement paths for different detection tasks, that can be generalized in underwater scenes.

3   Experiments

3.1   Implementation Details

The UDD dataset [18] is an underwater image dataset for robot target capture tasks, that was created by the Dalian University of Technology underwater robotics team. It contains three categories: sea urchin, sea cucumber, and scallops, with a training set of 1827 images and a testing set of 400 images. Original

Table 3. Feature/Calculation Formula/Value

Feature	Calculation Formula	Value
Gradient	$Gradient = \dfrac{1}{x * y} \sum_x \sum_y (G_x * I(x,y) + G_y * I(x,y))^2$	0–0.9
Saturation	$Saturation = (max(R,G,B) - min(R,G,B))/max(R,G,B)$	0.3–0.5
Entropy	$Entropy = -\sum_0^{255} P_i log_2 P_i$	0–0.9
Brightness	$Brightness = 0.299 * R + 0.587 * G + 0.114 * B$	0.4–0.6

images suffered from severe motion blurring and color degradation. In the following discussion, only sea urchins will be evaluated.

The Fish4knowledge dataset is derived from an official SeaCLEF competition. It contains eight species of fish: Chaetodon lunulatus, Pempheris vanicolensis, Amphiprion clarkii, Chaetodon trifascialis, Chromis chrysura, Dascyllus reticulatus, Plectrogly phidodon dickii and Dascyllus aruanus. The dataset provides images with 640×480 or 320×240 pixels. The training set covers 6436 images and validation set covers 1462 images and test set covers 2742 images.

Table 3 shows equations for image features corresponding to corrections. As described in Sect. 2.2, we can obtain ω by calculating feature values.

Specifically, the gradient value can reflect image sharpness and texture variation. The Tenengrad gradient function, where G_x and G_y are the kernels of the Sobel operators, employs the Sobel operators to extract gradient values in the horizontal and vertical directions, respectively. Image entropy represents the average amount of information in an image. In the calculation formula, P_i shows the proportion of pixels in the image with the gray value i. The entropy and gradient values can be increased by clarity correction and contrast correction, to enhance image utility quality by effectively restoring edges and contour information. Brightness and saturation can be characterized by a linear combination of three elements in the RGB color space. Brightness correction can properly enhance the overall image without introducing additional unfavorable information. Color correction can correct color detail information in the image.

Since the YOLOX model and the Centernet model perform well in accuracy and real-time performance among popular detection networks. Meanwhile, there are significant differences between the two models in the feature-extracting and feature-matching process. We carry out experiments based on these two models as illustrations.

According to Eq. 4, the image utility quality score corresponding to the detectors is obtained. And according to the formula in Table 3, image feature values are acquired. In this part, s and p here refers to the image utility quality score

Table 4. Contribution weight: $\xi(C, D)$

Feature	YOLOX	Centernet
Gradient	0.4229	0.3707
Saturation	0.3768	0.2808
Brightness	0.3222	0.2810
Entropy	0.1073	0.0933

Table 5. Time complexity: T

Correction	Time
Contrast	0.027
Color	0.033
Brightness	0.024
Clarity	0.021

and image feature values. ξ denotes the correlation between utility quality and image features, which is measured according to the following formula:

$$PLCC = \frac{\sum_{i=1}^{N}(s_i - \bar{s})(p_i - \bar{p})}{\sqrt{\left(\sum_{i=1}^{N}(s_i - \bar{s})^2 \sum_{i=1}^{N}(p_i - \bar{p})^2\right)}} \tag{7}$$

As a result, the contribution dictionary weights for features changed by corrections and detectors can be recorded in Table 4.

To measure the time complexity of each correction operation, this paper tests the corrections with the same image resolution and at the same computing device. Table 5 presents the time complexity of each correction.

After the above work, the B value can be easily obtained according to Eq. 6, and then the enhancement method can be finally settled down.

The backbone network CSPDarknet of the YOLOX network is a modified Darknet-53, which divides the input feature map into two channels, one of which is connected to the transition layer by residual convolution and 1×1 convolution, the other of which is connected directly to the transition layer by shortcut. More high-level features are extracted as useful features by the YOLOX model. Therefore, the detector is more concerned with gradient features overall. And the dynamic enhancement method is mainly constructed by contrast correction. The Centernet's backbone is ResNet-50. It adopts an anchor-free strategy, estimating the object's location by key points. Therefore, the Centernet model focuses on gradient features as well as saturation and brightness features. Its enhancement method automatically matches contrast correction and brightness correction and color correction cascades.

3.2 Performance Analysis

We conducted experiments on both UDD and Fish4knowledge for the same detection task. Figure 6 shows the enhanced results.

After image utility quality enhancement, the subsequent detection can be greatly improved. Enhanced images show a 15.86%/6.98% improvement in detection accuracy than original images at a speed of 105/126 frames per second (FPS), respectively. Figure 7 shows the increased result for each category.

(a) UDD   (b) Fish4knowledge

Fig. 6. Underwater object detection results based on our enhancement method. Raw images are in the top row, enhanced images are in the bottom row.

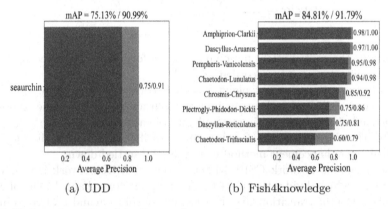

(a) UDD   (b) Fish4knowledge

Fig. 7. Underwater object detection performances based on our enhancement method

Furthermore, to verify that the dynamic enhancement method proposed in this paper can provide suitable solutions for various underwater object detection tasks, we train two detection models on UDD. $Ours_1$ is designed for the YOLOX model, and mAP_1 refers to the detection accuracy towards the YOLOX model; $Ours_2$ is designed for the Centernet model, and mAP_2 refers to the detection accuracy towards the Centernet model. The qualitative and quantitative analysis of our methods is shown in Fig. 8 and Table 6.

Our method provides different correction solutions for different detection tasks and therefore shows the most favorable improvement in detection tasks. Ablation experiments were conducted to study the contribution of low-level corrections to detection performance. Only one correction operation is carried out for each experiment. Performance comparisons are given in Table 7.

The results of the table show that the four aspects discussed in this paper are not redundant. In the four aspects of correction operations, contrast correction seems to be able to make the greatest contribution to the improvement of image utility quality while maintaining a low time complexity.

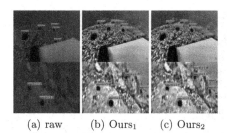

(a) raw   (b) Ours$_1$ (c) Ours$_2$

Fig. 8. Qualitative results comparison.

Table 6. Quantitative performances comparison

Method	mAP$_1$	mAP$_2$	FPS
Raw	75.13	71.83	
Ours$_1$	**90.99**		105
Ours$_2$		**91.22**	101

Table 7. Ablation performance

Correction	Contrast	Color	Clarity	Brightness	Ours
mAP$_1$/FPS	89.82/126	87.79/63	87.66/188	87.74/157	90.99/105
mAP$_2$/FPS	89.09/100	87.73/67	87.90/ 175	87.92/138	91.22/101

3.3   Comparison with State-of-the-Art Methods

We compare our proposed method to the advanced underwater enhancement methods, including deep learning-based methods: FUnIE-GAN [19], SCNet [20] and physical model-based methods: CLAHE [21], UNVT [22], and MLLE [23] on UDD. Although these excellent underwater image enhancement methods are mainly designed to improve image visual quality, the researchers state that these methods can be beneficial to help high-level vision tasks or feature-matching tasks which is similar to our goal. The enhanced results are shown in Fig. 9.

Compared to physical model-based enhancement methods, deep learning-based enhancement methods generally have weaker generalization ability. The deep convolutional neural network performs better in color correction, but less well at contrast correction which is precisely contrary to image utility quality tendency. FUnIE-GAN, for example, enhances image visual quality while weakening image gradient features, leading to a decrease in image utility quality instead. Table 8 provides the performance comparison of each enhancement method.

To additionally quantitatively evaluate image visual quality, we introduce two no-reference evaluation metrics: UIQM and UCIQE. Experimental data illustrate that the improvement in visual quality does not coincide with the improvement in utility quality. Our proposed method outperforms advanced enhancement methods by 3.61%. At the same time, the time complexity of our method makes it well-suited for underwater scenes.

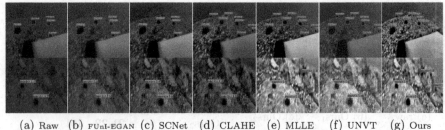

(a) Raw   (b) FUnI-EGAN   (c) SCNet   (d) CLAHE   (e) MLLE   (f) UNVT   (g) Ours

Fig. 9. Visual comparison of enhancement methods on UDD.

Table 8. Performance comparison of enhancement methods on UDD

Method	Raw	FUnIE-GAN	SCNet	CLAHE	UNVT	MLLE	Ours
mAP	75.13	69.67	80.41	86.36	83.42	87.38	**90.99**
UIQM	0.05	0.69	0.60	0.46	1.08	1.04	**1.09**
UCIQE	21.47	26.16	25.40	24.63	29.26	29.43	**29.47**
FPS		25	30	37	5	9	**105**

4 Conclusion

In this paper, we propose an underwater image enhancement method, that selectively enhances useful image features, and improves image utility quality. The task-oriented dynamic enhancement framework can be widely applied before various detection tasks. In comparison to the advanced underwater image enhancement methods, our method shows promising results. Since image utility quality can offer recommendations and guidance for boosting high-level vision task performance. Our work opens up many possibilities for further exploration. Inspired by reinforcement learning, in future work, we plan to develop a feedback-optimization enhancement strategy that uses image utility quality as supervision.

Acknowledgements. This work was supported in part by the National Natural Science Foundation of China under Grant 61901119, and in part by the Natural Science Foundation of Fujian Province under Grant 2022J05117.

References

1. Liu, R., Fan, X., Zhu, M., Hou, M., Luo, Z.: Real-world underwater enhancement: challenges, benchmarks, and solutions under natural light. IEEE Trans. Circuits Syst. Video Technol. **30**(12), 4861–4875 (2020). https://doi.org/10.1109/TCSVT.2019.2963772
2. Drews, J.P., Nascimento, E., Moraes, F., Botelho, S., Campos, M.: Transmission estimation in underwater single images. In: IEEE International Conference on Computer Vision Workshops (2013)

3. Song, W., Wang, Y., Huang, D., Tjondronegoro, D.: A rapid scene depth estimation model based on underwater light attenuation prior for underwater image restoration. In: Hong, R., Cheng, W.-H., Yamasaki, T., Wang, M., Ngo, C.-W. (eds.) PCM 2018. LNCS, vol. 11164, pp. 678–688. Springer, Cham (2018). https://doi.org/10.1007/978-3-030-00776-8_62

4. Liu, Y., Rong, S., Cao, X., Li, T., He, B.: Underwater single image dehazing using the color space dimensionality reduction prior. In: IEEE, p. 1 (2020)

5. Fabbri, C., Jahidul Islam, M., Sattar, J.: Enhancing underwater imagery using generative adversarial networks. arXiv (2018)

6. Li, J., Skinner, K.A., Eustice, R.M., Johnson-Roberson, M.: WaterGAN: unsupervised generative network to enable real-time color correction of monocular underwater images. IEEE Robot. Autom. Lett. 3(1), 387–394 (2018)

7. Uplavikar, P., Wu, Z., Wang, Z.: All-in-one underwater image enhancement using domain-adversarial learning. arXiv:1905.13342 (2019)

8. Li, C., Anwar, S., Hou, J., Cong, R., Ren, W.: Underwater image enhancement via medium transmission-guided multi-color space embedding. IEEE Trans. Image Process. 30, 4985–5000 (2021)

9. Zhang, J., Zhu, L., Xu, L., Xie, Q.: Research on the correlation between image enhancement and underwater object detection. In: 2020 Chinese Automation Congress (CAC), pp. 5928–5933 (2020). https://doi.org/10.1109/CAC51589.2020.9326936

10. Sharma, V., Diba, A., Neven, D., Brown, M.S., Stiefelhagen, R.: Classification driven dynamic image enhancement. In: 2018 IEEE/CVF Conference on Computer Vision and Pattern Recognition, pp. 4033–4041 (2018)

11. Tao, P., Kuang, H., Duan, Y., Zhong, L., Qiu, W.: BITPNet: unsupervised bio-inspired two-path network for nighttime traffic image enhancement. IEEE Access 8, 164737–164746 (2020)

12. Chen, L., et al.: Perceptual underwater image enhancement with deep learning and physical priors. IEEE Trans. Circuits Syst. Video Technol. 31(8), 3078–3092 (2021). https://doi.org/10.1109/TCSVT.2020.3035108

13. Gao, P., Tian, T., Li, L.F., Ma, J., Tian, J.: DE-CycleGAN: an object enhancement network for weak vehicle detection in satellite images. IEEE J. Sel. Top. Appl. Earth Obs. Remote Sens. 14, 3403–3414 (2021)

14. Liu, W., et al.: SSD: single shot multibox detector. In: Leibe, B., Matas, J., Sebe, N., Welling, M. (eds.) ECCV 2016. LNCS, vol. 9905, pp. 21–37. Springer, Cham (2016). https://doi.org/10.1007/978-3-319-46448-0_2

15. Tan, M., Pang, R., Le, Q.V.: EfficientDet: scalable and efficient object detection. In: 2020 IEEE/CVF Conference on Computer Vision and Pattern Recognition (CVPR) (2020)

16. Duan, K., Bai, S., Xie, L., Qi, H., Huang, Q., Tian, Q.: CenterNet: keypoint triplets for object detection. In: 2019 IEEE/CVF International Conference on Computer Vision (ICCV), pp. 6568–6577 (2019). https://doi.org/10.1109/ICCV.2019.00667

17. Ge, Z., Liu, S., Wang, F., Li, Z., Sun, J.: YOLOX: exceeding YOLO series in 2021. arXiv preprint arXiv:2107.08430 (2021)

18. Liu, C., et al.: A new dataset, Poisson GAN and AquaNet for underwater object grabbing. IEEE Trans. Circuits Syst. Video Technol. 32(5), 2831–2844 (2022)

19. Islam, M.J., Xia, Y., Sattar, J.: Fast underwater image enhancement for improved visual perception. IEEE Robot. Autom. Lett. 5(2), 3227–3234 (2020)

20. Fu, Z., Lin, X., Wang, W., Huang, Y., Ding, X.: Underwater image enhancement via learning water type desensitized representations. In: 2022 IEEE International

Conference on Acoustics, Speech and Signal Processing (ICASSP), ICASSP 2022, pp. 2764–2768 (2022). https://doi.org/10.1109/ICASSP43922.2022.9747758

21. Pizer, S.M., Johnston, R.E., Ericksen, J.P., Yankaskas, B.C., Muller, K.E.: Contrast-limited adaptive histogram equalization: speed and effectiveness. In: Proceedings of the First Conference on Visualization in Biomedical Computing (1990)

22. Xie, J., Hou, G., Wang, G., Pan, Z.: A variational framework for underwater image dehazing and deblurring. IEEE Trans. Circuits Syst. Video Technol. **32**(6), 3514–3526 (2022). https://doi.org/10.1109/TCSVT.2021.3115791

23. Zhang, W., Zhuang, P., Sun, H.H., Li, G., Kwong, S., Li, C.: Underwater image enhancement via minimal color loss and locally adaptive contrast enhancement. IEEE Trans. Image Process. **31**, 3997–4010 (2022). https://doi.org/10.1109/TIP.2022.3177129

Water Segmentation via Asymmetric Multiscale Interaction Network

Jianzhuo Chen[1], Tao Lu[1(✉)], Yanduo Zhang[1,3], Wenhua Fang[1], Xiya Rao[1], and Mingming Zhao[2]

[1] Wuhan Institute of Technology, Wuhan, China
`lut@wit.edu.cn`
[2] Wuhan Fiberhome Technical Services Co., Ltd., Wuhan, China
[3] Hubei Three Gorges Laboratory, Yichang, China

Abstract. It is important to observe and split water region to help acquire the water quality and supervise water environment. Water segmentation is a task to separate water region from images. Due to the specular nature of the water surface, various types of reflections usually appear on the water surface, which can change significantly with weather and lighting changes, it is difficult for general segmentation to work. According to the characteristics of waters, i.e. wide area and reflection, we propose a asymmetric interaction module (AIM) converge the features to a larger receptive field. Further, with this powerful module, we design the asymmetric multiscale interaction network, which can maintain the features of each scale and reassign the weights of features at different scales. We conduct extensive experiments on Hubei water dataset we constructed, The results show the framework effectively improves the accuracy of water segmentation and greatly improves the visual effect of segmentation, which is 5.9% higher in self-made dataset with advanced methods.

Keywords: Water segmentation · Hubei water dataset · Asymmetric interaction

1 Introduction

Inland water is one of the most protected resources. However, Water pollution threatens the health of the water quality, and will cause a large number of dead fish, cyanobacteria outbreaks and other ecological disasters. At the same time, floods and dry waters will also cause a huge threat to human society. Therefore, it is important to supervise the water surface situation. To monitor the water environment, identifying the water region and segment it from its surroundings is essential.

This work was supported by the Science and technology project innovation fund of Hubei Three Gorges Laboratory under Grant SC215002, National Natural Science Foundation of China under Grant 62072350, Grant 62171328; and the Hubei Technology Innovation Project under Grant 2019AAA045.

G. Zhai et al. (Eds.): IFTC 2022, CCIS 1766, pp. 217–228, 2023.
https://doi.org/10.1007/978-981-99-0856-1_16

As shown in Fig. 1, due to the specularity and indeterminacy of water, problems such as reflection on the water surface can, weather changes, and lighting changes will significantly change the feature distribution on the water surface. Hence, we thought of use semantic segmentation for water segmentation.

(a)   (b)

(c)   (d)

Fig. 1. Some common situation in water segmentation. The first row is two images of the water surface on a cloudy day. In (a), the severe reflection blurs the boundary between the water surface and the plants. In (b), Floating objects such as algae, garbage, and reflections coexist in the water, complicating the situation on the water surface. (c) and (d) show the conditions of the water surface on sunny days and in the toward evening, respectively, which make the distribution of water surface features more uncertain.

Semantic segmentation or pixel-level classification [1], which aims to assign each pixel if an image to one category, is one of the key problems in computer vision. Semantic segmentation is applied in many scenes such as geographic information systems and medical image analysis systems, advanced driver assistance systems (ADAS) and various applications in autonomous vehicles. Most of the semantic segmentation methods reproduce the details in a fine way [16,21], so that each pixel can be segmented under the condition of fuzziness and occlusion. However, in the task of water segmentation, many interference details (such as various reflections on the water surface and the appearance of various underwater plants) may lead to network learning irrelevant semantic to the nature of water, thus resulting the inaccurate segmentation. In order to solve the above problem, a natural idea is to learn features of a large area with the help of larger scale receptive field and reduce the interference of local harmful information Fig. 2.

In this paper, we analyze the characteristics of the task of water segmentation in the scene of inland rivers in Hubei Province under the monitoring video. We propose a asymmetric interaction module (AIM) to converge the water features to a larger receptive field and use this powerful module to construct asymmetric multiscale interaction network (AMINet). The proposed network uses AIM to fuse the features of various scales, so as to achieve the goal of accurate learning of large scale features to segment the water boundary more accurate.

Our contributions are mainly in the following folds:

(1) We propose a new semantic segmentation dataset, Hubei Water dataset, which includes water monitoring images of different time periods and weather in Hubei and annotations of the corresponding water surface and surrounding environment.

(2) We propose a novel multiscale semantic segmentation network, unidirectional feature finege network (AMINet), which converge features into large scale features with our proposed asymmetric interaction module (AIM). Within the scope of our knowledge, this is the first work on semantic segmentation of water surface in surveillance scenarios.

(3) We empirically demonstrate the superior key point detection performance the Hubei water dataset we collected. Compared with existing popular CNN-based semantic segmentation methods, we achieve a 5.9-point improvement. In addition, we have achieved unimaginable improvements in visual effects.

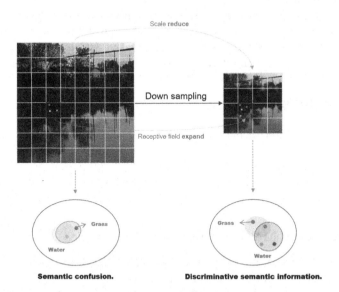

Fig. 2. With the same size red patch, the point in left image may confuse whether it belongs to water or grass. But in right one, grass point and water point can be will separate. Enriching images with large receptive fields is beneficial to water segmentation. (Color figure online)

2   Related Work

Semantic Segmentation. Due to the rapid development of deep learning [2–10], Fully Convolutional Networks (FCNs) [11] have been an dominated and fundamental work in the field of semantic segmentation. However, only convolution-based architectures are difficult to handle large objects due to the weak ability of convolution operations to process global information. To alleviate this problem and enhance the global correlation capability of convolution-based architectures, LC Chen et al. propose atrous convolution [12,13], Zhao et al. propose a pyramid pooling module [14]. Meanwhile, follow the [15], Huang et al. find that attention mechanism can effectively change the network preferences [16]. After that, Yuan et al. use the area contextual information to solve context aggregation problem [21].

Water Segmentation. Water segmentation plays a supporting role in water area monitoring and water quality warning. To achieve water segmentation of monitoring scenes, traditional methods mostly rely on low-level features. By using decision forests [17] or support vector machines [18] on low-level features, one can achieve simple water segmentation task. To improve the segmentation accuracy, Kristan proposed a method [19] to use inertial measurement unit to assist maximize expectations for water segmentation. Further more, Lopez-Fuentes et al. proposed a simple CNN method [20] to detect flooding in rivers by water segmentation.

The existing research on water segmentation in monitoring scenes is not yet mature. Our method aims to achieve high-precision water semantic segmentation in monitoring scenes. We choose the representative CCNet [16] and the strong semantic relevance network OCRNet [21] as the comparison objects.

3   Methodology

In this section, we first display the proposed asymmetric multiscale interaction Network (AMINet). Then, We introduce the core component of AMINet, asymmetric interaction module (AIM), shown in Fig. 3. After that, we introduce the loss we use. At last, we introduce the proposed water segmentation dataset, Hubei water dataset.

3.1   Asymmetric Multiscale Interaction Network

We focus on the design of the main body and introduce our asymmetric multiscale interaction network. The goal of this network is, given an input image with size of $H \times W \times 3$, we generate different scale feature map set F_i with a resolution of $\frac{H}{2^{i+1}} \times \frac{W}{2^{i+1}} \times C_i$, where $i \in 1, 2, 3, 4$. Then, By interacting information between layers, a mask with both semantic information and detailed information is generated. **Sequential Feature Enrichment Subnetworks.** Existing CNN semantic segmentation networks are constructed by concatenating sub-networks of different resolutions, where each sub-network forms a stage, which consists of a series of convolutions, and adjacent sub-networks are up-sampling or down-sampling to separate the resolution. The rate increases or decreases in multiples. In the next paragraphs of this section, we detailed the architecture of our proposed wide area enhanced multi-scale feature fusion network and the asymmetric interaction module.

Table 1. The architectures of AMINet.

	Output size	Asymmetric multiscale interaction network			
Stage1	1024×1024	3×3 32			
Stage2		3×3 32	$3 \times 3/2$ 64		
	1024×1024	3×3 32	3×3 64		
	512×512	3×3 32	3×3 64	x 2	
		Low to high fusion			
Stage3	1024×1024	3×3 32	$3 \times 3/2$ 64	$2 \times [3 \times 3/2]$ 128	
	512×512	3×3 32	$3 \times 3/2$ 64	$2 \times [3 \times 3/2]$ 128	
	256×256	3×3 32	3×3 64	$3 \times 3/2$ 128	
Stage4			$3 \times 3/2$ 64	$2 \times [3 \times 3/2]$ 128	$3 \times [3 \times 3/2]$ 256
		3×3 32	3×3 64	$3 \times 3/2$ 128	$2 \times [3 \times 3/2]$ 256
					$3 \times 3/2$ 256
	1024×1024	5×5 32	5×5 64	5×5 128	5×5 256
	512×512	Low to High fusion			
	256×256			$2 \times [3 \times 3/2]$ 128	$3 \times [3 \times 3/2]$ 256
	128×128	5×5 32	$3 \times 3/2$ 64	$3 \times 3/2$ 128	$2 \times [3 \times 3/2]$ 256
			5×5 64	5×5 128	$3 \times 3/2$ 256
					5×5 256
Output	1024×1024	Low to high fusion			

Network Construction. With a large-scale layer as the first layer, our network propagates construct layer by layer while maintaining high-resolution features. As a result, the layers in the later stage consists of resolution from the previous stage and an extra lower resolution. This process can be vividly described as a inverted triangle construction process. As the Table 1 shown, our network consist of four stages. They can be subjectively divided into two part, stage 1 to stage 3 can be considered as a whole to obtain effective features of each scale, and stage 4 is to integrate features of each resolution into low resolutions to obtain a wide-area enhancement scale feature. In this table, $K \times K/S$ represents a layer with a convolution kernel size of K, stride size of S and its supporting BN Layer and ReLU Layer. To be specific, given an image of size $H \times W \times 3$, we first resize the image scale into size 1024×1024. With a multi-resolution feature extraction network, the information of the image gradually convergence on low-resolution feature maps, i.e. feature maps with a wider receptive field.

3.2 Asymmetric Interaction Module

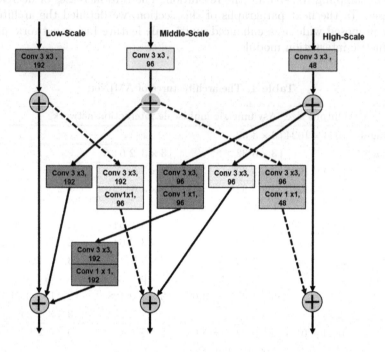

Fig. 3. The architecture of asymmetric interaction module. The ReLU and BN layers after every Conv are hidden.

An example of the detailed architectures of asymmetric interaction module is shown in Fig. 3. For a three-branched input, a series bottleneck is added at the end of each branch. The cross fusion includes fusing the high-scale branch into low-scale branch (high-to-low fusion) and fusing the adjacent low-scale branch into high-scale fusion (low-to-high fusion). For low-to-high fusion, low-scale feature maps are first compressed by a 3×3 convolution and then upsampled by a 1×1 convolution. For high-to-low fusion, high-scale feature maps are downsampled by a series of 3×3 convolution with a stride of 2 and 1×1 convolution. For the i-th size $N \times N$ feature map, the fusion feature map $X_{i,N}$ can be written as:

$$X_{i,N} = \sum FH(X_{i-1,N \times j}) + FL(X_{i-1,N/2}) + ConvBlock(Xi-1,N) \quad (1)$$

where FH and FL refer to the feature from high scale feature maps and low feature maps, the $ConvBlock$ represent a sequence of convolutional layer with BN and RELU.

3.3 Post Processing

In this part, we use the strategy used in OCRNet to make our. Unlike other secondary processing algorithm such as ASPP, etc. which sample around the target point, OCRNet use the object segmentation area to replace the sparse point. In this paper, This strategy is added after the AMINet to better focus on area context information.

3.4   Loss

In this paper, we only adopt simple extra supervision for a fair comparison with most of the methods. Following the PSPNet, we add the auxiliary loss and set the weight to 0.4. The final loss can be expressed as:

$$L_f = L_c + \alpha L_a ux \tag{2}$$

where L_f and L_c are the final loss and the cross-entropy loss, $L_a ux$ represents auxiliary loss with a weight $\alpha = 0.4$.

3.5   Hubei Water Dataset

Construction. The main types of water surface in the study area are rivers and lakes. To construct this dataset, we collected data from surveillance videos of different waters in Hubei Province. In order to obtain samples in different weather and at different times, we collected samples in three time periods in different weather, namely, 9:00 a.m.–11:00 a.m., 11:30 p.m.–1:30 p.m. and 6:00 p.m.–8:00 p.m.

Dataset Scale and Partition. Hubei water dataset consists of 896 images with a size of 2560 × 1440. images are evenly divided into training (598), verification (151) and test sets (147) according to the scene.

Pre-processing. The images with low imaging quality and the images after 7:30 pm cannot identify any effective information through human eyes or the network, so they are removed in this dataset.

Class Selection Rules. In order to maximize the difference between the reflection on the water surface and the entities out of the water, we selected other nine classes to help segment the water region. The Fig. 4 display the classes we select and the reason for choosing.

Dataset Label Generation. Labels are interpreted as a polygon shape file format showing the water area. We carefully separated the water surface boundary, summarized the common reflections and floating objects on the water surface, and then marked them manually.

4   Experiments

4.1   Dataset and Metrics

Dataset. In this part, We train and evaluate our model on the aforementioned Hubei water dataset.

id	class	discription	example
0	water	Refers to the inland waterways of the Yangtze River basin, including lakes and rivers. The target class	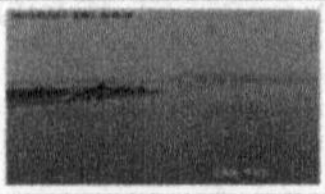
Major classes			
1	algae	A common floating object on the water surface. It has become a major pest of rivers and dams.	
2	sky	The sky above the water. The reflection of sky is always exists on water surface	
3	tree	Waterfront trees. The most difficult reflection is usually from a tree.	
Other classes			
4	bridge	A structure built to span the body of water. It always been the boundary of water and sky	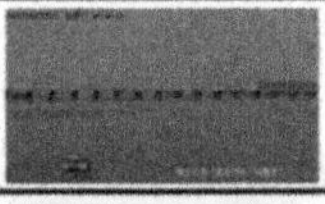
5	boat	Transportations on waterways such as rivers and lakes. Often appears in the dataset	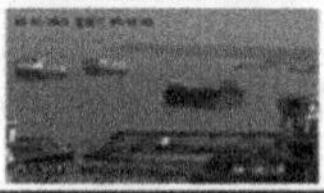
6	building	Waterfront buildings (such as houses). Often appears in the dataset	
7	shore	The fringe of land at the edge of a large body of water. Cause server reflection	
8	sluice	A movable gate allowing water to flow under it. Often appears in the dataset	
9	road	It is found in training that this kind of water is easily confused with water surface.	
10	grass	It is found in training that this kind of water is easily confused with water surface	

Fig. 4. Total classes of the Hubei water dataset. The class names and the choose reason are given. Examples are given in the end of each row.

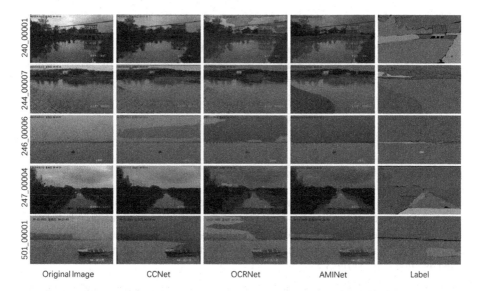

Fig. 5. Qualitative results on Hubei water dataset. compared to CCNet and OCRNet, our AMINet predicts masks with substantially finer details near water boundaries. And our network can better distinguish the reflection on the water surface.

Evaluation Metrics. Although the dataset labeled about eighteen categories, but the goal is to separate the water region. So we take the Intersection over Union (IOU) as the final inspection index.

4.2   Implementation Details

Training Sets. We trained with the input size of 1024×1024. The data augmentation includes random crop and random rotation. Only water is taken as positive sample. We use stochastic gradient descent (SGD). The base learning rate is set as $1e - 2$, and is dropped to $1e - 4$ and $1e - 5$ at the $130th$ and $176th$ epoch. The training processing is terminated within 200 epochs.

Test Sets. We binarize the labeled mask images of pixel classification results and test sets by whether they are water, and then calculate water IOUs.

4.3   Result on Test Set

We report the results of our method with other advanced methods. AS shown in Table 2, Our method get a 78.5% IOU and which surpasses other advanced method. Figure 5 shows qualitative results on Hubei water dataset, where AMINet provides better effect and details than CCNet and OCRNet.

Table 2. Comparison on the Hubei water test set. The best result is in bold.

Method	Backbone	Input size	IOU
CCNet	ResNet-101	2560 × 1440	43.2
HRNet	HRNet-W48	1024 × 1024	68.3
OCRNet	HRNet-W48	1024 × 1024	72.6
AMINet	AMINet	1024 × 1024	**78.5**

4.4 Ablation Study

In this part, we separate our network into three part: The AMINet (/) use a simple bilinear to replace low-to-high fusion and use only convolutional layer with BN+RELU to replace high-to-low; The core component asymmetric interaction module; The Conv5 × 5. We analyze the effect of these factors and the direct effect is shown in Table 3.

Effects of AIM. from the Table 3, it is easy to find that AIM greatly improves the IOU, which proves the effectiveness of this module and focuses more attention on the characteristics of larger receptive field to water segment.

Conv 5×5. After using 5 × 5 convolution in the last several layers, the IOU is 2.4 % and 1.8 % higher than that of AMINet (/) and AMINet (/)+AIM respectively. This proves that large convolution kernels will have better effect for large water areas with uneven characteristic distribution.

Table 3. The effects of factors in AMINet.

AMINet (/)	+AIM	+CONV5 × 5	IOU ↑
✓			71.4
✓	✓		76.7
✓		✓	73.8
✓	✓	✓	**78.5**

5   Conclusion

In this paper, we propose AMINet, a powerful water semantic segmentation method and introduce our dataset Hubei water dataset. With the effective asymmetric interaction module, our framework gradually aggregates information on the smallest feature layer with a larger perceptive field, and ultimately gets better performance on the Hubei water dataset. The disadvantage is that AMINet does not achieving good results in all categories. We leave it in the future.

References

1. Li, Z., Wang, R., Zhang, W., Hu, F., Meng, L.: Multiscale features supported DeepLabV3+ optimization scheme for accurate water semantic segmentation. IEEE Access **7**, 155787–155804 (2019)
2. He, K., Zhang, X., Ren, S., Sun, J.: Deep residual learning for image recognition. In: Proceedings of the IEEE Conference on Computer Vision and Pattern Recognition, pp. 770–778 (2016)
3. Simonyan, K., Zisserman, A.: Very deep convolutional networks for large-scale image recognition. arXiv preprint arXiv:1409.1556 (2014)
4. Li, X., Wang, W., Hu, X., Yang, J.: Selective kernel networks. In: Proceedings of the IEEE/CVF Conference on Computer Vision and Pattern Recognition, pp. 510–519 (2019)
5. Wang, W., Li, X., Yang, J., Lu, T.: Mixed link networks. arXiv preprint arXiv:1802.01808 (2018)
6. Lu, T., Wang, Y., Zhang, Y., Jiang, J., Wang, Z., Xiong, Z.: Rethinking prior-guided face super-resolution: a new paradigm with facial component prior. IEEE Trans. Neural Netw. Learn. Syst. (2022)
7. Wang, Y., Lu, T., Zhang, Y., Wang, Z., Jiang, J., Xiong, Z.: FaceFormer: aggregating global and local representation for face hallucination. IEEE Trans. Circuits Syst. Video Technol. (2022). https://doi.org/10.1109/TCSVT.2022.3224940
8. Lu, T., et al.: Face hallucination via split-attention in split-attention network. In: Proceedings of the 29th ACM International Conference on Multimedia, pp. 5501–5509 (2021)
9. Wang, Y., Lu, T., Zhang, Y., Fang, W., Wu, Y., Wang, Z.: Cross-task feature alignment for seeing pedestrians in the dark. Neurocomputing **462**, 282–293 (2021)
10. Wang, Y., Lu, T., Zhang, Y., Wu, Y.: Multi-scale self-calibrated network for image light source transfer. In: Proceedings of the IEEE/CVF Conference on Computer Vision and Pattern Recognition (CVPR) Workshops, pp. 252–259 (2021)
11. Long, J., Shelhamer, E., Darrell, T.: Fully convolutional networks for semantic segmentation. In: Proceedings of the IEEE Conference on Computer Vision and Pattern Recognition, pp. 3431–3440 (2015)
12. Chen, L.C., Papandreou, G., Kokkinos, I., Murphy, K., Yuille, A.L.: DeepLab: Semantic image segmentation with deep convolutional nets, atrous convolution, and fully connected CRFs. IEEE Trans. Pattern Anal. Mach. Itell. **40**(4), 834–848 (2017)
13. Chen, L.C., Papandreou, G., Schroff, F., Adam, H.: Rethinking atrous convolution for semantic image segmentation. arXiv preprint arXiv:1706.05587 (2017)
14. Zhao, H., Shi, J., Qi, X., Wang, X., Jia, J.: Pyramid scene parsing network. In: Proceedings of the IEEE Conference on Computer Vision and Pattern Recognition, pp. 2881–2890 (2017)
15. Hu, J., Shen, L., Sun, G.: Squeeze-and-excitation networks. In: Proceedings of the IEEE Conference on Computer Vision and Pattern Recognition, pp. 7132–7141 (2018)
16. Huang, Z., Wang, X., Huang, L., Huang, C., Wei, Y., Liu, W.: CCNet: criss-cross attention for semantic segmentation. In: Proceedings of the IEEE/CVF International Conference on Computer Vision, pp. 603–612 (2019)
17. Yao, T., Xiang, Z., Liu, J., Xu, D.: Multi-feature fusion based outdoor water hazards detection. In: 2007 International Conference on Mechatronics and Automation, pp. 652–656. IEEE (2007)

18. Achar, S., Sankaran, B., Nuske, S., Scherer, S., Singh, S.: Self-supervised segmentation of river scenes. In: 2011 IEEE International Conference on Robotics and Automation, pp. 6227–6232. IEEE (2011)
19. Kristan, M., Kenk, V.S., Kovačič, S., Perš, J.: Fast image-based obstacle detection from unmanned surface vehicles. IEEE Trans. Cybern. **46**(3), 641–654 (2015)
20. Lopez-Fuentes, L., Rossi, C., Skinnemoen, H.: River segmentation for flood monitoring. In: 2017 IEEE International Conference on Big Data (Big Data), pp. 3746–3749. IEEE (2017)
21. Yuan, Y., Chen, X., Chen, X., Wang, J.: Segmentation transformer: object-contextual representations for semantic segmentation. arXiv preprint arXiv:1909.11065 (2019)

Quality Assessment

MSPP-IQA: Adaptive Blind Image Quality Assessment Based on Multi-level Spatial Pyramid Pooling

Fangfang Lu[1], Yingjie Lian[1], Feng Qin[1], Guangtao Zhai[2], Xiongkuo Min[2(✉)], Wei Sun[2], and Jianye Zhang[3]

[1] College of Computer Science and Technology,
Shanghai University of Electric Power, Shanghai, China
lufangfang@shiep.edu.cn, lianyingjie@mail.shiep.edu.cn
[2] Institute of Image Communication and Network Engineering,
Shanghai Jiao Tong University, Shanghai, China
{zhaiguangtao,minxiongkuo,sunguwei}@sjtu.edu.cn
[3] Electricity Industry, China State Grid Xinjiang Electric Power Co.,
Wulumuqi, China

Abstract. The main reason why image quality assessment (IQA) for real distortion has not been well solved is that, first, after the training of CNN is completed, the parameters of the convolution kernel are fixed, but the image content is changeable, which limits the generalization performance of the model. Second, the real distortion often exists in the local area of the image, which puts higher requirements on the ability of the model to perceive local distortion. In this paper, a multi-level spatial pyramid pooling-based blind image quality assessment method (MSPP-IQA) for real distortion is proposed. First, ResNet50 is used as the backbone network. Next, a feature pyramid structure is used to combine features, and then the proposed adaptive local distortion perception (ALDP) module is used to improve the semantic features. The ALDP module is based on conditional parameter convolution to make sure that the model's scoring ability can handle different images in large datasets. Residual connectivity is used to improve the model's ability to learn. At the same time, the model uses the semantic feature understanding module for image content understanding and provides prediction guidance for the scoring module. The proposed model improved the generalization power as well as the evaluation accuracy of the quality assessment compared to the current more advanced models. The final experimental resulted demonstrate that the model can quickly and accurately evaluate the real image quality without reference.

Keywords: Image quality assessment · Real distortion · Pyramid structure

1 Introduction

The objective image quality assessment (IQA) is to make the scores predicted by the model consistent with the subjective human scores. Objective IQA methods

© The Author(s), under exclusive license to Springer Nature Singapore Pte Ltd. 2023
G. Zhai et al. (Eds.): IFTC 2022, CCIS 1766, pp. 231–245, 2023.
https://doi.org/10.1007/978-981-99-0856-1_17

can be divided into three categories: full reference (FR), half reference (RR), and no reference (NR). In realistic scenarios, it is impossible to obtain distortion-free reference images; the most practical one at present is the NR-IQA method.

According to the different sources of distortion in the image, the no reference image quality evaluation methods can be further divided into real distortion image quality evaluation and synthetic distortion image quality evaluation. Among them, synthetic distortion based image quality evaluation can also be divided into three categories: natural scene statistics (NSS) [1–7] models, artificial feature extraction models, and deep learning-based models. Xu et al. proposed a hybrid algorithm based on High Order Statistics Aggregation (HOSA [8]). Based on the NSS model of steerable pyramid decomposition (SPNSS), Lu et al. [9] proposed an NRIQA method suitable for natural images. In order to solve the TMI quality assessment, Wang et al. [10] processed the visual signal into a low-level visual layer, a middle-level visual layer, and a high-level visual layer and extracted corresponding features from these three layers for SVR for quality prediction. The goal of the model based on NSS and manual feature extraction is to first design methods that can effectively extract visual representations and then map the features to quality scores using methods such as SVR.

Influenced by Retinex theory, Li et al. [11] Modeled illumination and content by two factors, proposed a novel deep decomposition and bilinear pooling network (DDB-Net). In order to make full use of the visual information from low-level to high-level, Sun et al. [12] hierarchically fused features from the mid-level to the high-level, and then used an iterative hybrid database training (IMDT) strategy to train BIQA models on multiple databases simultaneously. Sun et al. [13] projected a 360-degree image into six viewport images, then trained with a multi-channel CNN and a quality regressor, and proposed a multi-channel convolutional neural network for blind 360-degree IQA.

For authentically distorted images, Zhang et al. [14] made two networks for synthetic distortion and real distortion. Su et al. [15] proposed an adaptive hyper network structure (HyperIQA) to predict the image quality of real scenes. Chen et al. [16] constructed the CSPP-IQA model based on the spatial pyramid without adjusting the input image, which will avoid destroying the original structure and content of the input image.

The main reason why IQA for real distortion has not been well solved is that, first, after the training of CNN is completed, the parameters of the convolution kernel are fixed, and as the data set becomes larger and larger, the image content in it also changes. It is complex and changeable, which limits the generalization performance of the model. Second, the real distortion often exists in the local area of the image, which puts higher requirements on the ability of the model to perceive local distortion. As shown in Fig. 1, since the size of the image input to the CNN for training is fixed, the input image needs to be cropped or deformed. These operations will cause the image to lose part of the area, and the lost part of the area may just exist as local distortion, resulting in an incorrect model evaluation.

In this paper, a real distorted IQA method based on multi-level spatial pyramid pooling is proposed. In general, the main contributions of the proposed model can be divided into the following three folds:

Fig. 1. Problems with existing models.

1. A multi-level spatial pyramid pooling structure named MSPP is proposed. The SPP structure using only three levels inevitably leads to partial loss of semantic information when processing feature maps with larger sizes at the bottom. The undesirable effects from semantic information loss can be reduced by a top-down progressively increasing SPP structure.
2. For the IQA task, an adaptive local distortion perception (ALDP) module based on conditional parameter convolution [17] is proposed, which adaptively adjusts the convolution kernel parameters according to the image content. Meanwhile, the module further enhances the learning capability through residual connectivity.
3. The model uses ResNet50 as the backbone network and uses a feature pyramid network (FPN) [18] structure to better fuse semantic information from the bottom to the top layer, helping the model to better perceive local distortions.

2   The Proposed Model Architecture

The multi-level spatial pyramid pooling-based blind image quality assessment method (MSPP-IQA) for real distortion is proposed in this paper. The method consists of three parts: multi-level semantic feature extraction, semantic feature understanding and quality scoring, as shown in Fig. 2. In the multi-level semantic feature extraction module, ResNet50 is improved as the backbone network for multi-level semantic feature extraction, and the feature maps are output using two paths, bottom-up and top-down, respectively. The multi-level semantic feature maps generated in the middle layer of the image during the transmission of the two paths are fused to obtain four semantic feature streams (U1, U2, U3, U4), and then the proposed adaptive local distortion perception (ALDP) module is used to enhance the distortion perception capability. Afterwards, the obtained features are combined using multi-level spatial pyramid pooling (SPP) to obtain the input features for the quality scoring module. The output of Stage 4 in ResNet50 is used as the input of the semantic feature understanding module, which dynamically generates weights and biases for the quality scoring module that are appropriate to the content of the corresponding image. Finally, the quality scoring module applies these weights and biases to the fully connected layer and predicts the quality score of the real distorted image to be tested.

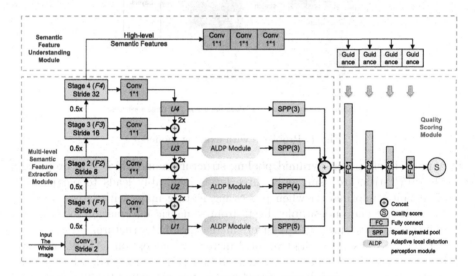

Fig. 2. The framework of the proposed model.

2.1   Multi-level Semantic Feature Extraction Module

The multi-level semantic feature extraction module adopts the deep learning-based semantic feature extraction method, and its performance is much better than the manual feature extraction method. This paper adopts ResNet50 [19] as the backbone model and pre-trains it on ImageNet in advance to optimize various parameters. The multi-level semantic feature extraction module, shown in the lower left part of Fig. 2, uses a combination of bottom-up and top-down approaches to extract feature maps.

For the bottom-up path, the path is part of the feed-forward backbone network. The input whole image, after the first convolutional layer, is downsampled in a way that each passing stage can be regarded as a step of 2. Thus, the output feature stream of Stage1–Stage4 is obtained, noted as $\{F1, F2, F3, F4\}$, which correspond to the downsampling multiples of $\{4, 8, 16, 32\}$ for the input image, respectively. The main reason why the feature streams after the first convolution are not used is that the semantics of the first stage is too low-level. Followed by, to facilitate the subsequent feature fusion, the $F1$-$F4$ are downsampled in parallel using 1×1 convolution to ensure the same dimensionality (set to 256 in this paper), while 1×1 convolution can reduce the model computation as well as enhance the model feature representation.

For the top-down path, the path up-samples the top-level small feature map to the same size as the output feature map of the previous stage. The up-sampling method used in the MSPP-IQA model is nearest-neighbor interpolation, which can preserve the semantic information of the feature map to the maximum extent during the up-sampling process compared to the linear interpolation method, and the feature map generated by the bottom-up path. The feature flow with more semantic information is obtained by fusing it with the feature map generated by the bottom-up path. The specific process is to use 1×1 convolution on $F4$ to obtain $U4$, then upsamples $U4$ and fuses the feature map of $F3$ after 1×1 convolution to obtain $U3$, and repeats the process twice more. The final output $\{F1, F2, F3, F4\}$ is obtained after two paths of the image.

Fig. 3. Adaptive local distortion perception (ALDP) module.

Then, in order to better perceive the distortion in real scenes, an adaptive local distortion perception (ALDP) module is proposed in this paper. As shown in Fig. 3, the module consists of two 1×1 convolutions and a 3×3 conditional parameter convolution. The first 1×1 convolution is used for dimensionality reduction, the second for dimensionality enhancement, and the middle 3×3 conditional parameter convolution (CondConv), which is mainly used to improve the generalization performance of the model by dynamically adapting the convolution kernel parameters to different image contents on the one hand, and to reduce the confounding effect caused by the upsampling process described previously to a certain extent on the other hand. Finally, the features before and after convolution are fused using residual connections to achieve feature enhancement.

In conventional convolution, its convolution kernel parameters are determined by training, which means that the rules for extracting features are the same for different image contents after the training is completed. In contrast, in conditional parameter convolution (CondConv), as shown in Fig. 4, the convolution kernel parameters are adjusted in time according to the image content, and the process can be described as follows:

$$Output(x) = \sigma((\alpha_1 \cdot W_1 + \cdots + \alpha_n \cdot W_n) * x) \qquad (1)$$

where σ denotes the activation function, n is the number of expert blends, W_i is the kernel dimension of the original convolutional layer in the network, and

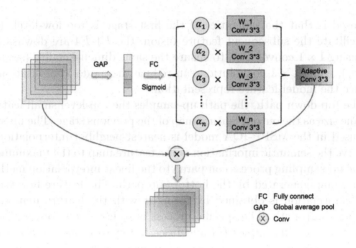

Fig. 4. The structure of CondConv.

$\alpha_i = \gamma_i(x)$ is a scalar weight dependent on the input feature map, computed from a routing function with the learning parameters.

$$\gamma(x) = Sigmoid(GlobalAveragePool(x)R) \qquad (2)$$

In Eq. (2), the global average pooling of the input feature map is done first, and then an n-dimensional vector (corresponding to the weighted values of n experts) is obtained by R (a fully connected layer with n neurons), and finally the values are constrained to [0, 1] by the sigmoid function to be used as the weighted weights of the convolution kernel parameters. The application of conditional convolution is equivalent to a linear combination of multiple expert formulas, which can be expressed as:

$$\sigma((\alpha_1 \cdot W_1 + \cdots + \alpha_n \cdot W_n) * x) = \sigma(\alpha_1(W_1 * x) + \cdots + \alpha_n(W_n * x)) \qquad (3)$$

where each expert corresponds to a traditional static convolution. Thus, conditional convolution has the same capacity as n experts linear mixing, but is more computationally efficient because only one convolution operation is required, and given the computational efficiency, this paper uses a linear combination of four experts instead of the highest 32 experts model used in the literature [17].

For the traditional IQA method, the size of its input image is fixed, so there is a need to crop the image to a fixed size in advance, but this will lead to the loss of some local distortion, and it is possible that the loss is exactly where the local distortion exists. Also, this will largely affect the effect of the model quality assessment, so the quality assessment should target the original distorted image. This paper proposed a convolutional spatial pyramid pooling (named CSPP) structure to replace the common pooling structure in image semantic feature extraction, so that the extracted multi-level semantic features have a fixed size and do not need to be cropped and also can meet the size requirements of the fully connected layer for image size. Then, pooling is performed for $U4$ using the SPP(3) structure. Meanwhile, to ensure that the share of the high-level semantic feature stream $U4$ in all extracted features is sufficiently large, $U3$, $U2$, and $U1$, which have undergone the adaptive local distortion perception module, are pooled using a multi-level spatial pyramid pooling structure in increasing order from top to bottom, SPP(3), SPP(4), and SPP(5), respectively. Figure 5 illustrates the structure of SPP(4). For each region of the feature map, pooling is performed using four pooling methods, the first of which directly pools the entire region; the second divides the region into $2 \times 2 = 4$ parts and pools each part; the third divides the region into $3 \times 3 = 9$ parts and pools each part; the fourth divides the region into $4 \times 4 = 16$ parts and pools each part, and finally the results obtained from the four divisions are stitched together. In this way, regardless of the size of the input feature map, the final feature vector is of fixed length 30×256. By analogy the output of SPP(5) is 55×256. Finally, the output of the Multi-level Semantic Feature Extraction module is obtained by pooling these four semantic feature vectors, denoted as Vec.

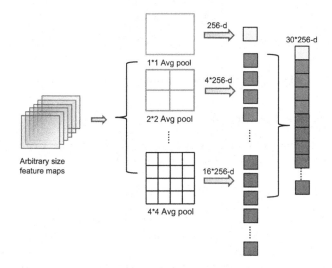

Fig. 5. The structure of SPP(4).

2.2 Semantic Feature Understanding Module

The model strictly follows HVS characteristics. First, the content of images is understood, and then different evaluation rules are customized according to the content of different images. The function of this module is to generate the network parameters θ_I of the quality scoring module, as shown in Eq. (4).

$$\theta_I = T(F_4, \lambda) \tag{4}$$

where T is the mapping from the advanced semantic feature F_4 output by Stage4 to the network parameter θ_I of the scoring module, λ is the network parameter of the semantic features understanding module.

As shown in Fig. 2, the semantic features understanding module is mainly composed of three 1×1 convolutional layers, and four weight generation branches. Its main role is to make sense of the image content and guide the quality scoring module. Since the fully connected layer is used as the basic target network component in the quality scoring module, this module only needs to generate the fully connected layer weights and biases in the quality scoring module. Specifically, as shown in Fig. 6, in the scoring guidance module, both fully connected layer weights and biases are generated by convolution. For the features after three convolutions, a 3×3 convolution is used, followed up by a deformation (Reshape) operation to generate the fully connected layer weights, while for the biases, a 2×2 maximum pooling is first used, followed up by a 1×1 convolution.

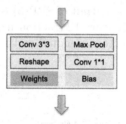

Fig. 6. The structure of scoring guidance module.

2.3   Quality Scoring Module

The task of the quality scoring module is shown in Eq. (5). Vec is the output features vector of multi-level semantic feature extraction module.

$$s = P(Vec, T(F_4, \lambda)) \tag{5}$$

The module consists of four full connection layers. The semantic feature vectors pooled by multi-level spatial pyramids are combined to get Vec, which is used as the input of the quality scoring module. The weight and bias (i.e. network parameter θ_I) of each full connection layer are generated by the scoring guidance module in the semantic feature understanding module. The final module outputs image quality score of the input image.

3   Experiment

3.1   Experimental Dataset

We used five real-world distortion datasets, Live-Challenge [20], KonIQ-10k [21], BID [22], SPAQ [23], FLIVE [24] to evaluate our model.

3.2   Training Strategies

Our experiments are coded using the Pytorch framework, using the windows 10 operating system with a GPU of 2080ti and using the single-size training method in literature [18] for model training. Optimization is performed using Adam, with weight decay set to 5×10^{-4} and learning rate set to 2×10^{-5}. We simultaneously randomly sample and flip each image to enhance the generalization ability of the model. For each training, we randomly select 80% of the images as the training set and 20% as the test set. In the testing process of the model, we take the whole image directly as input, and use SmoothL1Loss as the loss function, which can make the model converge very well, and has the advantages of L2Loss and L1Loss, and its definition is as follows:

$$smooth_{L_1}(x) = \begin{cases} 0.5t^2, & if \ |t| < 1 \\ |t| - 0.5, & otherwise, \end{cases} \tag{6}$$

The t in Eq. (6) is given by the following equation.

$$t = P(Vec, T(F_4, \lambda)) - Q \tag{7}$$

In Eq. (7), P($\cdot$) is the predicted score of the image obtained by the model, and Q is the subjective score of the image.

3.3   Evaluation Metrics

In our experiments, we adopted Spearman's rank-order correlation coefficient (SROCC) and Pearson's linear correlation coefficient (PLCC) as metrics to evaluate model performance. Among them, SROCC evaluates the monotonicity of model prediction, and PLCC evaluates the prediction accuracy of the model.

3.4   Experimental Results

Single Dataset Experiment. The algorithm is tested on the Live-Challenge dataset, KonIQ-10k dataset, BID dataset, SPAQ dataset and FLIVE dataset, respectively. From Table 1, it can be seen that the performance of the proposed algorithm is almost optimal by comparing the traditional hand-extracted feature IQA methods BRISQUE [1], CORNIA [7], ILNIQE [25], HOSA [8], synthetic distortion-based IQA methods BIECON [26], WaDIQaM [27], FRIQUEE [28] and real distortion-based IQA methods SFA [29], PQR [30], DBCNN [14], HyperIQA [15], CSPP-IQA [16]. Moreover, when the training dataset is large, the performance improvement of MSPP-IQA is more obvious compared with other algorithms. The main reason is that firstly, the model can better fuse the underlying and high-level semantic feature information, because the low enough underlying information will be helpful for detecting distortion in local areas. At the same time, with the help of conditional parameter convolution and semantic feature understanding modules, MSPP-IQA can make timely adjustments to the network parameters for different image contents, especially in the case of large datasets.

Table 1. Performance comparison of SROCC and PLCC on single dataset.

Database	Live challenge		KonIQ-10k		BID		SPAQ		FLIVE	
Criterion	SROCC	PLCC	SROCC	PLCC	SROCC	PLCC	SROCC	PLCC	SROCC	PLCC
BRISQUE [1]	0.608	0.629	0.665	0.681	0.574	0.540	0.802	0.806	0.320	0.356
CORNIA [7]	0.629	0.671	0.683	0.713	0.612	0.663	0.709	0.725	0.311	0.349
ILNIQE [25]	0.432	0.508	0.507	0.523	0.516	0.554	0.713	0.721	0.332	0.335
HOSA [8]	0.640	0.678	0.671	0.694	0.721	0.736	0.721	0.733	0.338	0.354
BIECON [26]	0.595	0.613	0.618	0.651	0.439	0.576	0.702	0.722	0.301	0.336
WaDIQaM [27]	0.671	0.680	0.797	0.805	0.725	0.742	0.837	0.845	0.452	0.433
FRIQUEE [28]	0.682	0.705	0.808	0.811	0.728	0.739	0.819	0.830	0.434	0.428
SFA [29]	0.812	0.833	0.685	0.872	0.826	0.840	0.906	0.907	0.542	0.626
PQR [30]	0.857	0.882	0.880	0.884	0.830	0.852	0.902	0.913	0.547	0.635
DBCNN [14]	0.851	0.869	0.875	0.884	0.845	0.859	0.910	0.913	0.554	0.652
HyperIQA [15]	0.859	0.882	0.906	0.917	0.869	0.878	0.916	0.919	0.535	0.623
CSPP-IQA [16]	0.882	0.898	0.912	0.921	0.875	**0.891**	0.916	0.922	0.556	0.649
MSPP-IQA	**0.895**	**0.913**	**0.919**	**0.931**	**0.876**	0.889	**0.921**	**0.927**	**0.560**	**0.667**

Generalization Performance Experiments. To test the generalization performance of the model, different datasets were used for training and testing in this paper, as shown in Table 2, where Live-C represents the dataset Live-Challenge and KonIQ represents the KonIQ-10k dataset. Compared with PQR, HyperIQA and DBCNN, the proposed algorithm is optimal. By using the feature pyramid network, more semantic feature information can be extracted, and with the convolution of conditional parameters, the algorithm model ensures better scoring accuracy with better generalization performance in the case of complex and variable image contents.

Table 2. SROCC performance comparison of model generalization ability.

Train	Tset	PQR	DBCNN	HyperIQA	CSPP-IQA	MSPP-IQA
Live-C	KonIQ	0.757	0.754	0.772	0.788	**0.803**
Live-C	BID	0.714	0.762	0.756	0.763	**0.782**
KonIQ	Live-C	0.770	0.755	0.785	0.797	**0.815**
KonIQ	BID	0.755	0.816	0.819	0.808	**0.931**

Conditional Parameter Convolution (CondConv). The MSPP-IQA model proposed in this paper uses a linear combination of four experts in the adaptive local distortion perception module, and to verify its effectiveness, it is performed using 1, 2, 4, 8 experts in the Live-Challenge, BID, KonIQ-10k, and SPAQ datasets, respectively, and the experimental results are shown in Fig. 7. According to the analysis of Fig. 7, in the case of small datasets (Live-Challenge and BID), the overall performance of the model improves with the increase of the number of experts, especially when the number of experts is increased from 1 to 2 and from 2 to 4, while the performance of the model is only slightly improved from 4 to 8. When the data set is large (KonIQ-10k and SPAQ), the

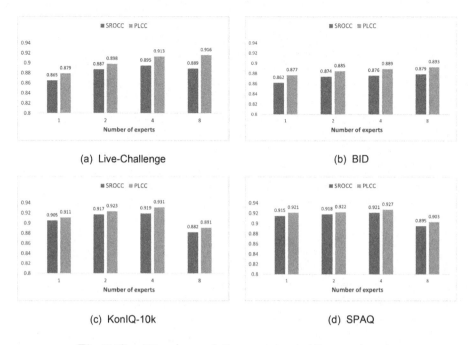

(a) Live-Challenge

(b) BID

(c) KonIQ-10k

(d) SPAQ

Fig. 7. Conditional convolution expert quantity experiment.

performance drops sharply when the number of experts is increased from 4 to 8. The reason is that when the data set is large and the image size is large, the tensor generated by the model after the input image is too large, and the experts use full connectivity in generating the weight parameters, which leads to a larger number of model parameters. This makes the model difficult to converge and eventually leads to poor scoring performance.

MOS and Predicted MOS Scatter Plot. We draw scatter plots for BIECON, FRIBQUEE, DBCNN, CSPP-IQA, HyperIQA and the MSPP-IQA method mentioned in this article, and the scatter plot can more intuitively show the performance of the model. In the scatter plot, the more the scatter points are clustered around the red fitted line, the better the model is. As shown in Fig. 8, the abscissa is the real MOS value, and the ordinate is the predicted MOS value obtained by the objective model. It can be seen that the scatter plot in Fig. 8(f) is more clustered than other methods, which indicates that our proposed model has better performance.

Algorithm Scoring Accuracy Comparison. In this section, we randomly select 5 images from the SPAQ dataset, as shown in Fig. 9. Three methods of BIECON, DBCNN, HyperIQA and CSPP-IQA are selected to compare with the MSPP-IQA method in this paper. The comparison results are shown in Table 3. It can be seen that the predicted score of our MSPP-IQA method for each image

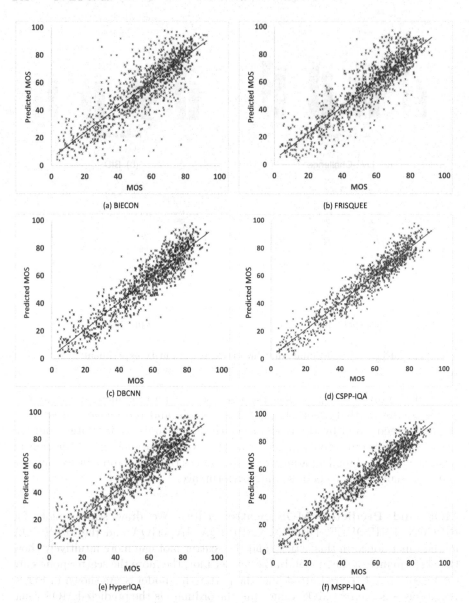

Fig. 8. Scatter plot of predicted MOS results of different IQA algorithms.

is closer to the real MOS value in the second row. Compared to other methods, our MSPP-IQA method better understands image content including animals, people, landscapes, buildings, etc., and thus predicts more realistic scores.

Ablation Study. To verify the effectiveness of the various components of the model proposed in this paper, an ablation study was conducted on the Live-

Table 3. Comparison of prediction MOS of several IQA algorithms.

Image number	(a)	(b)	(c)	(d)	(e)
MOS	49.73	82.38	85.33	91.95	75.50
BIECON [26]	28.79	89.36	75.99	83.78	59.20
DBCNN [14]	32.43	70.33	91.49	81.74	56.32
HyperIQA [15]	43.50	86.45	**86.77**	88.46	71.86
CSPP-IQA [16]	45.62	79.37	89.28	88.55	73.49
MSPP-IQA	**52.83**	**79.83**	83.24	**92.50**	**74.91**

Challenge and KonIQ-10k datasets. As shown in Table 4, adding the SPP structure alone to the base method HyperIQA, it can be seen that the performance of SROCC improves by 1.5% and that of PLCC improves by 0.7% on the Live-Challenge dataset. On the KonIQ-10k dataset, SROCC and PLCC improve by 0.4% and 0.5%, respectively. The last row indicates the complete effect of our model. Compared with the HyperIQA structure, SROCC and PLCC improve by 3.6% and 3.1% on the Live-Challenge dataset, and by 1.3% and 1.4% on the KonIQ-10k dataset, and the experimental structure fully validates the effectiveness of each part of our model.

(a)   (b)   (c)   (d)   (e)

Fig. 9. Randomly selected pictures in SPAQ.

Table 4. Ablation study results.

Dataset	Live challenge		KonIQ-10k	
Components	SROCC	PLCC	SROCC	PLCC
HyperIQA	0.859	0.882	0.906	0.917
HyperIQA+SPP	0.874	0.889	0.910	0.912
MSPP-IQA	**0.895**	**0.913**	**0.919**	**0.931**

4   Conclusion

In this paper, a multi-level spatial pyramid pooling-based blind image quality evaluation method (MSPP-IQA) for realistic distortion is presented. The method first uses ResNet50 as the backbone network, then uses a feature pyramid structure for feature fusion, followed immediately by the proposed adaptive local distortion-aware module to enhance the semantic feature information. The module is designed based on conditional parameter convolution to ensure the scoring ability of the model to cope with large datasets, while the learning ability of the model is further improved by means of residual connectivity. At the same time, the model uses the semantic feature understanding module for image content understanding and provides prediction guidance for the scoring module. The proposed method is experimentally validated to have better consistency with subjective assessment than other deep learning-based IQA methods.

References

1. Mittal, A., Moorthy, A.K., Bovik, A.C.: No-reference image quality assessment in the spatial domain. IEEE Trans. Image Process. **21**(12), 4695–4708 (2012)
2. Mittal, A., Soundararajan, R., Bovik, A.C.: Making a "completely blind" image quality analyzer. IEEE Signal Process. Lett. **20**(3), 209–212 (2012)
3. Moorthy, A.K., Bovik, A.C.: A two-step framework for constructing blind image quality indices. IEEE Signal Process. Lett. **17**(5), 513–516 (2010)
4. Moorthy, A.K., Bovik, A.C.: Blind image quality assessment: from natural scene statistics to perceptual quality. IEEE Trans. Image Process. **20**(12), 3350–3364 (2011)
5. Saad, M.A., Bovik, A.C., Charrier, C.: A DCT statistics-based blind image quality index. IEEE Signal Process. Lett. **17**(6), 583–586 (2010)
6. Mahmoudpour, S., Kim, M.: No-reference image quality assessment in complex-shearlet domain. Signal Image Video Process. **10**(8), 1465–1472 (2016). https://linkspringer.53yu.com/
7. Ye, P., Kumar, J., Kang, L., Doermann, D.: Unsupervised feature learning framework for no-reference image quality assessment. In: 2012 IEEE Conference on Computer Vision and Pattern Recognition, pp. 1098–1105. IEEE (2012)
8. Xu, J., Ye, P., Li, Q., Du, H., Liu, Y., Doermann, D.: Blind image quality assessment based on high order statistics aggregation. IEEE Trans. Image Process. **25**(9), 4444–4457 (2016)
9. Lu, F., Zhao, Q., Yang, G.: A no-reference image quality assessment approach based on steerable pyramid decomposition using natural scene statistics. Neural Comput. Appl. **26**(1), 77–90 (2015)
10. Wang, X., Jiang, Q., Shao, F., Gu, K., Zhai, G., Yang, X.: Exploiting local degradation characteristics and global statistical properties for blind quality assessment of tone-mapped hdr images. IEEE Trans. Multimed. **23**, 692–705 (2020)
11. Li, T., Min, X., Zhao, H., Zhai, G., Xu, Y., Zhang, W.: Subjective and objective quality assessment of compressed screen content videos. IEEE Trans. Broadcast. **67**(2), 438–449 (2020)
12. Sun, W., Min, X., Zhai, G., Ma, S.: Blind quality assessment for in-the-wild images via hierarchical feature fusion and iterative mixed database training. arXiv preprint arXiv:2105.14550 (2021)
13. Sun, W., Min, X., Zhai, G., Gu, K., Duan, H., Ma, S.: MC360IQA: a multi-channel CNN for blind 360-degree image quality assessment. IEEE J. Sel. Top. Signal Process. **14**(1), 64–77 (2019). https://ieeexplore.ieee.org/abstract/document/8910364/

14. Zhang, W., Ma, K., Yan, J., Deng, D., Wang, Z.: Blind image quality assessment using a deep bilinear convolutional neural network. IEEE Trans. Circuits Syst. Video Technol. **30**(1), 36–47 (2018)

15. Su, S., et al.: Blindly assess image quality in the wild guided by a self-adaptive hyper network. In: Proceedings of the IEEE/CVF Conference on Computer Vision and Pattern Recognition, pp. 3667–3676 (2020)

16. Chen, J., et al.: CSPP-IQA: a multi-scale spatial pyramid pooling-based approach for blind image quality assessment. Neural Comput. Appl. 1–12 (2022). https://doi.org/10.1007/s00521-022-07874-2

17. Yang, B., Bender, G., Le, Q.V., Ngiam, J.: CondConv: conditionally parameterized convolutions for efficient inference. Adv. Neural Inf. Process. Syst. **32** (2019)

18. Lin, T.Y., Dollár, P., Girshick, R., He, K., Hariharan, B., Belongie, S.: Feature pyramid networks for object detection. In: Proceedings of the IEEE Conference on Computer Vision and Pattern Recognition, pp. 2117–2125 (2017)

19. He, K., Zhang, X., Ren, S., Sun, J.: Deep residual learning for image recognition. In: Proceedings of the IEEE Conference on Computer Vision and Pattern Recognition, pp. 770–778 (2016)

20. Ghadiyaram, D., Bovik, A.C.: Massive online crowdsourced study of subjective and objective picture quality. IEEE Trans. Image Process. **25**(1), 372–387 (2015). https://ieeexplore.ieee.org/abstract/document/7327186/

21. Hosu, V., Lin, H., Sziranyi, T., Saupe, D.: KonIQ-10k: an ecologically valid database for deep learning of blind image quality assessment. IEEE Trans. Image Process. **29**, 4041–4056 (2020)

22. Ciancio, A., da Silva, E.A., Said, A., Samadani, R., Obrador, P., et al.: No-reference blur assessment of digital pictures based on multifeature classifiers. IEEE Trans. Image Process. **20**(1), 64–75 (2010)

23. Fang, Y., Zhu, H., Zeng, Y., Ma, K., Wang, Z.: Perceptual quality assessment of smartphone photography. In: Proceedings of the IEEE/CVF Conference on Computer Vision and Pattern Recognition, pp. 3677–3686 (2020)

24. Ying, Z., Niu, H., Gupta, P., Mahajan, D., Ghadiyaram, D., Bovik, A.: From patches to pictures (PaQ-2-PiQ): mapping the perceptual space of picture quality. In: Proceedings of the IEEE/CVF Conference on Computer Vision and Pattern Recognition, pp. 3575–3585 (2020)

25. Zhang, L., Zhang, L., Bovik, A.C.: A feature-enriched completely blind image quality evaluator. IEEE Trans. Image Process. **24**(8), 2579–2591 (2015)

26. Kim, J., Lee, S.: Fully deep blind image quality predictor. IEEE J. Sel. Top. Signal Process. **11**(1), 206–220 (2016)

27. Bosse, S., Maniry, D., Müller, K.R., Wiegand, T., Samek, W.: Deep neural networks for no-reference and full-reference image quality assessment. IEEE Trans. Image Process. **27**(1), 206–219 (2017)

28. Ghadiyaram, D., Bovik, A.C.: Perceptual quality prediction on authentically distorted images using a bag of features approach. J. Vis. **17**(1), 32 (2017)

29. Li, D., Jiang, T., Lin, W., Jiang, M.: Which has better visual quality: the clear blue sky or a blurry animal? IEEE Trans. Multimedia **21**(5), 1221–1234 (2018)

30. Zeng, H., Zhang, L., Bovik, A.C.: A probabilistic quality representation approach to deep blind image quality prediction. arXiv preprint arXiv:1708.08190 (2017)

Subjective and Objective Emotional Consistency Assessment for UGC Short Videos

Yubo Gui, Yucheng Zhu, Guangtao Zhai, and Ning Liu[✉]

Institute of Image Communication and Network Engineering,
Shanghai Jiao Tong University, Shanghai 200240, China
{guiyubo,ningliu}@sjtu.edu.cn

Abstract. Short video is one of the most popular forms of user generated contents and it is also a carrier of people's emotion. However, researches on the emotional consistency between audio and video are limited, and there is also a lack of relevant datasets. In this paper, we propose a multi-model fusion system for assessing emotional consistency between different types of action videos and audios with different emotions. We also build a new dataset and compare the early fusion and late fusion methods on this dataset. We use video features extracted by a pre-trained C3D network and audio features extracted by Librosa, a tool for audio analysis. In early fusion method, we concatenate video features and audio features and train a SVM with a linear kernel using the fused features. In late fusion method, video features and audio features are used for training separately to get their own decisions. Then we fuse these two kinds of decisions to get the classification result. Our best classifier attained 85.56% accuracy.

Keywords: Emotional consistency · Emotion recognition · 3D convolutional Network · Model fusion

1 Introduction

Music has played an important role since it was born [1,2]. With the advent of the information society, this importance has increased. It is deeply associated with our daily life and scientific research. When listening to music, people's emotion always changes accordingly. This emotional change may be related to the timbre, lyrics, rhythm of the music.

Emotion is described using dimensional space in dimensional approach. Russell [3] proposed a 2 dimension emotion model, one dimension is valence and the other dimension is arousal; The 2D emotion model is used in [4–6]. 3D emotion model is Pleasure-Arousal-Dominance (PAD). It was used in [7,8].

Short video is one of the most popular forms of entertainment nowadays. In fact, like music, short video is also a carrier of people's emotion. There are many types of short videos, in this paper we limit short videos' range to action videos.

Action short videos have a high proportion of short videos, and compared with other types of short videos, the video content and background music of action short videos are more emotionally consistent.

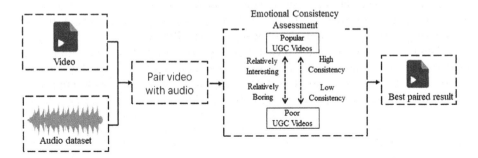

Fig. 1. We pair the video with audios in the audio dataset and then assess the emotional consistency score. Finally we get the short video with the best paired result.

We find that when watching different types of action videos, our emotion also changes accordingly. If a short video selects a suitable background music, we consider this short video has a high audio-video emotional consistency. It is necessary to propose a system to evaluate the emotional consistency between audio and video. It can help us choose a suitable background music for a short action video. Figure 1 shows us the process of using this system to make short videos.

The major challenge in emotional consistency assessing is the lack of dataset. The video content in the existing short video emotion datasets does not meet our requirements. Most of the content is about various speech and dialogue videos and the focus is on human facial expressions [9–11]. The video content required for this experiment is a variety of actions. Therefore, we first need to build a new dataset for our experiment.

In this paper, we propose a multi-model fusion architecture for audio and video emotional consistency evaluation. A pre-trained C3D model on sprots-1M [12] is used to extract video features. Librosa [13] is a tool for audio analysis. It is used to extract low level descriptors(LLDs) features and Mel Frequency Cepstral Coefficients (MFCC) features of audio. Similarly, we also train 2 CNNs to further extract features from MFCC. In early fusion experiment, we concatenate audio features and video features and train a SVM with a linear kernel as the classifier using concatenated features. In late fusion experiment, we train different SVMs with linear kernel using audio features and video features separately to get audio and video decisions. Then we fuse the two kinds of decisions to get the final classification result. The main contribution of this paper are listed below:

1. We propose a new labelled dataset for this experiment. It consists of 4260 action short videos, and each short video has three consistency scores ranging from 0 to 2.

2. We propose a multi-model architecture for audio and video emotional consistency assessing on this dataset. And we conducted 2 experiments of early fusion and late fusion respectively under this architecture.

The final results show that both methods achieve a good result on our dataset. In early fusion experiments, our best classifier attained 85.56% accuracy. In late fusion experiments, our best classifier attained 84.72% accuracy.

The rest of the paper is organized as follows. In Sect. 2, details of establishing our dataset are provided. The proposed modeling and prediction framework are described in Sect. 3. Section 4 gives the experimental result of the emotional consistency assessing experiment. Finally, we conclude the paper in Sect. 5.

2   Datasets

2.1   Audio Dataset

Several datasets have previously been proposed for music emotion analysis. Some datasets [14,15] follow the categorical model [16], providing several discrete categories of emotions, and other datasets [6,17] use the dimensional model [3] to represent emotion as a value in 2D valence and arousal space.

DEAM [18] dataset is a MediaEval Database for Emotional Analysis in Music. It consists of 1802 excerpts and full songs. It used the two-dimensional valence-arousal (V-A) model to measure emotions in music. The model (Fig. 1) consists of two independent dimensions of valence (horizontal axis) and arousal (vertical axis). Each song is annotated with valence and arousal values. Both of the two kinds of values range from 1 to 9.

We use K-means [19] to cluster valence and arousal over the whole dataset and choose the best K by Gap statistic [20]. It is defined as:

$$Gap(K) = E(logD_k) - logD_k \tag{1}$$

where D_k is the loss function and $E(logD_k)$ is the expectation of $logD_k$. This value is usually generated by Monte Carlo simulation. We randomly generate as many random samples as the original samples according to the uniform distribution in the area where the samples are located, and perform K-Means on this random sample to obtain D_k. So many times, usually 20 times, we can get 20 values of $logD_k$. Averaging these 20 values gives an approximation of $E(logD_k)$. Finally the Gap Statistic can be calculated. The K corresponding to the maximum value of Gap statistic is the optimal K. The results show that the best effect is when K is 4.

We divide the songs in DEAM into 4 categories according to the clustering results. Then we selected 3 songs that are closest to the center point of the category from each category. The selected 12 songs are used for subsequent pairings with video dataset. The amount of examples in quarters on the A-V emotion plane is presented in Table 1.

Table 1. DEAM dataset content

Arousal-valence	Amount of songs
High-high	412
High-low	491
Low-low	515
Low-high	426

Table 2. Video dataset content

Action type	Amount of videos
Football	15
Basketball	15
Skiing	8
Fitness	8
Skating	8
Horse riding	5
Boating	5
Surfing	5
Others	19
Total	88

2.2 Video Dataset

As we mentioned above, the existing video datasets about video emotion focus on the facial expressions of the people in the video, and classify the video emotion by people's expressions. These datasets don't meet the requirements of this experiment. So we decided to collect new videos. We select videos on Douyin according to the following requirements:

a. The content of video is action.
b. There is no reversal of the video content.
c. The length of the video is more than 10 s.

Following these requirements, we collected a total of 88 original short videos on Douyin. The amount of videos of different action types is displayed in the Table 2. We process these videos first, cut out the useless parts, and cut the longer videos and the videos converted by shots. The number of videos obtained after processing is 355.

2.3 Building Fused Dataset

We paired 12 chosen audios with these 355 processed videos, and got a total of 4260 pairing results. It is shown it Fig. 2. We adjust the audio based on the length

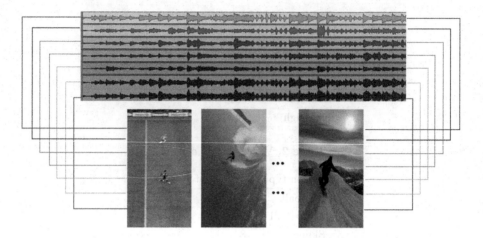

Fig. 2. Fused dataset obtained by pairing audio dataset with video dataset.

of the video when pairing. These paired short videos were divided into 4 parts, each part was annotated by 4 different people with a university education. Each annotator annotated all the dataset, which has a positive effect on the quality of the received data [21]. Consistency scores have three levels from 0 to 2. The scores of these 4 people will be averaged and rounded up as the score for the segment. The annotated criteria are as follows:

a. 2 if the emotions of the audio and video are consistent.
b. 1 if the emotions of the audio and video are irrelevant.
c. 0 if the emotions of the audio and video are conflicting.

When annotating, we do not consider those short videos that create a sense of contrast, but only consider whether the video content and audio emotion are consistent. In this way, our audio and video emotional consistency dataset is established.

3   Proposed Methods

The overview of the system is shown in Fig. 3. The hybrid network has three core parts: audio part, video part and fusion part. In this section we first introduce audio part, We extract two kinds of audio features and obtain audio decisions in this part. Then we introduce video part, We extract video features and obtain video decisions in this part. At last, we give the details of how to do early fusion and late fusion experiments.

3.1   Extracting Audio Features

We first extract audio features of all of the audios in DEAM. We use Librosa to extract audio features. Librosa is a python package for music and audio analysis.

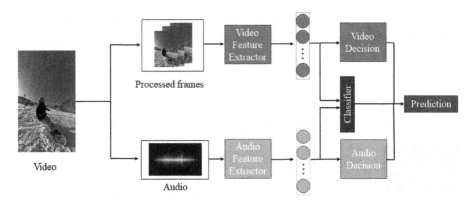

Fig. 3. The overview of the system.

It provides the building blocks necessary to create music information retrieval systems. Every audio we only select its first 15 s for extracting features. We extracted two kinds of audio features in this experiment: LLDs and MFCC.

LLDs include a total of 54-dimensional features including average loudness, barkbands kurtosis, barkbands spread (L), etc. We can directly extract these 54 features using Librosa. Then we trained two SVMs with linear kernel using LLDs features to regress each audio's valence and arousal separately.

When extracting MFCC features, We get the MFCC spectrum first. We set the window size and stride value to 100 milliseconds and finally the size of the MFCC spectrum of each audio is $\{100 \times 13 \times 5\}$.

Because MFCC spectrum is temporal but the video feature is not. So we need to process the MFCC spectrum. We train 2 CNNs to regress audios' valence and arousal separately. The two CNNs can both help us to process MFCC features and get audio decisions. The network model structure is shown in Fig. 4.

We obtain the valence and arousal of the audios predicted by the two kinds of audio features respectively. Then we calculate the distance from the valence and arousal to classify the audios. The classification results are considered as audio decisions.

Fig. 4. CNN architecture using MFCC spectrum.

In addition, we extract the output of the respective fc3 layers of the two CNN networks, a 2048-dimensional vector. Concatenate the two vectors to get the new audio features extracted by MFCC. We end up with these two kinds of audio features: LLDs (54) and MFCC (4096). The overview of the audio part is shown in Fig. 5.

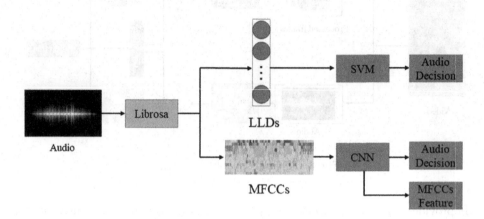

Fig. 5. The overview of the audio part.

3.2 Video Part

In recent years, C3D plays an important role in dealing with many video analysis tasks. C3D features have a good performance on various video analysis tasks [22,23] but a few works are given for video-based emotion recognition using CNN or RNN structures in recent papers [24,25]. The 3D convolutional framework is shown in Fig. 6. The input size of the frames is $\{H \times W \times L\}$. For the convolution layers, the kernel size is $\{K \times K\}$, and the kernel temporal depth is d.

In this experiment, We fine-tuned the pretrained sports-1m C3D model to help us extract video features. This C3D architecture has 8 convolutions, 5 maxpoolings, and 2 fully connected layers, followed by a softmax output layer.

Our video dataset needs to be processed to input to C3D network. Firstly, we should choose 16 frames from each video. We calculate the step size according to the total number of frames of the video to select the 16 frames equidistantly. Then, the selected 16 frames are compressed to a size of $\{116 \times 116\}$. We input the sequence of 16 frames into C3D network and get the output of fc6 layer as the video feature which is a vector of length 4096.

We also need to train a network to get video decisions. Video decisions dataset comes from our fused dataset. We average the consistency scores of the three songs under the same category for each video. Then take the nearest integer as the video's score on that category of music. Then a video gets 4 average scores. These 4 scores are considered as this video's decision. It is defined as:

$$S_n^a = round(\frac{a_0 + a_1 + a_2}{3}) \tag{2}$$

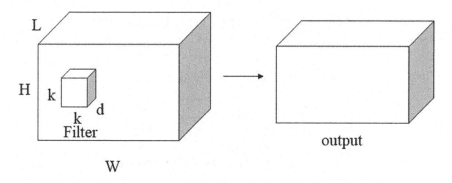

Fig. 6. 3D convolution on multiple frames.

where S_n^a is the The score of video n on the emotional category of a and a_0, a_1 and a_2 are the scores of the video with the three songs we chosen in a.

After extracting video features representation by the feature extraction module, we need to map these features to the 4 average scores with a regression model. In this paper, we use two fully connected (FC) layers as the regression model. The two FC layers consist of 4096 and 4 neurons respectively. Therefore, we can obtain the score via

$$s = W_{FC}(f) \tag{3}$$

where W_{FC} denotes the function of the two FC layers and s is the 4 scores of the video.

3.3 Fused Part

We now have two kinds of audio features and one kind of video feature and the respective decision for each kind of feature. In this part we fuse features and decisions to get the final results. There are two types of fusion: early fusion and late fusion.

In early fusion experiment, we fused audio features and video features. Because we have two kinds of audio features, we first concatenate each kind of audio feature with the video feature separately, then concatenate three kinds of features in series. Then we get three kinds of fused features. We train different SVMs with linear kernel as classifier using these 3 kinds of fused features.

In late fusion experiment, we fuse the audio decision and video decision to get the final result. Audio decision is the classification result of each audio. Video decision is the score of the video on four categories. Fusing these two decisions then we get the final classification result.

4   Experimental Results

In early fusion experiments, our results are the final classification results obtained using the fused features. We evaluated the effect of various combinations of feature sets: LLDs audio features (LLDs), audio features extracted by MFCC (MFCC) and C3D video features (C3D).

Table 3. Accuracy of early fusion result.

	Features	Accuracy
Early fusion	C3D+LLDs	61.32
	C3D+MFCC	82.47
	C3D+LLDs+MFCC	**85.56**

The obtained results, presented in Table 3, indicate that the use of three kinds of features resulted in the best performance. But it is very close to the result of using the set C3D+MFCC. We can see that audio features extracted using MFCC play a bigger role in early fusion experiments. This may be because this feature extraction method is closer to the video feature extraction method. Features are extracted by convolutional layers and fully connected layers.

In late fusion experiment, We first got the audio decision and the video decision. Each decision is a classification task and the results are shown in Table 4. We then fuse these two kinds of audio decisions and video decisions to get the final classification result (Table 5).

Table 4. Accuracy of different decisions

	Features	Accuracy
Audio features	LLDs	67.26
	MFCC	65.37
Video features	C3D	82.91

Table 5. Accuracy of late fusion result.

	Features	Accuracy
Late fusion	C3D+LLDs	83.34
	C3D+MFCC	78.53
	C3D+LLDs+MFCC	**84.72**

In addition, we also compare the effect of the audio model part of the late fusion experiment with some previous studies on musical emotion. It is shown in Table 6.

Table 6. Comparisons with past studies.

Method	Dataset	Emotion class	Score
RNN [26]	LastFM [27]	4	0.542 (accuracy)
SVM [28]	Own	4	0.764 (F1-score)
Our (LLDs+SVM)	DEAM	4	0.732 (accuracy)

Compared with existing research on music emotion classification, our audio part of the experiment may lack information about audio lyrics related aspects, which is also determined by our dataset. Because the audios we use for pairing are mostly absolute music and lack lyrics, this will also lead to a decrease in the final classification result.

We can see that the experimental results of early fusion are significantly better than late fusion. This may be due to the performance of our audio classification part. Emotion description is inherently subjective because the context of music corresponds to the associated emotion. In the early fusion experiments, we fused audio features and video features for training, focusing more on discovering the relationship between the two kinds of features. In this way we can avoid this problem and achieve better results.

5   Conclusion

Computing the emotional consistency of audio and video is extremely useful for both personal use and industrial applications. But few work has be done in this field. The reason may be the lack of related datasets and the difficulty of annotations.

In this paper, we jointly established an audio-video emotional consistency dataset by using the DEAM audio dataset and the video dataset we collected on Douyin. On this dataset we propose an architecture for multimodal fusion. We use Librosa to extract two kinds of audio features, LLDs and MFCC Spectrum features. Then we trained SVMs with linear kernel to get audio decisions. We use pre-trained C3D to extract video features and trained a FC to get the video decision. In early fusion experiments, we train a SVM using fused features for classification. In late fusion experiments, we fuse audio and video decisions to get classification results. The obtained results show that our experiment has achieved good results. It is believed that this experiment will also promote the development of the short video industry.

Acknowledgements. This work was supported by the National Natural Science Foundation of China (62101326, 62225112, 61831015, and 62271312), National Key R&D Program of China (2021YFE0206700), and China Postdoctoral Science Foundation (2022M712090).

References

1. Montagu, J.: How music and instruments began: a brief overview of the origin and entire development of music, from its earliest stages. Front. Sociol. **2**, 8 (2017)
2. Hallam, S., Cross, I., Thaut, M.: Oxford Handbook of Music Psychology. Oxford University Press, Oxford (2011)
3. Russell, J.A.: A circumplex model of affect. J. Pers. Soc. Psychol. **39**(6), 1161 (1980)
4. Grekow, J.: Music emotion maps in arousal-valence space. In: Saeed, K., Homenda, W. (eds.) CISIM 2016. LNCS, vol. 9842, pp. 697–706. Springer, Cham (2016). https://doi.org/10.1007/978-3-319-45378-1_60
5. Schmidt, E.M., Turnbull, D., Kim, Y.E.: Feature selection for content-based, time-varying musical emotion regression. In: Proceedings of the International Conference on Multimedia Information Retrieval, pp. 267–274 (2010)
6. Yang, Y.H., Lin, Y.C., Su, Y.F., Chen, H.H.: A regression approach to music emotion recognition. IEEE Trans. Audio Speech Lang. Process. **16**(2), 448–457 (2008)
7. Deng, J.J., Leung, C.H.: Dynamic time warping for music retrieval using time series modeling of musical emotions. IEEE Trans. Affect. Comput. **6**(2), 137–151 (2015)
8. Lin, Y., Chen, X., Yang, D.: Exploration of music emotion recognition based on MIDI. In: ISMIR, pp. 221–226 (2013)
9. Dhall, A., Goecke, R., Lucey, S., Gedeon, T.: Collecting large, richly annotated facial-expression databases from movies. IEEE Multimed. **19**(03), 34–41 (2012)
10. Douglas-Cowie, E., et al.: The HUMAINE database: addressing the collection and annotation of naturalistic and induced emotional data. In: Paiva, A.C.R., Prada, R., Picard, R.W. (eds.) ACII 2007. LNCS, vol. 4738, pp. 488–500. Springer, Heidelberg (2007). https://doi.org/10.1007/978-3-540-74889-2_43
11. Sneddon, I., McRorie, M., McKeown, G., Hanratty, J.: The belfast induced natural emotion database. IEEE Trans. Affect. Comput. **3**(1), 32–41 (2011)
12. Karpathy, A., Toderici, G., Shetty, S., Leung, T., Sukthankar, R., Fei-Fei, L.: Large-scale video classification with convolutional neural networks. In: Proceedings of the IEEE Conference on Computer Vision and Pattern Recognition, pp. 1725–1732 (2014)
13. McFee, B., et al.: librosa: audio and music signal analysis in python. In: Proceedings of the 14th Python in Science Conference, vol. 8 (2015)
14. Eerola, T., Vuoskoski, J.K.: A comparison of the discrete and dimensional models of emotion in music. Psychol. Music **39**(1), 18–49 (2011)
15. Aljanaki, A., Wiering, F., Veltkamp, R.C.: Studying emotion induced by music through a crowdsourcing game. Inf. Process. Manag. **52**(1), 115–128 (2016)
16. Ekman, P.: Basic emotions. Handb. Cogn. Emot. **98**(45–60), 16 (1999)
17. Aljanaki, A., Yang, Y.H., Soleymani, M.: Developing a benchmark for emotional analysis of music. PLoS One **12**(3), e0173392 (2017)
18. Soleymani, M., Aljanaki, A., Yang, Y.: DEAM: mediaeval database for emotional analysis in music (2016)
19. Hartigan, J.A., Wong, M.A.: Algorithm as 136: a k-means clustering algorithm. J. Roy. Stat. Soc. Ser. C (Appl. Stat.) **28**(1), 100–108 (1979)
20. Tibshirani, R., Walther, G., Hastie, T.: Estimating the number of clusters in a data set via the gap statistic. J. Roy. Stat. Soc.: Ser. B (Stat. Methodol.) **63**(2), 411–423 (2001)

21. Aljanaki, A., Yang, Y.H., Soleymani, M.: Emotion in music task: lessons learned. In: MediaEval. Citeseer (2016)
22. Tran, D., Bourdev, L., Fergus, R., Torresani, L., Paluri, M.: Learning spatiotemporal features with 3D convolutional networks. In: Proceedings of the IEEE International Conference on Computer Vision, pp. 4489–4497 (2015)
23. Liu, Z., Chai, X., Liu, Z., Chen, X.: Continuous gesture recognition with hand-oriented spatiotemporal feature. In: Proceedings of the IEEE International Conference on Computer Vision Workshops, pp. 3056–3064 (2017)
24. Liu, M., Wang, R., Li, S., Shan, S., Huang, Z., Chen, X.: Combining multiple kernel methods on Riemannian manifold for emotion recognition in the wild. In: Proceedings of the 16th International Conference on Multimodal Interaction, pp. 494–501 (2014)
25. Ebrahimi Kahou, S., Michalski, V., Konda, K., Memisevic, R., Pal, C.: Recurrent neural networks for emotion recognition in video. In: Proceedings of the 2015 ACM on International Conference on Multimodal Interaction, pp. 467–474 (2015)
26. Jakubik, J., Kwaśnicka, H.: Music emotion analysis using semantic embedding recurrent neural networks. In: 2017 IEEE International Conference on INnovations in Intelligent SysTems and Applications (INISTA), pp. 271–276. IEEE (2017)
27. Çano, E., Morisio, M., et al.: Music mood dataset creation based on last. FM tags. In: 2017 International Conference on Artificial Intelligence and Applications, Vienna, Austria, pp. 15–26 (2017)
28. Panda, R., Malheiro, R., Paiva, R.P.: Novel audio features for music emotion recognition. IEEE Trans. Affect. Comput. **11**(4), 614–626 (2018)

Few-Reference Image Quality Assessment with Multiple Information Measurement Fusion

Shuang Shi[1,2,3,4,5], Simeng Wang[1,2,3,4,5], Yuchen Liu[1],
Chengxu Zhou[1,2,3,4,5,6,7(✉)], and Ke Gu[1,2,3,4,5]

[1] Faculty of Information Technology, Beijing University of Technology,
Beijing, China
zhouchengxu@lnut.edu.cn

[2] Engineering Research Center of Intelligent Perception and Autonomous Control,
Ministry of Education, Beijing, China

[3] Beijing Laboratory of Smart Environmental Protection, Beijing, China

[4] Beijing Key Laboratory of Computational Intelligence and Intelligent System,
Beijing, China

[5] Beijing Artificial Intelligence Institute, Beijing, China

[6] School of Electronic and Information Engineering,
Liaoning University of Technology, Jinzhou, Liaoning, China

[7] Key Laboratory of Intelligent Control and Optimization for Industrial Equipment
of Ministry of Education, Dalian University of Technology, Dalian, China

Abstract. In the era of media information explosion, there is an urgent
need for a fast and reliable image quality assessment (IQA) model to
improve the actual application effect of images. To this end, we propose
the multiple information measurement fusion metric (MMFM), which
innovatively combines two types of information measures (IMs), i.e., local
IM and global IM, using only a small number of references for IQA. First,
inspired by the free energy theory, we combine 2-dimensional autoregressive model with sparse random sampling method as an inference engine
on an input image to generate its associated predicted image. Second,
by the inspiration of pixel-wise measurement, we obtain the local IM
by calculating the information entropy of the residual error between the
input image and its corresponding predicted one. Third, motivated by
the histogram-based measurement, we acquire the global IM by computing the two kinds of divergences between the input image and its
predicted one. Fourth, we systematically fuse three components, independently including one distance of local IM between the reference and
corrupted images and two distances of global IMs between the reference

This work was supported in part by the Beijing Natural Science Foundation under
Grant JQ21014; in part by the National Science Foundation of China under Grant
62273011 and Grant 62076013; in part by the Industry-University-Research Innovation
Fund for Chinese University - Blue Point Distributed Intelligent Computing Project
under 2021LDA03003; in part by the Ministry of Education of China under Grant
202102535002, Grant 202102535012; in part by the Key Laboratory of Intelligent Control and Optimization for Industrial Equipment of Ministry of Education, Dalian University of Technology under Grant LICO2022TB03.

and corrupted images, based on a linear function to derive the final IQA result. The results of experiment on the most popular LIVE database show that our designed algorithm with only one number used as few reference has achieved well performance as compared with several mainstream IQA models.

Keywords: Free energy theory · Image quality assessment · Few reference · Information measurement fusion

1 Introduction

Currently, the speed of information dissemination is extremely fast by various media, enabling everyone to obtain a huge number of images or video frames every minute. A vast quantity of visual data is easily corrupted by aliasing, blurring, noise, etc., in the process of generation, storage, transmission and consumption. In this case, it is too costly and inefficient to rely on a large amount of human labor for monitoring and controlling the quality of an image or a video frame. Therefore, an automatic system that can quickly and accurately evaluate visual data is urgently needed [1]. The image quality assessment (IQA) approach is considered as the best solution confronting this situation, which adopts computer techniques has excellent perception ability to obtain visual quality.

Generally, the IQA methods are divided into objective and subjective assessment methods [2–5]. The subjective IQA method is an accurate evaluation method that plays an important role, since it can provide the testing data and its truth quality scores (such as LIVE [6]) for corroborating the precision of objective IQA methods. However, subjective IQA method highly relies on human observers, and thus is laborious, time-wasting, high-costing and cannot be used in real-time applications. So, there is a growing promotion of the objective IQA methods to speed up and precisely evaluate the image quality by adopting multifarious mathematical models. Based on the utilization of the original image information, the objective IQA methods are further divided into three classes, that is full-reference (FR), reduced-reference (RR) and no-reference (NR). The FR IQA method is supposed to utilize complete original image information, like famous mean squared error (MSE), structural similarity index (SSIM) [7], feature similarity (FSIM) [8], etc. In the existing researches [9–20], the primary designing principle of the most FR IQA methods is based on extreme sensitivity of the human visual system (HVS) to the degradation of image structure. Nevertheless, we cannot guarantee that the entire original image information is always available, which makes the application scopes of FR methods greatly narrow. The RR IQA methods [21–26] use a portion of the referenced image information and the NR methods [15,27–38] rely on statistical rules without using any original information, attracting more and more attention. It is worth noting that the free energy-based IQA algorithm can highly simulate the process of human visual perception, so it has been widely studied by peers. For instance, the free energy based distortion metric (FEDM) gets inspirations from the free energy theory to estimate the human internal generative (IG) model [39,40].

Although a great quantity of IQA algorithms were proposed, only a minority of algorithms (such as MSE and SSIM) can be commendably embedded into pre-existing image/video image processing systems due to the restriction of computational complexity, portability and the demand of the whole referenced image [41]. Aiming at these limitations, we designed a valid IQA method, named multiple information measurement fusion metric (MMFM), considering both local and global information metrics (IMs). The designed MMFM has the characteristics of stronger portability and less computation, deserving great potential of development and wide application prospects. It is worth emphasizing that MMFM can be considered as a reference-free IQA model, since it just requires one number as an RR IQA feature and this number can be precisely encoded in a header file with relatively minor bits.

The remainder of this paper is arranged as follows. In Sect. 2, we present five specific steps of the MMFM model in detail. In Sect. 3, we conduct comparative experiments with typical FR and RR algorithms on the famous LIVE database. The results show that the proposed algorithm has comparable performance with some mainstream FR and RR algorithms. In Sect. 4, we introduce the areas where the model can be applied. In Sect. 5, we finally summarize all the work.

2   Methodology

In most cases, humans can perceive visual signals through specific mechanisms, which have been shown to be strongly associated with neural circuits in the primate visual cortex. This paper fuses a local IM and two global IMs to obtain MMFM. Its framework is shown in Fig. 1. The main rationale behind the proposed MMFM is that the image with more valuable information can help for evaluating image quality.

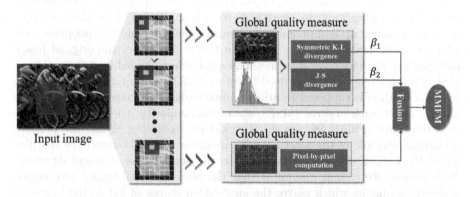

Fig. 1. Basic framework of our designed MMFM model.

2.1   Free Energy Measurement

The most mainstream IQA models focus on extracting low-level features, including structural information, image gradient, and phase congruency. We have faith that the image quality is highly related with the human brain's perception mechanisms on the psychological and physiological. During the past few years, Friston came up with a landmark theory called the free energy theory based on human perception, demonstrating multiple brain principles including human perception, thinking, behavior and learning from biological and physical scientific perspectives. The free energy theory depends on the IG model control to achieve accurate cognition, which is very like the Bayesian brain hypothesis extensively used in ensemble learning [42]. Specifically, the IG model indicates that the human brain can understand, interpret and forecast those external visual scenes in a constructive way. In effect, the IG model is a probabilistic model containing a likelihood term and a prior term, which can be utilized to categorize the input images into ordered part and unordered part. For the follow-up work, the two parts can be well embedded into the process of analysis, detection, and identification, etc.

First, we consider the internal generative model G as a parameterized model of visual perception. The IG model can explain the perceptual scenes by changing the vector $\mathbf{m}$ of parameters. The "surprise" of an input image I is assessed by joint distribution $J(I, \mathbf{m}|G)$ integral on the model parameters $\mathbf{m}$:

$$-\log J(I|G) = -\log \int J(I, \mathbf{m}|G) d\mathbf{m}. \tag{1}$$

Then, we add an auxiliary term $A(\mathbf{m}|I)$ into Eq. (1) to obtain:

$$-\log J(I|G) = -\log \int A(\mathbf{m}|I) \frac{J(I, \mathbf{m}|G)}{A(\mathbf{m}|I)} d\mathbf{m}. \tag{2}$$

By utilizing Jensen's inequality, Eq. (2) can be rewritten as

$$-\log J(I) \leq -\int A(\mathbf{m}|I) \log \frac{J(I, \mathbf{m})}{A(\mathbf{m}|I)} d\mathbf{m}. \tag{3}$$

So, the right-hand side of Eq. (3) is a maximum term called "free energy", which is defined as

$$F(\mathbf{m}) = -\int A(\mathbf{m}|I) \log \frac{J(I, \mathbf{m})}{A(\mathbf{m}|I)} d\mathbf{m}. \tag{4}$$

2.2 Sparse Random Sampling

Based on Attias research, the famous linear autoregressive (AR) model can minimize free energy, which is resemblance to the predictive coding [43]. The AR model can approximate a wide range of natural scenes by changing the parameters. Thus, we utilize the AR model to simply represent the IG model of the free energy theory for making analysis of the input image I. The location and value of pixel are defined as a and p_a. The relationship between this pixel information and its surrounding information can be expressed as

$$p_a = \Gamma_\theta(p_a)\mathbf{n} + \sigma_a \tag{5}$$

where $\Gamma_\theta(p_a)$ is an adjacent vector covering its neighborhoods θ pixels in the local $(\theta+1)^{\frac{1}{2}} \times (\theta+1)^{\frac{1}{2}}$ block, $\mathbf{n} = (\mathbf{n}_1, \mathbf{n}_2, ..., \mathbf{n}_\theta)^T$ is a vector of AR coefficients, and σ_a is the white noise with a mean of zero:

$$q_a = \mathbf{n}_{est}\Gamma_\theta(p_a) \tag{6}$$

where q_a is the predicted pixel value corresponded to p_a, and the $\mathbf{n}_{est}$ is the optimal predictive value of AR coefficient for p_a.

To obtain the optimal vector of AR coefficient, we consider the linear system as a matrix way:

$$\mathbf{n}_{est} = \arg\min_{\mathbf{n}} ||\mathbf{y} - \mathbf{Yn}||_2 \tag{7}$$

where $\mathbf{y}$ on behalf of the transpose vector of $(p_a^1, p_a^2,..., p_a^\gamma)$, and $\mathbf{Y}(l,:) = \Gamma_\theta(p_a, l)$, among which $l > 1$, $l \in [1,l]$ is spaced by one.

Then the least square approach is embedded into Eq. (7), and we finally obtain the best AR coefficient as follows:

$$\mathbf{n}_{est} = (\mathbf{Y}^T\mathbf{Y})^{-1}\mathbf{Y}^T\mathbf{y}. \tag{8}$$

The current proposed IQA model on the basis of free energy theory can obtain great performance, but requires a lot of CPU running time. To promote efficiency of implementation, we design a low time-consuming and high performance method by introducing the sparse random sampling method. In this work, the method of sparse random sampling is used to conduct 28 samplings from 1/1,000 pixels to an entire input image. It is particularly worthy to mention that the method of extremely sparse random sampling implements pretty quickly and is able to extensively inserted into the most image processing systems. The preponderance of the method of sparse random sampling makes the proposed IQA model more flexible and practical.

2.3   Local Information Measurement

Motivated by the pixel-wise measurement, we calculate the information entropy of the residual error between the input image and the predicted one. The r_a in the residual map r is related to p_a, which can be obtained by canceling the predicted pixel:

$$r_a = p_a - q_a. \tag{9}$$

To sum up, by calculating the entropy of the residual map, the free energy value F of the input image can be rewritten as

$$F = -\int_b r(b)\log r(b)db \tag{10}$$

where $r(b)$ indicates the probability density of grayscale b. Accordingly, we define the perceptual distance D between the reference image I_R and the corresponding corrupted image I_C. By using Eq. (10), we can obtain:

$$D = |F_R - F_C| \tag{11}$$

where F_R and F_C correspond to the free energy values of I_R and I_C, respectively.

2.4   Global Information Measurement

The entropy of image ignores the influence of pixel position and only considers the distribution of pixel values. The uniform degree of image's histogram distribution reflects the amount of information contained in the image. The image N' with completely uniform histogram distribution contains the most information. As the gap between the histogram of the input image N_I and that of the image N' decreases, the global information of N_I increases.

The difference of histogram information between N_I and N' is computed by

$$\Delta F = F(N_I) - F(N') = \sum N_I(b) \log N_I(b) - \sum N'(b) \log N'(b). \quad (12)$$

Since it cannot explain the interrelation between two images, we select a commonly used distance measure method named the Kullback-Leibler (K-L) divergence. N_O is the histogram of predicted image. The K-L divergence between the given two probability N_I and N_O can be calculated:

$$D_{KL}(N_I, N_O) = - \sum N_O(b) \log N_I(b) + \sum N_I(b) \log N_O(b). \quad (13)$$

By using K-L divergence, the interaction between N_I and N_O is also commendably considered. However, in practical applications, the order of K-L divergence's arguments may cause the results to change substantially [44]. Therefore, we introduce a symmetric variant of asymmetric K-L divergence to measure distance, which can be obtained by:

$$D'_{KL}(N_I, N_O) = \frac{D_{KL}(N_I, N_O) + D_{KL}(N_O, N_I)}{2}. \quad (14)$$

In addition to the symmetric variant of the K-L divergence, many symmetric forms have been proposed, such as Jensen-Shannon (J-S) divergence, arithmetic mean, geometric mean, harmonic mean and so on [40]. In our work, we select the typical J-S divergence because of its symmetric and smooth format:

$$D_{JS}(N_I, N_O) = \frac{D_{KL}(N_I, N) + D_{KL}(N_O, N)}{2} \quad (15)$$

where $N = (N_I + N_O)/2$. The testing results show that J-S divergence and 128-bin histograms can improve the performance by about 2%, in contrast to the symmetric form on the basis of arithmetic geometry and harmonic means.

2.5   Multiple Information Measurement Fusion

It is difficult to acquire ideal results by using one type of IM. In this paper, we systematically introduce one local IM and two global IMs, making the obtained IQA results close to the HVS perception. The final IQA result can be obtained via a linear function:

$$\text{MMFM} = \frac{D + \beta_1 [D'_{KL}(I_R) - D'_{KL}(I_C)] + \beta_2 [D_{JS}(I_R) - D_{JS}(I_C)]}{1 + \beta_1 + \beta_2} \quad (16)$$

with

$$D'_{KL}(I_R) = \frac{D_{KL}(N_R, N_O) + D_{KL}(N_O, N_R)}{2}, \tag{17}$$

$$D'_{KL}(I_C) = \frac{D_{KL}(N_C, N_O) + D_{KL}(N_O, N_C)}{2}, \tag{18}$$

$$D_{JS}(I_R) = \frac{D_{KL}(N_R, N) + D_{KL}(N_O, N)}{2}, \tag{19}$$

$$D_{JS}(I_C) = \frac{D_{KL}(N_C, N) + D_{KL}(N_O, N)}{2}, \tag{20}$$

where N_R and N_D correspond to the histogram of the reference image I_R and the corrupted image I_C respectively. By using the symmetric variant of the K-L divergence, we can obtain: 1) the distance $D'_{KL}(I_R)$ between the referenced image and its corresponding predicted image; 2) the distance $D'_{KL}(I_C)$ between the corrupted image and its corresponding predicted image. By using the J-S divergence, we can acquire: 1) the distance $D_{JS}(I_R)$ between the referenced image and its corresponding predicted image; 2) the distance $D_{JS}(I_C)$ between the corrupted image and its corresponding predicted image. β_1 and β_2 are constants, corresponding to the weight parameters of the symmetric variant of the K-L divergence and J-S divergence, respectively.

3   Experimental Results

We selected four famous IQA models, including PSNR, SSIM, FEDM and SDM, to conduct this experiment on the commonly used LIVE database. The LIVE consists of 29 reference images and 779 corrupted images destroyed by 5 distortion types. According to the suggestion introduced by the VQEG [45], we first adopt the nonlinear regression on the basis of the five-parameter logic function to acquire the objective quality value of the 5 IQA models:

$$\text{quality}(s) = \gamma_1 \left(\frac{1}{2} - \frac{1}{1 + \exp[\gamma_2(e - \gamma_3)]} \right) + \gamma_4 e + \gamma_5 \tag{21}$$

where quality(s) is the mapped value of the input value s. The e represents the value of the predicted image. The free parameters $\{\gamma_1, \gamma_2, ..., \gamma_5\}$ are ascertained in the process of curve fitting. We next exploit Pearson linear correlation coefficient (PLCC), Spearman rank-order correlation coefficient (SROCC), and root mean-squared error (RMSE) to identify the performance of these 5 IQA models on the most regularly utilized LIVE database. The experimental results are shown in Table 1, 2 and 3.

It is obvious that the proposed MMFM has obtained remarkable performance, which is superior to classical FR algorithms and RR algorithms. Beyond that, the proposed MMFM has high portability and low computational complexity, since both JPEG and JP2K compression can run fast and are widely integrated into most existing applications. First, we analyze the performance of MMFM on PLCC. Compared with FR IQA, the average performance of MMFM is only 0.8%

Table 1. PLCC values of typical models and our proposed MMFM model on 5 image subsets of distinct distortion types containing JP2K, JPEG, AGWN, Blur and Fast-fading in the database of LIVE.

Pearson linear correlation coefficient (PLCC)						
Algorithm	JP2K	JPEG	AGWN	Blur	FF	Average
PSNR	0.8896	0.8879	0.9858	0.8753	0.8895	0.8893
SSIM	0.9410	0.9504	0.9695	0.8743	0.9428	0.9356
FEDM	0.9262	0.9211	0.9256	0.7359	0.8532	0.8724
SDM	0.9447	0.9569	0.9789	0.9252	0.9316	0.9475
MMFM	0.9364	0.9353	0.9518	0.7339	0.8525	0.8820

Table 2. SROCC values of typical models and our proposed MMFM model on 5 image subsets of distinct distortion types containing JP2K, JPEG, AGWN, Blur and Fastfading in the database of LIVE.

Spearman rank-order correlation coefficient (SROCC)						
Algorithm	JP2K	JPEG	AGWN	Blur	FF	Average
PSNR	0.8954	0.8809	0.9854	0.7823	0.8907	0.8869
SSIM	0.9355	0.9449	0.9629	0.8944	0.9413	0.9358
FEDM	0.9200	0.9226	0.9152	0.7594	0.8229	0.8681
SDM	0.9439	0.9227	0.9729	0.9342	0.9384	0.9468
MMFM	0.9303	0.9323	0.9243	0.7627	0.8261	0.8751

Table 3. RMSE values of typical models and our proposed MMFM model on 5 image subsets of distinct distortion types containing JP2K, JPEG, AGWN, Blur and Fast-fading in the database of LIVE.

Root mean-squared error (RMSE)						
Algorithm	JP2K	JPEG	AGWN	Blur	FF	Average
PSNR	11.017	14.653	4.7027	11.478	13.015	10.973
SSIM	8.5349	9.9070	6.8533	8.9643	9.4963	8.7512
FEDM	9.5226	12.409	10.613	12.516	15.410	12.094
SDM	8.2737	9.2445	5.7166	7.0095	10.357	8.1202
MMFM	8.8515	11.274	8.5827	12.546	14.890	11.229

behind that of the full reference algorithm PSNR. Compared with RR IQA, the proposed MMFM achieves an average performance gain of 0.9% over FEDM. Then, the performance of MMFM on SROCC is analyzed. Compared to the FR IQA, MMFM is particularly close to the results of PSNR with an average performance, lagging only 1.3% in average performance. With respect to the RR IQA algorithm, the proposed MMFM achieves a maximum of 0.8% average performance gain over FEDM. Finally, we analyze the results obtained on RMSE. Compared with FR IQA, the average performance of MMFM algorithm is 2.3% lower than the PSNR. Compared with RR IQA, the proposed MMFM has a maximum average performance gain of 7.1% over FEDM.

Thus we would like to emphasize that: 1) MMFM obtains desirable results without increasing the computational complexity, 2) MMFM adaptively selects JPEG or JPEG2000 compression depending on the conditions of application, and 3) MMFM requires only one number and encodes that number precisely in the header file, allowing MMFM to be considered as a blind IQA model.

4   Application

Along with the speedy advancement of image processing technology, IQA models using a modest number of parameters can be expanded to various practical application scenarios. These include: 1) The monitoring methods of abnormal conditions, especially smoke monitoring in industrial scenarios, has emerged a lot of research achievements [46–48]. The detection of anomalies is extremely image dependent. The information provided by the images enables the staff to detect the target in time to avoid environmental pollution, safety accidents and a host of other problems. 2) The monitoring and early warning methods of air pollution [49,50] rely on the numerous visual features about the target provided by the images to facilitate real-time pollution monitoring. 3) 3-dimensional vision and display technologies [51] expand the image from a 2D plane to a 3D space, which can give the viewer a sense of immersion. As shown above, IQA has a wide range of applications, and in the future we will consider enhancing our algorithm to expand its applications and reap certain social and economic benefits.

5   Conclusion

In this paper, we have presented a novel IQA algorithm based on the fusion of multiple IMs from the local and global perspective. First, we have combined the AR model with sparse random sampling method to generate the predicted image corresponding to the input image. Second, we have obtained the local IM and two global IMs to measure the difference between the input image and the predicted image. Third, we have utilized the local IM and two global IMs to calculate the difference between the reference and corrupted image, and fuse the three components by a linear function. The final experimental results on the typically utilized LIVE database indicate that the MMFM has obtained competitive performance with the commonly used FR and RR IQA models.

References

1. Bovik, A.C.: Automatic prediction of perceptual image and video quality. Proc. IEEE **101**(9), 2008–2024 (2013)
2. Gu, K., et al.: Saliency-guided quality assessment of screen content images. IEEE Trans. Multimedia **18**(6), 1098–1110 (2016)
3. Gu, K., Wang, S., Zhai, G., Ma, S., Lin, W.: Screen image quality assessment incorporating structural degradation measurement. In: IEEE International Symposium on Circuits and Systems, pp. 125–128 (2015)
4. Sun, W., Gu, K., Ma, S., Zhu, W., Liu, N., Zhai, G.: A large-scale compressed 360-degree spherical image database: from subjective quality evaluation to objective model comparison. In: IEEE International Workshop on Multimedia Signal Processing, pp. 1–6 (2018)
5. Gu, K., Zhai, G., Lin, W., Liu, M.: The analysis of image contrast: from quality assessment to automatic enhancement. IEEE Trans. Cybern. **46**(1), 284–297 (2016)
6. Sheikh, H.R., Wang, Z., Cormack, L., Bovik, A.C.: LIVE image quality assessment database release 2. http://live.ece.utexas.edu/research/quality
7. Wang, Z., Bovik, A.C., Sheikh, H.R., Simoncelli, E.P.: Image quality assessment: from error visibility to structural similarity. IEEE Trans. Image Process. **13**(4), 600–612 (2004)
8. Zhang, L., Zhang, L., Mou, X., Zhang, D.: FSIM: a feature similarity index for image quality assessment. IEEE Trans. Image Process. **20**(8), 2378–2386 (2011)
9. Sheikh, H.R., Bovik, A.C.: Image information and visual quality. IEEE Trans. Image Process. **15**(2), 430–444 (2006)
10. Larson, E.C., Chandler, D.M.: Most apparent distortion: full reference image quality assessment and the role of strategy. J. Electron. Imaging **19**(1), 011006 (2010)
11. Wang, Z., Li, Q.: Information content weighting for perceptual image quality assessment. IEEE Trans. Image Process. **20**(5), 1185–1198 (2011)
12. Wang, Z., Simoncelli, E.P., Bovik, A.C.: Multi-scale structural similarity for image quality assessment. In: IEEE Asilomar Conference on Signals, Systems and Computers, pp. 1398–1402 (2003)
13. Liu, A., Lin, W., Narwaria, M.: Image quality assessment based on gradient similarity. IEEE Trans. Image Process. **21**(4), 1500–1512 (2012)
14. Gu, K., Zhai, G., Yang, X., Chen, L., Zhang, W.: Nonlinear additive model based saliency map weighting strategy for image quality assessment. In: IEEE International Workshop on Multimedia Signal Processing, pp. 313–318 (2012)
15. Xia, Z., Gu, K., Wang, S., Liu, H., Kwong, S.: Toward accurate quality estimation of screen content pictures with very sparse reference information. IEEE Trans. Ind. Electron. **67**(3), 2251–2261 (2020)
16. Wu, J., Lin, W., Shi, G., Liu, A.: Perceptual quality metric with internal generative mechanism. IEEE Trans. Image Process. **22**(1), 43–54 (2013)
17. Gu, K., Zhai, G., Yang, X., Zhang, W.: Self-adaptive scale transform for IQA metric. In: Proceedings of the IEEE International Symposium on Circuits and Systems, pp. 2365–2368 (2013)
18. Wang, S., Gu, K., Zhang, X., Lin, W., Ma, S., Gao, W.: Reduced reference quality assessment of screen content images. IEEE Trans. Circuits Syst. Video Technol. **28**(1), 1–14 (2018)
19. Gu, K., Zhai, G., Yang, X., Zhang, W., Liu, M.: Structural similarity weighting for image quality assessment. In: Proceedings of the IEEE International Conference on Multimedia and Expo Workshops, pp. 1–6 (2013)

20. Chen, W., Gu, K., Min, X., Yuan, F., Cheng, E., Zhang, W.: Partial-reference sonar image quality assessment for underwater transmission. IEEE Trans. Aerosp. and Electron. Syst. **54**(6), 2776–2787 (2018)

21. Zhai, G., Wu, X., Yang, X., Lin, W., Zhang, W.: A psychovisual quality metric in free-energy principle. IEEE Trans. Image Process. **21**(1), 41–52 (2012)

22. Gu, K., Zhai, G., Yang, X., Zhang, W., Liu, M.: Subjective and objective quality assessment for images with contrast change. In: Proceedings of the IEEE International Conference on Image Processing, pp. 383–387 (2013)

23. Narwaria, M., Lin, W., McLoughlin, I.V., Emmanuel, S., Chia, L.T.: Fourier transform-based scalable image quality measure. IEEE Trans. Image Process. **21**(8), 3364–3377 (2012)

24. Gu, K., Zhai, G., Yang, X., Zhang, W.: A new reduced-reference image quality assessment using structural degradation model. In: Proceedings of the IEEE International Symposium on Circuits and Systems, pp. 1095–1098 (2013)

25. Rehman, A., Wang, Z.: Reduced-reference image quality assessment by structural similarity estimation. IEEE Trans. Image Process. **21**(8), 3378–3389 (2012)

26. Soundararajan, R., Bovik, A.C.: RRED indices: reduced-reference entropic differencing for image quality assessment. IEEE Trans. Image Process. **21**(2), 517–526 (2012)

27. Gu, K., Zhai, G., Lin, W., Yang, X., Zhang, W.: No-reference image sharpness assessment in autoregressive parameter space. IEEE Trans. Image Process. **24**(10), 3218–3231 (2015)

28. Mittal, A., Moorthy, A.K., Bovik, A.C.: No-reference image quality assessment in the spatial domain. IEEE Trans. Image Process. **21**(12), 4695–4708 (2012)

29. Gu, K., Zhou, J., Qiao, J., Zhai, G., Lin, W., Bovik, A.C.: No-reference quality assessment of screen content pictures. IEEE Trans. Image Process. **26**(8), 4005–4018 (2017)

30. Gu, K., Lin, W., Zhai, G., Yang, X., Zhang, W., Chen, C.W.: No-reference quality metric of contrast-distorted images based on information maximization. IEEE Trans. Cybern. **47**(12), 4559–4565 (2017)

31. Min, X., Gu, K., Zhai, G., Liu, J., Yang, X., Chen, C.W.: Blind quality assessment based on pseudo-reference image. IEEE Trans. Multimedia **20**(8), 2049–2062 (2018)

32. Gu, K., Zhai, G., Yang, X., Zhang, W.: Deep learning network for blind image quality assessment. In: IEEE International Conference on Image Processing, pp. 511–515 (2014)

33. Gu, K., Tao, D., Qiao, J., Lin, W.: Learning a no-reference quality assessment model of enhanced images with big data. IEEE Trans. Neural Netw. Learn. Syst. **29**(4), 1301–1313 (2018)

34. Gu, K., Zhai, G., Yang, X., Zhang, W.: Using free energy principle for blind image quality assessment. IEEE Trans. Multimedia **17**(1), 50–63 (2015)

35. Zhang, L., Zhang, L., Bovik, A.C.: A feature-enriched completely blind image quality evaluator. IEEE Trans. Image Process. **24**(8), 2579–2591 (2015)

36. Gu, K., et al.: Blind quality assessment of tone-mapped images via analysis of information, naturalness, and structure. IEEE Trans. Multimedia **18**(3), 432–443 (2016)

37. Gu, K., Li, L., Lu, H., Min, X., Lin, W.: A fast reliable image quality predictor by fusing micro- and macro-structures. IEEE Trans. Ind. Electron. **64**(5), 3903–3912 (2017)

38. Gu, K., Zhai, G., Yang, X., Zhang, W.: Hybrid no-reference quality metric for singly and multiply distorted images. IEEE Trans. Broadcast. **60**(3), 555–567 (2014)

39. Friston, K., Kilner, J., Harrison, L.: A free energy principle for the brain. J. Physiol. Paris **100**, 70–87 (2006)
40. Friston, K.: The free-energy principle: a unified brain theory? Nat. Rev. Neurosci. **11**, 127–138 (2010)
41. Yue, G., Hou, C., Gu, K., Zhou, T., Zhai, G.: Combining local and global measures for DIBR-synthesized image quality evaluation. IEEE Trans. Image Process. **28**(4), 2075–2088 (2019)
42. Knill, D.C., Pouget, A.: The Bayesian brain: the role of uncertainty in neural coding and computation. Trends Neurosci. **27**(12), 712–719 (2004)
43. Attias, H.: A variational Bayesian framework for graphical models. Adv. Neural. Inf. Process. Syst. **12**, 209–215 (2000)
44. Johnson, D.H., Sinanovic, S.: Symmetrizing the Kullback-Leibler distance. IEEE Trans. Inf. Theory (2001)
45. VQEG: Final report from the video quality experts group on the validation of objective models of video quality assessment (2000). http://www.vqeg.org/
46. Gu, K., Zhang, Y., Qiao, J.: Ensemble meta-learning for few-shot soot density recognition. IEEE Trans. Ind. Informat. **17**(3), 2261–2270 (2021)
47. Gu, K., Xia, Z., Qiao, J., Lin, W.: Deep dual-channel neural network for image based smoke detection. IEEE Trans. Multimedia **22**(2), 311–323 (2020)
48. Liu, H., Lei, F., Tong, C., Cui, C., Wu, L.: Visual smoke detection based on ensemble deep CNNs. Displays **69**, 102020 (2021)
49. Gu, K., Liu, H., Xia, Z., Qiao, J., Lin, W., Thalmann, D.: $PM_{2.5}$ monitoring: use information abundance measurement and wide and deep learning. IEEE Trans. Neural Netw. Learn. Syst. **32**(10), 4278–4290 (2021)
50. Gu, K., Xia, Z., Qiao, J.: Stacked selective ensemble for $PM_{2.5}$ forecast. IEEE Trans. Instrum. Meas. **69**(3), 660–671 (2020)
51. Ye, P., Wu, X., Gao, D., Deng, S., Xu, N., Chen, J.: DP3 signal as a neuro indictor for attentional processing of stereoscopic contents in varied depths within the 'comfort zone'. Displays **63**, 101953 (2020)

L2RT-FIQA: Face Image Quality Assessment via Learning-to-Rank Transformer

Zehao Chen[1,2] and Hua Yang[1,2(✉)]

[1] Institute of Image Communication and Network Engineering,
Shanghai Jiao Tong University, Shanghai, China
{chenzehao0915,hyang}@sjtu.edu.cn
[2] Shanghai Key Lab of Digital Media Processing and Transmission, Shanghai, China

Abstract. Face recognition (FR) systems are easily constrained by complex environmental situations in the wild. To ensure the accuracy of FR systems, face image quality assessment (FIQA) is applied to reject low-quality face image unsuitable for recognition. Face quality can be defined as the accuracy or confidence of face images being correctly recognized by FR systems, which is desired to be consistent with recognition results. However, current FIQA methods show more or less inconsistency with face recognition due to the following four biases, including implicit constraint, quality labels, regression models, and backbone networks. In order to reduce such biases and enhance the consistency between FR and FIQA, this paper proposes a FIAQ method based on Learning to rank (L2R) algorithm and vision Transformer named L2RT-FIQA. L2RT-FIQA consists of three parts: relative quality labels, L2R framework, and vision Transformer backbone. Specifically, we utilize normalized intra-class and inter-class angular distance to generate relative quality labels; we employ L2R model to focus more on the quality order rather than the absolute quality value; we apply unpretrained vision transformer as our backbone to improve generalization and global information learning. Experimental results show our L2RT-FIQA effectively reduces the aforementioned four kinds of biases and outperforms other state-of-the-art FIQA methods on several challenging benchmarks.

Keywords: Face image quality assessment · Learning to rank · Vision transformer

1 Introduction

Face image contains a large amount of personal information, including appearance, gender, age, and skin color, which is the most important and effective

This research was partly supported by grants of National Natural Science Foundation of China (NSFC, Grant No. 62171281), Science and Technology Commission of Shanghai Municipality (STCSM, Grant No. 20DZ1200203, 2021SHZDZX0102).

G. Zhai et al. (Eds.): IFTC 2022, CCIS 1766, pp. 270–285, 2023.
https://doi.org/10.1007/978-981-99-0856-1_20

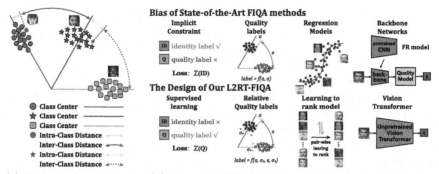

(a) Essence of Face Quality. (b) Bias of FIQA methods and Our Design Principles.

Fig. 1. The essence of face quality and bias of FIQA methods.

biometric information for identity authentication. With the rapid development of deep learning, high-performance face recognition (FR) methods [12,29,35] have been put forward and FR systems have been widely and irreplaceably utilized in all aspects of society. Although FR methods perform impressively in academic experiments, the application of FR systems still faces great challenges of unconstrained conditions. Complex environmental and personal factors (*e.g.* illumination, pose, focus, *etc.*) can easily affect the quality of face images, to which even robust FR systems are sensitive. Low-quality face images cause inaccurate face features extracted by FR models, making a negative influence on the recognition or verification accuracy of FR systems. Therefore, scholars pay more attention to face image quality assessment (FIQA) methods, which have been applied to FR systems to reject low-quality face images.

Face image quality can be defined as the accuracy or confidence of a face image being correctly recognized by FR systems. Early FIQA methods [1,16,34] focus on the hand-craft features based on non-reference image quality assessment, which are not always effective for face image quality assessment. To enhance the consistency between quality assessment and recognition, several works [2,22,29,33] discuss the essence of face quality based on FR methods. The training phase of mainstream FR methods [12,29,35] is a classification task, where the optimizing goal is to minimize intra-class distance and maximize inter-class distance of all samples in the latent space. Hence, face quality is related to intra-class and inter-class distance of the corresponding face embedding in the latent space, as shown in Fig. 1a. According to the aforementioned discussion, [2,22,33] directly utilize distance-based label to train regression models for FIQA. SER-FIQ [39] directly considers the distance between face embeddings as the face quality score. For the effectiveness of FR systems, some end-to-end methods [29,37] are designed for both FR and FIQA. PFE [37] estimates an uncertainty of face embedding to be face quality and MagFace [29] regards the feature magnitude of face embedding as the corresponding face quality.

However, such aforementioned FIQA methods still face the inconsistency problem with various FR methods due to the four bias illustrated in Fig. 1b. (1) Implicit constraint. The quality learning of [29,37] is based on implicit constraint and the constraint perfectly works only when the model converges to the global minimum. However, deep CNNs are hard to converge to the global minimum, which leads to the bias of learned quality assessment. (2) Quality labels. Several state-of-the-arts [2,22,33] generate quality labels by intra-class and inter-class distance. However, the sample distribution is easily biased by variations in age and pose of different identities. The absolute Euclidean or angular distances cannot represent the real quality of face samples. (3) Regression models. Most FIQA methods [2,22,23,33] directly employ regression models to learn from the quality labels. Therefore, the bias generated by quality labels is further amplified by regression learning. (4) Backbone networks. Recent FIQA methods [2,33,39] prefer to use a pre-trained FR method backbone as their own backbones. The pre-trained backbones result in the bias that the quality assessment suits the certain FR method but is not generalized for other FR methods. And due to the end-to-end methods for both FR and FIQA, the quality scores generated by [29,37] are also biased by the recognition part of themselves.

In order to reduce such bias in FIQA methods, we design our method following four principles, as illustrated in Fig. 1b. (1) Supervised learning. Because the implicit constraint of quality learning brings uncertainty, we apply the supervised way for quality learning. Supervised learning can provide a stronger constraint, which makes the quality model converge more to the desired optimum. (2) Relative quality labels. Due to the variations in age, pose, and other factors, the feature distributions in the latent space of different individuals are of big differences, leading to the inaccuracy of absolute-distance-based quality labels. To eliminate such bias, we consider utilizing normalized angular intra-class and inter-class distances to replace absolute distances as our training ground truth for face quality. (3) Learning to rank model. For FIQA task, the relative quality relationship among images is more important than the absolute quality score. Compared to the regression model, L2R model focuses more on the relative rank of quality labels but not their absolute value. Therefore, the L2R model is more skilled in learning a reasonable quality order of a series of labeled face images, which can effectively avoid the quality misordering bias caused by the regression model. (4) Vision Transformer. For the generalization ability, we decide to employ a randomly initialized backbone network without any pretraining. Also, compared to CNNs, vision transformers have better performance on global information learning and higher robustness to severe noise [32]. Therefore, we apply an unpretrained vision transformer as our backbone network.

According to the aforementioned four principles, this paper proposes a face image quality assessment method based on Learning to rank algorithm and vision Transformer called L2RT-FIQA. Our main contributions are as follows:

– We study state-of-the-art FIQA methods and conclude four kinds of biases causing the inconsistency problem and the lack of generalization, which are implicit constraint, quality labels, regression models and backbone networks.

- We put forward a Learning-to-rank transformer for face image quality assessment called L2RT-FIQA, which includes three main parts: relative quality labels, L2R framework for FIQA, and the backbone of vision Transformer.
- We train and evaluate our L2RT-FIQA on challenging benchmarks. The experimental results verify that L2RT-FIQA effectively reduces the aforementioned four biases and shows a great generalization ability over other state-of-the-art FIQA methods.

2   Related Works

2.1   Face Image Quality Assessment Methods

Face image quality is used to evaluate the accuracy or confidence of a face image being correctly recognized by FR systems. According to the development of FIQA methods, face quality can be divided into two aspects: image-based quality and identity-based quality. Image-based quality is similar to traditional image quality, which is mainly based on illumination, pose, camera focus, resolution, and other image characteristics. Several non-reference image quality assessment methods including BRISQUE [30], NIQE [31], and PIQE [41] can be used to evaluate image-based quality. Further, several works define hand-craft features for face quality assessment. Ferrara et al. [16] define 30 types of factors; Raghavendra et al. [34] employ two-stage features involving pose and GLCM features [20]; Bharadwaj [1] adopts Gist and HOG features. The development of deep learning makes learning-based FIQA methods become mainstream. FaceQnetv0 [23] utilizes image-based quality labels generated by human and BioLab-ICAO framework [16] to train Convolutional Neural Networks (CNN) for FIQA. Nevertheless, image-based quality is associated with a limited number of quality factors, which are biased for not always consistent with face recognition results. Therefore, image-based quality is not an effective direction for FIQA task.

In order to improve the consistency between FIQA and FR results, scholars turn to another direction which is identity-based quality. Identity-based quality is mainly based on intra-class and inter-class distance of face embedding features in the latent space, as discussed in Sect. 1. FaceQnetv1 [22] train CNN-based model by the average Euclidean distance of face embeddings generated by three different FR methods. SER-FIQ [39] calculates the distance of face embeddings generated by several random recognition subnetworks as the face quality score. SDD-FIQA [33] and CR-FIQA [2] add regression models to a pre-trained FR model and train the regression models by quality labels generated by both intra-class and inter-class distance. MagFace [29] considers the effect of embeddings' magnitude in angular-based softmax and regards magnitude as the representation of image quality. Compared to our methods, all of the aforementioned FIQA methods have biases in different ways including implicit constraint, quality label, regression model, and backbone networks.

2.2   Learning to Rank Methods

Learning to rank methods are a series of machine learning and deep learning methods for scoring and ranking candidate items, which are widely utilized in the field of search and recommendation. According to the training input and loss function, L2R methods can be classified into three categories: point-wise methods [10,11], pair-wise methods [3–5,17,25], and list-wise methods [7]. In our paper, we mainly focus on the pair-wise methods. RankSVM [25] and RankBoost [17] are machine learning methods for L2R by using date pairs for training. RankNet [3] firstly applies neural networks and the back propagation algorithm on the pair-wise L2R methods, which defines cross entropy as the loss function and abstracts the rank problem into a classification problem. RankNet has become a general framework for pair-wise L2R methods. Based on RankNet, LambdaRank [4] adds a cost term to the loss function to focus more on the top-k-ranked items. LambdaMART [5] combines MART algorithm with LambdaRank to further improve the rank performance. DIPIQ [28] utilizes the RankNet-based L2R method for image quality assessment.

2.3   Vision Transformer

Transformer [40] is first put forward in the field of natural language processing (NLP), whose main contribution lies in the multi-head self-attention mechanism. ViT [14] is the first work to apply pure transformer architecture in the field of computer vision (CV). Based on ViT, several improved vision Transformers [8,13,19,26,27] are put forward to enhance the capacity for local information and boost the local and global information exchange in the vision Transformers. Among them, Swin Transformers [13,27] propose a shifted window partitioning approach for cross-window connections and local attention, which has shown great ability on discriminative feature learning and impressive performance on classification, object detection, segmentation, and other downstream computer vision tasks. Based on the main architecture of [9,27] conducts a Neural architecture search (NAS) to search not only the architecture but also the search space for a more effective vision transformer architecture. The searched model Swin-Transformer-S3 shows superior performance on a series of CV tasks. The backbone network of our L2RT-FIQA is based on Swin-S3.

3   Methodology

Face image quality is the reflection of the confidence or the accuracy of face images to be recognized by FR systems. Therefore, the quality scores of face images are desired to be more consistent with recognition results and to reduce the misordering of quality. In this section, we propose our FIQA method based on learning-to-rank algorithm and vision Transformer called L2RT-FIQA. The architecture of L2RT-FIQA is illustrated in Fig. 2. Firstly, we generate relative quality labels for face samples by intra-class distance and inter-class distance in the latent space. Secondly, we utilize a vision Transformer as a quality model. The training of quality model is based on a pair-wise learning-to-rank method.

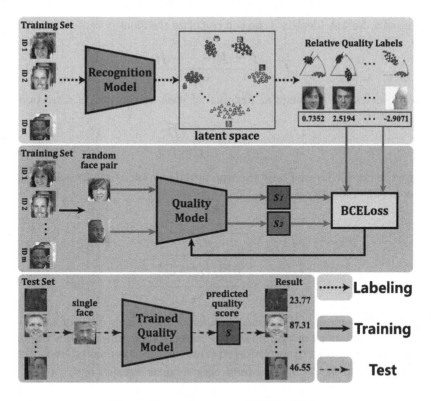

Fig. 2. The architecture of L2RT-FIQA.

3.1   Generation of Relative Quality Labels

As the essence of the face quality is that face samples with smaller intra-class distances and larger inter-class distances in the latent space are of higher identity-quality, we utilize intra-class angular distance and inter-class angular distance to generate the relative quality labels for face image samples.

Firstly, given a face image set $\mathcal{X}$ with m identities.

$$\mathcal{X} = \left\{ \mathbf{x}_1^1, \ \mathbf{x}_2^1, \ \cdots, \ \mathbf{x}_{n_1}^1, \mathbf{x}_1^2, \ \mathbf{x}_2^2, \ \cdots, \ \mathbf{x}_{n_2}^2, \ \cdots, \ \mathbf{x}_1^m, \ \mathbf{x}_2^m, \ \cdots, \ \mathbf{x}_{n_m}^m \right\}, \quad (1)$$

where $\mathbf{x}_i^j$ denotes i-th face image of j-th identity and n_k denotes the amount of face images for k-th identity. Given a face recognition model $\mathcal{R}$. We generate face embedding features via the recognition model: $\mathcal{F} = \mathcal{R}\left(\mathcal{X}\right)$, where $\mathcal{F}$ denotes the face feature set. Each image $\mathbf{x}_i^j \in \mathcal{X}$ has a corresponding feature $\boldsymbol{f}_i^j \in \mathcal{F}$. Therefore,

$$\mathcal{F} = \left\{ \boldsymbol{f}_1^1, \ \boldsymbol{f}_2^1, \ \cdots, \ \boldsymbol{f}_{n_1}^1, \boldsymbol{f}_1^2, \ \boldsymbol{f}_2^2, \ \cdots, \ \boldsymbol{f}_{n_2}^2, \ \cdots, \ \boldsymbol{f}_1^m, \ \boldsymbol{f}_2^m, \ \cdots, \ \boldsymbol{f}_{n_m}^m \right\}. \quad (2)$$

Secondly, for any identity j, we can calculate the identity center in the latent space,

$$\overline{f^j} = \frac{f_1^j + f_2^j + \cdots + f_{n_j}^j}{n_j}. \tag{3}$$

Then, we calculate the angular distance of each feature to its corresponding identity center,

$$a_i^j = \arccos \frac{f_i^j \cdot \overline{f^j}}{\|f_i^j\| \|\overline{f^j}\|}. \tag{4}$$

And we can get the mean $\overline{a^j}$ and the standard deviation σ^j of intra-class distances of the identity j,

$$\overline{a^j} = \frac{a_2^j + a_2^j + \cdots + a_{n_j}^j}{n_j}, \tag{5}$$

$$\sigma^j = \sqrt{\frac{\sum_{i=1}^{n_j} \left(a_i^j - \overline{a^j}\right)^2}{n_j}}. \tag{6}$$

We find that the mean and variance of different individuals differ greatly due to the different variations of age, pose, and other factors, which causes the biases and inaccuracy for directly regarding absolute distance as quality labels. Therefore, we calculate the normalized intra-class angular distance $a_i^{j'}$,

$$a_i^{j'} = \frac{a_i^j - \overline{a^j}}{\sigma^j}. \tag{7}$$

Thirdly, besides intra-class angular distance, we also need to calculate inter-class angular distance of each sample. For $\forall f_i^j \in \mathcal{F}$, we can obtain its angular distance to other identity k ($k = 1, 2, \cdots, m$ and $k \neq j$),

$$e_i^{jk} = \arccos \frac{f_i^j \cdot \overline{f^k}}{\|f_i^j\| \|\overline{f^k}\|}. \tag{8}$$

And we treat the minimum angular distance to other identities as the inter-class angular distance,

$$e_i^j = \min_{k \neq j} \left\{ e_i^{j1}, e_i^{j2}, \cdots, e_i^{jk}, \cdots, e_i^{jm} \right\}. \tag{9}$$

Similar to Eq. 7, we also normalize e_i^j to the normalized inter-class angular distance $e_i^{j'}$ by the corresponding mean and standard deviation of the identity which has the minimum angular distance to f_i^j.

Finally, we utilize intra-class angular distance a_i^j and inter-class angular distance e_i^j to generate relative quality label y_i^j for face image sample $\mathbf{x}_i^j$,

$$y_i^j = -a_i^{j'} + \alpha e_i^{j'}, \tag{10}$$

where α is a constant. Therefore, we generate a relative quality label set $\mathcal{Y}$ for the face image set $\mathcal{X}$, where each image corresponds to a relative quality label.

$$\mathcal{Y} = \left\{ y_1^1,\ y_2^1,\ \cdots,\ y_{n_1}^1, y_1^2,\ y_2^2,\ \cdots,\ y_{n_2}^2,\ \cdots,\ y_1^m,\ y_2^m,\ \cdots,\ y_{n_m}^m \right\}. \quad (11)$$

3.2   Learning-to-Rank Quality Model

After getting the relative quality label set $\mathcal{Y}$ of the face image set $\mathcal{X}$, we design a quality model $\mathcal{Q}$ to realize face image quality assessment called L2RT-FIQA. Given a face image $\mathbf{x}$, L2RT-FIQA can generate its corresponding quality score s: $s = \mathcal{Q}(\mathbf{x})$.

The training phase of our L2RT-FIQA is based on a pair-wise L2R algorithm RankNet [3], as illustrated in Fig. 2. Given a pair of face images $\mathbf{x}_{i_1}^{j_1}$ and $\mathbf{x}_{i_2}^{j_2}$. Two images are separately predicted by the quality model to generate the predicted quality score, $s_1 = \mathcal{Q}\left(\mathbf{x}_{i_1}^{j_1}\right)$ and $s_2 = \mathcal{Q}\left(\mathbf{x}_{i_2}^{j_2}\right)$. Denote P_{12} is the posterior probability of $\mathbf{x}_{i_1}^{j_1}$ having a higher quality rank than $\mathbf{x}_{i_2}^{j_2}$. We can model the P_{12} by s_1 and s_2 by using a logistic function [3].

$$P_{12} = \frac{e^{s_1 - s_2}}{1 + e^{s_1 - s_2}}. \quad (12)$$

Based on this, we can formulate the cross entropy loss as follow:

$$\mathcal{L}\left(P_{12}, \overline{P}_{12}\right) = -\overline{P}_{12} \log P_{12} - \left(1 - \overline{P}_{12}\right) \log \left(1 - P_{12}\right), \quad (13)$$

where $\overline{P}_{12}$ is the ground truth probability of the input image pair. Considering the face image pair $\mathbf{x}_{i_1}^{j_1}$ and $\mathbf{x}_{i_2}^{j_2}$ with the relative quality label pair $y_{i_1}^{j_1}$ and $y_{i_2}^{j_2}$,

$$\overline{P}_{12} = \begin{cases} 1, y_{i_1}^{j_1} > y_{i_2}^{j_2}, \\ 0, otherwise. \end{cases} \quad (14)$$

As $\overline{P}_{12} \in \{0,\ 1\}$, the training phase of L2RT-FIQA can be treated as to optimize a two-class classification problem. Therefore, the loss function for the whole model can be formulated as follow:

$$\mathcal{L}\left(\mathcal{Q}; \mathbf{x}_{i_1}^{j_1}, \mathbf{x}_{i_2}^{j_2}, \overline{P}_{12}\right) = -\overline{P}_{12}\left(\mathcal{Q}\left(\mathbf{x}_{i_1}^{j_1}\right) - \left(\mathbf{x}_{i_2}^{j_2}\right)\right) + \log\left(1 + \left(\mathcal{Q}\left(\mathbf{x}_{i_1}^{j_1}\right) - \left(\mathbf{x}_{i_2}^{j_2}\right)\right)\right) \quad (15)$$

After the training phase, we utilize the trained L2RT-FIQA to predict the quality score of a given face image $\mathbf{x}$. We just treat $\mathbf{x}$ as input of the quality model, and the output is the predicted quality score s:

$$s = \mathcal{Q}(\mathbf{x}). \quad (16)$$

The backbone of the quality model is based on Swin-Transformer-S3 [9], which has shown the superiority on several computer vision tasks. The lightest model in Swin-S3 family is Swin-S3-Tiny with the input size of 224×224. For further lightweight, we change the input size 112×112 and modify the overall architecture to 3 Swin blocks. The modified version is named Swin-S3-Tiny-112, whose specific structure is demonstrated in Table 1. We adopt Swin-S3-Tiny-112 as the backbone network of our method.

Table 1. The specific structure of Swin-S3-Tiny-112.

Layer	Input resolution	Window size	Depth	Head nums
Swin-Layer1	112×112	7	2	3
Swin-Layer2	56×56	7	18	12
Swin-Layer3	28×28	14	2	12

4   Experiments and Results

In order to evaluate the performance of our proposed L2RT-FIQA, we demonstrate several experiments of L2RT-FIQA and compare the results with state-of-the-arts in this section. Firstly, we introduce datasets, baselines, and experimental settings. Then, we provide experimental results and analysis. Last, we do some ablation studies to discuss different settings for our L2RT-FIQA.

4.1   Datasets

Training Data. MS-Celeb-1M [18] is one of the largest face image datasets consisting of about 10M images from 100k identities. Due to the large amount of incorrectly labeled data in MS-Celeb-1M, we choose to utilize a refined version MS1Mv2 [12] as our training set, which has 5.8M images of 81k identities and has been widely used in previous works [2,29,33].

Test Data. The test for FIQA methods is conducted on LFW [24], CFP [36], and Adience [15]. LFW [24] is the most classic and widely used benchmark for unconstrained face verification. CFP-FP [36] contains 7000 face images of 500 individuals with large poses and age variations. Adience [15] comprises 19370 images from 2284 identities, which is collected for age and gender classification, covering various variations in appearance, pose, focus, and illumination. Adience is one of the most popular datasets for FIQA methods evaluation.

4.2   Baselines

FIQA Methods. L2RT-FIQA is compared to eight state-of-the-art methods, which are three IQA methods including BRISQUE [30], NIQE [31], and PIQE [31], as well as six FIQA methods including FaceQnetv0 [23], FaceQnetv1 [22], SER-FIQ [39], SDD-FIQA [33], MagFace [29], and CR-FIQA [2]. BRISQUE [30], NIQE [31], and PIQE [41] are all non-deep-learning methods for image quality evaluation. FaceQnetv0 and v1 [22,23] are deep-learning FIQA methods by learning quality labels separately based on [16] and embedding distance. SER-FIQ [39] employs several sub-networks of a recognition model to generate quality scores. SDD-FIQA [33] and CR-FIQA [2] add regression networks to the recognition models for learning identity-based quality. MagFace [29] associates the magnitude of face embeddings with face quality, which can be employed

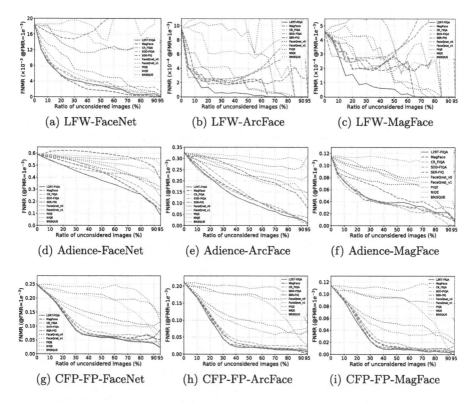

Fig. 3. EVRCs on different datasets based on different recognition results. EVRCs show the effectiveness of FIQA methods rejecting low-quality images.

for both FR and FIQA tasks. We utilize officially released codes or pretrained models for all state-of-the-art methods.

FR Methods. The evaluation of FIQA methods is based on face verification results. In order to evaluate the generalization of methods, we apply three different FR methods in our experiments, which are FaceNet [35], ArcFace [12], and MagFace [29]. All of them are officially released pretrained models. FaceNet [35] is trained on VGG-Face2 [6] with the backbone network of Inception-ResNet-V2 [38]. ArcFace [12] adopts ResNet50 [21] as the backbone network and is trained on MS1Mv2. MagFace [29] is also trained on MS1Mv2 but employs a deeper backbone of ResNet100.

4.3   Experimental Settings

Implementation Details. The recognition model $\mathcal{R}$ for generating relative quality labels is ArcFace [12] pretrained on MS1Mv2 with the backbone of ResNet-100. α in Eq. 10 is set as 0.1. The training phase of L2RT-FIQA is pairwise learning with the batch size of 256 pairs. We utilize Stochastic Gradient

Table 2. AOC results. Higher AOC indicates better FIQA performance.

DataSet		LFW [24]			Adience [15]			CFP-FP [36]		
FR	FIQA	FMR								
		1e−2	1e−3	1e−4	1e−2	1e−3	1e−4	1e−2	1e−3	1e−4
FaceNet [35]	BRISQUE [30]	0.0317	−0.0271	0.0639	0.1974	0.1093	0.0560	0.0802	0.0654	0.0483
	NIQE [31]	0.2335	0.2064	0.1272	0.0824	0.0355	0.0168	0.2787	0.2449	0.1911
	PIQE [41]	0.3414	0.2691	0.1620	0.1432	0.0469	0.0217	0.2106	0.1615	0.1155
	FaceQnetv0 [23]	0.7454	0.6323	0.4803	0.2975	0.1894	0.1173	0.4568	0.3937	0.3204
	FaceQnetv1 [22]	0.7832	0.7262	0.5812	0.3028	0.1724	0.0920	0.5188	0.4464	0.3467
	SER-FIQ [39]	0.0851	−0.0926	−0.0397	0.0952	0.0165	0.0124	0.7004	0.6067	0.4777
	SDD-FIQA [33]	0.7628	0.7249	0.5788	0.5183	0.2421	0.1199	0.6744	0.6021	0.4652
	MagFace [29]	**0.8627**	**0.8169**	0.6882	0.4890	0.2928	0.1656	0.6613	0.5883	0.4641
	CR-FIQA [2]	0.7578	0.7656	0.6561	0.4769	0.2486	0.1343	0.6498	0.5636	0.4452
	L2RT-FIQA	0.8340	0.7865	**0.7008**	**0.5739**	**0.3545**	**0.2063**	**0.7092**	**0.6290**	**0.5008**
ArcFace [12]	BRISQUE [30]	0.0113	0.0358	0.0287	0.2637	0.2095	0.1290	0.0988	0.0956	0.0667
	NIQE [31]	0.4288	0.2068	0.2018	0.0696	0.0558	0.0299	0.2913	0.2785	0.2631
	PIQE [41]	0.3757	0.3438	0.3936	0.1622	0.1201	0.0646	0.1798	0.1828	0.1778
	FaceQnetv0 [23]	0.6553	0.7738	0.8261	0.3570	0.2903	0.2110	0.4828	0.4774	0.4813
	FaceQnetv1 [22]	0.6377	0.7578	0.8219	0.2860	0.2907	0.1953	0.5209	0.5283	0.5246
	SER-FIQ [39]	0.5868	0.7092	0.7362	0.3798	0.2885	0.1785	0.7321	0.7302	0.7171
	SDD-FIQA [33]	0.4476	0.6585	0.7648	**0.6691**	0.5726	0.3738	0.7151	0.7078	0.6976
	MagFace [29]	0.7065	0.8160	0.8738	0.6365	0.5568	0.4096	0.7268	0.7219	0.7082
	CR-FIQA [2]	0.1939	0.5274	0.6980	0.6148	0.5229	0.3556	0.6844	0.6820	0.6757
	L2RT-FIQA	**0.8976**	**0.9035**	**0.8975**	0.6587	**0.6013**	**0.4492**	**0.7483**	**0.7421**	**0.7270**
MagFace [29]	BRISQUE [30]	0.1241	0.1801	0.2027	0.2266	0.2642	0.2357	0.0477	0.0518	0.0733
	NIQE [31]	0.3767	0.4577	0.4802	0.0192	0.0385	0.0401	0.2807	0.2871	0.2919
	PIQE [41]	0.4301	0.4657	0.4428	0.1909	0.1998	0.1553	0.2005	0.1848	0.1876
	FaceQnetv0 [23]	0.5595	0.6245	0.6729	0.3830	0.4151	0.4319	0.5042	0.5004	0.4935
	FaceQnetv1 [22]	0.4654	0.5118	0.5467	0.1213	0.2747	0.3580	0.5672	0.5590	0.5458
	SER-FIQ [39]	0.3598	0.4255	0.4287	0.4434	0.5312	0.5070	0.7340	0.7364	0.7344
	SDD-FIQA [33]	0.2419	0.2892	0.4094	**0.5829**	**0.6661**	0.6678	0.7291	0.7280	0.7278
	MagFace [29]	0.5853	0.6230	0.6935	0.5724	0.6511	**0.6798**	0.7238	0.7279	0.7314
	CR-FIQA [2]	−0.1317	0.0183	0.2380	0.5647	0.6533	0.6387	0.6915	0.6977	0.7008
	L2RT-FIQA	**0.8395**	**0.8062**	**0.7898**	0.5684	0.6475	0.6592	**0.7540**	**0.7608**	**0.7620**

Descent as the optimizer with the initial learning rate of 0.1. The learning rate decay is set as a factor of 0.1 for every 10 epochs during 50 epochs in total. All images are aligned and cropped by MTCNN [42] and resized to the required size according to each FIQA method.

Evaluation Protocols. We use Error-Versus-Reject-Curves (EVRC) and Area-Over-Curve (AOC) to quantitatively evaluate FIQA methods, following [33] and [2]. EVRC demonstrates the face verification error rates when getting rid of images with the lowest predicted quality scores in the current remaining images. As the face quality assessment is desired to be consistent with recognition results, the decrease of error rates with the increase of unconsidered ratio of images indicates effective FIQA results. The EVRC of a better-performance FIQA method is lower than other EVRCs of competitive methods. EVRCs are reported in terms of false non-match rate (FNMR) at a false match rate (FMR) threshold of 1e−3 with pair verification of all images. AOC is the area over EVRC, which is reported at FMR of 1e−2, 1e−3, and 1e−4 to further quantify the EVRC results. AOC is formulated as follow:

$$\text{AOC} = \frac{\int_l^u \left(r\left(0\right) - r\left(\phi\right) \right) \, d\phi}{\int_l^u r\left(0\right) \, d\phi}, \tag{17}$$

where ϕ is the ratio of unconsidered images, l and u are the lower and upper bound of ϕ, which are set as 0 and 0.95 respectively. $r\left(\phi\right)$ denotes the FNMR at the unconsideration ratio of ϕ.

4.4   Face Image Quality Assessment Results

The experimental results of EVRCs and AOCs are respectively reported in Fig. 3 and Table 2. Among nine sets of EVRCs, our L2RT-FIQA outperforms other state-of-the-art methods in seven sets. Especially in the range of rejecting ratio from 20% to 70%, our curves are apparently lower than curves of other methods, which indicates that L2RT-FIQA has outstanding quality assessment ability for medium-quality face images. As we know, medium-quality face images always have so tiny quality differences that they are easily misordered by other FIQA methods. Thanks to the L2R framework, our L2RT-FIQA can effectively decrease the quality misordering for medium-quality face images and show superior FIQA performance.

The AOC results listed in Table 2 further quantify the performance of all compared methods. L2RT-FIQA achieves 21 highest AOC of all 27 items, which verifies the strong generalization ability of our method when facing different challenging benchmarks, different FR methods with large variations, and different FMR rates. L2RT-FIQA shows superior performance than state-of-the-arts at most of conditions. Therefore, it is proven our method can deal with complex conditions in the wild and achieve a satisfying performance in public applications.

4.5   Ablation Study

Relative Quality Labels. Our relative quality labels are based on normalized intra-class and inter-class angular distance of face samples in the latent space. The big difference with other methods is that we utilize normalized distance rather than absolute distance. To prove such normalization can reduce the bias, we generate another quality label for each sample based on absolute distance. The AOCs are shown in the row of 'Absolute Distance' in Table 3. The AOCs of absolute labels are lower than relative labels, which verifies that relative labels can reduce the bias caused by the variations in age, pose, and other factors of different identities.

Pretrained CNN. The backbone of L2RT-FIQA is based on Vision Transformer without any pretraining. To prove the effectiveness of our backbone, we compare it with a pretrained CNN, which is the ResNet100 for FR method

Table 3. AOC results for ablation study.

DataSet	LFW [24]			Adience [15]			CFP-FP [36]		
Ablation	FR methods								
	FN	Arc	Mag	FN	Arc	Mag	FN	Arc	Mag
Absolute Distance	0.7803	0.7898	0.6228	0.3500	0.5908	0.6421	0.6191	0.7297	0.7422
Pretrained CNN	0.6809	0.7753	0.7868	0.2233	0.5013	0.5392	0.6086	0.7057	0.7412
Regression Model	0.6867	0.8348	0.7613	0.2838	0.4948	0.5152	0.6061	0.7114	0.7255
L2RT-FIQA	**0.7865**	**0.9035**	**0.8062**	**0.3545**	**0.6013**	**0.6475**	**0.6290**	**0.7421**	**0.7608**

MagFace [29] pretrained on MS1Mv2. The experimental results are shown in the row of 'Pretrained CNN' in Table 3. The results verify that pretrained backbone perform better when using the same FR method than other FR methods, which causes the bias of FIQA methods. Also, the results also prove that Vision Transformer is more suitable for FIQA task than CNN.

L2R Framework. We train another regression model with the same settings with L2RT-FIQA to verify the effectiveness of L2R framework in our method. The training loss is SmoothL1-Loss. The results are demonstrated in the row of 'Regression Model' in Table 3. L2R model outperforms the regression model on all nine AOCs. This study reveals that L2R effectively prevents the model from amplifying the bias and misordering the quality sequence caused by regression learning.

5   Conclusion

This paper studies state-of-the-art FIQA methods and finds their four typical biases, which affect the consistency between quality scores and recognition results. Aiming to reduce such biases, we propose a vision Transformer-based learning-to-rank algorithm called L2RT-FIQA. L2RT-FIQA contains three main parts, including relative quality labels, L2R framework, and vision Transformer backbone. Such three parts reduce the aforementioned biases in different ways and improve the consistency between our quality assessment with various FR methods. An abundance of experiments show the superior FIQA performance of L2RT-FIQA, especially the generalization performance when facing various FR methods. Therefore, our L2RT-FIQA is suitable for different FR systems without any fine-tuning.

References

1. Bharadwaj, S., Vatsa, M., Singh, R.: Can holistic representations be used for face biometric quality assessment? In: 2013 IEEE International Conference on Image Processing, pp. 2792–2796 (2013). https://doi.org/10.1109/ICIP.2013.6738575
2. Boutros, F., Fang, M., Klemt, M., Fu, B., Damer, N.: CR-FIQA: face image quality assessment by learning sample relative classifiability. arXiv preprint arXiv:2112.06592 (2021)

3. Burges, C., et al.: Learning to rank using gradient descent. In: Proceedings of the 22nd International Conference on Machine Learning, ICML 2005, pp. 89–96. Association for Computing Machinery, New York (2005)

4. Burges, C., Ragno, R., Le, Q.: Learning to rank with nonsmooth cost functions. In: Advances in Neural Information Processing Systems, vol. 19 (2006)

5. Burges, C.J.: From RankNet to LambdaRank to LambdaMART: an overview. Learning **11**(23-581), 81 (2010)

6. Cao, Q., Shen, L., Xie, W., Parkhi, O.M., Zisserman, A.: VGGFace2: a dataset for recognising faces across pose and age. In: 2018 13th IEEE International Conference on Automatic Face Gesture Recognition (FG 2018), pp. 67–74 (2018). https://doi.org/10.1109/FG.2018.00020

7. Cao, Z., Qin, T., Liu, T.Y., Tsai, M.F., Li, H.: Learning to rank: from pairwise approach to listwise approach. In: Proceedings of the 24th International Conference on Machine Learning, pp. 129–136 (2007)

8. Chen, C.F., Panda, R., Fan, Q.: RegionViT: regional-to-local attention for vision transformers. In: International Conference on Learning Representations (2021)

9. Chen, M., et al.: Searching the search space of vision transformer. In: Ranzato, M., Beygelzimer, A., Dauphin, Y., Liang, P., Vaughan, J.W. (eds.) Advances in Neural Information Processing Systems, vol. 34, pp. 8714–8726. Curran Associates, Inc. (2021)

10. Cossock, D., Zhang, T.: Subset ranking using regression. In: Lugosi, G., Simon, H.U. (eds.) COLT 2006. LNCS (LNAI), vol. 4005, pp. 605–619. Springer, Heidelberg (2006). https://doi.org/10.1007/11776420_44

11. Crammer, K., Singer, Y.: Pranking with ranking. In: Advances in Neural Information Processing Systems, vol. 14 (2001)

12. Deng, J., Guo, J., Xue, N., Zafeiriou, S.: ArcFace: additive angular margin loss for deep face recognition. In: Proceedings of the IEEE/CVF Conference on Computer Vision and Pattern Recognition, June 2019

13. Dong, X., et al.: CSWin transformer: a general vision transformer backbone with cross-shaped windows. In: Proceedings of the IEEE/CVF Conference on Computer Vision and Pattern Recognition, pp. 12124–12134 (2022)

14. Dosovitskiy, A., et al.: An image is worth 16 × 16 words: transformers for image recognition at scale. In: International Conference on Learning Representations (2021). https://openreview.net/forum?id=YicbFdNTTy

15. Eidinger, E., Enbar, R., Hassner, T.: Age and gender estimation of unfiltered faces. IEEE Trans. Inf. Forensics Secur. **9**(12), 2170–2179 (2014)

16. Ferrara, M., Franco, A., Maio, D., Maltoni, D.: Face image conformance to ISO/ICAO standards in machine readable travel documents. IEEE Trans. Inf. Forensics Secur. **7**(4), 1204–1213 (2012). https://doi.org/10.1109/TIFS.2012.2198643

17. Freund, Y., Iyer, R., Schapire, R.E., Singer, Y.: An efficient boosting algorithm for combining preferences. J. Mach. Learn. Res. **4**, 933–969 (2003)

18. Guo, Y., Zhang, L., Hu, Y., He, X., Gao, J.: MS-Celeb-1M: a dataset and benchmark for large-scale face recognition. In: Leibe, B., Matas, J., Sebe, N., Welling, M. (eds.) ECCV 2016. LNCS, vol. 9907, pp. 87–102. Springer, Cham (2016). https://doi.org/10.1007/978-3-319-46487-9_6

19. Han, K., Xiao, A., Wu, E., Guo, J., Xu, C., Wang, Y.: Transformer in transformer. In: Advances in Neural Information Processing Systems, vol. 34, pp. 15908–15919 (2021)

20. Haralick, R.M., Shanmugam, K., Dinstein, I.: Textural features for image classification. IEEE Trans. Syst. Man Cybern. **SMC-3**(6), 610–621 (1973). https://doi.org/10.1109/TSMC.1973.4309314

21. He, K., Zhang, X., Ren, S., Sun, J.: Deep residual learning for image recognition. In: Proceedings of the IEEE Conference on Computer Vision and Pattern Recognition (CVPR), June 2016

22. Hernandez-Ortega, J., Galbally, J., Fierrez, J., Beslay, L.: Biometric quality: review and application to face recognition with FaceQnet. arXiv preprint arXiv:2006.03298 (2020)

23. Hernandez-Ortega, J., Galbally, J., Fierrez, J., Haraksim, R., Beslay, L.: FaceQnet: quality assessment for face recognition based on deep learning. In: 2019 International Conference on Biometrics (ICB), pp. 1–8 (2019)

24. Huang, G.B., Mattar, M., Berg, T., Learned-Miller, E.: Labeled faces in the wild: a database for studying face recognition in unconstrained environments. In: Workshop on Faces in 'Real-Life' Images: Detection, Alignment, and Recognition, October 2008

25. Joachims, T.: Optimizing search engines using clickthrough data. In: Proceedings of the Eighth ACM SIGKDD International Conference on Knowledge Discovery and Data Mining, pp. 133–142 (2002)

26. Lin, H., Cheng, X., Wu, X., Shen, D.: CAT: cross attention in vision transformer. In: 2022 IEEE International Conference on Multimedia and Expo (ICME), pp. 1–6. IEEE (2022)

27. Liu, Z., et al.: Swin transformer: hierarchical vision transformer using shifted windows. In: Proceedings of the IEEE/CVF International Conference on Computer Vision, pp. 10012–10022 (2021)

28. Ma, K., Liu, W., Liu, T., Wang, Z., Tao, D.: dipIQ: blind image quality assessment by learning-to-rank discriminable image pairs. IEEE Trans. Image Process. **26**(8), 3951–3964 (2017)

29. Meng, Q., Zhao, S., Huang, Z., Zhou, F.: MagFace: a universal representation for face recognition and quality assessment. In: Proceedings of the IEEE/CVF Conference on Computer Vision and Pattern Recognition (CVPR), pp. 14225–14234, June 2021

30. Mittal, A., Moorthy, A.K., Bovik, A.C.: No-reference image quality assessment in the spatial domain. IEEE Trans. Image Process. **21**(12), 4695–4708 (2012)

31. Mittal, A., Soundararajan, R., Bovik, A.C.: Making a "completely blind" image quality analyzer. IEEE Sig. Process. Lett. **20**(3), 209–212 (2013). https://doi.org/10.1109/LSP.2012.2227726

32. Naseer, M.M., Ranasinghe, K., Khan, S.H., Hayat, M., Shahbaz Khan, F., Yang, M.H.: Intriguing properties of vision transformers. In: Advances in Neural Information Processing Systems, vol. 34, pp. 23296–23308 (2021)

33. Ou, F.Z., et al.: SDD-FIQA: unsupervised face image quality assessment with similarity distribution distance. In: Proceedings of the IEEE/CVF Conference on Computer Vision and Pattern Recognition (CVPR), pp. 7670–7679, June 2021

34. Raghavendra, R., Raja, K.B., Yang, B., Busch, C.: Automatic face quality assessment from video using gray level co-occurrence matrix: an empirical study on automatic border control system. In: 2014 22nd International Conference on Pattern Recognition, pp. 438–443 (2014). https://doi.org/10.1109/ICPR.2014.84

35. Schroff, F., Kalenichenko, D., Philbin, J.: FaceNet: a unified embedding for face recognition and clustering. In: Proceedings of the IEEE Conference on Computer Vision and Pattern Recognition (CVPR), June 2015

36. Sengupta, S., Chen, J.C., Castillo, C., Patel, V.M., Chellappa, R., Jacobs, D.W.: Frontal to profile face verification in the wild. In: IEEE Winter Conference on Applications of Computer Vision, pp. 1–9 (2016). https://doi.org/10.1109/WACV.2016.7477558

37. Shi, Y., Jain, A.K.: Probabilistic face embeddings. In: Proceedings of the IEEE/CVF International Conference on Computer Vision (ICCV), October 2019

38. Szegedy, C., Ioffe, S., Vanhoucke, V., Alemi, A.A.: Inception-v4, inception-ResNet and the impact of residual connections on learning. In: Thirty-First AAAI Conference on Artificial Intelligence (2017)

39. Terhorst, P., Kolf, J.N., Damer, N., Kirchbuchner, F., Kuijper, A.: SER-FIQ: unsupervised estimation of face image quality based on stochastic embedding robustness. In: Proceedings of the IEEE/CVF Conference on Computer Vision and Pattern Recognition (CVPR), June 2020

40. Vaswani, A., et al.: Attention is all you need. In: Advances in Neural Information Processing Systems, vol. 30 (2017)

41. Venkatanath, N., Praneeth, D., Maruthi, C.B., Channappayya, S.S., Medasani, S.S.: Blind image quality evaluation using perception based features. In: 2015 Twenty First National Conference on Communications (NCC), pp. 1–6 (2015)

42. Zhang, K., Zhang, Z., Li, Z., Qiao, Y.: Joint face detection and alignment using multitask cascaded convolutional networks. IEEE Sig. Process. Lett. **23**(10), 1499–1503 (2016). https://doi.org/10.1109/LSP.2016.2603342

Blindly Evaluate the Quality of Underwater Images via Multi-perceptual Properties

Yan Du[1], Xianjing Xiao[1], Runze Hu[1(✉)], Yutao Liu[3], Jiasong Wang[2], Zhaolin Wan[4], and Xiu Li[1]

[1] Tsinghua Shenzhen International Graduate School, Tsinghua University, Shenzhen, China
{duy21,xxj21}@mails.tsinghua.edu.cn,
{hurunze,li.xiu}@sz.tsinghua.edu.cn
[2] Changchun Institute of Optics, Fine Mechanic and Physics, Chinese Academy of Sciences, Changchun, China
[3] School of Computer Science and Technology, Ocean University of China, Qingdao, China
[4] College of Artificial Intelligence, Dalian Maritime University, Dalian, China
zlwan@dlmu.edu.cn

Abstract. The quality of underwater images can vary greatly due to the complexity of the underwater environment as well as the limitations of imaging devices. This can have an effect on the practical applications that are used in fields such as scientific research, the modern military, and other fields. As a result, attaining subjective quality assessment to differentiate distinct qualities of underwater photos plays a significant role in guiding subsequent tasks. In this study, an effective reference-free underwater image quality assessment metric is proposed by combining the colorfulness, contrast, sharpness, and high-level semantics cues while taking into account the underwater image degradation effect and human visual perception scheme. Specifically, we employ the low-level perceptual property-based method to characterize the image's visual quality, and we use deep neural networks to extract the image's semantic content. SVR is then used to create the quality prediction model by analyzing the relationship between the extracted features and the picture quality. Experiments done on the UWIQA database demonstrate the superiority of the proposed method.

Keywords: Image quality assessment (IQA) · Underwater images · High-level semantics · Human visual system

1 Introduction

The ocean, which covers approximately 71% of the Earth's surface area, is an important part of the global living system and is rich in biological and mineral resources, making it a valuable asset for the sustainable development of human society. The exploitation and utilization of such rich marine resources require large-scale, accurate data on the marine environment; however, images taken in underwater environments are characterized by low contrast, blurred targets, color cast, and loss of detail, and thus usually

---

Y. Du and X. Xiao—Contribute equally to this work.

G. Zhai et al. (Eds.): IFTC 2022, CCIS 1766, pp. 286–300, 2023.
https://doi.org/10.1007/978-981-99-0856-1_21

exhibit impaired visual quality. Therefore, determining a well-designed image quality assessment (IQA) metric to predict the quality of underwater images faithfully becomes a very urgent and beneficial endeavor for practical image processing systems.

With the increasing importance on marine resources, marine research places higher demands on the ability to capture images in underwater environments where image quality has a direct impact on their research value [1–3]. In this case, it can be measured using IQA metrics suitable for underwater images. Image quality evaluation is one of the basic techniques in image processing, mainly by characterizing and studying the image and then assessing its merit (the degree of image distortion). Image quality evaluation has an important role in image processing systems for algorithm analysis and system performance evaluation. In recent years, with the extensive research in the field of digital images, the study of image quality evaluation has received more and more attention from researchers, and many metrics and methods for image quality evaluation have been proposed and improved. Distinguished from the perspective of whether there is human involvement, there are two branches of image quality evaluation methods, subjective evaluation and objective evaluation. The subjective evaluation uses a human as the observer to evaluate the image quality subjectively, aiming to reflect the human visual perception faithfully. Objective evaluation methods [4,5] reflect the subjective perception of the human eye with the help of some mathematical models, giving results based on numerical calculations. This paper focuses on the study of quality evaluation algorithms for underwater images.

The last few years have seen an explosion of IQA research. However, to the best of our knowledge, there are few studies on the visual quality assessment of underwater images, which is a challenging and unresolved task. Many image quality evaluation algorithms designed for natural images (over watering) do not work well on underwater images. This is due to the apparent optical nature of seawater, where the irradiance of light attenuates with increasing depth of seawater, making the natural light underwater weaker, and the complex environment in seawater can cause the target not to be effectively acquired by the imaging equipment. There is also variability in the absorption and scattering of light by different types of dissolved substances and suspended particulate matter [6], with green and blue light having shorter wavelengths and stronger penetration capabilities, making underwater images often greenish and bluish.

To confront this challenge, we in this paper propose a new underwater IQA metric based on the low-level perceptual properties and semantics of underwater images. We first extract the perceptual features related to the colorfulness, sharpness, and contrast to characterize the low-level properties of underwater images effectively. Then, we leverage the powerful deep-learning network to extract the semantic features. These extracted features are eventually fed into a support vector machine to regress the quality score of underwater images. Figure 1 depicts the full procedure of the proposed NR IQA metric. The experimental results on the UWIQA database indicate that the performance of the proposed method is superior to that of other major IQA methods.

Our contributions can be summarized as follows.

1) We make use of a variety of important low-level image properties, such as colorness, contrast, and sharpness, which have the potential to be more all-encompassing than the currently utilized BIQA metrics for determining the quality of the image.

2) We explore the image's high-level semantics for quality assessment, which is rarely covered by the current BIQA metrics. A number of well-known DNN models, such as GoogleNet [7] and ResNet [8], etc., that extract the high-level semantics of the image for quality assessment are explored.
3) Thorough testing on a standard underwater image database shows that the proposed UIPQM significantly outperforms the existing state-of-the-art BIQA metrics.

The rest of this article is organized as follows. Section 2 presents the related works. Section 3 describes the proposed underwater images NR-IQA metric. Section 4 employs numerous experiments and detailed analysis to demonstrate the efficacy of the proposed strategy. Finally, in Sect. 5, we draw a conclusion to this article.

2   Related Work

IQA algorithms can be divided into two categories: subjective evaluation and objective evaluation. Subjective evaluation mainly relies on human subjective perception. The commonly used evaluation methods are Mean Opinion Score (MOS) and Differential Mean Opinion Score (DMOS). Subjective evaluation can actually reflect the subjective visual perception of people, and the evaluation results are direct, accurate and reliable. But it requires multiple iterations of experiments, which is time-consuming and costly. Objective evaluation uses the computer modeling to simulate human visual perception to evaluate image quality, with the advantages of simplicity and low cost. According to the extent of reliance on the reference image, it can be divided into Full Reference (FR), Reduced Reference (RR), and No Reference (NR). The objective of FR IQA is to predict the quality of a target image with full access to the original reference image. Most FR IQA measures follow a similar framework, feature extraction from both images followed by distance calculation. RR IQA measures is to predict the quality of image with limited access to the reference image. Generally, RR features of the reference are extracted at the sender side. NR IQA method, also known as blind-IQA is to evaluate the quality through the features of the image itself without requiring its pristine reference image.

According to the framework adopted, NR IQA methods can be divided into two categories: the framework of feature extraction followed by regression, and the end-to-end deep learning framework. In the first category, the features of the image are first extracted, and then the mapping model between the features and the quality score is established using a machine learning approach. Ye et al. [9] proposed Codebook Representation for No-Reference Image Assessment (CORINA) model, which divides the image into several patches for feature extraction, and then uses SVR for score prediction. The DeepBIQ model proposed by Bianco et al. [10] uses AlexNet as the backbone network for feature extraction and then SVR for score prediction. The second category, using the end-to-end deep learning framework, has been getting more attention recently. Kang et al. [11] proposed IQA-CNN network architecture, including 1 convolutional layer and 2 fully connected layers in 2014. Later, Hou et al. [12] proposed DLIQA, which firstly extracts the statistical feature NSS of the distorted images, then uses the deep classification model to map the NSS feature into five quality levels, and finally maps the distorted images marked with quality levels into quality scores. In 2018, Ma [13] proposed MEON and designed GDN to replace the ReLU activation function. In 2020, Ma [14] adopted deep learning technology to fuse the image features extracted through the convolutional layer and input them into the fully connected layer to obtain the quality score of the distorted image.

Most of the existing NR IQA methods are designed for in-air images. Due to the difference between underwater and in-air environments, some IQA methods for in-air images are not applicable to underwater images. To tackle this problem, researchers have proposed some specific IQA methods based on the characteristics of underwater images. Yang et al. [15] designed an underwater color image quality evaluation metric (UCIQE) based on CIELab color space to qualify chromaticity, contrast, and saturation, which are more consistent with human perception. Panetta et al. [16] proposed an underwater image quality measure (UIQM) inspired by human visual system. UIQM assesses image quality in terms of colorfulness, sharpness, and contrast. CCF [17] proposed by Wang et al. combines colorfulness, contrast, and fog density, performing well for color loss, blurring, and fog caused by underwater absorption and scattering. Afterward, Yang et al. [18] designed a reference-free underwater image quality assessment metric in frequency domain by combining the colorfulness, contrast and sharpness, called FDUM.

3   Methodology

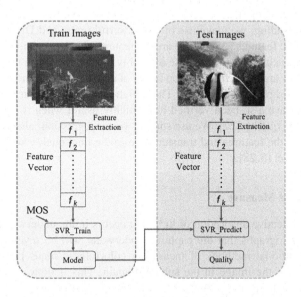

Fig. 1. Framework of the proposed underwater IQA metrics.

In this article, we propose a new no-reference metric to quantify the quality of the underwater images in order to address the concerns that were discussed earlier. We aim at simulating the way of the human vision system to judge the image quality. It is well known that the human brain has a hierarchical way of perceiving picture quality, beginning with the most basic visual perception and progressing all the way up to the most advanced level of semantic comprehension [19,20]. To be more exact, the human brain primarily sees the early properties of the input visual scenes, such as colorness, contrast, sharpness, and other similar characteristics, during the low-level visual perception that takes place in the primary visual areas. The following visual areas are responsible for the perception of information that is both more sophisticated and regional in nature, such as contour and shape. Thus, we propose to characterize the low-level visual perception to describe the visual quality of underwater images.

The human brain is able to see the high-level semantic information of a picture, such as objects and categories, when it has first integrated and abstracted the aspects gleaned through earlier phases of visual perception [21]. As a result of this, our proposal is to evaluate the quality of the image by characterizing both the preliminary visual perception as well as the semantic comprehension, which aligns with the process that occurs in the human brain during the perception of quality [22,23]. During the early stages of visual perception, the human brain has a tendency to pick up on certain low-level image properties, such as sharpness and other similar characteristics [24]. In contrast to the BIQA approaches, which only characterize a small subset of properties for the image's qualities, we characterize a large subset of the image's properties, including its colorness, contrast, and sharpness, and thus to provide a comprehensive description of the image's quality. These quality-related traits, which we consider to be low-level perceptual features, are represented by dedicated features that have undergone thorough design and development. On the other hand, for the purpose of characterizing the semantic understanding, we make use of the powerful pretrained DNNs to extract the matching semantic features [25]. These are the features that we consider to be the high-level perceptual features for the purpose of quality evaluation. To be more specific, the high-level features are taken from the top layers of a particular deep neural network that has been pretrained on ImageNet [26]. These high-level features that are related to the image category have also been verified to be highly useful when it comes to characterizing the image quality [27]. We use support vector regression, also known as SVR, to integrate all of the features and transfer them to the final quality score to derive the picture quality level [5,28].

3.1   Colorfulness Measure

Because of the selective absorption of light that occurs in the underwater medium, the colors of the photographs that are captured underwater will be severely distorted. In general, the traditional methods of measuring colorfulness focus primarily on conducting analysis of the image in the spatial domain. This is done so that the results may be used to quantify the influence of colorfulness distortion. In point of fact, the human visual system has distinct capabilities for perceiving high-frequency and low-frequency components of images. In addition, the high-frequency and low-frequency components of different quality levels of underwater photographs should be distinct from one another. To put it another way, the variations in colorfulness that were recorded are mirrored not just in the spatial domain, but also in the frequency domain.

The underwater image can be transformed from the spatial domain to the frequency domain using a technique called the discrete cosine transform (DCT). In this domain, the energy of the image is primarily concentrated in a certain local area, and the image characteristics can be described by a small amount of DCT coefficients. Theoretically, the low-frequency coefficients in the frequency domain reflect the flat area information in the image. This information is primarily concentrated in the upper left corner of the frequency domain map. On the other hand, the high-frequency coefficients typically describe the image boundary and texture information. These coefficients correspond to the other areas.

In order to more fully analyze the colorfulness of underwater photographs of varying quality, the final colorfulness measure is defined as the product of the colorfulness metric in the frequency domain and the colorfulness meter in the spatial domain. The following is the formula:

$$Colorfulness = Colorfulness_s \times Colorfulness_f \tag{1}$$

where $Colorfulness_s$ and $Colorfulness_f$ are, respectively, the colorfulness metrics in the spatial and frequency domains. As with the UCIQE [15], the colorfulness measure in the spatial domain is defined by the variance of chroma since it correlates well with how people perceive colors in underwater photographs:

$$Colorfulness_s = \sigma_{chr} = \sqrt{\frac{1}{MN} \sum_{i=1}^{M} \sum_{j=1}^{N} \left(I_{ij} - \bar{I}\right)^2} \tag{2}$$

where σ_{chr} indicates the chroma standard deviation, I_{ij} is the chroma component of the image in CIELab space, $\bar{I}$ represents the mean value of the chroma component in CIELab space, M and N are the height and width, respectively, of the underwater image. We calculate the standard deviation of the DCT map to get the colorfulness metric in the frequency domain. The standard deviation of the DCT map is defined as follows:

$$Colorfulness_f = \sigma_{DCT} = \sqrt{\frac{\sum_{i=1}^{M} \sum_{j=1}^{N} \left(DCT_{ij} - \overline{DCT}\right)^2}{MN}}, \tag{3}$$

where DCT_{ij} stands for the DCT coefficient at the coordinate (i, j) of the input image, and $\overline{DCT}$ is the mean value of the DCT map determined by the discrete cosine transform of the input underwater picture.

3.2 Contrast Measure

Aside from the color distortion caused by the selective absorption effect, light scattering in the underwater material can also generate poor contrast and blurring in the image. When non-target scattered light strikes water's suspended particles, it scatters erratically at a tiny angle before entering the camera lens, causing backscattering, an optical phenomenon. This results in the haze-like phenomena in underwater photographs, significantly reduces scene contrast, and degrades image quality [29]. As a result, measuring contrast is a crucial component of assessing the quality of underwater images.

The blurring of an underwater image was represented and the contrast measurement was defined by Wang et al. in their paper [17], and they did it by using the sum of contrast metric values from edge image blocks. First, the underwater image is cut up into several blocks of 64 by 64 pixels each, and then the Sobel operator is employed to produce an edge map from those blocks. Using the given edge map, we are able to determine if the block in question is an edge block or a flat block.

To be more specific, a block is determined to be an edge block if the number of edge pixels included within it constitutes a percentage of more than 0.2% of the total pixels [30]. Then, the contrast measure of the underwater image is defined as the total of the root mean square (RMS) contrast values of all of the edge blocks, which is as follows:

$$\text{Contrast } _{CCF} = \sum_{k=1}^{K} \sqrt{\frac{1}{XY} \sum_{i=1}^{X} \sum_{j=1}^{Y} \left(Ir_{ij}^{k} - \bar{Ir}\right)^2} \tag{4}$$

where Ir_{ij}^{k} is the value of the red intensity of each pixel in the kth edge block that is X by Y, K is the total number of edge blocks, and $\bar{Ir}$ is the average value of the red intensity of each pixel in the underwater image.

However, utilizing the contrast measure directly as described in [17] is not an effective method for differentiating between images of varying qualities. In light of this, our goals for this work are to improve the contrast measure and broaden the range of discernible values. Based on the observation that some pixels always have at least one color channel with a very low value in the vast majority of non-sky local areas, He et al. [30] presented a defogging technique. This prior is referred to as the dark channel prior (DCP). Therefore, the DCP map of an image without fog should have a lower intensity value, whereas the DCP map of an image with fog should have a value that is much higher. In point of fact, there are some similarities between the image of water and the image of fog, and the atmospheric scattering model can be used to model both. As a consequence of this, underwater photos of varying grades should likewise have varied dark channel prior maps. In a nutshell, when it comes to underwater photographs that have varying degrees of contrast, the DCP map becomes darker as the contrast level increases. In order to improve upon the performance of the conventional CCF contrast metric, we devise a DCP weighted contrast measurement.

First, the DCP method [30] is used to take the underwater image that was given as input and then the DCP map I^{dark} is generated from that.

$$I^{\text{dark}}(x) = \min_{y \in \Psi(x)} \left(\min_{c \in (r,g,b)} I^{c}(y) \right) \tag{5}$$

where $c \in r, g, b, \Psi(x)$ denotes a window centered on the pixel x, and the window width is set to 15. I^{c} stands for each channel of the underwater image. After that, taking into account that the contrast of the underwater image is inversely correlated to the intensity of the DCP map, we determine the DCP weighting coefficient by using an exp function of the DCP map's mean value, which is specified as:

$$W_{DCP} = \exp\left(-\frac{I^{\text{dark}}}{\sigma^2}\right) \tag{6}$$

where σ is a parameter and is set to 10 empirically.

Finally, the DCP coefficient-weighted global contrast measurement is presented in

$$\text{Contrast} = W_{DCP} * \text{Contrast}_{CCF} \tag{7}$$

The contrast in the enhanced image of the underwater scene is significantly higher than in the original picture. When comparing underwater photographs of varying quality, it has been found that a higher image quality results in a higher contrast measurement score, which in turn results in improved discrimination.

3.3 Sharpness Measure

Under the impact of the underwater scattering effect, forward scattering causes the underwater image to become extremely blurry. This has the effect of lowering the image's clarity and causing some details and edges of the image to become lost. Therefore, sharpness is the quality of an image that depicts changes in the details of the image, which is a more relevant parameter in the analysis of the quality of an underwater image. In a manner analogous to [31], the sharpness of the grayscale edge map is quantified using the enhancement measure estimation (EME) measure, defined as:

$$\text{Sharpness} = \sum_{c=1}^{3} \lambda_c EME\left(\text{grayscale edge}_c\right) \tag{8}$$

$$EME = \frac{2}{k_1 k_2} \sum_{l=1}^{k_1} \sum_{k=1}^{k_2} \log\left(\frac{I_{\max,k,l}}{I_{\min,k,l}}\right) \tag{9}$$

where the underwater image is partitioned into $k_1 k_2$ blocks, $\left(\frac{I_{\max,k,l}}{I_{\min,k,l}}\right)$ is the relative contrast of each block, and the EME measurements in the three RGB color components are linearly blended with their corresponding coefficient λ_c. In conjunction with the relative visual response of the red, green, and blue channels, the values $\lambda_R = 0.299$, $\lambda_G = 0.587$, and $\lambda_B = 0.114$ are utilized.

3.4 High-Level Semantics

As mentioned in [32], ignoring the high-level semantics of the image in the quality evaluation may lead to certain undesired results. One example of this would be the assignment of a low-quality score to a clear blue sky, which would be inconsistent with the subjective quality evaluation. Therefore, in order to more accurately assess the image quality, we further specify the image's high-level semantics. Because of this, we further characterize the high-level semantics of the image in order to provide a more accurate assessment of the image's quality. Feeding an image into a pretrained deep convolutional neural network (DCNN) model and then extracting the output of the top layers as the high-level features is one of the most common methods that can be found in the research literature. This helps to characterize the image semantics [32–34]. The DCNN model may imitate the human visual perception mechanism by cascading the convolutional layers and the pooling layers for the purpose of extracting the high-level semantics of the image [8].

To extract the high-level perceptual information, we make use of the DCNN-based methods in this work. Due to the fact that the pretrained DCNN model often needs an image patch of defined size as input [7,8], we take the center patch $\mathbf{p}_c$ of size $N \times N$ of the picture and feed it into the pretrained DCNN model to derive its high-level semantics, indicated as

$$\mathbf{f}_h = \mathrm{DCNN}\left(\mathbf{p}_c, L; \mathbf{W}\right) \tag{10}$$

where $\mathbf{f}_h$ stands for the high-level features, L for the layer from which the features are extracted, and $\mathbf{W}$ for the parameters of the DCNN model. Take note that the center patch may not actually represent the whole image. There are additional methods for extracting the patches, some of which can provide a more accurate representation of the image. For example, the image can be cut up into patches, and then the high-level characteristics of each patch can be extracted. This methodology, however, results in a high dimensional feature vector and a significant amount of processing time. Based on the following two factors, we only take into account the central patch in this case. First, the central patch, which contains the original quality data of the image, is immediately taken from the query image. The center portion of the image receives more visual attention from human eyes, according to research on visual saliency [6]. Additionally, only extracting the center patch's high-level properties can also lead to a comparatively good prediction performance. Consequently, it is a good and effective technique to extract the high-level feature of the center patch. In a subsequent study, we plan to look into other patch-extracting techniques that are more efficient and have the potential to better represent the image. When it comes to the actual implementation, we take the activations of the layer that comes before the last softmax layer. This gives rise to a vector with 1000 dimensions that describe the high-level semantics of the image. We use ResNet [8] to explain the extraction process of the high-level perceptual features in Fig. 2. Some example images in the UWIQA database are presented in Fig. 3.

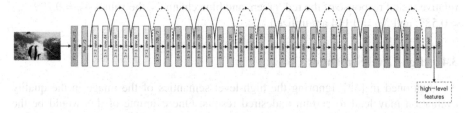

high–level
features

Fig. 2. Extraction of the high-level semantic features of underwater images using the ResNet.

Fig. 3. Examples of UWIQA database

4   Experiment Validation and Discussion

4.1   Performance Evaluation Protocols

In order to validate the proposed method's prediction performance, we apply it to the largest underwater public datasets available, namely the UWIQA [18] database. To thoroughly assess the efficacy of the suggested strategy, we develop a nonlinear regression model with a five-parameter logistic function according to the recommendation made by VQEG [35].

$$M(Y) = \gamma_1 \left(\frac{1}{2} - \frac{1}{1 + \exp\left(\gamma_2 \cdot (Y - \gamma_3)\right)} \right) + \gamma_4 \cdot Y + \gamma_5, \tag{11}$$

where M represents the subject's MOS value and Y represents the predicted score correspondingly. $\gamma_1, ..., \gamma_5$ are the parameters that have been fitted. The Pearson's linear correlation coefficient (PLCC), the Spearman rank order correlation coefficient (SRCC), the Kendall's rank correlation coefficient (KRCC), and the root mean square error (RMSE) are the four commonly used mathematical measures that are adopted. The SRCC and KRCC measure the rank correlation between M and Y. PLCC is a method for quantifying the linear correlation that exists between M and Y. RMSE can be utilized to quantify the error of the suggested method's prediction. The IQA approach has greater performance when the absolute value of these correlation coefficients (SRCC, KRCC, PLCC) is closer to 1 and the RMSE is closer to 0.

4.2   Performance Comparison

The performance of the proposed method is evaluated by contrasting it with the state-of-the-art methods of NR IQA, which are referred to as DBCNN [36], NFERM [37], MEON [13], BRISQUE [38] and BMPRI [39]. All of the methods use the same experimental settings, with each database randomly split into training and test sets. The model will be trained using 80% of the images in the database, which are located in the training set. The remaining 20% of the images are located in the test set, and they will be used to evaluate the performance of the model. In order to reduce the impact of the bias that might be caused by the randomness of data sampling, we repeat the experimental procedure a total of one thousand times, each time producing a set of evaluation results that includes SRCC, KRCC, PLCC, and RMSE. We take the average of all one thousand evaluation results and report it in Table 1, where the evaluation index with the highest performance result is highlighted in boldface.

Table 1. Prediction performance on the UWIQA database in terms of SRCC, KRCC, PLCC, and RMSE. The best result on each indicator is highlighted in boldface.

Database	Index	HyperIQA [40]	NFERM [41]	UCIQE [15]	NIQE [42]	SNP-NIQE [43]	NPQI [44]	Proposed
UWIQA	SRCC	0.6501	0.3486	0.6271	0.4347	0.5516	0.6078	**0.7610**
	KRCC	0.5040	0.2595	0.4863	0.3243	0.4199	0.4667	**0.6174**
	PLCC	0.6799	0.3925	0.6261	0.4687	0.5897	0.6361	**0.7902**
	RMSE	0.1114	0.1398	0.1185	0.1343	0.1228	0.1173	**0.0925**

In Table 1, it is easy to see that the proposed method achieves the greatest results when applied to the dataset, which is solid evidence of the proposed method's superiority and effectiveness. Since the learning-based method, like the HyperNet and NPQI, is able to obtain substantially superior results, this finding suggests that high-level perceptual information of images is an important component in the process of evaluating image quality.

4.3   Discussion

Ablation Study. The low-level perceptual properties and semantics of the underwater image are both taken into consideration while carrying out an analysis of an image's quality using the method that has been proposed here. It is important to investigate the specific role that each category of characteristics plays in the overall quality assessment. If there are certain aspects of the approach that are deemed insignificant, we have the option of omitting such aspects in order to make the process more efficient. In order to accomplish this, we first derive the quality model for each different kind of characteristic, and then we assess how well it performs on the UWIQA database. Experiments were carried out in accordance with the techniques described in Sect. 4.2. The experimental results with regard to SRCC, KRCC, PLCC, and RMSE are presented in Table 2.

It has been noticed that both low-level perceptual properties and high-level semantic features obtain moderate prediction performance when compared to the approach that was proposed, which unmistakably illustrates the significance of these two different kinds of features in terms of quality evaluation. Additionally, the high-level semantic features deliver relatively better performance than the low-level perceptual properties, which indicates that the high-level semantic features have a higher contribution to the proposed method than those low-level related features. In the end, the proposed method achieves the best prediction performance, which indicates that these two categories of attributes play roles in quality evaluation that are complementary to one another.

Table 2. Performance analysis of the various types of features included in the proposed method using the UWIQA database.

Feature type	UWIQA			
	SRCC	KRCC	PLCC	RMSE
Colorness	0.4826	0.3618	0.4983	0.1313
Sharpness	0.5444	0.4128	0.5424	0.1277
Contrast	0.5374	0.4047	0.5298	0.1307
High-level semantics	0.7441	0.5999	0.7728	0.0955
Proposed	0.7610	0.6174	0.7902	0.0925

Computational Efficiency. The proposed method's prediction accuracy has undergone a thorough analysis. Finally, we look at the method's computational effectiveness, which is very crucial for practice [45, 46]. The functionality of real-time systems may be facilitated by an IQA method that is computationally efficient. In this research, we use running time to calculate the efficiency of the suggested technique. We specifically count the running time of the suggested method on the full process of picture quality prediction given an input image. Matlab R 2019b was used for the research, and our machine was outfitted with a 3.0 GHz Intel Core i5-9500 CPU and 8 GB RAM.

Table 3 summarizes the experimental findings. As noted, the suggested method outperforms existing major IQA methods in terms of efficiency, and its running duration is less than one second, indicating considerable promise in practical applications. Despite the fact that some IQA methods, such as BRISQUE, are more efficient than the suggested method, their prediction accuracy remains inadequate. The trade-off between accuracy and computing efficiency is always there. Our future research will concentrate on increasing the efficiency of the proposed method while retaining excellent prediction accuracy. For example, we will investigate more effective approaches for characterizing image naturalness and look for alternatives to the SVR method to improve the quality prediction model's training process.

Table 3. Running time of NR IQA methods measured in seconds

HyperNet	NFERM	NPQI	BRISQUE	SNPNIQE	Proposed
1.03	77.38	5.08	0.33	9.20	0.2510

5 Conclusion

In this paper, the problem of assessing the quality of underwater images without the use of a reference image is addressed, and an efficient quality measure that takes into account both the low-level perceptual properties of the image and its high-level semantics is proposed as a solution. Specifically, the proposed method characterizes the low-level properties of underwater images, and it makes use of pre-trained deep convolutional neural networks to gather semantic information about an image. These extracted perceptual features are then mapped to a single quality score of the image using the SVR approach. A considerable number of experiments are carried out, and the experimental results demonstrate that the proposed technique is superior in terms of the prediction accuracy, the capability of its generalization, and computational efficiency. The experimental results also confirm the proposed method's capabilities in real-world applications.

Acknowledgments. This work is supported by the National Key R&D Program of China (No. 2021YFF0900503), the National Natural Science Foundation of China (No. 62102059 & 62201538), the Fundamental Research Funds for the Central Universities (No. 3132022225), and the Natural Science Foundation of Shandong Province under grant ZR2022QF006.

References

1. Liu, Y., Li, X.: No-reference quality assessment for contrast-distorted images. IEEE Access **8**, 84105–84115 (2020)
2. Liu, Y., Fan, X., Gao, X., Liu, Y., Zhao, D.: Motion vector refinement for frame rate up conversion on 3D video. In: 2013 Visual Communications and Image Processing (VCIP), pp. 1–6. IEEE (2013)
3. Liu, Y., Zhai, G., Zhao, D., Liu, X.: Frame rate and perceptual quality for HD video. In: Ho, Y.-S., Sang, J., Ro, Y.M., Kim, J., Wu, F. (eds.) PCM 2015. LNCS, vol. 9315, pp. 497–505. Springer, Cham (2015). https://doi.org/10.1007/978-3-319-24078-7_50
4. Liu, Y., Zhai, G., Liu, X., Zhao, D.: Perceptual image quality assessment combining free-energy principle and sparse representation. In: 2016 IEEE International Symposium on Circuits and Systems (ISCAS), pp. 1586–1589. IEEE (2016)
5. Hu, R., Liu, Y., Wang, Z., Li, X.: Blind quality assessment of night-time image. Displays **69**, 102045 (2021)
6. Hu, R., Monebhurrun, V., Himeno, R., Yokota, H., Costen, F.: A statistical parsimony method for uncertainty quantification of FDTD computation based on the PCA and ridge regression. IEEE Trans. Antennas Propag. **67**(7), 4726–4737 (2019)
7. Szegedy, C., et al.: Going deeper with convolutions. In: Proceedings of the IEEE Conference on Computer Vision and Pattern Recognition, pp. 1–9 (2015)
8. He, K., Zhang, X., Ren, S., Sun, J.: Deep residual learning for image recognition. In: Proceedings of the IEEE Conference on Computer Vision and Pattern Recognition, pp. 770–778 (2016)
9. Ye, P., Kumar, J., Kang, L., Doermann, D.: Unsupervised feature learning framework for no-reference image quality assessment, pp. 1098–1105 (2012)
10. Bianco, S., Celona, L., Napoletano, P., Schettini, R.: On the use of deep learning for blind image quality assessment. SIViP **12**(2), 355–362 (2018). https://doi.org/10.1007/s11760-017-1166-8
11. Kang, L., Ye, P., Li, Y., Doermann, D.: Convolutional neural networks for no-reference image quality assessment, pp. 1733–1740 (2014)
12. Hou, W., Gao, X., Tao, D., Li, X.: Blind image quality assessment via deep learning. IEEE Trans. Neural Netw. Learn. Syst. **26**(6), 1275–1286 (2014)
13. Ma, K., Liu, W., Zhang, K., Duanmu, Z., Wang, Z., Zuo, W.: End-to-end blind image quality assessment using deep neural networks. IEEE Trans. Image Process. **27**(3), 1202–1213 (2017)

14. Ma, Y., Cai, X., Sun, F.: Towards no-reference image quality assessment based on multi-scale convolutional neural network. Comput. Model. Eng. Sci. **123**(1), 201–216 (2020)
15. Yang, M., Sowmya, A.: An underwater color image quality evaluation metric. IEEE Trans. Image Process. **24**(12), 6062–6071 (2015)
16. Panetta, K., Gao, C., Agaian, S.: Human-visual-system-inspired underwater image quality measures. IEEE J. Oceanic Eng. **41**(3), 541–551 (2015)
17. Wang, Y., et al.: An imaging-inspired no-reference underwater color image quality assessment metric. Comput. Electr. Eng. **70**, 904–913 (2018)
18. Yang, N., Zhong, Q., Li, K., Cong, R., Zhao, Y., Kwong, S.: A reference-free underwater image quality assessment metric in frequency domain. Sig. Process. Image Commun. **94**, 116218 (2021)
19. Van Essen, D.C., Maunsell, J.H.: Hierarchical organization and functional streams in the visual cortex. Trends Neurosci. **6**, 370–375 (1983)
20. Hu, R., Liu, Y., Gu, K., Min, X., Zhai, G.: Toward a no-reference quality metric for camera-captured images. IEEE Trans. Cybern. (2021)
21. Hu, R., Monebhurrun, V., Himeno, R., Yokota, H., Costen, F.: Uncertainty analysis on FDTD computation with artificial neural network. IEEE Antennas Propag. Mag. (2021)
22. Liu, Y., Gu, K., Zhai, G., Liu, X., Zhao, D., Gao, W.: Quality assessment for real out-of-focus blurred images. J. Vis. Commun. Image Represent. **46**, 70–80 (2017)
23. Liu, Y., Zhai, G., Gu, K., Liu, X., Zhao, D., Gao, W.: Reduced-reference image quality assessment in free-energy principle and sparse representation. IEEE Trans. Multimedia **20**(2), 379–391 (2018)
24. Liu, Y., Gu, K., Wang, S., Zhao, D., Gao, W.: Blind quality assessment of camera images based on low-level and high-level statistical features. IEEE Trans. Multimedia **21**(1), 135–146 (2019)
25. Hu, R., Yang, R., Liu, Y., Li, X.: Simulation and mitigation of the wrap-around artifact in the MRI image. Front. Comput. Neurosci. **15**, 89 (2021)
26. Deng, J., Dong, W., Socher, R., Li, L.-J., Li, K., Fei-Fei, L.: ImageNet: a large-scale hierarchical image database. In: 2009 IEEE Conference on Computer Vision and Pattern Recognition, pp. 248–255. IEEE (2009)
27. Zhang, R., Isola, P., Efros, A.A., Shechtman, E., Wang, O.: The unreasonable effectiveness of deep features as a perceptual metric. In: Proceedings of the IEEE Conference on Computer Vision and Pattern Recognition, pp. 586–595 (2018)
28. Hu, R., Monebhurrun, V., Himeno, R., Yokota, H., Costen, F.: An adaptive least angle regression method for uncertainty quantification in FDTD computation. IEEE Trans. Antennas Propag. **66**(12), 7188–7197 (2018)
29. Schettini, R., Corchs, S.: Underwater image processing: state of the art of restoration and image enhancement methods. EURASIP J. Adv. Sig. Process. **2010**, 1–14 (2010). https://doi.org/10.1155/2010/746052
30. He, K., Sun, J., Tang, X.: Single image haze removal using dark channel prior. IEEE Trans. Pattern Anal. Mach. Intell. **33**(12), 2341–2353 (2010)
31. Panetta, K., Samani, A., Agaian, S.: Choosing the optimal spatial domain measure of enhancement for mammogram images. Int. J. Biomed. Imaging **2014**, 3 (2014)
32. Li, D., Jiang, T., Jiang, M.: Exploiting high-level semantics for no-reference image quality assessment of realistic blur images. In: Proceedings of the 25th ACM International Conference on Multimedia, pp. 378–386 (2017)
33. Gu, S., Bao, J., Chen, D., Wen, F.: GIQA: generated image quality assessment. In: Vedaldi, A., Bischof, H., Brox, T., Frahm, J.-M. (eds.) ECCV 2020. LNCS, vol. 12356, pp. 369–385. Springer, Cham (2020). https://doi.org/10.1007/978-3-030-58621-8_22

34. Hu, R., Monebhurrun, V., Himeno, R., Yokota, H., Costen, F.: A general framework for building surrogate models for uncertainty quantification in computational electromagnetics. IEEE Trans. Antennas Propag. **70**(2), 1402–1414 (2021)

35. Rohaly, A.M., Libert, J., Corriveau, P., Webster, A., et al.: Final report from the video quality experts group on the validation of objective models of video quality assessment. ITU-T Standards Contribution COM, pp. 9–80 (2000)

36. Zhang, W., Ma, K., Yan, J., Deng, D., Wang, Z.: Blind image quality assessment using a deep bilinear convolutional neural network. IEEE Trans. Circ. Syst. Video Technol. **30**(1), 36–47 (2020)

37. Gu, K., Zhai, G., Yang, X., Zhang, W.: Using free energy principle for blind image quality assessment. IEEE Trans. Multimedia **17**(1), 50–63 (2015)

38. Mittal, A., Moorthy, A.K., Bovik, A.C.: No-reference image quality assessment in the spatial domain. IEEE Trans. Image Process. **21**(12), 4695–4708 (2012)

39. Min, X., Gu, K., Zhai, G., Liu, J., Yang, X., Chen, C.W.: Blind quality assessment based on pseudo reference image. IEEE Trans. Multimedia **20**(8), 2049–2062 (2017)

40. Su, S., et al.: Blindly assess image quality in the wild guided by a self-adaptive hyper network. In: Proceedings of the IEEE/CVF Conference on Computer Vision and Pattern Recognition, pp. 3667–3676 (2020)

41. Gu, K., Zhai, G., Yang, X., Zhang, W.: Using free energy principle for blind image quality assessment. IEEE Trans. Multimedia **17**(1), 50–63 (2014)

42. Mittal, A., Soundararajan, R., Bovik, A.C.: Making a "completely blind" image quality analyzer. IEEE Sig. Process. Lett. **20**(3), 209–212 (2012)

43. Liu, Y., et al.: Unsupervised blind image quality evaluation via statistical measurements of structure, naturalness, and perception. IEEE Trans. Circ. Syst. Video Technol. **30**(4), 929–943 (2019)

44. Liu, Y., Gu, K., Li, X., Zhang, Y.: Blind image quality assessment by natural scene statistics and perceptual characteristics. ACM Trans. Multimedia Comput. Commun. Appl. (TOMM) **16**(3), 1–91 (2020)

45. Min, X., et al.: Quality evaluation of image dehazing methods using synthetic hazy images. IEEE Trans. Multimedia **21**(9), 2319–2333 (2019)

46. Zhang, J., et al.: HazDesNet: an end-to-end network for haze density prediction. IEEE Trans. Intell. Transp. Syst. **23**(4), 3087–3102 (2020)

Vidoeo Processing

Adaptive Amplitude Modulation and Recovery Method for Video Coding

Haiwu Zhao[✉], Xiwu Shang, Jianghong Yu, and Guozhong Wang

Shanghai University of Engineering Science, Shanghai, China
zhao.hw@avsgm.com, yujianghong@icloud.com, wanggz@sues.edu.cn

Abstract. With the explosive growth of video data, such as ultra-high definition and virtual reality videos, higher video coding schemes are urgently required to improve the compression efficiency. Currently, most methods focus on developing advanced coding techniques. This paper proposes a new method which co-designs the pre-process and post-process units for a codec system. At the encoder side, a pre-process is utilized to modulate the amplitude of an input frame of the input video, which blurs the picture. After the codec procedure, a corresponding decoder post-process recovers the blurred decoded picture by utilizing a demodulation filter. Experimental result demonstrates that the proposed method can improve the codec efficiency by 50.31% on average.

Keywords: Video coding · Pre-process · Post-process · Coding efficiency

1 Introduction

In the past decades, great and tremendous effects have been made to improve the coding efficiency for a codec system. From Moving Picture Experts Group (MPEG)-2 Video, H.264/AVC [1], H.265/HECV [2], to the newest H.266/VVC [3], the efficiency of the video codec systems has been improved a lot, especially in the circumstance of a low bitrate application.

All the codec systems mentioned above utilize the hybrid codec structure [4]. Different modes are adopted to do prediction, and the residue of the prediction is transformed to the frequency domain. In the frequency domain, a quantizer is utilized to adjust the transformed residue. Finally, the prediction information and quantized transformed resided are combined together through the entropy coding.

To improve the coding efficiency, more and more prediction modes are introduced into video codec systems. Here, the intra prediction is used as an example. The mode number of intra prediction increases from 9 modes in H.264/AVC to nearly 67 modes in H.266/VVC [5, 6]. This increased intra mode number makes the prediction much more accurate, and the prediction residue will be smaller. Therefore, the bit number resulted from the residue will be reduced.

However, this trend of increased mode number results in the tremendous increase of computing amount, especially at the encoding side [7, 8]. Compared with the H.264/AVC encoder, the computing amount of the H.265/HEVC encoder generally increase by

© The Author(s), under exclusive license to Springer Nature Singapore Pte Ltd. 2023
G. Zhai et al. (Eds.): IFTC 2022, CCIS 1766, pp. 303–314, 2023.
https://doi.org/10.1007/978-981-99-0856-1_22

5 times [9], and another computing amount increase by 18 times is brought by an H.266/VVC encoder [10]. Meanwhile, the coding efficiency improvement becomes less in the circumstance of high bit rate, compared with the circumstance of low bitrate.

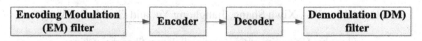

Fig. 1. Structure of the codec with AAMR codec system.

Pre-process and post-process are two widely used techniques to further improve the efficiency of a codec system. By a pre-processing technique [11, 12], such as de-noising, some details are removed from the input video, which will result in a smaller prediction residue and a reduced bitrate. Some post-preprocess techniques [13, 14] will reduce some artifacts of a codec system, and some other post-preprocess techniques carry out image enhancement to improve subjective quality of the decoded video.

However, there is not such a method which co-designs a pre-process unit and a post-preprocess unit at the same time. In this paper, we propose a method called adaptive amplitude modulation and recovery (AAMR) codec system shown in Fig. 1. In this method, an encoding modulation (EM) filter is used in the unit of pre-process, realizing the function of amplitude modulation. A demodulation (DM) filter is used as the post-preprocess unit at the decoder side, realizing the function of recovering blurred pictures. By co-designing all the filters at both the encoder and decoder side, the coding efficiency can be improved significantly [15].

The rest of this paper is organized as follows. Section 2 analyzes the effect of a codec system in the frequency domain. Section 3 describes the principle of AAMR method, and experimental results are show in Sect. 4. A conclusion is drawn in Sect. 5.

2   Frequency Response of a Codec System

For an image/video codec encoder, the loss is introduced by the quantization unit, or the quantizer [16]. There are many zeros generated by the quantizer in the frequency domain, and zeros first appear in the high frequency region. This phenomenon is quite similar to the effect of a low pass filter. However, the quantizer only deals with the transformed prediction residue, instead of the transformed input picture. This difference makes the quantization only affect parts of the input picture, instead of the whole picture. For the decoded picture, we have

$$P_R = P_{pred} + R. \qquad (1)$$

In Eq. (1), P_R represents the decoded picture, P_{pred} is the predicted picture, and R is the decoded prediction residue. Even R is totally removed, much of the frequency component can still be kept by the prediction part.

Therefore, the difference between the input picture and the decoded picture should not be similar to the frequency response of a lowpass filter. This is verified by the curve shown in Fig. 2.

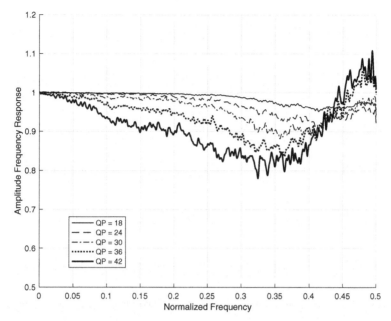

Fig. 2. Frequency response of an H.264/AVC codec

The sequence of "KristenAndSara" is coded by H.264/AVC encoder, and the FFT in the horizontal direction are carried for both an input picture and its corresponding decoded picture. The frequency response of the H.264 codec can be obtained and drawn. In Fig. 2, the results of five different quantization parameters (QP) are shown. From this figure, we can see that there is no zero point of the frequency response of the H.264 codec. We also tried different FFT directions, or different sequences, and similar result are obtained.

Another phenomenon is well known that re-encoded a decoded sequence will result in a low bit rate [17]. The frequency response curves and this phenomenon invoke us to think about what will happen if we do some modulation on the amplitude of the input picture by using an FIR filter to simulate the frequency response of a codec.

3   Principle of Adaptive Amplitude Modulation and Recovery Method

The key point of the frequency response is that there is no zero points in the frequency domain, which is quite different from a standard lowpass filter. It should have some zero points in the stopband.

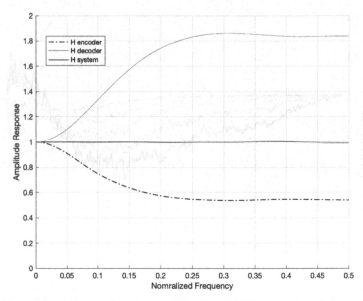

Fig. 3. Amplitude frequency response of EM filter, DM filter and the AAMR method.

Therefore, it is possible that an FIR filter can be utilized as a pre-process filter at the encoder side. There should be no zero points of the frequency response of this FIR filter. This filter is called EM filter. At the decoder side, another FIR can be designed to compensate the encoding modulation filter. This compensating filter is called DM filter. These two filters should satisfy the following condition.

$$\begin{cases} H_{EM} > 0 \\ H_{EM} \cdot H_{DM} \geq 1 \end{cases} \quad (2)$$

In Eq. (2), H_{EM} is the transfer function of the EM filter, and H_{DM} is the transfer function of the decoding demodulation filter. H_{EM} must be greater than 0 everywhere in the frequency domain, for fully recover the input signal at the decoder side. If there is a zero point of H_{EM} in the frequency domain, some frequency components of the input signal will be filtered out, and these frequency components cannot be recovered at the decoder side. The product of H_{EM} and H_{DM} should be equal or greater than 1 to ensure the input signal can be recovered. If the product of H_{EM} and H_{DM} is greater than 1, the decoded picture will have the effect of image enhancement.

To verify Eq. (2), we use a pulse signal and a step signal as the input signal, and do convolutions for a co-designed EM and DM filter, ignoring the codec step. The frequency response of the EM filter, the DM filter, and the AAMR system is show in Fig. 3. The signals of different types are shown in Figs. 4 and 5. For both signals, the max absolute value of error is no more than 1. That is to say, a signal can be fully recovered at the decoder side if errors caused by a codec system were ignored.

From Figs. 4 and 5, we can see that the blurred signal is blurred to some extends, and the basic shape of the pulse signal and step signal is still kept. When this blurring is applied to a picture, the basic structure and details should also be kept.

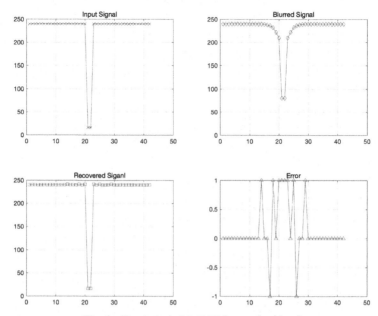

Fig. 4. Simulation of AAMR for a pulse signal

When a codec is taken into account, the artifact caused by the codec should be considered. Therefore, the following two conditions are satisfied to find the best EM and DM filters.

$$FA(QP, H_{EM}(f) \cdot H_{codec} \cdot H_{EM}(f)) \approx FA(QP, H_{codec}) \tag{3}$$

$$FA(QP, H_{EM}(f) \cdot H_{codec} \cdot H_{EM}(f)) \gg FA(QP + 1, H_{codec}) \tag{4}$$

In Eq. (3) and (4), FA is a subjective assessment function, which can assess the subject quality accurately, such as VMAF which is proposed by Netflix [18, 19].

Equation (3) means that when this EM and DM filters are included in the original codec system, the loss of details in a decoded picture in the AAMR codec system should be almost the same as the original codec system without the EM and DM filters. It will be better if loss of details in a decoded picture in the AAMR codec system is smaller. Equation (4) means that the loss of details in a decoded picture must be much smaller than the original codec system without the AAMR codec system while the QP is increased with 1. When these two requirements are fulfilled, the AAMR codec system is acceptable. The amplitude responses of EM and DE filters in Fig. 2 satisfy the requirements, which are adopted in this paper.

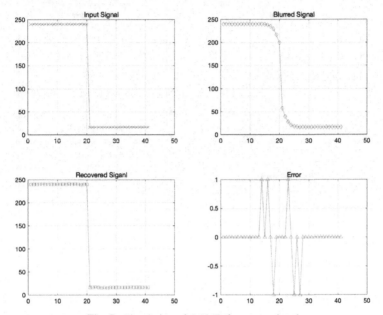

Fig. 5. Simulation of AAMR for a step signal

To yield linear phase filters, we utilize positive symmetry of impulse response $h(n)$, which is denoted by

$$h(n) = h(N - n - 1), \tag{5}$$

where N is the length of the filter. The frequency response can be calculated as

$$H(w) = |H(w)|e^{j\varphi(w)}, \tag{6}$$

where $|H(w)|$ and $\varphi(w)$ are the amplitude response and the phase response respectively. When the impulse response is positive symmetric, $\varphi(w)$ is computed as [20]

$$\varphi(w) = -(\frac{N-1}{2})w. \tag{7}$$

In this paper, N is set to 19. According to the amplitude response in Fig. 2, we can calculate $H(w)$. Taking the inverse DFT of $H(w)$ the impulse responses in the encoder and decoder $h_{en}(n)$ and $h_{de}(n)$ are derived as

$$h_{en}(n) = \frac{1}{256}[3, 3, 4, 4, 3, 3, 5, 9, 14, 160, 14, 9, 5, 3, 3, 4, 4, 3, 3], \tag{8}$$

$$h_{de}(n) = \frac{1}{256}[-6, -6, -6, -7, -6, -4, -7, -17, -29, 430, \\ -29, -17, -7, -4, -6, -7, -6, -6, -6]. \tag{9}$$

The filter operations for each row of the frames in the pre-process and the post-process are performed by

$$P_1(n) = P_0(n) * h_{en}(n), \tag{10}$$

$$P_3(n) = P_2(n) * h_{de}(n),   (11)$$

where $P_0(n), P_1(n), P_2(n)$ and $P_3(n)$ are the original video, pre-processed video, decoded video, and the post-processed video, respectively.

Table 1. The coding performance of different sequences

Sequence	H.265 BD-RATE	H.266 BD-RATE	H.264 + AAMR BD-RATE
Akiyo 355x288	−12.60%	−32.15%	−34.33%
BQMall 832X480	−31.05%	−53.21%	−14.87%
Four people 1280x720	−20.42%	−43.58%	−59.59%
Johnny 1280x720	−32.52%	−47.90%	−79.80%
KristenAndSara 1280x720	−27.05%	−48.43%	−68.96%
BQTerrace 1920x1080	−29.19%	−46.53%	−69.18%
Cactus 1920x1080	−25.35%	−36.10%	−25.43%
Average	−25.45%	−43.99%	−50.31%

4 Experimental Results

To validate the effectiveness of the proposed AAMR method, we integrate it into H.264/AVC codec JM19.0. Sequences with different resolutions and texture information are tested under the random access (RA) profile with four QPs (17, 22, 27, 32). BD-RATE of VMAF is exploited to measure the coding performance [21], where the negative number indicates the performance gain and the positive number indicates the performance loss.

Table 1 demonstrates the experimental results of the proposed AAMR method. Compared with the original encoder H.264/AVC, the AAMR + H.264 method can improve the coding performance by 50.13% in terms of BD-RATE. We also compare AAMR + H.264 with the reference software of H.265/HEVC and H.266/VVC (HM16.0 and VTM 11.0). It can be observed from Table 1 that the proposed method can achieve an additional coding gain of 24.86% and 6.32% on average compared with H.265/HEVC and H.266/VVC codecs, respectively. The reason is that with the proposed method, the high frequency components are suppressed, which is beneficial to improve the prediction accuracy. Thus, the coding efficiency can be improved.

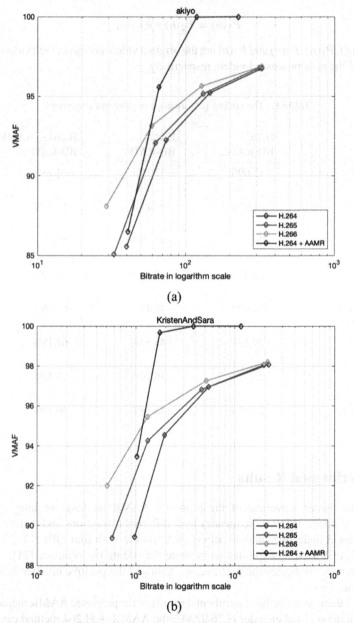

Fig. 6. Illustration of the BD-RATE curves. (a) Sequence "akiyo", (b) Sequence "KeristenAnd-Sara", (c) Sequence "Cactus".

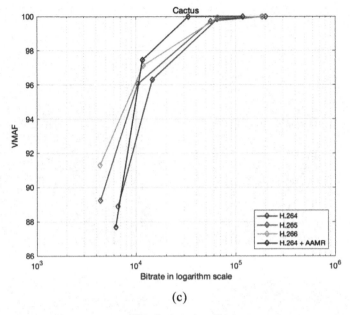

Fig. 6. (*continued*)

We also find that the coding performance of the proposed method is not always the optimal. For example, although the coding performance of "BQmall" of the proposed method is superior to H.264, with a coding gain of 14.87%, its performance is inferior to H.265/HEVC and H.266/VVC. This is because when the coding content are with more sharp edges, the proposed method can only relieve the gradients but not remove them. In this condition, more advanced coding techniques are required to develop to improve the coding performance. Thus, the coding performance of H.265/HEVC and H.266/VVC is better than the proposed method.

It can be seen from Fig. 6 that when the value of bit rate is high, the BD-RATE curve of the proposed method is significantly high. However, when the value of bit rate is low, the performance of the proposed method is not always the best.

During the coding process, a smaller QP corresponds to a higher bit rate. Therefore, the phenomenon in Fig. 6 indicates that the performance of the proposed method under smaller QPs is better than greater QPs. The reason is that the prediction accuracy improved by the proposed method is counteracted by higher QPs. Overall, the BD-RATE curve is significantly higher than other codecs.

Figure 7 shows the subjective quality comparison during the coding process of the proposed method. It can be seen from the right half of Fig. 7(a) that the frame is burred after filtering by EM filter. In the decoder side, the decoded frame is filtered by DM filter, which is almost the same with the original one. Thus, the AAMR system can realize the image enhancement to improve the subjective quality, which is preferred by many end users.

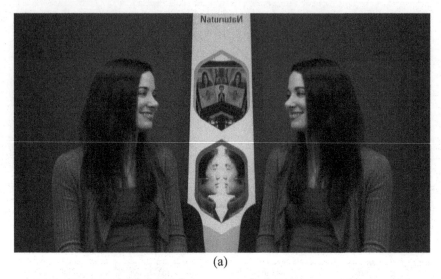

(a)

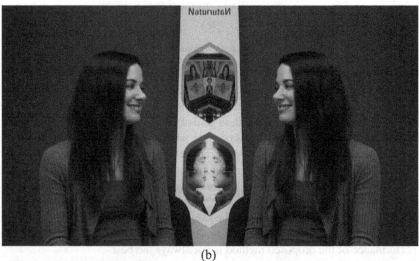

(b)

Fig. 7. Subjective quality comparisons: (a) the original fame VS the blur frame by EM filter; (b) the original frame VS the decoded frame by DM filter.

5 Conclusion

An adaptive amplitude modulation and recovery (AAMR) codec system is proposed in this paper. By blurring the input signal to an appropriate extent and reducing prediction residue, the AAMR methods can reduce the bitrate of an encoder significantly. Meanwhile, the AAMR methods can be applied to all the existing codec system. The AAMR methods only use FIR filters to modulate the amplitude of pictures, which requires ignorable computing resources to realize this method.

Acknowledgments. This work was supported by the National Natural Science Foundation of China under 62001283, National Key R&D Project of China under 2019YFB1802702.

References

1. Wiegand, T., Sullivan, G.J., Bjontegaard, G., Luthra, A.: Overview of the H.264/AVC video coding standard. IEEE Trans. Circuits Syst. Video Technol. **13**(7), 560–576 (2003)
2. Sullivan, G.J., Ohm, J., Han, W., Wiegand, T.: Overview of the high efficiency video coding (HEVC) standard. IEEE Trans. Circuits Syst. Video Technol. **22**(12), 1649–1668 (2012)
3. Bross, B., et al.: Overview of the versatile video coding (VVC) standard and its applications. IEEE Trans. Circuits Syst. Video Technol. **31**(10), 3736–3764 (2021)
4. Bross, B., Chen, J., Ohm, J.-R., Sullivan, G.J., Wang, Y.-K.: Developments in international video coding standardization after AVC, with an overview of versatile video coding (VVC). Proc. IEEE **109**(9), 1463–1493 (2021)
5. Pfaff, J., et al.: Intra prediction and mode coding in VVC. IEEE Trans. Circuits Syst. Video Technol. **31**(10), 3834–3847 (2021). https://doi.org/10.1109/TCSVT.2021.3072430
6. Wu, S., Shi, J., Chen, Z.: HG-FCN: hierarchical grid fully convolutional network for fast VVC intra coding. IEEE Trans. Circuits Syst. Video Technol. **32**(8), 5638–5649 (2022)
7. Tech, G., et al.: CNN-based parameter selection for fast VVC intra-picture encoding. In: 2021 IEEE International Conference on Image Processing (ICIP). IEEE (2021)
8. Wieckowski, A., Bross, B., Marpe, D.: Fast partitioning strategies for VVC and their implementation in an Open Optimized Encoder. In: 2021 Picture Coding Symposium (PCS). IEEE (2021)
9. Correa, G., Assuncao, P., Agostini, L., da Silva Cruz, L.A.: Performance and computational complexity assessment of high-efficiency video encoders. IEEE Trans. Circuits Syst. Video Technol. **22**(12), 1899–1909 (2012)
10. Tun, E., Aramvith, S., Onoye, T.: Low complexity mode selection for H.266/VVC intra coding. ICT Express (2021)
11. Chen, C., Han, J., Xu, Y.: Video denoising for the hierarchical coding structure in video coding. Data Compress. Conf. (DCC) **2020**, 362 (2020)
12. Chadha, A., Andreopoulos, Y.: Deep perceptual preprocessing for video coding. IEEE/CVF Conference on Computer Vision and Pattern Recognition (CVPR) **2021**, 14847–14856 (2021)
13. Zhao, H., He, M., Teng, G., Shang, X., Wang, G., Feng, Y.: A CNN-based post-processing algorithm for video coding efficiency improvement. IEEE Access **8**, 920–929 (2020)
14. Huang, Z., Sun, J., Guo, X., Shang, M.: One-for-all: an efficient variable convolution neural network for in-loop filter of VVC. In: IEEE Transactions on Circuits and Systems for Video Technology (2021)
15. Yu, J.: Image and video processing methods and systems. U.S. Patent 11,064,207 (13 Jul 2021)
16. Rao, K.R., Kim, D.N., Hwang, J.J.: Introduction. In: Video Coding Standards. SCT, pp. 1–36. Springer, Dordrecht (2014). https://doi.org/10.1007/978-94-007-6742-3_1
17. Li, M., Wang, B.: Hybrid H. 264 video transcoding for bitrate reduction in wireless networks. In: 2009 5th International Conference on Wireless Communications, Networking and Mobile Computing. IEEE (2009)
18. Li, Z., Aaron, A., Katsavounidis, I., Moorthy, A., Manohara, M.: Toward a practical perceptual video quality metric. Netflix Technol. Blog **62**(2) (Jun 2016). Accessed 21 Aug 2018
19. Li, Z., et al.: VMAF: The journey continues. Netflix Technol. Blog **25** (Oct 2018). Available: https://netflixtechblog.com/vmaf-the-journey-continues-44b51ee9ed12. Accessed 30 Nov 2018

20. Yan, S., Ma, Y.: A unified framework for designing FIR filters with arbitrary magnitude and phase response. Digital Signal Processing **14**(6), 510–522 (2004)
21. Bjontegaard, G.: Calculation of average PSNR differences between RD-curves. ITU-T VCEG-M33, April, 2001 (2001)

Tracking of Aerial Cooperative Target by Satellite-Based Optical Cameras

Qichang Zhao[1,2], Lian Chen[2], Houmao Wang[3], Yefei Li[2], Yubin Yuan[1], and Yiquan Wu[1(✉)]

[1] School of Electronic Information Engineering, Nanjing University of Aeronautics and Astronautics, Nanjing 211106, China
wuyiquan@163.com
[2] Shanghai Satellite Engineering Research Institute, Shanghai 201109, China
[3] National Space Science Center, Chinese Academy of Sciences, Beijing 100190, China

Abstract. In this paper, we propose a real-time window tracking algorithm for cooperative high-speed aerial targets via optical cameras on satellites. It includes three parts: (1) The relative motion relation between the predicted orbits of the satellite and the aerial target is constructed based on the orbital dynamic theory; (2) The relative position vector is projected to the camera coordinate system; (3) The angular deviation from the relative Line-of-Sight (LoS) between the target and the camera to the optical axis of the camera is calculated. Finally, the window tracking algorithm is implemented on a typical aerial target. Simulation results show that, by using the proposed window tracking algorithm, the angular dispersion of the target in the focal plane of the camera is lower than 0.11% when the swing mirror adjustable speed is less than 2.40 degree per second. The tracking precision is better than 0.53% during the whole tracking measurement process.

Keywords: Optical camera · Aerial target · Target measurement · Program tracking · Window tracking

1 Introduction

Real-time tracking and measurement of aerial targets, such as Unmanned Aerial Vehicles (UAVs), missiles et al. is crucial to national security and defense. Since aerial targets are characterized by fast speed, strong maneuverability and small sizes, it is hard to track it by on-the-earth stations due to non-line-of-sight. Therefore, optical remote sensing satellites are widely used to achieve real-time tracking and measurement in many countries [1].

Aerial targets can be divided into two types, non-cooperative targets and cooperative targets [1]. For non-cooperative target, the motion trajectory is unknown, so the autonomous tracking mode is often used for its tracking [2, 3]. For cooperative targets, the motion trajectory can be obtained through wireless communication, so the tracking mode can be autonomous tracking or programming tracking, which depends on whether the image is processed on board or not.

In autonomous tracking mode, on-board image processing obtains the deviation angle of the target relative to the camera optical axis, and then feeds it back to the camera

G. Zhai et al. (Eds.): IFTC 2022, CCIS 1766, pp. 315–325, 2023.
https://doi.org/10.1007/978-981-99-0856-1_23

tracking servo system, in order to guide the camera optical axis to the target. However, the autonomous tracking mode requires high-performance on-board information processing system, so the application is still limited now. In contrast, program tracking is often used for cooperative targets nowadays. In this mode, the camera's optical axis is controlled to track and measure the target by ground stations, which is based on the orbit and platform attitude of the target and satellite platform. As most data is processed on the ground, the onboard information processing system is easy to implement and is widely used in the optical surveillance systems [4–6].

For the tracking problem, the method measuring aerial targets on the ground without real-time prediction of their spatial positions has been proposed [7]. However, it is not applicable to the scene that both of the target and the measurement satellite are moving. Image-based ground target tracking methods have been proposed in [8–10]. However, they are not suitable for aerial target tracking, where the LoS of the measuring camera needs to be adjusted in real time. Target contour extraction and recognition using multiple features of the target at the same time are adopted in [11, 12]. However, they are not suitable for small-target recognition and tracking with insignificant morphological features.

In order to achieve real-time tracking and measurement of high-speed aerial targets, in this paper, we propose a window tracking algorithm that controls the camera swing mirror to achieve high-precision real-time tracking and measurement of on-orbit cooperative targets. The proposed algorithm can improve efficiency and expand engineering application of in-flight target tracking.

The left of the paper is organized as follows. Methods are introduced in Sect. 2. Results and discussion are presented in Sect. 3. Finally, the whole paper is concluded in Sect. 4.

2 Methods

2.1 System Model

The relation between the tracking window and the Field of View (FOV) is shown in Fig. 1. The red point represents the target, while FOV_h and FOV_v represent the horizontal and vertical field of view for the camera, respectively. The grey area encompassed by dotted frame refers to tracking window, the size of which is $2n_2FOV_h \times 2n_1FOV_v$, where n_1 and n_2 are restraint coefficients determining the size of the trace window.

When the target moves out of the agreed FOV, the swing mirror should be adjusted quickly to make sure that the target move into the FOV. The swing mirror repeats the process of 'keep-adjust-keep' to complete the window tracking of the cooperative target.

The moving process of swing mirror for the window tracking is illustrated in Fig. 2.

Let, t_{out}, t_{in}, T_{hold}^i, T_{move}^i denote the window serial number, the target leaving the field window; the target at the initial position in the FOV, the target holding time in the i-th field window, and the time required for the swing mirror adjusting from the i-th window to the $(i + 1)$-th window, respectively.

Therefore, we have the following relations:

$$T_{move}^i = m \cdot T_{hold}^i \qquad (1)$$

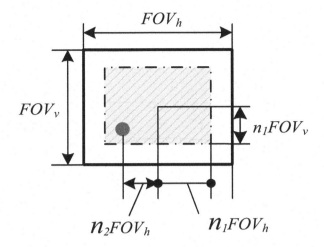

Fig. 1. The relation between the tracking window and the field of view

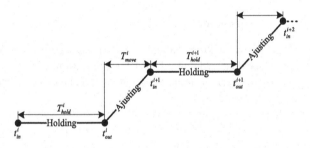

Fig. 2. The moving process of swing mirror or the window tracking

$$t_{in}^{i+1} = t_{out}^{i} + T_{move}^{i} \tag{2}$$

$$T_{hold}^{i} = t_{out}^{i} - t_{in}^{i} \tag{3}$$

where m denotes the coefficient for time adjustment.

To calculate the angular deviation between the relative LoS of the target and the measuring camera and the optical axis of the camera, we define the camera measurement coordinate system o-xyz which is illustrated in Fig. 3.

The origin of the coordinate is located in the center of the focal plane of the camera. The oz axis coincides with the optical axis of the camera. The ox axis is located in the main symmetry plane of the camera, perpendicular to the oz axis and pointing to the direction of satellite speed. The oy axis can be finally obtained since oy, ox and oz axes form a right-handed coordinate system.

When the camera is not working, the camera measurement coordinate system o-xyz coincides with the satellite body coordinate system.

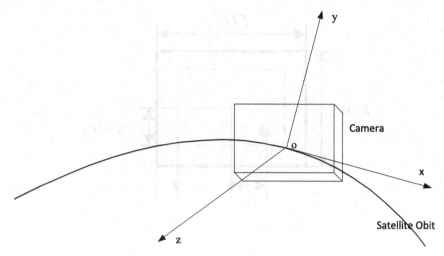

Fig. 3. The camera measurement coordinate system

2.2 Tracking Target Coordinate Conversion

To achieve real-time window tracking of aerial targets, the swing mirror of the measuring camera needs to be adjusted according to the tracking deviation, which is characterized by the angular deviation between the relative LoS of the target and the measuring camera and the optical axis of the camera.

Above all, we should transform the relative position of the target from the geocentric inertial system to the satellite body coordinate system. The process of coordinate conversion will be introduced in the following.

Firstly, it is transferred from the geocentric inertial system to the satellite orbital coordinate system by the matrix [13–15]:

$$M_{OG} = M_3[u] \cdot M_2[i] \cdot M_3[R] \tag{4}$$

where R, i, u are Right ascension, orbital inclination and latitude argument of ascending intersection point, M_1 and M_3 are rotation matrixes.

Secondly, it is transferred from satellite orbital coordinate system to the satellite body coordinate system by the matrix M_{BO} [13–15]

$$M_{BO} = M_2[\vartheta] \cdot M_1[\gamma] \cdot M_3[\Psi] \tag{5}$$

where θ, γ, Ψ are attitude angles, M_1, M_2 and M_3 are rotation matrixes.

Thirdly, it is transferred from the satellite body coordinate system to the camera measurement coordinate system by the matrix M_{OB} [13–15].

$$M_{OB} = M_1[v] \cdot M_2[\theta] \tag{6}$$

where v, θ are swing mirror pitch and azimuth, respectively. M_1 and M_2 are rotation matrixes.

Thus, the transfer matrix from the geocentric inertial system to the camera measurement coordinate system is

$$
\begin{aligned}
M_p &= M_{OB} \cdot M_{BO} \cdot M_{OG} \\
&= M_1[v] \cdot M_2[\theta] \cdot M_2[\vartheta] \cdot M_1[\gamma] \cdot M_3[\psi] \cdot M_3[u] \cdot M_1[i] \cdot M_3[R]
\end{aligned}
\tag{7}
$$

Assuming that the coordinates of the target and the observational satellite in the geocentric inertial system are (X_t, Y_t, Z_t) and (X_s, Y_s, Z_s), respectively, the relative coordinates of the target in the camera measurement coordinate system (x_p, y_p, z_p) will be.

$$
\begin{pmatrix} x_p \\ y_p \\ z_p \end{pmatrix} = M_p \cdot \begin{pmatrix} X_t - X_s \\ Y_t - Y_s \\ Z_t - Z_s \end{pmatrix}
\tag{9}
$$

2.3 Calculation of Relative LoS Angle Deviation

The angular deviation can be obtained based on the coordinate transformation, through the coordination transformation, we can obtain the motion of the target relative to the camera LoS.

When the swing mirror performs two-dimensional pointing tracking, the normal of the incident plane rotates α and the angle between the incident direction and the outgoing direction changes 2α. Therefore, the angular deviation of the target relative to the two-dimensional swing mirror can be written as

$$
\begin{cases}
\lambda_1 = \frac{1}{2} arctg\left(\frac{x_p}{z_p}\right) \\
\lambda_2 = \arcsin\left(\frac{y_p}{(x_p^2 + y_p^2 + z_p^2)^{1/2}}\right)
\end{cases}
\tag{9}
$$

where λ_1, λ_2 are azimuth angle and pitch angle of target in measuring coordinate system, which are illustrated in Fig. 4.

Because the dynamic data is a function of time, the time series of the relative angular position of the target can be obtained.

2.4 Window Tracking Algorithm

Let $f(t)$ denote the movement relation between the target and the swing mirror fitted by the time series of the relative angular positions. Generally, the functions in the quadratic polynomial form.

Thus, time of the target in the field of view can be described as:

$$
\begin{cases}
|f_h(t_{h,mid}^i) - f_h(t_{in}^i)| = n_1 \cdot FOV_h \\
|f_v(t_{v,mid}^i)| - f_v(t_{in}^i) = n_1 \cdot FOV_v \\
t_{mid}^i = \min(t_{h,mid}^i, t_{v,mid}^i)
\end{cases}
\tag{10}
$$

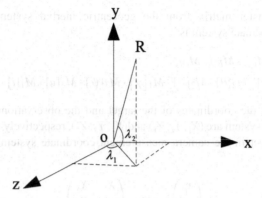

Fig. 4. Angular displacement of target relative line of sight and measuring coordinate system

where t^i_{mid} is the time duration at the center view of the FOV, $|\cdot|$ means the absolute calculation, t^i_{mid} equals to the minimum value of $t^i_{h,mid}$ and $t^i_{v,mid}$ considering that the target reaches the center of the window in every direction by way of pitch or roll.

Out-of-field time of the target can be described as

$$\begin{cases} |f_h(t^i_{h,out}) - f_h(t^i_{mid})| = n_1 \cdot FOV_h \\ |f_v(t^i_{v,out}) - f_v(t^i_{mid})| = n_1 \cdot FOV_v \\ t^i_{out} = \min(t^i_{h,out}, t^i_{v,out}) \end{cases} \tag{11}$$

where t^i_{out} is the time of the target out of field. The definition of absolute value is similar to (10).

Let $\Delta\theta^i_{g,h}$ and $\Delta\theta^i_{g,v}$ denote the movement angle of the swing mirror from the i-th window to the $(i + 1)$-th window, $\overline{\omega}^i_{g,h}$ and $\overline{\omega}^i_{g,v}$ the average angular velocity in both directions. The center position of the i-th FOV (that is, the pointing of the swing mirror) can be described as

$$\theta^i_{g,h} = \frac{1}{2}f_h(t^i_{mid}) \tag{12}$$

$$\theta^i_{g,v} = f_v(t^i_{mid}) \tag{13}$$

When the swing mirror is adjusted from the i-th position to the $(i + 1)$-th position, the average adjustment angular velocity is:

$$\Delta\theta_{g,h} = |f_h(t^{i+1}_{mid}) - f_h(t^i_{mid})| = 2\overline{\omega}^i_{g,h} \cdot T^i_{move} \tag{14}$$

$$\Delta\theta^i_{g,v} = |f_v()t^{i+1}_{mid} - f_v(t^i_{mid})| = \overline{\omega}^i_{g,v} \cdot T^i_{move} \tag{15}$$

When the swing mirrors holding, the average angular velocity of the target on the focal plane, i.e., $\overline{\omega}^i_{t,h}$ and $\overline{\omega}^i_{t,v}$, $\overline{\omega}^i_{t,h}$ and $\overline{\omega}^i_{t,v}$, can be solved by (16) and (17).

$$|f_h(t^i_{out}) - f_h(t^i_{in})| = \overline{\omega}^i_{t,h} \cdot T^i_{hold} \tag{16}$$

$$|f_v(t^i_{out}) - f_v(t^i_{in})| = \overline{\omega}^i_{t,v} \cdot T^i_{hold} \tag{17}$$

When the swing mirror is adjusted, the relative angular velocities of the target on the focal plane are $(2\overline{\omega}^i_{g,h} - \overline{\omega}^i_{t,h})$ and $(\overline{\omega}^i_{g,v} - \overline{\omega}^i_{t,v})$.

Let τ_{int} denote the integration time, and DAS denote the angular resolution of the detector pixel, then the size of the dispersion spot (n_{hold} and n_{move}) caused by the relative motion of the target can be calculated as:

Holding stage:

$$n_{hold} = \sqrt{(\overline{\omega}^i_{t,h})^2 + (\overline{\omega}^2_{t,v})} \cdot \tau_{int}/DAS \tag{18}$$

Adjustment stage:

$$n_{move} = \sqrt{(2\overline{\omega}^i_{g,h} - \overline{\omega}^i_{t,h})^2 + (\overline{\omega}^i_{g,v} - \overline{\omega}^2_{i,v})} \tau_{int}/DAS \tag{19}$$

As shown in Fig. 5, let λ denote the angle of the target relative to the optical axis of the measuring camera swing mirror (measuring coordinate system axis oz), it can be calculated by

$$\lambda = arcos\left(\frac{z}{(x^2 + y^2 + z^2)^{1/2}}\right) = g(x, y, z) \tag{20}$$

where x, y, z are coordinates of the target in the measurement coordinate system.

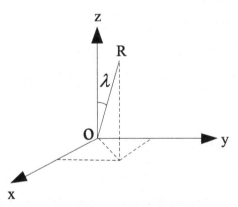

Fig. 5. Angular position relation between target's relative line of sight and measuring camera's optical axis

Assuming that the satellite attitude angle, camera LOS angle error, and the angle between the relative line of sight and the optical axis of the camera follow the normal distribution of zero mean value, the target tracking error $\Delta\lambda$ can be calculated by differentiate (20).

$$\Delta\lambda = \frac{\partial g}{\partial x} \cdot \Delta x + \frac{\partial g}{\partial y} \cdot \Delta y + \frac{\partial g}{\partial z} \cdot \Delta z \tag{21}$$

where σ_λ is the tracking precision defined as:

$$\sigma_\lambda = \sqrt{\left(\frac{\partial g}{\partial x}\right)^2 \cdot \sigma_x^2 + \left(\frac{\partial g}{\partial y}\right)^2 \cdot \sigma_y^2 + \left(\frac{\partial g}{\partial z}\right)^2 \cdot \sigma_z^2} \tag{22}$$

To sum up, the details of the proposed winding tracking algorithm are shown in Figure 6.

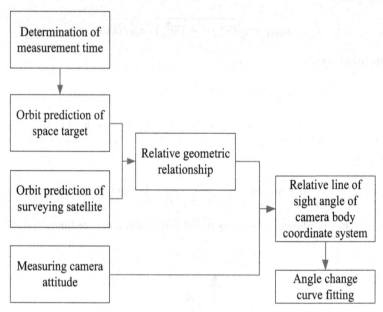

Fig. 6. Flowchart of the window tracking process

3   Results and Discussion

3.1   Simulation Setup

We use Systems Tool Kit (STK [16–21]) to evaluate the performance of the proposed tracking and measurement scheme of on-orbit aerial target. The orbit and attitude parameters of the satellite and the aerial target are set as shown in Table 1.

Table 1. Orbit parameters of measuring satellite and aerial target

Parameter	Measuring satellite	Aerial target
Orbit type	sun-synchronous orbit	circular orbit
Orbit height	600km	1000km
Orbit inclination	97.8°	45°
Ascending node Right ascension	279.1°	10°
Eccentricity	0	0
True perigee angle	0o	0o
Start and end time of measurement	1 Jul 2007 12:22:30.181–1 Jul 2007 12:30:57.064	

According to the optical camera design, horizontal field of view of camera is 4.4°, vertical field of view of camera is 5.5°, n = 1/3, τ_{int} = 20ms, DAS = 1'.

3.2 Window Tracking Results

Based on the simulated orbit data of the measured satellite and the aerial target, the angle sequence of the relative position of the target and satellite changing with time can be obtained by (4)–(8), and the functional relations between the change angle of the visual axis and time can be fitted. Then, the window tracking can be realized by (9)–(13), and the results are shown in Fig. 7. The blue box represents the tracking window. The red dot represents the target, and the blue line represents the fitting curve of pitch and roll angle of the target in the measurement coordinate system.

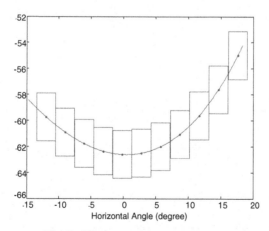

Fig. 7. Window tracking target process

It can be obtained that the number of adjustments of swing mirror are 11. The angular velocity ranges of the swing mirror adjustment in rolling direction and pitch direction can be calculated from Eq. (14)–(17), which are 0.0047–2.26 degree per second and 0.11–2.40 degree per second, respectively. Angular dispersion in holding stage and adjusting stage can be calculated from Eq. (18)–(19), which are 0.098%–0.11% and 0.086%–0.10%, respectively.

Thus, we can conclude that, when the maximum adjustable speed of the swing mirror in the roll direction is not less than 2.26 degree per second and in the direction angle is not less than 2.40 degree per second, the proposed window tracking algorithm can be guaranteed to track the target. These results present the constraint on the capability of the swing mirror, which is instructive to the design of the swing mirror control system.

3.3 Tracking Error Analysis

Tracking error can be calculated from Eq. (21)–(22), which is 2.40–2.72 pixels as shown in Fig. 8.

Thus, during the whole tracking process, the angle dispersion of the target on the focal plane is not greater than 0.11%, leading to good imaging quality. Since the tracking error is only 2.40–2.72 pixels, the tracking precision is better than 0.53% of the focal plane with 1024×512 pixels. In order to further improve the tracking precision, it is necessary to improve the satellite attitude measurement and control precision, and reduce the camera swing mirror pointing control error. From Figs. 5 and 6 and the simulation results, we can find that the number of swing mirror adjustments is rare during the tracking period, which can reduce the number of swings of the swing mirror and help to extend its life.

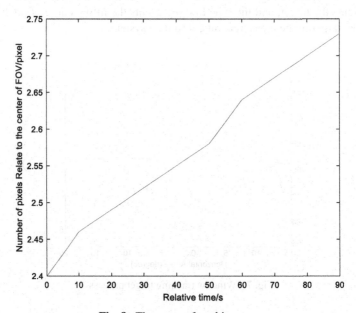

Fig. 8. The curve of tracking error

4 Conclusions

From the perspective of orbital dynamic theory, we propose a real-time window tracking algorithm for aerial targets via satellite-based optical camera. The window tracking of aerial targets in a typical orbit is simulated and analyzed. Simulation results show that when the speed constraints of the swing mirror are satisfied, the proposed window algorithm can track the target with good imaging quality and high tracking precision.

References

1. Che, R., Zhang, H.: Relative orbit design of tracking stars for tracking non cooperative targets in space. Aerospace Control **24**(5), 40–45 (2006)
2. Grant, H.S., von Curt, B., Ramaswamy, S., et al.: The space-based visible program. Lincoln Lab. J. **11**(2), 205–238 (1998)
3. Zhang, Y., Li, Q., Yu, F., et al.: Air to ground target detection and tracking method based on multi feature fusion. Electro Optics and Control **26**(06), 6–11 (2019)
4. Ge, Z., Liu, J., Zhang, R., et al.: Development and Status Quo of US Russian Missile Early Warning Satellite. Spacecraft Eng. **10**(4), 38–44 (2001)
5. DSP 1,2,3,4 (Phase 1). http://space.skyrocket.de/doc_sdat/dsp-1.htm
6. Beaulieu, R., Alfriend, T., Jerardi, T.: Launch detection satellite system engineering error analysis. J. Spacecr. Rocket. **35**(4), 487–495 (1998)
7. Xu, Z., Wu, L., Wang, X.: Real time automatic acquisition method of near earth and medium high orbit aerial targets. Invention patent, CN201110449365.92015.01
8. Ma, C., Huang, J.B., Yang, X., et al. Hierarchical convolutional features for visual tracking. In: ICCV, pp. 3074–3082 (2015)
9. Guang-Long, W., Jie, T., Wen-Jie, Z., et al.: HOGHS and zernike moments features-based motion-blurred object tracking. Int. J. Humanoid Rob. **16**(1), 1950004 (2019)
10. Zhang, Y., Tang, Y., Fang, B., et al.: Multi-object tracking using deformable convolution networks with tracklets updating. Int. J. Wavelets Multi-resolut. Inform. Process. **7**, 1–20 (2019)
11. Ke, B., Zheng, H., Chen, L., et al.: Multi-object tracking by joint detection and identification learning. Neural Process. Lett. **50**(1), 283–296 (2019)
12. Karunasekera, H., Wang, H., Zhang, H.: Multiple object tracking with attention to appearance structure motion and size. IEEE Access **7**, 104423–104434 (2019)
13. Xi, X., Wang, W.: Orbital Basis of Near Earth Spacecraft, pp. 66–68. National University of Defense Technology Press, Changsha (2003)
14. Li, J.: Spacecraft Orbit Determination, pp. 60–67. National Defense Industry Press, Beijing (2003)
15. Zhao, Y., Yi, D., Pan, X., et al.: Visibility analysis of aerial targets based on space-based optical observation. J. Aircraft Meas. Control **26**(3), 5–12 (2007)
16. Yang, Y., Wang, Q.: Application of STK in Computer Simulation. National Defense Industry Press, Beijing (2005)
17. Li, Y., Li, Z.: Simulation analysis of Starlink constellation coverage based on STK. The first network paper of Command, Control and Simulation, 12 Aug 2022
18. Xu, Z.: Simulation study of STK in GPS system. Value Eng. **31**(16), 178–179 (2012)
19. Wang, X.: Simulation and analysis of beidou satellite navigation system based on STK. Enterp. Sci. Technol. Dev. **3**, 79–80 (2018)
20. Ni, Y., Chen, J., Wei, B., et al.: Simulation and performance analysis of BDS constellation based on STK. Comput. Meas. Control **24**(1), 281–288 (2016)
21. Xu, J., Bai, X., Zhou, X.: Simulation analysis of reconnaissance satellite coverage based on STK. Softw. Guide **15**(8), 156–158 (2016)

Regression Augmented Global Attention Network for Query-Focused Video Summarization

Min Su[1,2], Ran Ma[1,2]([⊠]), Bing Zhang[1,2], Kai Li[1,2], and Ping An[1,2]

[1] School of Communication and Information Engineering, Shanghai University, 99 Shangda Road, Baoshan District, Shanghai 200444, China
maran@shu.edu.cn
[2] Shanghai Institute for Advanced Communication and Data Science, Shanghai University, 99 Shangda Road, Baoshan District, Shanghai 200444, China

Abstract. Video summarization compresses a long video into some keyframes or a short video, which enables users to quickly obtain important contents in the video and improves the user experience. However, generic video summarization generates a single summarization result for each video, ignoring the user subjectivity. Query-focused video summarization introduces the user subjectivity in the form of user query into the summary process, and takes into account the importance of the frames/shots selected in the summarization and their relevance to the query jointly, which solves the above problem well. For query-focused video summarization, we propose a Regression Augmented Global Attention Network (RAGAN), which is mainly composed of a global attention module and a query-aware regression module. The global attention module takes advantage of the key concept of multiple computational steps (which is termed as "hops") used in the memory network to continuously optimize the global attention information between hops. The query-aware regression module consists of a skip connection, a multi-modal feature fusion module and a two-layer fully connected network. The skip connection combines information from low and high layers. The multi-modal feature fusion module fuses visual features and textual features from three perspectives, i.e., the original information of each modality, the additive interaction between two modalities and the multiplicative interaction between two modalities. The two-layer fully connected network regresses the fused features to the importance scores to obtain the final video summarization result. Extensive experiments on the query-focused video summarization dataset demonstrate the effectiveness of our proposed RAGAN model.

Keywords: Video summarization · Query · Global attention · Multi-modal feature fusion

1 Introduction

For video summarization, we can classify it into query-focused video summarization and generic video summarization according to whether the summary process involves user query. Generic video summarization generates a single summarization result for each video, consisting of the most representative and diverse video contents. However, different users may have various preferences over the summaries, that is, generic video summarization has not taken into account the user subjectivity. Query-focused video summarization is an emerging research direction in the field of video summarization to solve the above problem in recent years. It introduces the user subjectivity in the form of user query into the summary process, and the generated summarization takes into account both the context importance of video frames/shots and their relevance to the query. When a user has need of customizing a video summarization for a long video to quickly obtain information of interest, query-focused video summarization will be very useful.

Recent researches on query-focused video summarization mainly use long short-term memory (LSTM) network to model the temporal dependencies between video frames/shots [1–3] or use global attention mechanism to generate the importance scores for frames/shots [4, 5]. However, there are some drawbacks in the above methods. In the case of a long input sequence, LSTM is not only time-consuming, but also loses the information from previous time steps. The global attention mechanism only performs one computational step and still contains some redundant information.

To this end, we propose a novel query-focused video summarization method called Regression Augmented Global Attention Network (RAGAN) in this paper. Our proposed approach is inspired by the end-to-end memory network (MemN2N) [6], which is a classic model in the task of question answering (QA) and has strong long-term memory modeling ability. The key concept of multiple hops in MemN2N performs multiple computational steps before producing an output, thereby enhancing the memory extraction.

Unlike another research that applies memory network to query-focused video summarization [7], which uses memory network to calculate the relevance between text query and each video shot, our proposed RAGAN uses memory network to obtain global attention between all video shots, and then predicts the probability of each shot being selected to form a summary through the query-aware regression module. Specifically, RAGAN is composed of two modules, i.e., the global attention module and the query-aware regression module. The global attention module obtains global attention by taking all shot features as input, and then performs multiple hops to continuously optimize the extracted long-term memory. And this module outputs a memory output sequence that contains context-important information in the video. The query-aware regression module is composed of a skip connection, a multi-modal feature fusion module, and a fully connected network. The skip connection combines the input and output of the global attention module, and then the multi-modal feature fusion module takes the combined representation and the text query as input to obtain the relevance between the video shot and the query. Finally, the fully connected network is used to regress the fused feature representation to the shot-level importance scores. Thus, the final obtained summarization result contains both context-important shots and shots related to the text query.

The key contributions are as follows:

1. We propose a novel query-focused video summarization method called Regression Augmented Global Attention Network (RAGAN). This network performs multiple hops to continuously optimize the extracted global attention information to obtain a memory output sequence, and then uses the query-aware regression module to perform multi-modal feature fusion between visual features and textual features. Finally, the importance score for each video shot is generated, simultaneously measuring the relevance to the query and the contextual importance.

2. To archive more sufficient fusion between the visual features from the output of the skip connection and the textual features from the input query, we combine the above features from three perspectives in the query-aware regression module, i.e., the original information of each modality, the additive interaction between two modalities and the multiplicative interaction between two modalities. Then the fused features are regressed to shot-level importance scores through a fully connected network.

3. Extensive experiments on the query-focused video summarization dataset demonstrate that our approach outperforms several state-of-the-art supervised approaches.

2   Related Work

Since Zhang et al. [8] introduced LSTM into the field of generic video summarization in 2016, more and more scholars have begun to research generic video summarization methods based on deep learning, including supervised [8–10], unsupervised [11, 12] and weakly-supervised methods [13, 14]. Compared with generic video summarization, query-focused video summarization takes a user query and a video as the input of the algorithm and outputs a summarization result related to the user query, taking into account the subjectivity of users. It is an emerging research direction in video summarization task, and can also be classified into supervised [4, 5, 7, 15–17], unsupervised [1, 2] and weakly-supervised [18] ones.

Sharghi et al. [15] first proposed the task of query-focused video summarization in 2016, and proposed a model called Sequential and Hierarchical Determinantal Point Process (SH-DPP) for this task. The model considered the shot's importance in the video context and relevance to the query when deciding whether to select a shot to form the summarization result. In 2017, Sharghi et al. [7] established a query-focused video summarization dataset on the basis of the UT Egocentric (UTE) dataset [19], which was later widely used in the field of query-focused video summary, and Sharghi et al. proposed a memory network parameterized sequential determinantal point process (seqDPP) for the query-focused video summarization task in [7]. In 2017, Vasudevan et al. [16] also proposed a dataset for query-focused video summary, the Relevance And Diversity (RAD) dataset, and a Quality-Aware Relevance (QAR) model for this dataset. Zhang et al. [1] proposed a three-player generative adversarial network in 2018, introducing a three-player loss to force the generator to learn better summarization. In 2019, Jiang et al. [2] designed a Hierarchical Variational Network (HVN), which improved the user-oriented diversity to some extent. Zhang et al. [3] introduced deep reinforcement learning into query-focused video summarization, and proposed a Mapping Network (MapNet) to jointly model relatedness, diversity and representativeness. In 2020, Huang et al. [17] proposed an end-to-end model for RAD dataset, which was composed of a controller, a generator and a output module. Xiao et al. [4] proposed a Convolutional Hierarchical Attention Network (CHAN), which consisted of a feature encoding network that learns visual representation of video shots and a query-relevance computing module that generates the final summary result. In the same year, Xiao et al. [5] proposed a Query-Biased Self-Attentive Network (QSAN), which first used the reinforced caption generator and the hierarchical self-attentive network to calculate the general importance scores of video shots, and then used the query-aware scoring module to select the query-related shots to generate a summary. In 2022, Cizmeciler et al. [18] proposed a weakly supervised model for the RAD dataset, where weakly supervision was semantic saliency maps predicted by pre-trained attribute/action classifiers.

The above methods have obtained meaningful query-focused video summarization results, which can be proved by the experimental results in the corresponding papers. However, they ignored the redundant information in the global attention under one computational step, and only employed element-wise multiplication when calculating the relevance between each video frame/shot and user query, resulting in insufficient fusion between multi-modal features. Our proposed RAGAN model makes multiple hops to continuously optimize the extracted information, and fuses visual features and textual features from multiple perspectives such as additive interaction and multiplicative interaction between two modalities, which effectively solves the above problems.

3 The Proposed Approach

In this section, we first describe the problem formulation. Then we give the details of our proposed RAGAN model, including the global attention module and the query-aware regression module. Finally, we explain the process of summarization generation.

3.1 Problem Formulation

Our proposed RAGAN model takes the feature sequence of video shots $\{x_i\}, i \in \{1, 2, \ldots, N\}, x_i \in \mathbb{R}^{D_1}$ as input, where N is the total number of shots in the video, x_i represents the extracted feature of i-th shot in the video, and D_1 is the feature dimension. The model outputs an importance score sequence $\{s_i\}, i \in \{1, 2, \ldots, N\}, s_i = [0, 1)$ for video shots, where s_i is the importance score corresponding to i-th video shot x_i. For each component of the model, as illustrated in Fig. 1, the global attention module takes $\{x_i\}$ as input, and outputs the memory output sequence $\{o_i\}, i \in \{1, 2, \ldots, N\}, o_i \in \mathbb{R}^{D_2}$, where D_2 is the feature dimension of the memory output o_i. The query-aware regression module takes the original feature sequence $\{x_i\}$, the memory output sequence $\{o_i\}$, and the text concept feature c as input, and outputs the shot-level importance score sequence $\{s_i\}$, where two text concepts form a user query [7].

3.2 Global Attention Module

We design this module for the purpose of obtaining the global attention between all video shots, thereby giving higher weight to the context-important video shots. However, there may be some redundant information in the feature representation obtained by global

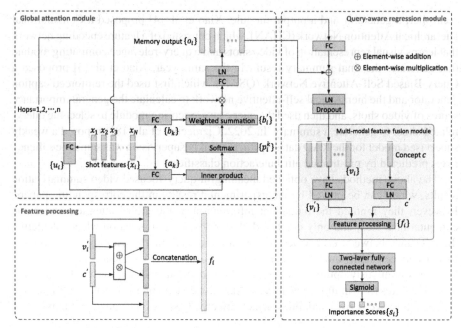

Fig. 1. The framework of our proposed regression augmented global attention network (RAGAN), which consists of a global attention module that performs multiple hops to extract global attention information between all video shots and a query-aware regression module that makes a fusion of visual representation and text query to generate importance score for each shot.

attention under one computational step, which affects the final summary result. In order to solve this problem, we perform multiple hops over the global attention extraction process, and input the memory output sequence of the current hop to the next hop. The extracted long-term memory information can be continuously optimized between hops to obtain more useful information.

Figure 1 shows the structure of the global attention module. Firstly, we pass the input shot feature sequence $\{x_i\}$ through three different fully connected layers to obtain the internal state sequence $\{u_i\}$, the input memory sequence $\{a_k\}$ and the output memory sequence $\{b_k\}$ respectively. Secondly, the inner product between $\{u_i\}$ and $\{a_k\}$ is calculated, and then through a softmax function, we get the attention weights $\{p_i^k\}$, where p_i^k represents the attention weight of each internal state u_i with respect to the input memory a_k. The above operation is expressed by the following equation:

$$p_i^k = Softmax\left(\alpha u_i^T a_k\right) \qquad (1)$$

where $i, k \in \{1, 2, \ldots, N\}$, $\alpha = 0.05$ is a scale parameter that reduces the inner product value, determined experimentally.

Then we perform summation over $\{b_k\}$ weighted by the attention weights $\{p_i^k\}$ to get $\{b_i'\}$:

$$b_i' = \sum_k p_i^k b_k \qquad (2)$$

After obtaining the weighted summation result, we make element-wise multiplication between $\{b_i'\}$ and $\{u_i\}$, and then the computing result is passed through a fully connected layer with layer normalization (LN) to get the memory output sequence $\{o_i\}$, which represents the global attention vector of other frames in the video to the current frame:

$$o_i = LN\left(FC\left(b_i' \otimes u_i\right)\right) \tag{3}$$

Finally, we use the memory output sequence $\{o_i\}$ of the current hop as the internal state sequence of the next hop:

$$u_i^{t+1} = o_i^t \tag{4}$$

where $t \in \{1, 2, \ldots, n-1\}$, n is the value of hops.

To reduce the number of parameters, we adopt the adjacent weight tying strategy used in MemN2N [6], that is, the fully connected layer of the output memory sequence for one hop is identical to that of the input memory sequence for the next hop, and the fully connected layer of the internal state sequence $\{u_i\}$ is identical to that of the input memory sequence for the first hop.

3.3 Query-Aware Regression Module

Based on the global attention visual representation obtained from the global attention module, the query-aware regression module aims to select video shots that are more relevant to the text query to form the final summary result. As illustrated in Fig. 1, the query-aware regression module consists of a skip connection, a multi-modal feature fusion module, and a fully connected network.

Skip Connection. The skip connection combines the input and output sequences of the global attention module, which increases the utilization of information in the original video shot features. Note that before performing skip connection, in order for the dimension of the original shot feature sequence to match with the memory output sequence, we use a fully connected layer to map the feature dimension of $\{x_i\}$ to the same value as $\{o_i\}$. After the skip connection, the obtained result is passed through a LN and a dropout to get the visual feature sequence $\{v_i\}$.

Multi-modal Feature Fusion Module. This module first maps the visual feature sequence $\{v_i\}$ and the text concept feature c to two feature spaces with the same dimension by using two different fully connected layers with LN, respectively, to get $\{v_i'\}$ and c', and then the feature processing is performed as follows to get the fused feature sequence $\{f_i\}$:

$$f_i = v_i' || c' || \left(v_i' \oplus c'\right) || \left(v_i' \otimes c'\right) \tag{5}$$

where $||$ represents vector concatenation, $\oplus$ represents element-wise addition, $\otimes$ represents element-wise multiplication. The fused feature sequence $\{f_i\}$ is a concatenation of the original feature representation, the additive interaction between two modalities and the multiplicative interaction between two modalities. Compared with using element-wise operation or concatenation operation alone, our feature processing makes the visual features and textual features more fully fused.

Fully Connected Network. After the fused feature sequence $\{f_i\}$ is obtained, a two-layer fully connected network is employed to regress it to the shot-level importance score sequence $\{s_i\}$, where the first layer is followed by a LN, a ReLU activation function and a dropout, and the second layer is a single fully connected layer whose output dimension is 1. Finally, a sigmoid function is used to limit the importance score for each shot to [0, 1).

3.4 Summarization Generation

A user query consists of two text concepts. In our proposed RAGAN model, these two concepts share all the parameters of the query-aware regression module. Firstly, for each concept, we calculate the corresponding shot-level importance score sequence. Then we merge the two sequences as the final importance score sequence by element-wise addition. After that, we sort the scores in the merged sequence from high to low, and take the first 2% shots to form the query-focused video summarization.

4 Experiments

In this section, we first give the experimental setup, including the details of the dataset, the evaluation metrics used in the experiments, and the implementation details. Then, we provide and discuss the experimental data including quantitative and qualitative results, as well as parameter analysis and ablation studies.

4.1 Experimental Setup

Dataset. Our RAGAN model is evaluated on the query-focused video summarization dataset [7]. The dataset is built upon the UTE dataset [19] and consists of four daily life videos captured by the head-mounted camera, and the duration of each video is 3–5 h. For each video, there are 46 user queries, each corresponding to a manually annotated summary. And a user query consists of two concepts from an expressive and comprehensive dictionary of 48 words [7]. These 46 queries cover the following different scenarios: 1) all concepts in the query appear in the same video shot, 2) concepts appear in different video shots, 3) only one concept appears in the video, and 4) none of the concepts appear in the video. The last scenario is same as the generic video summarization to certain degree. In addition, the dataset also provides dense per-video-shot concept annotations, that is, each video is uniformly partitioned to shots of 5 s long, and each video shot is labeled with several concepts.

Evaluation Metrics. Following [7], we first calculate the intersection-over-union (IOU) of the concepts corresponding to any two video shots as the similarity between them, and then take the IOU as the edge weights in the bipartite graph between the user summary and the machine summary to find the maximum weight matching of the bipartite graph. Finally, based on the number of matching pairs, we calculate precision, recall and F1-score as evaluation metrics.

Implementation Details. We first sample the input long video to 1 fps, then take 5 s as a shot. In each video shot, ResNet [20] pre-trained on ImageNet [21] is employed to extract the frame features, and then we obtain the shot feature by computing the average of the frame features. The dimension of each shot feature is 2048. The Glove vector [22] is used to extract the feature representation of the concept with a dimension of 300. We set batch size to 1. The weighted Binary CrossEntropy loss (BCELoss) is used as loss function, where the weight of the shot with label 0 is set to the ratio of the number of labels 1 to the total number of labels, and accordingly the weight of the shot with label 1 is set to the ratio of the number of labels 0 to the total number of labels. In the training phase, for each concept, we calculate the loss between the shot-level importance scores and the corresponding ground-truth, then the two loss values are added as the total loss. And we use Adam with learning rate 10^{-5} for parameter optimization. The size of the input memory and the output memory in the global attention module is the number of shots in the input video, and the feature dimension is 512, so the dimension of the memory output sequence is also 512. In the query-aware regression module, we use 50% dropout, and the dimensions of visual features and textual features in the feature processing are both 512. In the fully connected network, the dimensions of the hidden state for the first and second layer are 512 and 1, respectively. The value of hops is set to 4, which will be detailed in the parameter analysis of Sect. 4.2. We randomly selected two videos for training, one for validation, and the remaining last video for testing model performance. We do training over 300 epochs and the model with the highest validation F1-score is selected.

4.2 Experimental Results

Comparison with State-of-the-Art Approaches. We compare the performance of our proposed RAGAN model with other state-of-the-art supervised researches on the dataset described in Sect. 4.1, as shown in Table 1, where the last row is the average performance on four videos. From Table 1, we can observe that our method outperforms the existing state-of-the-art by 1.6% on average F1-score. Especially for Video4, our method is 7.9% higher than QSAN [5], which has the second highest F1-score on Video4. Such significant performance improvements show the superiority of our proposed RAGAN on obtaining global attention and multi-modal feature fusion.

Parameter Analysis. Figure 2 shows the impact of hops on the performance of our model. We can observe that the average F1-score increases with the value of hops, and reaches saturation when the value of hops is 4. Therefore, we can conclude that the global attention module can indeed continuously optimize the obtained information between hops, and the default value for hops is set to 4 in our proposed model.

Ablation Studies. Table 2 shows the ablation analysis. It should be noted that 1) for the global attention module, we set the value of hops to 1 to verify the impact of the multiple hops mechanism on model performance, 2) after removing the multi-modal feature fusion module, we use element-wise multiplication instead. From the table, we can see that after making only one hop in the global attention module, the model performance decreased by 5.0%. In the query-aware regression module, after removing the

Table 1. Comparison of our proposed RAGAN with other state-of-the-art supervised query-focused video summarization researches in terms of precision (Pre), recall (Rec) and F1-sore (F1). Best values (F1-score) are denoted in bold.

	SeqDPP [23]			QC-DPP [7]			QSAN [5]			CHAN [4]			RAGAN		
	Pre	Rec	F1	Pre	Rec	F1	Pre	Rec	F1	Pre	Rec	F1	Pre	Rec	F1
Video1	53.43	29.81	36.59	49.86	53.38	48.68	48.41	52.34	48.52	54.73	46.57	**49.14**	57.52	41.21	46.95
Video2	44.05	46.65	43.67	33.71	62.09	41.66	46.51	51.36	46.64	45.92	50.26	46.53	45.99	52.41	**48.61**
Video3	49.25	17.44	25.26	55.16	62.40	56.47	56.78	61.14	56.93	59.75	64.53	**58.65**	69.24	50.61	58.17
Video4	11.14	63.49	18.15	21.39	63.12	29.96	30.54	46.90	34.25	25.23	51.16	33.42	28.14	55.67	**36.96**
Avg	39.47	39.35	30.92	40.03	60.25	44.19	45.56	52.94	46.59	46.40	53.13	46.94	50.22	49.98	**47.67**

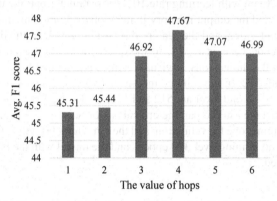

Fig. 2. The impact of hops on model performance, where the abscissa and ordinate represent the value of hops and the average F1-score, respectively. We set the default value as 4 in our proposed RAGAN model.

skip connection and replacing the multi-modal feature fusion module with element-wise multiplication, the performance of the model decreased by 2.2% and 1.8%, respectively. Therefore, it can be concluded that the multiple hops mechanism, the skip connection and the multi-modal feature fusion module do help to improve the model performance.

Table 2. Ablation study on average precision, recall and F1-score. Best values (F1-score) are denoted in bold.

Model	Pre	Rec	F1
RAGAN w/o multiple hops	47.80	47.48	45.31
RAGAN w/o skip connection	49.15	48.81	46.60
RAGAN w/o multi-modal feature fusion module	49.42	48.90	46.79
RAGAN	50.22	49.98	**47.67**

In the multi-modal feature fusion module, we fuse visual features and textual features from three perspectives, i.e., the original information of each modality, the additive interaction between two modalities and the multiplicative interaction between two modalities. In order to verify the effectiveness of these three parts, we remove them from our proposed RAGAN model respectively, and the average F1-scores are shown in Table 3. From Table 3, we can observe that after removing the above three parts respectively, the model performance has decreased to varying degrees, ranging from 0.9% to 4.1%, which proves that each part of the multi-modal feature fusion module does play an indispensable role in multi-modal feature processing.

Table 3. Ablation study about the multi-modal feature fusion module on average precision, recall and F1-score, where RARAN-B represents removing the original information of each modality during the feature processing of the multi-modal feature fusion module, and RAGAN-A and RAGAN-C represent removing the additive and multiplicative interaction between two modalities respectively. Best values (F1-score) are denoted in bold.

Model	Pre	Rec	F1
RAGAN-A	48.29	47.80	45.73
RAGAN-B	49.21	49.12	46.78
RAGAN-C	49.95	49.21	47.22
RAGAN	50.22	49.98	**47.67**

Qualitative Results. Figure 3 shows the visualization results. The query for Fig. 3(a) is "Desk Hands", and the query for Fig. 3(b) is "Sky Street". From the figure, we can see that the summarization generated by our model not only contains query-related shots, but also takes into account the importance of shots in video context, which proves that our proposed model can balance context-important and query-related information well.

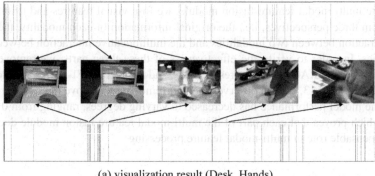

(a) visualization result (Desk, Hands)

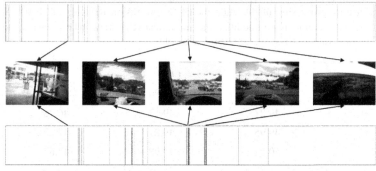

(b) visualization result (Sky, Street)

Fig. 3. The visualization results of our proposed model on Video1. The x-axis represents the temporal order of video shots, the green lines represent the shots in the oracle summarization, and the blue lines represent the shots in the summarization generated by our model. (a) The result for the query "Desk Hands". (b) The result for the query "Sky Street".

5 Conclusion

In this paper, we propose a novel query-focused video summarization method called regression augmented global attention network. It continuously optimizes the obtained global attention information through the multiple hops mechanism, and fuses textual features and different levels of visual features through the skip connection and the multi-modal feature fusion module. After that, a two-layer fully connected network is used to regress the fused features to the shot-level importance scores. Finally, the shots with higher scores are selected to form the query-focused video summarization result. Experiments on the query-focused video summarization dataset demonstrate the superiority of our model over other state-of-the-art researches.

Acknowledgments. This work was supported by the National Natural Science Foundation of China under Grant No. 62020106011, Chen Guang Project supported by Shanghai Municipal Education Commission and Shanghai Education Development Foundation under Grant No.17CG41.

References

1. Zhang, Y., Kampffmeyer, M.C., Liang, X., Tan, M., Xing, E.: Query-conditioned three-player adversarial network for video summarization. In: British Machine Vision Conference 2018, BMVC 2018, Northumbria University, Newcastle, UK, 3–6 September 2018, 288 p. BMVA Press (2018). https://researchr.org/publication/ZhangKLTX18/related

2. Jiang, P., Han, Y.: Hierarchical variational network for user-diversified & query-focused video summarization. In: Proceedings of the 2019 on International Conference on Multimedia Retrieval, pp. 202–206. Association for Computing Machinery, Ottawa ON, Canada (2019)

3. Zhang, Y.J., Kampffmeyer, M., Zhao, X.G., Tan, M.: Deep reinforcement learning for query-conditioned video summarization. Appl. Sci. Basel **9**, 16 (2019)

4. Xiao, S., Zhao, Z., Zhang, Z., Yan, X., Yang, M.: Convolutional hierarchical attention network for query-focused video summarization. In: AAAI, pp. 12426–12433 (2020)

5. Xiao, S.W., Zhao, Z., Zhang, Z.J., Guan, Z.Y., Cai, D.: Query-biased self-attentive network for query-focused video summarization. IEEE Trans. Image Process. **29**, 5889–5899 (2020)

6. Sukhbaatar, S., Szlam, A., Weston, J., Fergus, R.: End-to-end memory networks. In: Proceedings of the 28th International Conference on Neural Information Processing Systems, vol. 2, pp. 2440–2448. MIT Press, Montreal, Canada (2015)

7. Sharghi, A., Laurel, J.S., Gong, B.: Query-focused video summarization: dataset, evaluation, and a memory network based approach. In: 2017 IEEE Conference on Computer Vision and Pattern Recognition (CVPR), pp. 2127–2136 (2017)

8. Zhang, K., Chao, W.-L., Sha, F., Grauman, K.: Video summarization with long short-term memory. In: Leibe, B., Matas, J., Sebe, N., Welling, M. (eds.) ECCV 2016. LNCS, vol. 9911, pp. 766–782. Springer, Cham (2016). https://doi.org/10.1007/978-3-319-46478-7_47

9. Zhu, W., Lu, J., Li, J., Zhou, J.: DSNet: a flexible detect-to-summarize network for video summarization. IEEE Trans. Image Process. **30**, 948–962 (2021)

10. Liang, G., Lv, Y., Li, S., Wang, X., Zhang, Y.: Video summarization with a dual-path attentive network. Neurocomputing **467**, 1–9 (2022)

11. Jung, Y., Cho, D., Woo, S., Kweon, I.S.: Global-and-local relative position embedding for unsupervised video summarization. In: Vedaldi, A., Bischof, H., Brox, T., Frahm, J.-M. (eds.) ECCV 2020. LNCS, vol. 12370, pp. 167–183. Springer, Cham (2020). https://doi.org/10.1007/978-3-030-58595-2_11

12. Hu, M., Hu, R., Wang, X., Sheng, R.: Unsupervised temporal attention summarization model for user created videos. In: Lokoč, J., et al. (eds.) MMM 2021. LNCS, vol. 12572, pp. 519–530. Springer, Cham (2021). https://doi.org/10.1007/978-3-030-67832-6_42

13. Cai, S., Zuo, W., Davis, L.S., Zhang, L.: Weakly-supervised video summarization using variational encoder-decoder and web prior. In: Ferrari, V., Hebert, M., Sminchisescu, C., Weiss, Y. (eds.) Computer Vision – ECCV 2018. LNCS, vol. 11218, pp. 193–210. Springer, Cham (2018). https://doi.org/10.1007/978-3-030-01264-9_12

14. Fei, M., Jiang, W., Mao, W.: Learning user interest with improved triplet deep ranking and web-image priors for topic-related video summarization. Expert Syst. Appl. **166**, 114036 (2021)

15. Sharghi, A., Gong, B., Shah, M.: Query-focused extractive video summarization. In: Leibe, B., Matas, J., Sebe, N., Welling, M. (eds.) ECCV 2016. LNCS, vol. 9912, pp. 3–19. Springer, Cham (2016). https://doi.org/10.1007/978-3-319-46484-8_1

16. Vasudevan, A.B., Gygli, M., Volokitin, A., Gool, L.V.: Query-adaptive video summarization via quality-aware relevance estimation. In: Proceedings of the 25th ACM international conference on Multimedia, pp. 582–590. Association for Computing Machinery, Mountain View, California, USA (2017)

17. Huang, J.-H., Worring, M.: Query-controllable Video Summarization. In: Proceedings of the 2020 International Conference on Multimedia Retrieval, pp. 242–250. Association for Computing Machinery, Dublin, Ireland (2020)

18. Cizmeciler, K., Erdem, E., Erdem, A.: Leveraging semantic saliency maps for query-specific video summarization. Multimed. Tools Appl. **81**, 17457–17482 (2022)

19. Lee, Y.J., Ghosh, J., Grauman, K.: Discovering important people and objects for ego-centric video summarization. In: 2012 IEEE Conference on Computer Vision and Pattern Recognition, pp. 1346–1353 (2012)

20. Szegedy, C., Ioffe, S., Vanhoucke, V., Alemi, A.A.: Inception-v4, inception-ResNet and the impact of residual connections on learning. In: Proceedings of the Thirty-First AAAI Conference on Artificial Intelligence, pp. 4278–4284. AAAI Press, San Francisco, California, USA (2017)

21. Deng, J., Dong, W., Socher, R., Li, L.J., Kai, L., Li, F.-F.: ImageNet: A large-scale hierarchical image database. In: 2009 IEEE Conference on Computer Vision and Pattern Recognition, pp. 248–255 (2009)

22. Pennington, J., Socher, R., Manning, C.: GloVe: Global Vectors for Word Representation. In: Proceedings of the 2014 Conference on Empirical Methods in Natural Language Processing (EMNLP), pp. 1532–1543. Association for Computational Linguistics, Doha, Qatar (2014)

23. Gong, B., Chao, W.L., Grauman, K., Sha, F.: Diverse sequential subset selection for supervised video summarization. Adv. Neural. Inf. Process. Syst. **27**, 2069–2077 (2014)

Deep Video Matting with Temporal Consistency

Yanzhuo Li, Li Fang, Long Ye, and Xinyan Yang[✉]

Key Laboratory of Media Audio and Video, Communication University of China,
Ministry of Education, Beijing, China
xyyang@cuc.edu.cn

Abstract. Temporal consistency is a significant issue for video matting. In this study, we propose a temporal feature enhancement network for video matting. To enhance temporal feature propagation and alignment between video frames, recurrent pipelines are designed as our network architecture. In addition, an attention module is add to correct the temporal information of misaligned video frames. Finally revert the output video to the input resolution. We do the experiments on the benchmark which contains of VideoMatte240K (VM), Distinctions-646 (D646) and Adobe Image Matting (AIM) datasets. The experiment result shows that our method outperforms the state-of-the-art methods and prove that temporal consistency enhancement can make the video matting algorithm robust.

Keywords: Video matting · Temporal consistency · Attention mechanism

1 Introduction

Video matting is a technique for separating the video into foreground and background. It is a widely used technology in automatic video production, such as movie special effects, video conferences and live televisions. Video matting focuses on predicting continuous alpha mattes, which contains time domain features. So that unlike a single alpha map prediction in image matting, temporal consistency is the primary task for video matting. The existing algorithms are not always robust for videos with multiple people or complex backgrounds, because the extraction of foreground feature is inaccurate and artifacts will still occur. Therefore, our research centres around how to keep temporal coherence in the video matting.

For video matting, there is a straightforward solution, post-processing, which applies image matting on a single frame. It inevitably leads to extreme flickering artifacts on moving foreground edges. Hence, previous methods [1,2,8,10,26,37] solved this problem by finding local or non-local affinity among pixel colors and computing the movement of the foreground, but their results are prone to errors in computation especially when dealing with complex backgrounds. Some existing solutions [21,36] utilize optical flow to smooth frame-wise prediction and

G. Zhai et al. (Eds.): IFTC 2022, CCIS 1766, pp. 339–352, 2023.
https://doi.org/10.1007/978-981-99-0856-1_25

refine alpha mattes, whereas these solutions can not handle large area of semi-transparency so far. RVM [28] adopts ConvGRU module to aggregate temporal information by computing the hidden state of the current frame, but this neglects the interactions between frames. To obtain high-quality alpha mattes of video matting, we focus on preserving temporal consistency in the predicted alpha mattes by improving the propagation of adjacent frame's feature and aligning the feature after propagation.

In this paper, we propose a matting network which consists of a semantic encoder and a recurrent architecture decoder inspired by RVM [28]. The role of the encoder is to extract the features of the foreground in the video, it aims to locate the main part of the foreground firstly. Then refine the features through the decoder, aggregate the time information and output the final result. For temporal consistency, we refer to the second-order grid propagation [7], it allows more active bidirectional propagation arranged in a grid form and information can be aggregated from different spatial and temporal locations by setting a second-order connection. Within the propagation framework, the features of the current moment are optimized using features from neighboring moment or neighboring propagation branch. Moreover, our module employs the flow-guided deformable convolution to implement the feature aggregation after propagation. Deformable alignment has demonstrated its advantage in video tasks, but the training stage of deformable alignment module is instable [6]. Therefore, using optical flow as the base offset in module gives a specific guidance to deformable alignment. The network do not learn the deformable convolution networks offsets directly, in contrast, optical flow field refined by flow field residue as base offsets can reduce the instability of offset learning. After alignment, we still need to pay attention to the effect of feature channels alignment. Since some channels may be misaligned during the alignment process, we add an attention module to alleviate the misalignment. This module includes spatial attention and channel attention, generates weights for feature maps and feature channels, and alleviates channel misalignment by reducing the weight of misaligned channels.

In general, we propose a novel feature processing framework that can extract the time information of videos more accurately and obtain better temporal consistency. Compared to the existing video matting methods which either utilize trimaps or backgrounds as the additional input for modeling training, our auxiliary-free method achieves better performance against the state-of-the-art method on the composited datasets and real videos.

2   Related Works

2.1   Image Matting

Formally, image matting can be expressed as a compositing equation by frame I, foreground F, background B and coefficient α. Traditional image matting methods are mainly based on sampling [11,13,15,17] and propagation [1–3,8,26, 27,34,37], both of them use color or other relevant low-level image features for estimating alpha mattes, which often fail in complex scenes. Recently, with the progress of deep learning, methods based on the convolutional neural networks [5,9,12,18,41,43] have been proposed with notable successes. For example, Cho et al. [9] combine the classic algorithms with CNNs for alpha matte refinement. Cai et al. [5] suggest a trimap refinement process before matting and showed the advantages of using the refined trimaps. Most of aforementioned methods always require a manual trimap annotation to solve for the unknown regions of the trimap. Since creating trimaps also requires researcher's additional efforts and the quality of the annotations, researchers consider to avoid trimap or other external input like background image without objects. Auxiliary-free matting [32,43] has also been studied. However, most of them are trained specifically for portraits rather than the whole human body.

2.2   Video Matting

Compared with image matting, temporal consistency is the key point to generate high quality video mattes. Lee et al. [25] tackled the video matting by considering time as a third spatial dimension and developed an anisotropic kernel using optical flow. Bai et al. [4] first generate trimaps on some key frames, and then propagate the trimaps to all other frames. Few deep-learning based matting methods are designed specifically for video, and existing methods typically utilize post-processing modules or propagation modules to maintain temporal consistency. For instance, MODNet [24] proposes a post-processing step that compares the predictions of adjacent frames to reduce flicker, but it cannot handle fast moving body parts and the model itself still operates with frames as separate images. Sengupta et al. [33] explored a trimap-free approach using additional background images as input, but this work only provides temporal cues through several adjacent frames, the effect of which is not the focus of temporal consistency studies. DVM [38] applies to video matting, but it actually focused on utilizing temporal information to propagate trimaps. Hence, we focus on aggregating temporal information by improving the way we propagate and align features.

2.3   Recurrent Network

Recurrent neural network is a popular structure adopted in video processing tasks [14,19,20,22,28,31,44], it can largely maintain the temporal coherency of the video. Previous work has explored the use of recurrent architectures in various video sequence tasks and has shown better performance, such as video matting, super-resolution, frame-interpolation and deblurring. In our experiment, we focus on using recurrent architecture in matting tasks.

Deformable Alignment. Some works employ deformable alignment [6,39, 40,42]. TDAN [39] uses deformable convolution to align at the feature level. Basicvsr [6] shows that the performance gain over flow-based alignment comes from the offset diversity. Here we adopt the deformable alignment, which utilizes the deformable convolution to implement the feature aggregation.

High-Order Propagation. Higher-order propagation has been investigated to improve gradient flow [23,29,35], however, these methods do not take into account temporal alignment, which is crucial in video tasks. In order to perform temporal alignment in propagation, we add alignment to our propagation process by extending flow-guided deformable alignment to the second-order propagation scheme.

2.4   Attention Mechanism

Attention mechanism can be regarded as an adaptive selection process according to the input feature [30]. Attention in computer vision can be divided into four basic categories [16], including channel attention, spatial attention, temporal attention and branch attention, and their combinations such as channel & spatial attention. Each kind of attention has a different effect in visual tasks. According to the purpose of adding the attention module, we used the channel attention to refine the aligned features (Fig. 1).

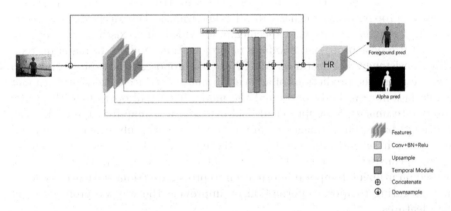

Fig. 1. Our network consists of a feature-extraction encoder, a recurrent architecture decoder, and a HR (High-Resolution) module. The HR module is used to upsample the result.

3   Method

The network architecture consists of a deep convolutional encoder-decoder network and an upsampling module. We refer to most of the matting networks and use a segmentation network as our encoder to extract foreground object's features, in fact, there is a same goal between matting and segmentation tasks that we have to determine the location of the object. The decoder part is based on a recurrent architecture, it's a prevalent structure adopted in various video processing tasks which helps us to aggregate spatio-temporal features. If your input is high resolution video and you need the output to maintain the same resolution, the last module ultimately accomplish high-resolution upsampling.

3.1   Recurrent Architecture

Video matting needs to keep temporal consistency when predicted alpha mattes. A post-processing solution may fatally cause severe flickering artifacts for moving details. Conversely, for video sequences, recurrent architecture can exploit the long-term dependencies by propagating the latent features. To improve matting quality, we decide to add two components to temporal module, namely propagation and alignment, and add an attention module after the alignment to mitigate feature misalignment during transmitting features in the recurrent framework. We use the encoder to obtain the original image $\frac{1}{2}$, $\frac{1}{4}$, $\frac{1}{8}$, $\frac{1}{16}$ four different scales of features. Then, the decoder extracts temporal information using low level features. When going through the temporal module, the optical flow is calculated using the input frames downsampled to the same scale, and then the resulting optical flow is warping with the input features of the same scale, and the offset between the warped features and the original features will be computed. After performing feature alignment, we use the output features for attention computation to further enhance the accuracy of features. Finally, the obtained features are passed to the next block for operation.

Propagation. Traditionally, for video sequences, the approach of unidirectional propagation is the mainstream method in information exchange, whereas this [7] work demonstrates the importance of bidirectional propagation over unidirectional propagation to better exploit features temporally. Grid propagation form ensures that spatial features can be reused for other frames refinement. Meanwhile, second-order connection can further enhance the robustness of matting. With this connection, temporal information can be aggregated from different temporal locations, improving robustness and effectiveness in complex matting and fine regions.

Formally, the propagation module is defined as follows. Let I_i be the input image, f_i be the feature extracted from I_i by encoder, and x_i^j be the feature computed at the i-th moment in the j-th propagation branch. We show the procedure for forward propagation, and the procedure for backward propagation is defined similarly. Firstly, to compute the feature x_i^j, we align x_{i-1}^j and x_{i-2}^j through deformable alignment guided by optical flow:

$$\hat{x}_i^j = A(f_i, x_{i-1}^j, x_{i-2}^j, y_{i \rightarrow i-1}, y_{i \rightarrow i-2}) \qquad (1)$$

where $y_{i \rightarrow i-1}$, $y_{i \rightarrow i-2}$ represent the optical flows from i-th frame to the $(i-1)$-th and $(i-2)$-th frames, and A denotes flow-guided deformable alignment respectively. Then, the features are concatenated and went through a stack of residual blocks:

$$x_i^j = \hat{x}_i^j + R(c(x_i^{j-1}, \hat{x}_i^j)) \qquad (2)$$

where R represents the residual blocks, and c represents concatenation at channel dimension. In next section, we discuss the flow-guided deformable alignment (Fig. 2).

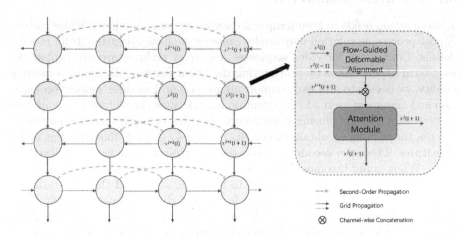

Fig. 2. In temporal module, we adopt second-order propagation to refine the features bidirectionally. Within each propagation branch, flow-guided deformable alignment increase the offset diversity while overcoming the offset overflow problem. Attention module aims to correct misaligned feature.

Alignment. In previous studies, it has been shown that deformable alignment outperforms flow-based alignment because of the diversity of offsets in deformable alignment. Utilizing optical flow to guide deformable alignment and benefit from the offset diversity, and by learning only the offset can significantly reduce the burden in deformable alignment network. The alignment process of forward propagation is certainly similar to the backward propagation.

For convenience, we just detail the j-th propagation branch, so that we omit the superscript j of the x_i^j. At the i-th moment, the original feature f_i computed from the i-th low resolution input image, the feature x_{i-1} computed for the previous moment (these initial time step like $x_{-1}, x_{-2}, y_{0\to-1}, y_{0\to-2}, y_{1\to-1}$ are zero), and the optical flow $y_{i\to i-1}$ to the previous frame, we first warp x_{i-1} with $y_{i\to i-1}$:

$$\bar{x}_{i-1} = W(x_{i-1}, y_{i\to i-1}) \tag{3}$$

where W denotes the operation of feature warping. $\bar{x}_{i-1}$ are then used to compute the deformable convolution offsets $o_{i\to i-1}$ and modulation masks $m_{i\to i-1}$. We compute the residue to the optical flow rather than computing offsets straightforward:

$$o_{i\to i-1} = y_{i\to i-1} + C^o(c(f_i, \bar{x}_{i-1})) \tag{4}$$

$$m_{i\to i-1} = \sigma(C^m(c(f_i, \bar{x}_{i-1}))) \tag{5}$$

where $C^{(o,m)}$ represents a heap of convolutions, and σ denotes the sigmoid function. A deformable convolution is then applied to the unwarped feature x_{i-1}:

$$\hat{x}_i = D(x_{i-1}; o_{i \to i-1}, m_{i \to i-1}) \qquad (6)$$

where D denotes deformable convolution. The aforementioned method is directly applicable to align one individual feature, as for the second-order propagation, we process alignment of two features simultaneously. Since, if we directly apply the above process to the two features, like x_{i-1}^j and x_{i-2}^j, it will take more computing time and unefficient. Moreover, independent alignment may ignore the supplementary information from the features. Hence, we concatenate the warped features and flows to compute the offsets o_{i-p} $(p = 1, 2)$:

$$o_{i \to i-p} = y_{i \to i-p} + C^o(c(f_i, \bar{x}_{i-1}, \bar{x}_{i-2})) \qquad (7)$$

$$m_{i \to i-p} = \sigma(C^m(c(f_i, \bar{x}_{i-1}, \bar{x}_{i-2}))) \qquad (8)$$

Then, a deformable convolution network is applied to the unwarped features:

$$o_i = c(o_{i \to i-1}, o_{i \to i-2}) \qquad (9)$$

$$m_i = c(m_{i \to i-1}, m_{i \to i-2}) \qquad (10)$$

$$\hat{x}_i = D(c(x_{i-1}, x_{i-2}); o_i, m_i) \qquad (11)$$

Attention Module. The features of the adjacent frames are propagated and then we align them on the channel. Video matting has an additional time dimension compared to image matting, so we use flow-guided deformable convolution to solve the temporal alignment. However, the optical flow estimation is not accurate for complex matting regions, and misalignment may occur even with the addition of deformable convolution. If some channels are aligned and some are not, then flickering artifacts may still exist. We therefore use the attention module to reduce the weight of those misaligned channels, thus mitigating misalignment cases. Attention module contains both spatial attention, which is useful for both segmentation and keying, and channel attention, which is used to generate weights for the feature channels. The aligned features are first subjected to a spatial local convolution to exploit local contextual information, and then undergo a spatial dilation convolution to further increase the perceptial field to obtain the long-range relationship. Finally the adaptability of the channel dimension is achieved by a channel convolution (1×1 convolution). The module can be written as

$$Attention = Conv_c(Conv_d(Conv(F))) \qquad (12)$$

$$Output = Attention \otimes F \qquad (13)$$

Here, F is the aligned feature, Attention denotes attention map, $\otimes$ means element-wise product. The value in attention map indicates the importance of each feature.

3.2 High-Resolution Module

We adopt an High-Resolution module which composed of multiple convolutions and pixel-shuffle operations to generate the output high-resolution prediction such as HD and 4k. When the network processes HR videos, we first downsample the patch size of the original video frames to 512px. After processing, the low-resolution prediction and the final features are provided to the HR module to produce high-resolution alpha and foreground through convolution and pixel-shuffling. Meanwhile, this module is a learnable module that can follow the entire network for end-to-end training.

4 Training and Experimental Evaluation

Table 1. Low-resolution comparison.

Dataset	Method	MAD	MSE	Grad	Conn	dtSSD
VM$_{(512\times288)}$	DeepLabV3	14.47	9.67	8.55	1.69	5.18
	FBA	8.36	3.37	2.09	0.75	2.09
	BGMv2	25.19	19.63	2.28	3.26	2.74
	MODNet	9.41	4.30	1.89	0.81	2.23
	RVM	6.08	1.47	0.88	0.41	1.36
	Ours	**5.77**	**1.13**	**0.87**	**0.36**	**1.35**
D646$_{(512\times512)}$	DeepLabV3	24.50	20.1	20.30	6.41	4.51
	FBA	17.98	13.4	7.74	4.65	2.36
	BGMv2	43.62	38.84	5.41	11.32	3.08
	MODNet	10.62	5.71	3.35	2.45	1.57
	RVM	7.28	3.01	2.81	1.83	1.01
	Ours	**7.03**	**2.86**	**2.65**	**1.73**	**0.98**
AIM$_{(512\times512)}$	DeepLabV3	29.64	23.78	20.17	7.71	4.32
	FBA	23.45	17.66	9.05	6.05	2.29
	BGMv2	44.61	39.08	5.54	11.6	2.69
	MODNet	21.66	14.27	5.37	5.23	1.76
	RVM	14.84	8.93	4.35	3.83	1.01
	Ours	**13.98**	**8.88**	**4.34**	**3.67**	**1.00**

4.1 Training Procedures

The training datasets we use are all from the pre-processed datasets in RVM [28] and we did not change the settings of the datasets. Our matting training is divided into four stages, we use Adam optimizer and all stages use batch size B = 1 on 4 Nvidia Geforce RTX2080 11G GPUs. First we first train on VM at low-resolution without the HR module for 18 epochs. We set a short sequence length T = 5 frames. We uses $5e^{-5}$ learning rate for encoder, while the rest of the network uses $5e^{-5}$. In stage 2, we increase T to 11 frames for 3 epochs, this is the longest we can fit on our GPUs. Keeping the learning rate of encoder and reduce others learning rate to $2e^{-5}$. Third, we attach the HR module and train on VM with high-resolution samples for 1 epoch. Because high resolution consumes more GPU memory, the sequence length must be set to very short. We set T = 8 frames for low-resolution and T = 3 frames for high-resolution. Specifically, all the learning rate of the network is $1e^{-5}$. Finally, we train on the combined dataset of D646 and AIM for 5 epochs and keep other settings from third stage.

4.2   Evaluation on Composition Datasets

We follow the RVM approach by compositing each test sample from the VM, D646 and AIM datasets onto 5 video and 5 image backgrounds to construct our benchmark. We use the motion augmentation scheme to increase the diversity of image samples. Every test clip has 100 frames. To show the effectiveness of the method, we evaluate the results on five quantitative metrics in Table 1, namely mean absolute differences (MAD), mean square error (MSE), the gradient error (Grad), the connectivity error (Conn) and temporal coherence (dtSSD). These metrics can be used to evaluate the accuracy of the alpha matte for every single frame and the temporal coherence within a video. The first four metrics are widely used for image matting evaluation. In addition to the experiments conducted by RVM [28] itself for comparison, our experiments are also directly compared with RVM [28]. In the same way, all experimental conditions and parameters of the comparison experiment were kept the same as before. Table 1 shows the test results obtained by all methods on low resolution frames. We can see that both the accuracy of the obtained alpha mattes and the temporal coherence are better than the results of RVM. Table 2 further compares the performance of our method and RVM at high resolution. Since the HR module must be trained end-to-end with the network, we modified RVM to use a non-learning fast guided filter (FGF) to upsample the predictions. Since it is too computationally large at high resolution, we remove Conn metric. Our method outperforms RVM on all metrics.

Table 2. High-resolution comparison.

Dataset	Method	SAD	MSE	Grad	dtSSD
$\mathbf{VM}_{(1920 \times 1080)}$	RVM+FGF	6.61	1.99	10.88	1.92
	Ours	**6.55**	**1.91**	**10.54**	**1.87**
$\mathbf{D646}_{(2048 \times 2048)}$	RVM+FGF	8.70	4.13	31.44	1.89
	Ours	**8.66**	**4.11**	**30.66**	**1.63**
$\mathbf{AIM}_{(2048 \times 2048)}$	RVM+FGF	15.03	9.11	35.11	1.79
	Ours	**14.88**	**8.96**	**34.97**	**1.65**

4.3   Evaluation on Real Videos

Figure 3 shows a comparison of real videos. We experiment on real videos and find that our approach is more robust to semantic errors. Our method can handle fast moving body parts better than RVM.

4.4   Ablation Studies

Role of Temporal Module's Quantity. We have tried adding different numbers of temporal modules to the decoder in our experiments and compared the results. Determine whether the model is feasible by observing the total loss size during the experimental training. When we add only one module, the total loss finally stabilizes at 0.02, which is clearly not enough precision. When two modules were added, the total loss finally stabilized at about 0.0175 after 25 epochs, and after testing the model, the first four of these evaluation metrics exceeded the RVM, but there was still a small gap in temporal coherence. Therefore we continued to increase the number of modules by adding three modules. After 13 epochs, the total loss is 0.0163, and the data tested with this model already exceeds the best result of adding only two modules. After this, we continued to try adding four temporal modules, but greatly increased the parameters and computation while making the training time much longer. We did not complete this case because our computational resources were not very sufficient (Table 3).

Table 3. Comparison of different quantities of temporal modules on VM dataset.

Method	MAD	MSE	Grad	Conn	dtSSD
Ours+1module	6.81	1.70	1.19	0.52	1.78
Ours+2modules	6.17	1.24	1.00	0.42	1.64
Ours+3modules	5.77	1.13	0.87	0.36	1.35

Role of Attention Module. The purpose of adding the attention module is to improve the accuracy of feature alignment. Compared to before adding the attention module, the total loss of the model after training decreases by 0.0036 after adding the attention module (Table 4).

Table 4. Comparison with and without attention modules with the addition of three time modules.

Method	MAD	MSE	Grad	Conn	dtSSD
No Attention	5.88	1.15	0.83	0.38	1.47
Attention	5.77	1.13	0.87	0.36	1.35

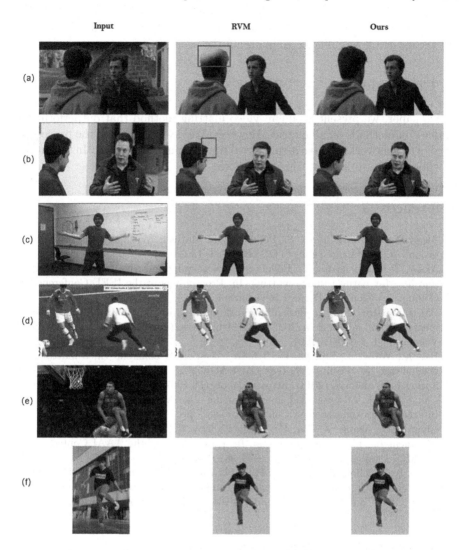

Fig. 3. Comparisons on real videos and movie clips. For (a) and (b), our method does not improve much when evaluating videos with little motion, but it gets a little boost in hair details. When dealing with other videos with large motion, such as ball games, dance videos, our method is more accurate in comparison and can extract more comprehensive semantic information of foreground details.

Role of Flow-Guided. We compared the effect of the experiment after adding and discarding the auxiliary part of optical flow guidance. The biggest improvement after discarding is in the processing speed, which is about 2 times faster than before discarding. In terms of experimental results, after dropping the optical flow guidance, we found that using only deformable convolution can only align features of small size, and when facing large size features, it is still necessary to add the optical flow guidance to maintain the accuracy of matting.

5   Conclusion

In this paper, we present a human video matting method that outperform the comparison methods on all metrics. However, We need to increase the processing speed of the network to make it run in real time as much as possible. In the future, we will continue to improve this framework.

References

1. Aksoy, Y., Oh, T.H., Paris, S., Pollefeys, M., Matusik, W.: Semantic soft segmentation. ACM Trans. Graph. (TOG) **37**(4), 1–13 (2018)
2. Aksoy, Y., Ozan Aydin, T., Pollefeys, M.: Designing effective inter-pixel information flow for natural image matting. In: Proceedings of the IEEE Conference on Computer Vision and Pattern Recognition, pp. 29–37 (2017)
3. Bai, X., Sapiro, G.: A geodesic framework for fast interactive image and video segmentation and matting. In: 2007 IEEE 11th International Conference on Computer Vision, pp. 1–8. IEEE (2007)
4. Bai, X., Wang, J., Simons, D.: Towards temporally-coherent video matting. In: Gagalowicz, A., Philips, W. (eds.) MIRAGE 2011. LNCS, vol. 6930, pp. 63–74. Springer, Heidelberg (2011). https://doi.org/10.1007/978-3-642-24136-9_6
5. Cai, S., et al.: Disentangled image matting. In: Proceedings of the IEEE/CVF International Conference on Computer Vision, pp. 8819–8828 (2019)
6. Chan, K.C., Wang, X., Yu, K., Dong, C., Loy, C.C.: Understanding deformable alignment in video super-resolution. In: Proceedings of the AAAI Conference on Artificial Intelligence, vol. 35, pp. 973–981 (2021)
7. Chan, K.C., Zhou, S., Xu, X., Loy, C.C.: BasicVSR++: improving video super-resolution with enhanced propagation and alignment. In: Proceedings of the IEEE/CVF Conference on Computer Vision and Pattern Recognition, pp. 5972–5981 (2022)
8. Chen, Q., Li, D., Tang, C.K.: KNN matting. IEEE Trans. Pattern Anal. Mach. Intell. **35**(9), 2175–2188 (2013)
9. Cho, D., Tai, Y.-W., Kweon, I.: Natural image matting using deep convolutional neural networks. In: Leibe, B., Matas, J., Sebe, N., Welling, M. (eds.) ECCV 2016. LNCS, vol. 9906, pp. 626–643. Springer, Cham (2016). https://doi.org/10.1007/978-3-319-46475-6_39
10. Choi, I., Lee, M., Tai, Y.-W.: Video matting using multi-frame nonlocal matting Laplacian. In: Fitzgibbon, A., Lazebnik, S., Perona, P., Sato, Y., Schmid, C. (eds.) ECCV 2012. LNCS, vol. 7577, pp. 540–553. Springer, Heidelberg (2012). https://doi.org/10.1007/978-3-642-33783-3_39
11. Chuang, Y.Y., Curless, B., Salesin, D.H., Szeliski, R.: A Bayesian approach to digital matting. In: Proceedings of the 2001 IEEE Computer Society Conference on Computer Vision and Pattern Recognition, CVPR 2001, vol. 2, p. II. IEEE (2001)

12. Ding, H., Jiang, X., Shuai, B., Liu, A.Q., Wang, G.: Context contrasted feature and gated multi-scale aggregation for scene segmentation. In: Proceedings of the IEEE Conference on Computer Vision and Pattern Recognition, pp. 2393–2402 (2018)
13. Feng, X., Liang, X., Zhang, Z.: A cluster sampling method for image matting via sparse coding. In: Leibe, B., Matas, J., Sebe, N., Welling, M. (eds.) ECCV 2016. LNCS, vol. 9906, pp. 204–219. Springer, Cham (2016). https://doi.org/10.1007/978-3-319-46475-6_13
14. Fuoli, D., Gu, S., Timofte, R.: Efficient video super-resolution through recurrent latent space propagation. In: 2019 IEEE/CVF International Conference on Computer Vision Workshop (ICCVW), pp. 3476–3485. IEEE (2019)
15. Gastal, E.S., Oliveira, M.M.: Shared sampling for real-time alpha matting. In: Computer Graphics Forum, vol. 29, pp. 575–584. Wiley Online Library (2010)
16. Guo, M.H., et al.: Attention mechanisms in computer vision: a survey. Comput. Vis. Media **8**, 331–368 (2022). https://doi.org/10.1007/s41095-022-0271-y
17. He, K., Rhemann, C., Rother, C., Tang, X., Sun, J.: A global sampling method for alpha matting. In: CVPR 2011, pp. 2049–2056. IEEE (2011)
18. Hou, Q., Liu, F.: Context-aware image matting for simultaneous foreground and alpha estimation. In: Proceedings of the IEEE/CVF International Conference on Computer Vision, pp. 4130–4139 (2019)
19. Huang, Y., Wang, W., Wang, L.: Bidirectional recurrent convolutional networks for multi-frame super-resolution. In: Advances in Neural Information Processing Systems, vol. 28 (2015)
20. Huang, Y., Wang, W., Wang, L.: Video super-resolution via bidirectional recurrent convolutional networks. IEEE Trans. Pattern Anal. Mach. Intell. **40**(4), 1015–1028 (2017)
21. Ilg, E., Mayer, N., Saikia, T., Keuper, M., Dosovitskiy, A., Brox, T.: FlowNet 2.0: evolution of optical flow estimation with deep networks. In: Proceedings of the IEEE Conference on Computer Vision and Pattern Recognition, pp. 2462–2470 (2017)
22. Isobe, T., Jia, X., Gu, S., Li, S., Wang, S., Tian, Q.: Video super-resolution with recurrent structure-detail network. In: Vedaldi, A., Bischof, H., Brox, T., Frahm, J.-M. (eds.) ECCV 2020. LNCS, vol. 12357, pp. 645–660. Springer, Cham (2020). https://doi.org/10.1007/978-3-030-58610-2_38
23. Ke, N.R., et al.: Sparse attentive backtracking: temporal credit assignment through reminding. In: Advances in Neural Information Processing Systems, vol. 31 (2018)
24. Ke, Z., et al.: Is a green screen really necessary for real-time portrait matting? arXiv preprint arXiv:2011.11961 (2020)
25. Lee, S.Y., Yoon, J.C., Lee, I.K.: Temporally coherent video matting. Graph. Models **72**(3), 25–33 (2010)
26. Levin, A., Lischinski, D., Weiss, Y.: A closed-form solution to natural image matting. IEEE Trans. Pattern Anal. Mach. Intell. **30**(2), 228–242 (2007)
27. Levin, A., Rav-Acha, A., Lischinski, D.: Spectral matting. IEEE Trans. Pattern Anal. Mach. Intell. **30**(10), 1699–1712 (2008)
28. Lin, S., Yang, L., Saleemi, I., Sengupta, S.: Robust high-resolution video matting with temporal guidance. In: Proceedings of the IEEE/CVF Winter Conference on Applications of Computer Vision, pp. 238–247 (2022)
29. Lin, T., Horne, B.G., Tino, P., Giles, C.L.: Learning long-term dependencies in NARX recurrent neural networks. IEEE Trans. Neural Netw. **7**(6), 1329–1338 (1996)

30. Mnih, V., Heess, N., Graves, A., et al.: Recurrent models of visual attention. In: Advances in Neural Information Processing Systems, vol. 27 (2014)
31. Nah, S., Son, S., Lee, K.M.: Recurrent neural networks with intra-frame iterations for video deblurring. In: Proceedings of the IEEE/CVF Conference on Computer Vision and Pattern Recognition, pp. 8102–8111 (2019)
32. Qiao, Y., et al.: Attention-guided hierarchical structure aggregation for image matting. In: Proceedings of the IEEE/CVF Conference on Computer Vision and Pattern Recognition, pp. 13676–13685 (2020)
33. Sengupta, S., Jayaram, V., Curless, B., Seitz, S.M., Kemelmacher-Shlizerman, I.: Background matting: the world is your green screen. In: Proceedings of the IEEE/CVF Conference on Computer Vision and Pattern Recognition, pp. 2291–2300 (2020)
34. Shahrian, E., Rajan, D., Price, B., Cohen, S.: Improving image matting using comprehensive sampling sets. In: Proceedings of the IEEE Conference on Computer Vision and Pattern Recognition, pp. 636–643 (2013)
35. Soltani, R., Jiang, H.: Higher order recurrent neural networks. arXiv preprint arXiv:1605.00064 (2016)
36. Sun, D., Yang, X., Liu, M.Y., Kautz, J.: PWC-Net: CNNs for optical flow using pyramid, warping, and cost volume. In: Proceedings of the IEEE Conference on Computer Vision and Pattern Recognition, pp. 8934–8943 (2018)
37. Sun, J., Jia, J., Tang, C.K., Shum, H.Y.: Poisson matting. In: ACM SIGGRAPH 2004 Papers, pp. 315–321 (2004)
38. Sun, Y., Wang, G., Gu, Q., Tang, C.K., Tai, Y.W.: Deep video matting via spatio-temporal alignment and aggregation. In: Proceedings of the IEEE/CVF Conference on Computer Vision and Pattern Recognition, pp. 6975–6984 (2021)
39. Tian, Y., Zhang, Y., Fu, Y., Xu, C.: TDAN: temporally-deformable alignment network for video super-resolution. In: Proceedings of the IEEE/CVF Conference on Computer Vision and Pattern Recognition, pp. 3360–3369 (2020)
40. Wang, H., Su, D., Liu, C., Jin, L., Sun, X., Peng, X.: Deformable non-local network for video super-resolution. IEEE Access 7, 177734–177744 (2019)
41. Xu, N., Price, B., Cohen, S., Huang, T.: Deep image matting. In: Proceedings of the IEEE Conference on Computer Vision and Pattern Recognition, pp. 2970–2979 (2017)
42. Xu, X., Li, M., Sun, W., Yang, M.H.: Learning spatial and spatio-temporal pixel aggregations for image and video denoising. IEEE Trans. Image Process. 29, 7153–7165 (2020)
43. Zhang, Y., et al.: A late fusion CNN for digital matting. In: Proceedings of the IEEE/CVF Conference on Computer Vision and Pattern Recognition, pp. 7469–7478 (2019)
44. Zhou, S., Zhang, J., Pan, J., Xie, H., Zuo, W., Ren, J.: Spatio-temporal filter adaptive network for video deblurring. In: Proceedings of the IEEE/CVF International Conference on Computer Vision, pp. 2482–2491 (2019)

Deep Flow-Guided Video Dehazing Based on Multi-scale Recurrent Network

Shiyan Sun[1], Yongfang Wang[1(✉)], Tengyao Cui[1], and Zhijun Fang[2]

[1] School of Communication and Information Engineering, Shanghai University,
Shanghai 200444, China
yfw@shu.edu.cn

[2] School Computer Science and Technology, Donghua University, Shanghai 201620, China

Abstract. We present a deep flow-guided video dehazing method based on multi-scale recurrent network dehazing. First, optical flow estimation is used for extracting inter-frame information between adjacent frames. Next, the adjacent frames and the target frames are aligned after deformation operation. Finally, the aligned frames are fed into a multi-scale recurrent network for dehazing, which employs an encoder-decoder structure that incorporates residual blocks. Moreover, this method introduces a hybrid loss method including hard flow example mining loss, contrastive regularization loss and bright channel loss to improve the training accuracy. To further improve the generalization ability, we added real datasets to train the network, which is different from the previous training method that used only synthetic datasets. Extensive experimental results demonstrate that the proposed video defogging algorithm outperforms other mainstream algorithms.

Keywords: Video dehazing · Optical flow · Multi-scale recurrent · Bright channel prior

1 Introduction

The goal of video dehazing tasks is to restore original features such as colors and contours to images or videos obscured by fog layers so as to achieve a fog-free or near-fog-free state. Dehazing algorithms play an integral role in services such as satellite map analysis, environmental monitoring, cameras and surveillance, and photography optimization, which drive the further development of advanced dehazing technologies. With the wide application of video services in various industries, it has important theoretical and practical significance to explore efficient video dehazing techniques under the influence of harsh environments.

Most of the early dehazing methods are designed based on traditional algorithms, which can be divided into image enhancement methods and physical model dehazing methods. The former ones achieve the dehazing effect by optimizing image contrast or removing image noise. Some representative methods include histogram equalization (HLE) [1], Retinex algorithm [2], and adaptive histogram equalization (AHE) [3], which can only remove part of the haze. As another important path, physical model methods

G. Zhai et al. (Eds.): IFTC 2022, CCIS 1766, pp. 353–364, 2023.
https://doi.org/10.1007/978-981-99-0856-1_26

perform fog removal based on the priori principle of atmospheric degradation models and fog maps [7, 23, 24]. This kind of methods performs better than the former ones. In general, traditional algorithms are easy to implement but weak in generalizability, and such methods are difficult to perform high-quality dehazing tasks in complex environments with multiple scenarios. With the fast evolution of deep learning, it has also been applied to image and video dehazing. Most methods are based on the idea of end to end, which means to get the image after fog directly through the input fog image. DehazeNet developed by B. Cai et al. is an early network that uses deep learning to dehaze [4]. It uses convolutional neural network (CNN) to estimate the transmittance in the atmospheric degradation model. Boyi Li et al. proposed an All-in-One Dehaze Network structure (AOD-NET) [5]. Zhang et al. presented a Densely Connected Pyramid Dehazing Network (DCPDN) to maximize the flow of information at different levels of characteristics [6]. These ways are effective and outperform traditional prior-based algorithms. But most of them rely on synthetic datasets and sometimes cannot perform well on real hazy pictures.

For video dehazing, different kinds of convolutional neural networks (CNN) are added to take advantage of inter-frame information, such as deformable alignment [15, 21] and multi-scale [25]. These methods can achieve good results but still have room for improvement.

To achieve better dehazing results, we propose a video dehazing network on the basis of a multi-scale recurrent network with fused optical flow estimation. This is an end-to-end and supervised video dehazing algorithm. Inspired by deformable alignment, we propose an optical flow estimation module for extracting inter-frame motion information. It can warp neighboring frames towards the target frame. Multi-scale recurrent network is used for image dehazing. It can fully exploit scales information to supplement the details of the frame.

The contributions of our work are summarized as follows:

1. We propose a compact deep convolutional model that simultaneously estimates the optical flow and latent frames for video dehazing.
2. Bright channel prior is proposed to enhance the performance of dehazing.
3. The mixed loss function is used to train the model, which improves its performance.

Different from the previous video dehazing algorithms trained only on synthetic datasets, the proposed method uses real datasets to achieve more realistic results.

2   Related Work

2.1   Image Dehazing

A classical algorithm of traditional image dehazing algorithms is based on the dark channel prior (DCP) proposed by Kaiming He et al. in 2011 [7]. This method is founded on an important prior knowledge: for an outdoor fog-free image, excluding the sky region, each local region is likely to have a very low-intensity value on at least one color channel, which tends to zero. According to this prior, the estimate of transmittance can be calculated, and finally the clear image can be restored according to the fog map formation model. This method can be applied to both image and video dehazing. It is simple and convenient, but it requires extensive calculations and a long time, and it cannot remove the fog from indoor and outdoor sky areas well. Tan [23] et al. dahaze by establishing the cost equation of Markov model based on fog maps. Tarel [24] et al. white balance the image for color restoration, and then calculate the clean image using the atmospheric veil inference and median filtering. But these ways cannot remove the haze near the strong edge well.

Deep learning image dehazing methods have developed rapidly in recent years with diverse network structures. Xu et al. presented a Feature Fusion Attention Network (FFA) [8]. It can keep shallow information and directly transfer it to deeper layers to achieve better dehazing effect. H et al. proposed a Multi-Scale Boosted Dehazing Network (MSBDN) on the basis of U-Net architecture, in which two modules, SOS enhancement and dense feature fusion, were integrated [9]. Shao et al. proposed a domain adaptation paradigm, which uses a bidirectional transformation network to complete the conversion from the synthetic domain to the real domain and improve the dehazing effect on the real fog map [10]. Li et al. introduced a semi-supervised image dehazing method, which adopted a CNN with a supervised learning branch and an unsupervised one [11]. The network model and weight of the two branches are the same, but the loss function is different.

2.2 Video Dehazing

Video dehazing is an extension of image dehazing. First, the video is processed by frame, and then sent to the dehazing network. After all processing, the video is integrated, that is, there is a more video processing module in comparison to image dehazing.

The earlier video dehazing algorithm is a frame-by-frame video dehazing algorithm proposed by Zhang et al., which uses optical flow based on Markov Random Field (MRF) to improve the temporal coherence of adjacent frames [12]. Later, Li et al. proposed an algorithm to recover a clear potential frame from a hazy video sequence by estimating the image depth [13]. Ren et al. proposed a synthetic video dehazing dataset and developed a deep learning approach to gather abundant data across frames [14]. Nevertheless, their network did not meet expectations in real foggy scenarios. Later, a video restoration network (EDVR) is proposed by Wang et al. that integrates deformable convolutional network and attention mechanism [15]. This network performs well on multiple video recovery tasks, but it cannot handle frames with large resolution well. Zhang et al. produced a real-world dataset containing indoor scenes and proposed a method fusing deformable convolutional network containing enhancement and Multi-Scale Boosted Dehazing Network with Dense Feature Fusion [21]. We note that most methods use large capacity models. Different from these models, we propose a more compact CNN model for video defogging.

3 Proposed Method

In this section, the overall structure of the proposed method is presented first, followed by a description of the architecture of the optical flow estimation network and the video dehazing network, respectively. Finally, the details of the loss function are presented.

3.1 Overall Network Structure

The proposed network structure is shown in Fig. 1, including two parts of the optical flow estimation network and video dehazing network (Dehazing-net). Firstly, three consecutive frames of the video are taken as input. They are fed into the optical flow estimation network to calculate the optical flow from the middle frame to the two before and after frames. Finally, the optical flow results with final resolution are obtained step by step. The resulting two optical flow images and the original intermediate frames are combined into three new frames and sent to Dehazing-net. Defog-net uses a multi-scale recurrent network, which is a codec network with residual blocks. The codec is a symmetric structure. In the case of the encoder, it includes three parts, each of which has one convolutional layer and three residual blocks. In the final two convolutional layers, they downsampled the feature mapping by half and meanwhile doubling the channel. The final output of the decoder is the result of dehazing.

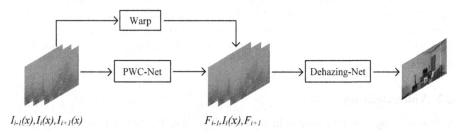

$I_{i-1}(x),I_i(x),I_{i+1}(x)$ $F_{i-1},I_i(x),F_{i+1}$

Fig. 1. Structure of deep flow-guided video dehazing based on multi-scale recurrent network

3.2 Optical Flow Estimation Network

Here we select PWC-Net [16] as the optical flow estimation network, which is a CNN model used for optical flow estimation. It uses the classic feature pyramid structure as the feature extraction network and a multi-layer CNN as the optical flow estimator for estimating the optical flow of the current pyramid layer. The optical flow can be estimated by:

$$F_{i \to i+1} = N_f(I_i, I_{i+1}) \tag{1}$$

where $F_{i \to i+1}$ is the optical flow vector of the neighboring frames, N_f represents the network for calculating optical flow.

We use bilinear interpolation to warp the features of the second image to the first image [27], so that the adjacent frames are aligned with the target frame. It can be defined by:

$$P = W_j(I_i, F_{i \to i+1}) \tag{2}$$

where P denotes the warped frame, W_j denotes the warping process, I_i denotes the adjacent frame.

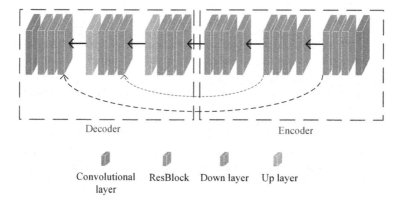

Decoder   Encoder

<table>
<tr><td>▯</td><td>▯</td><td>▯</td><td>▯</td></tr>
<tr><td>Convolutional
layer</td><td>ResBlock</td><td>Down layer</td><td>Up layer</td></tr>
</table>

Fig. 2. Structure of multi-scale recurrent network

3.3 Video Dehazing Network

The video dehazing network of this method is a multi-scale recurrent network, which is a cross-scale recurrent architecture consisting of multiple encoders and decoders. As shown in Fig. 2, the encoder has three coding blocks, each of which includes a convolutional layer and three ResBlocks. The first coding block generates a feature map with 32 channels, and the convolutional layers of the last two coding blocks with downsampling operation, named Down layer here, which doubles the number of kernels of the preceding layer and samples the feature mapping to half the size. Symmetrically, the decoder contains three decoding blocks, and the position of the Down layer corresponding to the encoder is the Up layer, which first performs the deconvolution operation and then upsampling to bring the image back to its original size. Here the upsampling and downsampling are implemented using the discrete wavelet transform and the integer wavelet transform. The last decoding block uses the preceding feature mapping as input and generates the output image. The number of kernels for the encoding block are 64 and 128; the number of kernels for the decoding block is 128 and 64; additionally, all the convolution layers have the same quantity of kernels. The size of all inner convolution kernels is set to 5, and all step sizes are set to 1.

In this method, the multi-scale recurrent network considers the process of generating clear images at different scales as a subproblem of image dehazing. The hazy image and the initial dehazing results are fed into the network to estimate a clear image at the current scale. The defogged image at that scale is estimated as:

$$I^i = Net_{SR}\left(B^i, I^{i+1}, \theta_{SR}\right) \tag{3}$$

where i indicates the scale index and $i = 1$ indicates the best scale. B^i and I^i are the input fogged and defogged potential images on the scale i. Net_{SR} is the multi-scale recurrent network which has the training parameters θ_{SR}. $(\cdot)^\uparrow$ is the operator that adjusts the feature or image from scale $i - 1$ to the scale i.

3.4 Loss Function

The selection of loss function incorporates the traditional bright channel prior algorithm, the contrastive regularization loss to enhance the input and output contrast, and HFEM loss to strengthen the boundary. This hybrid loss function is used as a constraint to improve the dehazing effect. The overall loss function is calculated as follows:

$$L = \lambda_1 L_{MS} + \lambda_2 L_{HFEM} + \lambda_3 L_{CR} + \lambda_4 L_{BC} \tag{4}$$

where $L_{MS}, L_{HFEM}, L_{CR}, L_{BC}$ are the mean squared loss, hard flow example mining loss, contrastive regularization loss, and bright channel loss, respectively. $\lambda_1, \lambda_2, \lambda_3, \lambda_4$ indicating the respective weights. Here $\lambda_1 = 1, \lambda_2 = 2, \lambda_3 = 0.1, \lambda_4 = 0.00005$ are taken empirically.

Mean Squared Loss. We use the mean squared loss to measure the absolute difference between the target values and the predicted values. It is functioned by:

$$\mathcal{L}_{MS} = \|X^{\text{defogged}} - X^{\text{gt}}\| \tag{5}$$

where $X^{defogged}$ is the recovered image and X^{gt} is the clear image.

Hard Flow Example Mining Loss. We employ a hard flow example mining loss [17] to automatically focus more on hard regions, thus encouraging the model to produce sharper boundaries. Specifically, we arrange all pixels in a descending order of loss. The first 50% of pixels are marked as hard examples while a random 10% of pixels are marked as random samples. HFEM loss is defined as:

$$\mathcal{L}_{HFEM} = \left\| \left(M^h + M^r\right) \odot \left(X^{\text{defogged}} - X^{\text{gt}}\right) \right\| \tag{6}$$

where M^h, M^r represent binary masks of the hard flow areas and random flow areas, $\odot$ indicates element-wise multiplication.

Contrastive Regularization Loss. The contrastive regularization loss inspired by [18] constructs positive and negative pairs, where the positive ones consist of the clear image J and the recovered image $\hat{J}$; the negative ones are generated by the clear image J and the fogged image I. The two pairs are compared simultaneously so that the output is as close as possible to the clear image and away from the fogged image. For the potential feature space, common intermediate features are selected from the same fixed pre-training model G (VGG-19) [19]. The contrastive regularization loss is defined as follows:

$$\sum_{i=1}^{n} w_i \frac{D(G_i(J), G_i(\phi(I, w)))}{D(G_i(I), G_i(\phi(I, w)))} \tag{7}$$

To enhance the comparison ability, hidden features need to be extracted from different layers in a fixed pre-trained model. $i = 1, 2, \ldots n$ denotes the i-th hidden feature extracted from this pre-trained model. $D(x, y)$ indicates the mean squared difference of x and y. ω_i indicates a weighting factor, which is taken here as 0.1 based on empirical values [18].

Bright Channel Loss. Bright channel prior [26] means light source area pixels typically have a high-intensity value on at least one color channel that converges to 1. Due to the lack of light for indoor video, there will be a darker picture after dehazing, so we use the bright channel loss to solve this problem. It calculates the mean squared loss between the bright channel of the image and 1, and is calculated as follows:

$$L_{BC} = \|1 - J^{Bright}\|_1 \tag{8}$$

where L_{BC} indicates bright channel loss and J_{Bright} indicates the image bright channel.

4 Experimental Results

In this section, we introduce the datasets and evaluation metrics first, next comparison experiments with other advanced methods on synthetic dataset and real dataset, and finally ablation experiments to prove the effectiveness of each part.

Our network is trained using Pytorch on a PC with a Geforce GTX 1080 GPU. The batch size and epoch are set to 4 and 200, respectively. Initial learning rate is set to 0.0001, which decays by half every 40 epochs.

4.1 Datasets and Evaluation Metrics

To improve training accuracy, synthetic and real-world datasets are used together to train the network. The pre-trained model is first trained on the synthetic dataset and then trained on the real dataset for tuning. The synthetic dataset is chosen from NYU2 [20], which is the more commonly used fog removal dataset and contains 464 videos of different indoor scenes, and the real dataset is chosen from REVIDE [21] with higher resolution. The training set contains 42 indoor fog videos with 1697 images and their corresponding fog-free videos, and the test set includes 6 videos with 284 images.

Here, commonly-used evaluation metrics Peak Signal-to-Noise Ratio (PSNR) and Structural Similarity (SSIM) [22] are employed to objectively evaluate the recovery results.

4.2 Comparison with other Mainstream Dehazing Algorithms

The average PSNR and SSIM values on two datasets with different methods are given in Table 1. As can be observed the proposed method performs much better than DCP and FFA. Compared with EDVR, the proposed method gets better result on PSNR in synthetic dataset and on SSIM in real dataset. The experimental data show that the proposed method performs better in objective metrics.

The visual comparison results of the proposed method with others on the synthetic dataset are given in Fig. 3. It can be observed that the images processed by the DCP [7] method based on the dark channel theory are severely distorted. We infer that the proposed dark channel theory for outdoor fog-free images cannot cope with indoor dehazing scenes. It can also be observed that FFA [8] and EDVR [15] exhibit more

Table 1. Average PSNR (dB) and SSIM values on two datasets with different methods

Dataset	Metric	DCP [7]	FFA [8]	EDVR [15]	Proposed
NYU2	PSNR	22.71	34.30	36.68	**39.41**
	SSIM	0.8987	0.9363	0.9515	**0.9632**
REVIDE	PSNR	11.03	16.65	21.22	**22.38**
	SSIM	0.7285	0.8133	0.8707	**0.8979**

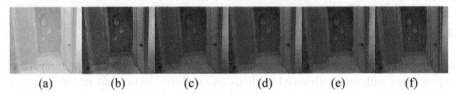

(a)   (b)   (c)   (d)   (e)   (f)

Fig. 3. Visual comparison of dehazing results on NYU2 (a) Input (b) DCP (c) FFA (d) EDVR (e) Proposed (f) Ground Truth

(a)   (b)   (c)   (d)   (e)   (f)

Fig. 4. Visual comparison dehazing results on REVIDE (a) Input; (b) DCP; (c) FFA; (d) EDVR; (e) Proposed; (f) Ground Truth

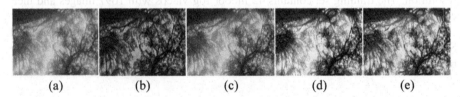

(a)   (b)   (c)   (d)   (e)

Fig. 5. Visual comparison dehazing results on real outdoor videos (a) Input; (b) DCP; (c) FFA; (d) EDVR; (e) Proposed

desirable dehazing effects, but residual fog can still be observed in the image. In contrast, the fog removal effect and color reproduction of the proposed method are more significant, which implies that the proposed method has better fog removal performance.

The visual comparison results of the proposed method with others on the real dataset are given in Fig. 4, it can be seen that each method degrades in performance on the real data set. Specifically, DCP is able to remove most of the fog, but the results are darker and the overall image tones change significantly. FFA has poor results on the real fog map: the color distortion is obvious and the fog at the white walls is not well removed.

EDVR is able to remove most of the fog, but color distortion and black blocks appear at the white walls. In comparison to the above methods, the proposed method achieves the closest fog removal to ground truth, which implies a superior performance.

To assess the practical performance of the method, we acquired real outdoor foggy videos and processed them using different methods, the visual comparison results are presented in Fig. 5. It can be observed that DCP can remove the fog but the overall tone of the picture changes. FFA and EDVR can only remove the fog from near areas. The proposed method can remove the haze well, and can retain the location information of different objects. In summary, the proposed method performs better on both synthetic and real-world datasets.

4.3 Ablation Study

Validity of Optical Flow Estimation Network. To verify the effectiveness of the optical flow estimation network (OFEN), it is removed and three consecutive frames of images are allowed to go directly to the dehazing network. Through Table 2, we can learn that the optical flow estimation network improves the PSNR by 1.20 dB and the SSIM by 0.0293, which shows that this module is effective and also proves that the utilization of inter-frame correlation improves the performance of dehazing.

Table 2. Results of ablation study on optical flow estimation module

	PSNR	SSIM
Without OFEN	21.18	0.8686
With OFEN	**22.38**	**0.8979**

Validity of the Mixed Loss Function. The proposed network uses four loss functions, and to prove the effectiveness of each, respectively this ablation experiment has the following control groups: 1) without hard flow example mining (HFEM) loss, 2) without contrastive regularization (CR) loss, 3) without bright channel (BC) loss, and 4) Proposed.

The results of the ablation experiments with mixed loss functions are presented in Table 3, and the visual comparison results of the ablation study on the mixed loss function are given in Fig. 6. It can be seen that the lack of HFEM loss causes the PSNR to drop 0.94 dB and SSIM to drop 0.0312, with obvious demarcation lines outside the object boundaries and color distortion on the white walls at the corners; the lack of CR loss causes the PSNR to drop 1.80 dB and SSIM to drop 0.0340, with changes in the picture tones and multiple color distortion on the white walls. The lack of BC loss causes the PSNR to drop by 1.17 dB and the SSIM to drop by 0.0152, and the overall picture color becomes dark. The experimental results show that all the above loss functions play an effective role, and the proposed hybrid loss function exhibits the best objective performance.

Table 3. Results of ablation study on the mixed loss function

Group	Methods	PSNR	SSIM
1	Without HFEM loss	21.44	0.8667
2	Without CR loss	20.58	0.8639
3	Without BC loss	21.21	0.8827
4	Proposed	**22.38**	**0.8979**

(a)   (b)   (c)   (d)   (e)   (f)

Fig. 6. Visual comparison results of the ablation study on the mixed loss function. (a) Input (b) Without HFEM loss (c) Without CR loss (d) Without BC loss (e) Proposed (f) Ground Truth

5 Conclusion

In this paper, a video dehazing method based on a multi-scale recurrent network with fused optical flow estimation is proposed. The proposed method uses an optical flow estimation module to estimate the optical flow maps of the current frame and adjacent frames, and a multi-scale recurrent network takes the above three frames as input to fully utilize the optical flow information of video frames. These two links effectively compensate for the lack of utilization of inter-frame correlation in existing work. To further improve the dehazing accuracy, a hybrid loss function incorporating the bright channel prior, the contrastive regularization loss and the HFEM loss is employed. Different from the established work, this paper uses synthetic and real-world datasets to train the network together, which effectively improves the generalization ability. Experimental results demonstrate the proposed method improves 1.16dB in PSNR and 0.0272 in SSIM compared to the latest algorithm.

Acknowledgement. This work was supported by Natural Science Foundation of China under Grant No. 61671283, U2033218.

References

1. Gonzalez, R.C., Woods, R.E.: Digital Image Processing. Prentice Hall Press (2002). ISBN: 0-201-18075-8
2. Wang, L., Xiao, L., Liu, H., Wei, Z.: Variational bayesian method for Retinex. IEEE Trans. Image Process. **23**(8), 3381–3396 (2014)
3. Kim, J.Y., Kim, L.S., Hwang, S.H.: An advanced contrast enhancement using partially overlapped sub-block histogram equalization. IEEE Trans. Circuits Syst. Video Technol. **11**(4), 475–484 (2001)

4. Cai, B., Xu, X., Jia, K., Qing, C., Tao, D.: DehazeNet: an end-to-end system for single image haze removal. IEEE Trans. Image Process. **25**(11), 5187–5198 (2016)

5. Li, B., Peng, X., Wang, Z., Xu, J., Feng, D.: An All-in-One Network for Dehazing and Beyond. arXiv:1707.06543 (2015)

6. Zhang, H., Patel, V.M.: Densely connected pyramid dehazing network. In: IEEE/CVF Conference on Computer Vision and Pattern Recognition, pp. 3194–3203 (2018)

7. He, K., Sun, J., Tang, X.: Single image haze removal using dark channel prior. IEEE Trans. Pattern Anal. Mach. Intell. **33**(12), 2341–2353 (2010)

8. Qin, X., Wang, Z., Bai, Y., Xie, X., Jia, H.: FFA-Net: feature fusion attention network for single image dehazing. In: AAAI, pp. 11908–11915 (2020)

9. Dong, H., et al.: Multi-scale boosted dehazing network with dense feature fusion. In: 2020 IEEE/CVF Conference on Computer Vision and Pattern Recognition (CVPR), pp. 2154-2164. Seattle, WA, USA (2020)

10. Shao, Y., Li, L., Ren, W., Gao, C., Sang, N.: Domain adaptation for image dehazing. In: 2020 IEEE/CVF Conference on Computer Vision and Pattern Recognition (CVPR), pp. 2805-2814. Seattle, WA, USA (2020)

11. Li, L., et al.: Semi-supervised image dehazing. IEEE Trans. Image Process. **29**, 2766–2779 (2020)

12. Jiawan, Z., Liang, L., Yi, Z., Yang, G., Cao, X., Sun, J.: Video dehazing with spatial and temporal coherence. The Visual Comput. **27**(6–8), 749–757 (2011)

13. Li, Z., et al.: Simultaneous video dehazing and stereo reconstruction. In: IEEE CVPR (2015)

14. Ren, W., et al.: Deep video dehazing with semantic segmentation. IEEE Trans. Image Process. **28**(4), 1895–1908 (2019)

15. Wang, X., Chan, K.C.K., Yu, K., Dong, C., Loy, C.C.: EDVR: video restoration with enhanced deformable convolutional networks. In: 2019 IEEE/CVF Conference on Computer Vision and Pattern Recognition Workshops (CVPRW), pp. 1954–1963 (2019)

16. Sun, D., Yang, X., Liu, M.Y., Kautz, J,: PWC-Net: CNNs for optical flow using pyramid, warping, and cost volume. In: 2018 IEEE/CVF Conference on Computer Vision and Pattern Recognition, pp. 8934–8943 (2018)

17. Xu, R., Li, X., Zhou, B., Loy, C.C.: Deep flow-guided video inpainting. In: 2019 IEEE/CVF Conference on Computer Vision and Pattern Recognition (CVPR), pp. 3718–3727. Long Beach, CA, USA (2019)

18. Wu, H., et al.: Contrastive Learning for Compact Single Image Dehazing. In: 2021 IEEE/CVF Conference on Computer Vision and Pattern Recognition (CVPR), pp.10546–10555 (2021)

19. Simonyan, K., Zisserman, A.: Very deep convolutional networks for large-scale image recognition. Comput. Sci. (2014)

20. Silberman, N., Hoiem, D., Kohli, P., Fergus, R.: Indoor segmentation and support inference from RGBD images. In: Fitzgibbon, A., Lazebnik, S., Perona, P., Sato, Y., Schmid, C. (eds.) ECCV 2012. LNCS, vol. 7576, pp. 746–760. Springer, Heidelberg (2012). https://doi.org/10.1007/978-3-642-33715-4_54

21. Zhang, X., et al.: Learning to restore hazy video: a new real-world dataset and a new method. In: 2021 IEEE/CVF Conference on Computer Vision and Pattern Recognition (CVPR), Nashville, TN, USA, pp. 9235–9244 (2021)

22. Li, M., Cao, X., Zhao, Q., Zhang, L., Meng, D.: Online rain/snow removal from surveillance videos. IEEE Trans. Image Process. **30**, 2029–2044 (2021)

23. Tan, R.T. :Visibility in bad weather from a single image. In: 2008 IEEE Computer Society Conference on Computer Vision and Pattern Recognition (CVPR 2008), pp. 24–26. IEEE, Anchorage, Alaska, USA (2008)

24. Tarel, J.-P., Hautière, N.: Fast visibility restoration from a single color or gray level image. In: 2009 IEEE 12th International Conference on Computer Vision, pp. 2201–2208 (2009)

25. Xue, M., Ji, Y., Yuyan, Z., Weiwei, L., Jiugen, Z.: Video image dehazing algorithm based on multi-scale retinex with color restoration. In: 2016 International Conference on Smart Grid and Electrical Automation (ICSGEA), pp. 195–200. Zhangjiajie, China (2016)
26. Fu, X., Zeng, D., Huang, Y., Ding, X., Zhang, X.-P.: A variational framework for single low light image enhancement using bright channel prior. In: 2013 IEEE Global Conference on Signal and Information Processing, pp. 1085–1088 (2013)
27. Li, M., Wang, Y., Fang, Z.: Optical flow-guided multi-level connection network for video deraining. In: Zhai, G., Zhou, J., Yang, H., An, P., Yang, X. (eds.) Digital TV and Wireless Multimedia Communications. IFTC 2021. Communications in Computer and Information Science, vol. 1560. Springer, Singapore (2022). https://doi.org/10.1007/978-981-19-2266-4_29

Fast Skip Inter Coding Decision Algorithm for VVC

Xiangkai Hu[1(✉)], Yue Li[1(✉)], and Wenbin Lin[2(✉)] (iD)

[1] School of Computer Science, University of South China, Hengyang 421001, China
kait@stu.usc.edu.cn
[2] School of Mathematics and Physics, University of South China,
Hengyang 421001, China
lwb@usc.edu.cn

Abstract. Versatile Video Coding (VVC), which mainly introduces the QTMT partition structure and introduces new technologies in inter coding and intra coding, greatly improves the coding efficiency compared with the previous generation video coding standard. However, the improvement in coding efficiency comes at the cost of a huge increase in coding complexity. In order to reduce the computational complexity of VVC, this paper proposes a fast skip coding unit (CU) inter prediction algorithm in the VVC encoder. The algorithm mainly uses the difference between the original pixel value of the CU and its predicted value. After obtaining the difference between the original pixel value and the predicted value and performing a series of calculations, a threshold is set to weigh the loss of coding efficiency and the reduction of coding complexity. Extensive experimental results show that the proposed algorithm reduces the inter coding time by 12% to 60% while BD-Rate improves by less than 1% on average.

Keywords: Versatile Video Coding · QTMT · Inter prediction

1 Introduction

With the development of multimedia technology, new types of videos such as UHD, 4 K, and 360° have emerged. These new types of videos bring a better experience to people's visual perception. At the same time, these new types of videos also have a huge amount of data, which brings great challenges to the storage and transmission of videos. The previous generation of video standards, High Efficient Video Coding (HEVC), is difficult to meet the compression requirements of explosive video data [1]. In order to improve the compression efficiency of video, the Joint Video Experts Group (JVET) released a proposal for a new generation of video coding standards, and then started the standardization process of Versatile Video Coding (VVC), and completed the finalization of the first version of the standard in 2020. Compared with HEVC, VVC has higher coding efficiency and quality, but also greatly increases coding complexity.

G. Zhai et al. (Eds.): IFTC 2022, CCIS 1766, pp. 365–374, 2023.
https://doi.org/10.1007/978-981-99-0856-1_27

On the basis of the QT block partition structure of HEVC, VVC adds a binary tree partition structure and a ternary tree partition structure, which include horizontal binary tree partition, vertical binary tree partition, horizontal ternary tree partition, and vertical ternary tree partition, which are collectively referred to as multi-type tree (MTT), as showed in Fig. 1. VVC has a more advanced and flexible partition structure by using QT plus nested MTT (QTMT) partition structure, for example, sub-blocks can be square or rectangular, so as to achieve better compression coding effect. But at the same time, due to this more flexible partition structure, the coding complexity is also greatly increased.

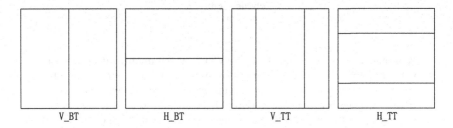

V_BT   H_BT   V_TT   H_TT

Fig. 1. MTT partition structure

In VVC, the QTMT partition structure determines the optimal partition structure for all blocks through a rate-distortion optimize (RDO) process [2]. It first regards the coding tree unit (CTU) as an undivided coding unit (CU), and after dividing the CTU with QT structure, the quad-tree leaf nodes are further divided by the recursive QT structure or recursive MTT structure. Figure 2 shows an example of dividing a CTU into multiple CUs with the QTMT structure. Note that if a node is divided with MTT structure, its child node can not be divided with QT structure. Due to this flexible QTMT partition structure, the complexity of the VVC Test Model (VTM) is many times that of the HEVC Test Model (HM), which greatly hinders the application of the VVC coding standard to real-time video coding [3,4]. Therefore, simplifying the QTMT structure can greatly reduce the coding complexity of VVC. In addition, VVC also introduces many advanced prediction technologies to improve inter prediction accuracy and VVC compression efficiency, such as Merge mode, affine transformation technology, adaptive motion precision technology, and so on. While these advanced prediction modes improve the accuracy of inter prediction, they also increase the computational complexity of inter prediction. Therefore, within the acceptable coding loss range, implementing some algorithms to conditionally skip the inter prediction mode can also effectively reduce the VVC coding complexity.

At present, the block-based inter prediction method used in mainstream video coding. The principle of this method is to find the reference block with the smallest difference from the current coding block in the adjacent reference reconstructed frames through motion estimation (ME). And take the reconstructed value of the reference block as the predicted value of the current block.

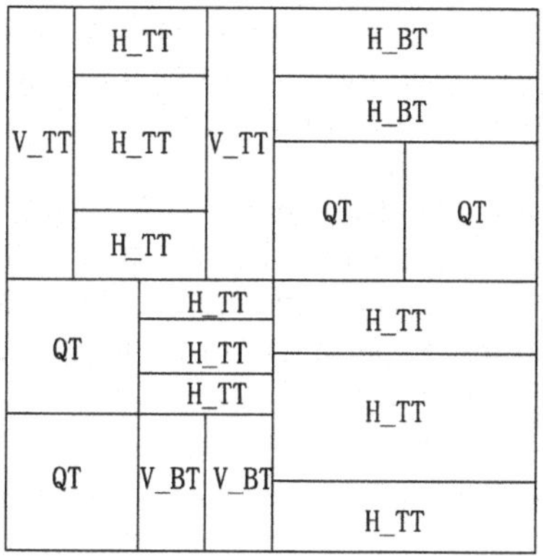
H_TT
H_BT
H_BT
V_TT
H_TT
V_TT
QT
QT
H_TT
H_TT
QT
H_TT
H_TT
H_TT
H_TT
QT
V_BT
V_BT
H_TT

(a) Coding tree unit (CTU) partition structure

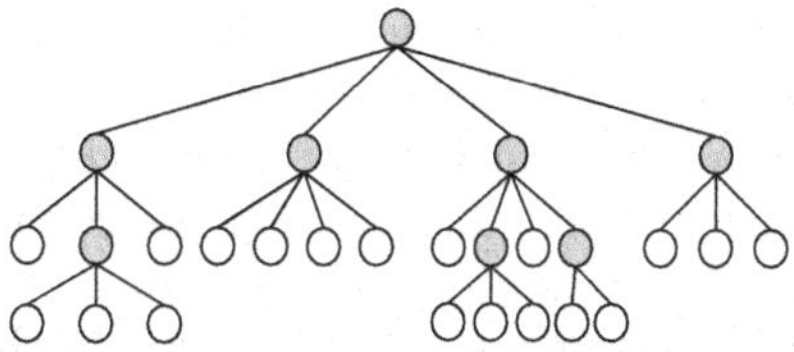

(b) Example of the hierarchy of the (a)

Fig. 2. Example of the optimal CTU partition structure

The displacement from the reference block to the current block is called a motion vector (MV). The process of using the reconstructed value of the reference block as a predicted value of the current block is called motion compensation (MC). Since there are generally many moving objects in the video, the prediction accuracy of simply using the value of co-located pixels block in the reference frame as the prediction value of current block is not high, so motion estimation is usually used to obtain the best matching block in the reference frame. Then the motion vector of the reference block and the current block are obtained, and finally the prediction value of the current block is obtained through motion compensation. The basic idea of the inter prediction technology in VVC is to use the temporal correlation between consecutive images of the video, which mainly use the block-based method to perform inter prediction by using the encoded image as the reference image of the current encoded image to remove the temporal redundancy of the image and improve the compression efficiency. The inter prediction in VVC follows and modifies some related technologies such as motion estimation, motion vector prediction and motion compensation in HEVC, and also introduces some new technologies to improve the performance of inter coding. For example, technologies such as extended merge prediction and merge mode with motion vector difference (MVD) are introduced to improve the accuracy of MV prediction. Bi-directional optical flow technology, CU Bi-prediction with CU-level weight and other technologies improve the accuracy of motion compensation. Affine motion compensated prediction technology is introduced to represent non-translational motion. So as to improve such as zoom-in, zoom-out, Motion under various viewing angles such as rotation and various irregular motion inter prediction performance.

This paper is composed of five parts. The Sect. 2 reviews some methods for reducing complexity in inter mode. In Sect. 3, a description of the proposed algorithm for fast skipping inter prediction mode. Then Sect. 4 gives the reference experimental results and test experimental results and their comparison results, and concludes this paper in Sect. 5.

2   Related Work

By inheriting and extending some of the inter prediction technologies in the previous generation video coding standard HEVC and introducing some new technologies, VVC improves the accuracy of its motion estimation and motion compensation, but also greatly increases the inter coding complexity. Based on this, some related methods of reducing the complexity of inter coding studied on HEVC can be applied to VVC, and most of the complexity problems of CU inter coding are related to motion estimation and motion compensation, and also related to the number of reference frames. Due to the complex and diverse motion of objects in the real world, the increase in the number of reference frames can effectively improve the accuracy of the coding results, but the corresponding computation and memory space will also be more complex, resulting in an increase in coding complexity. In order to effectively reduce the complexity of VVC inter coding, many research works have proposed various algorithms for inter coding. These algorithms can be roughly divided into the following three directions: simplifying the search pattern, adjusting the search range, and terminating motion estimation early [5]. The first two methods have been studied for many years, and corresponding experiments have been carried out in previous video coding standard test models. In the previous generation video coding standard HEVC, a diamond search algorithm [6] based on block matching motion estimation was proposed. This algorithm effectively simplifies the search mode on the premise of ensuring the coding quality, and has now become a core component of the motion estimation algorithm in VVC Test Model (VTM) and HEVC Test Model (HM). Reducing the number of searched reference frames is also an effective way to reduce the complexity of motion estimation. [7] proposed a fast reference frame selection method based on content similarity, which is used in the motion estimation of HM and effectively reduces the coding complexity of HM. [8] proposed a method for generating reference frames using a convolutional neural network structure, the basic idea of which is to use the encoded frames to generate virtual reference frames with neural networks instead of the reference frames selected from the reference frame sequence, to achieve the purpose of improving coding efficiency. Early termination of unnecessary motion estimation is also a simple and effective method to reduce coding complexity. Both [5,9] proposed methods to terminate motion estimation early. Among them, [5] skips some CUs' affine motion estimation (AME) by using the statistical features of MTT partition structure and AME to achieve the effect of reducing the spatial and temporal complexity of inter prediction with almost no coding loss. In [9], the texture space structure and temporal correlation of the image are used to terminate the further division of the CU in advance and optimize the affine motion, which saves the inter-coding time by reducing the complexity of motion estimation. Li, Lanlan, et al. [10] proposed a deep neural network structure model to predict motion vectors to reduce the complexity of motion estimation.

In order to reduce the computational complexity of VVC inter coding, a fast skip inter prediction decision algorithm is proposed in this paper. Unlike the previously discussed ways to reduce the computational complexity of inter-coding, this algorithm decides whether to skip inter-prediction for the current CU. When the CU's inter prediction is skipped, various inter prediction techniques including motion estimation, motion compensation, etc. will also be skipped at the same time, so the inter coding time can be greatly saved. The corresponding experimental reference software and test software in this paper have chosen VTM16.0 version. Compared with previous versions, many new methods are integrated in VTM16.0 to reduce the complexity of inter coding. However, the inter-coding complexity of the CU in VTM can still be further reduced by using the fast decision algorithm discussed in the next section. The main contributions and innovations of this paper are as follows:

1) A fast decision algorithm for skipping CU inter coding is proposed for VVC inter coding. To the best of our knowledge, our work is the first algorithm that attempts to skip the entire inter encoding mode of CU.
2) Compared with the work based on machine learning that needs to extract multiple features, the proposed algorithm only needs two features and can be directly obtained from CU. Because feature acquisition is more convenient and feature dimensions are reduced a lot, the decision algorithm is easier to implement in VVC and integrate into different video coding standards.
3) The proposed algorithm of fast skip inter mode is integrated into VTM, and the experimental results show that the inter coding time can be greatly reduced while the rate distortion performance can be neglected.

3   Proposed Method

In this part, a fast skip CU inter prediction decision algorithm is proposed to determine whether to skip the inter mode of the current CU, in order to achieve the goal of reducing the computational complexity of inter coding in VTM. For this algorithm, we mainly use the luminance difference between the original luminance value and the predicted luminance value of the CU as a feature to perform a series of computations. Then an algorithm model is constructed by using the obtained results as one of the decision conditions. Algorithm 1 shows the fast skip CU inter prediction decision algorithm in pseudo code. The feature selection and its calculation method are discussed in Sect. 3.1, and the decision algorithm is established in Sect. 3.2 and the overall flow chart of the algorithm is described.

Algorithm 1: Fast skip inter prediction decision algorithm

   Input: μ, threshold, bestCS->cu[0]->skip
  Output: skip inter prediction or not
    if μ>=threshold **then**

       return not skip inter prediction ;
    else if bestCS->cu[0]->skip == TRUE **then**

       return skip inter prediction ;
    else

       return not skip inter prediction ;
    end if
  final ;

3.1 Feature Calculation

In order to make the coding loss of the fast skip CU inter prediction decision algorithm within an acceptable range, it is very critical to select appropriate CU features for calculation. In VVC, the optimal partition structure of a CU is related to the rate distortion (RD) cost. The CU with the smallest RD cost will be selected as the optimal partition structure. Therefore, if the current CU is the optimal partition structure, the minimum RD cost value can be obtained by calculation for its inter coding. However, when the CU has a high probability of not being the optimal partition structure, its inter coding is likely not to obtain the minimum RD and the inter coding should be skipped. Therefore, the selected features should be able to well reflect the optimal partition structure of CU. Since VVC uses a more flexible QTMT partition structure, the selected features should be more relevant to this new partition structure. Different from machine learning-based methods that need to use multiple feature information, and also different from previous work on fast inter coding that directly uses image texture or directly uses original CU luminance values, we try to select more efficient and more relevant features from CU. In previous work, the luminance value of a CU is usually selected as a feature to predict whether the partition of a CU is the best partition structure. Therefore, we decide to select the features related to the CU luminance value, and finally we choose the absolute difference between the CU's original luminance value and its predicted luminance value as the feature of the decision algorithm for calculation. At the same time, because the RD cost value calculated by the coding of the CU is related to the QP initial value of the experimental configuration parameter, the QP is also calculated as a feature of the decision algorithm. We then construct a temporary CU called Predicted CU with the same width and height as the original CU and its per-pixel value calculated from formula (3). Since the mean value can well reflect the concentration of a set of data, we use the mean value (μ) of the predicted CU as an effective decision condition for the fast skip inter prediction decision algorithm. It is calculated as:

$$Res_{abs\_i} = |pixel_{org\_i} - pixel_{pred\_i}| \tag{1}$$

$$QP_{level} = QP/RESIDUAL\_QP\_LEVEL \tag{2}$$

$$Pre\_CU_{pixel\_i} = Res_{abs\_i} \, QP_{level} \tag{3}$$

$$\mu = \frac{\sum_0^{h-1} \sum_0^{w-1} Pre\_CU_{pixel\_i}}{h \times w} \tag{4}$$

where $pixel_{org\_i}$ represents the original luminance value of the i-th pixel of the current CU, and $pixel_{pred_i}$ represents the predicted luminance value of the i-th pixel of the current CU. QP is the initial parameter value configured before VTM encoding. h and w represent the height and width of the CU respectively. In order to assign different levels to the initial QP parameter values, we introduced a parameter $Residual\_QP\_Para$ and set its value as 9 in the experiment. Finally, μ represents the average pixel value of the predicted CU, which is used to determine whether the decision algorithm will skip the inter coding.

3.2   Established Decision Algorithm Model

According to formula (1–4), the average μ of the predicted CU can be calculated. When μ value is large, it indicates that the current encoded CU may be the smallest RD cost value, and then the current CU inter coding mode performs. Therefore, we set a threshold value of 10 to define μ. When μ is greater than or equal to the threshold, we continue to execute the current CU inter encoding. In order to ensure that the coding loss is within the acceptable range, the algorithm should be more careful to decide whether to skip the inter prediction. Therefore, we also select the skip attribute of the first CU in the best coding structure as another condition for building the decision algorithm model. When μ is less than the threshold, if Skip is True, the current CU inter encoding mode is skipped; otherwise, the current CU inter coding mode is continued. The overall flow chart of the algorithm is shown in Fig. 3. Because the proposed decision algorithm is used to determine whether to skip the inter mode, the algorithm is executed when the CU encoding mode is ETM_INTER_ME.

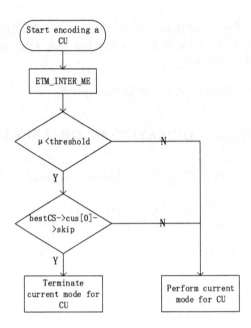

Fig. 3. Flowchart of the proposed method.

4   Experiments and Results

4.1   Experimental Configurations

In order to verify the effectiveness of the proposed decision algorithm for fast skip CU inter prediction, the experiment was integrated into VTM16.0 and performed under Random Access(RA) configuration. A total of 20 standard test video sequences from Class A to Class E were used for experimental testing. Note that the resolution of the video sequence file varies in different class. The encoded standard test video sequences all use four Quantization Parameters (QP), whose QP values are set to 22, 27, 32, and 37. All the experimental results were obtained by encoding a 30-frame video sequence, and the widely used BD-Rate [11] and encoding time saving rate were used to measure the performance of the proposed algorithm. The encoding time saving rate is defined as:

$$TS = \frac{T_{ref} - T_{test}}{T_{ref}} \times 100\% \tag{5}$$

where T_{ref} and T_{test} represent the total inter coding time of the four QP values of the original VTM16.0 and the total inter coding time of the four QP values of the VTM16.0 using the proposed algorithm respectively.

4.2   Performance Comparison

Tested in Table 1 shows the comparison between the proposed decision algorithm and VTM16.0. Tested represents the fast skip inter prediction decision algorithm proposed in this paper. The results show that the fast skip inter coding decision algorithm can save inter coding time from 12.44% to 60.67%, the average saving inter coding time is 35.17%, while the BD-rate only increases 0.98%. Experimental results show that the proposed algorithm can effectively save CU inter coding time while the increase of BD-rate is almost negligible. In order to further prove the effectiveness of the proposed decision algorithm, the fast skipCU affine motion part of the proposed method [5] was integrated into VTM16.0 for testing, and Park [5] showed its experimental results. It can be seen that although the fast skip affine motion method does not increase the BD-Rate, the time saved by inter coding is only from 6.72% to 8.98%, with an average of 7.74%. This further proves that the proposed method can greatly reduce the complexity of inter coding.

Table 1. Performance of proposed method compared with VTM 16.0 (UNIT: %)

Class	Sequence	Park [5]		Tested	
		BD-rate	TS	BD-rate	TS
A	BasketballPass	0.00	8.44	0.64	37.06
	BlowingBubbles	0.00	8.00	1.17	33.32
	BQSquare	0.00	7.85	1.28	49.12
	RaceHorses	0.00	7.17	1.41	25.09
B	BasketballDrill	0.00	8.45	1.04	25.68
	BQMall	0.00	7.82	0.87	36.61
	PartyScene	0.00	6.72	0.56	23.62
	RaceHorsesC	0.00	6.98	1.25	22.67
C	ChinaSpeed	0.00	7.41	0.98	22.35
D	FourPeople	0.00	8.92	0.66	52.44
	Johnny	0.00	8.47	2.49	59.60
	KristenAndSara	0.00	8.29	1.48	51.00
	SlideEditing	0.00	6.91	0.34	60.67
	SlideShow	0.00	7.69	-0.05	38.52
E	BasketballDrive	0.00	7.77	0.95	25.38
	BQTerrace	0.00	6.78	1.64	44.46
	Cactus	0.00	7.80	0.59	31.98
	Kimono	0.00	8.03	0.48	21.09
	ParkScene	0.00	7.13	0.79	44.03
	RitualDance	0.00	8.19	0.99	12.44
	Average	**0.00**	**7.74**	**0.98**	**35.17**

5   Conclusions

In the above work, this paper proposed a fast algorithm to skip CU inter prediction for VVC. In order to reduce the coding complexity of VVC, the algorithm uses two conditions to decide whether to skip the inter prediction mode of the current coding block. The experimental results show that the fast skip inter prediction algorithm can effectively reduce the VVC coding complexity and save the inter coding time, while the BD-Rate only increases slightly.

In the following work, the fast skip inter prediction algorithm can be combined with other modes such as intra mode to further reduce the VTM encoding time; It can also be combined with deep learning and other methods to quickly determine the CU partition structure, so as to further reduce the coding complexity and reduce the coding time while ensuring a small coding loss.

References

1. Yun, S., et al.: An efficient low-complexity block partition scheme for VVC intra coding. J. Real-Time Image Process. **19**(1), 161–172 (2022)
2. Tang, N., et al.: Fast CTU Partition Decision Algorithm for VVC Intra and Inter Coding. In: IEEE Asia Pacific Conference on Circuits and Systems (APCCAS), vol. 2019, pp. 361–364 (2019). https://doi.org/10.1109/APCCAS47518.2019.8953076
3. Tissier, A., et al.: Complexity reduction opportunities in the future VVC intra encoder. In: 2019 IEEE 21st International Workshop on Multimedia Signal Processing (MMSP). IEEE (2019)
4. Pan, Z., et al.: Low complexity versatile video coding for traffic surveillance system. Int. J. Sens. Netw. **30**(2), 116–125 (2019)
5. Park, S.-H., Kang, J.-W.: Fast affine motion estimation for versatile video coding (VVC) encoding. IEEE Access **7**, 158075–158084 (2019)
6. Zhu, S., Ma, K.-K.: A new diamond search algorithm for fast block-matching motion estimation. IEEE Trans. Image Process. **9**(2), 287–290 (2000)
7. Pan, Z., et al.: Fast reference frame selection based on content similarity for low complexity HEVC encoder. J. Vis. Commun. Image Representation **40**, 516–524 (2016)
8. Lee, J.-K., et al.: Deep video prediction network-based inter-frame coding in HEVC. IEEE Access **8**, 95906–95917 (2020)
9. Guan, X., Sun, X.: VVC fast ME algorithm based on spatial texture features and time correlation. In: 2021 International Conference on Digital Society and Intelligent Systems (DSInS). IEEE (2021)
10. Li, L., et al.: Deep motion vector prediction for versatile video coding. In: 2021 7th International Conference on Computer and Communications (ICCC). IEEE (2021)
11. Gisle, B.: Calculation of average PSNR differences between RD-curves. In: VCEG-M33 (2001)

Machine Learning

SMA-Net: Sobel Operator Combined with Multi-attention Networks for COVID-19 Lesion Segmentation

Fangfang Lu[✉], Chi Tang[✉], Tianxiang Liu, and Zhihao Zhang

College of Computer Science and Technology, Shanghai University of Electric Power,
Shanghai, China
lufangfang@shiep.edu.cn, tangchi9710@163.com,
{liutianxiang,zhangzhihao}@mail.shiep.edu.cn

Abstract. Coronavirus disease 2019 (COVID-19) has been spreading since late 2019, leading the world into a serious health crisis. To control the spread rate of infection, identifying patients accurately and quickly is the most crucial step. Computed tomography (CT) images of the chest are an important basis for diagnosing COVID-19. They also allow doctors to understand the details of the lung infection. However, manual segmentation of infected areas in CT images is time-consuming and laborious. With its excellent feature extraction capabilities, deep learning-based method has been widely used for automatic lesion segmentation of COVID-19 CT images. But, the segmentation accuracy of these methods is still limited. To effectively quantify the severity of lung infections, we propose a Sobel operator combined with Multi-Attention networks for COVID-19 lesion segmentation (SMA-Net). In our SMA-Net, an edge feature fusion module uses Sobel operator to add edge detail information to the input image. To guide the network to focus on key regions, the SMA-Net introduces a self-attentive channel attention mechanism and a spatial linear attention mechanism. In addition, Tversky loss function is adopted for the segmentation network for small size of lesions. Comparative experiments on COVID-19 public datasets show that the average Dice similarity coefficient (DSC) and joint intersection over Union (IOU) of proposed SMA-Net are 86.1% and 77.8%, respectively, which are better than most existing neural networks used for COVID-19 lesion segmentation.

Keywords: Lesion segmentation · Deep learning · COVID-19 · Multi-attention

1 Introduction

Coronavirus disease 2019 (COVID-19) is an epidemic disease caused by a new coronavirus (formerly known as 2019 nCoV). This new coronavirus has strong adaptability, so far, it has produced eleven different mutant strains [1]. According to the latest statistics from the Johns Hopkins Center for Systems Science and Engineering (CSSE) (updated October 8, 2022), the number of confirmed COVID-19 cases worldwide has reached 621 million, including 6.56 million

© The Author(s), under exclusive license to Springer Nature Singapore Pte Ltd. 2023
G. Zhai et al. (Eds.): IFTC 2022, CCIS 1766, pp. 377–390, 2023.
https://doi.org/10.1007/978-981-99-0856-1_28

deaths. Currently, reverse transcription-polymerase chain reaction (RT-PCR) is the standard test for diagnosing COVID-19 disease [2]. However, the RT-PCR test has the possibility of false negatives when the nucleic acid content of the new coronavirus is too low in the test sample. The missed diagnosis cases caused by false negatives will lead to more widespread transmission, which is extremely unfavorable for the prevention and control of the epidemic [3].

In order to better suppress the spread of the coronavirus, chest computed tomography (CT) images have become an important tool for diagnosing COVID-19. Studies in [4,5] show that CT scan has high sensitivity, and abnormal features such as ground-glass opacity (GGO), consolidation and rare features in CT images can reflect the severity of infection in patients. However, it takes a lot of time to manually segment the lesion area in CT images, and for an experienced radiologist, it needs about 21.5 min to get the diagnostic results of each case by analyzing CT images [6]. Therefore, it is necessary to propose an automatic lesion segmentation method to assist doctors in diagnosis. Recently, with the powerful feature extraction capability of deep convolutional neural networks, deep learning-based method has been widely used in medical image processing [1,7]. Wang et al. [8] developed a deep learning method combined with CT classification and segmentation that can extract CT image features of COVID-19 patients and provide medical diagnosis for doctors. Matteo et al. [9] proposed a lightweight convolutional neural network for distinguishing CT images of COVID-19 patients from healthy CT images.

It is worth noting that the encoder-decoder structure is the most common used in lesion segmentation models. Many studies [10,11] have confirmed that this structure has good segmentation performance and robustness. As a result, a number of studies have been conducted on segmentation of COVID-19 lesions by using encoder-decoder structures. FCN [12], SegNet [13], Unet [14] and deeplav3 [15] are applied to the COVID-19 segmentation task. In addition, Unet and its variants have also been applied to the COVID-19 segmentation task. Chen et al. [16] used Unet combined with residual network to achieve automatic segmentation of COVID-19 lesions. Bhatia et al. [17] proposed a U-Net++-based segmentation model for identifying 2019-nCoV pneumonia lesion on chest CT images of patients. A large number of deep learning-based methods [18,19] have been applied to the lesion segmentation of COVID-19. Although these methods are more efficient than manual segmentation, they still have shortcomings in segmentation accuracy. They tend to have the following problems. (1) Although the encoder-decoder structure can extract high-level features with rich semantics, it will lose spatial detail information such as the edge information of the lesion area when the encoder performs down sampling. (2) These networks lack an effective mechanism to learn the channel information and spatial information of features. (3) The previous loss function of semantic segmentation is not suitable for the lesion segmentation task of COVID-19, which makes the network insensitive to small lesion areas.

To solve the above problems, we propose a Sobel operator combined with Multi-Attention networks (SMA-Net) to segment the lesions of COVID-19. Different from previous methods, we pay more attention to the edge information of images. We propose self-attentive channel attention mechanism and spatial attention mechanism to guide the network in the concatenation of low-level and high-level features for feature extraction. The Tversky loss function adopted by SMA-Net can take into account the small lesion area and improve its sensitivity.

Our contributions are summarized as follows:

1) We propose a module for fusing COVID-19 CT images and their edge features to provide more detailed information for the network. This module uses the Sobel edge detection operator to obtain edge information.
2) We propose a self-attentive channel attention mechanism with a spatial linear attention mechanism module that is independent of the resolution size of the feature map, which we apply to each layer of the low-level feature and high-level feature splicing. It enables the network to focus on important semantic information, thereby improving the segmentation performance of the network.
3) SMA-Net has a suitable loss function for the small lesion area of COVID-19. Compared with other segmentation methods, SMA-Net has better segmentation accuracy in small lesion.

2   Dataset and Data Enhancement

Public COVID-19 segmentation dataset: The public dataset used in this paper is from zendo [20]. The dataset contains 20 COVID-19 CT scans, including lung and lesion segmentation labels. The dataset was annotated by two radiologists and examined by an experienced radiologist. In this study, 2237 CT images were selected for the experiment. To speed up the convergence of the network and improve efficiency, some preprocessing operations were performed on this dataset. We cropped the CT images to a resolution of 512*512 size to reduce the amount of calculation in the training process. The CT images are then normalized. Image normalization is the process of centering the data by de-meaning, which can improve the generalization of the network.

3   The Proposed Method

In this section, we first propose the overall structure of SMA-Net. Then the core modules of the network are introduced in detail, including edge feature fusion, self-attentive channel attention mechanism and spatial linear attention mechanism. Finally, the loss function used for training is described.

3.1   Network Structure

The structure of proposed SMA-Net is shown in Fig. 1. It can be seen that the original CT image is first fused with its corresponding edge features to obtain the input tensor of the network. Then the input feature map is divided into two directions after convolution and activation operations. Feature map is sent to the SCAM module, and it is also sent to the next layer by pooling for further

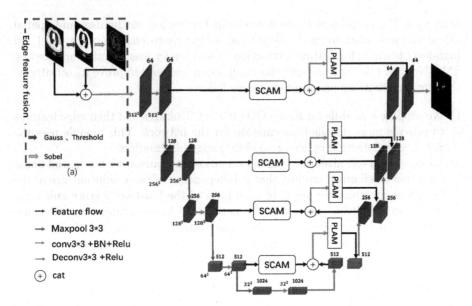

Fig. 1. The network structure of SMA-Net. The part (a) in the blue dashed box is the edge feature fusion. After the edge feature fusion is completed, the image is fed into the segmentation network. The segmentation network has four layers. Each layer has a corresponding channel attention mechanism and a spatial linear attention mechanism. The input image and the segmentation result output by the network have the same resolution size. (Color figure online)

feature extraction. SMA-Net performs 4 times down-sampling for the features. The feature map is reduced from a resolution size of 512*512 to 32*32. Then, the feature map is begun up-sampling. After up-sampling, the feature map is concatenated with the encoder feature map in the same layer after it passing through SCAM module, and then the obtained feature map is sent to the PLAM module to get a feature map with rich semantic information. Next, the feature map is further upsampled, and then repeat the above operation to upsample the feature map to the original image size. Finally, compress the channel to get the final segmentation result.

3.2   Edge Feature Fusion

In the semantic segmentation models applied to medical images, most of them use encoding-decoding structure as the overall architecture. The encoder extracts the feature maps from the images through convolution and pooling operations. The low-level feature maps are often containing more edge information of the lesions in the CT images. But in the process of downsampling, the edge details in the feature map will be partially lost. To solve the loss of edge information, we propose to fuse CT images with their edge features to add spatial detail information from the source of the model input. As shown in Fig 1(a), we first do a Gaussian filtering process on the CT image. The idea of Gaussian filtering is to suppress noise and retain detail information by weighted average of pixels. Then, a thresholding process is done to obtain a binary map U.

$$U = T(G(X, k = 3), t = 127) \tag{1}$$

where G denotes Gaussian filtering operation, k is the filter size and X is the grey scale map of the input CT image. t denotes image thresholding and it is set to 127 in this paper. The Sobel operator is then used to calculate the gradient in the X and Y directions for the binary map, and the two gradients are combined to obtain the edge feature map. Finally, the model input Z is obtained by fusing the extracted edge feature map with its CT image.

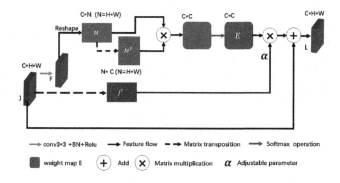

Fig. 2. SCAM: Self-attentive channel attention mechanism

3.3   Self-attentive Channel Attention Mechanism (SCAM)

To improve semantic segmentation performance, U-shaped networks concatenate high-level features with low-level features to obtain richer semantic information. In the process of concatenation, a redundancy channel of feature map often occurs. So, channel attention modules (such as the classical SE module) are usually added to the network in order to emphasize the meaningful features of channel axis. SE module obtains the compressed feature vectors by global average pooling of the feature maps, and then the obtained compressed feature vectors go through the full connection layer to generate the weight of each channel of the feature map. The SE module is simple and easy to apply it to the model. However, the global averaging pooling operation in the SE module results in a loss of semantic information.

In order to solve this problem, we propose a self-attentive channel attention mechanism (SCAM) module as shown in Fig. 2. Instead of compressing the feature map by global average pooling, the module first performs a convolution operation on the feature map J input to the SCAM module to obtain the feature map $F \in R^{C \times H \times W}$ as shown in Eq. 2. The feature map F is then reshaped to obtain the matrix $M \in R^{C \times N}$, and then the transpose of matrix M and M are calculated as matrix product. Finally, using softmax to activate the matrix product yields the channel attention weight map E.

$$F = f(J, k = 3) \tag{2}$$

$$E_{ji} = \frac{\exp(M_i \cdot M_j)}{\sum_{i=1}^{C} \exp(M_i \cdot M_j)} \tag{3}$$

where E_{ji} denotes the effect of the i-th channel on the j-th channel. After obtaining the weight map E, E and the transpose of matrix J are calculated as matrix product. This assigns the values in the weight map to each channel of J. Given on the idea of residual networks, the result of the product is multiplied by the adaptive coefficient α and then summed with J to obtain the final output L of the SCAM module.

$$L = \alpha \sum_{i=1}^{c} \left(E_{ji} J^{\top} \right) + J \tag{4}$$

where the initial value of α is set to 0 and it can be changed with the needs of the network during the training process. L is used as the output of the input J passing through the SCAM module. L is then connected in series with its corresponding high-level features in the decoder.

3.4   Spatial Linear Attention Mechanism (PLAM)

After completing the concatenation of low-level features with high-level features, the decoder obtains a semantic rich feature map. However not all regions of this rich semantic information are equally important for lesion segmentation. To enhance the representation of key regions, we introduce the spatial linear attention module as shown in Fig. 3. Before introducing the spatial linear attention module, we first review the principle of the compressed dot product attention mechanism (Scaled-Dot Attention, SDA), as given in Eq. 5.

$$\text{Attention}(Q, K, V) = \text{softmax}\left(\frac{QK^T}{\sqrt{d_k}}\right) V \tag{5}$$

where Q, K and V denote the query matrix, the key matrix and the value matrix respectively. These three matrices are obtained by convolving the input feature map by compressing the number of channels and then reshaped the feature map. $\sqrt{d_k}$ denotes the scaling factor. The overall dot product attention

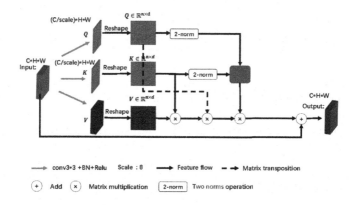

Fig. 3. PLAM Spatial linear attention mechanism structure

mechanism can be summarized as modeling the similarity between pixel points by matrix multiplication and the softmax function is used to activate the matrix multiplication result.

However, since $Q \in \mathbb{R}^{n \times d}$, $K \in \mathbb{R}^{n \times d}$, $V \in \mathbb{R}^{n \times d}$ where $n = W * H$, W and H represent the width and height of the feature map respectively. The complexity of the dot product attention mechanism is $\mathcal{O}\left(n^2\right)$, which makes SDA limited by the image resolution. Moreover, the resolution of CT images is usually large and if SDA is used directly, it will exceed the computational power of the computer. If the resolution of the CT image is scaled by scaling, much detailed information is lost in the image.

In order to improve SDA, we propose a spatial linear attention mechanism module. The complexity of the module is reduced from $\mathcal{O}\left(n^2\right)$ to $\mathcal{O}(n)$, which allows the module to be flexibly applied to segmentation networks. We start by equivalently rewriting Eq. 5 as Eq. 6. Because PLAM does not use a scaling factor, $\sqrt{d_k}$ is removed from Eq. 6. Equation 6 represents the result of the i-th row of the matrix obtained from the feature map after feeding into the dot product attention mechanism.

$$\text{Attention}\left(Q, K, V\right)_i = \frac{\sum_{j=1}^{n} e^{q_i^\top k_j} v_j}{\sum_{j=1}^{n} e^{q_i^\top k_j}} \tag{6}$$

where $e^{q_i^\top k_j}$ is essentially a weighted average over v_j, so Eq. 6 can be generalized to a general form by replacing the softmax function with the general function as given in Eq. 7.

$$\text{Attention}(Q, K, V)_i = \frac{\sum_{j=1}^{n} \text{sim}\left(q_i, k_j\right) v_j}{\sum_{j=1}^{n} \text{sim}\left(q_i, k_j\right)} \tag{7}$$

where $\text{sim}\left(q_i, k_j\right) \geq 0$. In order to reduce the complexity of Eq. 7, the order of concatenation of q_i, k_j, v_j needs to be changed and the normalization of q_i, k_j

needs to be solved. In the construction of linear attention mechanism, we start with Taylor expansion. Turn $e^{q_i^T k_j}$ into $1 + q_i^T k_j$.

$$e^{q_i^T k_j} \approx 1 + q_i^T k_j. \tag{8}$$

According to the Taylor expansion of Eq. 7, $\text{sim}(q_i, k_j) = 1 + q_i^T k_j$. Since we need to normalize q_i, k_j and ensure that $\text{sim}(q_i, k_j) > 0$. We can use the two norms of the matrix for normalization. Following this Eq. 6 can be equated to Eq. 9.

$$\text{Attention}(Q, K, V)_i = \frac{\sum_{j=1}^{n} \left(1 + \left(\frac{q_i}{\|q_i\|_2}\right)^T \left(\frac{k_j}{\|k_j\|_2}\right)\right) v_j}{\sum_{j=1}^{n} \left(1 + \left(\frac{q_i}{\|q_i\|_2}\right)^T \left(\frac{k_j}{\|k_j\|_2}\right)\right)} \tag{9}$$

By modifying the original form of the attention mechanism, we have completed the construction of a spatial linear attention mechanism.

3.5   Loss Function

Due to the exist of small lesions in the CT images of COVID-19, and the early clinical manifestations of COVID-19 are not obvious. The small lesion part of the CT images can be used as a basis for the early diagnosis of COVID-19. When the proportion of pixels in the target region is small, network training becomes more difficult, so small lesions are easily ignored in the network training process. Therefore, after the network has been built, it is important to choose a suitable loss function that is appropriate for the segmentation task. The Dice Loss function, which is often used in segmentation tasks, cannot meet the segmentation needs of small lesions in COVID-19. In order to fit the segmentation task, we chose the Tversky loss. As given in Eq. 10.

$$TL(\alpha, \beta) = \frac{\sum_{i=1}^{N} p_{0i} g_{0i}}{\sum_{i=1}^{N} p_{0i} g_{0i} + \alpha \sum_{i=1}^{N} p_{0i} g_{1i} + \beta \sum_{i=1}^{N} p_{1i} g_{0i}} \tag{10}$$

where α, β are hyper parameters, set to 0.3 and 0.7 respectively in this paper. p_{0i} represents the probability of a pixel point being diseased. g_{0i} is 1 and g_{1i} is 0 when the pixel point is diseased. p_{1i} represents the probability of a pixel point being non-diseased. When the pixel point is non-lesioned, g_{0i} is 0 and g_{1i} is 1. As can be seen from the Eq. 10, the trade-off between false negatives and false positives can be controlled when adjusting the values of α, β. The value of β is taken to be 0.7 greater than α, improving sensitivity by emphasizing false negatives. This allows the network to focus on small lesion areas during training, thus addressing the problem of data imbalance in CT images of patients with neocoronary pneumonia.

4   Experiment

4.1   Experimental Setup

Baseline: In the lesion segmentation experiments, our proposed SMA-Net is compared with the classical network Unet and Unet++. In addition, we also refer to the advanced semantic segmentation networks Deeplabv3, FCN, SegNet. Moreover, we also compare three newly proposed COVID-19 lesion segmentation networks: AnamNet, JCS, and Inf-Net.

AnamNet [21]: A lightweight CNN based on deformation depth embedding for segmentation network of COVID-19 chest CT image anomalies, can be deployed to mobile terminals.

JCS [22]: A novel combined classification and segmentation system for real-time and interpreted COVID -19 chest CT diagnosis.

Inf-Net [23]: A semi-supervised segmentation framework based on a random selection propagation strategy for a network with a fully supervised form, which we have selected for its fully supervised approach.

Table 1. Comparison of lesion segmentation performance

Methods	DSC	IOU	SEN	SPE
Unet	0.797	0.701	0.869	**0.998**
Unet++	0.754	0.687	0.836	0.993
Deeplabv3	0.773	0.646	0.861	0.997
FCN	0.689	0.612	0.795	0.876
Segnet	0.731	0.634	0.854	0.993
AnamNet	0.808	0.71	0.846	0.979
JCS	0.847	0.754	0.852	0.989
Inf-Net	0.818	0.723	0.871	0.985
Ours	**0.861**	**0.778**	**0.915**	0.997

4.2   Segmentation Results

To compare the segmentation performance of SMA-Net, we refer to the classical medical image segmentation network Unet and its variant Unet++. In addition we also refer to the advanced semantic segmentation networks Deeplabv3, FCN, SegNet. For the three recently proposed COVID-19 lesion segmentation networks (AnamaNet, JCS, Inf-Net), we have also conducted comparative experiments. The quantitative results are shown in Table 1. It can be seen that for the other methods our proposed SMA-Net achieves a significant improvement in IOU metric, with a 7.8% improvement compared to Unet. The DSC coefficient also achieves the best. We attribute this improvement to our edge feature fusion

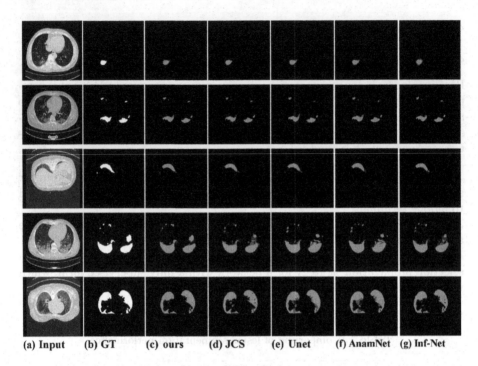

(a) Input   (b) GT   (c) ours   (d) JCS   (e) Unet   (f) AnamNet (g) Inf-Net

Fig. 4. Visual comparison of lesion segmentation results using different networks. (a) represents CT images (b) represents ground truth. (c), (d), (e), (f) and (g) represent the segmentation results of SMA-Net, JCS, Unet, AnamNet and Inf-Net, respectively. The green, blue, and red regions refer to true positive, false negative and false positive pixels, respectively. (Color figure online)

module as well as to self-attentive channel attention mechanism and spatial linear attention mechanism. Thanks to the two attention mechanisms guiding SMA-Net, SMA-Net can sample a richer feature map of semantic information during feature extraction.

Figure 4 shows a visual comparison of SMA-Net with Unet and the three newly proposed COVID-19 lesion segmentation networks (AnamaNet, JCS, Inf-Net). The green, blue, and red regions refer to true positive, false negative and false positive pixels, respectively. It can be seen that SMA-Net is closest to the ground truth. In contrast, many false positive pixels appear in the Unet and AnamNet segmentation results. Thanks to our choice of Tversky loss function, SMA-Net achieves good results in the segmentation of small lesions. Compared to the other networks, our increased sensitivity of the loss function to the small lesion region allows the network to segment the small lesion region well.

4.3   Ablation Studies

In this section, we experimentally demonstrate the performance of key components of SMA-Net, including the edge feature fusing module, the self-attention channel attention mechanism module (SCAM), and the spatial linear attention mechanism module (PLAM). In Table 2, A is the SMA-Net without the SCAM module, B is the SMA-Net without the PLAM module, C is the SMA-Net with the edge feature fusion module removed and D is the complete SMA-Net. E is the SMA-Net without SCAM, PLAM and the feature fusion module.

Table 2. Results of the ablation experiment

Model	DSC	IOU	SEN	SPE
A	0.846	0.756	0.903	0.997
B	0.837	0.732	0.897	0.983
C	0.783	0.697	0.884	0.997
D	**0.861**	**0.778**	**0.915**	0.997
E	0.797	0.701	0.869	**0.998**

- Effectiveness of **SCAM**: To explore the SMA-Net's self-attentive channel attention module, we propose two benchmarks: as shown in Table 2, A (SMA-Net without SCAM), D (SMA-Net), and the results show that SCAM is effective in improving network performance.
- Effectiveness of **PLAM**: From Table 2, it can be observed that the IOU values decrease more between B (SMA-Net without PLAM) compared to D. This indicates that the spatial linear attention mechanism has an important role in guiding the network to learn to segment the lesion area, allowing the network SMA-Net to focus more on the pixels in the lesion area.
- Effectiveness of edge feature stitching: After the fusing of edge features is completed, the encoder obtains richer semantic information. As can be seen from Table 2, C has the lowest IOU metric compared to A, B and D, which indicates that edge features are important for the detail complement of CT images.

5   Comparison of Loss Function

5.1   Selection of Loss Function

After the construction of the network SMA-Net is completed, the selection of the loss function has a great impact on the performance of the network. Therefore, for different semantic segmentation tasks, the selection of the loss function is based on the characteristics of the task. Commonly used loss functions such as Dice loss (DL) function, Balanced cross-entropy loss function BCE for binary classification task, Weighted cross-entropy loss function WCE. In addition, we also selected excellent loss functions that have been used for semantic segmentation in recent years, namely Asymmetric Loss Functions (AL), Tversky Loss (TL), PenaltyGDiceLoss (PL).

1) Asymmetric Loss Functions (AL): A novel loss function is designed to address the problem of positive and negative sample imbalance in classification tasks. Adaptive methods are proposed to control the asymmetric rank.
2) Tversky Loss (TL): In order to solve the problem of data imbalance, a new loss function is proposed to improve the sensitivity of small lesion areas by adjusting the hyper parameters of the tversky index.
3) PenaltyGDiceLoss (PL): improves network segmentation performance by adding false negative and false positive penalty terms to the generalized dice coefficients (GD).

Table 3. Comparison of SMA net results under different loss functions

Loss	DSC	IOU	SEN	SPE
BCE	0.834	0.743	0.979	0.896
WCE	0.823	0.726	0.983	0.852
DC	0.783	0.697	0.997	0.884
GD	0.799	0.689	0.973	0.854
AL	0.824	0.727	**0.998**	0.897
TL	**0.861**	**0.778**	0.997	**0.915**

5.2   Comparison Results

As can be seen from Table 3, Tversky Loss (TL) performed the best among the three indicators of IOU, DSC and SPE. Compared to the BCE loss function IOU and DSC coefficients improved by 6.8% and 7% respectively. Among them, AL performed the best in sensitivity. We also made a visual comparison of the output results of SMA-Net with different loss functions. The results from TL are more sensitive for small lesion regions and can do well in segmenting small lesions. In contrast, the lack of segmentation for small lesion regions can be observed from the segmentation results of BCE as well as AL.

6   Conclusion

To improve the efficiency of diagnosis of COVID-19, we have developed a COVID-19 lesion segmentation network. In our network, we propose the first edge feature fusion module, which allows the network to capture more edge feature information. In addition, we introduce a self-attentive channel attention mechanism and a spatial linear attention mechanism to improve the network performance. Two attention mechanisms guide SMA-Net, which captures lesion areas more accurately during feature extraction. Compared with the classical medical image segmentation network Unet, the DSC and IOU of SMA-Net are improved by 7% and 7.8% respectively. Although our method achieves good results in terms of performance, it still has the following shortcomings. (1) the network has a high computational complexity, and (2) the network does not perform the classification task simultaneously. Therefore, our future work will try to start with the light weighting of the model and to achieve simultaneous network classification and segmentation as a way to improve the diagnosis of neocrown pneumonia.

References

1. Shi, F., et al.: Review of artificial intelligence techniques in imaging data acquisition, segmentation, and diagnosis for COVID-19. IEEE Rev. Biomed. Eng. **14**, 4–15 (2020)
2. Ai, T., Yang, Z., Hou, H., Zhan, C., Chen, C., Lu, W., et al.: Correlation of chest CT and RT-PCR testing for coronavirus disease 2019 (COVID-19) in china: a report of 1014 cases. Radiology **296**(2), E32-40 (2020)
3. Fang, Y., et al.: Sensitivity of chest CT for COVID-19: comparison to RT-PCR. Radiology **296**(2), E115–E117 (2020)
4. Ankur, G.-W., et al.: False-negative RT-PCR for COVID-19 and a diagnostic risk score: a retrospective cohort study among patients admitted to hospital. BMJ Open **11**(2), e047110 (2021)
5. Swapnarekha, H., Behera, H.S., Nayak, J., Naik, B.: Role of intelligent computing in COVID-19 prognosis: a state-of-the-art review. Chaos Solitons Fractals **138**, 109947 (2020)
6. Wang, Y., Hou, H., Wang, W., Wang, W.: Combination of CT and RT-PCR in the screening or diagnosis of COVID-19 (2020)
7. Rajinikanth, V., Dey, N., Raj, A.N.J., Hassanien, A.E., Santosh, K.C., Raja, N.: Harmony-search and otsu based system for coronavirus disease (COVID-19) detection using lung ct scan images. arXiv preprint arXiv:2004.03431 (2020)
8. Wang, B., et al.: Ai-assisted CT imaging analysis for COVID-19 screening: Building and deploying a medical AI system. Appl. Soft Comput. **98**, 106897 (2021)
9. Polsinelli, M., Cinque, L., Placidi, G.: A light CNN for detecting COVID-19 from CT scans of the chest. Pattern Recogn. Lett. **140**, 95–100 (2020)
10. Chen, J., Qin, F., Lu, F., et al.: CSPP-IQA: a multi-scale spatial pyramid pooling-based approach for blind image quality assessment. Neural Comput. Appl. pp. 1–12, (2022). https://doi.org/10.1007/s00521-022-07874-2
11. Xiaoxin, W., et al.: Fam: focal attention module for lesion segmentation of COVID-19 CT images. J. Real-Time Image Proc. **19**(6), 1091–1104 (2022)
12. Long, J., Shelhamer, E., Darrell, T.: Fully convolutional networks for semantic segmentation. In: Proceedings of the IEEE Conference on Computer Vision and Pattern Recognition, pp. 3431–3440 (2015)
13. Badrinarayanan, V., Kendall, A., Cipolla, R.: SEGNET: a deep convolutional encoder-decoder architecture for image segmentation. IEEE Trans. Pattern Anal. Mach. Intell. **39**(12), 2481–2495 (2017)
14. Ronneberger, O., Fischer, P., Brox, T.: U-Net: convolutional networks for biomedical image segmentation. In: Navab, N., Hornegger, J., Wells, W.M., Frangi, A.F. (eds.) MICCAI 2015. LNCS, vol. 9351, pp. 234–241. Springer, Cham (2015). https://doi.org/10.1007/978-3-319-24574-4_28

15. Chen, L.-C., Zhu, Y., Papandreou, G., Schroff, F., Adam, H.: Encoder-decoder with atrous separable convolution for semantic image segmentation. In: Ferrari, V., Hebert, M., Sminchisescu, C., Weiss, Y. (eds.) ECCV 2018. LNCS, vol. 11211, pp. 833–851. Springer, Cham (2018). https://doi.org/10.1007/978-3-030-01234-2_49

16. Chen, J., et al.: Deep learning-based model for detecting 2019 novel coronavirus pneumonia on high-resolution computed tomography. Sci. Rep. **10**(1), 1–11 (2020)

17. Bhatia, P., Sinha, A., Joshi, S.P., Sarkar, R., Ghosh, R., Jana, S.: Automated quantification of inflamed lung regions in chest CT by UNET++ and SegCaps: a comparative analysis in COVID-19 cases. In: 2022 44th Annual International Conference of the IEEE Engineering in Medicine & Biology Society (EMBC), pp. 3785–3788. IEEE (2022)

18. Tang, S., et al.: Release and demand of public health information in social media during the outbreak of COVID-19 in China. Front. Pub. Health **9**, 2433 (2021)

19. Gao, K., et al.: Dual-branch combination network (DCN): towards accurate diagnosis and lesion segmentation of COVID-19 using CT images. Med. Image Anal. **67**, 101836 (2021)

20. Ma, J., et al.: Toward data-efficient learning: a benchmark for COVID-19 CT lung and infection segmentation. Med. Phys. **48**(3), 1197–1210 (2021)

21. Paluru, N., et al.: Anam-net: anamorphic depth embedding-based lightweight CNN for segmentation of anomalies in COVID-19 chest CT images. IEEE Trans. Neural Netw. Learn. Syst. **32**(3), 932–946 (2021)

22. Kimura, K., et al.: JCS 2018 guideline on diagnosis and treatment of acute coronary syndrome. Circ. J. **83**(5), 1085–1196 (2019)

23. Fan, D.-P., et al.: INF-net: Automatic COVID-19 lung infection segmentation from CT images. IEEE Trans. Med. Imaging **39**(8), 2626–2637 (2020)

ViT-Siamese Cascade Network for Transmission Image Deduplication

Zhenyu Chen[1]([✉]), Siyu Chen[1], Xuan Peng[2], Jingchen Bian[1], Lina Jiang[1], and Xiaoyu Zhang[1]

[1] Big Data Center, State Grid Corporation of China, Beijing, China
czy9907@163.com
[2] Institute of Microelectronics, Chinese Academy of Sciences, Beijing, China

Abstract. With the large-scale use of various inspection methods such as drones, helicopters, and robots, the generated power inspection images have increased significantly, which has brought huge pressure on data storage and transmission. At the same time, with the rapid development of artificial intelligence technology in the electric power field, the cost of manual labeling required for model training has become a major pain point. This paper studies a transmission image deduplication technology based on ViT-Siamese cascade network, which reduces the amount of data and the cost of data annotation. This paper first investigates the research status of image similarity at home and abroad, and then studies the transmission image deduplication technology based on the ViT-Siamese cascade network, which greatly reduces the complexity of similarity calculation, and finally trains the model on the transmission image data set. Firstly, this paper investigates the research status of image similarity at domestic and international. Next, transmission image deduplication technology based on ViT-Siamese cascade network is studied, which greatly reduces the complexity of similarity calculation. And finally, the AI model is trained on transmission image dataset, and effectiveness and feasibility of the technology in transmission scene processing are verified by experiments.

Keywords: Transmission · Vision transformer · Siamese network · Image deduplication

1 Introduction

Power inspection is a vital warranty for secure and non-stop power transmission. The traditional inspection of transmission lines depends on a massive range of authorities' on-site inspection, resulting in excessive inspection fees and low inspection efficiency. With the in-depth application of drones and helicopters in transmission line inspections, the pressure of manual inspections has been greatly reduced, but a large amount of data generated by inspections still requires manual inspection [1]. The combination of artificial intelligence technology and power inspection can notably enhance the efficiency of inspection. However, drones and helicopter inspections will generate a large amount

of data [2], and the influx of large amounts of inspection data will bring two problems:
(1) Huge amounts of data will deliver increased strain on data transmission and storage.
(2) Training artificial intelligence models requires a large amount of labeling data, and
there is a large amount of duplicate data in the image data of each inspection, which
will lead to duplicate labels and increase labeling costs. Therefore, this paper proposes
a transmission image de-duplication technology based on the ViT(Vision Transformer)-
Siamese cascade network. Using this technology, the repeated data in the data set can
be removed and the overall data volume can be reduced.

At present, there has been a lot of research on data deduplication technology, which
is mainly divided into two aspects: one is traditional deduplication methods, including histogram method, cosine similarity method, mean hash method, complete file
detection technology, and block-level duplicate detection technology. The second is
the deduplication method based on deep learning.

Traditional deduplication methods usually compare multi-level data such as file-level
and block-level to achieve the purpose of identifying whether the data is duplicated [3].
This type of method first uses hash algorithms such as MD4, MD5 and SHA-1 to mine
the duplicate data in the file, or calculates the similarity of the photos by calculating the
cosine distance and color distribution between the two pictures. This kind of method
produces a very complicated calculation process in the data detection process, which
reduces the detection speed [4], or the calculation accuracy is not high enough, and the
calculation efficiency and recognition accuracy are difficult to balance.

The deduplication method based on deep learning firstly extracts global features
through wavelet transform, Gabor transform, etc., or directly obtains image features
through CNN, then obtains the real number matrix of the image through feature hashing feature engineering technology, and finally through binary features Comparison to
achieve repeated inspection of the data [5]. Such methods combine machine learning
techniques and feature engineering techniques to achieve complex implementations.

Siamese network was first proposed by LeCun to verify whether the signature on the
check is consistent with the signature reserved by the bank [6]. Siamese Network [6] is
the most classic in the similarity determination of face image pairs. Siamese Network
combines CNN and Euclidean distance to determine the similarity of face image pairs.
The CNN part adopts GoogLeNet, but there are still problems such as large model and
environmental impact [7]. With the development of this technology, by 2010, Hinton
used the Siamese architecture structure to build a model [8], to achieve face recognition
verification, and obtained good experimental results. In 2015, Sergey Zagoruyko et al.
improved the Siamese Network [9] to calculate the image similarity, which made the
system performance better. However, the Siamese networks proposed in these documents
are all comparisons of two images. If they are directly used for similarity analysis of a
large number of transmission images, the efficiency will be greatly reduced, and it is not
suitable for transmission inspection scenarios.

The current mainstream target detection algorithms based on convolutional neural
networks are divided into one-stage and two-stage types. At present, the Trans-former
[11] network has been deeply applied to natural language processing (NLP), and has
achieved success, and some scholars have migrated it to the CV field. In 2018, Parmar first
applied Transformer to image generation and proposed the Image Transformer model

[12]. In 2020, Carion et al. combined CNN and Transformer to propose a complete end-to-end DETR target detection framework [13], applying Transformer to target detection for the first time. In 2021, Zhu [14] and others proposed the Deformable DETR model based on the variable convolutional neural network; in the same year, Zheng [15] and others proposed the ACT algorithm to reduce the computational complexity of the self-attention module; Google research used only Transformer to propose the ViT model [21] and apply it to image classification with high performance. In addition, the training process is greatly simplified due to the unique advantage of the deep learning method [17–20] that it can automatically learn features from the data, thus eliminating the feature extraction process.

In this paper, through the study of the ViT-Siamese cascade network, the image deduplication in the power transmission inspection scene is realized. First, the technology classifies the inspection images through ViT to obtain image sub-data sets un-der each background; then uses the Siamese Network technology to perform similarity indexing analysis on the sub-data to obtain the similarity analysis results; The effectiveness and feasibility of this deduplication technique in power transmission scenarios.

2   ViT-Siamese Cascade Network Principle

2.1   Basic Structure of ViT-Siamese Cascade Network

For the deduplication of massive transmission lines, the basic structure of the cascade network proposed in this paper is shown in Fig. 1. The basic structure mainly includes two parts of the processing process. (1) The classification process of video transmission based on ViT, this process classifies the cluttered data obtained by each inspection according to the requirements, for example, according to the tower, foundation and channel as shown in the Fig. 1. (2) The similarity calculation based on Siamese Network is performed in each classified sub-data set, and compared with the threshold to obtain duplicate data, and finally the duplicate data is deleted to achieve the purpose of image deduplication.

2.2   Classification of Input Image Data Based on ViT

Transformer architectures have become common network components in natural language processing tasks, but still have limited applications in computer vision. Pure Transformers utilized immediately to sequences of image patches can efficiently accomplish image classification tasks. When pre-trained on a large amount of data and migrated to multiple small and medium image recognition benchmarks, Vision Transformer achieves higher image classification accuracy while requiring fewer training resources than traditional convolutional neural network approaches.

Inspired by the scaling concept of Transformers in natural language processing tasks, standard Transformers are directly applied to image classification tasks. The image is split into patches [21], and the linear embedding sequence of these patches is used as the input to the Transformer to train an image classification model in a super-vised manner.

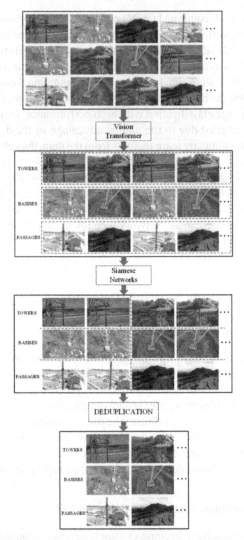

Fig. 1. Schematic diagram of the basic structure of ViT-Siamese cascade network.

Image Block Embedding. In order to meet the data input format of the standard Transformer architecture, the three-dimensional image data is reconstructed into a two-dimensional block sequence, where the image data dimension can be regarded as $\in R^{(H*W*C)}$. The reconstructed block sequence is $x_p \in R^{N*(P^2*C)}$, , where, (H, W) represents the resolution of image data, C represents the number of channels of the image data, P^2 represents the resolution of the image block data. The number of image blocks is expressed as $N = \frac{H*W}{P^2}$, that is, the effective input sequence length in the Transformer architecture.

The image block embedding process is similar to the word embedding process in NLP. As shown in Fig. 2, the image is flattened into multiple image blocks to achieve the purpose of being similar to a word in NLP.

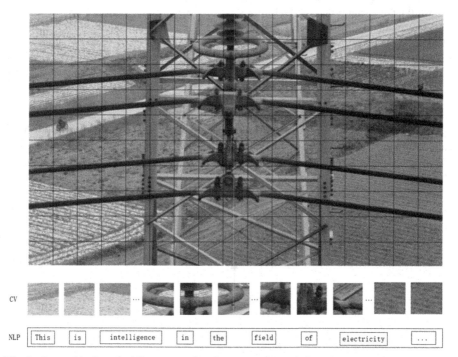

Fig. 2. Image block embedding processing for power transmission pictures, CV is the corresponding image block processing, NLP is word embeddings.

The essence of image block embedding is to perform a linear transformation on each image block data to obtain $E \in R^{(P^2 * C) * D}$, and then, after dimensionality reduction, we get $x_p E \in R^{N * D}$ from $P^2 * C$ to D dimension. This process realizes the standard data input format conversion of image data in the Transformer architecture.

Learnable Embedding. Add a learnable embedding block $z_0^0 = x_{class}$ to the image block embed sequence, and the states or features output by Transformer encoder are represented by z_L^0 as images. During the pre-training and parameter fine-tuning stages, a classification head is attached to z_L^0 for image classification.

Position Embedding. Position embedding $E_{pose} \in R^{(N+1) * D}$ is also an important content of image block embedding, which is used to retain the position information between input image blocks. If the location information of image blocks is not provided to the model, the model needs to learn the puzzle through the semantics of image blocks, which is easy to increase the learning cost of image classification model.

The Encoder. After integrating category vector, image block embedding and position coding into one input embedding vector, Transformer Encoder can be fed. Transformer Encoder Blocks are continuously stacked forward, and finally features corresponding to learnable category embedding vectors are extracted for image classification. The over-all forward calculation process is as follows:

The embedded input vector z_0 is composed of image embedding block $x_p^i E, i \in 1, 2, ..., N$, category vector x_{class} and position code E_{pose}.

$$z_0 = \left[x_{class}; x_p^1 E; x_p^2 E; ......; x_p^N E \right] + E_{pose} \tag{1}$$

Among them, $E \in R^{(P^2*C)*D}$, $E_{pose} \in R^{(N+1)*D}$.

MSA (Multi-head Self-Attention) blocks shown in Fig. 3 composed of multi-head attention mechanism, Layer normalization and Layer Norm & Add can be repeated L. Among them, the l-th output z_l' is calculated as follows, and the MSA diagram is shown below.

$$z_l' = MSA(LN(z_{l-1})) + z_{l-1}, l \in 1, ..., L \tag{2}$$

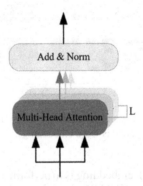

Fig. 3. MSA block diagram

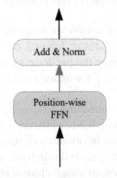

Fig. 4. MLP block diagram

MLP Block (Multilayer Perceptron Block) shown in Fig. 4, consisting of feedforward network (FFN), Layer normalization and jump connection (Layer Norm & Add), can be repeated L, in which the output l is z_l, and the calculation method is as follows:

$$z_l = MLP\left(LN\left(z_l'\right)\right) + z_l', l \in 1, ..., L \tag{3}$$

The output image represents y by Layer Norm and classification header (MLP or FC), and the calculation process is as follows:

$$y = LN\left(z_L^0\right) \tag{4}$$

Transmission image data based on ViT batch processing is classified into tower, infrastructure and image.

2.3 Similarity Analysis Based on Siamese Network

Siamese network, also known as Siamese neural network, is derived from hand-writing contrast and later developed in face recognition. In this paper, Siamese net-work is introduced into the field of power transmission inspection to check duplicate images and reduce the number of duplicate data. The main idea is to first map the two images through feature extraction technology to obtain low-dimensional data vector, and then calculate the similarity of the data vector and output the similarity or 0 and 1.

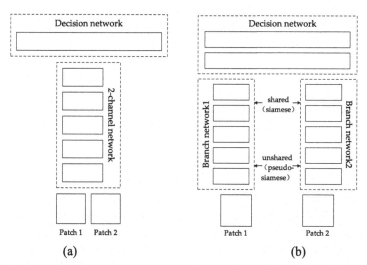

Fig. 5. Two basic structures of Siamese network. (a) 2-channel network structure; (b) Pseudo-Siamese network structure.

Siamese network is a double-branch structure composed of two sub-networks with shared weights. Paired image data sets are input to the branch network. After a series of steps such as convolution, activation and pooling, the branch network outputs the results and sends them to the top-level decision network for similarity calculation. The branches of the Siamese network can be considered as descriptor computation modules, and the top network can be viewed as similarity functions. At present, this network has been developed into two basic structures: pseudo-Siamese network and 2-channel network, as shown in Fig. 5 respectively.

Based on the network shown in Fig. 5(a), this paper integrates ResNet50 for feature extraction. The Siamese network structure of integrating ResNet50 is shown in Fig. 6.

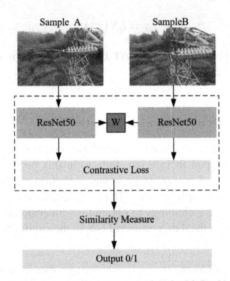

Fig. 6. Siamese network structure fused with ResNet50.

In the process of model training, images processed in advance are respectively sent to ResNet50 network for feature extraction to obtain the data set after dimensionality reduction, and then sent to Contrastive Loss network for Loss function calculation to train the model in a strongly supervised way. The following contains loss term and L2 norm regularization term are used as learning objective function:

$$\min_{w} \frac{\lambda}{2} \|w\|_2 + \sum_{i=1}^{N} \max\left(0, 1 - y_i o_i^{net}\right) \tag{5}$$

In the above formula, the first part is the regularization term, using L_2 regularization term, and the second part is the error loss part, where w is the weight of neural network, o_i^{net} is the output neuron of the i-th training image, and y_i is the corresponding label (with -1 and 1 respectively indicating input image mismatch and input image matching).

Model Training Process:

Step 1: Data preparation. The training data set is divided into positive sample data pairs and negative sample data pairs, as shown in the Fig. 7.

Step 2: Feature extraction. For each scenario, feature extraction was carried out through ResNet50 network to obtain low-dimensional data sets, as shown in the Fig. 8.
Step 3: Training network.

The training neural network trains positive and negative samples respectively (Fig. 9).

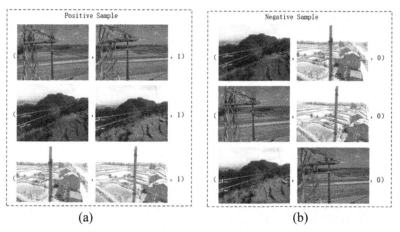

(a)   (b)

Fig. 7. Positive and negative sample datasets. (a) is similar image dataset, we label similar image pairs with "1"; (b) is dissimilar image dataset, we label the dissimilar image pairs with "0".

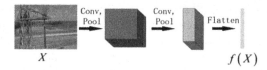

Fig. 8. Schematic diagram of the feature extraction process, after the image is convolved and pooled, it is straightened into a one-dimensional vector.

3   Basis of Model Training

3.1   Software and Hardware

The test conditions of this paper are: Centos 6, 64-bit operating system, TensorFlow framework. Computer configuration: Desktop COMPUTER, NVIDIA TESLA P100, 16 GB video memory; E5-2680 V4 CPU processor, maximum main frequency 3.30 GHz, disk capacity 500 GB, Python programming language.

3.2   Experimental Data

In this paper, the original data set is used to take images for the inspection of the transmission line UAV, and a total of 5742 images of transmission business scenes are captured

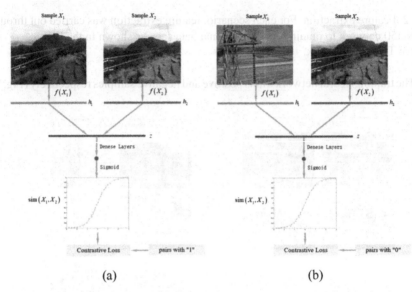

(a) (b)

Fig. 9. Training process. (a) is Positive sample training process; (b) is Negative sample training process. The loss function adopts Contrastive Loss, which can effectively deal with the relationship of paired data in the Siamese neural network.

(Fig. 10). 5% of all images (that is, 300 images) are randomly selected as the final test data, and the remaining 5442 images are used as the training data set as well as the input of ViT-Siamese neural network. The original image contains three types of targets, including channel, infrastructure and tower. They are not evenly dis-tributed in the image, and the image of the same scene is shot from multiple angles. The three types of transmission image data used in this paper are shown as follows.

Accuracy (P), Recall (R) and Average Precision (AP) are used as evaluation indexes to evaluate the proposed method. Among them, the calculation method of AP value refers to the calculation method of Everingham et al. [9]. The calculation formula of accuracy and recall rate is as follows:

$$P = \frac{TP}{TP + FP} \tag{6}$$

$$R = \frac{TP}{TP + FN} \tag{7}$$

where TP (True Position) is a positive sample that is predicted to be a positive sample, FP (False Position) is a Negative sample that is predicted to be a positive sample, and FN (False Negative) is a positive sample that is predicted to be a Negative sample.

In this paper, ResNet50 is pre-trained in the data set of power transmission scenarios to improve the image classification and recognition effect of ResNet50 in power transmission scenarios. The data set of the transmission scene contains 5742 samples, and the sample number of each type of target is shown in the following table. During the

Fig. 10. Power Transmission Image Dataset. (a) Passage Images; (b) Tower Images; (c) Basis Images.

training, the learning rate is set to 0.001, the momentum is 0.9, and the weight attenuation is 10-4, with a total of 60K training times. The pre-trained ResNet50 is used in the image classification training of the transmission scene in this paper (Table 1).

Table 1. Number of pretrained transmission samples.

Type	Passage	Tower	Basis
Number	2177	1943	1622

This paper first tests the difference of image replay in the original sample and the expanded sample, so the original data set and the expanded data set are used to train the

ViT-Siamese cascading network model and the Siamese neural network model respectively. The training data set of Experiment 1 consists of 2100 original images. For the data of this experiment, 70% is selected as the training set and the remaining 30% as the verification set. During training, the learning rate is initialized to 0.01 and momentum is to 0.9, and the learning rate is changed every 2000 iterations and gradually decreased to 0.0001. At the same time, this paper also compares with the traditional CV domain deduplication method, and the experimental results are shown in the Table 2 (Fig. 11, 12 and 13).

Table 2. Accuracy comparison table.

Type	Passage	Tower	Basis
ViT-Siamese	84.3%	87.1%	78.5%
Siamese Net	80.6%	82.7%	74.4%
Histogram	75%	76.5%	68%
Average Hash	77%	79.5%	75.2%
Cosine	83%	86.7%	77%

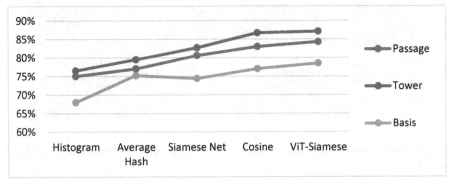

Fig. 11. Compared with the other four types of algorithms, the accuracy of the ViT-Siamese method is better than other algorithms for different power transmission scenarios. For the tower scene target, the target is more prominent, so the accuracy rate can reach 87.1%.

It can be seen from Table 2, Table 3 and Table 4 that the accuracy, precision and recall rate of ViT-Siamese cascade network are higher than those of common Siamese neural network, and have a great improvement. Compared with other traditional CV field methods, the accuracy, precision and recall rate are higher than histogram method and mean hashing method, and slightly higher than cosine similarity.

In experiment 2, transmission data sets with different data volumes were set respectively. Data subsets N1 = 500, N2 = 2000 and N3 = 4000 were set in transmission image data sets. The time of transmission image checking was compared based on ViT-Siamese cascade network, Siamese neural network and histogram, mean hash and cosine similarity (Fig. 14).

Table 3. Precision comparison table.

Type	Passage	Tower	Basis
ViT-Siamese	83.1%	84.6%	80.2%
Siamese Net	80.7%	81.1%	74.2%
Histogram	77.2%	83.3%	74.8%
Average Hash	79.3%	84%	78.5%
Cosine	82.8%	84.2%	79.6%

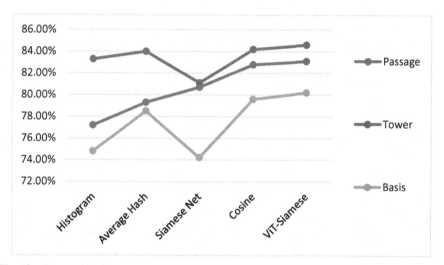

Fig. 12. Compared with the other four types of algorithms, the accuracy of the ViT-Siamese method is better than other algorithms for different power transmission scenarios. For the tower scene target, the target is more prominent, so the accuracy rate can reach 87.1%.

Table 4. Recall comparison table.

Type	Passage	Tower	Basis
ViT-Siamese	83.4%	78.9%	83.3%
Siamese Net	82.7%	77.3%	81.8%
Histogram	71.2%	70.5%	79.3%
Average Hash	75.2%	72.1%	75.6%
Cosine	80.1%	79.3%	80.3%

As can be seen from Table 5 above, although the repetition speed of ViT-Siamese cascade network is higher than the histogram and cosine similarity of the traditional method, it is lower than that of Siamese neural network and mean hash. Based on the

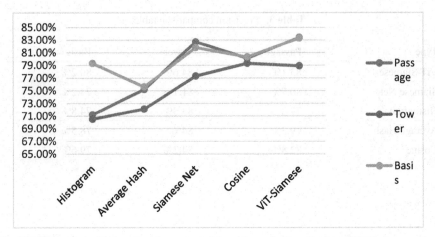

Fig. 13. Compared with the other four types of algorithms, the Recall of the ViT-Siamese method is better than other algorithms for different power transmission scenarios.

Table 5. About the comparison of the duplication check time of the three data sets.

Time (s)	N1	N2	N3
ViT-Siamese	482.3	1947.5	5429.9
Siamese Net	510.9	2249.3	6891.1
Histogram	470.2	1871.6	5120.1
Average Hash	530.8	2173.4	5532.3
Cosine	480.1	1944.3	5421.8

analysis of Table 2, Table 3 and Table 4, it can be seen that ViT-Siamese cascade network can sacrifice a smaller replay speed for a larger recognition rate improvement, which is close to the cosine similarity index.

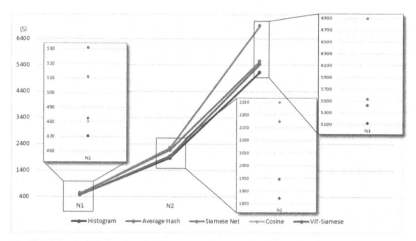

Fig. 14. Compared with the other four algorithms, although ViT-Siamese is slower than Histogram algorithm and Cosine algorithm on different data sets, it is much faster than Average Hash algorithm and traditional Siamese algorithm.

4   Conclusion

In this paper, a transmission image deduplicating technology based on ViT-Siamese cascading network is proposed to solve the problems of repeated inspection data images, limited storage space of side acquisition equipment and limited model recognition data in power business. Firstly, the collected transmission image data are classified based on Transformer network architecture to provide data preprocessing and data availability for subsequent transmission image de-duplication and solve the problem of uneven classification distribution in transmission image. Secondly, the image de-duplication processing method of ViT-Siamese cascade network is used to improve the transmission image de-duplication efficiency. The transmission image de-weighting technology based on ViT-Siamese cascading network proposed in this paper can effectively achieve the classification and de-weighting of transmission image data, and provide a good data basis for intelligent diagnosis of power transmission.

Acknowledgment. This work was funded by the "Research on the key technologies of zero sample knowledge transfer learning and defect recognition for fine-grained goals" program of the Big Data Center, State Grid Corporation of China.

References

1. Zhaoyun, Z., Guanfeng, H., Shihong, H., Zhi, Z.: Target detection in power checking the application and development trend of. J. Hubei Univ. Nat. (Natural Science edn.) **33**(3) 6, 305-314 (2021). https://doi.org/10.13501/j.carolcarrollnki.42-1908/n.2021.09.012
2. Mingmin, F.: Design and application of cloud storage subsystem for power equipment inspection data. Sci. Technol. Wind **30**, 157 (2019). https://doi.org/10.19392/j.cnki.1671-7341.201 930136

3. Zhijian, S.: Research on Massive Image De-Duplication Algorithm. Chongqing Jiaotong University (2016)
4. Fengqing, H., Zhijian, S., Rui, Y.: Fast deduplication for massive images. J. Comput. Appl. **36**(07), 1797–1800 (2016)
5. Tengfei, P.: The aurora image retrieval based on convolution neural network research. Nanjing University of Posts and Telecommunications (2021). 10.27251
6. Bromley, J., et al.: Signature verification using a "siamese" time delay neural network. Int. J. Patt. Recogn. Artif. Intell. **07**(04), 669–688 (1993)
7. Chopar, S., Hadsell, R., Lecun, Y.: With application to face verification. In: 2005 IEEE Computer Society Conference on Computer Vision and Pattern Recognition, pp. 113–119. IEEE, San Diego(2005)
8. Nair, V., Geoffrey, E.H.: Rectified linear units improve restricted boltzmann machines. In: Proceedings of the 27th International Conference on Machine Learning, Haifa, Israel, 21–24 Jun 2010
9. Zagoruyko, S., Komodakis, N.: Learning to compare image patches via convolutional neural networks. In: 2015 IEEE Conference on Computer Vision and Pattern Recognition (CVPR). IEEE (2015)
10. Everingham, M., Van Gool, L., Williams, C.K.I., Winn, J., Zisserman, A.: The pascal visual object classes (VOC) challenge. Int. J. Comput. Vis. **88**(2), 303–338 (2010)
11. Vaswani, A., Shazeer, N., Parmar, N.: Attention is all you need. Adv. Neural Inform. Process. Syst. Long Beach 6000–6010 (2017)
12. Parmar, N., et al.: Image Transformer. ArXiv: 1802.05751 [cs. CV]. 15 Feb 2018. https://arxiv.org/abs/1802.05751
13. Carion, N., Massa, F., Synnaeve, G., Usunier, N., Kirillov, A., Zagoruyko, S.: End-to-end object detection with transformers. In: Vedaldi, A., Bischof, H., Brox, T., Frahm, J.-M. (eds.) ECCV 2020. LNCS, vol. 12346, pp. 213–229. Springer, Cham (2020). https://doi.org/10.1007/978-3-030-58452-8_13
14. Zhu, X.Z., Su, W.J., Lu, L.W., Li, B., Wang, X., Dai J.: Deformable DETR: Deformable Transformers for End-to-End Object Detection. https://arxiv.org/ABS/2010.04159 (2020)
15. Zheng, M.H., Gao, P.; Wang, X.G., et al.: Adaptive Clustering Transformer with end-to-end Object Detection. ArXiv. https://arxiv.org/ABS/2011.09315 V1 (2022)
16. Liu, L., et al.: Deep learning for generic object detection: a survey. Int. J. Comput. Vision **128**(2), 261–318 (2019). https://doi.org/10.1007/s11263-019-01247-4
17. Gao, X.Y., Hoi, S.C.H., Zhang, Y.D., Zhou, J.S., Wan, J.: Sparse online learning of image similarity. ACM Trans. Intell. Syst. Technol. **8**(5), 641–6422 (2017)
18. Zhang, Y., Gao, X., Chen, Z., Zhong, H., Xie, H., Yan, C.: Mining spatial-temporal similarity for visual tracking. IEEE Trans. Image Process. **29**, 8107–8119 (2020)
19. Xia, Z.X., Hong, X.P., Gao, X.Y., Feng, X.Y., Zhao, G.Y.: Spatiotemporal recurrent convolutional networks for recognizing spontaneous micro-expressions. IEEE Trans. Multimed. **22**(3), 626–640 (2020)
20. Gao, X.Y., Xie, J.Y., Chen, Z.Y., Liu, A.A., Sun, Z., Lyu, L.: Dilated convolution-based feature refinement network for crowd localization. ACM Trans. Multimedia Comput., Commun. Appl. (2022)
21. Dosovitskiy, A., et al.: An Image is Worth 16x16 Words: Transformers for Image Recognition at Scale. arXiv:2010.11929 (2020)

Adversarial Example Defense via Perturbation Grading Strategy

Shaowei Zhu[1], Wanli Lyu[1], Bin Li[2], Zhaoxia Yin[3]([⊠]), and Bin Luo[1]

[1] Anhui Provincial Key Laboratory of Multimodal Cognitive Computation,
Anhui University, Hefei, China
[2] Guangdong Key Laboratory of Intelligent Information Processing and Shenzhen
Key Laboratory of Media Security, Shenzhen University, Shenzhen, China
libin@szu.edu.cn
[3] School of Communication and Electronic Engineering,
East China Normal University, Shanghai, China
zxyin@cee.ecnu.edu.cn

Abstract. Deep Neural Networks have been widely used in many fields. However, studies have shown that DNNs are easily attacked by adversarial examples, which have tiny perturbations and greatly mislead the correct judgment of DNNs. Furthermore, even if malicious attackers cannot obtain all the underlying model parameters, they can use adversarial examples to attack various DNN-based task systems. Researchers have proposed various defense methods to protect DNNs, such as reducing the aggressiveness of adversarial examples by preprocessing or improving the robustness of the model by adding modules. However, some defense methods are only effective for small-scale examples or small perturbations but have limited defense effects for adversarial examples with large perturbations. This paper assigns different defense strategies to adversarial perturbations of different strengths by grading the perturbations on the input examples. Experimental results show that the proposed method effectively improves defense performance. In addition, the proposed method does not modify any task model, which can be used as a preprocessing module, which significantly reduces the deployment cost in practical applications.

Keywords: Deep Neural Network · Adversarial examples · JPEG compression · Image denoising · Adversarial defense

1 Introduction

Deep neural networks (DNNs) have achieved widespread success in modern life, including image classification [14], medical image segmentation [11], and vehicle detection [27]. Research [28] has shown that attackers can add carefully crafted tiny perturbations to normal examples to mislead the model into making bad decisions. The new input generated by deliberately adding tiny perturbations to

G. Zhai et al. (Eds.): IFTC 2022, CCIS 1766, pp. 407–420, 2023.
https://doi.org/10.1007/978-981-99-0856-1_30

408   S. Zhu et al.

normal examples is called adversarial examples, which can lead to misjudgment of the model and cause great harm.

However, existing studies have shown that there are also adversarial examples in real physical scenarios, so there is a significant safety problem in the practical application of DNN, such as automatic driving [22] and face recognition [7]. The safety requirements are higher in such case task scenarios.

Researchers have proposed various defense methods to reduce the impact of such adversarial perturbations, including adversarial training [8,25], defense distillation [21], and preprocessing of input transformations [12,17,32]. Among them, adversarial training and defensive distillation require retraining or modification of the classifier. At the same time, input transformation-based methods focus on denoising/transforming the input before feeding it into the classifier, making it easier to deploy in practical applications. For these reasons, many input transformation-based methods have emerged in recent years. For example, ComDefend [12], Deep Image Prior (DIP) [29], and DIPDefend [3] directly reconstruct adversarial examples into normal images. Similarly, DefenseGAN [24] uses generative adversarial networks (GANs) to remove the effects of adversarial perturbations. However, these defense methods heavily depend on the dataset size and training time for training models and are computationally expensive, limiting their real-life applications. Therefore, some researchers [17,32] turn to study how to denoise through image processing techniques.

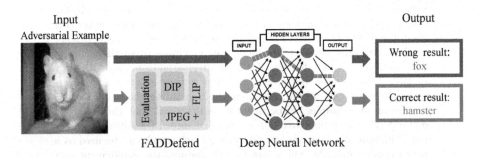

Fig. 1. An example of the proposed FADefend. It removes the perturbations in the adversarial examples before feeding them into the classifier.

Yin et al. [33] found that the image compression method based on image processing technology can remove the perturbation from the small-perturbed image, and combined with the mirror flip, the defense effect can be improved. However, as the adversarial perturbation increases, the defense effect becomes worse. Furthermore, DIP [29] can be obtained from a single low-dimensional robust feature extracted from the input image to reconstruct the image without additional training cost. The reconstructed images of this method can significantly reduce the aggressiveness of large-perturbed adversarial examples. Therefore, we propose a perturbation grading strategy-based defense method called FADDefend, which classifies adversarial perturbations and performs different operations on different levels of perturbations to improve the defense performance. The proposed method's adversarial example defense process is shown in Fig. 1.

The main contributions of our paper are:

- We propose an effective adversarial defense method that takes different defensive operations on adversarial examples with different perturbations.
- The proposed method uses a perturbation grading strategy to divide adversarial examples into large and small-perturbed examples.
- Experimental results show that the proposed method not only improves the performance of the adversarial defense but also reduces the computational cost.

2   Related Works

2.1   Adversarial Attack Methods

Adversarial examples are input images to which tiny perturbations are maliciously added to fool the neural network classifier. Common adversarial attack algorithms can be divided into attack methods based on white-box settings and attack methods based on black-box settings. Under the white-box attack, the attacker can fully understand the structure and parameters of the target model, while under the black-box attack, the attacker knows nothing about the relevant information of the target model.

White-Box Attacks. Szegedy et al. generate adversarial examples using L-BFGS [28], and Goodfellow et al. proposed a method to generate adversarial examples with only a one-step attack called the Fast Gradient Sign Method (FGSM) [9]. In order to improve the attack performance of FGSM, iteration-based multi-step attack methods are proposed, such as the Basic Iterative Method (BIM) [13], Momentum-based Iterative FGSM (MIFGSM) [5], and Projected Gradient Descent (PGD) [18]. DeepFool [19] attack method proposed to generate adversarial examples by finding the minimum perturbation on the hyperplane. The C&W attack [2] is another way to find adversarial examples through optimization. JSMA [20] is a sparse attack method that only modifies a small number of pixels. Athalye et al. proposed an attack method called Backward Pass Differentiable Approximation [1] by approximating the gradient of the defense to break this stochastic defense method.

Black-Box Attacks. Black-box attacks usually generate black-box adversarial examples on surrogate models and then exploit the transferability of adversarial examples to attack the target model. Various methods are proposed to improve the adversarial transferability of black-box attacks, such as query-based attacks [7,30] and transfer-based attacks [6].

2.2   Adversarial Defense Methods

Many adversarial defense methods have been proposed, including adversarial training and input transformation methods. The first method improves the robustness of the model by adding some adversarial examples to the normal training dataset, but this method slightly reduces the accuracy of normal examples. The second method modifies the input examples by preprocessing before entering the model to eliminate the adversarial perturbations in the examples. Classic digital image processing techniques, such as color depth reduction [31], image stitching [4], and JPEG compression [17], are used to improve model accuracy. However, these methods perform unsatisfactorily in defending against large-perturbed adversarial examples.

Later, model-based image reconstruction methods are proposed, including 1) denoising adversarial examples and 2) restoring them to clean images through CNN networks. Liao et al. proposed a high-level representation-guided denoiser [15] to remove adversarial perturbation. However, it requires a large dataset and more iterations to train a denoising model that transforms adversarial examples into clean images, limiting its practical scope.

Our work focuses on improving the unsatisfactory robustness of these defenses to large-perturbed adversarial examples. Since previous defense methods have shown better defense against small-perturbated adversarial examples, this problem can be solved by transforming large-perturbed images into small-perturbed images through the DIP [29] network.

3   Proposed Method

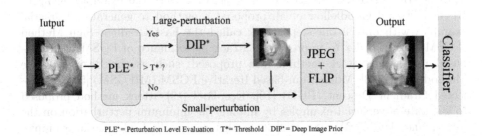

PLE* = Perturbation Level Evaluation   T* = Threshold   DIP* = Deep Image Prior

Fig. 2. FADDefend defense framework.

This paper proposes a new defense method FADDefend. FADDefend is divided into three modules. The first module is an evaluation module used to evaluate the noise level in the example. The second module is a JPEG compression and mirror flip module used to process the small-perturbed examples after perturbation grading. The third module is the DIP reconstruction module used to process large-perturbed examples after perturbation grading. Specifically, when an example is fed into FADDefend, the evaluation module evaluates its perturbation level. If the perturbation level is less than a pre-set threshold, it is defined as a small perturbation. It is denoised using a JPEG compression algorithm with a quality factor (QF) of 95, then mirror flipped and fed into the classifier. Otherwise, it is defined as a large perturbation and sent to the DIP image restoration module, which is sent to the JPEG compression and mirror flip module after processing. Figure 2 shows the framework of FADDefend.

The basic idea of the proposed method to resist adversarial perturbation is introduced in this section. Then the pros and cons of the JPEG compression and DIP defense methods are revealed. Finally, the proposed method combines the advantages of the two defense methods through the perturbation level evaluation module to achieve a better defense effect.

3.1   Image Perturbation Level Evaluation

Defenders assume a known perturbation level and conduct targeted defenses, but this assumption is unrealistic. When the model is deployed, it is attacked by an unknown perturbation strength, and its perturbation level cannot be judged based on the input image. Therefore, this problem can be solved by evaluating the perturbation level of the input image by blind image perturbation level evaluation.

Liu et al. proposed a blind image perturbation level assessment algorithm [16] to select low-level patches without high-frequency information from noisy images. The Principal Component Analysis technique estimates the perturbation level based on the selected patches. The eigenvalues of the image gradient covariance matrix are used as the standard to measure the texture intensity. A stable threshold is selected to distinguish the perturbation level through an iterative method.

In this section, the experimental examples are composed of 500 examples from the data set and the expected accuracy of the default is set to 50%: A choice that balances detection accuracy and defense time consumption. Therefore, the threshold is chosen by comparing the defense accuracies of adversarial examples with different perturbation levels, as shown in Fig. 3 (Threshold is 2.13). Those smaller than the threshold are defined as small-perturbed adversarial examples, and those greater than the threshold are defined as large-perturbed adversarial examples.

The perturbation strength can be divided into different intervals by selecting different thresholds, convenient for subsequent selection of different image processing modules.

3.2   Defense Methods Based on Image Processing Technology

Most existing defense methods cannot defend well against large-perturbed adversarial examples. For example, the standard JPEG compression algorithm can remove the high-frequency information in the image well to retain the low-frequency information. Just as research [15] shows that adversarial perturbations can be viewed as high-frequency information with a specific structure so that this image compression can achieve a specific denoising effect. However, as

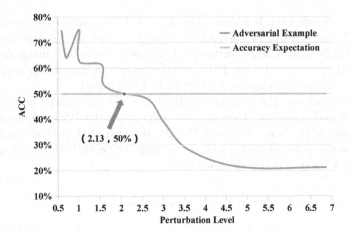

Fig. 3. Different thresholds can be chosen by the intersection of expected accuracy and adversarial example defense accuracy.

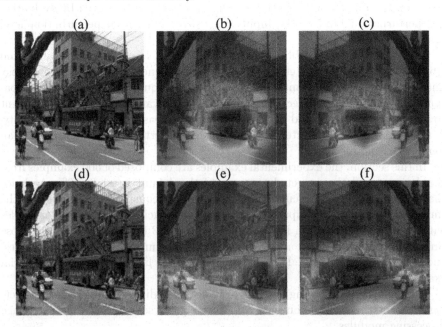

Fig. 4. (a) original example; (d) corresponding adversarial example. (b)(c)(e)(f) used class activation mapping of the images. (b) original example-bus; (c) flipped original example-bus; (e) adversarial example-bike; (f) flipped adversarial example-bus. The redder the class activation mapping of the image, the more the model pays attention to this area.

the perturbation strength increases, the adversarial perturbation may enter the low-frequency range. Even after removing some high-frequency information, the adversarial perturbation still exists.

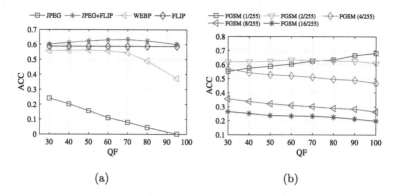

Fig. 5. Comparison of defense effects of preprocessing methods under different QFs. (a) Defense accuracy of various preprocessing methods under FGSM (2/255), (b) Defense accuracy using JPEG compression combined with mirror flip under different perturbations.

We strengthen JPEG's defense against small perturbations by breaking the adversarial structure by mirror flipping [33]. As shown in Fig. 4, the model's attention is observed by flipping the original and adversarial examples and using the class activation map. For the original example, the model's attention is focused on the object's main part before and after the flip. At the same time, for the adversarial example, the model is distracted, and the flipped adversarial example can correct the model's attention so that it can be classified correctly.

Figure 5(a) shows the defense accuracy of different defense methods under the QFs. As the QF increases, the compression rate decreases, reducing the defense effect of JPEG compression against adversarial examples. In contrast, JPEG compression combined with mirror flip has better defense accuracy and stability. Figure 5(b) shows that the defense of JPEG compression combined with mirror flip is unsatisfactory under the large-perturbation (FGSM, $\epsilon = 8/16$).

The compressed image loses semantic information by using a smaller QF (the smaller the QF, the worse the image quality), making it more difficult for the model to distinguish accurately. Although such methods defend well on small-perturbed adversarial examples and low computational cost, they cannot effectively deal with adversarial examples with large perturbations. Consider using image reconstruction methods to process large perturbations in adversarial perturbations into small perturbations, followed by JPEG and flip processing, which is introduced in the next section.

(a) 635/0   (b) 442/100   (c) 276/300   (d) 274/500   (e) 773/900   (f) 370/1500   (g) Target

Fig. 6. The above figures show the image reconstruction process of DIP and the image classification results (predicted category ID/iteration number) at different stages. The Top-5 predictions containing the correct label are marked in red (true labels: 274). PGD (8/255) is used to generate untargeted adversarial examples. (Color figure online)

3.3   Defense Methods Based on Deep Image Priors

Many model-based defense methods can achieve good defense results, such as image reconstructions [3], image denoising [15], image super-resolution [29], or GANs [24] recovering images for large-perturbed adversarial examples.

However, these methods require image reconstruction by learning a large amount of prior knowledge of external training data during the training stage. These defense methods consume a lot of computational and hardware costs. The CNN model itself has specific image prior capability. A clean image can also be reconstructed using prior internal knowledge of the image itself. Therefore, an untrained convolutional neural network is used in this module to generate denoised images through the DIP-based [29] generator network. Specifically, an adversarial example x_{adv} adds random noise z as the input example of the generator, which is solved by the following constraints by

$$\min_{\theta} \| f_\theta(z) - x_{adv} \|_2^2, \tag{1}$$

where f is a randomly initialized network, random but fixed noise z and adversarial examples x_{adv} as learning targets, each iteration input is a fixed noise z, and the parameter θ is updated by gradient descent. As the number of iterations increases, the output is closer to x_{adv}.

Consistent with the conclusions drawn [29], the DIP-based image reconstruction method restores the low-frequency information of the image in the early iterative stage and restores the high-frequency information (including adversarial perturbation) as the number of iterations increases. Figure 6 shows the image reconstruction process of DIP and the image classification results. In the early stage, the network recovered the image's low-frequency information (main contours). The high-frequency information of the image will also be recovered in later iterations. It can be seen that the visual quality of the image is very high at this time. Unfortunately, adversarial perturbations are also recovered, leading to overfitting. Therefore, reconstructed images with few adversarial perturbations are obtained by stopping in an early stage. Finally, the DIP module transforms the large-perturbed example into a small-perturbed example. The small perturbation adversarial examples can increase the classification model's defense accuracy through JPEG and flip processing.

4   Experiments

4.1   Experimental Settings

Our experiments are tested on the ImageNet dataset. 10,000 test images are selected randomly from the whole test set, and 8,850 clean example sets are screened for experiments. ResNet152 [10] is used to test robustness against various attack strengths of FGSM [9], PGD [18], BIM [13], and MIFGSM [19] ($\epsilon = 2/4/8/16$, using the L_∞ distance metric). ResNet152 [10] and VGG19 [26] are used to test cross-model defense robustness.

The DIP module adopts the U-Net [23] structure as the generative network and skip-connections to connect outputs of layers with the same spatial dimension. Specifically, LeakyReLU is used as the nonlinear activation function. Moreover, convolution operation and bilinear interpolation are used for downsampling and upsampling. An adversarial example is input as the target image. The generator network parameters are randomly initialized, random noise is used as input, and the target image is reconstructed by gradient descent training, stopping after 400 iterations.

4.2   Comparison with Image Compression Defenses

FADDefend combines image compression, mirror flip, and reconstruction modules with perturbation level evaluation modules. Since the image reconstruction module has a better processing effect on the large-perturbed adversarial examples, the image compression method is used as an auxiliary. It makes up for the disadvantage of the image compression defense method that the defense effect is unsatisfying when dealing with large-perturbed adversarial examples.

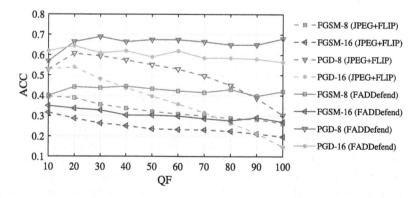

Fig. 7. The dotted part is the defense method of JPEG Compression combined with mirror flip. The solid part is the FADDefend defense method, showing the recognition accuracy curves under different QFs.

As shown in Fig. 7, compared with the defense method of JPEG image compression combined with mirror flip, FADDefend has better performance under different QFs and maintains stable defense performance with the increase of QF.

Table 1. Accuracy results (%) of defense methods on ResNet152 under attacks of different types and strengths (ImageNet, $\epsilon = 2/4/8/16$)

Method	Clean	FGSM	MIFGSM	PGD	BIM
Normal	100	0 / 0 / 0 / 0	0 / 0 / 0 / 0	0 / 0 / 0 / 0	0 / 0 / 0 / 0
JPEG [17]	86	47/45/24/13	74/64/40/14	59/64/50/37	56/68/56/63
War [32]	86	60/**59**/36/21	79/72/53/27	65/68/59/51	61/75/63/72
ComDefend [12]	94	32/19/ 5 / 5	56/30/ 9 / 1	44/32/ 7 / 2	37/48/21/23
DIPDefend [3]	79	55/45/26/14	80/67/43/25	60/69/60/38	61/71/59/77
FADDefend	94	**62**/55/**43**/**32**	**81**/**75**/**60**/**44**	**66**/**72**/**66**/**65**	**68**/**78**/**70**/**84**

Table 2. Accuracy results (%) of defense methods on attacks on the VGG19, the source model is ResNet152. (ImageNet, $\epsilon = 4/8/16$)

Method	Clean	FGSM	MIFGSM	PGD	BIM
Normal	89	48/40/22	66/40/23	62/42/28	70/51/60
War [32]	74	**57**/42/26	65/54/39	52/50/37	67/56/62
ComDefend [12]	86	52/38/22	70/50/31	66/47/41	**75**/60/62
DIPDefend [3]	86	50/44/31	69/54/46	66/**65**/44	73/61/72
FADDefend	86	50/**46**/31	**70**/**57**/46	66/61/44	73/**62**/72

4.3 Results on Attacks of Different Types and Strengths

To verify the effectiveness of the proposed FADDefend method, other state-of-the-art defense methods are compared, including JPEG compression [17], War (WebP compression and resize) [32], ComDefend [12], and DIPDefend [3]. The classification accuracy on ImageNet is shown in Table 1. In contrast, the image reconstructed methods have high defense accuracies, such as DIPDefend [3] and the proposed method. Under the FGSM attack($\epsilon = 8/16$), compared with the other four methods, the proposed method improves accuracy by at least 10%. Compared with the image compression method of ComDefend [12], the defense accuracy can even exceed 20%. The image compression methods are generally ineffective due to the large perturbation, which destroys the image structure and causes the loss of semantic information.

4.4   Results on Migration Attacks Under Different Models

Under cross-model attacks, assume that the attacker does not have access to the specific parameters of the target classifier or defense model. Attackers can only attack by exploiting the transferability of adversarial examples. The attacker acts as a surrogate model by training a model with a different structure than the target classifier. Then, adversarial examples generated by attacking the surrogate model may also lead to misclassification of the target classifier. Adversarial examples are generated under various attack algorithms ($\epsilon = 4/8/16$) using the ResNet152 model as surrogate and VGG19 as the target model. The test results are shown in Table 2. It can be seen that the recognition accuracy of the VGG19 model drops significantly on the adversarial examples generated by ResNet152. The larger the perturbation, the lower the recognition accuracy, which is the same result tested on the surrogate model and verified the attack transferability of adversarial examples. The recognition accuracy of the target model under different strengths and attack algorithms is significantly improved after adopting the proposed defense method. Compared with War [32], Comdefend [12], and DIPDefend [3] defense methods, the proposed method achieves the same or even better performance under various attacks.

The data in Table 2 shows that the defense performance of the proposed method is almost equal to that of DIPDefend under specific attack strengths, but this does not mean that the proposed method has no advantages. At the same time, we also conduct comparative experiments on the running speed, and memory consumption with the image reconstruction method [29] and the method [3] with the defense accuracy close to the proposed method. Randomly select 1000 images from the same dataset in Table 2 to form an example dataset for experimentation. Table 3 shows that the proposed method is less than the other two methods in running time and memory consumption because the other two methods reconstruct all the examples. Due to the number of iterations required to guarantee the generation of normal examples, the DIP method takes about 900 iterations, and DIPDefend takes about 500 iterations. We allow the generated examples to contain fewer perturbations, so only 400 iterations are needed for large-perturbed examples, and image compression algorithms are used for small-perturbed examples. Therefore, compared with other methods, the proposed method has certain advantages in defense accuracy and computational cost.

Table 3. Compared with the running time and memory consumption of other existing image reconstruction methods.

Method	Run-time (s)	Memory (MB)
DIP [29]	52.896	153.9
DIPDefend [3]	31.038	146.8
FADDefend	**13.616**	**121.1**

5   Conclusion and Future Work

This paper proposes an effective adversarial defense method. Different defenses are performed according to the perturbation grading strategy by evaluating the adversarial perturbation strength. The proposed method achieves better defensive performance against the ImageNet dataset under different perturbation strengths and attack algorithms, as well as in cross-model attacks. Because this classification strategy ensures defense accuracy, it also improves the running speed and reduces the computational cost.

Since the proposed method uses mirror flip, it is well defensive against real-world adversarial examples. However, in special scenarios such as numbers, mirror flip leads to semantic information changes, which need improvement.

Acknowledgments. This research work is partly supported by National Natural Science Foundation of China No. 62172001 and No. 61860206004 Guangdong Basic and Applied Basic Research Foundation (Grant 2019B151502001) and Shenzhen R&D Program (Grant JCYJ20200109105008228).

References

1. Athalye, A., Carlini, N., Wagner, D.: Obfuscated gradients give a false sense of security: circumventing defenses to adversarial examples. In: International Conference on Machine Learning, pp. 274–283 (2018)
2. Carlini, N., Wagner, D.: Towards evaluating the robustness of neural networks. In: IEEE Symposium on Security and Privacy, pp. 39–57 (2017)
3. Dai, T., Feng, Y., Chen, B., Lu, J., Xia, S.T.: Deep image prior based defense against adversarial examples. Pattern Recogn. **122**, 108249 (2022)
4. Ding, L., et al.: Delving into deep image prior for adversarial defense: a novel reconstruction-based defense framework. In: Proceedings of the 29th ACM International Conference on Multimedia, pp. 4564–4572 (2021)
5. Dong, Y., et al.: Boosting adversarial attacks with momentum. In: Proceedings of the IEEE/CVF Conference on Computer Vision and Pattern Recognition, pp. 9185–9193 (2018)
6. Dong, Y., Pang, T., Su, H., Zhu, J.: Evading defenses to transferable adversarial examples by translation-invariant attacks. In: Proceedings of the IEEE/CVF Conference on Computer Vision and Pattern Recognition, pp. 4312–4321 (2019)
7. Dong, Y., et al.: Efficient decision-based black-box adversarial attacks on face recognition. In: Proceedings of the IEEE/CVF Conference on Computer Vision and Pattern Recognition, pp. 7714–7722 (2019)
8. Ganin, Y.: Domain-adversarial training of neural networks. J. Mach. Learn. Res. **17**(1), 2030–2096 (2016)
9. Goodfellow, I.J., Shlens, J., Szegedy, C.: Explaining and harnessing adversarial examples. In: International Conference on Learning Representations (2014)
10. He, K., Zhang, X., Ren, S., Sun, J.: Identity mappings in deep residual networks. In: Leibe, B., Matas, J., Sebe, N., Welling, M. (eds.) ECCV 2016. LNCS, vol. 9908, pp. 630–645. Springer, Cham (2016). https://doi.org/10.1007/978-3-319-46493-0_38
11. Ji, W., et al.: Learning calibrated medical image segmentation via multi-rater agreement modeling. In: Proceedings of the IEEE/CVF Conference on Computer Vision and Pattern Recognition, pp. 12341–12351 (2021)

12. Jia, X., Wei, X., Cao, X., Foroosh, H.: Comdefend: an efficient image compression model to defend adversarial examples. In: Proceedings of the IEEE/CVF Conference on Computer Vision and Pattern Recognition, pp. 6084–6092 (2019)
13. Kurakin, A., Goodfellow, I.J., Bengio, S.: Adversarial examples in the physical world. In: Artificial Intelligence Safety and Security, pp. 99–112. Chapman and Hall/CRC (2018)
14. Lanchantin, J., Wang, T., Ordonez, V., Qi, Y.: General multi-label image classification with transformers. In: Proceedings of the IEEE/CVF Conference on Computer Vision and Pattern Recognition, pp. 16478–16488 (2021)
15. Liao, F., Liang, M., Dong, Y., Pang, T., Hu, X., Zhu, J.: Defense against adversarial attacks using high-level representation guided denoiser. In: Proceedings of the IEEE/CVF Conference on Computer Vision and Pattern Recognition, pp. 1778–1787 (2018)
16. Liu, X., Tanaka, M., Okutomi, M.: Single-image noise level estimation for blind denoising. IEEE Trans. Image Process. 22(12), 5226–5237 (2013)
17. Liu, Z., et al.: Feature distillation: DNN-oriented jpeg compression against adversarial examples. In: Proceedings of the IEEE/CVF Conference on Computer Vision and Pattern Recognition, pp. 860–868 (2019)
18. Madry, A., Makelov, A., Schmidt, L., Tsipras, D., Vladu, A.: Towards deep learning models resistant to adversarial attacks. In: International Conference on Learning Representations (2018)
19. Moosavi-Dezfooli, S.M., Fawzi, A., Frossard, P.: Deepfool: a simple and accurate method to fool deep neural networks. In: Proceedings of the IEEE/CVF Conference on Computer Vision and Pattern Recognition, pp. 2574–2582 (2016)
20. Papernot, N., McDaniel, P., Jha, S., Fredrikson, M., Celik, Z.B., Swami, A.: The limitations of deep learning in adversarial settings. In: IEEE European Symposium on Security and Privacy, pp. 372–387 (2016)
21. Papernot, N., McDaniel, P., Wu, X., Jha, S., Swami, A.: Distillation as a defense to adversarial perturbations against deep neural networks. In: IEEE Symposium on Security and Privacy, pp. 582–597 (2016)
22. Quinonez, R., Safaoui, S., Summers, T., Thuraisingham, B., Cardenas, A.A.: Shared reality: detecting stealthy attacks against autonomous vehicles. In: Proceedings of the 2th Workshop on CPS&IoT Security and Privacy, pp. 15–26 (2021)
23. Ronneberger, O., Fischer, P., Brox, T.: U-net: convolutional networks for biomedical image segmentation. In: International Conference on Medical Image Computing and Computer-Assisted Intervention, pp. 234–241 (2015)
24. Samangouei, P., Kabkab, M., Chellappa, R.: Defense-GAN: protecting classifiers against adversarial attacks using generative models. In: International Conference on Learning Representations (2018)
25. Shafahi, A., et al.: Adversarial training for free! In: Advances in Neural Information Processing Systems, vol. 32 (2019)
26. Simonyan, K., Zisserman, A.: Very deep convolutional networks for large-scale image recognition. In: International Conference on Learning Representations (2015)
27. Srivastava, S., Narayan, S., Mittal, S.: A survey of deep learning techniques for vehicle detection from UAV images. J. Syst. Architect. 117, 102–152 (2021)
28. Szegedy, C., et al.: Intriguing properties of neural networks. In: International Conference on Learning Representations (2014)
29. Ulyanov, D., Vedaldi, A., Lempitsky, V.: Deep image prior. In: Proceedings of the IEEE/CVF Conference on Computer Vision and Pattern Recognition, pp. 9446–9454 (2018)

30. Wang, J., Yin, Z., Jiang, J., Du, Y.: Attention-guided black-box adversarial attacks with large-scale multiobjective evolutionary optimization. Int. J. Intell. Syst. **37**(10), 7526–7547 (2022)
31. Wang, L.Y.: Adversarial perturbation suppression using adaptive gaussian smoothing and color reduction. In: International Symposium on Multimedia, pp. 158–165 (2021)
32. Yin, Z., Wang, H., Wang, J.: War: An efficient pre-processing method for defending adversarial attacks. In: International Conference on Machine Learning for Cyber Security, pp. 514–524 (2020)
33. Yin, Z., Wang, H., Wang, J., Tang, J., Wang, W.: Defense against adversarial attacks by low-level image transformations. Int. J. Intell. Syst. **35**(10), 1453–1466 (2020)

Audio and Speech Processing

Perceptual Quality Assessment
of TTS-Synthesized Speech

Zidong Chen[1(✉)] and Xiongkuo Min[2(✉)]

[1] Department of Computer Science and Engineering, Shanghai Jiao Tong University,
Shanghai 200240, China
czd96715@sjtu.edu.cn
[2] Institute of Image Communication and Network Engineering, Shanghai Jiao Tong University,
Shanghai 200240, China

Abstract. The evaluation of a Text-to-Speech (TTS) system is typically labor-intensive and highly biased because there is no golden standard of the generated speech or objective evaluation metrics. To improve the performance of TTS systems, it is highly desirable to explore the perceptual quality assessment of TTS-synthesized speech and propose a relatively valid evaluation method. In this paper, we introduce a deep-learning-based approach to predict human labeled perceptual quality scores of the generated speech. Our approach is based on ResNet and self-attention, where the former addresses the issue of deep feature extraction and integration and the latter takes advantage of the natural relationship between the input sequences. The experiment results indicate that the proposed method performs better on test tasks in terms of various accuracy evaluation criteria than the state-of-the-art methods. Additionally, the experiment demonstrates a strong correlation between the predicted scores and the true (human) MOS scores.

Keywords: Text-To-Speech (TTS) · Speech quality assessment · Mean opinion score

1 Introduction

Speech quality assessment is critical for improving the final performance of the Text-to-Speech (TTS) system. However, the current evaluation metrics of human-based work are labor-intensive and biased. This is because personal perceptions affect the objectivity and accuracy of the evaluation results. On the other hand, a set of evaluation metrics for similar tasks (e.g., automatic speech recognition, speaker recognition, etc.) are fairly objective but hard to apply to TTS directly. Therefore, it is necessary to explore a perceptual quality assessment method for TTS. There are a group of evaluation metrics of widely adopted that based on the evaluation of the synthesized speech. However, personal perceptions affect the objectivity and accuracy of the evaluation results. Most TTS systems that are based on deep learning use maximal likelihood (or minimum error) of acoustic parameters and phoneme duration to train and optimize. However, these criteria are unavailable when using TTS to synthesize text beyond the dataset and immeasurable to the subjective perception of the synthesized speech. Assessing the quality of

G. Zhai et al. (Eds.): IFTC 2022, CCIS 1766, pp. 423–435, 2023.
https://doi.org/10.1007/978-981-99-0856-1_31

the generated speech has been a problem for a long time, not just in TTS but also in speech enhancement and voice conversion (VC). Objective measurements such as the mel-cepstral distortion (MCD) [1] are often used in the VC field to measure the quality of converted speech, but these metrics mainly measure distortion of acoustic parameters and do not provide a good measure of the listener's subjective perception. By classifying listeners' subjective perceptions and specifying graded evaluation criteria, the mean opinion score (MOS) and other subjective evaluation methods can quantify listeners' subjective evaluations of speech into ratings, which can well measure both the naturalness of speech and listeners' subjective perceptions of speech. However, MOS scores need to be collected through a subjective speech quality assessment test, which will require significant time and labor cost when there are many audio samples, as the test needs multiple listeners to be able to cover all the speech with their measurements and scores.

There is a line of works proposed to overcome the above difficulties. Perceptual evaluation of speech quality (PESQ) [2] published by ITU-T (ITU Telecommunication Standardization Sector) is often used in industrial applications to evaluate speech quality. However, this method requires high quality reference speech, a limitation that makes it not directly applicable to the evaluation of synthesized speech, since the synthesized speech may not have a corresponding original speech, and the method evaluates results that do not focus on the naturalness of the synthesized speech. Like PESQ, traditional metric methods) [3–5] use standard signal processing blocks, such as short-time Fourier transforms, or perceptual excitation blocks, together with further processing blocks to build rule-based systems, but these methods can't measure the listener's subjective perception of speech appropriately. Classification and regression trees (CART) were used to predict speech quality scores [6] and used a large count of manual features. Better prediction results were achieved, but features and prediction models are not jointly optimized. Since features can be extracted out of speech and human audiometric evaluation results can be generated by subjective quality evaluation tests, an alternative is to use machine learning models to learn the quality of speech from the dataset and use that to predict evaluation scores [7–19]. Quality-Net [16] predicts the speech quality of enhanced speech by adding frame-by-frame error detection based on a bidirectional long and short-term memory (BLSTM) network, and the prediction scores are highly correlated with PESQ scores, providing an effective non-intrusive evaluation of speech enhancement. However, for purely predicting synthetic speech quality, the PESQ score used as a metric for speech enhancement does not serve as a measure of naturalness of synthesized speech. MOS-net [17] employs a CNN-LSTM-based model trained on the Voice Conversion Challenge (VCC) 2018 [20], allowing the model to predict the quality of converted speech. The model did a good job of predicting the quality of the system, but the main goal of this work is to evaluate VC systems, which is different from our goal of evaluating the perceptual quality of TTS synthesized speech.

In this paper, we propose a deep learning-based method for predicting the perceptual quality of the speech synthesized by TTS systems. Our method consists of two parts, dataset building and prediction model. Since our goal is to purely predict the perceptual quality of the synthesized speech, rather than to measure the effect of voice conversion or speech enhancement, the audio samples in our dataset are all TTS synthesized speech, and the data labels are human MOS scores. To get the audio samples in the dataset, we used several TTS systems trained with different speakers to generate speech. The text used for synthesis is usually used to train the TTS model, which includes both short and long sentences. To ensure data diversity, some of these TTS systems synthesize better and some worse. The data labels are the results of how different listeners judged the quality of the speech in the dataset. These results are shown as MOS scores. We conducted a statistical analysis of the dataset to make sure that the quality of speech in the dataset could be predicted. The analysis results show that for the speeches in the dataset, although there are high and low results for each speech rated by the listeners, there is an intrinsic correlation between the distinction of the quality of different speech by different listeners, and the system-level rating results of different raters have higher stability than that of utterance-level. We also predicted the objective evaluation method on the dataset, and the results showed that the objective evaluation method is not applicable in our task, because in the case that the reference speaker is not used as the speaker of the training set of our TTS system, the reference speaker does not act as standard to evaluate quality of the synthesized speech, and the objective evaluation method does not reflect the naturalness of the synthesized speech well in our dataset. We also propose a synthesized speech MOS score prediction model based on ResNet [21] and self-attention [22]. After training the model with our dataset, it can accurately predict the quality of both utterance-level and system-level TTS synthesized speech, with better performance at the system level. The strong correlation between the prediction results and the manual scoring results, and the higher correlation at the system level, indicate that our model can better predict the trend of the listeners' evaluation results for different TTS models. We also tried some other deep learning-based models and the results showed that although objective evaluation methods did not work in our task, prediction by neural network models could provide better results and our model performed best in them. By trying different model inputs, we found that using F-bank feature as model input gives the best results compared to using temporal information and raw magnitude spectrogram.

2 Dataset

2.1 Dataset Establishment

We create a dataset containing both synthesized speech and human MOS scores with the aim of predicting MOS scores for synthesized speech by TTS systems. Based on the aim of evaluating synthesized voices, the original voices of texts are not included in the audio dataset. The utterances are taken from the VCTK training set [23], and we choose 100 sentences from it, 50 of which are longer and 50 of which are shorter. We use 10 different TTS systems to generate 1000 training audio samples, where 8 systems are deep-learning based while the other 2 systems are not. More specifically, the 8 systems used in our dataset are tacotron2 [24], fastspeech 2 [25], glow-tts [26], speedy-speech [27], tactron with double decoder consistency, vits [28], fastpitch [29], and yourtts [30]. We synthesized 100 texts using each TTS system that were each trained with a different speaker, yielding a total of 1000 synthesized speeches.

The 1000 synthesized speech sentences in the dataset are evaluated by 10 listeners for MOS scores. We use the Webmushra scoring system [31] to make sure the results of perceptual quality assessment are accurate. All audios were re-sampled to 16 kHz, 16bit. The order of the speakers corresponding to each of the 10 audios is also randomized as the 100 sentences of text are randomly interrupted and 10 speech voices synthesized from the same text are presented as signals. We won't compare the synthesized speech to the original speech anymore because our goal is to judge the perceptual quality of the synthesized speech, not how similar it is to the original speech. Scores will be converted to MOS scores on a scale of 0 to 100, with a minimum of 1 (Very bad - I don't understand what you're saying), one to five stars, with five being the best (Excellent - The announcer's voice. I feel at ease hearing it). In the end, the dataset has 100 texts and 1,000 audio samples. Ten people evaluate each audio sample, for a total of 10,000 manual evaluation scores. Each evaluation's MOS score is an integer between 1 and 5, with a minimum score of 1 and a maximum score of 5. The average of the 10 evaluations gives the real MOS rating for each voice.

2.2 Dataset Analysis

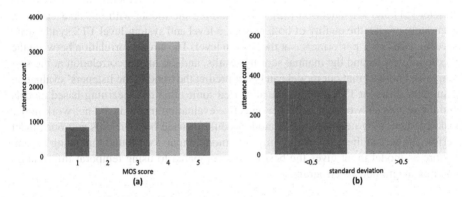

Fig. 1. The distribution of MOS scores and s.t.d (standard deviation) in our dataset. (a) report the distribution of MOS scores of all utterances in the dataset. Most MOS scores are concentrated at 3. (b) shows the standard deviation of the MOS score of each audio. About 2/3 s.t.d are over 0.5, that indicates the different rating on the same audio example of people.

The distribution and standard deviation of human MOS ratings of all synthesized speech in our dataset are reported in Fig. 1. The figure shows that the MOS scores for our dataset are mainly concentrated at 3. About two-thirds of the texts have a standard deviation of more than 0.5, which shows how different people are in how they rate same audio sample. Since each listener has different tastes and tolerance levels for accents, mispronunciations, etc., this is a natural and expected occurrence. After that, we need to ensure that the a human MOS scored for the speech the TTS system made is predictable. Thus, we use a bootstrapping method inspired by [16, 17] to take random samples from the experimental data with replacement, measure the change in the resampled MOS scores, and then confirm that the data in our dataset is naturally predictable and that listeners are naturally linked. The method of calculation is as follows.

1. Get the real MOS score sequence of all voices as MOS_{all},
2. Set the counter $k = 1$,
3. When k is not greater than K, for all MOS scores, split by N listeners, randomly extract n listeners' scores, extract duplicates and put them back, and merge the extracted scores into a new MOS score sampling set,
4. Then calculate the true MOS score sequence on the sample set as MOS_k by calculating the average value and taking the maximum or minimum value,
5. Calculate the linear correlation coefficient (LCC_k), mean squared error (MSE_k), etc. of MOS_k and MOS_{all} on utterance level and system level,
6. k is incremented by 1, jump back to step 3,
7. Perform statistics for all LCC_k, MSE_k, etc.

Table 1. The statistical result of bootstrapping method on our dataset.

	Utterance-level			System-level		
	LCC	SRCC	MSE	LCC	SRCC	MSE
Mean	0.977	0.967	0.129	0.989	0.966	0.119
Max	0.957	0.906	0.391	0.976	0.961	0.321
Min	0.952	0.914	0.354	0.976	0.921	0.246

In our dataset, N is 10. We let n be 5 and K be 1000, i.e., the ratings of five listeners are randomly selected for each sample and 1000 samples are made. Table 1 shows the results of bootstrap experiment. The linear correlation coefficients (LCC) and Spearman's rank correlation coefficient (SRCC) between the scores of all subsets resampled and the true MOS scores are high (greater than 0.9) and the mean squared error (MSE) is low (less than 0.4), regardless of whether the mean, maximum or minimum values are taken for the subset of MOS scores. The MSE obtained when taking the maximum or minimum value of the MOS scores in the subset is higher than that obtained when taking the average value, and the LCC, SRCC are lower. This indicates that for an audio sample, the scores given by all reviewers may not all converge to the mean, but may have discrete high or low scores. At the same time, the performance of results of system-level MOS scores is higher than that of utterance-level ones, which shows that for different texts, the performance of the speech synthesized by a TTS system may be good or bad, while from the perspective of the whole TTS system, the level of TTS synthesis is more stable for each system. The results indicate a good agreement across listeners in our dataset. Therefore, the human MOS ratings are predictable in our dataset.

2.3 Objective Evaluation Results

To test the performance of objective evaluation methods in our dataset, we used the PESQ and STOI [32] to score the speech in the dataset and compared the results with the human MOS ratings, and all scores are mapped between zero and five. For each

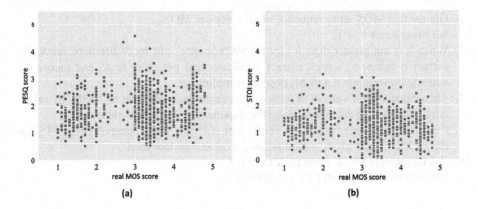

Fig. 2. Scatterplot of PESQ scores and STOI scores with respect to the true MOS rating. (a) and (b) show the mapping of PSEQ scores and STOI scores to real human MOS scores, respectively. Most of the scores are less than 3 in both (a) and (b), and there is no significant linear correlation between either PESQ scores or STOI scores and true MOS scores.

Table 2. The statistical result of bootstrapping method on our dataset.

Method	Utterance-level			System-level		
	LCC	SRCC	MSE	LCC	SRCC	MSE
PESQ	0.103	0.072	2.932	0.279	0.310	2.554
STOI	−0.054	−0.080	5.256	−0.121	−0.345	4.940

audio sample, Fig. 2 indicates the relationship between true MOS score and PESQ score, STOI score. It can be clearly seen that most of the scores are less than 3, i.e., for our dataset, the PESQ and STOI methods consider most of the synthesized speech to be of low quality. The average LCC, SRCC, and MSE values are shown in Table 2. It is clear from the result that neither the PESQ scores nor the STOI scores correlate well with the real MOS scores and have significant errors. Such a result is reasonable on our dataset. Since our goal is not for the synthesized speech to sound like the original speech, the TTS system we used to make the speech in our dataset did not use the original speech as training set. Moreover, the synthesized speech differs from the original speech in terms of acoustic features like fundamental frequency, tone color, and the length of each word or factor. Therefore, using objective evaluation methods to achieve our goal of predicting subjective MOS scores for TTS-synthesized speech in our dataset is ineffective.

3 Model

3.1 Model Input

Our goal is to predict MOS score for the input audio samples, and we want the process to be end-to-end. Therefore, for the input audio samples, we need to extract acoustic features as input to the prediction model. We chose to extract the F-Bank (Filter bank) feature because it conforms to the human hearing principle and has proven its effectiveness by being widely used. Compared with another widely used feature MFCC (Mel-frequency cepstral coefficients), F-Bank does not perform the last step of discrete cosine transform (lossy transform), so F-Bank features retain more original speech information.

The audio samples are pre-emphasized, split into frames, windowed, and then do STFT (Short-Time Fourier Transform) on the windowed signal of each frame. Thereafter, the Mel filter set is applied on the energy spectrum. Each filter in the filter bank is triangular having a response of 1 at the center frequency and decrease linearly towards 0 till it reaches the center frequencies of the two adjacent filters where the response is 0. The frequency response of the triangular filter is defined as:

$$H_m(k) = \begin{cases} 0, & k < f(m-1) \\ \frac{k-f(m-1)}{f(m)-f(m-1)}, & f(m-1) \le k < f(m) \\ 1, & k = f(m) \\ \frac{f(m+1)-k}{f(m+1)-f(m)}, & f(m) < k \le f(m+1) \\ 0, & k > f(m+1) \end{cases} \tag{1}$$

Applying the Mel filter bank on the energy spectrum, the equation is:

$$Y_t(m) = \sum_{k=1}^{N} H_m(k) |X_t(k)|^2 \tag{2}$$

where k denotes the index of frequency bin and m denotes the index of Mel filter. Thereafter we obtain the F-Bank features.

3.2 Model Structure

We propose a model based on ResNet and self-attention. The residual network solves the challenge of optimization in deep networks, while self-attention can better exploit the intrinsic relationship of the input sequences. Based on such characteristics, combining these two models is effective in our task.

The structure of our model is shown in Fig. 3. We use the ResNet18 model as a reference, and the 40-dimensional F-Bank feature extracted from the padded audio samples is input to conv1 layer. Shape of input tensor is (batch size, number of frames, 40). The conv1 layer contains two basic blocks, each containing two convolutional layers with a convolutional kernel shape of 3×3 and output channel number of 64. The conv2, conv3 and conv4 layer have similar shapes, but the number of output channels of the convolutional layers in the included basic block is 128, 256 and 512, respectively.

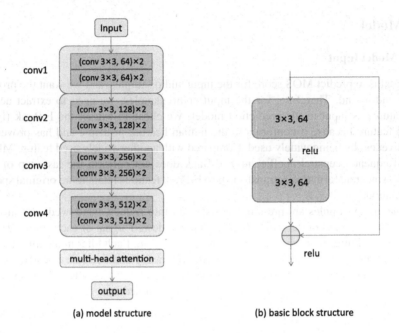

(a) model structure   (b) basic block structure

Fig. 3. Structure of our model. (a) shows the structure of our model. (b) shows the structure of a basic block of a convolutional layer in our model.

The shape of the basic block is shown on the right in Fig. 3. In the down-sampling process of the residual network, we use a 1×2 down-sampling, not in the time series dimension but only in the feature dimension. Therefore, the output tensor of the conv4 layer keeps the time length as same as the F-Bank feature and reduces the feature dimension by a factor of 16, i.e. from 40 to 3, so its shape is (batch size, number of frames, 512, 3). The output of the conv4 layer is reshaped to (batch size, number of frames, 1536) and then fed into the multi-head attention layer. The structure of the multi-head attention layer is shown in Fig. 4. We use a 8-head self-attention model. In the input of the multi-head attention layer, V and K are the tensor reshaped by the output of the conv4 layer, while Q is the tensor obtained by averaging the tensor over the frame dimension, i.e., the time dimension. In this way, we make the multi-head attention layer get the information at the frame level and the average information at the utterance level. Inspired by [16, 17], in addition to the utterance-level error, the frame-level error is also informative for predicting the utterance-level error. Therefore, the following objective function is used to train our model:

$$O = \frac{1}{S} \sum_{s=1}^{S} \left[\left(\hat{Q}_s - Q_s \right)^2 + \frac{1}{T_s} \sum_{t=1}^{T_s} \left(\hat{Q}_s - q_{s,t} \right)^2 \right] \tag{3}$$

S represents the number of utterances in a training batch. $\hat{Q}_s$ and Q_s denote the ground-truth and predicted MOS scores of the s-th speech, respectively. The total number of frames in the s-th speech is represented by T_s. $q_{s,t}$ indicates the predicted score of

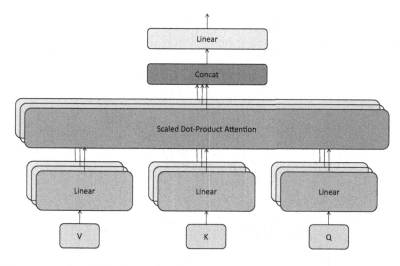

Fig. 4. Structure of multi-head attention. V and K are the tensor reshaped by the output of the ResNet, while Q is generated by averaging the tensor over the time dimension.

the s-th speech at frame t. It can be seen that the objective function in equation above contains both utterance-level error and frame-level error, and the frame-level MSE is averaged over the time series.

4   Experiments

The above-mentioned dataset consisting of human MOS scores and speeches generated by different TTS systems was used to train and test. For each voice in the dataset, the average of the ratings of the ten listeners was used as the true MOS score to calculate the loss with the predicted score. All the audio samples were resampled to 16 kHz, 16bit, generated by 10 different TTS systems, and for each TTS system we randomly selected 5 utterances as the test set, 50 in total, and the remaining 950 sentences were used to train the model. To extract the features of audio sample, we used a 20 ms window, 10 ms frame shift and 40 triangular filters to extract the F-bank features. We set the mini-batch to 24, the dropout rate of ResNet to 0.3, and the dropout rate of multi-head attention to 0.1. The Adam optimizer was used to train our model, and the learning rate was set to 0.00005. Figure 5 shows the relationship between the predicted results of our model and the true MOS scores for the synthesized speeches in our dataset. It can be clearly concluded that there is a strong linear relationship between the predicted scores and the true MOS scores. This is in line with our results on the predictability of the speech MOS scores in the dataset after statistical analysis. In addition to the objective assessment methods PESQ and STOI, we also selected some deep learning-based models to be trained on our dataset to predict MOS scores. The CNN-BiLSTM-based MOS-net [17], BiLSTM-based Quality-net [16], and CNN-based model [15] were applied to our dataset. We tested MOS-net by replacing raw magnitude spectrogram used as input

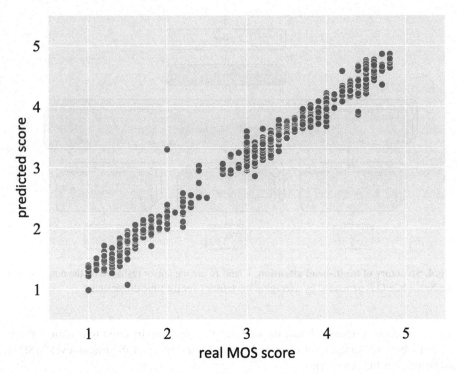

Fig. 5. Scatterplot of scores predicted by our model and the true MOS rating. This figure shows that the mapping of predicted scores to real human MOS scores. As can be seen from the figure, the scores predicted by our model have a significant linear correlation with the true MOS scores and are concentrated toward the true MOS scores.

with F-Bank features. We also used the original ResNet18 model. By a method of mapping time-domain information to higher dimensions [33], we conducted experiments using time-domain feature as the input to our model. Table 3 shows our experimental results on calculated accuracy(ACC), LCC, SRCC, and MSE on utterance level and system level of the true MOS scores with the predicted scores of all models.

The two objective evaluation methods, PESQ and STOI, predict scores with low accuracy, high MSE, and very low linear correlation with true MOS scores. This indicates that the objective evaluation criteria do not measure the subjective evaluation scores of the listeners in our dataset, and thus the task of predicting speech quality cannot be accomplished by objective evaluation methods in our dataset. Although the objective assessment methods PESQ and STOI do not work in our task, the deep learning-based models are able to have better prediction results. It can be seen that the accuracy of the predicted scores of each model can reach 0.89. Among them, our model has the highest accuracy, the lowest MSE, and a good performance in the degree of linear correlation. Our results show a 5% relative decrease in error rate on utterance level over ResNet's results, indicating that the multi-head attention layer is helpful for prediction accuracy. Using F-Bank features as the input to our model provides better

Table 3. The results of our experiment

Method	Utterance-level				System-level			
	ACC	LCC	SRCC	MSE	ACC	LCC	SRCC	MSE
PESQ	0.559	0.103	0.072	2.932	0.592	0.279	0.310	2.554
STOI	0.410	−0.054	−0.080	5.256	0.430	−0.121	−0.345	4.940
CNN	0.894	0.984	0.955	0.129	0.901	0.990	0.980	0.114
Quality-Net	0.899	0.980	0.955	0.083	0.903	0.984	0.963	0.061
Mos-Net	0.907	0.988	0.950	0.071	0.910	0.997	0.985	0.061
F-Bank Mos-Net	0.911	**0.990**	**0.972**	0.065	0.915	0.994	0.964	0.059
ResNet18	0.911	0.989	0.954	0.067	0.920	**0.997**	0.988	0.045
TResNet-attention	0.906	0.982	0.956	0.075	0.915	0.995	**0.988**	0.063
ResNet-attention (Our method)	**0.917**	0.988	0.961	**0.053**	**0.923**	0.994	0.979	**0.038**

prediction results compared to using time-domain feature as the model input, indicating that F-Bank is more suitable for our task compared to time-domain feature. MOSnet prediction accuracy using F-Bank is higher than MOSnet, indicating that F-Bank features are more suitable as feature inputs than raw magnitude spectrogram on our dataset. The system-level results are mostly better than the utterance-level results for all evaluation metrics, which indicates that the predictability is higher at system level than at utterance level. This is consistent with our idea that the speech quality of a TTS system cannot be exactly the same for speeches synthesized by different text, but the overall ratings for different TTS should be more easily distinguishable from the system level.

5   Conclusion

We propose a deep learning-based method for evaluating the perceptual quality of speech synthesized by TTS systems based on ResNet and self-attention. Moreover, we build a dataset containing TTS synthesized speech and listener-rated MOS scores, and we train our model on this dataset for predicting the real MOS scores. The experiments results prove that the true MOS scores in the dataset were predictable, and the proposed method achieves best performance in terms of the accuracy both in utterance level and system level across diverse baseline methods. Meanwhile, we prove that there is a high linear correlation between the predicted scores and the true MOS scores, and system-level prediction outperforms utterance-level prediction.

References

1. Kubichek, R.: Mel-cepstral distance measure for objective speech quality assessment. In: Proceedings of IEEE Pacific Rim Conference on Communications Computers and Signal Processing, vol. 1, pp. 1:125–128 (1993)
2. Methods for objective and subjective assessment of quality perceptual evaluation of speech quality (PESQ) : an objective method for end-to-end speech quality assessment of narrow-band telephone networks and speech codecs (2002)

3. Kim, D.-S.: Anique: an auditory model for single-ended speech quality estimation. IEEE Trans. Speech Audio Process. **13**, 821–831 (2005)
4. Falk, T.H., Zheng, C., Chan, W.Y.: A non-intrusive quality and intelligibility measure of reverberant and dereverberated speech. IEEE Trans. Audio Speech Lang. Process. **18**, 1766–1774 (2010)
5. Malfait, L., Berger, J., Kastner, M.: P.563–the ITU-T standard for single-ended speech quality assessment. IEEE Trans. Audio Speech Lang. Process. **14**, 1924–1934 (2006)
6. Sharma, D., Meredith, L., Lainez, J., Barreda, D., Naylor, P.A.: A non-intrusive PESQ measure. In: 2014 IEEE Global Conference on Signal and Information Processing (GlobalSIP), pp. 975–978 (2014)
7. Rahdari, F., Mousavi, R., Eftekhari, M.: An ensemble learning model for single-ended speech quality assessment using multiple-level signal decomposition method. In: 2014 4th International Conference on Computer and Knowledge Engineering (ICCKE), pp. 189–193 (2014)
8. Mittag, G., Möller, S.: Non-intrusive speech quality assessment for super-wideband speech communication networks. In: ICASSP 2019–2019 IEEE International Conference on Acoustics, Speech and Signal Processing (ICASSP), pp 7125–7129 (2019)
9. Gamper, H., Reddy, C.K., Cutler, R., Tashev, I.J., Gehrke, J.: Intrusive and non-intrusive perceptual speech quality assessment using a convolutional neural network. In: 2019 IEEE Workshop on Applications of Signal Processing to Audio and Acoustics (WASPAA), pp. 85–89 (2019)
10. Catellier, A.A., Voran, S.D.: Wenets: a convolutional framework for evaluating audio waveforms. ArXiv, abs/1909.09024 (2019)
11. Patton, B., Agiomyrgiannakis, Y., Terry, M., Wilson, K., Saurous, R.A., Sculley, D.: Auto-MOS: learning a non-intrusive assessor of naturalness-of-speech. ArXiv, abs/1611.09207 (2016)
12. Manocha, P., Finkelstein, A., Zhang, R., Bryan, N.J., Mysore, G.J., Jin, Z.: A differentiable perceptual audio metric learned from just noticeable differences. In: INTERSPEECH (2020)
13. Mittag, G., Naderi, B., Chehadi, A., Möller, S.: NISQA: a deep CNN-self-attention model for multidimensional speech quality prediction with crowdsourced datasets. In: Interspeech (2021)
14. Serrà, J., Pons, J., Pascual, S.: SESQA: semi-supervised learning for speech quality assessment. In: ICASSP 2021–2021 IEEE International Conference on Acoustics, Speech and Signal Processing (ICASSP), pp. 381–385 (2021)
15. Yoshimura, T., Henter, G.E., Watts, O., Wester, M., Yamagishi, J., Tokuda, K.: A hierarchical predictor of synthetic speech naturalness using neural networks, In: INTERSPEECH (2016)
16. Fu, S.W., Tsao, Y., Hwang, H.T., Wang, H.M.: Quality-net: an end-to-end non-intrusive speech quality assessment model based on blstm. ArXiv, abs/1808.05344 (2018)
17. Lo, C.C., et al.: Mosnet: deep learning based objective assessment for voice conversion. ArXiv, abs/1904.08352 (2019)
18. Jayesh, M.K., Sharma, M., Vonteddu, P., Shaik, M.A.B., Ganapathy, S.: Transformer networks for non-intrusive speech quality prediction. In: INTERSPEECH (2022)
19. Liu, W., Xie, C.: MOS prediction network for non-intrusive speech quality assessment in online conferencing. In: INTERSPEECH (2022)
20. Lorenzo-Trueba, J., et al.: The voice conversion challenge 2018: promoting development of parallel and nonparallel methods. ArXiv, abs/1804.04262 (2018)
21. He, K., Zhang, X., Ren, S., Sun, J.: Deep residual learning for image recognition. In: 2016 IEEE Conference on Computer Vision and Pattern Recognition (CVPR), pp. 770–778 (2016)
22. Vaswani, A., et al.: Attention is all you need. ArXiv, abs/1706.03762 (2017)
23. Yamagishi, J., Veaux, C., MacDonald, K.: CSTR VCTK corpus: english multi-speaker corpus for CSTR voice cloning toolkit (version 0.92) (2019)

24. Shen, J., et al.: Natural TTS synthesis by conditioning wavenet on MEL spectrogram predictions. In: 2018 IEEE International Conference on Acoustics, Speech and Signal Processing (ICASSP), pp. 4779–4783 (2018)
25. Ren, Y., et al.: Fastspeech 2: fast and high-quality end-to-end text to speech. ArXiv, abs/2006.04558 (2021)
26. Kim, J., Kim, S., Kong, J., Yoon, S.: Glow-TTS: a generative flow for text-to-speech via monotonic alignment search. ArXiv, abs/2005.11129 (2020)
27. Kuhn, D.: Speedy speech: efficient service delivery for articulation errors. Perspect. School-Based Issues **7**, 11–14 (2006)
28. Kim, J., Kong, J., Son, J.: Conditional variational autoencoder with adversarial learning for end-to-end text-to-speech. ArXiv, abs/2106.06103 (2021)
29. La'ncucki, A.: Fastpitch: parallel text-to-speech with pitch prediction. In: ICASSP (2021)
30. Casanova, E., Weber, J., Shulby, C. D., Júnior, A., Gölge, E., Ponti, M. A.: Yourtts: towards zero-shot multi-speaker TTS and zero-shot voice conversion for everyone. In: ICML (2022)
31. Bartoschek, S., et al.: webMUSHRA - a comprehensive framework for web-based listening tests. J. Open Res. Softw. **6**(1), 8 (2018)
32. Taal, C.H., Hendriks, R.C., Heusdens, R., Jensen, J.: An algorithm for intelligibility prediction of time-frequency weighted noisy speech. IEEE Trans. Audio Speech Lang. Process. **19**, 2125–2136 (2011)
33. Luo, Y., Mesgarani, N.: Conv-tasnet: Surpassing ideal time-frequency magnitude masking for speech separation. IEEE/ACM Trans. Audio Speech Lang. Process. **27**, 1256–1266 (2019)

An Adaptive Musical Vibrotactile System (MuViT) for Modern Smartphones

Tianqiang Yan[1](✉) and Yuwei Liu[2]

[1] The Chinese University of Hong Kong, Shenzhen, Shenzhen, China
222010015@link.cuhk.edu.cn
[2] Nanjing University of Science and Technology, Nanjing, China
Liuyw@njust.edu.cn

Abstract. Multimedia is a must-have for almost every person in daily life nowadays, but the truth is that most of the existing ways of enjoying multimedia sources are limited to listening to music or watching videos. In pursuit of the next-level experience, multimodal or multisensory entertainment has arisen in recent years, yet most of which involves special equipment and are designed for extremely limited scenarios that makes them hard to reach the populace. In this article, we propose a software-based, device-independent way to interact with audio contents on the smartphones involving another human sense besides hearing and vision, which is tactile sensation. We provide a system prototype, called MuViT, an adaptive musical vibrotactile system that allows users to feel the vibrations only by holding their phones while playing multimedia contents. The system is designed as a mobile application so that users can easily obtain and use it, and it's designed to adapt most of the popular multimedia applications found in apps market, such as YouTube and Apple Music. Furthermore, the system is fully open source on GitHub, so that interested individuals are welcomed to further tap its potential.

Keywords: Linear motor · Vibrotactile · Haptics · Onset detection · Onset event · Subjective evaluation

1 Introduction

As smartphones are updated and popularized at tremendous speed under the promotion of manufacturers and operators, the advancement of software ecosystem has been a heavy demand, and multimedia technologies and contents are a matter of great concern. In addition to ensuring visual and auditory needs, research and development on multimodal interactivity is blooming these years.

Haptics is an important dimension giving information as a position and force. For example, when people learn how to play musical instruments, not only visual and auditory feedback, but also tactile feedback from the instruments is momentous. Tactile information integrated into existing audio-visual scenarios can bring more immersive experience to human, such as movie experience [1], Virtual Reality [2, 3], music learning [3, 4] and accessibility for impaired listeners [4, 5]. Generally speaking, haptic interaction can make the audience feel the power of music and increase the reality for the auditory experience. Accordingly, we believe that multimodal perception including haptics has great potential to improve multimedia interaction experience.

In recent years, a growing corpus of studies explores how to use haptic stimulation to enhance the experience related to audio. Along the same lines, a broad range of musical haptics systems have been proposed in the literatures. Some of these systems are embedded on fixed equipment while listening to music or watching videos with soundtracks. For example, L. Hayes in [6] created an audio haptic work named Skin Music. By lying on a piece of bespoke furniture, the listener perceives the music both through the usual auditory channels, as well as by different types of haptic sensation, through their body. However, this is not a portable project. In addition, the project was optimized for just one special music, which is of no practical significance. Other proposed techniques rely on wearable accessories. Mazzoni et al. in [1] developed a wearable prototype system named Mood Glove to annotate the emotions of movie soundtracks through haptic sensation, thus enriching the viewing experience. Hwang et al. in [7] developed a haptic music player for mobile devices. They used two types of actuators attached to the handheld model (LRA and DMA), among which the DMA can generate vibrations composed of two main frequencies, which can lead to greater diversity in vibrotactile perception. The truth is that, the above-mentioned systems are all divided structures, which makes them hard to be integrated into daily life. To achieve a high-quality overall experience, we believe higher integration, or an all-in-one software platform, is more capable of creating seamless and on-the-go experience. Smartphones are the most widely used mobile devices, and their potential for haptic usability has been explored continuously.

Several attempts have been introduced based on similar concepts. QQ Music carries out a sound effect called Super-Hyped DJ which extracts upbeats and downbeats through artificial intelligence. Then it generates templates suitable for tracks according to the beat features. Super-Hyped DJ combines with the sound-track to produce rhythmic vibration and flash effects, enhancing the atmosphere for the users especially when someone is holding a party and playing some music. Although it is capable of fully-automatic vibrotactile generation based on audio features, the actual experience is not so desirable, and it only adapts to a fraction of songs. SONY also presents a dedicated Digital Vibration System (DVS) for its mobile phones, the Xperia series. The software and hardware operate in coordination, which can adaptively detect beat features and match vibration signals with great precision and elaboration. Nevertheless, it is a closed source system optimized solely for SONY's flagship phones and cannot be applied to others.

Driven by the same idea, we introduce an Adaptive Musical Vibrotactile System (MuViT), an upper-level software-based musical haptics extension compatible to any smartphones. Our scheme has the following advantages. First of all, we design an adaptive algorithm to extract the low-frequency features of music, which does not require manual settings for specific contents. The system can realize the real-time output of vibrotactile effect, producing vibration signals directly from audio sources without prior knowledge of the entire soundtrack, also protecting the user privacy. Furthermore, our vibration generation algorithms satisfy the functional requirements using digital signal processing techniques with very low computational complexity, while the vibration of the motor is generated jointly by two different control functions, which can still lead to delicate vibrotactile perception. More importantly, the system extends its usability to even more scenes, mobile gaming in particular. Meanwhile, we designed an application for MuViT, which is an open-source program for Android smartphones, and users can freely adjust the parameters to achieve better haptic experience according to their hardware environment.

Our research exploits the usability of haptics on arbitrary smartphone models. In the second section, the MuViT architecture is discussed in detail and by part. To further verify the functionality and performance, we proposed a subjective evaluation for the system and received reasonable feedback in our offline surveys, the results and analysis of which is delivered in Sect. 3. Section 4 is a conclusion of the paper.

2 System Description

The MuViT is designed fully based on subjective evaluations from real-world smartphone users. Therefore, some of the given parameters and algorithms are based on our experience gained during testing and may be inexplicable. However, the entire system is not designed to be a black box. Low-complexity signal processing and analysis methods are utilized to make the system mechanism as simple and interpretable as possible, and most of the values and expressions are customizable in some degree, the influence of which on our system as well as the user's somatosensory experience can be explained. As most of the existing technical means are still not capable enough to achieve full adaptation, we believe that appropriate system transparency and customizability should be left for users and further optimization. Generally speaking, the concept of this system is mainly delivered throughout the paper, and all technical details in this section are for annotating our implementation of this concept.

The following content of this section will be divided into two parts. The overall architecture will be introduced in the first part, while the second part decomposes the system process, and key technicalities are discussed.

2.1 Introduction to System Architecture

The following image (see Fig. 1) shows the overall architecture of MuViT.

MuViT does not require any peripheral equipment and is fully and well functioned with just a single smartphone. Compared with traditional smartphones equipped with rotator motors, the popularity of linear motors has driven the texture of haptic feedback on modern smartphones to a brand-new level, enough to set users free from sundry gadgets or specially-designed environments [1, 5–7] that generate vibration for audio signals. Besides that, we've seen more and more manufacturers paying attention to the vibration experience of smartphones, and integrating more advanced haptics tuning algorithms and stronger third-party application adaptability into the newly-launched models or the system upgrading of relatively old models. The mobile linear motors are generally divided into Z-axis (vibrate vertically) and X/Y axis (vibrate horizontally). The Z-axis linear motor was put into use earlier, possessing the advantages of occupying less interior space and lower cost. However, compared with the horizontal linear motor, which has two symmetrical spring coils, the Z-axis motor integrates only one lower-side spring, which enables the horizontal type to have a more delicate touch feedback experience. Due to the fact that the above two types of linear motors can be found in the market today, the parameters of MuViT are optimized for both of them. The respective settings will be given later.

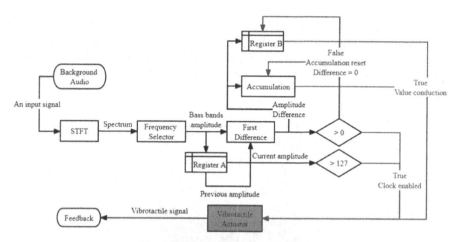

Fig. 1. The schematic flow of MuViT

The complete mechanism involves as few complicated calculations and delays as possible to meet satisfactory real-time performance. In addition, in the following analysis, you will see that MuViT requires low energy consumption on our test devices. When the audio signal is detected and obtained, short-time Fourier transform (STFT) is performed to convert discrete-time signals (DTS) to spectrums in real time. A frequency selector is utilized to filter out high frequency signals, and the output is a value ranging from 0 to 255, proportional to the instantaneous strength of the retained bass bands. Then, the time-domain first backward difference of the current amplitude is calculated in order to find the onset point and its strength. A dual-channel threshold is connected behind to let pass the high-enough amplitude with nonzero difference. When both the amplitude and the difference value meet the conditions for passing the threshold, the difference value is accumulated to compute the initial vibration intensity, the clock is enabled, and all required values are transmitted to the vibrotactile actuator, where two major functions are embedded for producing haptic signals. Otherwise, the clock is disabled and no tactile feedback is output. Suppose a vibration behavior is ready to be evoked, the clock driver function dynamically adjusts the clock interval before the clock starts. The feedback, delivered as the timer ticks, the strength of which is manipulated by a vibrotactile control function with the aim of providing sufficiently delicate texture.

The whole process is jointly realized and tested on two mobile devices, of which the specification list is shown in Table 1. Please note that the two models are equipped with two different types of linear motors.

An Android application, namely Viv Beats, is the instance of our MuViT system. The application does not perform as an audio player. Instead, it monitors the audio played in

Table 1. The specification list of smartphones for development and testing

Model name	Processor	RAM	Battery size	Motor type
Huawei Mate 20 Pro	HiSilicon Kirin 980	8 GB	4200 mAh	Z-Axis Linear
Sony Xperia XZ2	Qualcomm SDM845	4 GB	3180 mAh	X-Axis Linear

the background and applies the MuViT model to generate vibrotactile feedback based on the retrieved audio signals in real time. Figure 2 displays a screenshot of the application running in the foreground together with a popular multimedia application playing in the background.

Fig. 2. As is shown, the Viv Beats application is running in the split-screen mode in the foreground, and the audio source is being fed by YouTube Music, a widely-used multimedia streaming platform on Android.

The application is developed using an online Android development platform called Kodular. All the source file as well as the APK file (installation package) can be found and downloaded on its exclusive GitHub repository [8]. Table 2 demonstrates the basic information (size, permissions, etc.) of Viv Beats.

2.2 System Disassembly

Short-Time Fourier Transform (STFT). The Fourier transform only reflects the characteristics of the signal in the frequency domain, it cannot analyze the signal in the time

Table 2. Basic information of Viv Beats

Platform	API level	APK size	Storage required	Permissions
Android	29 (Android 10)	5.52 MB	At least 18 MB	Recording

domain. Therefore, the Fourier transform is only suitable for processing stationary signals. The frequency characteristics for non-stationary signals vary with time, in order to capture this time-varying characteristics, we need to perform time-frequency analysis of the signal. Gabor proposed the short-time Fourier transform (STFT) in 1946, which is essentially a windowed Fourier transform.

The process of STFT is as follows: before the Fourier transform, the signal is multiplied by a time-limited window function. The non-stationary signal is assumed to be stationary in the short interval of the analysis window subsequently. Through the movement of window function $h(t)$ on the time axis, the signal is analyzed segment by segment to obtain a set of spectrums of the signal.

The short-time Fourier transform of a signal is defined as:

$$STFT(t,f) = \int_{-\infty}^{\infty} x(\tau)h(\tau - t)e^{-j2\pi f\tau}d\tau \tag{1}$$

The short-time Fourier transform of the signal $x(t)$ at time t is equal to the Fourier transform made by multiplying the signal with an "analysis window" $h(\tau - t)$.

Frequency Selector. The frequency selector outputs the average amplitude of low frequency segment, i.e. the bass bands, since a significant increase in the strength of low band can usually be observed when it comes to a moment or a period with strong impact in a piece of music, mostly generated by percussion instrument. Hwang et al. in [7] separate bass and treble with a 200 Hz boundary. However, Merchel et al. [9] pointed out that pseudo-onsets are likely to be detected and converted into false vibration patterns when the dividing line is set to 200 Hz, and they further suggest a 100 Hz low-pass filter for broadband impulsive events.

Due to the limited frequency-domain sampling points with approximately 43 Hz spacing, 86 Hz (corresponding to 100 Hz), 129 Hz, and 172 Hz (corresponding to 200 Hz) are selected as the upper bound of the frequency selector respectively for testing. There is no need to examine even higher upper bounds for highly-noticeable spurious feedback ruining the experience. Eventually, our subjective assessment result indicates that the 129 Hz frequency limit can help the system achieve relatively first-rate experience in overall situations.

After the frequency selector finished its job, a value showing the present amplitude of bass bands, ranging from 0 to 255, is stored each round for later use.

Time-Domain First Difference. When the instantaneous amplitude of bass bands is acquired, the time-domain first difference plays the role of a preparation for the upcoming onset detection. The previous deposited amplitude value is regained to complete the calculation, which is given by (2).

$$\Delta \hat{y}[k, t_n] = \hat{y}[k, t_n] - \hat{y}[k, t_{n-1}]$$ (2)

Note that this is a backward difference. Here, $\hat{y}$ stands for the amplitude of bass bands (from 0 Hz to 129 Hz. k equals 129) sampled at the t_n-th time. We have also evaluated the effect of replacing this step with second difference, as second difference are widely used for extracting delicate edge features in the spatial domain of an image. A one-dimensional edge sharpening operator given by (3) was designed, in an attempt to depict subtle onset features.

$$\Delta \left(\Delta \hat{y}[k, t_n] \right) = \hat{y}[k, t_n] - 2\hat{y}[k, t_{n-1}] + \hat{y}[k, t_{n-2}]$$ (3)

Unfortunately, it turns out to be disappointing. As is shown in Fig. 3, the operator catches fallback signals while still returning positive values sometimes which are useless for producing vibration but are hard to filter within a few steps, and the exact opposite situation can happen either. In addition, compared with the first difference, the operation of second difference needs to wait for two additional input signals after the system starts to calculate the first value and output a vibration signal. That is to say, enabling second difference will waste about more than twice the initial time as the first difference, losing more onset information if an onset event happens to be located at the beginning.

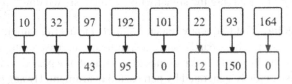

Fig. 3. As it's seen, some of the results of second backward difference are faulty, which are marked red in the picture. The '22-to-12' is a typical pseudo-onset, while the '164-to-0' is a wrongly-ignored onset point. (Color figure online)

Every output difference value in each process is summated, by which the envelope of the time-variant bass intensity level can be characterized. Yet not all features of such an envelope are demanded for perceiving and portraying remarkable onset events. More specifically, a noteworthy onset event contains a prominent signal take-off and, in some cases, a slope (usually rough) behind, reaching the local peak. Thus, it is essential to sort out an approach to determine whether the difference value should be reserved, and whether the accumulation is allowed. For this purpose, we introduced a dual-channel threshold to solve the problem.

Dual-Channel Threshold. The dual-channel threshold identifies the onset initiation point to the nearest onset peak as an onset event. It has two inputs, including the current bass amplitude and its first difference, each of which corresponds to a judging condition, namely a threshold. Figure 4 demonstrates the internal mechanism.

For the bass amplitude, values that are excessively low can be ignored, especially when the difference result of which is positive. A low-amplitude signal with positive onset strength is, in most cases as we've tested, a tactile disturbance when it comes to vibration formation. The threshold for bass amplitude is set to 127 (max. 255), an empiric value which facilitates relatively better haptic experience comparing to other alternatives examined.

For the difference value, the result of which is negative when a decline in bass intensity is detected. Such negative results make no more use for further steps, so they are set to zero after passing through the threshold. Likewise, declines are needless for the summation of differences, as summations are operated only when an onset event is being portrayed, the definition of which is aforementioned. Under such circumstances, the accumulation process should also be reset and remain inactive until the next onset point approaches.

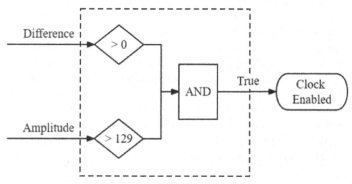

Fig. 4. The dual-channel threshold mainly acts as a conditional switch of the clock. Here in this image, the value transfer operations as well as the false condition are not drawn for involving too many external components.

The clock is used to actuate motor at appropriate intervals. By default, the clock is off, and remains off until inputs in both channels are greater than their corresponding thresholds. When the conditions are satisfied, the inputs are retained and are ready to be delivered into two key functions that drive the vibrotactile feedback on the basis of audio signals. The two functions are described right after.

Clock Driver Function and Vibrotactile Control Function. Delivering vivid and accurate vibration feedback is no easy job. Depending on these two functions, we try to provide tactile experience as excellent as possible. The combination of them matches the proper vibration frequency and intensity for each onset event in no time. Since whether the feedback texture is pleasant or not is decided by users, the two functions are designed mainly based on subjective experience, yet the parameters presented in the functions are mostly tunable, and the logic behind is explicated hereinafter.

Clock Driver Function. The clock driver function (4) allocates the length of intervals for the clock in real time, which determines the frequencies of vibration outputs. It is a composite function consisting of a constant coefficient and an exponential decay function.

$$t_{interval} = t_c \cdot a^{-s} \tag{4}$$

In the expression, $t_{interval}$ represents the clock interval in milliseconds. t_c is a constant, which stands for the maximum clock interval value. a is an attenuation factor greater than 1, deciding the attenuation rate of the curve. s is the dependent variable in this function, equal to the current difference which is always a positive value. As difference s becomes larger, $t_{interval}$ decays along the curve. The experience values of t_c and a are 280 and 1.06 respectively, which fit both two types of linear motors. Higher t_c requires more powerful onset to drive the clock within a single sampling period, allowing the system to better resist forged onsets, while resulting in greater attenuation rate and possibility of omitting effective strikes, so it should be adjusted with caution. To mitigate the excessive attenuation of the interval with the increase of the onset strength, appropriately lowering the value of a is recommended. Moreover, we suggest that after tuning the above parameters, the interval can be less than or equal to the minimum interval acceptable when s exactly reaches a high-enough value. It can be utilized to check if the attenuation rate is suitable or not. This high-enough value in our test platform is set between 70 to 80, and the maximum value 255, based on subjective sensation, is generally not suitable.

Vibrotactile Control Function. The basic idea behind the vibrotactile control function is to offer vibration feedback whose strength is proportional to the current impact of bass bands while providing a sense of damped oscillation during the sampling gap. The expression of the function is presented in (5):

$$A = A_{init} \cdot e^{-\left(\frac{\alpha}{255} \sum \Delta\right)^2 t} \tag{5}$$

In (5), A_{init} is the initial amplitude of vibrotactile signal transferred to the palm. It is a compound variable, the expansion of which is shown in (6) where A_{max} is the maximum vibration amplitude. α is the vibration attenuation factor that helps compensate or weaken the damping ratio. $\sum \Delta$ is the difference cumulative sum representing the current cumulative impact. t is the major argument of A. It changes with the clock.

$$A_{init} = \frac{A_{max}}{255} \sum \Delta \tag{6}$$

As it's shown in (5) and (6), the value of $\sum \Delta$ determines the initial amplitude of the vibration feedback, and as t grows larger, amplitude A attenuates. In the next paragraph, an example is given and described in order to provide a more intuitive impression of a complete vibrotactile event based on a typical onset event.

An onset event is made up of at least one onset point, the duration of which is a multiple of the signal sampling interval. Consider encountering an onset event formed by an initial onset point and a series of gradually rising signals before the upcoming peak which is also captured and contained, while the initial point has the largest difference compared with its followers, a period of high-frequency vibration feedback are delivered at the very beginning.

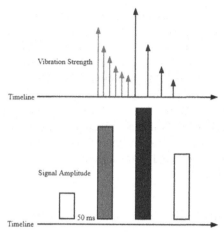

Fig. 5. This image demonstrates a vibration event synchronized with an onset event including two onset signals. The light green arrows constitute the feedback flow of the light green onset, while the dark green arrows form the feedback flow of the dark green onset. (Color figure online)

As the clock ticks within a sampling interval, the vibration amplitude decays along curve A, which is the same with the tactile significance. For the next signal, the clock is reset as soon as it arrives. According to what we've defined and functions (4)–(6), this signal has a relatively smaller difference but greater amplitude compared with the last one, which delivers more powerful initial vibration strength and lower feedback frequency. In addition, according to (5), the damping of vibration power should be comparatively faster. The above process lasts until the peak signal finally passes. The difference of the next signal is supposed to be negative, and the clock returns to standby mode, no vibrotactile event is to be triggered before the next onset event arrives. Figure 5 illustrates a vibrotactile event from its beginning to the end.

3   Evaluation Framework, Results and Analysis

3.1   Framework

We designed a HAPTIC framework with six subjective metrics (H, A, P, T, I, C) to evaluate the MuViT system based on offline survey results. First four of the metrics are listed as follows: Happiness (H)—The degree of the extra pleasure provided by the sensory extension; Adoption (A)—User's adaptability to such a novel function; Precision (P)—The onset detection accuracy reflected by actual multisensory impression, and Touch Sensation (T)—The overall comfort level of vibrotactile feedback during one's evaluation process regardless of Precision P. These four dimensions of metrics are graded in A (90–100), B (75–89), C (60–74), and D (0–59). Of the remaining metrics, Interaction (I) appraises the significance of the system, i.e. the willingness to use it in daily life, which is a binary option of 'yes' or 'no'. Compatibility (C) evaluates the compatibility ratio of MuViT to the most popular multimedia interactive platforms on Android, and the score is expressed in terms of a percentage. It is the only objective metric and is

446   T. Yan and Y. Liu

removed from our real-world assessment (HAPTI), the score of which is later obtained by ourselves.

Five CD-quality music clips of five music genres are chosen as the testing soundtracks, the details of which are shown in Table 3. Sixteen volunteers are selected randomly to participate in the HAPTI survey. Two versions of Viv Beats with minor configuration differences are installed separately on our two testing smartphones (as shown in Table 1), and the volunteers are divided into two groups, with eight testers in each, to partake in the same hands-on session and evaluation process on the two devices respectively. At the end of the hands-on session, participants are required to grade the MuViT system according to the HAPTI metrics and their subjective feeling. A questionnaire is designed for the grading procedure.

Table 3. Genre and music clips used for evaluation

Music title	Genre	Music clips
Harder, Better, Faster, Stronger	Electronics	1:36–2:36
Firework	Hip-pop	0:00–0:50
Nope!!!!!	ACG	0:00–1:00
Sunflower	R&B	0:00–0:27
H.O.L.Y.	Country	0:00–0:26

3.2 Results and Analysis

Figure 6 displays the gained HAPTI results. Since I (Interaction) is a binary option, it is not drawn in the chart. We take the average value of each grade (i.e. B denotes 82) and

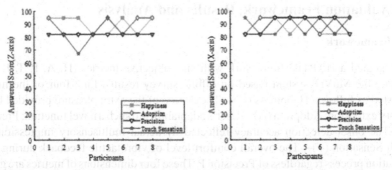

Fig. 6. The numbers of participants constitute the horizontal axis, while the gradings for four metrics (HAPT) constitutes the vertical axis. The two charts respectively show the evaluation results collected by the two test devices respectively (left: Huawei Mate 20 Pro's, right: Sony Xperia XZ2's).

draw the two graphs. On the whole, almost all the scores fall to or above Grade B (75–89), and Table 4 shows the average evaluation results of HAPTI collected respectively from the two testing smartphones.

The concept of bringing haptics to multimedia interaction is solid, as 100% of our volunteers recognize the prospect of MuViT as a product (see Interaction in Table 4). As for the other four markers, Xperia XZ2 wins a relatively better set of results, which doesn't surprise us, since the X-axis linear motor carried by Xperia XZ2 is superior to the Z-axis linear motor in Mate 20 Pro on the transient responsivity as well as the dynamic range. Additionally, Xperia XZ2 achieves more than 90 points in P (Precision), which embodies the outstanding adaptability of our algorithms. As it turns out, the idea behind MuViT is well-accepted, and it has shown fairly good performance as a tangible product prototype.

Table 4. HAPTI evaluation results in mean values

Model	H (Happiness)	A (Adoption)	P (Precision)	T (Touch Sensation)	I (Interaction)
Sony Xperia XZ2	85.3	91.8	90.1	88.5	100
Huawei Mate 20 Pro	90.1	88.5	82.0	81.8	100

Finally, the Compatibility (C) of HAPTIC is evaluated on ten mainstream multimedia platforms, including YouTube, YouTube Music, Apple Music, Spotify, TikTok, Netflix, Tidal Music, SoundCloud, QQ Music, and Bilibili. MuViT (Viv Beats) has achieved 90% compatibility ratio on these ten software platforms, among which only Tidal Music is incompatible with our system. This is to say that, unlike most of the other solutions, MuViT is a musical haptics extensible component on your smartphone in the true sense.

4 Conclusion

In this paper, we propose a musical haptics system called MuViT which is built for modern smartphones. The system takes an Android application (Viv Beats) as a carrier, and can provide vibrotactile feedback following the audio playing in the background in real time without any prior knowledge of the soundtrack data and regardless of the audio sources. We also design a HAPTIC evaluation method and conduct a real-world survey to let real participants help us assess the concept as well as the performance of MuViT, and the evaluation results indicate the usefulness and the prospectiveness of the proposed system.

Multimodal, or multisensory multimedia interaction, is one of the emerging areas, and we believe such kind of techniques will guide a prevailing and even essential way of multimedia interaction in the future, as long as both the technology providers and content providers work together to make this concept more and more mature.

References

1. Mazzoni, A., Bryan-Kinns, N.: Mood glove: a haptic wearable prototype system to enhance mood music in film. Entertainment Comput. **17**, 9–17 (2016)
2. Lin, X., Mahmud, S.: Virtual reality-based musical therapy for mental health management. In: Chakrabarti, S., Paul, R. (eds.) Computing and Communication Workshop and Conference (CCWC) 2020, pp. 948–952. IEEE, Las Vegas (2020)
3. Elvezio, C., Amelot, P.: Hybrid UIs for music exploration in AR and VR. In: IEEE International Symposium on Mixed and Augmented Reality Adjunct (ISMAR-Adjunct) 2020, pp. 411–412. IEEE, Munich (2018)
4. Kobayashi, N., Matsumoto, M.: Music learning support system using blocks. In: Matsuo, T., Takamatsu, K. (eds.) 12th International Congress on Advanced Applied Informatics (IIAI-AAI) 2022, pp. 164–169. IEEE, Kanazawa (2020)
5. Nanayakkara, S., Taylor, E.: An enhanced musical experience for the deaf: design and evaluation of a music display and a haptic chair. In: Proceedings of the Conference on Human Factors in Computing Systems, pp. 337–346. ACM (2009)
6. Hayes, L.: Skin music (2012): an audio-haptic composition for ears and body. In: Proceedings of the Conference on Creativity and Cognition, pp. 359–360. ACM, Glasgow (2015)
7. Hwang, I., Lee, H., Choi, S.: Real-time dual-band haptic music player for mobile devices. IEEE Trans. Haptics **6**(3), 340–351 (2013)
8. Project's GitHub Repository. https://github.com/henryyantq/MuViT. Accessed 6 Oct 2022
9. Merchel, S., Altinsoy, M.E.: Auditory-tactile experience of music. In: Papetti, S., Saitis, C. (eds.) Musical Haptics. SSTHS, pp. 123–148. Springer, Cham (2018). https://doi.org/10.1007/978-3-319-58316-7_7

Big Data

Big Data

A Random Forest-Based Model for Fusion of Organization Master Data

Jun Wang[✉] and Li Bai

Big Data Center of State Grid Corporation of China, Beijing, China
wj96006@163.com

Abstract. The organization master data is the most important data asset of an enterprise, representing the most basic organization structure, and is the data consistent and shared among systems. In order to solve the problem of inconsistency of organization master data across systems, establish a sparse table of mapping of each business system and serve the downstream application requirements, a random forest-based organization master data fusion model is built to automatically process organizational master data of each business system and fuse it to form a set of consistent and shared organization master data among business systems. The experiments show that the average matching rate of the model is 56.34% and the accuracy rate is 95.89% through data fusion of organization master organization data of 11 core business systems, which can effectively improve the efficiency of data fusion, reduce the labor cost and have high credibility, and has high practical value.

Keywords: Big data for electricity · Master data · Random forest · Data fusion

1 Introduction

Master data is the most important data asset of an enterprise, the data that is consistent and shared among various systems, the basis for information system construction and big data analysis, and the cornerstone of digital transformation of an enterprise [1]. Organizational master data is the most important data asset of an enterprise, the "golden data" of master data, representing the most basic organizational structure of an enterprise, and is the consistent and shared data among various business systems. At present, the new-generation master data management platform of State Grid Corporation has incorporated enterprise-level organization master data, but due to the different construction periods of each business system within the company, the organization master data has inconsistent management standards and imperfect data standards, and there are data barriers between each system, which makes it difficult to accurately and efficiently carry out cross-business system data application and multi-dimensional data analysis.

In recent years, industry scholars have extensively applied machine learning methods to data fusion penetration to improve the efficiency and accuracy of data fusion. Weiping Lai et al. [2] proposed a smart grid data fusion method based on PCA-MP_BP, and used a data fusion algorithm combining principal component analysis method and back propagation network to analyze the smart grid big data power prediction problem and improve the data processing efficiency and fusion accuracy. Jinlong Liu et al. [3] proposed an optimized text information extraction scheme and knowledge graph construction scheme based on Bi-LSTM and conditional random field model to realize the support of multi-source heterogeneous data fusion modeling work. Mao Xiangyin et al. [4] selected Hermite orthogonal basis forward neural network algorithm based on Map Reduce framework to solve the current problems of numerous power system automation systems, diverse data standards and duplicated information content, reduce data collection cost and improve data utilization value. Yan Wang et al. [5] introduced a power consumption data mining architecture combined with data fusion algorithms to analyze electricity consumption data, which improved the speed and accuracy of data analysis.

In order to promote the construction of the "good and easy to use" project of organization master data, solve the problems of cross-professional and cross-system association difficulties and inconsistent caliber of organization master data, this paper selects the random forest algorithm, builds the organization master data fusion model, and establishes the wide table of organization mapping of each business system in order to serve the downstream data application needs. In this paper, we choose Random Forest algorithm to build a fusion model of organizational master data and establish a wide table of organizational mapping for each business system in order to serve the downstream data application needs.

2   Problem Description

Organizational master data is the indispensable basic data of each business system. At present, the data storage between each business system within the State Grid Corporation is independent and does not have a uniform data format, coding system and organization name naming rules, there are data barriers, resulting in each business system can't be through the organization code for horizontal data penetration, it is difficult to unified query and hierarchical classification control of business scenarios data under the organization.

The existing organizational fusion method is to manually establish a mapping relationship between business organizations and administrative divisions. This method is highly dependent on manual work, inefficient, with limited matching capability, and overly dependent on business knowledge and high communication costs. Therefore, constructing an automatic organization mapping model, improving the efficiency of organization master data fusion, and solving the problem of automating the mapping of a large number of organizations, especially grassroots organizations at the county level and below, have become important problems that need to be tackled urgently.

Researching machine learning algorithms to build an automated fusion model for organizational master data will bring multiple implications. Firstly, the automated fusion model will significantly improve the efficiency of organizational fusion penetration and reduce the labor cost investment. Secondly, the model can automatically handle the grassroots organizations that are difficult to be handled manually, and fill the gap of this part of data. Thirdly, the model uses various features such as organization level, field and type for data fusion with high credibility. Finally, it solves the master data fusion problem from the perspective of organization mapping, and precipitates the technical foundation for the construction of the knowledge map of power system (Table 1).

Table 1. Experimental hardware environment

System	Organization code	Organizational hierarchy path	Remarks
Cooperative office system	505DSCS	/State Grid Sichuan Electric Power Corporation /Sichuan Siji Technology Co.	Inconsistent organization linkage, inconsistent organization name, unable to determine whether the same organization
Business Travel Cloud	3179	/State Grid Information and Communication Industry Group Corporation /State Grid Siji Innovation Technology (Sichuan) Co.	
Master Data Management Platform	2019371	/State Grid Corporation /State Grid Sichuan Electric Power Company /Siji Technology Co.	
Master Data Management Platform	10456727	/State Grid Corporation /State Grid Hubei Electric Power Co.	Organization name is inconsistent, and the superior linkage is missing, so it is impossible to determine whether it is the same organization
Cooperative office system	501XEZED	/Ezhou Electric Power Group Co.	

3 Organization Master Data Fusion Model

Construct the organization master data fusion model, which can receive the organization data of each business system, output the organization fusion result wide table. The model includes data pre-processing, feature extraction, model training and prediction processes. To support model iteration optimization and result correction, the model can also receive feedback from downstream workflows on the wide table of mapping results and the results of manual verification. The model structure is shown in Fig. 1. The main workflow of the model is shown in Fig. 2.

3.1 Data Pre-processing

This section performs data pre-processing for the organization master data of each business system, including deactivation word deletion, special character processing, data

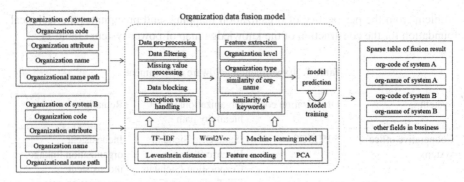

Fig. 1. Schematic diagram of organization data fusion model

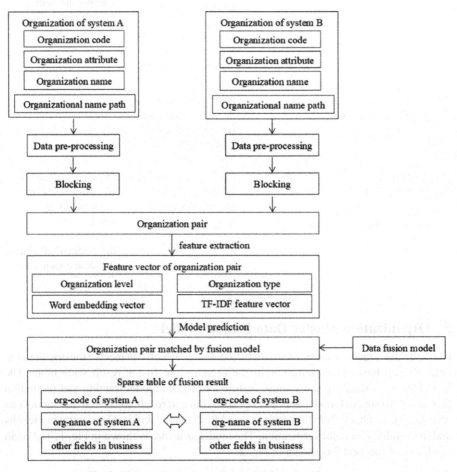

Fig. 2. Schematic diagram of organization matching process

conversion, and null value filling. For organization names, deactivation word deletion and special character processing are performed using the dictionary of deactivation words and special characters. For organization type, data encoding conversion is used, and null filling is performed by regular matching of "organization name" and organization hierarchy information. In particular, for organization data, "island" organizations are screened and valid fields are filtered. "Orphaned" organizations are organizations that have no parent organization other than the company headquarters and are isolated from the organizational system. Since the organization name path cannot be generated and the information features of the parent organization are missing, it is difficult to match and fuse the "silo" organizations and needs to be screened out.

3.2 Data Blocking

With the expansion of data size, the size of candidate set for organization data matching will increase significantly, resulting in the reduction of model efficiency. In order to efficiently match organizations, a candidate set needs to be built first. Otherwise, the candidate set will be the result of Cartesian product calculation of data organized by two sets of business systems, which brings unacceptable costs. To reduce the complexity, reducing the number of candidate set elements is an important data filtering process, and also a key point of performance optimization. At present, the mainstream technologies to solve this problem are blocking technology and indexing technology.

In this paper, the candidate set is screened by the blocking technology. Blocking technology is to remove those organization pairs that are obviously mismatched from the organization candidate matching set, and retain the entity pairs that are relatively likely to match, so as to reduce the size of the candidate matching set. The algorithm flow is shown in Fig. 3. First, organizations from different business systems are divided into several entity blocks using the same blocking technology. Then, the candidate set is generated by matching two pairs within the block. For each candidate, the model is used for prediction.

For the blocking technology, Zhang [6] proposed three solutions: content-based approach, structure based approach and a hybrid approach. Our model adopts a content-based approach, using a named entity recognition model CRF++ and regular matching to identify the administrative division information of the organization. Due to poor organizational mobility, a pair of matching organizations exist in the same region. We build each block set according to the administrative division information, and match each other to form a candidate set. Based on the candidate set, the trained machine learning model is used for binary prediction of matching and mismatching to achieve the goal of data fusion.

3.3 Feature Extraction

Due to the weak linguistic nature of the text of the main data of the organization, there are often missing subjects and abbreviations, and it is difficult to extract the text features. The data in the field of power system contains a large number of specialized vocabulary, and the naming rules and presentation habits of each business system are different, so it

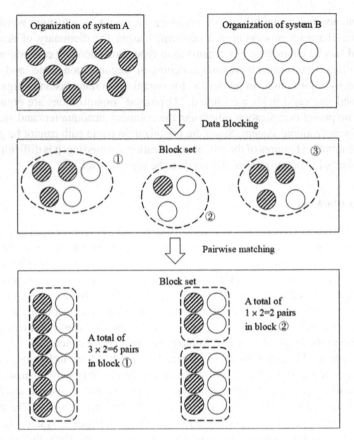

Fig. 3. Schematic diagram of organization matching process

is crucial to parse and enhance data features, identify specialized vocabulary, and extract hierarchical structure for data fusion and coherence.

There are many studies on text feature parsing and enhancement in the field of natural language processing. In order to perform automated data fusion and concatenation, features need to be extracted from organizational data, specifically, valid fields need to be identified and deep features need to be extracted using algorithms. The model selects TF-IDF algorithm to extract the key feature vocabulary of organization master data, selects pre-training tool Word2Vec to do text data vectorization processing, and uses Levenshtein distance to determine similar semantic strings.

(1) TF-IDF algorithm

TF-IDF algorithm is a statistical method to evaluate the importance of a word to one of the corpus in a document set or corpus [7].TF refers to word frequency and IDF refers to inverse text frequency.TF-IDF is a common weighting technique used in information retrieval and data mining to evaluate the importance of a word to a document in a document set or a corpus. The more a word appears in an article, while the less it appears in all articles, the more it can represent the central meaning of that article. The importance of a word increases proportionally with its number of occurrences in a document, but decreases inversely with its frequency in a corpus. The TF-IDF algorithm can perform a vector representation of text, and vectors can be used as features of text or to perform similarity calculation, reflecting the similar features of keywords. The formula is as follows. The number of occurrences of word A in the text is denoted as count(A). The total number of words in the text is denoted as Num.

$$TF_A = \frac{count(A)}{Num}.$$
(1)

The total number of texts in the corpus is denoted as Num_{all}. The number of documents containing the word A is denoted as Num_A.

$$IDF_A = \log\left(\frac{Num_{all}}{Num_A + 1}\right),$$
(2)

$$TFIDF_A = TF_A \times IDF_A.$$
(3)

The model uses the TF-IDF algorithm to calculate the keyword word frequencies of organization names and organization paths to form keyword vectors, and calculates the keyword vector cosine similarity between the baseline organization and the business organization as keyword similarity features.

(2) Word2Vec model

Word2vec model is a typical distribution coding model proposed by Google in 2013, which maps text into a numerical vector space, represented as a fixed-length vector, to learn semantic structure by unsupervised way [8]. Word2vec is divided into continuous bag-of-words model (CBOW) or Skip-gram model, which analyzes contextual relationships by different inputs and trains word generation vectors. CBOW is a three-layer neural network with word vectors of input contexts, intermediate vectors computed by the implicit layer, and a Huffman tree in the third layer for classification to get the prediction of the next word. The Skip-gram model is the opposite of the CBOW model, where the intermediate word is input and the prediction of its contextual word vector is output.

The model uses Word2Vec encoding of the "Organizational Attribute" and "Organizational Type" fields as organizational type features.

(3) Levenshtein distance

The distance between strings can be calculated as a quantitative measure of the degree of difference between two strings by looking at the minimum number of operations required to change one string into another [9]. The allowed edit operations include replacing one character with another, inserting a character, and deleting a character. It can measure the similarity of two strings from the editing point of view and is widely used in entity similarity judgment, entity linking, and entity merging tasks. The mathematical formula of Levenshtein distance is as follows.

$$
lev_{a,b}(i,j) = \begin{cases} \max(i,j) & if \ \min(i,j) = 0. \\ \min \begin{cases} lev_{a,b}(i-1,j)+1 \\ lev_{a,b}(i,j-1)+1 \\ lev_{a,b}(i-1,j-1)+1_{(a_i \neq b_j)} \end{cases} & otherwise. \end{cases} \tag{4}
$$

The model calculates the string edit distance of the organization name and organization path in the organization master data as the similarity feature of the organization name.

In order to define the effective fields and standardize the read in data table, covariance, information entropy and other correlation analysis algorithms are used to analyze the organizational fields of each business system to extract organizational characteristics, select regions, levels, types, organizational name similarity, keyword similarity characteristics, etc. The model adopts rule-based regular matching method, named entity identification [10] Principal component analysis [11] is used to extract the deep features of each field of the organization's master data.

3.4   Model Training and Prediction

The core of organization master data fusion is the short text binary classification problem, and the pre-processed business system organization master data are extracted by rule-based regular matching method, and the data are divided into regions based on this information, and the data are fully connected within each region, and each data is binary classified as "matching" and "not matching". "Finally, the classification results are grouped and counted to obtain a wide table of the results of organization master data fusion.

The key to the fusion process is the use of machine learning models for dichotomous classification training. A variety of mainstream classification machine learning algorithms such as decision tree, random forest, XGBoost, LightGBM, and support vector machine are selected to fuse the organizational data, and the classification results are evaluated using the common evaluation metrics of classification models. Based on the evaluation results, the model with better fusion effect, lower model resource consumption and higher model operation efficiency is selected for further tuning and model iteration, and finally a binary classification machine learning model is trained for organization master data fusion.

(1)   Decision tree [12]

A decision tree is a flowchart-like tree structure, where each node inside the tree represents a test of a feature, the branches of the tree represent each test result of the feature, and each leaf node of the tree represents a category. The highest level of the tree is the root node. The learning process of decision tree is divided into the process of feature selection, decision tree generation, pruning, etc. The core is the sample division process in the generation link. If all samples in the node belong to the same category, then the node becomes a leaf node and the node is marked as the category with the largest number of samples; otherwise, the information gain method is used to select the features used to divide the samples, which are the test features, and each value of the feature corresponds to the branch and the subset of the node that is divided. The above process is performed recursively until all nodes become leaf nodes, that is, the decision tree model is obtained.

(2) Random Forest, XGBoost, LightGBM

Random forest consists of multiple decision trees. When constructing a decision tree, a portion of samples are selected randomly from the training data in a put-back manner and a portion of features are selected randomly for training. Each tree uses different samples and features, and the trained results are different. Random forest is built on the basis of decision trees by the idea of model fusion, which significantly improves the robustness of the model and the prediction effect. XGBoost [13] and LightGBM [14] also improve the prediction effect by model fusion of basic or traditional machine learning algorithms.

(3) Support vector machines [15]

Compared with the traditional BP neural network [16], support vector machine is a new machine learning method based on the statistical learning theory created by Vapnik, which uses the structural risk minimization criterion to improve the generalization ability of the model and has no restriction on the number of data dimensions. Support vector machines can solve binary classification problems. When performing linear classification, support vector machines take the classification surface at a larger distance from the two classes of samples. When carrying out nonlinear classification, the nonlinear classification problem is transformed into a linear classification problem in high-dimensional space through high-dimensional space transformation [17].

4   Experimental Results and Analysis

4.1 Evaluation Indicators

In order to evaluate the effect of organization master data fusion model, the model prediction results can be classified into the following four cases.

True Positive: Organization A has corresponding organization B, and the model gives matching result also as B, which is recorded as TP (True Positive).

False Negative: Organization A has a corresponding organization B, but the model gives a matching result other than B, or the model does not give a matching result, which is called FN (False Negative).

False Positive: Organization A does not have a corresponding organization, and the model gives a matching result of organization B, which is denoted as FP (False Positive).

True Negative: Organization A does not have a corresponding organization, and the model does not give a matching result, which is denoted as TN (True Negative).

Based on the above four categories, accuracy rate, precision rate, recall rate, and F1 value are calculated as evaluation indexes.

Accuracy rate refers to the percentage of correct results of the sample to the total sample, i.e.

$$Accuracy = \frac{TP + TN}{TP + TN + FP + FN}. \tag{5}$$

Precision rate refers to the probability that the actual sample is positive among all the samples with positive predictions, and measures the prediction accuracy of positive sample results, i.e.

$$Precision = \frac{TP}{TP + FP}. \tag{6}$$

Recall rate is for the original sample and refers to the probability that a positive sample is predicted among the samples that are actually positive, i.e.

$$Recall = \frac{TP}{TP + FN}. \tag{7}$$

The F1 score considers both the precision and recall rates and is the arithmetic mean of the precision and recall rates, i.e.

$$F1 = \frac{2 \times Precision \times Recall}{Precision + Recall}. \tag{8}$$

For the organizational matching problem of sample imbalance, the recall rate and F1 value should be used as the main comparison index, and the accuracy rate and precision rate should be used as important indexes for reference.

4.2 Experimental Environment

The experiment is done on a PC with Windows 10, 64-bit operating system for programming and testing. The hardware environment for this experiment is shown in Table 2.

Table 2. Experimental hardware environment

Hardware section	Performance parameters
RAM	Samsung DDR4 3200 MHz 16 GB
CPU	Intel® Core™ i5-8265U CPU @ 1.80 GHz

The software environment for this experiment is shown in Table 3. The programming language is Python and its modules is used for data processing, model training and model prediction. The data fusion model can also be deployed and applied on the data platform of State Grid Corporation of China where PyODPS is Python SDK.

Table 3. Experimental software environment

Software section	Performance parameters
Operating system	Windows 10
Development tools	PyCharm, Jupyter notebook
Programming environment	Python 3.60, Numpy 1.19.5, Pandas 1.0.5, Sklearn 0.23.1, PyODPS 2

4.3 Experimental Result

The experiment selects the organization master data of 11 core business systems such as the marketing business system of State Grid Corporation of China, the new generation master data management platform (MDM3.0) as the model experiment data set. Manually sort out the mapping relationship of the organization, and divide the training set and test set according to the proportion of 3:1 to train the fusion model and evaluate the effect of the model. On the basis of this dataset, the experiment compares the classification effect of machine learning algorithms such as decision tree, naive Bayes, random forest, support vector machine, etc. The evaluation results of each model on test data are shown in Table 4 and Fig. 4. After comparison, the effect of random forest is the best. Grid search method is used to adjust parameters for random forests. Finally, the random forest model is selected as the model of organization master data fusion. Grid search method is used to adjust parameters for random forests. See Table 5 for random forest parameters when the model effect is optimal.

Table 4. Evaluation index of machine learning models

	Accuracy	Precision	Recall	F1
Decision Tree	75.37%	81.56%	70.31%	75.52%
Naive Bayes	84.32%	82.31%	87.33%	84.74%
Random Forest	96.74%	96.11%	96.76%	96.43%
Support vector machines	86.86%	90.15%	86.87%	88.48%

Table 5. Optimal parameters of fusion model

Parameters	Parameters meaning	Optimal value
n_estimators	Number of internal base tree learners	10
max_depth	Maximum depth of tree	15
max_features	Number of features to consider when searching for the best segmentation	10
min_samples_leaf	Minimum sample number of leaf nodes	3
min_samples_split	Number of features to consider when searching for the best segmentation	4

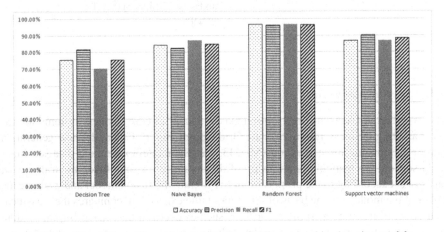

Fig. 4. Comparison of experimental results of different machine learning models

4.4 Model Application

Serving the data application needs, the organization master data fusion penetration model has supported the organization data fusion of 11 sets of business systems of State Grid Corporation, such as marketing business application, economic law and planning plan, with an average matching rate of 56.34% and an accuracy rate of 95.89%. The matching rate and accuracy statistics of each business system are shown in Fig. 5. The high accuracy of model fusion matching reduces the manual matching workload to a large extent and has high practical value. The public organization data set formed by the fusion has been put into use on the discipline inspection and supervision internal investigation platform of State Grid Corporation. Through the fusion of organization data, the business data of each business system can be queried through a unique organization tree, which greatly improves the user experience.

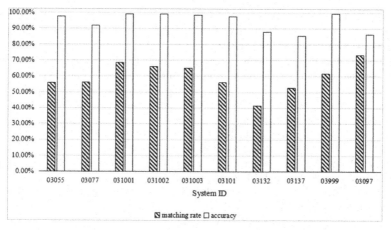

Fig. 5. Matching rate and accuracy of organization fusion model in each business system

5   Conclusion

For the problem of horizontal penetration of the main data of organizations of each business system, the experimental random forest algorithm was selected to carry out the data fusion model research, and a model construction process including data pre-processing, feature extraction and model training was proposed. The model is trained, tested and tuned based on the organizational master data of the core business systems of the State Grid Corporation, and its feasibility is verified in the process of serving the real data application requirements. According to the experimental comparison and application results, the organization master data fusion model can automatically process the corresponding data of each business system of State Grid Corporation, output a set of consistent and shared organization master data among systems, break the data barriers among systems, serve the data application needs of downstream systems, and has high practical value.

References

1. Luo, L.: Application of master data management in information construction. Electron. World **2012**(07), 105–109 (2012)
2. Lai, W., Lin, B.: Data fusion for smart grid based on PCA-MP-BP. Microcomput. Appl. **38**(01), 198–201 (2022)
3. Liu, J., Ma, J., Zou, S., et al.: Research on fusion of electric power industry data and external data based on knowledge graph. Sichuan Electr. Power Technol. **43**(06), 26–30+38 (2020). https://doi.org/10.16527/j.cnki.cn51-1315/tm.2020.06.006
4. Mao, X., Wen, Y., Ma, X., et al.: Research and application of multi-source heterogeneous data fusion technology based on power big data. Power Syst. Big Data **23**(08), 33–39 (2020). https://doi.org/10.19317/j.cnki.1008-083x.2020.08.005
5. Wang, Y., Lu, H., Yang, Y., et al.: Data analysis method of grid power consumption based on data fusion algorithm. Energy Conserv. Technol. **39**(02), 153–158 (2021)

6. Zhang, Y., Tang, J., Yang, Z., et al.: COSNET: connecting heterogeneous social networks with local and global consistency. In: ACM SIGKDD International Conference on Knowledge Discovery & Data Mining. ACM (2015)

7. Gongye, X., Lin, P., Ren, W., et al.: A method of extracting subject words based on improved TF-IDF algorithm and co-occurrence words. J. Nanjing Univ. (Nat. Sci.) **53**(06), 1072–1080 (2017)

8. Tang, M., Zhu, L., Zou, X.: Document vector representation based on Word2Vec. Comput. Sci. **43**(06), 214–217+269 (2016)

9. Zang, R., Sun, H., Yang, F., et al.: Text similarity calculation method based on Levenshtein and TFRSF. Comput. Modernization **2018**(04), 84–89 (2018)

10. Sun, Z., Wang, H.: Overview on the advance of the research on named entity recognition. Data Anal. Knowl. Discov. **2010**(06), 42–47 (2010)

11. Li, J., Guo, Y.: Principal component evaluation—A multivariate evaluate method expanded from principal component analysis. J. Ind. Eng. Eng. Manag. **2002**(01), 39–43+3 (2002)

12. He, Q., Li, N., Luo, W., et al.: A survey of machine learning algorithms for big data. Pattern Recogn. Artif. Intell. **27**(04), 327–336 (2014). https://doi.org/10.16451/j.cnki.issn1003-6059.2014.04.009

13. Chen, Z., Liu, J., Li, C., et al.: Ultra short-term power load forecasting based on combined LSTM-XGBoost model. Power Syst. Technol. **44**(02), 614–620 (2020). https://doi.org/10.13335/j.1000-3673.pst.2019.1566

14. Zhang, D.: Research on the prediction of fan blade icing based on LightGBM, XGBoost, ERT hybrid model.Shanghai Normal University (2018)

15. Zhang, X.: Introduction to statistical learning theory and support vector machines. Acta Automatica Sinica **2000**(01), 36–46 (2000). https://doi.org/10.16383/j.aas.2000.01.005

16. Liu, T.: The research and application on BP neural network improvement. Agricultural Mechanization Engineering (2011)

17. Rong, H., Zhang, G., Jin, W., et al.: Selection of kernel functions and parameters for support vector machines in system identification. J. Syst. Simul. **2006**(11), 3204–3208+3226 (2006)

The Effects of Air Pollution and Meteorological Factors in the Transmission and Lethality of COVID-19

Ting Shi[1($\boxtimes$)], Ailin Qi[1], Wu Yang[1], Pengyu Li[1], Chengxu Zhou[2], and Ke Gu[1]

[1] Faculty of Information Technology, Beijing University of Technology,
Beijing 100000, China
tingshi@bjut.edu.cn, s202173076@emails.bjut.edu.cn
[2] School of Electronic and Information Engineering,
Liaoning University of Technology, Jinzhou 121000, China

Abstract. The COVID-19 epidemic continues to have a negative impact on the economy and public health. There is a correlation between certain limits (meteorological factors and air pollution statistics) and verified fatal instances of Corona Virus Disease 2019 (COVID-19), according to several researchers. It has not yet been determined how these elements affect COVID-19. Using air pollution data and meteorological data from 15 cities in India from 2020 to 2022, Convergent Cross Mapping (CCM) is utilized to set up the causal link with new confirmed and fatal cases of COVID-19 in this study. Our experimental results show that the causal order of the factors influencing the diagnosis of COVID-19 is: humidity, PM_{25}, temperature, CO, NO_2, O_3, PM_{10}. In contrast to other parameters, temperature, PM_{25}, and humidity are more causally associated with COVID-19, while data on air pollution are less causally related to the number of new COVID-19 cases. The causal order of the factors affecting the new death toll is as follows: temperature, PM_{25}, humidity, O_3, CO, PM_{10}, NO_2. The causality of temperature with new COVID-19 fatalities in India was higher than the causation of humidity with new COVID-19 deaths, and O_3 also showed higher causality with it.

Keywords: COVID-19 · Air pollution · Causation · Meteorological factors · Convergent cross-mapping

This work was supported in part by the Organization Department of Beijing Municipal Committee under Grant Z2020549, in part by the National Science Foundation of China under Grant 62273011 and Grant 62076013; in part by the Ministry of Education of China under Grant 202102341001, 202102165002, 202102535002, Grant 202102535012; in part by the Beijing Natural Science Foundation under Grant JQ21014; in part by the Industry-University-Research Innovation Fund for Chinese University - Blue Point Distributed Intelligent Computing Project under 2021LDA03003; in part by the Key Laboratory of Intelligent Control and Optimization for Industrial Equipment of Ministry of Education, Dalian University of Technology under Grant LICO2022TB03.

G. Zhai et al. (Eds.): IFTC 2022, CCIS 1766, pp. 465–477, 2023.
https://doi.org/10.1007/978-981-99-0856-1_34

1   Introduction

In addition to causing public health problems, epidemics also have a devastating impact on the socio-economic structure of countries. Recent pandemics have plagued human society, causing hundreds of millions of deaths, diseases and expenditures. At the end of 2019, the new epidemic of COVID-19 threatened the earth. Despite the efforts of the Chinese government to isolate Wuhan from other regions, the epidemic is still widespread, and the World Health Organization has declared it a global pandemic [1]. As of October 21, 2022 Central European Time, there are 62383894 confirmed cases globally, 294250 more than the previous day, and 6553936 deaths. Therefore, in order to combat the epidemic, scientists are investigating relevant factors, including environmental factors such as weather and air pollution (Fig. 1).

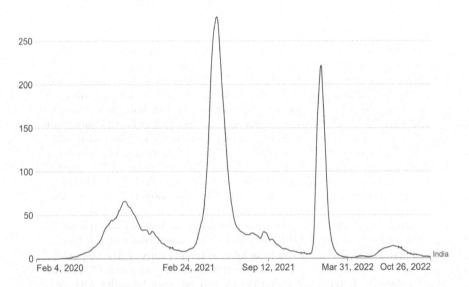

Fig. 1. Daily new confirmed COVID-19 cases per million people in India - image extracted from https://ourworldindata.org/.

The COVID-19 pandemic and air pollution have been connected in multiple epidemiological investigations [2]. To solve the problem of air pollution, Gu et al. proposed a new air quality predictor to infer air quality [3]. Some researchers also used temperature as an additional weather factor to study the correlation between new daily cases and new deaths. For instance, Kampf et al. investigated the duration of coronavirus survival on various surfaces. According to their findings, the novel coronavirus can survive for 9 days, depending on the surface of the substance and the ambient temperature [4]. The majority of studies on humidity is related to temperature. Chan et al. studied the effect of temperature and humidity on SARS (Severe Acute Respiratory Syndromes), another coronavirus. It is found that when the temperature rises, the ability of the virus to survive on the surface will be shortened, leading to a decline in the transmission ability [5].

However, Bashir's [6] survey showed that the prevalence of COVID-19 was negatively correlated with the concentration of $PM_{2.5}$. According to Zhu's research, these two factors have a positive association [7]. From January 25 to April 7, 2020, in Wuhan, China, Pearson and Poisson regression models were used to test the relationship between COVID-19 mortality and many risk factors. According to this study, $PM_{2.5}$ is the only pollutant that is positively related to the mortality of COVID-19. Gu et al. estimated the concentration of $PM_{2.5}$ in the atmosphere in real time by designing a variety of image-based $PM_{2.5}$ prediction models and monitors [8–11]. Some of the relationships found by using correlation analysis may still need to be supported by other elements, so the correlation tests conducted by Spearman and Kendall may not yield reliable evidence. It is very challenging to draw the conclusion of a single standard, because the research on the influencing factors of COVID-19 uses different standards for its observation unit, research period and the assessed exposure time of air pollution. In order to influence the results, many studies usually include additional risk factors or potential confounding factors in the statistical model. To obtain an accurate prediction of $PM_{2.5}$ concentration, Gu et al. designed a variety of model networks based on image quality assessment [12–14]. In contrast, CCM does not require any prior knowledge and is suitable for non separable systems with weak to medium coupling strength. CCM can effectively identify the interference of confounding factors and extract the true causal relationship.

In this study, a causal analysis of meteorological factors and air quality on the number of deaths and confirmed cases of neocrown pneumonia under the optimal embedding dimension was performed using the CCM technique. Using the CCM analysis, causal coefficients for air quality, climatic factors, and the number of New Coronary Pneumonia infections and deaths were calculated separately for different cities and ranked using standardized criteria to draw general conclusions. India does not have the same extensive urban closure policy as China, which makes it easier to study the transmission pattern of New Coronary Pneumonia in its natural environment. Studying the Indian New Coronary Pneumonia epidemic will help China to develop an outbreak prevention and control strategy, as both countries have large populations. Reduce air pollution to help the COVID-19 pandemic's effects be lessened. Research on the connection to human health is essential. It could limit the spread of pandemic viruses and diseases in the future. The remainder of this paper will be organized as follows: First, we will introduce the database and methods in Sect. 2. Then, the experimental results are given in Sect. 3. Finally, we conclude the study in Sect. 4.

2   Materials and Methods

2.1   Database

The dataset provided by the World Air Quality Index Project (WAQI) contains air quality datasets from more than 130 countries, covering 2,000 major cities, and is updated three times a day from January 2020. The dataset contains minimum, maximum, median and standard deviation values for each air pollutant CO, NO_2, O_3, SO_2, PM_{10}, PM_{25}; and meteorological data including humidity and temperature [15].

The data from January 1, 2020 to December 31, 2021 is chosen from the COVID-19 dataset on the Google Cloud platform, which includes the number of newly confirmed cases and newly added deaths per day. This data set was gathered directly from several national governments. The upstream data, which includes the data on administrative regions and cities from different countries, is maintained by the Center for Systems Science and Engineering (CSSE) at Johns Hopkins University. The data set is separated into data files for each nation by cutting and dicing it [16].

2.2   Data Processing

The final database for this project consists of three sections: data on pollutant concentrations, climate variables, and COVID-19 information. There are two steps in the processing of the data for pollutant concentrations and climate variables. In the first part, annual averages of these two types of data were calculated for each city for a simple and efficient denoising process to facilitate subsequent analysis of the experimental results, which were already in tabular form and did not require specific preprocessing or coordination techniques. The information from COVID-19 is processed in parallel with the second stage of the process.

Finally, a new overall data platter is created by matching the same dates between the daily averages of pollution concentrations and climate variables for each city and the corresponding daily additions and deaths from COVID-19. After removing duplicate data, cities with more missing information are eliminated, cities with less missing information are interpolated, and the interpolated data are then replaced with the median of the data before and after the missing information.

2.3   The Principle of Convergent Cross-Mapping

The Convergent Cross Mapping (CCM) method was put forth by Sugihara in 2012, and received a lot of interest from academics both domestically and internationally [17]. This approach examines the nonlinear causal relationship between two systems based on the reconstruction of nonlinear state space. The causal connection between the systems can be found by examining the correlation between the system X and system Y reconstructed manifolds.

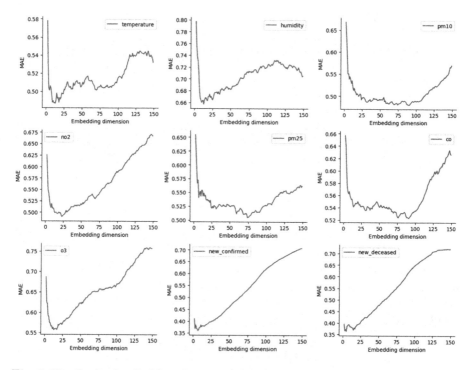

Fig. 2. The Optimal embedding dimension calculation result graph. It can be seen that the embedding dimension E has been iterated to the minimum value of MAE, so it can be taken as the optimal embedding dimension.

Assume that the two time series created by the projection of system M on one-dimensional space are $X(t)$ and $Y(t)$. Let the delay time be τ, the embedding dimension of the rebuilt manifold be E for the time series $X(t)$ and $Y(t)$, and the reconstructed state space be

$$X(t) = [X(t), X(t - \tau), \ldots, X(t - (E - 1)\tau)] \tag{1}$$

$$Y(t) = [Y(t), Y(t - \tau), \ldots, Y(t - (E - 1)\tau)] \tag{2}$$

The state-space reconstruction theory states that system M, reconstruction manifolds X and Y are diffeomorphic. Find the E nearest neighbors of the sample $X(i)$ in the system X, $X(i,k) = X(i,1), X(i,2), \ldots, X(i,E)$, and set it is mapped to the manifold Y, the corresponding sample point is $Y(i,k)$, and the estimated value of $Y(i)$ is calculated (Table 1)

$$\hat{Y}(i) = \sum_{k=1}^{E} w_k Y(i,k) \tag{3}$$

$$u_k = \exp\left(-\frac{\|X(i) - X(i,k)\|}{\|X(i) - X(i,1)\|}\right) \tag{4}$$

Table 1. Correlations between COVID-19 and factors

Environmental variables	Pearson (new cases)	Pearson (new deaths)	CCM (new cases)	CCM (new deaths)
Temperature	0.2	0.25	0.26897	0.28752
Humidity	−0.43	−0.38	0.57611	0.57675
PM_{10}	0.08	−0.01	0.1793	0.19075
PM_{25}	0.02	−0.05	0.27462	0.31491
CO	−0.02	−0.1	0.40214	0.44533
NO_2	0.02	−0.03	0.28338	0.31717
O_3	0.19	0.27	0.41555	0.50839

$$w_k = \frac{u_k}{\sum_{k=1}^{E} u_k} \tag{5}$$

$\|\cdot\|$ represents the Euclidean distance between samples. Define $\hat{Y}(i)$ as the cross mapping of $Y(i)$ from manifold X to Y, and calculate the correlation coefficient between $\hat{Y}(i)$ and $Y(i)$. And the formula for calculating the correlation coefficient is

$$r = \frac{\sum_{i=1}^{L}(Y(i) - \bar{Y}(i))(\hat{Y}(i) - \overline{\hat{Y}(i)})}{\sqrt{\sum_{i=1}^{L}(Y(i) - \bar{Y}(i))^2 \sum_{i=1}^{L}(\hat{Y}(i) - \overline{\hat{Y}(i)})^2}} \tag{6}$$

As the sample length L increases, $\hat{Y}(i)$ gradually converges to $Y(i)$, and finally the correlation coefficient converges to [0, 1], indicating that there is a causal relationship from system Y and system X.

To assess the association between novel coronavirus pneumonia and environmental conditions, we used standard correlation measures. For such nonlinear systems with weakly coupled interactions, correlation analysis is subject to some limitations. We can now identify causes of death and confirmed cases of novel coronavirus pneumonia, but exclude some unintegrated environmental factors. Table 2 compares the CCM and correlation coefficients. The correlation coefficient method is more suitable than the CCM method for non-separated systems with weak to moderate coupling strength, because the correlation coefficient method uses relatively small values and is therefore more likely to lead to inaccurate calculations.

3   Experiments and Results

3.1   Experiments

To determine the optimal embedding dimension for each array, the new confirmed and dead cases of COVID-19, CO, NO2, O3, PM10, PM25, temperature and humidity are first normalized for each city.

Table 2. The value of optimal E

	E	MAE
Temperature	13.0	0.486910
Humidity	13.0	0.657316
PM_{10}	90.0	0.479957
PM_{25}	74.0	0.504740
CO	91.0	0.523057
NO_2	23.0	0.490265
O_3	13.0	0.556216
New cases	7.0	0.359420
New deaths	5.0	0.363500

Next, the optimal embedding dimension corresponding to each type of dataset is calculated separately. Using Delhi, India as an example, the optimal embedding size for each type of data is shown in Fig. 2. The optimal embedding dimension allows the attractor to expand sufficiently to characterize the behavior of the original dynamic system without adding unnecessary computation.

The choice of the embedding dimension E of the manifold is crucial because the CCM method is based on the state-space reconstruction of the time-lag embedding of the attractor manifold. For each point under a particular dimension E, the E+1 nearest neighbor points and the corresponding weights are calculated, and then the value of the point is predicted and the difference between the predicted and the actual value is calculated. This process is repeated for a different embedding dimension E. The best embedding dimension for this set of data is the value of E corresponding to the smallest of these errors. To determine the best value of E, different embedding dimensions were included in the experiment using univariate simplex projections, and the mean absolute error (MAE) was used as the measurement variable to assess the predictability of the sample. The optimal E value should be examined between 1 and 365 because our data set comes from a once-per-day measurement (356 points per year), but for computational reasons, most of the data were able to iterate to the minimum value within 150. The selection range of the best E is 1–150.

Then, the causal relationships between each dataset were determined by calculating the CCM for CO, NO_2, O_3, PM_{10}, PM_{25}, temperature, humidity, and COVID-19 for new diagnoses and fatalities using the optimal embedding dimension. Finally, by excluding some cities without convergent relationships and rating the results of the convergent interactions for the remaining cities, we can obtain a causal ranking of the factors affecting COVID-19 deaths and confirmed cases. Figure 3 shows the CCM diagram of Delhi as an example.

3.2   Results

We can now determine the causes of the deaths and confirmed cases of the COVID-19, excluding some environmental elements that did not converge.

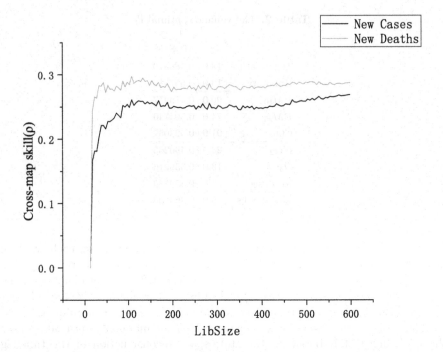

Fig. 3. The CCM graphic was created using the example of the correlation between temperature and new COVID-19 cases in Delhi. The graph's strong convergence trend, which denotes a consistent causal link between temperature and new COVID-19 instances, is visible.

An interval plot was created after the causation of CO, NO_2, O_3, PM_{10}, PM_{25}, temperature, humidity, and COVID-19 newly diagnosed cases and deaths in 15 cities was combined. Figure 4 displays the order of causality between several factors and newly confirmed COVID-19 cases in 15 Indian cities. Temperature, humidity, and PM_{25} all have quite high causalities while other pollutants have relatively low causalities. The pattern of the number of diagnoses and the factors in Fig. 5 is essentially in accordance with the trajectory of the causation of the number of fatalities and the influencing factors. However, due to the involvement of many medical care conditions, etc., the causality of the number of fatalities with regard to the factors is lower than that of the diagnoses with respect to the factors.

After calculating the annual mean of each factor for each city and the causal relationship between each factor and its corresponding factor, scatter plots were drawn. The points in the plot were then fitted linearly, and the following findings were reached. The causality of temperature, NO_2, and CO with new confirmed diagnoses increased with increasing annual mean temperature and concentration, but the causality of these factors with new deaths decreased, as shown in Fig. 6 below. Temperature and the dissemination of COVID-19 had a strong correlation, according to a case study in Brazil [18]. The majority of Brazilian

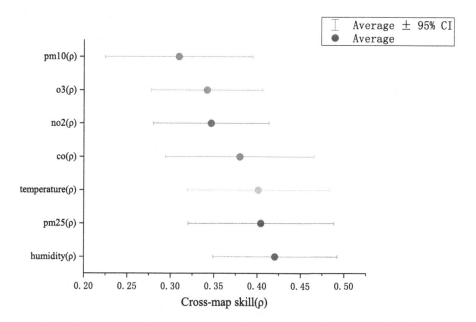

Fig. 4. Pollutants like CO and NO_2 have a relatively low causation compared to pollutants like humidity, PM_{25}, and temperature.

cities have shown that COVID-19 is spreading favorably in the tropical climate. Second, secondary reactions of aerosols with gaseous pollutants are enhanced at lower temperatures and higher relative humidity conditions, which increase the hazard of aerosols. First, exposure to high levels of gaseous pollutants can lead to airway inflammation, which can affect lung function and respiratory symptoms.

With new confirmed diagnoses and deaths, the causation of PM_{10} and PM_{25} decreased with concentration. Using Spearman and Kendall correlation tests, the relationship between air quality indicators and COVID-19 cases in California was examined [19]. The results showed that only the synergistic effect of CO was positively associated with COVID-19, and environmental pollutants, such as mass concentrations of PM10 and $PM_{2.5}$, SO_2, were negatively associated with the prevalence of COVID-19. This agrees with the findings of the Wuhan study that was previously highlighted.

With new confirmed illnesses and more deaths, the causation of humidity and O3 grew as concentrations rose. Copat et al. evaluated research examining the part that PM and NO_2 play in the spread and fatality of neocrown pneumonia [20]. The major conclusions emphasize the critical roles played by $PM_{2.5}$ and NO_2 in initiating the spread and fatality of neocrown pneumonia. However, more research is needed to determine whether pollutants like polycyclic aromatic hydrocarbons (PAHs) or volatile organic compounds (VOCs), which are typically released by dangerous industrial sites, have an effect on the severity and spread of neocrown pneumonia.

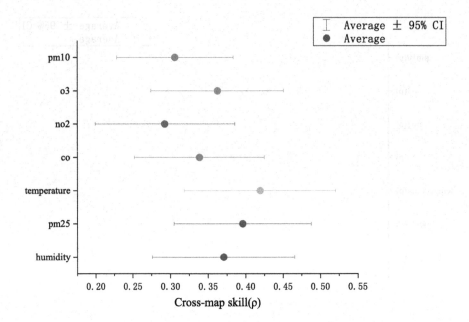

Fig. 5. Temperature, humidity, and PM_{25} all have quite high causalities while CO and NO_2 pollutants have relatively low causalities.

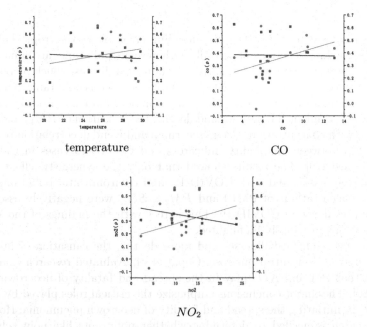

Fig. 6. The black line corresponds to the fit to the black dots, while the red color corresponds to the red color. The black dots show the causality of new verified diagnoses, while the red color reflects the causality of new fatalities. (Color figure online)

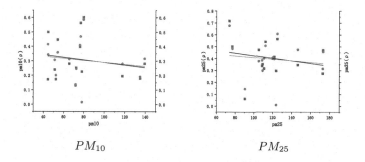

PM_{10} PM_{25}

Fig. 7. The black line corresponds to the fit to the black dots, while the red color corresponds to the red color. The black dots show the causality of new verified diagnoses, while the red color reflects the causality of new fatalities. (Color figure online)

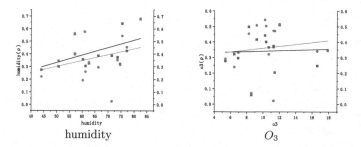

humidity O_3

Fig. 8. The black line corresponds to the fit to the black dots, while the red color corresponds to the red color. The black dots show the causality of new verified diagnoses, while the red color reflects the causality of new fatalities. (Color figure online)

4   Conclusion

Humidity, PM_{25}, and temperature had a stronger impact than other influencing elements, according to a research of the causal association between meteorological parameters and air quality, as well as the number of new instances of new coronary pneumonia and new deaths per day in 15 Indian cities in 2020–2022.

This study has several limitations. First, individual-level exposure to meteorological environment or air pollution is difficult to obtain and quantify. The results of the study are presented at the population level, which may lead to the ecological fallacy of inferring the situation of a particular individual based on the analysis of data from the population to which a particular individual belongs. However, given the current urgency of understanding novel coronaviruses, ecological studies are a necessary and valuable tool. Second, since COVID-19 is caused by the SARS CoV-2 virus, additional factors such as viral resistance, population mobility, population immunization levels, public interventions, and medical resources need to be investigated as well. Notably, public health interventions implemented by the government, such as traffic restrictions, social diversion measures, household isolation and centralized isolation, extensive health education, and strict measures in public places, also played an important role in mitigating the spread of COVID-19 (Figs. 7 and 8).

Overall, this study suggests that meteorological factors, air pollutants may influence the spread of COVID-19, varying between provinces. Nevertheless, we emphasize the need for further studies on the transmissibility of COVID-19 and its relationship with meteorological factors and air pollutants. For future work, some of the main factors influencing neocrown pneumonia can be used to create predictive models and guide future research efforts. A thorough causal analysis by sub-season can also be performed based on specific time series.

References

1. Covid-19 dataset. https://github.com/datasets/covid-19. Accessed 10 Oct 2022
2. World air quality index project. https://aqicn.org/data-platform/covid19/. Accessed 10 Mar 2021
3. Gu, K., Qiao, J., Lin, W.: Recurrent air quality predictor based on meteorology- and pollution-related factors. IEEE Trans. Industr. Inform. **14**(9), 3946–3955 (2018)
4. Auler, A., Cássaro, F., Silva, V.D., Pires, L.: Evidence that high temperatures and intermediate relative humidity might favor the spread of COVID-19 in tropical climate: A case study for the most affected Brazilian cities. Sci. Total Environ. **729**, 139090 (2020)
5. Bashir, M.F., et al.: Correlation between environmental pollution indicators and COVID-19 pandemic: a brief study in Californian context. Environ. Res. **187**, 109652 (2020)
6. Bashir, M.F., Ma, B., Komal, B., Bashir, M.A., Tan, D., Bashir, M.: Correlation between climate indicators and COVID-19 pandemic in New York, USA. Sci. Total Environ. **728**, 138835 (2020)
7. Chan, K.H., Peiris, J.M., Lam, S., Poon, L., Yuen, K., Seto, W.H.: The effects of temperature and relative humidity on the viability of the SARS coronavirus. Adv. Virol. (2011)
8. Copat, C., et al.: The role of air pollution (PM and NO2) in COVID-19 spread and lethality: a systematic review. Environ. Res. **191**, 110129 (2020)
9. Gu, K., Qiao, J., Li, X.: Highly efficient picture-based prediction of $PM_{2.5}$ concentration. IEEE Trans. Ind. Electron. **66**(4), 3176–3184 (2019)
10. Gu, K., Xia, Z., Qiao, J.: Stacked selective ensemble for $PM_{2.5}$ forecast. IEEE Trans. Instrum. Meas. **69**(3), 660–671 (2020)
11. Gu, K., Liu, H., Xia, Z., Qiao, J., Lin, W., Thalmann, D.: $PM_{2.5}$ monitoring: use information abundance measurement and wide and deep learning. IEEE Trans. Neural Netw. Learn. Syst. **32**(10), 4278–4290 (2021)
12. Yue, G., Gu, K., Qiao, J.: Effective and efficient photo-based $PM_{2.5}$ concentration estimation. IEEE Trans. Instrum. Meas. **68**(10), 3962–3971 (2019)
13. Gu, K., Wang, S., Zhai, G., Ma, S., Lin, W.: Screen image quality assessment incorporating structural degradation measurement. In: Proceedings of the IEEE International Symposium on Circuits and Systems, pp. 125–128 (2015)
14. Yue, G., Hou, C., Gu, K., Zhou, T., Zhai, G.: Combining local and global measures for DIBR-synthesized image quality evaluation. IEEE Trans. Image Process. **28**(4), 2075–2088 (2019)

15. Gu, K., Zhai, G., Yang, X., Zhang, W.: Deep learning network for blind image quality assessment. In: Proceedings IEEE International Conference on Image Processing, pp. 511–515 (2014)

16. Angelis, E.D., et al.: COVID-19 incidence and mortality in Lombardy, Italy: an ecological study on the role of air pollution, meteorological factors, demographic and socioeconomic variables. Environ. Res. **195**, 110777 (2021)

17. Kampf, G., Todt, D., Pfaender, S., Steinmann, E.: Persistence of coronaviruses on inanimate surfaces and their inactivation with biocidal agents. J. Hosp. Infect. **104**(3), 246–251 (2020)

18. Stieb, D.M., Evans, G.J., To, T.M., Brook, J.R., Burnett, R.T.: An ecological analysis of long-term exposure to PM2. 5 and incidence of COVID-19 in Canadian health regions. Environ. Res. **191**, 110052 (2020)

19. Sugihara, G., et al.: Detecting causality in complex ecosystems. Science **338**(6106), 496–500 (2012)

20. Zhu, Y., Xie, J., Huang, F., Cao, L.: Association between short-term exposure to air pollution and COVID-19 infection: evidence from china. Sci. Total Environ. **727**, 138704 (2020)

A Defect Detection Method for Small Fittings of Power Transmission Based on Improved SLIC

Zhenyu Chen[1]([✉]), Lutao Wang[1], Siyu Chen[1], Junda Ren[1], and Meng Xue[2]

[1] Big Data Center, State Grid Corporation of China, Beijing, China
czy9907@163.com
[2] Anhui Jiyuan Software Co., Ltd., Hefei, Anhui, China

Abstract. There are a large number of small-sized hardware such as nuts, washers and pins in power transmission equipment. The inspection image of power transmission has high resolution and large image size, which makes it difficult to detect defects distributed on such small-sized hardware. This is a major pain point in transmission line inspections. In response to this pain point, Ontology researches a defect detection model for small power transmission fittings based on improved SLIC (Simple Linear Iterative Clustering) and ViT (Vision Transformer). First, the improved SLIC is used to perform superpixel segmentation and clustering on the image, highlighting the position of small fittings in the entire image, and then using the visual Transformer deep learning network trains and learns the inspection images collected by drones at the power transmission inspection site, and obtains a model capable of stably and accurately identifying the defects of small power transmission fittings. The experimental results show that the method proposed in this paper can efficiently identify the defects of small power transmission fittings under the premise of ensuring stability, with an average recognition accuracy rate of 89.2%, which has high practicability and improves the detection and identification ability of small fittings defects.

Keywords: Power transmission · Small size fittings · Improve SLIC · Vision Transformer

1 Introduction

With the increase of domestic transmission lines, the line operation and maintenance environment are diverse and complex, and the requirements for the operation and maintenance of transmission lines are becoming more and more strict. The traditional manual inspection method has many limitations, resulting in low inspection efficiency and inspection costs. If it is too high, it cannot effectively guarantee the safe operation of the power grid [1, 2]. In recent years, unmanned aerial vehicle (UAV) has been widely used in transmission line inspection, which makes up for the deficiency of manual inspection method [3]. However, a large number of inspection images captured by drones still need to be reviewed manually. This front-line inspection team brings greater work pressure and cost, and artificial intelligence technology can solve this problem. In the process of

(a) Nuts are not properly installed

(b) Missing nuts

(c) Missing pins

(d) Pins out

(e) Rust

Fig. 1. Examples of five types of small-size fittings defects

inspection of transmission lines, there are a large number of small hardware [4], including bolts, nuts, pins and gaskets. The current target detection technology is often difficult to detect such small hardware, and the recognition rate is not high [5, 6]. Small hardware defects are shown in the Fig. 1.

2 Related Works

At present, there are few researches on the defect identification of small power transmission fittings. The paper [7] proposes to use the hierarchical model "AND-OR" to detect the defects of missing pins. Compared with the traditional image recognition algorithm, the algorithm is improved, but it cannot meet the detection needs in the actual inspection process. In [8], the algorithm based on RetinaNet is proposed to detect missing pins and loose pins. The detection speed of this method has been greatly improved, but the accuracy needs to be further improved.

For the detection of transmission line defects, researchers generally use the target detection algorithm based on deep learning. A large number of statistics show that the defect recognition algorithm based on geometric features has better detection effect on large target defects such as towers and large fittings, and the MAP can reach 80%. The above, while the recognition rate of small hardware defects is low, and the detection speed is slow, the false detection rate is high, and the false detection rate even exceeds 50%.

Then, superpixel generation algorithms can be roughly divided into two categories: superpixel algorithms based on graph theory and superpixel algorithms based on gradient ascent [9]. The core idea of the former is to take the generation method of superpixels as a point in the graph, the line between the two points as the weight, then respectively weighted the two points, and finally generate all the superpixels by minimizing the cost function. Such as the Graph-based method proposed by Felzenswalb et al. [10]; while the superpixel algorithm based on the gradient ascent method first performs simple clustering of pixels, and then through continuous iterative clustering, finally generates a superpixel, such as the well-known SLIC (Simple Linear Iterative Clustering) method proposed by Achanta et al. [11]. The representative algorithms of superpixels include NC algorithm, GS algorithm, SL algorithm, GCa and GCb algorithm, MS algorithm, QS algorithm, WS algorithm, TP algorithm and SLIC algorithm [12]. In [11], it is proved that the segmentation shape of SLIC superpixels is gentler, the boundary attachment rate is higher, and the speed is faster.

Additionally, in the year of 2017, Vaswani et al. [13] first proposed Transformer to build a new encoder-decoder architecture based on multi-head self-attention mechanism and feedforward neural network, which can easily solve sequence-to-sequence natural language tasks. Inspired by the Transformer in NLP, researchers have introduced Transformer into the CV field in recent years. Wu et al. [14] adopted ResNet as a baseline and used convolutional layers to extract image features, which were then fed into Vision Transformer. Previously, researchers introduced Transformer into the CV field, all using CNN network for feature extraction, while Dosovitskiy et al. proposed a ViT [15], which is a complete Transformer, when directly applied to image patch sequences, the performance of image classification tasks superior. In addition, the constructed detector is able to reduce certain computing time and improve the detection efficiency, and the training process is greatly simplified due to the unique advantage of the deep learning method [16–19].

From the perspective of practicality, this paper considers the relationship between small fittings and components, and improves the SLIC algorithm to highlight the larger parts from the original inspection pictures, and then builds five types of small fitting defect models, and then use this type of parts. Visual Transformer is used to detect small hardware defects. The detection process is shown in the Fig. 2.

Fig. 2. Small fittings defect detection process

3 Defect Detection of Small Fittings Based on Improved SLIC Algorithm and ViT

3.1 Laplace Sharpening

In order to improve the edge detection ability of SLIC, Laplacian sharpening is used to enhance image edge details before SLIC superpixel segmentation. The Laplacian sharpening of the image is a method of using the Laplacian operator to enhance the edge of the image.

The Laplacian operator is based on the calculation of the pixel grayscale in the image neighborhood, and is derived through the second-order differential. An image neighborhood enhancement algorithm. The basic idea is: when the gray level of the central pixel in the neighborhood is lower than the average gray level of other pixels in its neighborhood, the gray level of this central pixel should be further reduced. When the gray level of the central pixel in the neighborhood is higher than the average gray level of other pixels in its neighborhood, the gray level of this central pixel should be further improved.

The Laplacian mask center coefficient is:

$$\nabla^2 f = 4f(x, y) - f(x - 1, y) - f(x, y + 1) \\ -f(x + 1, y) - f(x, y - 1) \tag{1}$$

This results in a Laplace-sharpened four-direction template matrix:

$$\begin{pmatrix} 0 & -1 & 0 \\ -1 & 4 & -1 \\ 0 & -1 & 0 \end{pmatrix} \tag{2}$$

In the same way, the representation of the eight-neighborhood is:

$$\nabla^2 f = 8f(x, y) - f(x - 1, y - 1) - f(x - 1, y) \\ -f(x - 1, y + 1) - f(x, y - 1) - f(x, y + 1) \\ -f(x + 1, y - 1) - f(x + 1, y) - f(x + 1, y + 1) \tag{3}$$

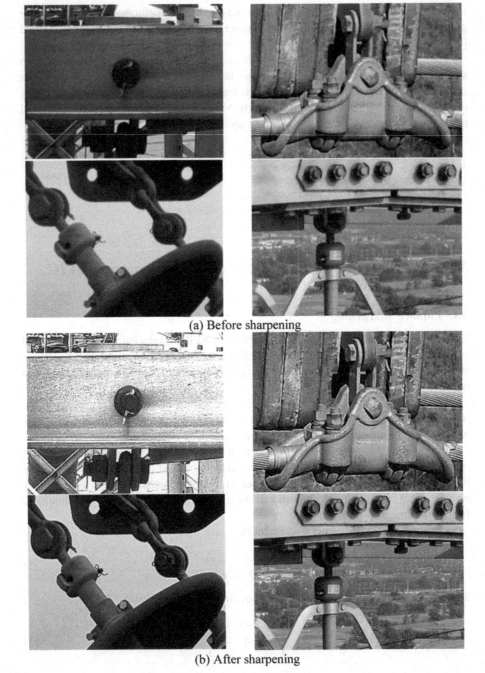

(a) Before sharpening

(b) After sharpening

Fig. 3. Laplace sharpening map comparison

This results in a Laplace-sharpened eight-direction template matrix:

$$\begin{pmatrix} -1 & -1 & -1 \\ -1 & 8 & -1 \\ -1 & -1 & -1 \end{pmatrix} \tag{4}$$

It can be concluded from the above two template matrices that if there is a white point in a 3 × 3 plane, and its neighbors are all black, then the template matrix can increase the brightness of the white point.

Convolve the template matrix with the power transmission inspection image, and use the following formula to update the pixel value of the original image:

$$g(x) = \begin{cases} f(x, y) - \nabla^2 f(x, y) & \nabla^2 f(x, y) < 0 \\ f(x, y) + \nabla^2 f(x, y) & \nabla^2 f(x, y) \geq 0 \end{cases} \tag{5}$$

Using the above formula to replace the pixel value of the original (x, y) with the calculated value, the sharpened image can be obtained. Figure 3 is the image after sharpening.

3.2 SLIC Superpixel Segmentation

The SLIC algorithm was proposed by Achanta et al. It is an algorithm with simple ideas, convenient implementation and fast calculation speed. Use this for superpixel segmentation. The algorithm first converts the color image to a 5-dimensional feature vector in the CIELAB color space and XY coordinates, then constructs a metric for the vector, and performs local clustering on the pixels of the inspection image. SLIC follows the following formula:

$$d = d_{lab} + \frac{m}{S} d_{xy} \tag{6}$$

Table 1. SLIC superpixel segmentation process

SLIC algorithm	Steps
1	Initialize, divide the regular grid according to the image size, and initialize the cluster center
2	Move the cluster center to the minimum gradient point in the $n \times n$ neighborhood
3	Assign a cluster label to each pixel according to the distance metric
4	Update the cluster center, calculate the new cluster center and error *Error*; until *Error* ≤ threshold
5	Iterative optimization
6	Enhance connectivity

For each pixel in the neighborhood of the inspection image cluster center, the color feature distance from the cluster center is:

$$d_{lab} = \sqrt{(l_k - l_i)^2 + (a_k - a_i)^2 + (b_k - b_i)^2} \tag{7}$$

Spatial feature distance between each pixel and the cluster center

$$d_{xy} = \sqrt{(x_k - x_i)^2 + (y_k - y_i)^2} \tag{8}$$

In the above formula, d is the distance from the pixel to the cluster center, m is the spatial distance influence factor, and S is the distance between the cluster centers.

The following SLIC segmentation steps are shown in Table 1, and the segmentation results of SLIC inspection images are shown in Fig. 4.

Fig. 4. Superpixel segmentation results

It can be seen from the figure that the edge of the part containing the small hardware can be well described through SLIC, which is beneficial to determine the position of the part, improve the detection of the small hardware, and reduce the false alarm rate.

3.3 Defect Detection of Small Fittings Based on ViT

The traditional Transformer is mainly composed of two parts: encoding and decoding. The multi-head attention mechanism is the core of the Transformer, which enables the model to remember the key information in the picture like human visual attention. Transformer uses an encoder-decoder structure, which consists of multiple layers of encoder layers and decoder layers. The encoder has two sublayers: the self-attention layer is followed by a position feedforward layer. The decoder has three sublayers: self-attention followed by an encoder-decoder attention layer, followed by a position feedforward layer. Each sublayer uses residual connections after layer normalization. The decoder uses a mask in its self-attention to prevent a given output location, gaining information about future output locations during training.

This paper builds a detection model for small fittings based on the ViT-FRCNN model [20]. The model first divides the inspection image into N sub-graphs, which will be arranged in order and converted into serialized data, similar to each word in a sentence in NLP, and then the serialized data is input into the ViT network, and processed by location After encoding, it is input to the encoder module, and the output is reassembled into a feature map, and then the feature map is input into the detection network containing the RPN module for category prediction and location prediction. The entire small fitting defect detection model is divided into three parts. The backbone network extracts image features, the encoder-decoder performs information fusion, and the feedforward network performs prediction. As shown in the figure below, the backbone network is used to learn to extract the features of the original image (Fig. 5).

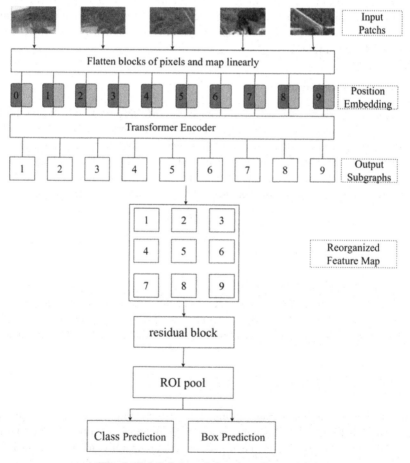

Fig. 5. Small fittings defect detection model

4 Experiment

4.1 Software and Hardware

The experimental setups of this paper are: Centos 6, 64-bit operating system, TensorFlow framework. Server, NVIDIA TESLA V100, video memory is 16 GB; E5-2680 V4 CPU processor, maximum frequency 3.30 GHz, disk capacity 500 GB, configuration CUDA10.1, cuDNN7.6 deep neural network acceleration library, deep learning framework using PyTorch.

4.2 Experimental Data

The original data set in this paper is transmission line inspection images, with a total of 4,000 image data of power transmission business scenarios, of which small hardware defects account for 80% of the total sample. This paper randomly selects about 4% of the 400 images from these 4000 images as the final test data, and the remaining 4600 images are used as the training dataset. In the model training stage, data enhancement processing such as rotation, flipping, and brightness adjustment is performed on the samples of the training set.

4.3 Evaluation Indicators

According to experience, the IoU in this paper is uniformly set to 0.3. When the IoU is set to 0.3, the precision (P), recall (R) and average accuracy (AP) of the model are calculated. The precision rate measures the false positives output by the model, the recall rate measures the practical level of the model, and the average accuracy rate can measure the comprehensive performance of the model. The calculation method of AP value refers to the calculation method of Everingham et al. The formula is as follows:

$$P = \frac{TP}{TP + FP} \tag{9}$$

$$R = \frac{TP}{TP + FN} \tag{10}$$

In the above formula, TP (True Position) is a positive sample that is predicted as a positive sample, FP (False Position) is a negative sample that is predicted to be a positive sample, and FN (False Negative) is a positive sample that is predicted to be a negative sample.

4.4 Experiment

In order to measure the performance of the defect detection model of small fittings based on improved SLIC and ViT, this paper conducts comparative experiments based on the self-built data set of transmission line inspection. The comparative models include Faster-RCNN and traditional Transformer. In the SLIC algorithm, we take the fixed constant $m = 10$ to replace the maximum space distance in the class. In transformer algorithm, since all images are of high resolution, the number of image blocks $N = 30$ should be adjusted. After the model training is completed, 400 test images are used. Three models are tested, the precision rates of the three models are shown in Table 2 below, the recall rates are shown in Table 3 below, and the average accuracy AP is shown in Table 4. It can be seen from Table 2, Table 3 and Table 4 that the three indicators of Faster-RCNN and Transformer are relatively close, and the method in this paper is better than these two methods, and the indicators are significantly improved. Table 5 shows the calculation time of each type of model. Table 5 shows the calculation time of each type of model. From the data in Table 5, we can see that our method is faster than Faster-RCNN and Transformer.

Table 2. Precision of small fitting defect model. Unit: %

Classes	Improper nuts installation	Missing nuts	Missing pins	Pins out	Rust
Faster-RCNN	73.1	80.4	78.5	77.5	76.2
Transformer	74.3	82.7	79.6	79.9	78.7
Our method	82.6	87.8	85.3	84.7	82.9

Table 3. Recall of small fitting defect model. Unit: %

Classes	Improper nuts installation	Missing nuts	Missing pins	Pins out	Rust
Faster-RCNN	80.1	93.6	92.1	86.5	82.7
Transformer	78.2	92.5	93.8	89.9	84.3
Our method	85.8	94.8	96.6	90.2	84.4

Table 4. Average accuracy of small fitting defect model. Unit: %

Classes	Improper nuts installation	Missing nuts	Missing pins	Pins out	Rust
Faster-RCNN	82.8	86.6	85.9	80.7	87.1
Transformer	83.3	85.2	84.6	84.1	89.3
Our method	86.5	89.8	88.2	87.9	93.7

4.5 Analysis of Detection Effect

The sample set used in this paper contains the original inspection images in various scenarios, and the quality characteristics of the images are also different. The following picture shows the defect recognition results of small fittings. It can be seen that the detection method of small fittings based on improved SLIC and ViT power transmission

Table 5. Mean computation time of small fitting defect model. Unit: s

Classes	Improper nuts installation	Missing nuts	Missing pins	Pins out	Rust
Faster-RCNN	4.2	4.17	5.35	5.31	5.33
Transformer	5.22	5.3	5.42	5.43	5.38
Our method	3.92	3.86	4.46	4.58	4.94

can effectively detect the defect area from the original inspection picture, and it still performs well in the case of large scenes and small targets. In the process of model training and detection, the enhancement processing of image sharpening is added, which optimizes the problems of low shooting quality and blurred pictures in some scenes, and further improves the detection accuracy of the model (Fig. 6).

Fig. 6. Results of small fitting defect recognition

5   Conclusions

Aiming at the problem of small defect targets and many types of defects in the UAV power transmission inspection images, which leads to the low detection accuracy of the model, this paper proposes a defect detection method for small power transmission fittings based on improved SLIC and ViT. First of all, the improved SLIC algorithm is used to sharpen and super-resolution the parts containing small hardware. While improving the texture features of the small hardware, the super-resolution segmentation of the parts is carried out to highlight the part area and reduce the detection range of the small hardware, and then use the ViT-FRCNN recognition model to build a small fitting defect recognition model to detect the small fittings. Experiments show that the average recognition accuracy of the defect detection method for small power transmission fittings based on improved SLIC and ViT is 89.2%, which further verifies the effectiveness of the algorithm in this paper. The defect detection method of transmission small fittings based on improved SLIC and ViT proposed in this paper can effectively identify small fittings defects in transmission line inspection images, and has a certain reference value for intelligent defect diagnosis of power inspection.

Acknowledgment. This work was funded by the "Research on the key technology of intelligent annotation of power image based on image self-learning" program of the Big Data Center, State Grid Corporation of China.

References

1. Peng, X., Qian, J., Mai, X., et al.: Automatic power line inspection technology of large unmanned helicopter and its application. South. Power Syst. Technol. **10**(2), 24–31, 76 (2016)
2. Liu, Z., Du, Y., Chen, Y., et al.: Simulation and experiment on the safety distance of typical ±500 kV DC transmission lines and towers for UAV inspection. High Voltage Eng. **45**(2), 426–432 (2019)
3. Sun, Y.: Research on 3D imaging system of UAV line laser scanning. Harbin Institute of Technology, Harbin, China (2017)
4. Liu, Z., Miao, X., Chen, J., et al.: Review of visible image intelligent processing for transmission line inspection. Power Syst. Technol. **44**(3), 1057–1069 (2020)
5. Xu, H., Yu, J., Liang, C., Zhang, X.: Detection method for small metal defects of improved RPN transmission line based on GAN. Chin. J. Electron Dev. **44**(06), 1409–1416 (2021)
6. Fang, Z., Lin, W., Fan, S., et al.: A defects recognition method for small fittings in power transmission towers based on hierarchical recognition model. Electr. Power Inf. Commun. Technol. **18**(9), 9 (2020)
7. Fu, J., Shao, G., Wu, L., et al.: Defect detection of line facility using hierarchical model with learning algorithm. High Voltage Eng. **43**(1), 272–281 (2017)
8. Wang, K., Wang, J., Liu, G., et al.: Using improved strategies to improve the smart recognition rate of defects in pin on power fittings. Electr. Power Eng. Technol. **38**(4), 80–85 (2019)
9. Song, X., Zhou, L., Li, Z., et al.: Review on superpixel methods in image segmentation. J. Image Graph. **5**, 599–608 (2015)
10. Felzenswalb, P.F., Huttenloche, R.D.P.: Efficient graph-based images segmentation. Int. J. Comput. Vis. **59**(2), 167–181 (2004)
11. Achanta, R., Shaji, A., Smith, K., et al.: SLIC superpixels compared to state-of-the-art superpixel methods. IEEE Trans. Pattern Anal. Mach. Intell. **34**(11), 2274–2282 (2012)
12. Dong, Q., Yan, K., Sun, T., Zhang, S.: Improvement of grab cut algorithm based on SLIC superpixel algorithm. Huazhong Univ. Sci. Tech. (Nat. Sci. Edn.) **44**, 43–47+66 (2016)
13. Vaswani, A., Shazeer, N., Parmar, N., et al.: Attention is all you need. In: Advances in Neural Information Processing Systems, vol. 30 (2017)
14. Wu, B., et al.: Visual transformers: token-based image representation and processing for computer vision. arXiv:2006.03677 (2020)
15. Dosovitskiy, A., et al.: An image is worth 16×16 words: transformers for image recognition at scale. In: ICLR (2021)
16. Gao, X., Hoi, S.C.H., Zhang, Y., et al.: Sparse online learning of image similarity. ACM Trans. Intell. Syst. Technol. **8**(5), 64:1–64:22 (2017)
17. Zhang, Y., Gao, X., Chen, Z., et al.: Mining spatial-temporal similarity for visual tracking. IEEE Trans. Image Process. **29**, 8107–8119 (2020)
18. Li, W., Chen, Z., Gao, X., et al.: Multimodel framework for indoor localization under mobile edge computing environment. IEEE Internet Things J. **6**(3), 4844–4853 (2019)
19. Gao, X., Xie, J., Chen, Z., et al.: Dilated convolution-based feature refinement network for crowd localization. In: ACM Transactions on Multimedia Computing, Communications, and Applications (2022)
20. Beal, J., Kim, E., Tzeng, E., et al.: Toward transformer based object detection [J/OL]. arXiv: 2012.09958 [cs.CV] (2020). https://arxiv.org/abs/2012.09958

Federated Learning for Industrial Entity Extraction

Shengze Fu, Xiaoli Zhao[✉], and Chi Yang

School of Electronic and Electrical Engineering, Shanghai University of Engineering Science, Shanghai, China
1012439688@qq.com

Abstract. Entity extraction in the industrial field is an important part of the realization of digital transformation in the industrial field. The construction of entity extraction model in the industrial field requires a large amount of data from various parties. However, due to the security and privacy issues of the data, the data in the industrial field often exists in the form of islands, so it is almost impossible to integrate the data scattered among various parties. Therefore, this paper proposes a federated learning framework to assist parties in industry to overcome data silos and collaborate in building entity extraction models. The solution to the Non-IID problem in federal learning is to find an index to measure the data performance of all participants. Participants with relatively good data performance have a higher weight in the aggregation stage, while participants with relatively poor data performance have a lower weight in the aggregation stage. In this paper, an aggregation update method FedData is proposed to improve the performance of federated learning in data Non-IID scenarios. The method measures the data performance of each participant based on the aggregate test performance of each participant's local model on the private data of other participants and assigns aggregate weights to each participant based on this. The experimental results show that the framework can make the participants who cannot cooperate in modeling jointly build the entity extraction model without being constrained by data security and privacy issues, so as to achieve better results. Moreover, the aggregation update method proposed in this paper has better performance than FedAvg in the scenario where the data is not independent and equally distributed.

Keywords: Industrial field · Entity extraction · Federated learning · Non-IID

1 Introduction

Knowledge graph is a visualization technology to display knowledge architecture and knowledge points in information [1], which is originally intended to improve users' search experience. The basic unit of knowledge graph is the triplet composed of "entity-relation-entity", which is also the core of knowledge graph, and its essence is a huge semantic network graph. In recent years, more and more fields are interested in using knowledge graph technology. As the society attaches more and more importance to knowledge graph technology, people have made a lot of progress in the research of

G. Zhai et al. (Eds.): IFTC 2022, CCIS 1766, pp. 490–501, 2023.
https://doi.org/10.1007/978-981-99-0856-1_36

knowledge graph [2–4]. Entity extraction is the first and key step in the construction of knowledge map, so this paper mainly studies the entity extraction in the industrial field, which will be helpful to the construction of knowledge map in the industrial field.

Entity extraction is also known as named entity recognition [5], whose main task is to identify named entities in text and classify them into predefined entity categories. Entity extraction is an important part of knowledge graph construction. The key problem is how to build a high-quality entity extraction model to extract the desired entity information from massive data sources. Therefore, the research on entity extraction in industrial domain is conducive to the construction of industrial domain knowledge graph.

The industrial field involves a large number of data acquisition and analysis operations such as industrial equipment fault monitoring and pattern sensing. The real time and complexity of industrial equipment data are not qualified by traditional database technology. Therefore, knowledge graph, a technology to show the relationship between data structures, has been applied more and more widely in industry. The construction of knowledge graph in the industrial field requires a large amount of data from all parties. However, as oil in the industrial field, data is an important resource, and the data of all parties often cannot be shared due to the business competition and security and privacy concerns of the industry itself, thus forming data islands [6]. Traditional machine learning methods integrate data for unified machine learning training, but this approach has the risk of data leakage. In order to solve this problem, Google proposed a federated learning solution to jointly model and share computing results under the premise of protecting the privacy and security of the original data [7, 8]. Although federated learning can effectively solve the problem of data islanding, in many practical scenarios, the data of all parties in federated learning are usually non-independent and identically distributed (called Non-IID). Literatures [9, 10] have shown through various experiments that Non-IID data will seriously affect the performance of federated learning.

Aiming at the problem of data islanding in the industrial domain, this paper proposes a federated learning framework for entity extraction in the industrial domain, which makes the parties that cannot cooperate with each other due to data security and privacy issues participate in modeling jointly, thus improving the model. In the experimental part, BERT + BiLSTM + CRF model is used as the entity extraction model, which verifies the feasibility of the federated learning framework applied to entity extraction in the industrial field, and an aggregation update method FedData is proposed to improve the performance of federated learning in Non-IID scenarios. The method adjusts the weight of the local model in the global model according to the comprehensive test accuracy of each participant's local model on the private data of all other participants. This paper uses the industrial equipment failure order data of an automobile group. The main contributions are as follows:

(1) The effectiveness of the federated learning framework is verified on the failure work order data of industrial equipment of an automobile group, and the feasibility of FedData method is verified under two Non-IID scenarios.
(2) Aiming at the Non-IID problem of data in the industrial field, this paper proposes a federated learning aggregation update algorithm FedData to improve the performance of the federated learning framework in the face of non-independent and identically distributed data in the industrial field.

(3) The federated learning is applied in the industrial field, and a federated learning framework is proposed to jointly construct entity extraction models under the premise of ensuring data security, which lays a foundation for the construction of knowledge graph in the industrial field.

2 Relevant Content

2.1 Entity Extraction

Entity extraction aims to automatically identify desired entities from unstructured text and label them into predefined categories, such as people, places, and organizations. Common annotation methods are BIO annotation: B-begin, I-inside, O-outside; B represents the beginning of the entity, I represents the content of the entity, and O represents the non-entity part. Since entity is the most basic element in knowledge graph, the completeness and accuracy of its extraction will directly affect the quality of knowledge base. Therefore, entity extraction is the most basic and key step to construct knowledge graph.

In the early days, entity extraction methods were based on statistical learning and rules. Although the traditional methods have achieved good results, they are highly dependent on professional domain knowledge and difficult to construct artificial features. Aiming at the problems existing in traditional methods, Hammerton et al. [11] first applied neural networks to the research of named entities. They used one-way long short-term memory network (LSTM), which has good sequence modeling ability, so LSTM-CRF is considered as the infrastructure of entity extraction. Later, on the basis of this architecture, Guillaume Lample et al. [12] proposed a neural network model combining Bidirectional Long Short-Term Memory (BiLSTM) and conditional random field (CRF). This architecture can extract the sequence information of the context, so it is widely used in the field of entity extraction. However, this method pays attention to the feature extraction of words, characters or between words, but ignores the context or semantics of words, which leads to the poor effect of entity extraction. In order to solve the above problems, Jacob Devlin et al. [16] used BERT (Bidirectional Encoder Representation from Transformers) language preprocessing model to represent word vectors. BERT can fully describe the relationship characteristics between characters, words and even sentences, and better represent the contextual and semantic information in different contexts.

In recent years, deep learning-based methods have been widely applied to Chinese named entity recognition research [13–16]. Compared with traditional methods, deep learning-based methods can learn independently from original data and find deeper and more abstract features, which has the advantage of stronger generalization.

2.2 Federated Learning

With the rapid development of digital society, technologies related to artificial intelligence and big data have been attached great importance, which not only bring new development opportunities for traditional industries, but also inevitably bring data security and privacy problems, and data island problem is one of the key problems. Federated

Learning provides a solution to the current problems faced by artificial intelligence and big data industry. This technology can complete joint modeling while protecting the data privacy of all parties.

Federated learning is a basic technology of artificial intelligence, which is essentially a machine learning framework. Its original intention is to assist multiple participants or multiple computing nodes to carry out machine learning to achieve the purpose of security modeling on the premise of ensuring data of all parties, protecting privacy and security, and ensuring legitimacy. Federated learning adheres to the idea of "only passing model parameters or gradients". Data of all parties only needs to be kept locally, thus avoiding data leakage.

As a user-based distributed machine learning method, federated learning has many advantages. It can directly train effective machine learning models based on users' local data, and make full use of high-quality data from various parties. The federated learning framework mainly includes data holders and central servers. The federated learning framework is mainly divided into the following steps, as shown in Fig. 1:

(1) Initialization: All users get an initialization model from the central server, they can join the federated learning, and determine the same task and model training objectives.

(2) Local computation: In the communication process of each round of federated learning, federated learning users first get the global model parameters from the central server, and then use their private training samples to train the model, update the model, and send these updates to the central server.

(3) Central aggregation: the global model of the next round can be obtained by aggregating the models trained by different users and updating them.

(4) Model update: The central server updates the global model once according to the aggregated results, and returns the updated model to the data holders participating in federated learning.

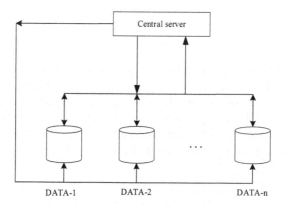

Fig. 1. Federal learning framework

Federated Average Algorithm (FedAvg) [17] is the most common algorithm scheme in the federated learning framework. The improvement and theoretical analysis of FedAvg algorithm is an important research direction in current federated learning [18–21]. Federated learning still faces some problems and challenges [22].

3 Federated Learning Framework for Industrial Entity Extraction

3.1 Entity Extraction Model

At present, methods based on deep learning can achieve better results, so this study uses BERT + BiLSTM + CRF as the entity extraction model, and uses the industrial equipment failure order data of an automobile group as corpus data. The model is divided into three modules: BERT (Bidirectional Encoder Representation from Transformers), namely Encoder of bidirectional Transformer; BiLSTM is composed of forward LSTM and backward LSTM. CRF is a conditional random field. The model structure is shown in Fig. 2.

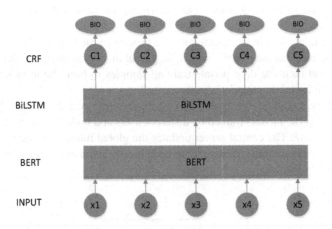

Fig. 2. Structure diagram of BERT + BiLSTM + CRF model

The workflow of the whole model is as follows: Input the corpus data of the industrial equipment fault order of the automobile group as the training data. Firstly, the BERT pre-training model is used to obtain the word vector and extract the important features of the text. Then, BiILSTM deep learning context feature information is used for named entity recognition. Finally, CRF layer processes the output sequence of BiLSTM to get a predicted annotated sequence, and then extracts and classifies each entity in the sequence.

3.2 FedData

In each round of FedAvg, the server first sends the global model to each participant, then each party updates the model with its local data set, and then sends the updated model back to the server. Finally, the server receives the local model and performs aggregation update, and finally gets the next round of global model. In the model aggregation stage of FedAvg, the weight of each participant is determined according to the proportion of its own data volume in the total data volume. However, the contribution of each participant to the global model is not necessarily positively correlated with the data volume, but also affected by data distribution and data quality. Since the principle of "only model parameters or gradients are passed" is always held in the process of federated learning, the method in this paper takes advantage of this feature to propose the FedData method, which can only pass the local model between different participants without data leakage. The starting point was to find a better metric to guide weight allocation in the model aggregation phase instead of data volume. Before the federal learning framework is fully developed, each participant uses the initial model for training and transmits the local training model to each other. The comprehensive test performance of each participant's local model on the private data of other participants is used to measure the data performance of each participant. Participants with relatively good data performance have a higher weight in the aggregation stage, while participants with relatively poor data performance have a lower weight in the aggregation stage. The FedData method is described as follows:

There are n participants in total. First, participant i trains the local model w_i, which is transmitted to all other participants through the central server, and the model testing accuracy is $v_{i,j}$ on the data of participant j. Then the data index of participant i can be expressed as the average value of all $v_{i,j}$ values, as shown in Eq. (1):

$$T_i = \frac{\left(v_{i,1} + v_{i,2} + \ldots + v_{i,n-1}\right)}{n - 1} \tag{1}$$

$D(i)$ represents the weight of participant i in the federated learning model aggregation stage. In FedData, the weight of each participant is shown in formula (2):

$$D(i) = \frac{T_i}{(T_1 + T_2 + \ldots + T_n)} \tag{2}$$

The overall federated learning algorithm is shown in Algorithm 1.

Algorithm 1 : FedData

Input: number of participants n, number of global model update rounds T, number of local iteration rounds M, Global model W, local model w, learning rate η

Output: the final model W_T

Server:
    initialize the global model W_0
    for t= 1, 2, ..., T **do**
        global model W_t is sent to each participant
        for participant $i \in n$ **do**
            initial model of the participant $w_t^i = W_t$
            $w_{t+1}^i \leftarrow w_t^i$ local update
        end

        $W_{t+1} \leftarrow \sum_{i=1}^{i=n} D(i)\, w_{t+1}^i$
    end

Client:
w_t^i local update:
    for m=1,2, ..., M **do**
        $w_{m+1}^i \leftarrow w_m^i - \eta \triangledown f(w_m^i)$
    return W_{t+1} to the server to get a new round of global model

---

The federated learning framework for entity extraction in the industrial domain is shown in Fig. 3, which shows the process of the framework and the help of using the framework to build the knowledge graph in the industrial domain. The work of the framework is mainly divided into the following steps.

(1) Initialization: First, the central government and all participants determine the common training objectives, and the central server initializes the original model. This framework adopts the BERT + BiLSTM + CRF joint model.
(2) Distribution model: the central server sends its own model to each participant, and each participant receives the model from the central server.
(3) Local training: Participants in federated learning get the global model from the central server, then use their private data to train the model locally and update the model parameters, and send these updates to the central server.
(4) Model aggregation: the central server uses FedData to aggregate and update the model parameters sent by each participant to obtain the global model of the next round; The above steps 2, 3 and 4 were repeated to optimize the global model. After the training, the joint model trained by all parties was obtained.

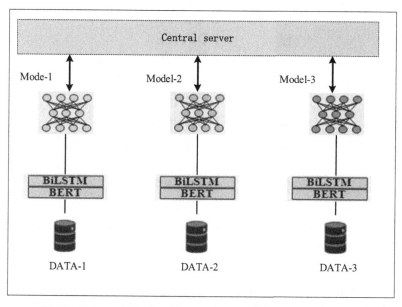

Fig. 3. Federated learning framework for industrial entity extraction

4   Experiment

4.1   Introduction of Data

The data in the experiment is the work order data of industrial equipment failure of an automobile group. Firstly, entities are annotated. There are six entity labels: ATTRIBUTE, NORMAL, UNNORMAL, FAULT, DEVICE, OPERATION, and non-entity label 0. The sample is shown in Fig. 4. In traditional machine learning, the data is distributed on the same machine, and it is assumed that the data are sampled independently from the same distribution, that is, the data in traditional machine learning is independent and identically distributed. However, in the federated learning scenario in the industrial field, because the equipment belongs to a certain enterprise, factory, or department, the data distribution is often very different, that is, the data is not independent and identically distributed. The amount of data owned by different data holders and the label category of data are very different, so the experiment in this paper will process the data from the perspectives of data amount and label category to simulate the scenario of Non-IID.

In this paper, two different processing methods are used to select data from the training set to construct two kinds of Non-IID scenarios, indicating the different degree of heterogeneity of data, which are named as low Non-IID and high Non-IID respectively. Among them, the selection method of low Non-IID is to randomly intercept multiple blocks of data from the original data set and distribute them to different participants, and the total amount of data of each participant is significantly different. The high Non-IID selects the data of partial labels from the original data and assigns them to each

机	B-DEVICE
械	I-DEVICE
手	I-DEVICE
无	B-UNNORMAL
法	I-UNNORMAL
上	I-UNNORMAL
电	I-UNNORMAL
，	O
检	B-OPERATION
查	I-OPERATION
后	O

Fig. 4. Data sample

participant. There are obvious differences in the total amount of data contained by each participant and the types of labels.

For the low Non-IID scenario, three sub-datasets low1, low2 and low3 are set to represent the private data of the three parties, among which low1 has 1000 rows of data, low2 has 875 rows of data, and low3 has 525 rows of data. For the high Non-IID scenario, three sub-datasets, high1, high2 and high3, are set up to represent the private data of the three participants. high1 has 100 lines of data, and only the data of O, DEVICE, and UNNORMAL labels are available. There are 125 lines of data in high2, only the data of O, DEVICE, NORMAL and OPERATION labels; There are 150 lines of data in high3, and only five labels of O, DEVICE, FAULT, OPERATION, and ATTRIBUTE are available.

4.2 Experimental Result

In order to verify the reliability of the federated learning framework and the effect of FedData, the experiment compares the effects of the participant training alone and each participant using the federated learning framework, and the effects of using FedAvg and FedData respectively in two scenarios: low Non-IID and high Non-IID.

Based on the experiment and formula (1), in low Non-IID and high Non-IID scenarios, the data indexes T_1, T_2, T_3 are shown in Table 1. These indexes are used to represent the data quality of each participant.

Table 1. Data index

Compare objects	T_1	T_2	T_3
Low Non-IID	0.65	0.60	0.63
High Non-IID	0.24	0.51	0.50

As can be seen from the data indicators, the data indicators of all participants in the low Non-IID scenario are close, and the weight of each participant is similar in the aggregation stage. In the high Non-IID scenario, for example, if the data index of Participant 1 is low, the weight of Participant 1 will be reduced in the aggregation phase. According to Formula (2), the aggregated weight values $D(1)$, $D(2)$ and $D(3)$ of each participant using FedAvg and FedData in the two data scenarios are shown in Table 2.

Table 2. Weight parameter value

Compare objects	$D(1)$	$D(2)$	$D(3)$
FedAvg-low Non-IID	$\frac{1000}{2400}$	$\frac{875}{2400}$	$\frac{525}{2400}$
FedData-low Non-IID	$\frac{65}{188}$	$\frac{60}{188}$	$\frac{63}{188}$
FedAvg-high Non-IID	$\frac{100}{375}$	$\frac{125}{375}$	$\frac{150}{375}$
FedData-high Non-IID	$\frac{24}{125}$	$\frac{51}{125}$	$\frac{50}{125}$

As can be seen from Table 2, the model aggregation weight of FedData is quite different from that of FedAvg. The amount of data of participants cannot well reflect the data quality of each participant, and the method allows participants with relatively good data performance to have higher weight in the aggregation stage. Table 3 and Table 4 record the experimental results under low Non-IID and high Non-IID scenarios respectively.

Table 3. Experimental evaluation of low Non-IID scenarios

Compare objects	Accuracy
low1	64.9
low2	69.6
low3	66.7
FedAvg	72.7
FedData	73.2

It can be seen from the experimental results that after using the federated learning framework, the effect of joint modeling of all parties is significantly better than that

Table 4. Experimental evaluation of high Non-IID scenarios

Compare objects	Accuracy
high1	37.9
high2	53.4
high3	67.1
FedAvg	69.4
FedData	70.2

of individual modeling of all parties in both low Non-IID and high Non-IID scenarios. In addition, the accuracy of FedData in low Non-IID and high Non-IID scenarios is improved by 0.5% and 0.8% compared with FedAvg, respectively. Experiments show that this method has better performance than FedAvg in Non-IID scenarios, and can alleviate the impact of Non-IID on federated learning.

5   Conclusion

In order to help all parties in the industrial domain to jointly model under the premise of protecting data privacy, this paper proposes a federated learning framework for entity extraction in the industrial domain, and puts forward FedData method to improve the performance of federated learning on Non-IID data. Experiments on different datasets show that the proposed framework and method are effective in industrial entity extraction. Although federated learning can be widely applied in the industrial field, it still faces many problems and challenges, which can be summarized as the following aspects: first, the heterogeneity of federated learning; Second, communication efficiency; Third, privacy and security. In the future, federal learning research in the industrial field needs to further explore these issues.

References

1. Singhal, A., et al.: Introducing the knowledge graph: things, not strings. Official Google Blog **5**, 16 (2012)
2. Cai, H., Zheng, V.W., Chang, K.C.-C.: A comprehensive survey of graph embedding: problems, techniques, and applications. IEEE Trans. Knowl. Data Eng. **30**(9), 1616–1637 (2018)
3. Zhang, Z., Han, X., Liu, Z., Jiang, X., Sun, M., Liu, Q.: Ernie: enhanced language representation with informative entities. arXiv preprint arXiv:1905.07129 (2019)
4. Liu, W., et al.: K-BERT: enabling language representation with knowledge graph. In: Proceedings of the AAAI Conference on Artificial Intelligence, vol. 34, pp. 2901–2908 (2020)
5. Zhao, S., Cai, Z., Chen, H., Wang, Y., Liu, F., Liu, A.: Adversarial training based lattice LSTM for Chinese clinical named entity recognition. J. Biomed. Inform. **99**, 103290 (2019)
6. Jolfaei, A., Ostovari, P., Alazab, M., Gondal, I., Kant, K.: Guest editorial special issue on privacy and security in distributed edge computing and evolving IoT. IEEE Internet Things J. **7**(4), 2496–2500 (2020)

7. Kairouz, P., et al.: Advances and open problems in federated learning. Found. Trends Mach. Learn. **14**(1–2), 1–210 (2021)

8. Chen, Y., Sun, X., Jin, Y.: Communication-efficient federated deep learning with layerwise asynchronous model update and temporally weighted aggregation. IEEE Trans. Neural Netw. Learn. Syst. **31**(10), 4229–4238 (2019)

9. Zhao, Y., Li, M., Lai, L., Suda, N., Civin, D., Chandra, V.: Federated learning with non-IID data. arXiv preprint arXiv:1806.00582 (2018)

10. Sattler, F., Wiedemann, S., Müller, K.-R., Samek, W.: Robust and communication-efficient federated learning from non-IID data. IEEE Trans. Neural Netw. Learn. Syst. **31**(9), 3400–3413 (2019)

11. Hammerton, J.: Named entity recognition with long short-term memory. In: Proceedings of the Seventh Conference on Natural Language Learning at HLT-NAACL 2003, pp. 172–175 (2003)

12. Lample, G., Ballesteros, M., Subramanian, S., Kawakami, K., Dyer, C.: Neural architectures for named entity recognition. arXiv preprint arXiv:1603.01360 (2016)

13. Devlin, J., Chang, M.-W., Lee, K., Toutanova, K.: BERT: pretraining of deep bidirectional transformers for language understanding. arXiv preprint arXiv:1810.04805 (2018)

14. Li, J., Sun, A., Han, J., Li, C.: A survey on deep learning for named entity recognition. IEEE Trans. Knowl. Data Eng. **34**(1), 50–70 (2020)

15. Huang, Z., Xu, W., Yu, K.: Bidirectional LSTM-CRF models for sequence tagging. arXiv preprint arXiv:1508.01991 (2015)

16. Dong, C., Zhang, J., Zong, C., Hattori, M., Di, H.: Character-based LSTM-CRF with radical-level features for Chinese named entity recognition. In: Lin, C.-Y., Xue, N., Zhao, D., Huang, X., Feng, Y. (eds.) ICCPOL/NLPCC -2016. LNCS (LNAI), vol. 10102, pp. 239–250. Springer, Cham (2016). https://doi.org/10.1007/978-3-319-50496-4_20

17. McMahan, B., Moore, E., Ramage, D., Hampson, S., Arcas, B.A.: Communication-efficient learning of deep networks from decentralized data. In: Artificial Intelligence and Statistics, pp. 1273–1282. PMLR (2017)

18. Wu, W., He, L., Lin, W., Mao, R., Maple, C., Jarvis, S.: SAFA: a semi-asynchronous protocol for fast federated learning with low overhead. IEEE Trans. Comput. **70**(5), 655–668 (2020)

19. Lu, X., Liao, Y., Lio, P., Hui, P.: Privacy-preserving asynchronous federated learning mechanism for edge network computing. IEEE Access **8**, 48970–48981 (2020)

20. Wang, H., Yurochkin, M., Sun, Y., Papailiopoulos, D., Khazaeni, Y.: Federated learning with matched averaging. arXiv preprint arXiv:2002.06440 (2020)

21. Chai, Z., Chen, Y., Anwar, A., Zhao, L., Cheng, Y., Rangwala, H.: FedAT: a high-performance and communication-efficient federated learning system with asynchronous tiers. In: Proceedings of the International Conference for High Performance Computing, Networking, Storage and Analysis, pp. 1–16 (2021)

22. Li, T., Sahu, A.K., Talwalkar, A., Smith, V.: Federated learning: challenges, methods, and future directions. IEEE Signal Process. Mag. **37**(3), 50–60 (2020)

Interactive Sharing Method of Power Grid Dispatching and Control Operation Data Based on Data Classification and Grading

Lin Xie[1]([✉]), Ruili Ye[1], Yan Wang[1], Chaohan Feng[1], Dapeng Li[1], Xiangyu Zhang[2], Can Cui[1], Qiong Feng[1], Zhoujie Zhang[1], and Xinxin Sheng[1]

[1] Beijing Key Laboratory of Research and System Evaluation of Power Dispatching Automation Technology, China Electric Power Research Institute, Beijing, China
xielin519@163.com

[2] Economic and Technological Research Institute, State Grid Shanxi Electric Power Company, Taiyuan, China

Abstract. The era of big data is characterized by rapid information change, large volume of data, many dimensions, and various types, which requires enterprises to classify and grade data management. Especially in the critical period of new power system construction, a method is needed to classify and share power grid dispatching and operation data safely. This paper analyzes the business characteristics of power grid dispatching and control data, and designs the classification principle of power grid dispatching and control operation data, and builds a data sharing open directory based on this principle, and proposes a method of interaction and sharing of power grid dispatching and control operation data. Finally, this paper realizes the internal sharing and external circulation of power grid dispatching and control data through the interaction process.

Keywords: Power grid dispatching and control operation data · Data classification and grading · Data sharing and open directory · Data interaction and sharing

1 Instruction

With the speeding up of the construction of extra-high voltage AC/DC interconnection grid, the centralized access of large-scale new energy, the deepening of power market reform, and the goal of "carbon peaking, carbon neutral" and "building a new power system", the grid operation has formed and accumulated rich data resources. These data resources have become important assets of the enterprise [1, 2]. The full exploitation of the value of these data assets can greatly promote the grid intelligent perception, internal control capabilities and customer service efficiency. Power grid dispatching and operation data sharing can also bring convenience to power production and marketing, etc. However, as the national critical infrastructure, power data is related to national security, and it is be easy to become the target of network attacks and theft. Once with these business data loss, damage or leakage, it may cause power system failure or

G. Zhai et al. (Eds.): IFTC 2022, CCIS 1766, pp. 502–511, 2023.
https://doi.org/10.1007/978-981-99-0856-1_37

major security incidents, and bring huge economic losses to the country and enterprises. Therefore, power enterprises must strengthen the security protection of power sensitive data assets and solve the security problems of value data exchange and sharing and data mining.

Data classification and grading is the cornerstone for promoting data sharing and data security construction, and sorting out data with different attributes and implementing differentiated opening strategies is the premise of data security sharing [3]. In February 2020, the Ministry of Industry and Information Technology issued the Guide to Industrial Data Classification and Grading (for Trial Implementation), which divides industrial data into three security levels and guides enterprises to comprehensively sort out their own industrial data and improve data grading management capabilities, but the guide is a guideline for the whole industrial field, which is relatively broad in rule design and has limitations for guiding the practical operation of the electric power industry [4]. In addition, various industries have successively proposed principles for data classification and grading. In September 2020, the People's Bank of China released JR/T0197–2020 "Financial Data Security Data Security Grading Guide", which gives principles for data security grading and divides financial data into 5 levels. In December 2020, the Ministry of Industry and Information Technology released YD/T3813- 2020 "Data Classification and Grading Methods for Basic Telecommunications Enterprises", which stipulates the principles of data classification and grading for basic telecommunications enterprises as well as the workflow and methods of data classification. at the end of 2020, the "Technical Specification for General Data Security Requirements of Southern Power Grid (for Trial Implementation)" was released, which puts forward the basic principles for data classification and grading work. The goal of data classification and grading is to ensure that information is appropriately protected and open according to its importance to the organization, so proposing a classification and grading method for grid dispatching and operation data is an important basis for open data sharing.

Based on the characteristics of instantaneous, reusable and multi-attributed power grid operation data, a scientific and reasonable classification of power grid dispatching and operation data and the design of "different and equal" sharing methods are indispensable tools to promote data sharing and data protection in the digital economy. This paper proposes a sharing and interaction method for power grid dispatching and control cloud data through a data sharing open directory to classify and display dispatching and operation data, and realize internal sharing and external circulation of enterprise data.

2 Grid Dispatching and Control Operation Data Classification and Classification

2.1 Principles of Wide-Area Service Proxy

Grid dispatching and control operation data are various historical data generated during the operation of the grid to reflect the operating status of the grid and related primary and secondary equipment [5]. Referring to the existing domestic and international data classification system standards, the paper presents the data asset classification principles for power grid dispatching and control operation with reference to the dispatching and control operation business data generation process and object-oriented principles. The data asset classification of power grid dispatching and control operation covers horizontally to each business information system, and vertically extends from business functions to specific power grid dispatching and control operation activities. Grid dispatching and control operation data comes from Supervisory Control and Data Acquisition, Operations Management System, Tele Meter Reading, Power Generation Plan, and other data assets. Reading, generation planning system, and other types of dispatching and control business systems [6].

In this paper, the data classification is carried out according to the idea of total division of business lines, and the business data are subdivided into 28 categories such as load, generation, current, voltage, etc., and then converged into 8 major categories such as power, electricity, planning, forecasting, alarm, event, environment, and market according to the business categories.

According to the above rules, combined with the 8 categories and 28 sub-categories of data objects, the data classification system for power grid dispatching and control operation data is designed, as shown in Fig. 1.

2.2 Data Security Intensity Grading

Data should be graded according to legal requirements, value, importance and its sensitivity to unauthorized leakage or modification [7, 8]. According to the core idea of ISO27001 system, security includes three elements of confidentiality, integrity and availability, and data asset evaluation can be judged by the assignment of the three elements, which can be calculated to reflect the business value of data according to the assignment and weight of CIA (Confidentiality, Integrity, Availability). Based on the classification, the data security grading of power grid control operation data takes the smallest data class as the grading object, takes into account the factors of power grid production and operation and dispatching professional management, and builds the data grading model from three evaluation dimensions according to the degree of damage and impact after the data is tampered, damaged, leaked or illegally obtained or illegally used, as shown in Fig. 2.

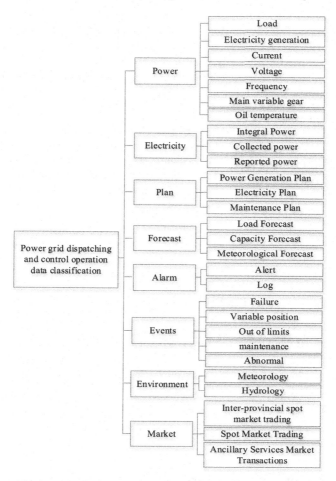

Fig. 1. Classification system of power grid dispatching and control operation data

Based on the data classification model, business data is identified and evaluated to determine the reasonable valuation of the data, and finally the data level is divided into three levels from high to low. If the first level data is tampered, damaged, leaked or illegally obtained or used, it may affect the safe operation of the power grid or the economic interests of the market players, such as remote telemetry, generation plan, protection value, market clearing data, etc. Once the secondary data is tampered with, damaged, leaked or illegally obtained or illegally used, it may affect the monitoring and analysis of the power grid, such as power consumption, telematics and telemetry data. If the tertiary data is tampered, damaged, leaked or illegally obtained or illegally used, it will not have a direct impact on the power grid operation and monitoring, such as secondary equipment operation and monitoring, meteorological data, etc. According to the above classification principles, the grid control operation data security grading control strategy matrix is formed, as shown in shown as Table 1.

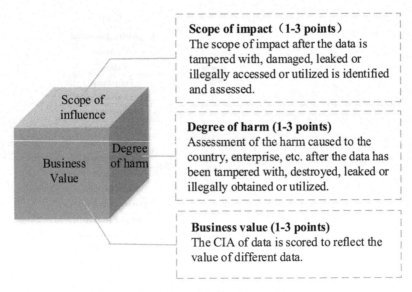

Scope of impact （1-3 points）
The scope of impact after the data is tampered with, damaged, leaked or illegally accessed or utilized is identified and assessed.

Degree of harm (1-3 points)
Assessment of the harm caused to the country, enterprise, etc. after the data has been tampered with, destroyed, leaked or illegally obtained or utilized.

Business value (1-3 points)
The CIA of data is scored to reflect the value of different data.

Fig. 2. Data classification model

Table 1. Data security classification and control strategy

Data grading	Impact level	Encryption principle	Desensitization principle
Level 1	Serious	Need to encrypt	Need to desensitize
Level 2	Moderate	/	Need to desensitize
Level 3	None or slight	/	/

3   Method of Sharing and Interacting with Data of Power Grid Dispatching and Control Operation

3.1   Data Sharing and Open Directory

Data sharing and open cataloging can clarify the scope and conditions of data resources for sharing and opening, and reduce the threshold for understanding system data. The shared open catalog for power grid dispatching and control cloud line data customizes the construction of data asset catalog hierarchy and describes data asset-related attributes in accordance with business requirements and enterprise standards. The shared open catalog of dispatching and operation data is organized in the form of metadata, which is a set of data sorted and coded according to certain classification methods to describe the characteristics of each data resource [9]. Then, according to different data classifications and data attributes, corresponding types of data topics are established, and different types of data catalogs are cataloged into the corresponding data topics, taking into account information such as resource dimension, security dimension and sharing dimension, which not only improves the ability to manage data, but also greatly enhances the efficiency of users in retrieving, locating and accessing data. It includes resource dimension, security dimension and sharing dimension, etc. The process of publishing the data sharing open catalog is generally divided into three steps: data catalog archiving, data catalog auditing, and data catalog publishing, and the flow chart is shown in Fig. 3.

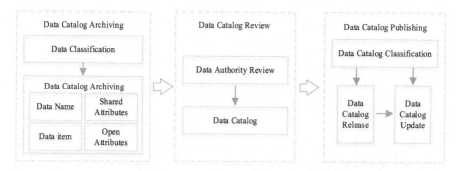

Fig. 3. Flow chart of data sharing and open catalog publication

Data catalog archiving is the process of open data archiving. Open data sources with file uploading and parsing, data sharing, data disclosure, etc. require unified data archiving functions. After data archiving, auditors from data providing departments are required to review and form data catalogs before publishing. When the data catalog is released, it needs to be classified and released according to different topics to facilitate data users to browse. After the data catalog is published, new data will be added and the data catalog will be continuously updated and maintained.

3.2 Data Sharing Methods

Grid dispatching and control operation data sharing, on the one hand, is oriented to the flow of data within the enterprise, and on the other hand, it is the act of providing data to external users such as government departments, external enterprises, organizations and individuals. This paper combines the data classification and grading principles and data opening forms, and proposes the interaction sharing method and interaction process for power grid dispatching and operation data. Users can get data from the data platform after authentication, but the content and way of data access are different for users with different authority. The internal sharing of data is the exchange of data across organizations and departments within the enterprise, which can be done through data services, database access, data files, etc.; the external sharing of data is mostly the exchange of data between enterprises, and due to the special nature of power grid dispatching and operation data, the original data is often not directly opened, and the primary and secondary data need to be protected and provided through data services. The data is provided through data services. For the data that can be provided to the public, it needs to be audited for information leakage. The interaction process for sharing data on power grid dispatching and operation is shown in Fig. 4.

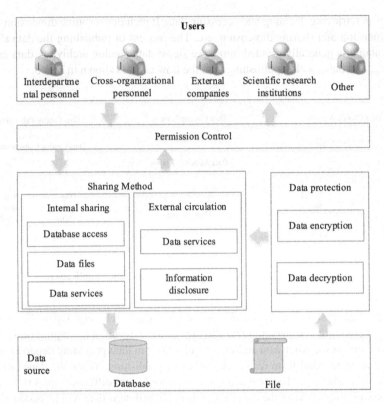

Fig. 4. Interaction flow of data sharing for grid dispatching and operation

(1) Permission control

Data permissions are a mapping relationship between users and data. Because different users enjoy permissions to different data resources, a many-to-many mapping relationship is formed. By introducing the Role-Based Access Control model [10], a mapping relationship is established between roles and data, as shown in Fig. 5(a). However, it is inappropriate to generate roles for each individual, as the mapping relationship is too large and redundant. In this paper, the control of permissions is combined with data levels, and the control of data permissions is performed by comparing user levels and data levels. Data and users are mapped to data levels to determine the data permissions that users have, as shown in Fig. 5(b). For different levels of users, the access content, access mode and data access frequency of data need to be controlled to ensure the security of data sharing.

(2) Sharing method

On the basis of classification and grading of power grid dispatching and operation, the data sharing mode is opened by following the principle of minimum authority and dynamic authorization. Data internal sharing is the exchange of data across organizations and departments within the enterprise, and data can be shared through data services,

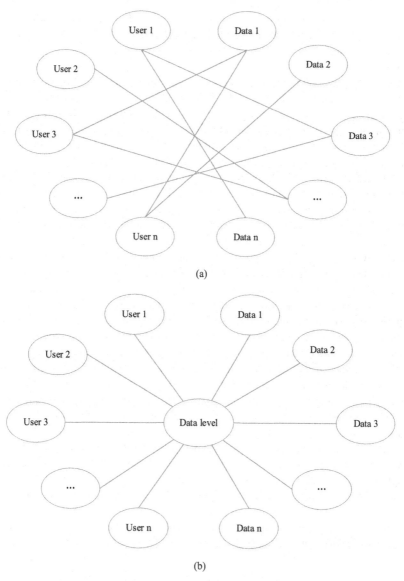

(a)

(b)

Fig. 5. User access control model

database access, data files, etc. Data services are encapsulated in the form of API inter-faces for data protection of security level data. The data file approach allows data to be exported offline, encrypted, and then shared. After the data visitor obtains the data per-mission through permission authentication, the sharing platform provides the choice of sharing methods according to the permission. The external sharing of data is mostly for data exchange between enterprises. Due to the special nature of power grid dispatching and operation data, the original data is often not opened directly, and for primary and secondary data, data protection processing is required and the data is provided through data services. For the data that can be provided to the public, it needs to be audited for information leakage, and the public can download and use the data.

(3) Data protection

In the data protection module, data with high security level will be encrypted and decrypted to key authorization, which enhances the security of sensitive data in the usage chain. By constructing an asymmetric encryption service AEMS, it provides an additional layer of protection for the asymmetric encryption public key in the hybrid encryption mechanism, and later uses a hybrid AES symmetric encryption algorithm and RSA encryption scheme to improve the confidentiality of data.

For sensitive data, static desensitization policy and dynamic desensitization policy are designed to realize the configuration of desensitization policy for each type and scenario. Static desensitization policy is generally used in non-production environment or in cases where data is used separately from the native business system, such as development testing and scientific research process [11]. In development and testing scenarios, such as power grid regulation and operation and other sensitive information systems contain sensitive information such as names, identities, and account numbers, but development and testing need to use these real data, so it is necessary to ensure that sensitive data are not leaked through desensitization means. Secondly, the data sharing scenario is usually under some specific needs to share the data with other departments or external enterprises. At this time, some sensitive data needs to be retained and specific sensitive data needs to be processed. Finally, scientific research scenarios usually center on the statistical analysis of data and the use of the results for scientific research, requiring the data to be desensitized while still retaining the original characteristics and content necessary for scientific research. Dynamic data desensitization is often used in the case of accessing sensitive data for immediate desensitization, and different levels of desensitization are required depending on the situation when the same sensitive data is read. In the case of interface call or data flow between business systems, the actual call can be executed and the desensitized data returned after receiving the data access request through dynamic desensitization agent conversion to ensure data security. In this paper, we design the desensitization policy configuration by considering the permission control and sharing methods, judge the data users according to the user's permission, and use the desensitization algorithm dynamically and senselessly by the selected sharing method to ensure the security of data sharing.

4 Conclusions

In order to solve the security sharing of power grid dispatching and control operation data, this paper combines the business characteristics of power grid dispatching and control data, designs the principle of grading and classification of power grid dispatching and control operation data, and builds a data sharing open directory based on the grading and classification of data, proposes a dynamic interaction sharing method of power grid dispatching and control operation data, and finally realizes the internal sharing and external circulation of power grid dispatching and control data through the interaction process. The paper puts forward some ideas and methods for grading and classification of power grid dispatching and control operation data as well as safe sharing, and the next step will be to continue the research on safe sharing of dispatching and control operation data with new technologies such as blockchain.

Acknowledgment. This work is supported by Science and Technology Program of State Grid Corporation of China under Grant No. 5442DZ210027 (Research on Asset Value Assessment Method for Power Grid Dispatching and Control Operation Data).

References

1. Hongqiang, X., Cai, Y., Xiong, W., et al.: Architecture and key technologies for big data platform in power grid. Power Syst. Technol. **45**(12), 4798–4807 (2021)
2. Ming, Z., Chi, S., Chenghua, W., et al.: Research on power data security classification algorithm under the Internet of things environment. Mach. Des. Manuf. Eng. **50**(4), 52–56 (2021)
3. Chang, W., Ya, Z.: Discussion on classification and classification of tobacco industry data and security protection methods. Inner Mongolia Sci. Technol. Econ. 1(443), 31–32+57 (2020)
4. Qiongli, Z., Yi, C.: Research of data classification model and practice. Technol. Market **29**(8), 150–153 (2022)
5. Hongqiang, X.U.: Structured design and application of power dispatching universal data object for dispatching and control cloud. Power Syst. Technol. **42**(7), 2248–2254 (2018)
6. Hongqiang, X.U.: Architecture of dispatching and control cloud and its application prospect. Power Syst. Technol. **41**(10), 3104–3111 (2017)
7. ZhenWei, T.: Discussion on classified management strategy of enterprise sensitive confidential data. Mod. Ind. Econ. Informationization 9(10), 79–80 (2019)
8. Jie, C., Tingyun, W., Wang, Qian, et al.: Research on the path of enterprise data classification and hierarchical management. Netw. Secur. Technol. Appl. (04), 70–71 (2022)
9. Vilminko-Heikkinen, R., Pekkola, S.: Master data management and its organizational implementation. J. Enterp. Inf. Manage. (3) 2017
10. Damiani, M.L., Bertino, E., Catania, B., Perlasca, P.: GEO-RBAC. ACM Trans. Inf. Syst. Secur. (TISSEC),(1) (2007)
11. Yiping, L., Chen, W.: Research on sensitive data protection of big data platform. Telecom Eng. Tech. Stand. **30**(11), 35–38 (2017)

On the Robustness of "Robust Reversible Data Hiding Scheme Based on Two-Layer Embedding Strategy"

Wen Yin[1], Zhaoxia Yin[2]($\boxtimes$)(iD), Xinpeng Zhang[3], and Bin Luo[1]

[1] Anhui University, Hefei, China
e20301241@stu.ahu.edu.cn, luobin@ahu.edu.cn
[2] East China Normal University, Shanghai, China
zxyin@cee.ecnu.edu.cn
[3] Fudan University, Shanghai, China
zhangxinpeng@fudan.edu.cn

Abstract. In the paper "Robust reversible data hiding scheme based on two-layer embedding strategy" published in INS recently, Kumar et al. proposed a robust reversible data hiding (RRDH) scheme based on two-layer embedding. Secret data was embedded into the most significant bit-planes to increase robustness, and a sorting strategy based on local complexity was adopted to reduce distortion. However, Kumar's reversible data hiding (RDH) scheme is not as robust against joint photographic experts group (JPEG) compression as stated and can not be called RRDH. This comment first gives a brief description of their RDH scheme, then analyzes their scheme's robustness from the perspective of JPEG compression principles. JPEG compression will change pixel values, thereby destroying auxiliary information and pixel value ordering required to extract secret data correctly, making their scheme not robust. Finally, the changes in both bit-plane and pixel value ordering after JPEG compression are shown and analyzed by different robustness-testing experiments.

Keywords: Robustness · Reversible data hiding · Least significant bit · Prediction error expansion · Steganography

1 Introduction

For some sensitive scenarios such as medical and military images, lossless recovery of original images and accurate secret data extraction are necessary. To solve this issue, reversible data hiding (RDH) is proposed to losslessly recover both the original image and the secret data [9]. The RDH technique reversibly embeds secret data into the original image to obtain a marked image. However, lossy procedures, such as JPEG compression, may cause irreversible damage to the marked image in some situations. The secret data can still be extracted correctly from the damaged image, even though the original image cannot be recovered reversibly, called robust reversible data hiding (RRDH) [9].

De Vleeschouwer et al. [5] introduced the first RRDH scheme, which proposed the histogram rotation technique. Their scheme suffered from salt-and-pepper noise because of modulo-256 addition, resulting in poor image quality after embedding a watermark. To avoid that in [5], Ni et al. [8] proposed an RRDH scheme using a robust parameter (difference value of all pixels in the block) to embed data and adopting error correction coding to achieve reversibility. Zeng et al. [14] increased the robustness of the scheme [8] by using the arithmetic difference of blocks as robust features and embedding secret data using two thresholds and a new histogram modification scheme. In [6], Gao et al. improved Zeng et al.'s scheme by designing a more stable framework to increase the embedding capacity and robustness. The RRDH scheme has also been developed in the wavelet domains. Based on the characteristics of the laplacian distribution of block mean values in the wavelet domain, Zou et al. [15] designed an RRDH scheme. Later, An et al. [1,2] improved the robustness by using histogram shifting and clustering, and efficiently dealing with overflow and underflow to achieve reversibility. Coltuc et al. [3,4] proposed a two-stage framework for RRDH. The first stage was the robust embedding stage for extracting the secret data accurately, and the second stage was used to restore the original image reversibly. However, the watermarking extraction may fail because both the robust embedding step and the reversible embedding stage were operated on the same embedding domain. To address this problem, Wang et al. [12] offered an independent embedding domain scheme to preserve robustness. Coltuc's scheme was improved by splitting the original image into two distinct domains, one for robust watermarking and the other for reversible embedding. Xiong et al. [13] proposed a multi-security protection RRDH scheme that used patchwork robust watermarking to provide the scheme's robustness and prediction error expansion to ensure the scheme's reversibility by exploiting the two-stage framework.

Recently, Wang et al. [11] proposed a lossless RRDH scheme based on significant-bit-difference expansion, in which secret data was embedded into higher significant bit-planes of the image to improve the embedding capacity. Inspired by the work of [11], Kumar et al. [7] first decomposed the original image into two planes, the most significant bit (MSB) (Here, MSB is equivalent to higher significant bit (HSB) in [7], but since the more general term is MSB, we use MSB instead.) planes and the least significant bit (LSB) planes. Then, the MSB planes of the original image were used to embed secret data by making a prediction error expansion with two-layer embedding. In this way, Kumar et al. achieved the robustness of their scheme against minor modification attacks like JPEG Compression. However, this paper demonstrates that the scheme [7] is not robust. The contributions of this paper are as follows:

1. This paper tests the percentage of bits changed in each bit-plane after JPEG compression and finds that JPEG compression will also cause the contents of MSB planes to be damaged.

2. This paper investigates the scheme [7] and analyzes the changes in both each bit-plane and pixel value ordering caused by JPEG compression to show that secret data can not be extracted correctly, thus proving their scheme is not robust.

The rest of the paper is organized as follows. In Sect. 2, the scheme [7] is briefly reviewed. In Sect. 3, a theoretical analysis is conducted from the perspective of JPEG compression principles. Section 4 shows the experimental results and analysis. Finally, the paper is concluded in Sect. 5.

2   Brief Description of Kumar's RDH Scheme [7]

For a self-contained discussion, we briefly review the scheme [7] and recommend [7] to readers for more detailed information about it.

To facilitate the introduction of the scheme [7], secret data is denoted as S, and an original image of size $h \times w$ is denoted as I. The pixel values of I vary in the range of 0–255. The eight main steps of the embedding scheme are summarized as follows:

1. Divide I into two parts, I_{MSB} and I_{LSB}, calculated as

$$p_{i,j} = x_{i,j} + l_{i,j}, \quad i = 0, ..., h-1, \quad j = 0, ..., w-1, \tag{1}$$

where

$$x_{i,j} = \sum_{k=n}^{7} b_k \times 2^k, \tag{2}$$

$$l_{i,j} = \sum_{k=0}^{n-1} b_k \times 2^k, \tag{3}$$

where $p_{i,j}$ represents the pixel value at the coordinate (i, j) of I, $x_{i,j}$ represents the pixel value in MSB planes of the pixel (I_{MSB}), $l_{i,j}$ represents the pixel value in LSB planes of the pixel (I_{LSB}), and b_k is the bit value in the k-th location. n represents the number of planes of LSB planes, and n varies from 1 to 8.
2. Preprocess I_{MSB}, construct a location map and compress it to achieve a compressed location map.
3. Save the least significant bit of pixels of I_{MSB} and attach the saved bits and compressed location map to the end of S.
4. Make use of the pattern in Fig. 1(a) to divide the image as in [7]. Sort the grey pixels by local complexity and use two-layer embedding in [11] to embed the first part of S. The local complexity of $x_{i,j}$ is calculated according to the variance ($\mu_{i,j}$) of surrounding pixels ($y_{i,j-1}, y_{i-1,j}, y_{i,j+1}, y_{i+1,j}$) (see Fig. 1(b)) by

$$\mu_{i,j} = \frac{1}{4} \sum_{t=1}^{4} (M_{i,j} - v_t)^2, \tag{4}$$

where $v_t (1 \le t \le 4)$ is the ascending sequence of the surrounding pixels, $M_{i,j}$ is the mean value of $v_t (1 \le t \le 4)$.

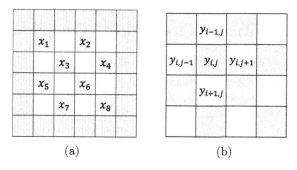

(a)   (b)

Fig. 1. (a) Chessboard pattern; (b) Prediction pattern.

5. Sort the white pixels based on local complexity, and the remaining part of S is embedded using prediction error expansion and two-layer embedding. The first prediction error (e_1) is calculated by $e_1 = x_{i,j} - \hat{p}_1$ where $\hat{p}_1 = \lfloor \frac{v_1 + v_2 + v_3}{3} \rfloor$ if $N = 3$ and $\lfloor \cdot \rfloor$ represents floor operators. N is the predictor number. The secret data bit $s_1 \in \{0, 1\}$ is embedded using

$$x'_{i,j} = \begin{cases} x_{i,j} + s_1, & e_1 = 1, \\ x_{i,j} + 1, & e_1 > 1, \\ x_{i,j}, & e_1 < 1, \end{cases} \tag{5}$$

where $x'_{i,j}$ is the obtained pixel value after the first layer embedding. The second prediction error (e_2) is calculated by $e_2 = x'_{i,j} - \hat{p}_2$ where $\hat{p}_2 = \lfloor \frac{v_2 + v_3 + v_4}{3} \rfloor$ if $N = 3$. The secret data bit $s_2 \in \{0, 1\}$ is embedded using

$$x''_{i,j} = \begin{cases} x'_{i,j} - s_2, & e_2 = -1, \\ x'_{i,j} - 1, & e_2 < -1, \\ x'_{i,j}, & e_2 > -1, \end{cases} \tag{6}$$

where $x''_{i,j}$ is the obtained pixel value after the second layer embedding.
6. Combine the resultant MSB planes and LSB planes to obtain the marked image.

7. Repeat Step 4 to Step 6 for all the three predictors, and select the most suitable predictor number (N) and the marked image according to application requirements.
8. Replace the $(n+1)$-th least significant bit of border pixels of the marked image to save auxiliary information (N and the coordinate of the last pixel to embed the secret data (C_{end})) using the least significant bit substitution scheme.

3   Theoretical Analysis from JPEG Compression Principles

Since Kumar et al. [7] only mentioned the robustness of their scheme against JPEG compression, we will focus on analyzing robustness against JPEG compression. This section first briefly reviews the JPEG compression process and then analyzes how this process changes the pixel value and destroys the robustness of the scheme [7].

3.1   Overview of JPEG Compression

JPEG compression is the most widely used lossy image compression method on the Internet. It uses the characteristics of the human visual system and uses the combination of quantization and lossless compression coding to remove the redundant information of the original image itself. Figure 2 shows the JPEG compression process, which is executed by three parts: Discrete Cosine Transform (DCT), Quantizer, and Entropy encoder [10].

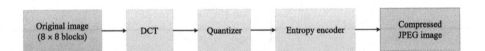

Fig. 2. JPEG compression encoding process.

Applying two-dimensional DCT transformation to the non-overlapping 8×8 blocks, the original DCT coefficients are obtained by

$$o\left(u, v\right) = \frac{1}{4}\alpha\left(u\right)\alpha\left(v\right)\sum_{i=0}^{7}\sum_{j=0}^{7}p_{i,j}\cos\frac{\left(2i+1\right)u\pi}{16}$$

$$\cos\frac{\left(2j+1\right)v\pi}{16}, u = 0, ..., 7, v = 0, ..., 7, \tag{7}$$

where

$$\alpha\left(u\right) = \left\{ \begin{array}{ll} \frac{1}{\sqrt{2}}, & u = 0, \\ 1, & else, \end{array} \right. \tag{8}$$

and $p_{i,j}$ represents the pixel value of a block at the position (i,j), and $o(u,v)$ is the original DCT coefficient at the position (u,v) of the block. Then the original image in the spatial domain is converted into an image in the frequency domain.

Next, the original DCT coefficients are quantized by a quantizer, which is the main reason for image quality deterioration. In the quantizer, the original DCT coefficients are processed by

$$r(u,v) = \text{round}\left(\frac{o(u,v)}{q(u,v)}\right), \tag{9}$$

where $r(u,v)$ is the quantized DCT coefficient, $q(u,v)$ is the predetermined quantization step of the position (u,v) in the quantization tables for different quality factors (QFs), round(t) means round to nearest integer to t. Through this step, the floating values of the original DCT coefficients are rounded to an integer, resulting in the loss of information, which is irreversible. It can be seen from Eq. 9 that the larger the quantization step $q(u,v)$ is, the rounding process introduces the larger error. Different quantization tables can be selected depending on the compression ratio of JPEG images. Generally speaking, the larger the compression rate (that is, the smaller the QF), the larger the quantization step in the quantization table, as shown in Fig. 3. As can be seen, the quantization step of the quantization table with QF = 70 is larger. Therefore, compared with QF = 80, the pixel value after JPEG compression with QF = 70 is tempered more seriously. Next, this variation is visualized to analyze the robustness of the scheme [7].

10	7	6	10	14	24	31	37
7	7	8	11	16	35	36	33
8	8	10	14	24	34	41	34
8	10	13	17	31	52	48	37
11	13	22	34	41	65	62	46
14	21	33	38	49	62	68	55
29	38	47	52	62	73	72	61
43	55	57	59	67	60	62	59

(a)

6	4	4	6	10	16	20	24
5	5	6	8	10	23	24	22
6	5	6	10	16	23	28	22
6	7	9	12	20	35	32	25
7	9	15	22	27	44	41	31
10	14	22	26	32	42	45	37
20	26	31	35	41	48	48	40
29	37	38	39	45	40	41	40

(b)

Fig. 3. Quantization tables: (a) QF = 70; (b) QF = 80.

3.2 Pixel Value Variation

We randomly select an 8×8 block of an image in Fig. 5 to calculate the change of pixel values before and after JPEG compression. Figure 4(b) and (c) illustrate the absolute values of the modifications on the compressed pixels compared to the original when QF = 70 and QF = 80, respectively. As we can see, QF = 70 causes a larger variation in pixel values than QF = 80, and the like, with QF decreases, this variation will become more and more apparent. The reason why pixel values vary so much is that, from Eq. 7, one DCT coefficient of a block is calculated by all pixel values of the block in the spatial domain. Therefore, the pixel values will be severely tampered with after rounding all DCT coefficients in the block, which is irreversible. As shown in Fig. 4(b) and (c), the pixel values required to extract secret data accurately will be greatly modified after JPEG compression, which will lead to errors when the receiver extracts secret data. Next, we will show robust testing experiments for the scheme [7] to illustrate how variation in pixel values affects the robustness of their scheme.

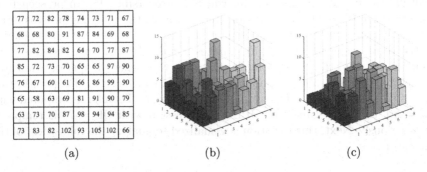

77	72	82	78	74	73	71	67
68	68	80	91	87	84	69	68
77	82	84	82	64	70	77	87
85	72	73	70	65	65	97	90
76	67	60	61	66	86	99	90
65	58	63	69	81	91	90	79
63	73	70	87	98	94	94	85
73	83	82	102	93	105	102	66

(a)   (b)   (c)

Fig. 4. Effect of different quantization tables on pixel values: (a) Pixel block; (b) QF = 70; (c) QF = 80.

4   Robust Testing

As described in Step 4 of Sect. 2, the scheme [7] used the partition pattern in Fig. 1(a) to generate independent cells, then rearranged the grey pixels in ascending order according to the local complexity of MSB planes (Step 1 of Sect. 2). Secret data can be embedded into pixels with lower local complexity. To extract the secret data correctly, the receiver sorts the pixels based on local complexity and then processes them in order. Therefore, we will show the changes in both bit-planes and pixel value ordering after JPEG compression to analyze the robustness of the scheme [7].

4.1   Changes in MSB Planes

Kumar et al. [7] showed that embedding secret data in MSB planes can improve the robustness of the scheme as slight attacks like JPEG compression make modifications in the lower bit-planes, so the content of MSB planes is intact. In fact, JPEG compression results in image pixels changing not only in LSB planes but also in MSB planes. The experiments were carried out on eight standard grey-scale images used by Kumar et al., as shown in Fig. 5. Each size is 512×512 pixels, including Lena, Baboon, Jetplane, Peppers, Barbara, Lake, Elaine, and Boat.

(a)   (b)   (c)   (d)

(e)   (f)   (g)   (h)

Fig. 5. Original images: (a) Lena; (b) Baboon; (c) Jetplane; (d) Peppers; (e) Barbara; (f) Lake; (g) Elaine; (h) Boat.

We perform JPEG compression with different QFs on the original images. The dissimilarity between the original image $(\boldsymbol{I})$ and the processed image $(\boldsymbol{I'})$ after JPEG compression has been observed by the number of bit change rates (NBCR). The NBCR indicates the percentage of bits in each bit-plane changed after JPEG compression. NBCR is formulated as

$$\text{NBCR} = \frac{1}{h \times w} \left[\sum_{i=1}^{h} \sum_{j=1}^{w} \left(\boldsymbol{I}_k(i,j) \oplus \boldsymbol{I}'_k(i,j) \right) \right] \times 100\%, \tag{10}$$

where "$\oplus$" represents exclusive-or (XOR) operation, $\boldsymbol{I}_k(i,j)$ and $\boldsymbol{I}'_k(i,j)$ represent the position (i,j) of the k-th bit-plane of the image $\boldsymbol{I}$ and $\boldsymbol{I}'$ respectively.

The testing results are shown in Fig. 6, where the horizontal axis represents different QFs, and the vertical axis represents the average NBCR of eight original images. The 1-st bit-plane represents the least significant bit-plane, and the 8-th bit-plane represents the most significant bit-plane. As described in Step 8 in Sect. 2, in the scheme [7], auxiliary information necessary to accurately extract secret data is embedded into the $(n+1)$-th LSB. Therefore, if we set $n = 3$ as an example, the auxiliary information will be stored in the 4-th bit-plane, so we will focus on the 4-th bit-plane. From Fig. 6, the 4-th bit-plane

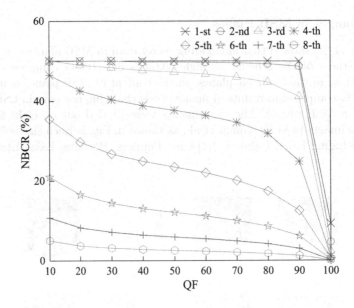

Fig. 6. Average NBCR of 8 original images on different bit-planes. n-th represents the n-th bit-plane.

has an average NBCR of about 25% when QF $=$ 90, which can damage the auxiliary information seriously. AS the compression QF decreases, the possibility of MSB being destroyed increases. So the auxiliary information is more likely to be damaged. With the damaged N, the prediction method will be wrong. Minor modifications will also have a huge impact on the entire scheme. As a result, the receiver will be unable to extract secret data accurately.

4.2   Changes in Pixel Value Ordering

In addition, in Step 4 in Sect. 2, before embedding the secret data, the scanned pixels are arranged according to the order of their local complexity (i.e., ascending order). However, according to the calculation formula of local complexity, as shown in Eq. 4, changes in pixel value will cause errors in the local complexity value, which affect the arrangement order of the pixel. Thus, JPEG compression will cause the secret data cannot be extracted correctly. The experimental results of the pixel sequence sorted by local complexity before and after compression are shown in Figs. 7, 8, 9, and Table 1. To demonstrate the change of pixel ordering clearly, we randomly select an 8×8 pixel block from Lena, as shown in Fig. 7(a). The matrix of the selected area is then divided into two parts by Eqs. 2 and 3, namely MSB and LSB matrix, under $n = 3$. The MSB matrix is shown in Fig. 7(b). Because the processing of white pixels is similar to that of grey pixels, only grey pixels are taken as an example here to calculate the local complexity and observe the pixel value ordering changes before and after compression. To better illustrate the local complexity of each grey pixel, we number it as shown in Fig. 8.

(a)

111	108	110	111	114	116	119	114
110	110	111	113	113	115	120	114
113	112	111	113	118	118	119	117
110	110	112	114	117	114	117	117
109	104	108	113	113	117	117	114
109	108	115	111	111	115	117	116
112	112	111	117	111	110	114	112
107	112	117	109	114	113	118	115

(b)

13	13	13	13	14	14	14	14
13	13	13	14	14	14	15	14
14	14	13	14	14	14	14	14
13	13	14	14	14	14	14	14
13	13	13	14	14	14	14	14
13	13	14	13	13	14	14	14
14	14	13	14	13	13	14	14
13	14	14	13	14	14	14	14

Fig. 7. Randomly select a pixel block with size 8×8 from Lena and its corresponding pixel value matrix: (a) Selected pixel block; (b) MSB matrix with $n = 3$.

	A1	B1	A2	B2	A3	B3	
	B4	A4	B5	A5	B6	A6	
	A7	B7	A8	B8	A9	B9	
	B10	A10	B11	A11	B12	A12	
	A13	B13	A14	B14	A15	B15	
	B16	A16	B17	A17	B18	A18	

Fig. 8. The pixel number of grey pixels.

Original pixel blocks are compressed with different QFs, e.g., QF = 100, 90, 85. Then the compressed pixel blocks are divided into two parts, namely LSB and MSB matrix under $n = 3$. MSB matrixes under different QFs are shown in Fig. 9. The pixels in red boxes in Fig. 9 indicate the pixels that have been changed after JPEG compression. We calculate the local complexity of the uncompressed and compressed MSB grey pixels, shown in Table 1.

We arrange the pixels according to the ascending order of their local complexity. From Table 1, the order of the uncompressed pixel block in Fig. 7 would be O = (A5, A8, A9, A12, A16, A1, A3, A4, A10, A14, A18, A2, A13, A15, A17). When the pixel block is compressed with QF = 100 (Fig. 9(a)), it is found that the value of (A17, B14) changes from (13, 13) to (14, 14). As the value of white pixel B14 changes, the local complexity of the surrounding pixels (A11, A14,

(a)

13	13	13	13	14	14	14	14
13	13	13	14	14	14	15	14
14	14	13	14	14	14	14	14
13	13	14	14	14	14	14	14
13	13	13	14	14	14	14	14
13	13	14	13	14	14	14	14
14	14	13	14	14	13	14	14
13	14	14	13	14	14	14	14

(b)

13	13	13	13	14	14	14	14
13	13	13	14	14	14	14	14
14	13	14	14	14	14	14	14
14	13	14	14	14	14	14	14
13	13	13	14	14	14	14	14
13	13	13	14	13	14	14	14
14	13	14	14	13	14	14	13
13	13	14	14	14	14	14	14

(c)

13	13	13	13	14	14	14	14
13	13	13	14	14	14	14	14
13	13	13	14	14	14	14	14
13	13	13	14	14	14	14	14
13	13	13	14	14	14	14	14
13	13	13	14	14	14	14	14
13	13	14	14	14	14	14	14
13	14	14	13	14	14	14	14

Fig. 9. MSB matrix of compressed pixel blocks: (a) QF = 100; (b) QF = 90; (c) QF = 85. (Color figure online)

Table 1. Changes in local complexity of grey pixels because of JPEG compression: (a) grey pixels A1–A9; (b) grey pixels A10–A18.

QF	A1	A2	A3	A4	A5	A6	A7	A8	A9
Original	0.1875	0.2500	0.1875	0.1875	0	0.1875	0.2500	0	0
100	0.1875	0.2500	0.1875	0.1875	0	0.1875	0.2500	0	0
90	0.1875	0	0.2500	0	0	0.2500	0	0	0.2500
85	0	0.1875	0	0.1875	0	0	0	0.1875	0

(a)

QF	A10	A11	A12	A13	A14	A15	A16	A17	A18
Original	0.1875	0.1875	0	0.2500	0.1875	0.2500	0	0.2500	0.1875
100	0.1875	0	0	0.2500	0	0.1875	0	0.1875	0.1875
90	0.1875	0	0	0.2500	0.1875	0.2500	0.1875	0.1875	0.1875
85	0.1875	0	0	0	0.1875	0	0.2500	0	0

(b)

A15, A17) changes from (0.1875, 0.1875, 0.2500, 0.2500) to (0, 0, 0.1875,0.1875), which results in a change in pixel ordering. As a result, the order of compressed pixels under QF = 100 is changed to O_{100} = (A5, A8, A9, A11, A12, A14, A16, A1, A3, A4, A6, A10, A15, A17, A18, A2, A7, A18, A2, A7, A13). Only A5, A8, and A9 are still in the same place. The order of compressed pixels under QF = 90 is changed to O_{90} = (A1, A3, A5, A6, A8, A9, A12, A11, A15, A17, A18, A4, A7, A10, A14, A16). None of the pixels is in their original position. The order of compressed pixels under QF = 85 is changed to O_{85} = (A1, A3, A5, A6, A7, A9, A11, A12, A13, A15, A17, A18, A2, A4, A8, A10, A14, A16). As with a QF of 85, all the pixels are out of place. Since JPEG compression causes changes in pixel value, and the local complexity of pixels depends on the pixel value, JPEG compression will lead to errors in calculating local complexity, resulting in confusion in pixel value ordering. As a result, the secret data extracted by the receiver is grossly inconsistent with the original secret data.

5   Conclusion

In the paper "Robust reversible data hiding scheme based on two-layer embedding strategy" published in INS recently, Kumar et al. proposed an RRDH scheme based on two-layer embedding. However, JPEG compression leads to a change in MSB planes, which leads to auxiliary information being damaged, which in turn leads to a change in the predictor. As a result, the secret data extracted by the receiver will be significantly different from the original secret data. The damaged pixel values caused by JPEG compression change the pixel value ordering, so the receiver extracts the secret data in the wrong order. From the above analysis, the secret data cannot be accurately extracted from compressed images, so Kumar et al.'s scheme is not robust.

References

1. An, L., Gao, X., Li, X., Tao, D., Deng, C., Li, J.: Robust reversible watermarking via clustering and enhanced pixel-wise masking. IEEE Trans. Image Process. **21**(8), 3598–3611 (2012)
2. An, L., Gao, X., Yuan, Y., Tao, D., Deng, C., Ji, F.: Content-adaptive reliable robust lossless data embedding. Neurocomputing **79**, 1–11 (2012)
3. Coltuc, D.: Towards distortion-free robust image authentication. In: Journal of Physics: Conference Series, vol. 77, p. 012005. IOP Publishing (2007)
4. Coltuc, D., Chassery, J.M.: Distortion-free robust watermarking: a case study. In: Security, Steganography, and Watermarking of Multimedia Contents IX, vol. 6505, p. 65051N. International Society for Optics and Photonics (2007)
5. De Vleeschouwer, C., Delaigle, J.F., Macq, B.: Circular interpretation of bijective transformations in lossless watermarking for media asset management. IEEE Trans. Multimedia **5**(1), 97–105 (2003)
6. Gao, X., An, L., Yuan, Y., Tao, D., Li, X.: Lossless data embedding using generalized statistical quantity histogram. IEEE Trans. Circuits Syst. Video Technol. **21**(8), 1061–1070 (2011)
7. Kumar, R., Jung, K.H.: Robust reversible data hiding scheme based on two-layer embedding strategy. Inf. Sci. **512**, 96–107 (2020)
8. Ni, Z., Shi, Y.Q., Ansari, N., Su, W., Sun, Q., Lin, X.: Robust lossless image data hiding designed for semi-fragile image authentication. IEEE Trans. Circuits Syst. Video Technol. **18**(4), 497–509 (2008)
9. Shi, Y.Q., Li, X., Zhang, X., Wu, H.T., Ma, B.: Reversible data hiding: advances in the past two decades. IEEE Access **4**, 3210–3237 (2016)
10. Wallace, G.K.: The jpeg still picture compression standard. IEEE Trans. Consum. Electron. **38**(1), xviii–xxxiv (1992)
11. Wang, W., Ye, J., Wang, T., Wang, W.: Reversible data hiding scheme based on significant-bit-difference expansion. IET Image Proc. **11**(11), 1002–1014 (2017)
12. Wang, X., Li, X., Pei, Q.: Independent embedding domain based two-stage robust reversible watermarking. IEEE Trans. Circuits Syst. Video Technol. **30**(8), 2406–2417 (2019)

13. Xiong, L., Han, X., Yang, C.N., Shi, Y.Q.: Robust reversible watermarking in encrypted image with secure multi-party based on lightweight cryptography. IEEE Trans. Circ. Syst. Video Technol. **32**, 75–91 (2021)
14. Zeng, X.T., Ping, L.D., Pan, X.Z.: A lossless robust data hiding scheme. Pattern Recogn. **43**(4), 1656–1667 (2010)
15. Zou, D., Shi, Y.Q., Ni, Z., Su, W.: A semi-fragile lossless digital watermarking scheme based on integer wavelet transform. IEEE Trans. Circuits Syst. Video Technol. **16**(10), 1294–1300 (2006)

Latent Energy Based Model with Classifier Guidance

Weili Zeng and Jia Wang[✉]

Shanghai Jiao Tong University, Shanghai 200240, China
`zwl666@sjtu.edu.cn`

Abstract. Energy-based generation models have attracted plenty of attention in last few years, but there is a lack of guidance on how to generate a condition-specific samples. In this work, we propose an energy based framework with an autoencoder and a standard discriminative classifier. Within this framework, we demonstrate that classifier can be reinterpreted as an EBM and we can accelerate sampling with fast MCMC in latent space of autoencoder. Both latent EBM and autoencoder can be learned jointly by maximum likelihood. Ultimately, our experimental results show that the trained model exhibits decent performance in both unconditional and conditional generation.

Keywords: Energy based model · Classifier guidance · Autoencoder · Latent MCMC · Image generation

1 Introduction

In recent years, the research on generative models has attracted increasing interest. The core of generative model is to use the generated sample distribution $x \sim p_\theta(x)$ to fit the real data distribution $x \sim q(x)$. Although GAN [1] exhibits higher generative quality, it requires a very specific design to stabilize training, and may collapse without carefully selected optimization and architecture. The ConvNet parameterized EBMs [3–5] framework addresses the attendant demands of representation, production, efficiency, and scalability in generative models. Specifically, it differs from existing popular generative models such as variational autoencoders (VAEs) [2] and generative adversarial networks (GANs), energy-based generative models can integrate bottom-up representations and top-down generation are unified into one framework and trained by maximum likelihood estimation. No need to recruit additional auxiliary models. Therefore, energy-based generative models are now used in many computer vision tasks [6,7] due to their major advantages over traditional models.

EBM models the data density via Gibbs distribution, which can be explicitly optimized via maximum likelihood, and the energy function $E(x)$ maps input variables x to energy scalars. However, the main drawback of EBM training is the need to generate negative samples using Markov Chain Monte Carlo (MCMC) for

G. Zhai et al. (Eds.): IFTC 2022, CCIS 1766, pp. 525–537, 2023.
https://doi.org/10.1007/978-981-99-0856-1_39

each iteration. This requires heavy computation, especially for high-dimensional data.

Moreover, the performance gap between generative modeling approaches for relevant downstream tasks and manually designed models for each concrete problem is still very large. One possible reason is that most downstream tasks are inherently discriminatory. This is often ignored in current generative models, with most attention focused on the quality of generation based on metrics. Therefore, the degradation in discriminative performance far outweighs the benefits brought by the generative component of the model. Inspired by [5], we attempted to reinterpret the classifier in latent space where the energy based model will be jointly trained.

In this work, we design a novel energy based framework based on autoencoder and a standard classifier to realize its potential on downstream specific tasks. Although EBMs are difficult to use at present, compared with other generative models, EBMs fit specific classification frameworks more naturally, and they can improve the performance of classifier architectures. Combined with specific downstream classification tasks, we define the latent space energy and implement fast MCMC. Because the latent pace is low-dimensional, we can traverse the data manifold more quickly. Learning latent energy in a low-dimensional latent space can help to traverse the data manifold quickly, and it is much easier to sample from a conditional distribution than a marginal distribution. Finally, our contribution can be summarized as follows:

1) We propose a new framework of EBM, where the latent energy is combined with specific downstream classification tasks.
2) Our method can take full advantage of the AE structure to speed up sampling and stabilize maximum likelihood training by first performing MCMC in the latent space.

2 Related Work

2.1 Energy Based Model

With the development of deep learning, a lot of works [3,5,8] has started using bottom-up structured deep convolutional neural networks to learn energy functions that map input images to energy scalars. However, due to the long mixing time of MCMC sampling for high-dimensional data, it is actually more difficult to implement and requires some practical skills, such as replay buffer [3] or coarse-to-fine strategy [8].

EBGAN [16] use an autoencoder as a discriminator, hoping that the generated image has the same low reconstruction error as the real image. Although EBGAN calls the reconstruction error "energy", the formulation is obvious different from our model. EBGAN does not model a distribution with Gibbs formulation, actually, it generates samples through an extra generator network. DSEBM [17] interpret the distance between input data and its reconstruction as the gradient of logarithmic density.

To reduce the complexity of sampling high-dimensional data, [9,10] introduces an adversarial learning framework with additional generators to learn the distribution under the energy model . However, maximizing the entropy of the generator is a difficult problem. MCMC sampling, on the other hand, is performed in latent space instead of data space. Mixing MCMC is more efficient because the latent space is low-dimensional and usually unimodal. This often leads to the need to jointly sample in latent space and data space [11–15].

2.2 Autoencoders

Some attempts have been made to formulate probabilistic models from autoencoders. VAE models the true distribution by leading into a prior $p(z)$. But this prior distribution may deviate from the true distribution in Z, which will cause some troubles in practice. GPND [18] models the data distribution by decomposing the probability density into on-manifold and off-manifold parts, but some certain assumptions about the prior distribution is still required. $\mathcal{M}$-flow [19] defines the probability density based on the a decoder manifold, and samples outside the manifold will be assigned extremely low probabilities. DAE models the data distribution by fitting the gradient of the log-likelihood under constraints [20].

2.3 Guidance

An interesting property of GAN and flow-based generative models is the ability to control the diversity of generated samples by limiting the original noise distribution at sampling time. The purpose of this is to generate samples under specific conditions, or to use sample diversity as a cost in exchange for generation quality of each individual sample. For example, truncation in BigGAN [21] produces a trade-off curve between FID scores and inception scores for low and high truncation amounts, respectively. Similar effect can found when implement low temperature sampling in Glow [22]. Unfortunately, straightforward attempts of implementing truncation or low temperature sampling in energy models are ineffective. For example, scaling model gradients or decreasing the variance of Gaussian noise in the MCMC process cause the model to generate blurry, low quality samples [23].

3 Background

Notation: let x, z be two random variables with joint probability density $p(x, z)$, and marginal distributions $p(x)$, $p(z)$. We will use the following notation:

1) Entropy: $H(x) = \mathbb{E}_{p(x)}[-\log p(x)]$.
2) Conditional entropy: $H(z \mid x) = \mathbb{E}_{p(x,z)}[-\log p(z \mid x)]$.
3) KL divergence: $D_{KL}(p\|q) = \mathbb{E}_{p(x)}\left[\log \frac{p(x)}{q(x)}\right]$.

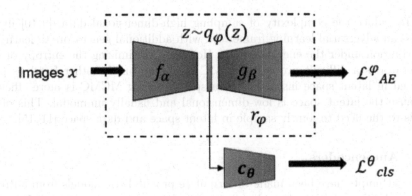

Fig. 1. The architecture of latent EBM. $r_\varphi = g_\beta \circ f_\alpha$ donate the autoencoder; c_θ denote the discriminative classifier mapping the code in latent space $\mathbb{R}^{D_z}$ to $\mathbb{R}^K$.

3.1   Autoencoder

Let the distribution of real data (image) be $x \sim q(x)$, the autoencoders r_φ denote the parametric network optimized to reconstruct the input data $x \in \mathcal{X} \subset \mathbb{R}^{D_x}$. For an input x, the reconstruction error $l_\varphi(x)$ is to measure its reconstruction quality, where φ denotes the parameter of autoencoder r_φ. L_{AE} is the loss function of r_φ, it is represented by the expected reconstruction error on input x. The optimization of the model parameters φ is performed by gradient descent:

$$\mathcal{L}_{AE} = \mathbb{E}_{x \sim q(x)} \left[l_\varphi(x) \right], \tag{1}$$

$$\nabla_\varphi \mathcal{L}_{AE} = \nabla_\varphi \mathbb{E}_{x \sim q(x)} \left[l_\varphi(x) \right], \tag{2}$$

where ∇_φ is the gradient operator on φ.

Architecture. There are two important components inside r_φ: encoder $f_\alpha(x)$ and decoder $g_\beta(z)$. Encoder $f_\alpha(x)$ maps the input x to low-dimensional latent representation $z \in \mathcal{Z} \subset \mathbb{R}^{D_z}$. And decoder $g_\beta(z)$ will map the latent representation z back to the data space. Then, $l_\varphi(x)$ can be formulated as:

$$l_\varphi(x) = dist(x, g_\beta(f_\alpha(x))), \tag{3}$$

where $\varphi = (\alpha, \beta)$ and $dist(\cdot, \cdot)$ acts as a distance function to measure the deviation between input x and its reconstruction $g_\beta(f_\alpha(x))$. For example, L^2 : $dist(x_i, x_j) = ||x_i - x_j||_2^2$ is a kind of typical distance function. Some other typical distance functions are $L_1 : dist(x_i, x_j) = |x_i - x_j|$ and structural similarity (SSIM) [24,25]. It should be noted that minimizing the reconstruction error does not correspond to maximizing the likelihood because the reconstruction error in Eq. (3) does not indicate the likelihood of data. As a result, autoencoder can not directly act as a probabilistic model per se and without modification [15].

3.2   Energy Based Model

Consider the observed example $x_1, x_2, \ldots, x_N \sim p(x)$. It is inspired by the physical point of view or the principle of maximum entropy, the energy-based model (EBM) aims to approximate $p(x)$ with a Gibbs model, defined as follows:

$$p_\theta(x) = \frac{1}{Z(\theta)} \exp\left(-U_\theta(x)\right), \tag{4}$$

where θ is the parameter of energy function U_θ and $Z(\theta) = \int_x \exp\left(-U_\theta(x)\right) dx$ is the partition function. There are no restrictions on the specific form of $U_\theta(x)$. To find the parameter θ, the model is optimized using MLE. The objective function for MLE learning is:

$$L(\theta) = \mathbb{E}_{p(x)}\left[-\log p_\theta(x)\right] \approx \frac{1}{N}\sum_{i=1}^{N} -\log p_\theta\left(x_i\right). \tag{5}$$

The gradient of the $L(\theta)$ is:

$$\nabla_\theta L(\theta) = \mathbb{E}_{p(x)}\left[\nabla_\theta U_\theta(x)\right] - \mathbb{E}_{p_\theta(x)}\left[\nabla_\theta U_\theta(x)\right]$$
$$\approx \frac{1}{N}\sum_{i=1}^{n} \nabla_\theta U_\theta\left(x_i\right) - \frac{1}{\tilde{N}}\sum_{i=1}^{\tilde{N}} \nabla_\theta U_\theta\left(\tilde{x}_i\right). \tag{6}$$

where the $\{\tilde{x}_1, \tilde{x}_2, \ldots, \tilde{x}_{\tilde{N}}\} \sim p_\theta(x)$ is approximated by Markov chain Monte Carlo (MCMC). Langevin Monte Carlo (LMC) is an MCMC method for obtaining random samples from probability distributions that are difficult to sample directly, which iterates

$$x_{t+1} = x_t - \eta\nabla_x U_\theta\left(x_t\right) + \sqrt{2\eta}e_t, \quad e_t \sim \mathcal{N}(0, I). \tag{7}$$

where η corresponds to the step-size. As $x \to 0$ and $t \to \infty$, the distribution of x_t converges to $p_\theta(x)$.

MCMC convergence is theoretically independent of its initialization, but in practice the initialization method can be important. In particular, when sampling with high-dimensional multimodal distributions, the initial states can deviate significantly from $p_\theta(x)$, making convergence difficult and generating poor MCMC sampling performance.

4   Methodology

In this section we describe how to build latent energy based model. As shown in Fig. 1, our model can be decomposed into two parts: autoencoder and a standard discriminative classifier. The overall learning procedure are trained via Maximum Likelihood Estimation (MLE).

Fig. 2. Randomly generated image. Left: SVHN samples ($32 \times 32 \times 3$). Right: CIFAR-10 samples ($32 \times 32 \times 3$).

4.1 Latent Energy with Classifier Guidance

In modern machine learning, the K-classes classification problem is usually solved by using a neural network. Here, let's consider a parametric classification network c_θ, and we can optimize it by minimizing the standard cross-entropy loss,

$$\mathcal{L}_{cls} = -\mathbb{E}_{(z,y)\sim q(z,y)} \sum_k q_k \log p_\theta(k|z), \tag{8}$$

where q is the one-hot encoding for the label y, that is to say, only the position q_k of the correct class is "1", while the position of the wrong class is encoded "0". $c_\theta : \mathbb{R}^{D_z} \to \mathbb{R}^K$ maps the latent representation $z \in \mathbb{R}^{D_z}$ to logits, which is a K-dimensional real-valued vector. Further, these logits can be normalized by the Softmax activation function, so that it has the form of a probability distribution to represent the classification:

$$p_\theta(y|z) = \frac{\exp\left(c_\theta(\mathbf{z})[y]\right)}{\sum_{y'} \exp\left(c_\theta(\mathbf{z})[y']\right)}, \tag{9}$$

where $c_\theta(\mathbf{z})[y]$ indicate the yth index of $c_\theta(z)$. To further improve the discriminability of latent codes, we also employ label smoothing technique at the same time, since it can maintain the intra-class distribution and help improve the inter-class distribution. With LS, the q_k in Eq. (8) is changed to $q_k^{ls} = (1-\alpha)q_k + \alpha/K$.

Following the work in [5] that we can reinterpret the logits obtained from c_θ and use it to define $p(z,y)$ and $p(z)$. Based on the standard classification network c_θ, we rewrite the logits to fit the Gibbs distribution and use it to represent the joint distribution of latent codes z and labels y:

$$p_\theta(\mathbf{z}, y) = \frac{\exp\left(c_\theta(\mathbf{z})[y]\right)}{Z(\theta)}, \tag{10}$$

where $Z(\theta)$ is the intractable partition function and $E_\theta(\mathbf{z}, y) = -c_\theta(\mathbf{z})[y]$.

Next, by accumulating y, we can obtain the Gibbs distribution model for z,

$$p_\theta(\mathbf{z}) = \frac{\sum_y \exp\left(c_\theta(\mathbf{z})[y]\right)}{Z(\theta)}, \tag{11}$$

It can be noticed that for any classifier, the LogSumExp($\cdot$) of its logits can be reused to explain the energy function of data x as

$$U_\theta(\mathbf{z}) = -\log \text{SumExp}_y\left(c_\theta(\mathbf{z})[y]\right) = -\log \sum_y \exp\left(c_\theta(\mathbf{z})[y]\right) \tag{12}$$

For standard classifiers, shifting the logits $c_\theta(z)$ to any scalar scale does not affect the performance of the model. But in our framework, the logits of a shifted latent code z will affect its corresponding likelihood $logp_\theta(z)$. In this case, we revisiting the expression form of logits. And then, we can define the marginal density function of the latent code and the joint density function between it and its corresponding label. Finally, dividing the Eq. (10) by the Eq. (11), we can calculate $p_\theta(y|z)$ by $p_\theta(z,y)/p_\theta(z)$, the tricky partial function cancellation, yielding the standard Softmax form in Eq. (9). Therefore, we can successfully build latent generative models based on any standard discriminative model.

Algorithm 1. Training and sampling algorithm

Input: (1) Training examples $x_1, x_2, \ldots, x_N \sim q(x)$, (2) numbers of MCMC steps K and T and step-size η_1, η_2, (3) reconstruction training steps L during per epoch.
Output: Parameter φ, θ, synthetic samples Y.

1: **while** not converged **do**
2:     **for** $l = 1 \rightarrow L$ **do**
3:         randomly sample a mini-batch examples $\{x_i, y_i\}_{i=1}^n$.
4:         compute $\Delta\varphi = \nabla_\varphi \mathcal{L}_{AE}^\varphi$, $\Delta\theta = \nabla_\gamma \mathcal{L}_{cls}^\theta$.
5:         update φ, θ based on $\Delta\varphi, \Delta\theta$ using Adam optimizer.
6:     **end for**
7:     **for** $t = 0 \rightarrow K - 1$ **do**
8:         $z^{t+1} = z^t - \eta_1 \nabla_z U_\theta^s\left(z^t\right) + \sqrt{2\eta_1} e_t$.
9:     **end for**
10:     let $x^0 = g_\beta(z^K)$.
11:     **for** $t = 0 \rightarrow T - 1$ **do**
12:         $x^{t+1} = x^t - \eta_2 \nabla_x U_\varphi^c\left(x^t\right) + \sqrt{2\eta_2} e_t$.
13:     **end for**
14:     $\Delta\theta = \sum_{i=1}^n \left[\nabla_\theta U_\theta^s\left(z_i\right)\right] - \sum_{i=1}^n \left[\nabla_\theta U_\theta^s\left(z_i^K\right)\right]$.
15:     $\Delta\varphi = \sum_{i=1}^n \left[\nabla_\varphi U_\varphi^c\left(x_i\right)\right] - \sum_{i=1}^n \left[\nabla_\varphi U_\varphi^c\left(x_i^T\right)\right]$.
16:     update φ, θ based on $\Delta\varphi, \Delta\theta$ using Adam optimizer.
17: **end while**
18: $Y = x^T$.
19: **return** φ, γ, Y.

4.2   Energy with Autoencoder

Here we propose the energy based on an autoencoder. The probability density of $p_\varphi(x)$ is formulated as a Gibbs distribution (Eq. (4)). Specifically, we use the reconstruction error of autoencoder to define the energy of probabilistic model:

$$U_\varphi(x) = l_\varphi(x) = ||x - r_\varphi(x)||_2^2. \tag{13}$$

Since the reconstruction error of observe data is small, it will be assigned a lower energy, while the generated data under the model will be penalized and given higher energy.

4.3   Model and Learning

Given the training samples $x_1, x_2, \ldots, x_N \sim q(x)$, consider the generative structure $z \to x$, we have $p_\varphi(x, z) = p_\theta(z)p_\varphi(x|z)$. Our model are trained by maximizing the marginal log-likelihood on the observed data x:

$$
\begin{aligned}
\nabla_{\varphi,\theta} \log p_\varphi(x) &= \frac{1}{p_\varphi(x)} \nabla_{\varphi,\theta} p_\varphi(x) \\
&= \frac{1}{p_\varphi(x)} \nabla_{\varphi,\theta} \int p_\varphi(x, z) dz \\
&= \frac{1}{p_\varphi(x)} \int p_\varphi(x, z) \nabla_{\varphi,\theta} \log p_\varphi(x, z) dz \\
&= \int \frac{p_\varphi(x, z)}{p_\varphi(x)} \nabla_{\varphi,\theta} \log p_\varphi(x, z) dz \\
&= \int q_\varphi(z \mid x) \nabla_{\varphi,\theta} \log p_\varphi(x, z) dz \\
&= \mathbb{E}_{q_\varphi(z|x)} \left[\nabla_{\varphi,\theta} \log p_\varphi(x, z) \right]
\end{aligned}
\tag{14}
$$

And then the gradient can be calculated according to

$$
\begin{aligned}
&\mathbb{E}_{q(x)} \nabla_{\varphi,\theta} - \log p_\varphi(x) \\
&= \mathbb{E}_{q(x)} \mathbb{E}_{q_\varphi(z|x)} \left[\nabla_{\varphi,\theta} - \log p_\varphi(x, z) \right] \\
&= \mathbb{E}_{q(x)} \mathbb{E}_{q_\varphi(z|x)} \left[-\nabla_\theta \log p_\theta(z) - \nabla_\varphi \log p_\varphi(x \mid z) \right]
\end{aligned}
\tag{15}
$$

Fig. 3. Class-conditional samples with classifier guidance.

For the discriminative classifier c_θ, the first term in Eq. (15) is to optimize:

$$\mathbb{E}_{q(x,z)} \nabla_\theta \left[-\log p_\theta(z) \right]$$
$$= \mathbb{E}_{q(z|x)} \left[\nabla_\theta U_\theta(z) \right] - \mathbb{E}_{p_\theta(z|x)} \left[\nabla_\theta U_\theta(z) \right]. \qquad (16)$$

And for the autoencoder, it is sufficient to learn the gradient of $\mathbb{E}_{q(x,z)} \left[\log p_\varphi(x|z) \right]$:

$$\mathbb{E}_{q(x,z)} \nabla_\varphi \left[-\log p_\varphi(x|z) \right]$$
$$= \mathbb{E}_{q(x)} \left[\nabla_\varphi U_\varphi(x) \right] - \mathbb{E}_{p_\varphi(x|z)} \left[\nabla_\varphi U_\varphi(x) \right]. \qquad (17)$$

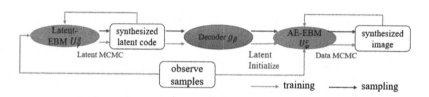

Fig. 4. Overview of our framework.

The expectations of the Eqs. (16) and (17) require MCMC of the latent marginal $p_\theta(z)$ in $\mathcal{Z}$ and latent-based conditional distribution $p_\varphi(x|z)$ in $\mathcal{X}$. To approximate $p_\theta(z)$, we iterate Eq. (18) from the fixed initial Gaussian distribution. Specifically, $\mathcal{Z}$ is low-dimensional, so MCMC only needs to iterate a small number of K steps, e.g., $K = 20$,

$$z^{t+1} = z^t - \eta_1 \nabla_z U_\gamma \left(z^t \right) + \sqrt{2\eta_1} e_t, \quad e_t \sim \mathcal{N}(0, I). \qquad (18)$$

To approximate $p_\varphi(x|z)$, we perform a two-stage sampling. The first-stage iterative Eq. (18) is to get $z^K \sim \hat{p}_\gamma(z)$ ($\hat{p}$ is the approximate distribution obtained by MCMC), and the second stage is to iterate Eq. (19) from the initial state $x^0 = g_\beta(z^K)$.

$$x^{t+1} = x^t - \eta_2 \nabla_x U_\varphi \left(x^t \right) + \sqrt{2\eta_2} e_t, \quad e_t \sim \mathcal{N}(0, I). \qquad (19)$$

It is worth noting that the initial state x^0 actually produced roughly what we wanted, hence we name it semantic image. However, the latent model is relatively simple and lacks detailed texture information, so the second stage is supplemental. Since the initial distribution of MCMC in the second stage is close to the model distribution that needs to be sampled, we only need to do a fixed number of T steps, such as $T = 90$, and the whole training framework is also very fast and stable. The training and sampling process is summarized in Algorithm 1. And the overview of our framework is shown in Fig. 4 (Table 1).

Table 1. Mean square error (MSE) of testing reconstructions and FID of random generated samples for SVHN ($32 \times 32 \times 3$), CIFAR-10 ($32 \times 32 \times 3$).

Models		VAE	RAE	SRI	Ours
SVHN	MSE	0.019	0.014	0.011	**0.009**
	FID	46.78	40.02	**35.23**	38.12
CIFAR-10	MSE	0.057	0.027	–	**0.015**
	FID	106.37	74.16	–	**69.47**

5 Experiment

Experimental setting: We used CIFAR-10 [26], SVHN [27] in our experiments. For autoencoder, we adopt the structure of ResNet [28,29]. On hyper parameter selection, we choose $L = 3, K = 20, T = 70$. Step-size $\eta_1 = 0.1$, $\eta_2 = 0.01$. All training experiments use Adam optimizer with learning rate of 5×10^{-5}. We used batch normalization 2D and batch normalization 1D during implementation. For CIFAR-10 32×32, SVHN 32×32, our model used 4 feature map resolution. All models had two convolutional residual blocks at each resolution level and adopt ELU as activation function. For the classifier we use 3 fully connected layers to implement and the detailed autoencoder structures were shew in Table 2.

Generation. Figure 2 shows random samples from the learned models on the SVHN and CIFAR-10 datasets. The left is the semantic map, and the right is the final generated samples after refinement of autoencoder energy. We evaluated $50k$ synthetic samples after training on the CIFAR-10 and SVHN datasets with FID [30] as quantitative metrics. As summarized in Table 2, our model achieves an FID of 69.47 on CIFAR-10 and 38.12 on SVHN. And we can also find that our model can perform better generatively than most baseline models.

Reconstruction. Here we evaluate the objective truth of the posterior inference by evaluating the reconstruction error of images. A suitable latent MCMC should not only facilitate learning the latent EBM model, but also match the corresponding true posterior distribution $p_\theta(z|x)$. In experiments, our model is compared with VAE [2] and SRI [31]. They both use a fixed Gaussian prior to assume a latent encoding distribution. Our model is also compared with RAE [32], which is a recent and powerful variant of VAE with prior and posterior sample learning. We quantitatively compare the reconstruction of test images with the aforementioned baseline models in terms of mean squared error (MSE). From Table 2, we can see that our proposed model not only achieves high generation quality, but also achieves accurate reconstruction.

Table 2. Autoencoder architecture.

Resolution 32 × 32
3 × 3 Conv2D, 64
ResBlocks Down, 128
2 ResBlocks, 128
ResBlocks Down, 256
2 ResBlocks, 256
ResBlocks Down, 512
2 ResBlocks, 512
linear 4 × 4 × 512→512
Batch normalization 1D, ELU()
linear 512→4 × 4 × 512
Batch normalization 1D
1 ResBlocks, 256
ResBlocks Up, 256
1 ResBlocks, 128
ResBlocks Up, 128
1 ResBlocks, 64
ResBlocks Up, 64
3 × 3 Conv2D, 3
tanh()

Conditional Sampling with Classifier Guidance. Different from normal EBMs, our model can generate conditional samples easily with discriminative classifier guidance. Starting from gaussian noise, we generate latent codes to maximize $p(y = \text{"car"}|z)$ through MCMC. Results are shown in Fig. 3.

6   Conclusion and Further Work

In this work we presented a latent energy based model with classifier guidance. By reinterpreting classifier as an energy model, we can generate semantically latent code through fast MCMC. Finally, our model exhibits strong performances in terms of unconditional generation and conditional generation. In the future, we need to improve the network structure to generate higher quality samples.

Acknowledgments. This work is supported by the National Science Foundation of China (NSFC) under grant 61927809. Here, the authors thank all anonymous reviewers as well as the processing area chair for their valuable comments on an earlier version of this work.

References

1. Goodfellow, I., Pouget-Abadie, J., Mirza, M., et al.: Generative adversarial networks. Commun. ACM **63**(11), 139–144 (2020)
2. Kingma, D.P., Welling, M.: Auto-encoding variational bayes. arXiv preprint arXiv:1312.6114 (2013)
3. Du, Y., Mordatch, I.: Implicit generation and modeling with energy based models. In: Advances in Neural Information Processing Systems, vol. 32 (2019)
4. Gao, R., Song, Y., Poole, B., et al.: Learning energy-based models by diffusion recovery likelihood. arXiv preprint arXiv:2012.08125 (2020)
5. Grathwohl, W., Wang, K.C., Jacobsen, J.H., et al.: Your classifier is secretly an energy based model and you should treat it like one. arXiv preprint arXiv:1912.03263 (2019)
6. Pang, B., Wu, Y.N.: Latent space energy-based model of symbol-vector coupling for text generation and classification. In: International Conference on Machine Learning, pp. 8359–8370. PMLR (2021)
7. LeCun, Y., Chopra, S., Hadsell, R., et al.: A tutorial on energy-based learning. Predicting Struct. Data **1**(0) (2006)
8. Zhao, Y., Xie, J., Li, P.: Learning energy-based generative models via coarse-to-fine expanding and sampling. In: International Conference on Learning Representations (2020)
9. Geng, C., Wang, J., Gao, Z., et al.: Bounds all around: training energy-based models with bidirectional bounds. In: Advances in Neural Information Processing Systems, vol. 34, pp. 19808–19821 (2021)
10. Kumar, R., Ozair, S., Goyal, A., et al.: Maximum entropy generators for energy-based models. arXiv preprint arXiv:1901.08508 (2019)
11. Arbel, M., Zhou, L., Gretton, A.: Generalized energy based models. arXiv preprint arXiv:2003.05033 (2020)
12. Pang, B., Han, T., Nijkamp, E., et al.: Learning latent space energy-based prior model. In: Advances in Neural Information Processing Systems, vol. 33, pp. 21994–22008 (2020)
13. Xiao, Z., Kreis, K., Kautz, J., et al.: VAEBM: a symbiosis between variational autoencoders and energy-based models. arXiv preprint arXiv:2010.00654 (2020)
14. Xie, J., Lu, Y., Gao, R., et al.: Cooperative learning of energy-based model and latent variable model via MCMC teaching. In: Proceedings of the AAAI Conference on Artificial Intelligence, vol. 32, no. 1 (2018)
15. Yoon, S., Noh, Y.K., Park, F.: Autoencoding under normalization constraints. In: International Conference on Machine Learning, pp. 12087–12097. PMLR (2021)
16. Zhao, J., Mathieu, M., LeCun, Y.: Energy-based generative adversarial network. arXiv preprint arXiv:1609.03126 (2016)
17. Zhai, S., Cheng, Y., Lu, W., et al.: Deep structured energy based models for anomaly detection. In: International Conference on Machine Learning, pp. 1100–1109. PMLR (2016)
18. Pidhorskyi, S., Almohsen, R., Doretto, G.: Generative probabilistic novelty detection with adversarial autoencoders. In: Advances in Neural Information Processing Systems, vol. 31 (2018)
19. Brehmer, J., Cranmer, K.: Flows for simultaneous manifold learning and density estimation. In: Advances in Neural Information Processing Systems, vol. 33, pp. 442–453 (2020)

20. Alain, G., Bengio, Y.: What regularized auto-encoders learn from the data-generating distribution. J. Mach. Learn. Res. **15**(1), 3563–3593 (2014)

21. Brock, A., Donahue, J., Simonyan, K.: Large scale GAN training for high fidelity natural image synthesis. arXiv preprint arXiv:1809.11096 (2018)

22. Kingma, D.P., Dhariwal, P.: Glow: generative flow with invertible 1x1 convolutions. In: Advances in Neural Information Processing Systems, vol. 31 (2018)

23. Dhariwal, P., Nichol, A.: Diffusion models beat GANs on image synthesis. In: Advances in Neural Information Processing Systems, vol. 34, pp. 8780–8794 (2021)

24. Wang, Z., Bovik, A.C., Sheikh, H.R., et al.: Image quality assessment: from error visibility to structural similarity. IEEE Trans. Image Process. **13**(4), 600–612 (2004)

25. Bergmann, P., Löwe, S., Fauser, M., et al.: Improving unsupervised defect segmentation by applying structural similarity to autoencoders. arXiv preprint arXiv:1807.02011 (2018)

26. Krizhevsky, A., Hinton, G.: Learning multiple layers of features from tiny images (2009)

27. Netzer, Y., Wang, T., Coates, A., Bissacco, A., Wu, B., Ng, A.Y.: Reading digits in natural images with unsupervised feature learning (2011)

28. He, K., Zhang, X.: Shaoqing Ren, and Jian Sun. deep residual learning for image recognition. In: Proceedings of the IEEE CVPR, pp. 770–778 (2016)

29. He, K., Zhang, X., Ren, S., Sun, J.: Identity mappings in deep residual networks. In: Leibe, B., Matas, J., Sebe, N., Welling, M. (eds.) ECCV 2016. LNCS, vol. 9908, pp. 630–645. Springer, Cham (2016). https://doi.org/10.1007/978-3-319-46493-0_38

30. Heusel, M., Ramsauer, H., Unterthiner, T., et al.: GANs trained by a two time-scale update rule converge to a local Nash equilibrium. In: Advances in Neural Information Processing Systems, vol. 30 (2017)

31. Nijkamp, E., Hill, M., Zhu, S.C., et al.: Learning non-convergent non-persistent short-run MCMC toward energy-based model. In: Advances in Neural Information Processing Systems, vol. 32 (2019)

32. Ghosh, P., Sajjadi, M.S., Vergari, A., Black, M., Scholkopf, B.: From variational to deterministic autoencoders. In International Conference on Learning Representations (2020)

Evaluation Technology of Power Regulation Data Assets

Yan Wang[1]([✉]), Can Cui[1], Ruili Ye[1], Fangchun Di[1], Lei Tao[1], Lin Xie[1], Chaohan Feng[1], Qiong Feng[1], Zhibin Song[2], Huiwen Qi[2], and Xiangyu Zhang[2]

[1] Beijing Key Laboratory of Research and System Evaluation of Power Dispatching Automation Technology, China Electric Power Research Institute, Beijing 100192, China
wangyan2@epri.sgcc.com.cn

[2] State Grid Shanxi Electric Power Company Economic and Technological Research Institute, Taiyuan 030602, Shanxi, China

Abstract. With the rapid development of the Internet and big data technology and the in-depth application in the field of power regulation, power regulation data shows explosive growth. Power regulation data runs through all aspects of power dispatching production and management. After years of operation, various business systems have accumulated rich information resources, which can bring huge profits to power grid enterprises. At present, the management and operation mode of data is relatively rough, and it is still used and managed by various business departments. As an intangible asset, the value of data has not been paid enough attention and deeply explored. Based on the characteristics of power regulation data and the factors affecting the value of data assets, combined with traditional evaluation algorithms, this paper studies the data asset value evaluation methods applicable to the field of power regulation; Based on the improved value evaluation method, a data asset evaluation model covering the cost, intrinsic value and use value of power regulation data is established to provide basic support for reasonable determination of big data asset value.

Keywords: Data asset value evaluation · Grid regulatory data · Improved cost method

1 Introduction

As an asset of an enterprise, when big data is fully utilized, it can create economic profits for the enterprise. In addition to helping enterprises obtain economic profits by improving production efficiency and innovation ability, as an asset with commercial value, you can directly gain profits by selling big data to other organizations. It is precisely because the value of big data has been continuously exploited and has brought considerable profits that many enterprises have regarded big data as assets. However, not all big data is of use value. To realize the transformation of big data into assets, enterprises should first clarify the goal of applying big data.

As the current accounting standards define assets, only things that can bring economic benefits to the enterprise can meet the recognition conditions of assets. The value of data assets is generally reflected when the data is consumed. Generally, the value of data assets is reflected through two ways: first, it is applied by the enterprise itself, thus the core competitiveness of the enterprise will be greatly improved; Second, data assets can also provide corresponding services for other enterprises through the market.

Different foreign scholars have put forward different big data asset value evaluation models according to the characteristics of big data assets and the practicality of evaluation methods. Berkman [1] once proposed that the income method is the best method for data asset valuation, but did not give a specific model. For the evaluation method of data assets, Long staff and Schwartz [2] began to use the Least Squares Monte Carlo Approach (LSM for short) to evaluate the data value and price in 2001, and used LSM to study the dependence of American option prices on historical data and the flexibility of option pricing, which opened a new era for people to evaluate data assets. Stentoft [3] made quantitative analysis on LSM method and proposed that the method can be extended to multiple application fields; Cortazar and Gravet [4] used the improved LSM method to evaluate multi-dimensional American real options, expanding the scope of LSM to evaluate real options. One of the important application fields of LSM is R&D project venture capital; Villani et al. [5] believed that R&D investment has great uncertainty, and in 2014, LSM method was used to solve the problem of multi-stage investment budget and flexible project valuation of R&D projects.

China has also accumulated a lot of research achievements in data asset valuation. Liu Qi et al. [6] assumed that the big data trading market would be very active in the future, and built a model to evaluate big data assets using the market approach. First, look for similar comparable transaction cases in the market, then introduce the analytic hierarchy process to modify the technology, value density, date, capacity and other factors of big data assets, and finally make differentiation adjustments to obtain the value of the big data assets being evaluated. Li Yonghong and Zhang Shuwen [7] introduced Analytic Hierarchy Process (AHP) on the basis of the market approach to determine the weight of the influencing factors of data assets. They used the grey relational analysis method to solve the quantitative data asset value influencing factors, and calculated the value of the appraised data assets. Zhang Zhigang et al. [8] determined the value of data assets through data asset costs and data asset expenses, and determined the weight of various factors by introducing the analytic hierarchy process, and then further calculated the evaluation value of data assets in combination with expert scoring. Shi Aixin et al. [9] built a data asset value evaluation model from the perspective of collecting, processing and maintaining three cost factors. Huang Le et al. [10] put forward the value evaluation model of platform data assets by combining cost method, market method and income method. The model takes into account such factors as the total income of data assets, data commodity cost, data operation cost, average market return, market adjustment coefficient, platform activity coefficient, and data realization factor, and comprehensively reflects the value of platform data assets.

2   Influencing Factors of Data Asset Value

The factors that affect the value of data assets are mainly considered from the two dimensions of income and risk of data assets. The income of data assets depends on the quantity, quality and application value of data assets. The quality of data assets is the basis of application value. A reasonable evaluation of data quality is conducive to accurate prediction of data application value (Fig. 1).

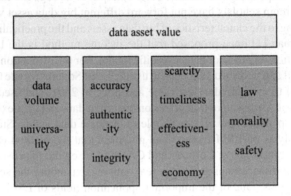

Fig. 1. Influencing factors of data asset value

From the data dimension, the influencing factors of data asset value include data volume and universality. Data volume is the most direct factor to image the value of data assets in the process of data trading. Generally, the more regulated data, the higher the asset value.

From the quality dimension, the influencing factors of data asset quality value include authenticity, integrity, accuracy, data cost, security, etc.

Authenticity indicates the authenticity of data. If there is deviation in the data, the results may be lost by a hair's breadth; If the data is falsified, it will lose the significance of data statistics. Real data is valuable.

Integrity indicates the integrity of all relevant indicators of the recorded object. The absence of key data will affect the value contribution of the data in the application, or increase the cost to supplement the data. The wider the data collection scope, the higher the integrity, and the greater the value of data assets.

Accuracy indicates the accuracy of data recorded. In the process of work, the obtained data needs to be cleaned first to eliminate abnormal values, blank values, invalid values, duplicate values, etc. This work is likely to take nearly half of the time of the entire data analysis process. The emergence of full-time "data cleaning engineer" also shows the complexity of data cleaning. The higher the accuracy of data, the lower the cost of data cleaning, and the greater the value of data.

The influencing factors of application value of application dimension data assets include scarcity, timeliness, effectiveness and economy.

Scarcity refers to the extent to which data asset owners have exclusive access to data. The essence of business competition comes partly from the competition for scarce resources. In the case of the flattening of manufacturing differentiation, the potential business information behind the scarce data resources is more prominent. Timeliness: The timeliness of data determines whether a decision is effective within a specific time. Validity refers to the function and effect of data. The value of data lies in the combination with application scenarios. Under different application scenarios, the economic value of data is different.

From the perspective of risk, the influencing factors of data asset value include legal restrictions, moral constraints and security risks. There are different risk factors in the data management circulation link, which affect the final value of the data.

3   Influencing Factors of Data Asset Value

The traditional appraisal method is to analyze the overview assets. Intangible assets appraisal started in China in the 1980s. In the early stage of asset appraisal, the enterprise value appraisal was mainly based on real estate, equipment and other physical assets. However, for enterprises with good benefits, good reputation and advanced patented technology, the value impact of intangible assets cannot be ignored. In order to ensure the equity transaction is fair and reasonable, objectively put forward the requirements for intangible asset value evaluation. In industry practice, the valuation methods of intangible assets include cost method, income method and market method and their derivatives.

3.1   Cost Method

The theoretical basis of the cost method is that the value of intangible assets is determined by the necessary labor time to produce the intangible assets. It is a valuation method from the perspective of asset replacement, that is, investors will not pay higher costs to purchase assets than they would need to spend to build the asset. Under the cost method, the value of intangible assets is equal to the replacement cost minus the depreciation of intangible assets. Replacement costs usually include reasonable costs, profits and relevant taxes, among which, in addition to direct and indirect costs, opportunity costs should also be considered. The depreciation of intangible assets usually needs to be considered from three aspects: functional depreciation, physical depreciation and economic depreciation. When applying the cost method, it is necessary to focus on the correlation between asset value and cost.

For the data assets generated and collected within the company, the explicit costs mainly include the human cost and equipment cost of data collection, storage and processing, while the implicit costs mainly include the R&D cost and human cost of the business to which the data is attached; For purchased data assets, the replacement cost is the amount to be paid to re acquire the same data asset under the current market conditions; Depreciation Factors In traditional cost method evaluation, the depreciation factors of physical assets are mainly divided into economic depreciation, physical depreciation and functional depreciation. However, for data assets that have no physical form and are not used as functional assets, the depreciation factors mainly come from the economic depreciation caused by the loss of timeliness of data assets.

3.2   Income Method

The theoretical basis of the income method is that the value of intangible assets is reflected by their expected earning capacity after being put into use. It is a valuation method to calculate the present value of future economic benefits based on the expected application scenario of target assets. The valuation methods of intangible assets derived from the income method mainly include: the royalty saving method is a valuation method based on the cost saving perspective of holding the asset without paying royalties.

Under this method, it is necessary to estimate a royalty rate, which is used to calculate "cost savings". The royalty rate usually adopts profit sharing or is linked to product sales; Multi period excess income method is a valuation method by calculating the present value of the net cash flow or excess income contributed by the intangible asset.

Under this method, it is necessary to reasonably estimate the increase in income or decrease in cost arising from holding the intangible asset; Incremental income method is a valuation method by comparing the cash flow difference generated by the use of the intangible assets, which is usually used for the valuation of exclusive agreements.

3.3 Market Method

The market method is a valuation method based on market comparable transaction cases of the same or similar assets. On the basis of obtaining the market transaction price, the market value of the target intangible assets is calculated by adjusting factors such as the nature of the intangible assets or differences in market conditions.

The market approach is applied on the premise that there is an open and active trading market for the underlying asset or its similar assets, and the trading price is easy to obtain.

At present, China has set up several data trading centers in Guizhou and other places, and the data trading valuation will continue to improve with the exploration of data trading centers.

3.4 Data Assets Evaluation Method of Power Regulation Data

The power regulation data asset has the characteristics of value and shareability, and the factors affecting the value of data asset are complex and diverse. The premise for the application of the market approach is to have a perfect data trading system, but for regulatory data, data trading is still in the primary stage, so there is a lack of similar assets as a reference.

The income method needs to predict the future data income, so it is difficult to determine the future cash flow of the assets to be assessed, and the assessment is subjective. Therefore, based on the characteristics of power regulation data and the factors affecting the value of data assets, combined with traditional cost evaluation algorithms, this paper studies the data asset value evaluation methods applicable to the field of power regulation; Based on the improved cost evaluation method, a data asset evaluation model covering the cost, intrinsic value and use value of power regulation data is established to provide basic support for reasonably determining the value of big data assets (Fig. 2).

The total cost of power regulation data assets mainly includes tangible asset investment, intangible asset investment and operation and maintenance costs. Intangible asset investment refers to software development and update iteration costs, tangible asset investment refers to the purchase of relevant equipment, and operation and maintenance

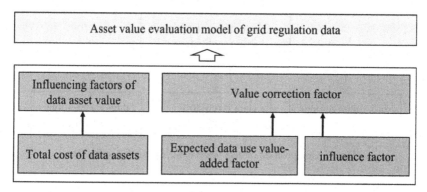

Fig. 2. Asset value evaluation system of regulation data

costs refer to the costs incurred from the maintenance and technical services of data assets in daily production. The total cost composition of data assets is shown in Fig. 3.

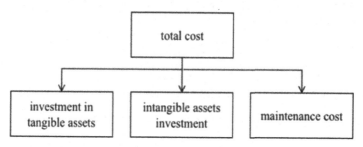

Fig. 3. Total cost composition of data assets

The expected data use the value-added coefficient to represent the ratio of the total value of the output of the data asset in the life cycle to the total cost. The coefficient is determined according to the historical income data of similar data assets and scored by experts.

There are different risk factors in various links such as data management, circulation and value-added application, which affect the final value of data. The risk coefficient of data value realization is quantified based on the analytic hierarchy process (Fig. 4).

The data circulation coefficient is determined by calculating the proportion of tradable data in the total data volume.

Data quality evaluation dimensions include data integrity, timeliness, accuracy, consistency, etc. Integrity checks whether the data access within the scope of each object model is complete, determines the scope of each object model through the object model information table, performs statistical analysis on the number of data accesses according to the scope of the object model, detects the data measurement points that have not been submitted, conducts integrity statistical analysis by day, and quickly checks the integrity of the daily access number of the platform.

Record the time period and missing points of missing data in a timely manner. Read the daily incremental data of the database, traverse each record of running data,

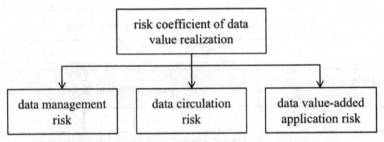

Fig. 4. Composition of data value realization risk coefficient

judge whether the measured value is empty, and record the time period and quantity of continuous empty measured values.

The accuracy detection is based on the grid operation business logic and operation specification, and the received data of the grid operation data is detected by object to see whether it conforms to the business logic and specification. Power grid business logic and operation specifications generally include power imbalance, grid aggregation accuracy, etc. (Fig. 5).

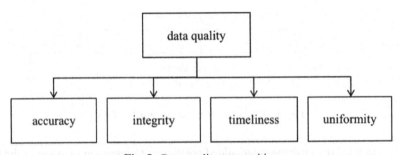

Fig. 5. Data quality composition

Based on the above analysis results, build the asset value evaluation index system. AHP is introduced to evaluate data asset. Divide the decision-making objectives, factors (decision-making criteria) and decision-making objects into the highest level, middle level and lowest level according to their interrelationships, and draw a hierarchy diagram. The highest level refers to the purpose of decision-making and the problems to be solved. The lowest level refers to alternatives in decision-making. The middle tier refers to the factors considered and the criteria for decision-making. For the two adjacent layers, the upper layer is called the target layer and the lower layer is the factor layer.

Firstly, the weight of the factors influencing the value of data assets is calculated by the analytic hierarchy process. Then the grey correlation analysis method is used to quantify the factors affecting the value of data assets and calculate the correlation coefficient between data assets. Then the correlation degree is calculated by combining the weight of the factors affecting the value of data assets, and the data assets with higher correlation degree are selected as the comparable data assets. Finally, on the basis of the cost method, we use the correlation degree to determine the expected data use value-added coefficient and build a data asset value evaluation model.

There are differences in the importance of indicators to the value of data assets, and the differences can be quantified through the judgment matrix. Assume that there is an expert who studies data assets to evaluate the importance of the factors affecting the value of data assets in a scale, and that the importance of each industry expert is equal, and then build a comparison judgment matrix A between each two levels.

$$A = \begin{bmatrix} a_{11} & \cdots & a_{1j} \\ \vdots & \ddots & \vdots \\ a_{i1} & \cdots & a_{ij} \end{bmatrix} \tag{1}$$

During the analysis of AHP, the most important step is to establish the hierarchical structure model of indicators, and construct the judgment matrix according to the structure model. Only after the judgment matrix passes the consistency test can the analysis and calculation be carried out. Among them, the structural model can be designed into three levels, the highest level is the daily standard level, which is the purpose of decision-making and the problem to be solved, the middle level is the factor to be considered in decision-making, which is the criteria for decision-making, and the lowest level is the alternative for decision-making. In this paper, the hierarchical model refers to the hierarchical model constructed by the factors that contribute to the value of data assets. In the process of construction, value influencing factors need to be considered. It can be considered by consulting experts, references and other methods. The hierarchical model is the basis for building the data asset evaluation model.

After building the hierarchical model, establish a judgment matrix based on the indicators in the hierarchical model. The judgment matrix represents the relative importance of all factors of this layer to a factor of the previous layer. The judgment matrix has an important influence on the subsequent results, and is also the embodiment of the quantitative nature of the analytic hierarchy process. The construction of the judgment matrix can refer to expert opinions, and relevant professionals can assign values to the elements of the judgment matrix. When assigning values to the elements of the judgment matrix, the nine-level scaling method can be used (that is, the numbers 1 to 9 and their reciprocal are used to indicate the relative importance of indicators), which is also the most commonly used method in the analytic hierarchy process.

The calculation formula of data asset value is as follows.

$$V = C * (1 + R) * (1 - r) * a * b \tag{2}$$

C refers to the total cost of data assets, including asset investment and operation and maintenance management, and R refers to the expected value-added coefficient, r is the data value realization risk coefficient, b is the application coefficient, a is the data quality coefficient.

For the data quality dimension, we construct a judgment matrix, as shown in Table 1.

Table 1. Data quality comparison judgment matrix

	A_1 accuracy	A_2 integrity	A_3 timeliness	A_4 uniformity
A_1 accuracy	A_{11}	A_{12}	A_{13}	A_{14}
A_2 integrity	A_{21}	A_{22}	A_{23}	A_{24}
A_3 timeliness	A_{31}	A_{32}	A_{33}	A_{34}
A_4 uniformity	A_{41}	A_{42}	A_{43}	A_{44}

For the data quality dimension, weight of data quality value evaluation index is shown in Table 2.

Table 2. Weight of data quality value evaluation index

1st indices	2nd indices	Weight
Data quality	Accuracy	W_{a1}
	Integrity	W_{a2}
	Timeliness	W_{a3}
	Uniformity	W_{a4}

The scoring criteria for the value of data quality are shown in Table 3.

Table 3. Scoring criteria of data quality value evaluation index

	Description	Scoring criteria
Accuracy	The degree to which data measurements conform to business logic and prescriptivity	S_{a1}
Integrity	The extent to which data is missing from the data range set	S_{a2}
Timeliness	The extent to which data is missing in the data point set	S_{a3}
Uniformity	How consistent the data measurements are from different data sources	S_{a4}

Calculate data quality score through weighted publicity.

$$S_a = W_{a1} \times S_{a1} + W_{a2} \times S_{a2} + W_{a3} \times S_{a3} + W_{a4} \times S_{a4} \tag{3}$$

For the apply dimension, we construct a judgment matrix, as shown in Table 4.

Table 4. Apply comparison judgment matrix

	B_1 scarcity	B_2 timeliness	B_3 effectiveness	B_4 economy
B_1 scarcity	B_{11}	B_{12}	B_{13}	B_{14}
B_2 timeliness	B_{21}	B_{22}	B_{23}	B_{24}
B_3 effectiveness	B_{31}	B_{32}	B_{33}	B_{34}
B_4 economy	BA_{41}	B_{42}	B_{43}	B_{44}

Table 5. Weight of apply value evaluation index

1st indices	2nd indices	Weight
Apply	Scarcity	W_{b1}
	Timeliness	W_{b2}
	Effectiveness	W_{b3}
	Economy	W_{b4}

Table 6. Scoring criteria of apply value evaluation index

	Description	Scoring criteria
Scarcity	The number of data provided and the number of providers	S_{b1}
Timeliness	Satisfaction of time characteristics of data to application	S_{b2}
Effectiveness	The extent to which data is missing in the data point set	S_{b3}
Economy	Economic value of data in specific scenarios	S_{b4}

For the apply dimension, weight of data quality value evaluation index is shown in Table 5.

The scoring criteria for the value of data quality are shown in Table 6.

Calculate data quality score through weighted publicity.

$$S_b = W_{b1} \times S_{b1} + W_{b2} \times S_{b2} + W_{b3} \times S_{b3} + W_{b4} \times S_{b4} \tag{4}$$

For the risk coefficient dimension, we construct a judgment matrix, as shown in Table 7.

Table 7. Risk coefficient comparison judgment matrix

	R_1 data management	R_2 data circulation	R_3 data value-added application
R_1 data management	R_{11}	R_{12}	R_{13}
R_2 data circulation	R_{21}	R_{22}	R_{23}
R_3 data value-added application	R_{31}	R_{32}	R_{33}

For the apply dimension, weight of risk coefficient value evaluation index is shown in Table 8.

Table 8. Weight of risk coefficient value evaluation index

1st indices	2nd indices	Weight
Risk coefficient	Data management	W_{r1}
	Data circulation	W_{r2}
	Data value-added application	W_{r3}

The scoring criteria for the value of data quality are shown in Table 9.

Table 9. Scoring criteria of risk coefficient value evaluation index

	Description	Scoring criteria
Data management	Data update frequency	S_{r1}
Data circulation	Risk of data security	S_{r2}
Data value-added application	Degree of data development	S_{r3}

Calculate data quality score through weighted publicity.

$$S_r = W_{r1} \times S_{r1} + W_{r2} \times S_{r2} + W_{r3} \times S_{r3} \tag{5}$$

4   Conclusions

Based on the data ontology attribute in the power dispatching system and the power grid operation mechanism, this paper studies the influencing factors of the value of power regulation data assets, analyzes the data characteristics in the data assets, constructs the element system of data asset value evaluation, and proposes a data asset value evaluation method covering the cost, intrinsic value and use value of power regulation data.

Acknowledgment. This work is supported by Science and Technology Program of State Grid Corporation of China under Grant No. 5442DZ210027.

References

1. Berkman, M.: Valuing intellectual property assets for licensing transactions. Licensing J. **22**(4), 16–23 (2002)
2. Longstaff, F.A., Schwartz, E.S.: Valuing credit derivatives. J. Fixed Income **5**(1), 6–12 (1995)
3. Stentoft, L.: Convergence of the least squares Monte Carlo approach to american option valuation. Manag. Sci. **50**(2), 129–168 (2004)
4. Gonzalo, C.S., Alexis, G.G.M., Jorge, U.: The Valuation of Multidimensional American Real Options Using the LSM Simulation Method. Elsevier Science Ltd. (2007)
5. Villani, G.: Application of market approach to evaluating big data assets. Comput. Econ. (2008)
6. Liu, Q., Tong, Y., Wei, T., at al.: Application of market approach to evaluating big data assets. J. Assets Appraisal (11), 33–37 (2016)
7. Li, Y., Zhang, S.: Construction of data asset value evaluation model. Financ. Account. Monthly **9**, 30–35 (2018)
8. Zhang, Z., Yang, D., Hongxia, W., et al.: Research and application of data assets valuation model. Mod. Electron. Tech. **20**, 44–47 (2015)
9. Shi, A., Gao, D., Xie, J., et al.: Construction of data assets value evaluation system for internet enterprises. Financ. Times **14**, 109 (2017)
10. Huang, L., Liu, J., Huang, Z.: Research on the value of platform data assets in the age of big data. J. Fuzhou Univ. **32**(4), 50–54 (2018)

Author Index

Printed in the United States
by Baker & Taylor Publisher Services